acadia 22

the **association for computer aided design in architecture** welcomes you to the end of its **twenty-second** year.

2003conference ***host:***

Ball State University
College of Architecture and Planning
Muncie Indiana

Department of Architecture
765.285.1908

BALL STATE UNIVERSITY®

Library of Congress Control Number: 2003097353

PRINTED BY
Bookmasters, Inc.
http://www.bookmasters.com
Mansfield, OH 44905

ISBN 1-8880250-12-8

ACADIA 2003 : CONNECTING--CROSSROADS OF DIGITAL DISCOURSE

Kevin R. Klinger, Editor

Includes bibliographic references.

I. Kevin R. Klinger; II. Association for Computer Aided Design in Architecture

Manufactured with pride in America's Heartland

Printed and bound in the United States of America

Credits

>>2003 Conference Chair:
Kevin R. Klinger, Ball State University

>>2003 Site Chair:
Frederick Stacy Norman, Ball State University

>>ACADIA22 Conference 2003 Administrative Support:
Bhavana Mokha, Graduate Student, Ball State University

>>ACADIA22 Conference 2003 Graphics, Web, and Exhibit Development: Aaron Brakke, Graduate Student, Ball State University

>>ACADIA22 Conference 2003 Proceedings Layout:
Christopher Reiter, Graduate Student, Ball State University

>>ACADIA22 Conference 2003 Brochure Layout:
Joshua Vermillion, Graduate Student, Ball State University

>>2003 | 4 Officers:
president: Kevin R. Klinger
vice-president: Ganapathy Mahalingam
treasurer: Kostas Papamichael
secretary: Carmina Sanchez
newsletter editor: Mark Clayton
webmaster: Kirk Martini
membership officer: Kostas Papamichael

>>2002 | 3 Officers:
president: Ganapathy Mahalingam
vice-president: Mark Clayton
treasurer: Kostas Papamichael
secretary: Carmina Sanchez
newsletter editor: Mark Clayton
webmaster: Kirk Martini
membership officer: Kostas Papamichael
outreach officers: Kevin R. Klinger, Murali Paranandi, Tina Sarawgi

>>2003 - 2005 Steering Committee:
Julio Bermudez
Wassim Jabi
Brian Johnson
Loukas Kalisperis
Mahesh Senagala

>>2002 - 2004 Steering Committee:
Peter Anders
Michael Berk
Volker Mueller
Carmina Sanchez
John Tector

alternates:
Theodore W. Hall

>>Paper Reviewers

Rodrigo Gracia Alvarado
Head Dept. Diseño y Teoria de la Arquitectura
Facultad De Arquitectura, Construcción Y Diseño
Universidad del Bio-Bio

Peter Anders
Director
MindSpace.net

Julio C. Bermudez, Ph.D.
Associate Professor
College of Architecture and Planning
University of Utah

Oscar A. Blazquez
Senior Lecturer
Department of Architecture
The University of Arizona

Mark Cabrinha, R.A.
Lecturer
Architecture Department
California State Polytechnic, San Luis Obispo

Sonia Carmena, Arq.
Director, CIAD
Faculty of Architecture
Rosario National University

Cristiano Ceccato
Research & Development
Gehry Partners, LLP

Nancy Y. Cheng
Associate Professor
Department of Architecture
University of Oregon

Renee Cheng
Associate Professor and Director of Design
Department of Architecture
University of Minnesota

Mao-Lin Chiu
Professor
Department of Architecture
National Cheng Kung University

Mark J. Clayton
Executive Associate Dean, College of Architecture
Texas A&M University

Pierre Côté
Professor
École d'architecture
Université Laval

Karl Daubmann
Assistant Professor of Practice
Taubman College of Architecture and Urban Planning
The University of Michigan

Bharat Dave, Ph.D.
Professor
Faculty of Architecture, Building & Planning
The University of Melbourne

Madhu C. Dutta
Assistant Professor
School of Architecture
University of Texas, San Antonio

Maia Engeli
Guest Professor
Architecture
TU Delft

Stefano Foresti
Director
CROMDI
University of Utah

Thomas Fowler IV
Associate Professor & Associate Director
Architecture Department
California State Polytechnic University

Glenn Goldman
Professor and Director of Imaging Laboratory
School of Architecture
New Jersey Institute of Technology

Wassim Jabi
Assistant Professor
School of Architecture
New Jersey Institute of Technology

Shailesh Jain
Doctoral Student
Ph.D. Program, College of Architecture
Georgia Institute of Technology

Mitsuo Morozumi
Professor
Department of Architecture and Civil Engineering,
Faculty of Engineering
Kumamoto University

Volker Mueller
Design Technology Manager
IT Department
NBBJ

Douglas Noble
Associate Professor
School of Architecture
University of Southern California

F. Stacy Norman
Assistant Professor
Department of Architecture
Ball State University

Filiz Ozel
Associate Dean and Professor
College of Architecture and Environmental Design
Arizona State University

Konstantinos Papamichael
Staff Scientist
Lawrence Berkeley National Laboratory

Murali Paranandi
Associate Professor
Department of Architecture
Miami University

Marcelo Paysse
Director of Informatics Department
Facultad de Arquitectura
Universidad del la Republica

Celine Pinet, Ph.D.
Co-Chair, Interior Design Program
Applied Arts and Sciences
West Valley College

George Proctor
Associate Professor
Department of Architecture
California State Polytechnic University

Carmina Sanchez-del-Valle
Associate Professor
Department of Architecture
Hampton University

Thomas Seebohm
Associate Professor
School of Architecture
University of Waterloo

Mahesh Senagala
Assistant Professor
School of Architecture
University of Texas, San Antonio

Aron P. Temkin, R.A.
Assistant Professor
School of Architecture
Florida Atlantic University

Andrew C. Thurlow
Assistant Professor
University of Tennessee
College of Architecture + Design

Lisa Tilder, R.A.
Assistant Professor
Knowlton School of Architecture
The Ohio State University

Raffi Tomassian
Design Architect
GlaserWorks

Jin Yeu Tsou
Professor
Department of Architecture
The Chinese University of Hong Kong

Guillermo P. Vasquez de Velasco
Associate Professor
Department of Architecture
Texas A&M University

Jerzy Wojtowicz
Professor of Architecture
School of Architecture
The University of British Columbia

Rob Woodbury, Ph.D.
Graduate Program Chair
Interdisciplinary Studies
Simon Fraser University

>>Topic node chairs:

Peter Anders
Director
MindSpace.net

Julio C. Bermudez, Ph.D.
Associate Professor
College of Architecture and Planning
University of Utah

Cristiano Ceccato
Research & Development
Gehry Partners, LLP

Nancy Y. Cheng
Associate Professor
Department of Architecture
University of Oregon

Mark J. Clayton
Executive Associate Dean
College of Architecture
Texas A&M University

Madhu C. Dutta
Assistant Professor
School of Architecture
University of Texas, San Antonio

Stefano Foresti
Director
CROMDI
(Center for the Representation of Multi-Dimensional Information)
University of Utah

Wassim Jabi
Assistant Professor
School of Architecture
New Jersey Institute of Technology

Kevin R. Klinger
Assistant Professor
Department of Architecture
Ball State University

Branko Kolarevic
Associate Professor
Department of Architecture
University of Pennsylvania

Loukas N. Kalisperis, Ph.D. A.D.E.
Professor
School of Architecture
Pennsylvania State University

Gregory A. Luhan
Professor
College of Design, School of Architecture
University of Kentucky

Ganapathy Mahalingam
Associate Professor
Department of Architecture and Landscape Architecture
North Dakota State University

Marta Male-Alemany
Architect / Design Faculty SCI-ARC (Southern California Institute of Architecture)

John F. Marx, AIA
Design Principal
Form4 Architecture

F. Stacy Norman
Assistant Professor
Department of Architecture
Ball State University

George Proctor
Associate Professor
Department of Architecture
California State Polytechnic University

Thomas Seebohm
Associate Professor
School of Architecture
University of Waterloo

Mahesh Senagala
Assistant Professor
School of Architecture
University of Texas- San Antonio

Aron P. Temkin, R.A.
Assistant Professor
School of Architecture
Florida Atlantic University

Special Thanks

ACADIA22 Conference2003: *Merci!*
Kevin R. Klinger, Conference Chair

ACADIA is a volunteer organization that depends upon the rigor and dedication of its membership to sustain an ongoing discourse on issues of digital technology in architecture. To this end, we are grateful for the hard work of countless individuals who have contributed to upholding the highest standards for this conference and organization.

112 abstracts were received from 17 countries. This resulted in 39 accepted papers. This year, to add an additional rigor, the abstracts were reviewed, and the final papers were reviewed. A double blind review process was employed to ensure the integrity of the review scholarship. We owe a special thanks to the volunteer efforts of the international review team of 70 reviewers (which include 20 topic node chairs) whose comments to the authors are largely responsible for tightening of the scholarship and focusing the discourse of the conference. Additionally, we are indebted to the 20 topic node chairs for their expertise and scholarly contributions in outlining the issues and raising the significant questions for each topic node area. I greatly appreciate their perseverance amidst a barrage of emails, deadlines, and requests. The shape of the discourse in this conference is determined in large part by these topic node chairs.

Thanks to the ACADIA Officers and Steering Committee for their advice and suggestions throughout the planning phases of this conference. Also, thanks to the previous Conference Chairs: George Proctor, Wassim Jabi, Julio Bermudez, and Mark Clayton for their counsel and guidance. The conferences at Quebec, Salt Lake City, Washington DC, Buffalo, and Pomona were considered as a gauge for the development of venues in Indianapolis, and the very well-crafted proceedings of ACADIA'98: Quebec City (Seebohm, Van Wyk) was a guide for organizing these proceedings. I only hope we came close to matching the quality of the many events and sessions ACADIA has historically provided its conference attendees.

We owe a special thanks to Wassim Jabi, who developed an online paper review system unmatched in its quality and ease of use (plus, its graphical interface design is quite rich). The creation of this system will serve as an infrastructure for ACADIA conferences for many years to come and will ensure the timely collection of data and information from reviewers and authors that will be invaluable for successful future conferences. Wassim's volunteer efforts and counsel helped facilitate a depth of quality and rigor of the review for ACADIA2003.

I am deeply indebted to the administration, colleagues, and students of Ball State University for a supportive environment whose consistent backing and enthusiasm for ACADIA has provided a platform for the careful evolution of all aspects of this event. Thanks to the College of Architecture and Planning, most specifically, Dean of our College, Dr. Joseph J. Bilello, Associate Dean, Michel A. Mounayar, and former Architecture Department Chair, Brian Sinclair, who encouraged me to bring this event to Ball State and Indiana, and provided us with space and resources to facilitate its development. I am grateful to Brian Sinclair, a former ACADIA participant, and Interim Architecture Department Chair Michele Chiuini for their research support allowing me to focus efforts on administering this event. Also, we are much obliged to Dr. Wesley R. Janz, Director of the Master of Architecture program for his administration of graduate student assistance. A great deal of thanks to the iCommunications initiative at Ball State University and the Lilly Endowment, Inc. for funding conference travel to pitch the BSU 2003 conference in 2002 at Pomona, as well as supporting over 700 hours of graduate student time to help organize the event. Thanks additionally to both the College of Architecture and Planning, and Department of Architecture support staff, Dave Bartle, Cheryl Duffy, Julie Kratzner, Patricia Quinn, Melanie Smith, Scott Truex, Candace Walker, Lu Ann Whitehair, and Roger Whitted for their quick answers to periodic requests as we developed the venue for this conference. It almost goes without mention that the Conference Site Chair, Frederick Stacy Norman, shouldered a significant portion of the conference planning, and like many ACADIAns earned his stripes as a dutiful and meticulous volunteer. Most importantly, we are grateful to the devotion and excitement for ACADIA of these most helpful graduate students: Aaron Paul Brakke, Bhavana Mokha, Christopher Reiter, and Joshua Vermillion. *Merci!*

The volunteer efforts of Dr. Cheryl Bove from the English Department at Ball State University ensured that every paper consistently adhered to the "ACADIA style and formatting." She also proofread the majority of the papers for grammar, punctuation, and bibliographic references. Dr. Stacy Mulder and Dr. Geralyn Strecker also deserve much credit for volunteering their services by proofreading papers. We are deeply appreciative of the volunteer efforts of Ball State University's English Department for ACADIA, and ensuring the paper formatting, style, and standards are of the highest quality. Stephanie, my wife, has been everlasting with patience for my endless hours of "volunteer" time, and for this steadfastness, I am truly grateful.

This conference is devoted to our tireless students who fully represent the future of ACADIA.

Kevin R. Klinger

ACADIA 2003
Sponsors

BALL STATE UNIVERSITY

<< 2003 conference **host**

form·Z 4

autodesk

acadia
BALL STATE
UNIVERSITY
<<2003 conference host
acadia conference 2003 october 23 24 25 26 indianapolis indiana
connecting >> the crossroads of digital discourse

ACADIA 2003
Digital*Content*

Introduction

ACADIA22 Conference2003: Introduction
Digital Architecture:
Defining Digital Discourse
Kevin R. Klinger

Architecture is presently engaged in an impatient search for solutions to critical questions about the nature and the identity of the discipline. Meanwhile, evolving digital technology continues to serve as a key agent for prevailing innovations and **new ideas** in architecture. Still, this feels familiar, as technology *has always been* a catalyst for new ideas in architecture. A positive digital future in architecture requires a clearer definition of principles and skills necessary to maintain a rigor in emerging digital projects/ projections. At the same time, recognition about the significance of the already existing digital scholarship in architecture must be connected with emerging lines of inquiry evolving within the discipline. Healthy disciplines remain tolerant of a state of flux by constantly questioning the inclusion|exclusion, import|export, and collaboration|isolation to|from new ideas, new techniques, new disciplines, and new technology. At the perimeter of this nebulous exchange, an innovative new **digital discourse** is emerging that offers some unexpected new conduits to an attentive discipline of architecture. **Topic nodes** have evolved which augment this discourse with overlapping issues, as well as a particular set of important distinctions from one another: *Digital Pedagogy, Digital Tools, Digital Production/ Fabrication, Digital Visualization, Digital Projects, Digital Design, Digital Representation, Digital Thinking, and Digital Practice.*

What is digital architecture? Architectural ideas have found new forms of digital representations, as information reconfigures into digital visualizations within the space of the screen. In contrast, some projects emerge into the physical world as digital fabrications, where the computer participates in the process from conception through manufacture. However, using digital technology doesn't necessarily constitute creating digital architecture. Ideas are still scrutinized by the author(s). Thus, a responsibility for a **critical dimension** still falls upon the author(s) of any project/projection. Any new categorizations of architecture must connect equally with the critical as well as the technological skill base of the authors. Just as there is a difference between building and architecture, there is also a distinct difference between digitally generated projects and digital architecture. The underlying scholarship of a solid digital discourse serves as the foundation, that ensures a solid critical rigor in digital architecture.

digital principles: We must invent new languages to continue this conversation about digital architecture on any meaningful level. Is this morph better than that warp? Does the tool path limit the density of the ripple? Did I choose a suitable instance for freezing the motion-animated surface? Amidst these new adjectives|verbs|nouns, clear and critical definitions of **new principles** have yet to materialize in the wake of new tool driven digital languages. I submit that digital architecture projects still come to life through the lens of a familiar architectural process—as a critical problem solving activity that results in projects represented with a rigor and depth of idea and intention, albeit with a highly sophisticated digital tool skill set. Collectively, we can help build these new principles with our critical research and scholarship and provide a clearer definition of the digital discourse. Without new principles, many projects remain impenetrable and thus intimidating, or merely "interesting." Without a rigor and critical dimension, the projects will remain only exercises in software.

digital skills: Digital architecture requires proficiency with a specific foundation set of **digital skills** such as: *2D composition, vector graphics, image manipulation, 3D modeling: surface modeling, solid modeling, video editing, motion graphics, rendering, animation, parametrics, VRML, drafting, communications, layout, printing, presentation, database operations, GIS, web interface, CAM-based fabrication, performance analysis, lighting simulation, structural performance, systems performance, etc.* A clear aim of the emerging digital discourse is to outline these skill sets and demonstrate effective employment of these skills to create innovative digital architecture. Innovative digital projects will not sacrifice the development of this skill set at the expense of a critical problem-solving dimension.

Through patient hard work and the collective expertise of the volunteer organization of ACADIA, and its sister organizations, we will continue the path for a rigorous digital discourse that will facilitate the evolution of solid scholarly contributions toward digital issues in architecture; a foundation for a critical digital architecture; an architecture of our new century.

01 >> Connecting Digital Design

Chairs: Wassim Jabi, Peter Anders

Digital Design

Wassim Jabi

Describing design as a sequence of steps cannot convey the complexity of social interactions that it embodies. Design is not merely a process, but a co-evolution of efforts and events in various places and times—both synchronous and asynchronous. Designers share their values, effort and expertise within design settings via artifacts that further the design process. Increasingly, these design settings in academia, research, and professional practice combine physical and virtual modalities such as immersion, projection, and a range of interaction technologies. Peter Anders has described such spaces as cybrids: hybrids that integrate virtual and physical space. In these settings, designers use overlapping physical and virtual artifacts and tools to arrive at a co-operative design resolution. Within collaborative design, these artifacts take on an additional role. As embodiments of design ideas and actions, they become media for communication. Donald Schon asserts that design should be considered a form of making, rather than primarily a form of problem solving, information processing or research. Indeed the line separating creation from design is becoming increasingly blurred. For the design artifact itself may become a part of the design proposal—its virtual presence incorporated within a cybrid structure or object. We may in the future see a proliferation of cybrid settings that support collaborative, digital design. The technologies for this already exist in collaborative tools, networked computing, scanning and immersive media. However, it will take a creative vision to see how these disparate tools and devices can integrate within the ideal design setting.

Wassim Jabi is an Assistant Professor of Architecture at the New Jersey Institute of Technology. Jabi is a Ph.D. candidate and holds an M.Arch with distinction from the University of Michigan. Jabi is currently the coordinator of the third year undergraduate design studios at NJIT and teaches electives on computer-aided design. He has published several articles on computer-supported collaborative design. Jabi is a long-time member of the Association for Computer Aided Design in Architecture (ACADIA). He is also a member of the editorial board of the International Journal of Architectural Computing (IJAC).

Four Degrees Of Freedom

Peter Anders

Letting go is hard to do. Remember back to when, after months of trying, you let go of the handlebars of your bicycle and sailed down the street, effortless and assured. It was a freedom born of mastery, balance and technique. You had let go, but were in control. Technique extends to other devices as well and we are here to discuss architectural computation. Here too, as we will see, mastery is shown by letting go.

These papers explore new degrees of freedom in design computation. Each is on a separate aspect of architecture, whether it be aesthetics, process, or structure. Two papers inquire into the entities of design and the processes by which they are manifested. They pose important questions. If we can affect the course of design going forward, are we free to change its past? By defining the characteristics of objects at the outset, are we through automation free to choose from a refined spectrum of outcomes? From the evidence of these papers, the answer to both questions is yes. Through the agency of parametric design we can affect the future and past of architectural processes and their products. Rather than being locked into rigid, linear decisions we are temporally free to choose, tweak and modify.

Choice and chance play an important role in aesthetics as well. This has become emblematic of design trends as we have seen in recent years. One of our papers addresses the indeterminacy of particle systems in the design of a monument to the victims of 9/11. By letting go of the handlebars of the computer, the author has been freed to new, poetic forms and processes. Another paper opens urban design to its client community by use of a sophisticated web site. In the tradition of populist innovators like Charles Moore and Lucien Kroll, the authors have extended the design process beyond the office walls to the city itself. The designers, by loosening their grip on the project have made the effort democratic and participatory. Intriguingly, at the end of the paper, they note that this use of cyberspace opens the door to a non-physical architecture. Could architecture, then, let go its materialist biases as well? We hope to engage this and other questions shortly.

We are pleased then, to share with you these insights and projects. Wassim and I hope that these presentations will be as liberating for you as they were for us.

Peter Anders is an architect, educator, information design theorist and author of Envisioning Cyberspace. He is currently a fellow of the University of Plymouth CAiiA-Star Ph.D. Program. Anders is director of Mindspace.Net, an architectural practice specializing in media/information environments and has presented his research and projects in a variety of international venues.

Undo Reinterpreted

Wilson Chang, Rob Woodbury
Simon Fraser University

Abstract

The class of operations known as "undo" has proven to be a valuable addition to most professional work tools. In practice though, its use is frustrating: undo often undoes too much. Its essential informal semantics are that it returns the user to a prior state by recapitulating all intervening states. Why not give the user greater control over which aspects of a design to undo? An alternative is to seek to reuse prior work in any logically-coherent pattern—user input is a precious commodity. The area of generative systems provides insights in a search for alternatives to undo, in particular that prior user and system actions can be changed and reused in new contexts. We contingently introduce a concept we label as design promotions to describe system designs that demonstrate a tight coupling between interactive authorship and system-led generation, that treat past user actions as valuable intentional statements, and that treat alternative user choices as first-class objects of concern. In practice these three properties emphasize reuse. We briefly survey the current state of undo-like operations and potential candidates for implementing design promotions strategies. Through examples, we demonstrate approaches to realizing undo-like operations over specific representations, especially that of constructive solid geometry.

Undo Reinterpreted

Wilson Chang, Rob Woodbury, Simon Fraser University

1 Introduction

Research in generative systems shows how alternative designs can be generated through the application of formal devices such as ontologies (Woodbury et al. 1999) and rules (Heisserman 1994). Realistic generative systems must work in vast solution spaces that defeat any attempts at completely automatic search. This is why the most convincing demonstrations of generative systems involve the user as an integral part of the process. There have been several intriguing interfaces developed for generative systems, and some of these are exemplars of the crafts of user-interface design and programming. There is, however, little theory to guide future development in how users can interact with generative capabilities.

Extant CAD systems present surprisingly similar problems. They provide the user with an often large array of design modification operators and relatively weak mechanisms for recovery of past states of a representation. Reuse is typically limited to insertion of previously saved files and a symbol instancing facility such as the symbols of Form Z (Form Z 2003b), the Xref of AutoCAD (AutoCAD 2003b), or the Reference File of MicroStation (MicroStation 2003a). Some advanced systems such as Bentley's CustomObjects (in the AEC industry) or CATIA (largely in the mechanical engineering industry) support the user in building parametric design representations, in which design variables are interrelated through relations (typically equations and inequations) and the system computes settings for the variables that are consistent with the relations. Such systems support reuse of work through quick recomputation of design variables after user changes, but remain largely silent on both higher levels of system assistance and on the capture and presentation of choices to the designer.

A key, perhaps the key, concept here is intent. Under an interpretation of designer action as intent, the undo/redo operators of conventional CAD systems can be seen as a means to return to prior intended states of a design. They are the main (perhaps the only) explicit record of design intent stored in a conventional system. Undo/redo was a powerful addition to most interactive authoring systems in the late 1980s and early 1990s. In its most frequently supported form it allows a user to undo to prior states of a design and to redo the undone operators provided that no new operations interceded between the undo and redo steps. In programming concept it is a pair of simple LIFO stacks. When a state is popped from the undo stack, it is pushed onto the redo stack. The redo stack is emptied on every new user operation. Of course, this simple mechanism can and has been implemented in a variety of ways, for instance through undoable operators and journaling mechanisms (Berlage 1994). Undo was lauded at the time, and most users of any sophistication rely on it today. It is clearly inadequate as a means to recover past work, as conversations with any group of users will reveal. It is typical that an operation to be undone lies well down the undo stack. Deletion of previous valuable work is often necessary, including related sub-concepts that the user would want to retain in future versions. Users are forced to delete valuable data in the undo process, making it necessary to reconstruct information back into the design. Sophisticated users develop idioms of use around undo. For example, they use the clipboard as a way of storing data that will be undone but that needs to be restored; they use a manual process of using existing data to build a scaffold for constructing new data prior to emulating undo through the manual deletion of data; and they manually patch existing data to approximate past data. These idioms are workarounds for a situation that seems obvious: undo as it is presently implemented in most systems is overly constraining. It often deletes more of a user's prior intent than is logically necessary.

Parametric design systems support designer intent in a fundamentally different way than do conventional CAD systems. Their main strategy is shared with a very familiar class of software: the spreadsheet. A parametric model is a template for a design expressed as a data structure containing variables, a set of relations amongst the variables that must be met in any instance of the template, and a set of assignments of values to the variables that comprise an instance of the design. Users of parametric modeling systems develop all three aspects of the model, and this can be a technically complex task. The payoff for all of this work is that a model can be varied. Changing one (or some) of the instance variables of a model causes the system to rewrite the other variables to be consistent with the expressed relations. (Some parametric modelers, for instance, most spreadsheets and CustomObjects, implement a model of computational flow from independent to dependent variables. Others, for instance, those of Gross (1990) and Borning and Freeman-Benson (1998), allow change to virtually any instance variable.) The intent here is the set of relations between variables in a model. In concept, parametric systems add a second level of undo to a system. One can (or should be able to) undo changes to the relations independent of changes to the values of the design variables. Both though recapitulate the problems encountered in conventional CAD systems: it often seems that more needs to be undone than is logically necessary. This creates extra work for the user.

Clearly, promoting designs to more complex states, demoting them to previous states, and reusing aspects of design work are all important to users. We contingently advance a concept we call design promotions as a combination of three features. It labels system designs in which generative tools are directly linked to interactive authorship and act to both promote and demote designs between less and more organized forms. It views past user actions as statements of intent, which may be edited to alter designs and reused in new contexts. Promotion/demotion and reuse imply that a fine-grained notion of choice and presentation of alternative choices be a part of the interface.

Design promotions embodies the idea that users' choices and actions are, in themselves, valuable objects and that users should be free to edit, reuse, and reflect on past choices and freely make new choices. The concept stresses the user—demonstration of its utility will be at the level of user tasks. Any number of well-known symbolic devices for supporting design change could well be used to implement design promotions. For example, the rules or type hierarchies of generative systems could be seen as a substrate for generalizing past experience. Extant systems are exemplars of choice in the moment—they typically provide many different ways to model designs, ranging in grain from global to local details of a representation. They are, however, primitive in their support of past operations, mostly limiting themselves to simple forms of undo. This paper begins with demonstrating the undo devices of current systems and shows how the information usually captured in undo stacks can be used in more powerful ways. For example, it is generally the case that the order of operations specified by a user provides more information than is necessary to model an object—it is a serialization of a process that has significant logical parallelism. Users should be free to revise models by undoing and redoing operations in any logically feasible order. Thus, in undoing or redoing, users may arrive at designs that they have never before made. Extant CAD systems provide hints at such capability. For example, in 3D Studio Max, primitive objects, such as box, allow undo of parametric modifiers in any order.

Undo though is only a synecdoche of a broader class of objects in CAD systems that would be amenable to reinterpretation under the concept of design promotions. In principle, any data structure created through the action of a user can be interpreted as a (partial) statement of the user's intent, and it may well be worthwhile to see if there are ways to rewrite the data structure to produce other models. If such other models contain less data than the original, that is, something is deleted from them, what the user will see will be related to undo in that it removes information, yet, unlike undo does not follow the strict logic of recapitulating the user's sequence of operations. A consequence of such a strategy is that the user will be able to "undo" operations to "return" to places never before encountered.

To implement a design promotions system it seems clear that at least two things are needed: a representation over which fine-grained change can be recorded and edited; and user interfaces for working with such fine-grained representations; neither are well-evidenced in the literature. Fine-grainedness is a necessary property for a system that does design promotions—the intent is to be able to alter literally every conceivable designer action. There is a literature on the related idea of selective undo, for example, "UNDO and REDO Operations for Solid Modeling" (Toria et al. 1986).

Woodbury et al. (1999) have developed a representation for design space exploration that appears to be suitable for implementing design promotions. This representation is an augmentation of typed feature structures (Carpenter 1994). It displays properties of partiality and intentionality that give it the requisite fine-grained structure.

Partiality is important because it allows us to have a representation of something without having all properties of the thing to hand. For example, we can know of the existence of a line without knowing the precise locations of its endpoints. We can know it has a colour without knowing its colour. A representation displaying this property comes with a way of incrementally changing properties, one by one. An intentional representation has the property that two identical representations do not necessarily model the same object. This allows us to make incremental decisions about how objects relate—we can, for instance, decide at any time that columns in two separate structural systems are, in fact, the same column.

Woodbury et al. (2000) show that there exists a natural operator over typed feature structures called hysterical undo. This operation allows a user to unwind operations done on a feature structure representation in every feasible order. The term hysterical refers not to an emotional state, but to the scientific sense of the word as designating the lagged entry of an effect into a system. In this case the cause is a statement of designer intent. Its effect as a design enters the system only when a particular subset of prior declared intentions is chosen. Over this one representation system, there appears to be a suitable algorithm for design promotions.

Revisiting undo and redo operations reveals how we might actually give a user control over such an algorithm. A first idea is to tie the notion of selection to that of undo. In such a scheme, undo would apply to the user-selected set of objects. With each selection, the system generates probable state transformations. Hysterical undo proposes possible demoting paths to a less organized state. The new state opens up opportunities for design reuse and promotion again into a more desirable design. Undo and redo operations provide specific and partial realization of design promotions. The undo mechanism provides a safety net for user to freely navigate the design space. The redo mechanism provides the liberty of reusing any feasible concepts. It is not clear that this is the only, or even a workable scheme for user interaction with a system supporting design promotions. An investigation of current undo/redo mechanisms reveals limitations and hints at richer interpretations of undo/redo operations for design promotions.

2 Extant examples of UNDO

Most applications incorporate variations of a linear undo model. In such a model, all executed commands are stored in a history list. To undo a command pop it out from the history list and push it into a redo list (Berlage 1994). The current linear undo models restrict the flow of design by documenting only a single working path. It limits the exploration nature of the design task and hinders reuse of past effort.

2.1 AutoCAD 2000i

AutoCAD (AutoCAD 2003a) incorporates a simple linear undo model. It records a history list and offers the user the possibility to redo one operation. Undoing sequentially will step backwards in the history list one operation at time, effectively returning to prior states. The history list can be switched off, or contain only one undo step to save computing resources. Users can group several commands as a single operation in the history list. For grouping to work, the user is required to set BEGIN and END pairs of checkpoints. The grouping operation is not intuitive. Users often cannot foresee the need for such grouping utility until several commands have been executed. A MARK feature is provided. When BACK is called, the history list returns to the state where the last MARK was set.

2.2 Form Z 3.8

Form Z (Form Z 2003a) incorporates a linear undo/redo model. Undo returns the project to its state before the most recent operation. Undo may be executed sequentially until all operation items are popped from the history list. Redo cancels the immediately precedent undo. As with sequential undo, redo may also be executed sequentially. The ability to sequentially redo after undo is an advantage over AutoCAD's single redo function. Users are able to visit previous states and use the Redo-All function to return to the state before the last sequential undo. Reset-Undo/Redo clears both history and redo lists to avoid overwhelming system memory. When a non-undo command is issued, the redo list is cleared and the new command is push into the history list. Clearing of redo list presents a problem since designers might need to return to previous designs during an undo/editing process.

2.3 Microsoft Word 2002

MS Word (Microsoft Word 2002 2003) provides a linear undo/redo model similar to the one in Form Z. User can undo sequentially as many actions as needed. The redo list contains all the actions that have been undone as long as no new command is issued. MS Word has an interface that allows the user to see both the history list and redo list. The visual representation of the history list provides clarity and predictability to the undo/redo process. One notable attribute is MS Word's extension to its redo function (Ctrl+Y). The redo function works as repeat function when there is no item in redo list.

2.4 Non-linear undo

3D Studio Max implements a limited form of selective undo, but only within the values of independent variables in its parametric primitive subsystem. It is one of a very small number of systems that implement a non-linear undo logic in any way. It demonstrates well that selective undoing of a parametric modifier at a lower part of modifier stack can result in forms never before encountered. In fact, the differences with prior forms can be dramatic indeed.

2.5 Scenarios in Microsoft Excel 2002

Some systems (e.g., spreadsheets, parametric modelers) model data dependencies as intentional acts (the user builds the dependencies with the expectation of their maintenance). Even in such systems, the maintenance of scenarios (prior settings of properties) is an issue. Note that MS Excel (Microsoft Excel 2002 2003) has a scenario system by which states of independent variable sets can be checkpointed. Excel's scenario tool is, in UI terms, quite removed from direct interaction with a spreadsheet.

3 Reinterpreting undo as design promotions

In this section we demonstrate two kinds of undo-like operations. Both treat prior user actions as serious statements of intent. Both support the reuse of user-created data structures to "return" a user to states never before seen. This makes them no longer undo operations. They are rather instances of a design promotions strategy—since they remove information we might well call them design demotions, but we will use the positive term promotions to describe both information adding and information removing operations.

3.1 Simple properties

The properties of objects exist or do not. Objects can have other objects as properties (all objects within a document can be considered properties of the document). Typically a property adopts all its sub-level properties as well. For example, selecting wood veneer as a surface property inherent the color, grain, reflection, and smoothness sub-properties of such surface type. Every change to an object introduces a new property of the object and undoes an old property. All old properties are potentially available to be reset. A selection of objects defines a set of old properties that may be reset. In the process, the generative mechanism proposes possible property combinations that the user might have missed. One simple example is choosing contrasting color pairs. Black and red is the first pair. Deep blue and bright orange is the second pair. An alternative combination might be black and bright orange. A user interface for such resetting would make old properties available based on user selection of objects. For example, clicking on an object pops up a list of properties appropriate for resetting. Moving over a property item display attributes for the property. A simple click resets the object with the selected property.

The independent variables of a parametric system are essentially simple properties of a model. They can be freely set without respect to other properties. In the parametric case, the system is responsible for tracking the effects of such change. We propose a scenario setting tools for CustomObjects (MicroStation 2003b). CustomObjects framework by Bentley Systems supports an object-oriented and parametric approach to modeling complex designs. Properties are propagated automatically through relationships built into a model. Designers as model programmers build relationships between parts and explore designs interactively. The design freedom of the system is commendable, yet designers are not able to document favorable model states. The proposed scenario setting tools would record independent variable sets for fast retract of design states. A user interface of the scenario manager would allow naming states for selected objects. A mouse click of such selection displays past scenarios to which a user might return.

3.2 Promotions in Boolean expressions

Constructive Solid Geometry (CSG) uses binary trees (with unary transformation nodes) as the data structure to store Boolean operations for a solid. The Boolean operators over solid models define a language of solids in which each object is (at least implicitly) associated with the CSG tree of operations used to create the solid. Of course, there are multiple CSG trees defining every solid. The particular choice of modeling operations defines one for each created solid. Further, every CSG tree corresponds to an algebraic expression that can be reduced to equivalent expressions by equivalence operations. The particular expression actually used in a modeling sequence represents, in some way, the intention of the user in a design process. Figure 4 illustrates the associations of CSG tree to the combinations of primitive shapes to form a simple massing model for a building (for the sake of rhetorical clarity, it omits the unary transformation nodes, the purpose of which is to locate primitive objects in space).

One definition of a design promotion in such a representation is that an operation can be simply removed from the expression. The results are independent expressions, no longer joined by an operation. Any of the operations in a Boolean expression can be undone—the result, using policy of treating the first operand as primary, is always two Boolean expressions yielding well-formed objects. Figure 5 shows examples of deleting selected operators from a Boolean expression.

A second strategy for Boolean expressions is to remove a chosen solid. Since every solid in a CSG tree identifies a path to the root of the tree and every path consists of zero or more operations, such a move provides opportunities to suggest different alternatives. Figure 6 shows examples of primitive deletion. By traversing up from the primitive nodes at the leaves of the tree, alternative choices can be generated.

A user interface for undoing primitives can be structured around picking a face—every face comes from a primitive object, and every primitive defines a path of operations leading to the root of the CSG tree. Any such choice is a candidate to undo a given face. A choice of multiple faces produces a path from the join of the argument paths to the root of the CSG tree. Upon selection, the system would prompt for the available alternatives.

4 Conclusions

Undo remains a highly useful and widely implemented idea. Its utility here is to suggest more general forms of reuse of designer actions. In concept every representational structure created by a user embodies an aspect of intent. The system design problem is to bring such past intent to the surface for present consideration. Such a process is not, in general, deterministic, and so is complicated by requiring user choice. The examples presented in this paper aim at specific representations, while it is clear that commonality across representations is important if an interface idea is to be broadly applicable. Nonetheless, the awkwardness of contemporary undo makes worthwhile a search for more logically sensible alternatives.

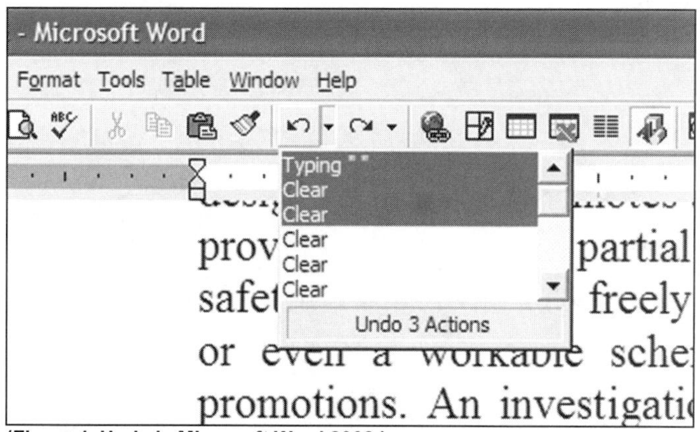

(Figure 1. Undo in Microsoft Word 2002.)

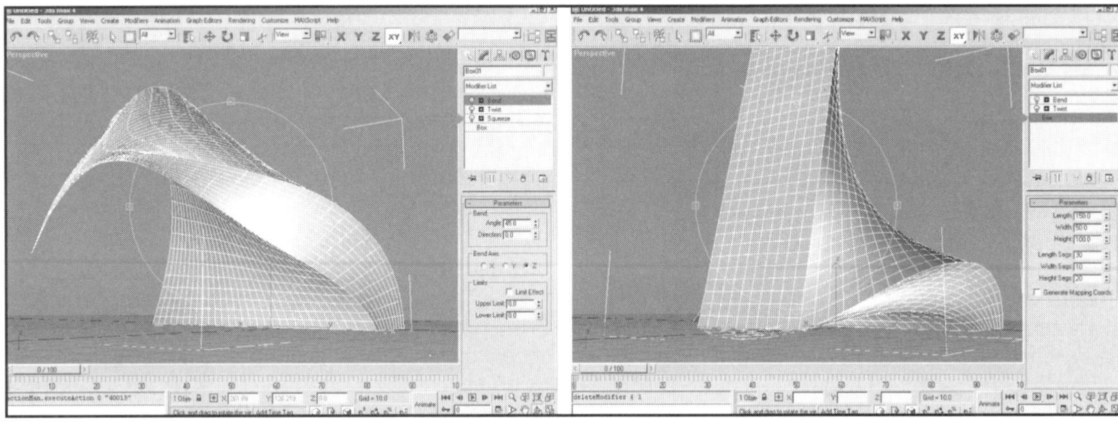

(Figure 2. Unexpected result of undoing a parametric modifier.)

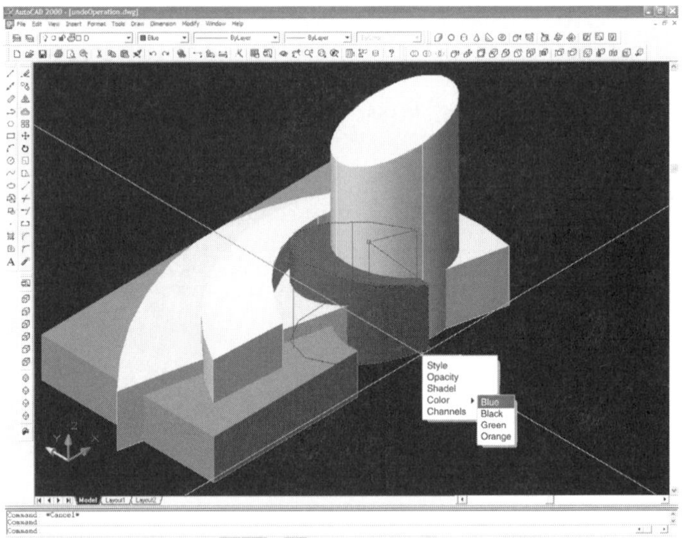

(Figure 3. Reusing simple properties.)

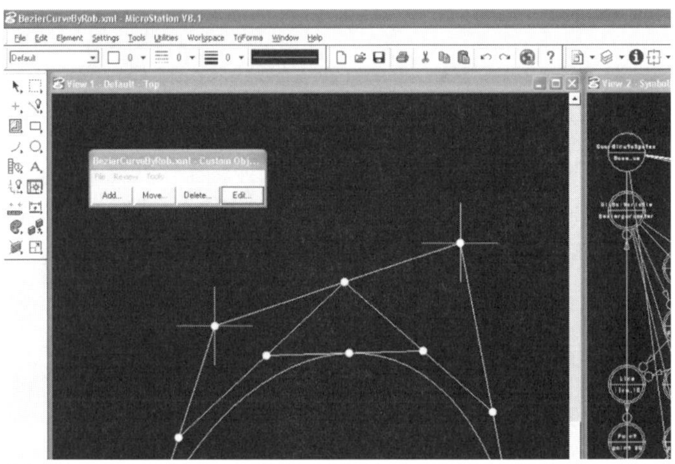

(Figure 4. Proposed Scenario Manager for CustomObjects.)

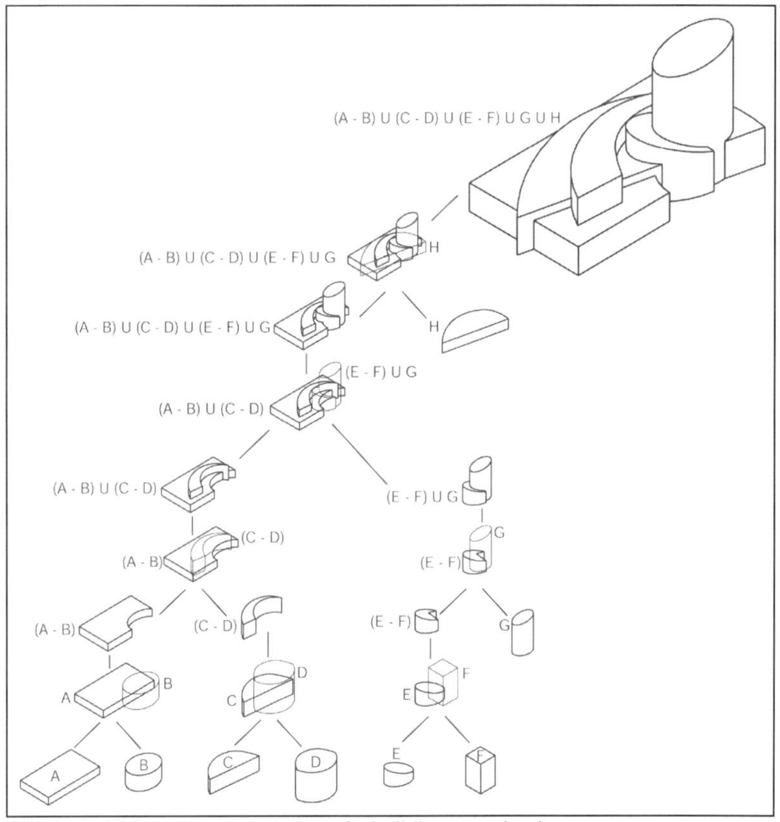

(Figure 5. CSG tree representation of a building massing.)

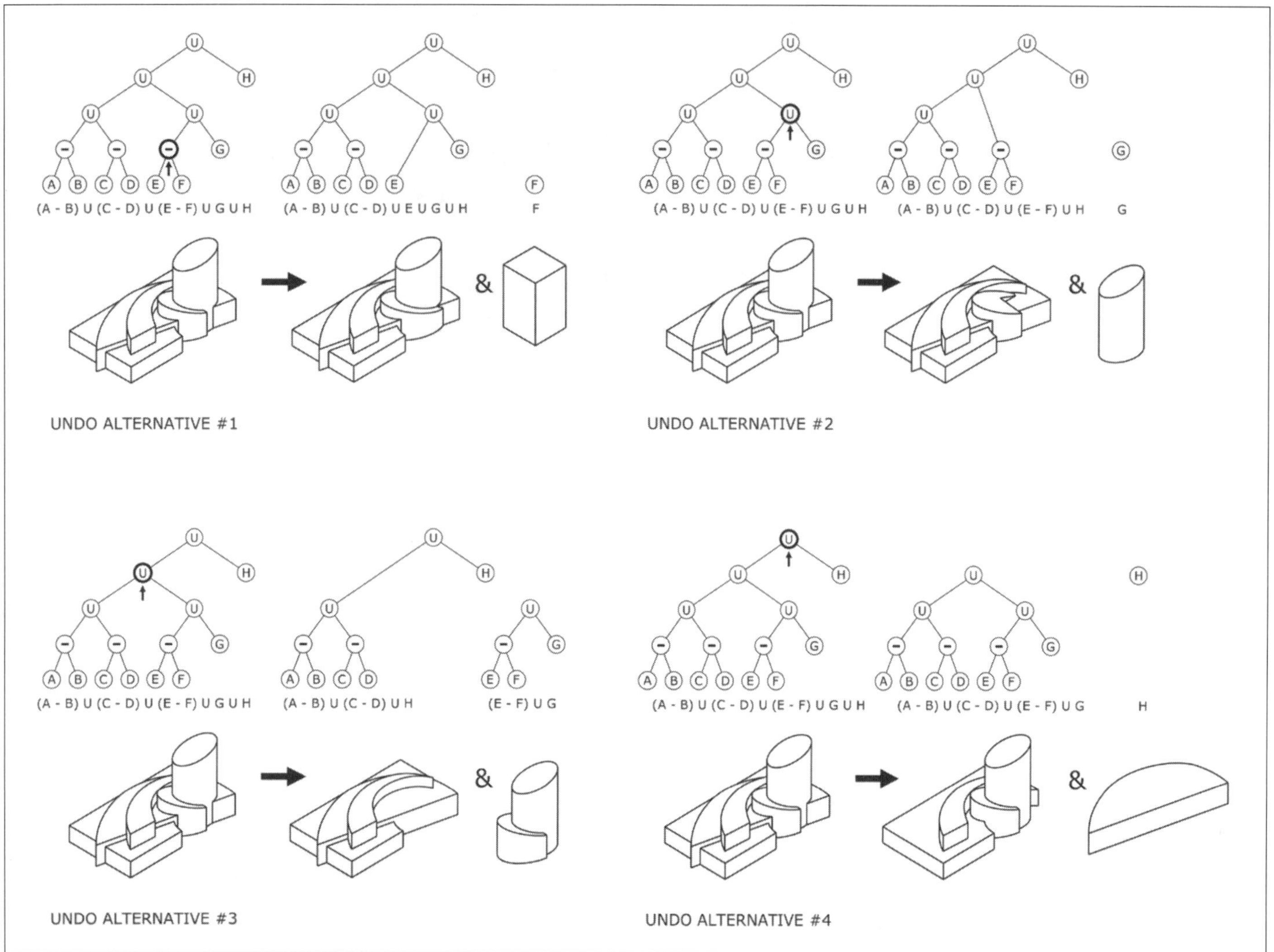

(Figure 6. Effect of deleting operators from a CSG representation of a building massing.)

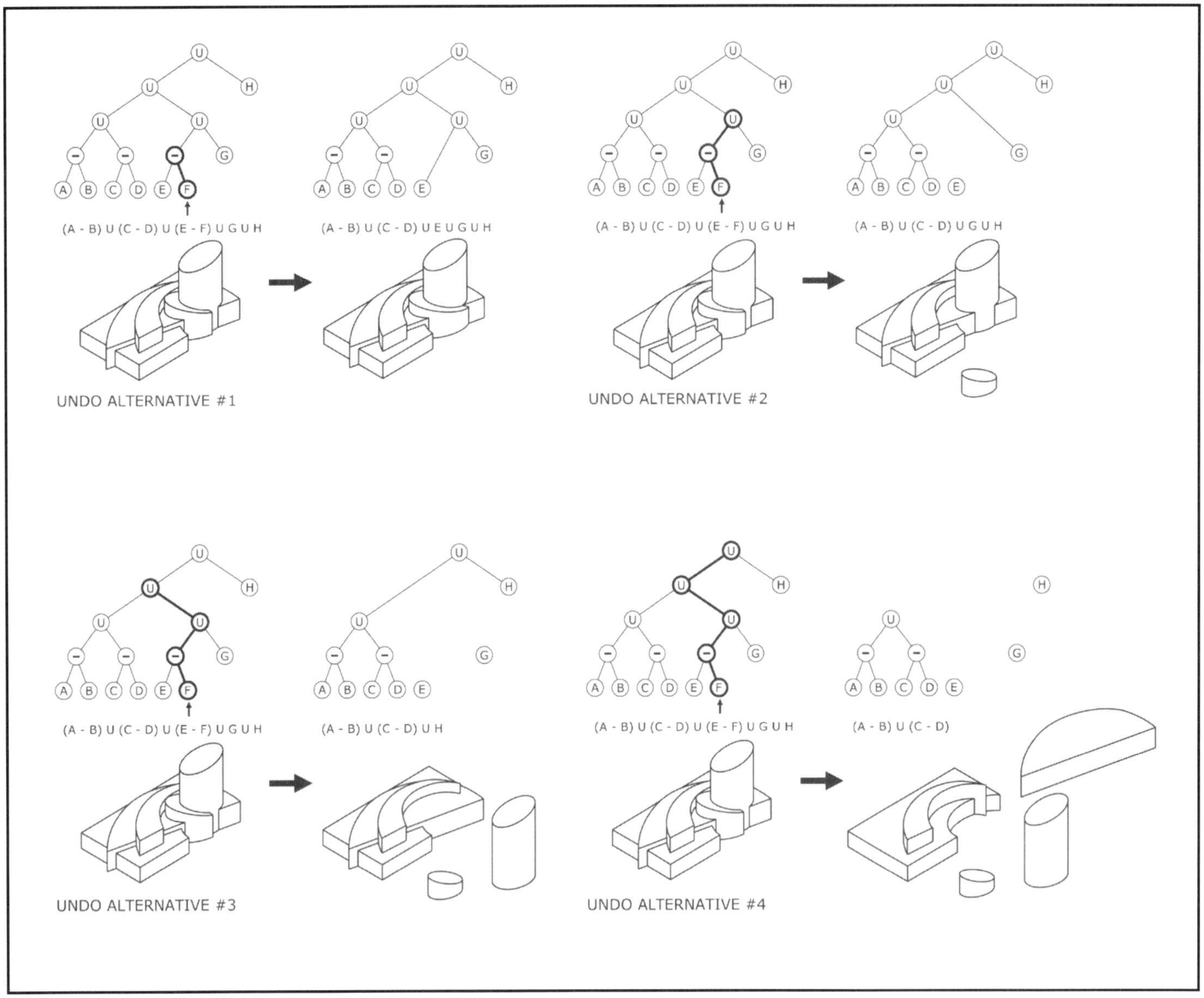

(Figure 7. Effect of deleting primitives from a CSG representation of a building massing.)

References

AutoCAD, Found on the WWW at *http://www.ids-cad-software.co.uk/arch_con_AutoCAD2000i.shtml* on 16 May 2003.

AutoCAD Xref, Found on the WWW at *http://www.laep.ced.berkeley.edu/classes/la132/htdocs/x_2002/x-10/ex10.html* on 16 May 2003.

Borning, A., and B. Freeman-Benson. (1998). Ultraviolet: A constraint satisfaction algorithm for interactive graphics. In *CONSTRAINTS: An international journal*, Special Issue on Constraints, Graphics, and Visualization 3(1): 9-32. New York: Kluwer Academic Publishers.

Berlage, T. (1994). A selective undo mechanism for graphical user interfaces based on command objects. *ACM transactions on computer-human interaction*, vol. 1(3):269-294. New York: ACM Press.

Carpenter, B. (1992). *The logic of typed feature structures*. Cambridge: The Cambridge University Press.

Form Z, Found on the WWW at http://www.autodessys.com/ on 16 May 2003.

Form Z Symbols, Found on the WWW at *http://www.mmhk.com/e/products/autodessys/symbols.htm* on 16 May 2003.

Gross, M. (1990). Relational modeling: A basis for computer-assisted design. In *The electronic design studio: architectural knowledge and media in the computer era*. CAAD Futures '89 Conference Proceedings, 123-136. Cambridge

Heisserman, J. (1994). Generative geometric design. *IEEE* 37-45. New York: The Institute of Electrical and Electronic Engineers.

Microsoft Excel 2002, Found on the WWW at http://www.microsoft.com/office/excel/default.asp on 16 May 2003.

Microsoft Word 2002, Found on the WWW at http://www.microsoft.com/office/word/default.asp on 16 May 2003.

MicroStation Reference File, Found on the WWW at http://selectservices.bentley.com/technotes/technotes/8235.htm on 16 May 2003.

MicroStation CustomObjects, Found on the WWW at http://www.bentleyuser.org/LarsWord/larsMar2003.htm on 16 May 2003.

Toria, H., T. Satoh, K. Ueda, and H. Chiyokura. (1986). UNDO and REDO operations for solid modeling. In *IEEE computer graphics and applications* 6:35-42. New York: The Institute of Electrical and Electronic Engineers.

Woodbury, R., A. Burrow, S. Datta, and T-W. Chang. (1999). Typed feature structures and design space exploration. In *Artificial intelligence for engineering design, analysis and manufacturing (AIEDAM) special issue on generative system in design* 13:287-302.

Woodbury, R., S. Datta, and A. Burrow. (2000). Erasure in design space exploration. *Artificial intelligence in design 2000*, 521-544. Worcester: Key Centre for Design Computing.

Process and Individuation: Designing for Controlled Indeterminacy

R. Shane Williamson
University of Toronto

Abstract

Through the presentation of the design of a memorial, this paper intends to introduce an iterative design process that incorporates particle-based animation, parametrically constrained operations, and a variety of rapid-prototyping techniques. This is a project rooted in the generation and interpretation of physical artifacts dependent upon both the generative potential of digital media and the subjective modifications associated with design authorship

It is stated in the brief for this ACADIA topic node that "the maturity of design, modeling, visualization, manufacturing and collaboration tools has allowed them to be naturally and comfortably integrated into the design process at all stages." As such, the design statement for this memorial makes no mention of the incorporation of digital media. Process is subordinate to its result. Simply, the victims' families would not find the range of technology incorporated in this design pertinent to the matter at hand: the design of a memorial to honor the victims of the attack on the Pentagon.

Within the context of this "Digital Design" topic node, though, it is my intention to expose the digital underpinnings of this project and position it within a discourse somewhere between *ars accidentalis* and the constraints of fully parametric and geometrically-associative design.

Process and Individuation: Designing for Controlled Indeterminacy

R. Shane Williamson
University of Toronto

1 Introduction

The animation industry has developed a set of tools for the simulation of life, which is effected by a mosaic of fluctuating external and invisible forces. Although architecture has been understood as static, fixed, ideal and inert, there is a shift going on from this determinism to directed indeterminacy through the incorporation of external constraints and environmental forces. Conventional architectural design software seems not suitable for the development of topological geometries that are capable of being changed and differentiated. For researching the possibilities of computer aided process and biological models of growth and transformation, architects should therefore rather discover the use of animation software (Lynn 1998).

Within Greg Lynn's discourse of animate form, the computer becomes a tool of indeterminacy. The abstract space of design is populated by virtual forces of deformation, with which the architect must join forces, to which he or she must yield in order to yield newness. The design process takes on certain autonomy, a life of its own (Massumi 1997). Perhaps this is not a question of authorship but rather a question of an author's role. The sophistication of digital animation is based upon a foundation of parameters and constraints. A perceived indeterminate process begins within a controlled set of actions. Design is instigation. Authorship is relegated to the initial establishment of control, or lack thereof, through programming. The generative potential of such a process is rooted in the creation of multiple artifacts, unique in form yet bound to a common set of instructions.
At one extreme, processes invested in animation and simulation emphasize the role of chance to the detriment of that of authorship. The introduction to the DEAF98 Catalogue boldly states that "a world that is open to continuous change and to becoming different, requires an *ars accidentalis*" and continues to say that "the creativity and the productivity of the accident, the break and the fall, have to be understood as the potential to achieve new forms of heterogeneity and of the disjunctive synthesis" (Brouwer 1998). The Art of the Accident accepts non-conclusive answers in defiance of deterministic formal agendas. Mark Burry has rebuked this "perverse giving-up of authorship" and argues that an "an object that has been designed reflects deliberate decision-making, not a serendipitous occurrence" (Burry 1999). He proposes parametric design through associative geometry as the "anathema to the accidental formalist." The logic of parametric design is pure formal determinism. It is deliberate and void of chance.

Perhaps a reference to the work of artists like John Cage would suffice as defense for chance-driven processes, but rather than validating or vilifying any particular design methodology, this paper intends to outline a specific process of individuation and interaction. It is a process that is purposefully open to chance and recognizes the importance of choice. It is not arbitrary, but it is subjective. It does recognize authorship, but it also recognizes process. Designing for controlled indeterminacy seeks to synthesize rather than polarize certain aspects of *ars accendentalis* and parametric design.

2 A Memorial to Honor the Victims of the Attack on the Pentagon

"One aspect of a nationwide bereaved community is the sense of being 'together' with millions of others in that expressions of mourning bypass or transcend the many ways in which people are divided . . ." (Linenthal 2003).

Figure 1. View of the collective memorial looking toward the Pentagon.

The attack on the Pentagon was unparalleled and is still so fresh in our minds that the event calls for a special way to hold in memory the lives lost. This memorial intends to address loss as both an individual experience and as a collective reality. To accomplish this, one hundred eighty four individual memorials totaling the number of victims of the attack will be dispersed

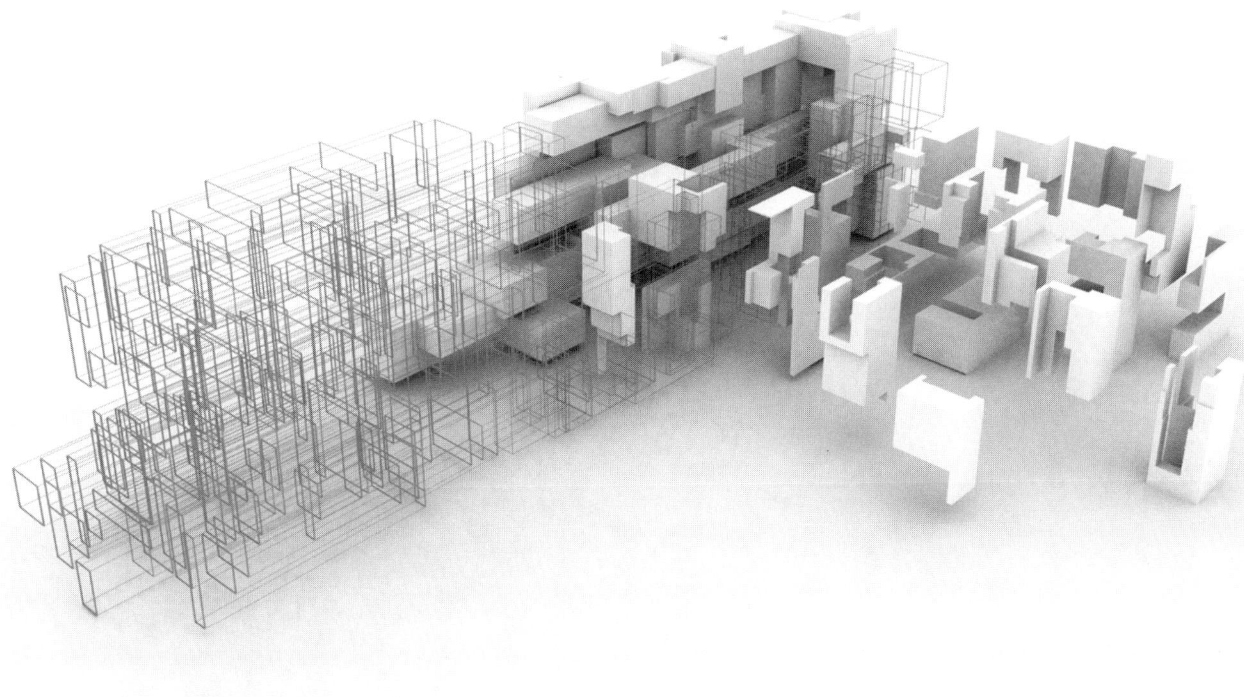

Figure 2. Conceptual Diagram showing the interaction of the individual memorials.

Figure 3. Conceptual sites for select memorials.

throughout the world and one collective memorial (Figure 4) will remain on the Pentagon site.

Recognizing that "loss is inseparable from what remains and that what is lost is known only by what remains of it "(Eng 2002), the collective memorial stands in contrast to the seamless renovation of the Pentagon in which the physical void created by the attack was filled within a year's time. Given that each void in the collective memorial stands in place of an absent individual memorial, a visitor is left with the indelible impression that the

Figure 4. Niches in the collective memorial serve as placeholders for mementos.

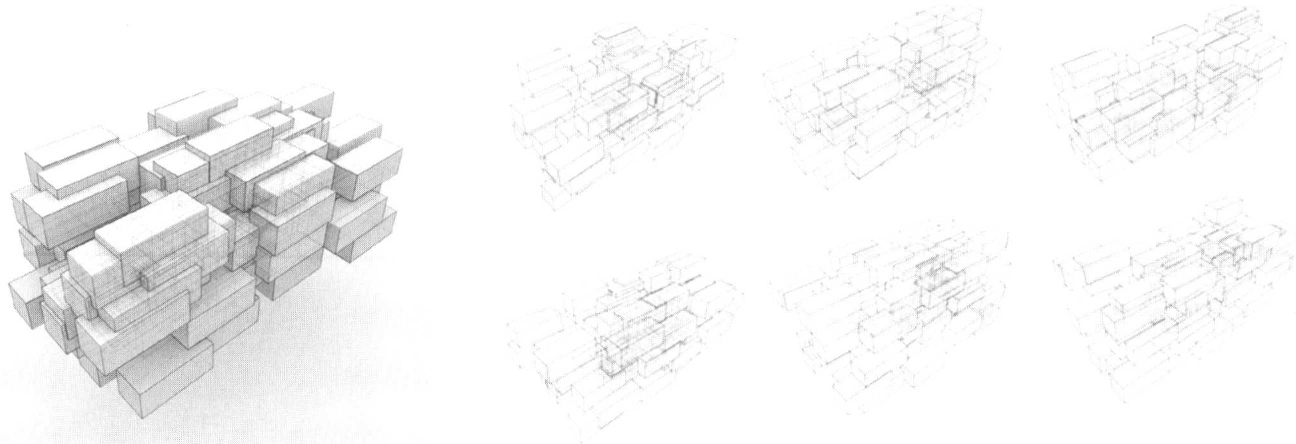

Figure 5. Particle-based simulations of the interaction of the individual memorials.

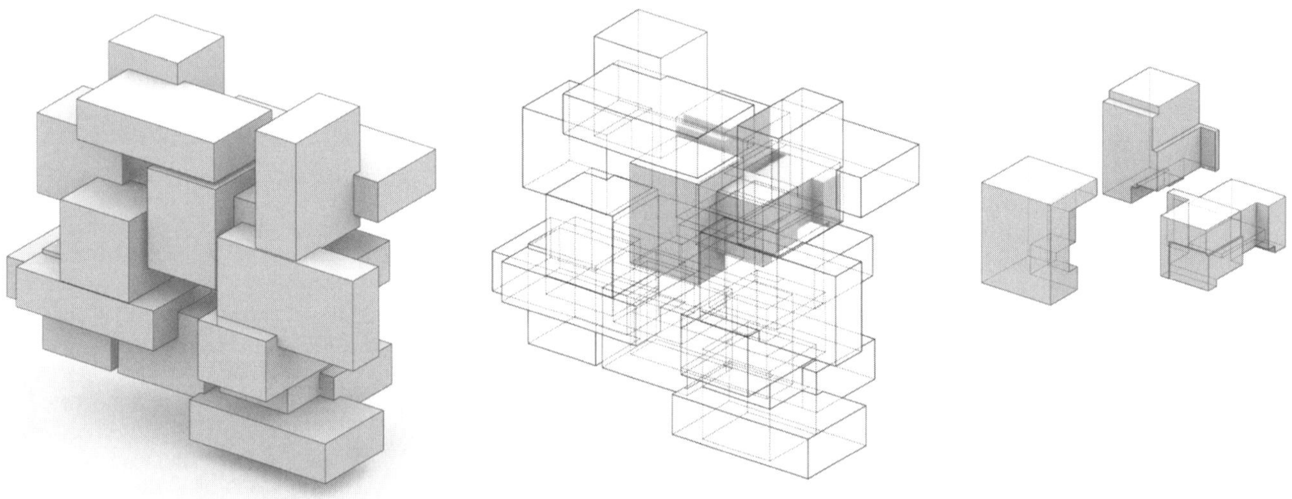

Figure 6. Diagram showing the varied orientation and size of the individual memorials and the resultant forms of three volumes following the subtractive process.

events of 9/11 reached far beyond the immediate site of the terrorist attack.

Physically the individual memorials represent the positive form of a subtraction from the collective memorial. They link together in complex ways, sharing volume as they overlap, making specific niches in the wall. The subtractive interaction (Figure 2) between them results in unique forms representative of the victim's individuality and of the inevitable convergence of personal loss experienced by the victim's friends and families. Each victim's family will be offered a unique piece, and we wish that each family will find a way of expressing the memory of their loved one. It is important to remember that there is no right or wrong way for the family to interpret this individual memorial. We imagine that some of the memorials will find a home within the intimate setting of a garden or yard while others will be located in more public contexts like town squares and urban centers (Figure 3). They can be inscribed with the family name, a favorite quote, or a meaningful image. They may be left anonymously in a field, by the shore, or in the woods. We cannot be prescriptive, but only inspired and taught by the many different ways that these memorials will be interpreted.

The niches and ledges (Figure 4) in the collective memorial are not only markers for the one hundred eighty four individuals, but places in which visitors can leave mementos honoring those who

Figure 7. One hundred eight-four unique memorials

died and marking empathy for the enormity of the event. The victim's families can find the place from which their individual memorial came and leave personal reflections. The existence of the voids within the collective memorial draws people to fill them with tokens of love and remembrance.

3 The Design Process

This project began with the intention of establishing random interactions between 184 discreet volumetric forms (i.e. the individual memorials).The interaction between these forms was driven by the parameters and constraints of a particle-based system (Figure 5). Initially, this system incorporated a simplified and uniform version of each memorial. By changing the algorithmic seed of the particle system, unique and random interactions were generated.

Within this animated particle system, each volume was scripted to subtract from other volumes upon intersection. The real-time nature of these Boolean operations allowed for a quick study of the potential resultant forms of the individual memorials when subjected to the interactive nature of the particle system. Later conceptual studies saw the variation of shape and orientation of the individual memorials, but the volume of each remained unchanged prior to any subtractions (Figure 6).

Certain rules were scripted into the interactions of the volumes. For example, each volume must intersect with at least two other volumes at all times. Also, Boolean operations were restricted

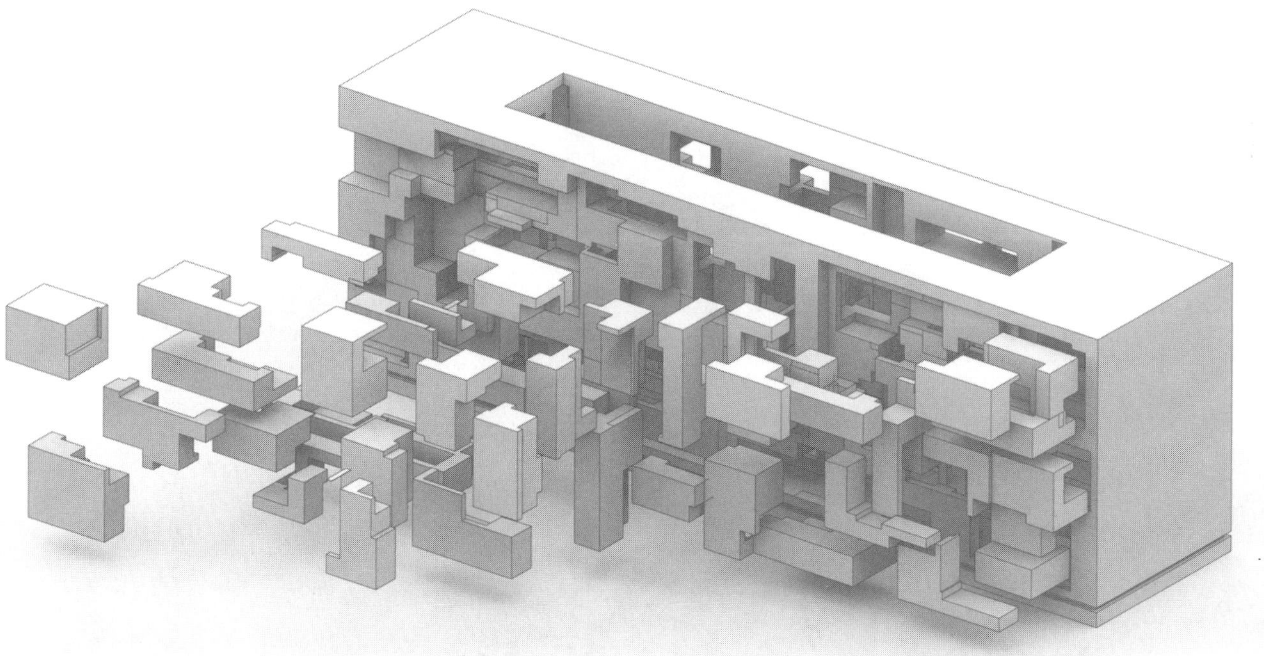

Figure 8. Diagram showing the subtractive relationship of the individual memorials and the collective memorial.

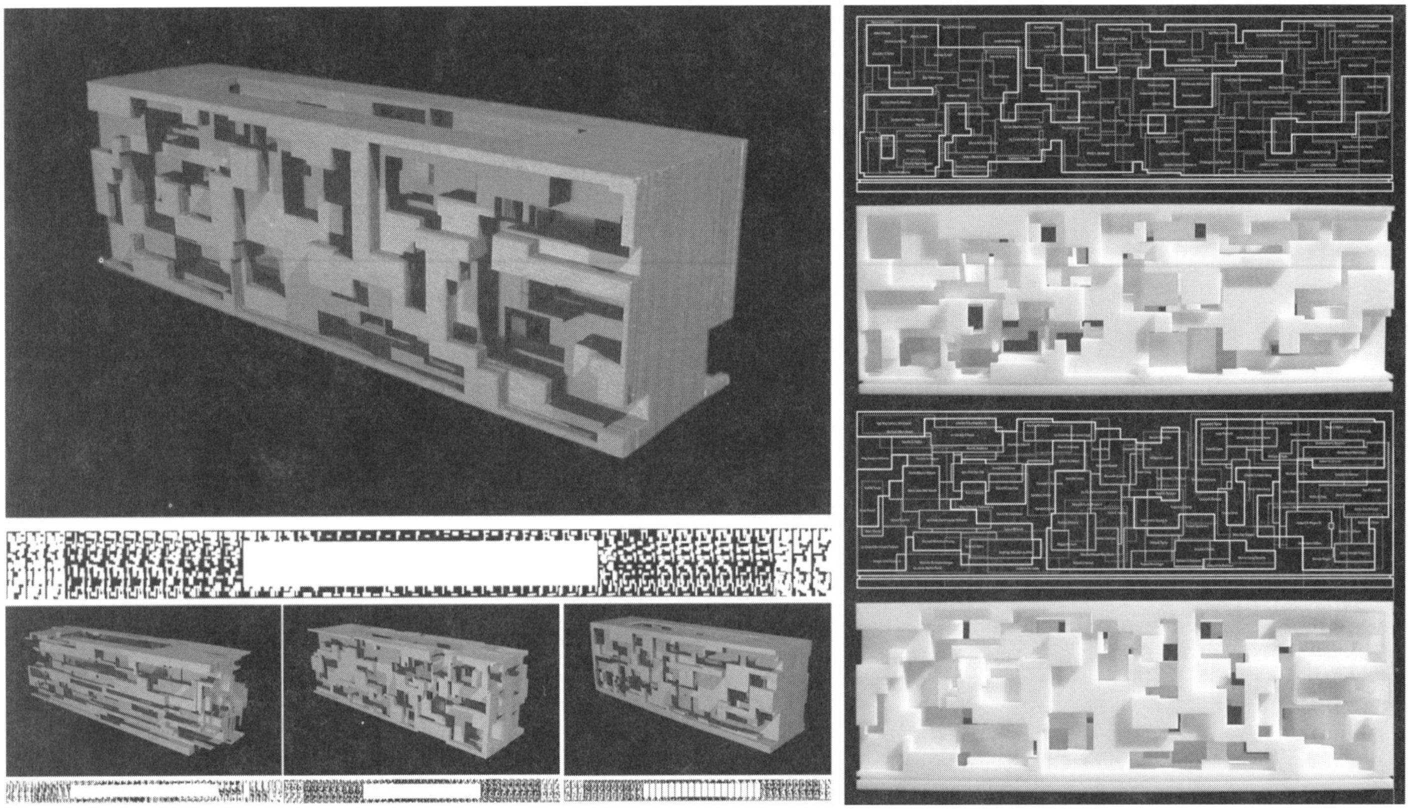

Figure 9. A few of the study models. Laser-cut (left) and FDM-based rapid-prototypes (right).

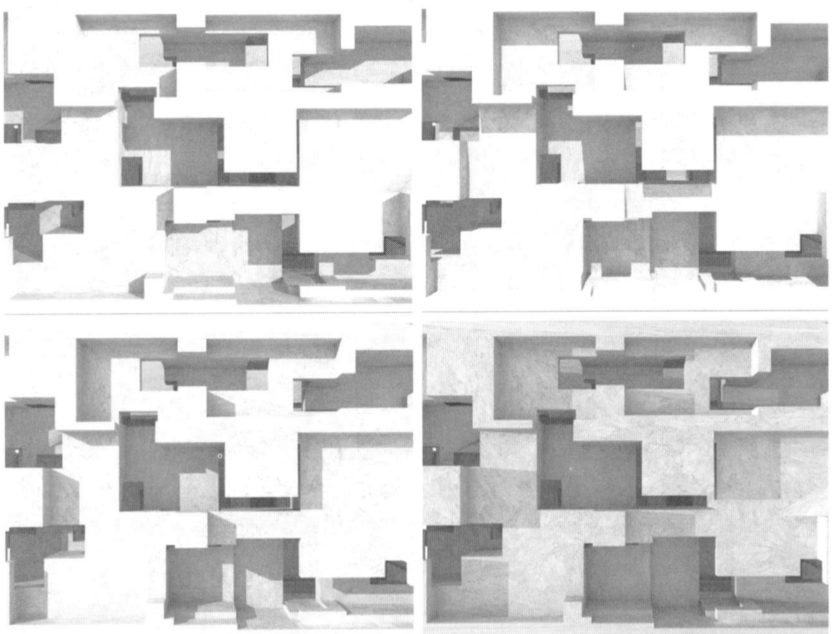

Figure 10. Lighting studies, morning to dusk (clockwise from the top-left)

Figure 11. The internal lighting of the collective memorial

to maximum depths within each volume in order to avoid the dissection of any particular volume. These rules became a primary organizational device for the positioning and hierarchy of the memorials and their respective subtractive operations. Although subtraction was a key element in the design process, it was equally important that an adequate amount of each memorial remain following each interaction. An initial volume of 25 cubic feet was set for each memorial. In conjunction with the aforementioned rules, this set volume allowed for the estimation of space required for the interaction of all 184 memorials (Figure 7).

The overall size of the larger collective memorial is driven by the cumulative volume of the massed individual memorials. The idea is that the collective memorial participates in the subtractive operations already established between the individual memorials. As each individual memorial subtracts from each other, it also subtracts from the collective memorial (Figure 8). A large singular subtraction within the collective memorial guarantees that all of the resultant voids will have an exposed niche or ledge no more than two feet from the outer surface of the memorial and provides a clearly defined interior which will be internally lit at night. The subtractions of the individual memorials occur along the

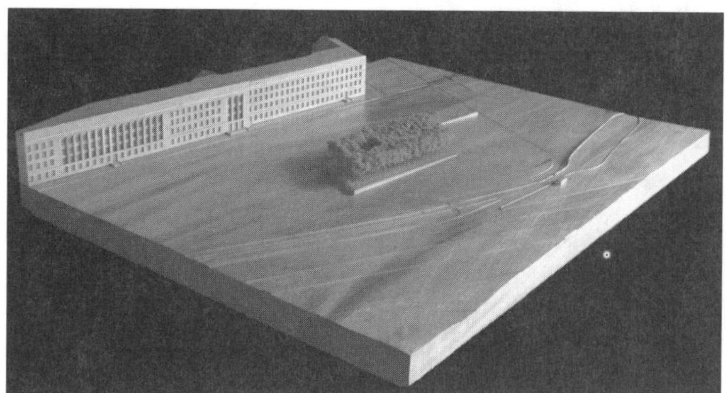

Figure 12. Site model

longitudinal faces of the collective memorial. The concentration of the individual subtractions along these faces became a new rule of interaction within the particle system. The individual volumes were not allowed to penetrate the full depth of either of the faces. This limitation guaranteed that no individual volume would be fully embedded within the larger volume; therefore, the record of each subtraction would be readily visible and accessible.

The second-stage of the competition permitted a more thorough examination of the resultant memorial forms. Throughout this stage many study models were generated (Figure 9). The 3D digital model of the collective memorial was sliced longitudinally and translated into 2D sectional profiles. The profiles were laser-cut to scale and assembled. It was at this stage that the form of the memorial was evaluated and altered by hand. The altered model was subsequently digitized and compared to the existing digital model. At this point, the rules of the particle system became subordinate to the alterations of the laser-cut model. Each change to this model required a manual change to the digital model. The particle system was *frozen* thus freeing the individual volumes to be moved accordingly.

Further subjective design decisions were made as rendered images of the digital models were composited into site photographs. Through the use of global illumination techniques, the memorial was studied under various lighting conditions (Figures 10,11). Again, the digital model was altered as necessary to reflect the desired changes respective of these lighting studies. In the latter stages of the design, several FDM-based rapid prototypes were created. Lacking the strong reading of striations found in the laser-cut models, the rapid-prototype models more closely reflected the monolithic intentions of the actual memorial. These models underwent the same process as that of the prior study models in which alterations were made and subsequently digitized.

4 Conclusion

The design of this memorial culminated with a synthesis of representation that included rapid prototyping for various scaled models, 3-axis milling for the site model (Figure 12), particle-based animation and parametrically constrained operations for the initial generation of form, and the study of light and shadow through image-based lighting techniques. It was a process of both chance and choice. The initial parameters set for the particle system were open-ended and the design was literally set into motion. Repeatedly, the animation was stopped for evaluation and change. Often change would come simply through the addition or alteration of parameters within the animated system. As physical models were made from the digital data, the design process became manual, in the sense that parametric changes could no longer accommodate subjective critical evaluations of the physical model. Physical alterations were digitized, and the digital model was modified accordingly. The maturity of technology permits the exchange of data between analogue and digital worlds. Clearly, a notion of *digital design* does not have to preclude iterative processes based upon normative analogue methods. The capabilities of rapid-prototyping provide tremendous opportunities relative to the physical production of artifacts that are no less abstract than their virtual counterparts. The oscillation between the digital and the analogue is the means by which critical subjectivity mitigates accidental occurrence.

Ars accidentalis and parametric design present a dialectic opposition. The issue is that of instigation and control, respectively, for the designer. *Ars accidentalis* positions the designer at the beginning of a process that otherwise runs an indeterminate course. Parametric design denies indeterminacy through the absolute control of the designer. It is in the vast middle ground between these oppositions, where the role of authorship assumes variable responsibility for instigation and control. The in-between constitutes an opportunity for chance, choice and perhaps the control of indeterminacy.

Project Credits
Design Team: Shane Williamson and Betsy Walker, design principals; Stephen Griffin, Ronen Bauer, Alex Horber and Steve Sestic, assistants.
Consultants: James Roche, site engineering, Dave Bowick, Blackwell Engineering, structural engineering and Gary Steffy, Gary Steffy Lighting Design, lighting design
Models: Peter McCann Architectural Models Inc., Jim Marshall and Simon Cooper, Two Degrees North and Magid Mikhail, Accurate Models and Prototypes Inc.
Contributors: Stratasys Inc.
Special Thanks: Brigitte Shim and Howard Sutcliffe, Betty Julian and Robert Wright

References

Brouwer, J., ed. (1998). Introduction of *The art of the accident*. Netherlands: NAI Publishers/V2_Organisatie Netherlands.

Burry, M. (1999). Paramorph: Anti-accident methodologies. In *Hypersurface Architecture 2*, ed. Stephen Perella, 78-83. New York: John Wiley and Sons Inc.

Lynn, G. (1998). Animate. In *The Art of the accident*. ed. Joke Brouwer, 159. Netherlands: NAI Publishers/V2_Organisatie Netherlands.

Massumi, B. (1997). Sensing the virtual, building the insensible. In *Hypersurface architecture*, ed. Stephen Perella, 16-25. New York: John Wiley and Sons Inc.

Eng, D. L., and D. Kazanjian, eds. (2002). Loss: The politics of mourning, 2. Berkeley: University of California Press.

Linenthal, D. (2003). The unfinished bombing: Oklahoma City in American memory, 111. Oxford: Oxford University Press.

The Parametric Bridge: Connecting Digital Design Techniques in Architecture And Engineering

Andrew Maher, Mark Burry
RMIT University

Abstract

New design opportunities that are facilitated by cross-disciplinary collaboration in both practice and research are available through the use of high level design software that simultaneously offers real time access to both analysis and design geometry in shared three-dimensional digital models. Here we present a collaborative research project between architects and structural engineers for the design of a pedestrian bridge, conceived to test current digital design processes in architectural and structural engineering practice with those in research through the use of models of parametrically defined associative geometry.

In this project, the digital model's architectural design geometry was constrained by the bridge's fabrication methods and linked with its engineering analysis. Iterations of the design geometry were then optimised or 'solved' to produce variations according to the design parameters offered up for change.

The shift of the professions from the plane to digital space exposes the possibilities of new design techniques with the exchange of design parameters potentially operating as a digital dialogue between the disciplines—a kind of digital version of Antoni Gaudi's funicular hanging model—a metaphor of the digital space that has been developed for this project.

The Parametric Bridge: Connecting Digital Design Techniques in Architecture And Engineering

Andrew Maher, Mark Burry
RMIT University

1 Introduction

This paper describes work undertaken for a parametric solution to an Arup bridge design. Concurrent with the design and construction of an actual bridge, the research was conceived as an attempt to test current design processes in architectural and engineering practice with those in research through the use of models of parametrically defined associative geometry. This approach sponsored a collaborative study across the disciplines of structural engineering and architecture through a system using a single digital model that shared geometrical constraints linked to its fabrication method, and material and loading analyses which could then be iteratively regenerated or optimised towards targeted solutions. The use of a single model significantly differentiates the research from other investigations into architect/engineer collaboration such as Klercker (2002).

Cross-disciplinary and *collaboration* are both widely used terms with an inferred interdependence, and both have positive as well as negative connotations. With ever increasing specialisation in design, much is to be gained from developing ways of broaching the traditional barriers of disciplines (Gann 2000). In distinguishing our research as collaborative we recognise that in fact it is more likely to be *co-operation,* the premise of the relationship between professionals, occurring across disciplines far more often and equally deserving in research (Kvan 2000). It is interesting to note though, that much research in cross-disciplinary thinking presupposes that the disciplines to be bridged are those already within a professional coterie. While this is in no way to be discouraged, there is much potential in drawing from outside sources. Our project used high-end software intended for the manufacturing and aerospace industries which necessitated a renewed approach to the design from both disciplines. This process of technological transfer facilitated a system of parallel and mutually dependant actions which were cross-disciplinary yet not essentially of either discipline.

In broadening the framework of the interaction entailed in this research project it has been helpful to review terms which approximate the activity in research from other fields. In interaction design "joint activity," a close-coupled interaction which is procedurally based might be useful in describing the "collaborative" result of our visual optimisation. While "mixed initiative," a responsive dialogue between human and machine, might better describe our 'cross-disciplinary' system, expanded in this project to interact discipline to discipline via machine. In that context the declarative process used to inform the parametric model is the common language local to the project, and the exchange of design parameters, the digital dialogue between the disciplines—a digital version of Antoni Gaudi's funicular hanging model, a metaphor for the digital space that has been developed in this project.

The research was undertaken in both Melbourne and London. The parametric model was developed in Melbourne, remotely from the project team and the periods of intensive collaboration were undertaken "on site" in London. This was partly due to the infancy of design spaces for online collaboration and partly due to its secondary role as a forerunner for an "embedded" research strategy where well equipped mobile post graduate students will spend part of their project based research collocated in practice, the other reflecting outside it.

1.1 Project description

The project is for the pedestrian bridge at the new Selfridges store in Birmingham UK. Future Systems are the architects. The bridge links the store with an adjoining carpark, over a busy road, which circumscribes the larger inner urban development known as the Bullring, in which the store is located (Figure 01).
The curved and seamless bridge is a difficult form to realise. Arup London Group Four was supplied with a digital model by the architects, and a fabrication method was sought through the tendering process. A revised model was then built which conformed to the selected fabricator's requirements. It was transformed into an analysable mesh by Arup's Advanced Technology Group and analysed in Arup's structural analysis package, a procedure taking one person working exclusively, three months to complete. While it could be expected subsequent iterations would not take as long, a considerable investment in time would still be required, and at a significant cost.

The aim of the research was to investigate the above process with a parametric model, so that in close to real time, iterations of the bridge could be generated thereby realising the design space that using explicit modelling would have been rendered opaque and unexplored. The project was undertaken with Arup London Group Four and facilitated by Arup Research and Development.

2 Parametric Design

The architectural historian Robin Evans noted the resistance of form to the architectural medium imposed upon it. He contrasted the rejection of perspective by modern painters with the adoption of standard orthographic projection in architecture and detailed near extinct traits such as stereotomy to illustrate the richness in translation through representation (Evans 1995). In this regard

Figure 01. The bridge in on site March 2003, without canopy.

the use of the computer to augment the description of form is well founded where that form resists conventional architectural description.

Three dimensional digital models in architecture are not yet well established beyond visualisation tools. Digital modelling, simultaneously and interactively, as an immersive editing process in practice is virtually unknown. Parametric design however, through the association of geometry, allows form to be controlled through the definition of parameters and application of constraints, which when manipulated can generate families of forms (Burry 1999). In proposing strategies for design structure in digital environments such high end software, developed for the aerospace and manufacturing industries, offers as many challenges as well as opportunities in its adoption to architectural design. In cost alone it is out of the reach of most architectural practices and being antithetical in approach to explicit "one off" modelling (Wittenoom 1999), it requires at the outset the development of an initial declarative schema, which then drives the design.

Research into applying parametric techniques to architecture has been led by Burry through the ongoing construction of The Sagrada Familia Church in Barcelona (Burry 1993). Here the process is informed through the research into the codex of ruled surfaces Gaudi developed during his final twelve years. Similarly the complex digital modelling undertaken by the architectural office of Gehry Partners LLP (Calf. USA) is determined through the primacy of the physical modelling methods used in the office. Glymph et al. (2002) show how Gehry Partners has used parametric design to describe freeform glass structures.

In our research a number of suites of parametric modelling software are utilised, and parametric techniques are often applied through programming. This project uses CATIA by Dassault Systemes, software developed originally for aerospace, but now used widely in the automotive industry. Parametric modelling in CATIA has been introduced in its current incarnation, version 5. In addition, CATIA offers a range of analysis methods and a set of tools for manipulating the information known as *Knowledgeware*, all exploited in this project.

2.1 Building the parametric model

The purpose of the parametric model for the bridge was to constrain its geometry to the fabrication methods selected for its construction. The bridge's underside or tray is steel, and the canopy is polycarbonate supported by steel hoops at varying angles from the deck which rises and falls gently to suit disabled access. The successful tender for the bridge was based on bending steel tubes (side tubes at the deck's edge and a main tube on the underside), in two directions to achieve the three dimensional curves that form the bridge's tray. The tubes were then to be cut down along their bi-tangent intersection and the sides infilled with steel plate. This method was preferred to another proposal which would have approximated the tray's surface to facets (Figures 02 and 03).

The hierarchical database of the parametric model was constructed by first interrogating the explicit model, supplied by Arup from Rhino NURBS modelling software, to gain an understanding of the geometry. Three guiding curves were extracted from the edges of the tubes in the original model and resided at the top of this database, so the parametrically variable tray could be varied to suit different tube sizes while maintaining the bi-tangency of the sides within the boundaries of its perimeter. The polycarbonate canopy followed suit, depending on the successful regeneration of the tray but also operating within its own fabrication constraints.

At any point along the tray an intersection made with the surface by a plane normal to the curve will be found to be circular in profile and of the same dimension as the ends, confirming the topology of a tube.

Bi-tangent lines between these tubes form the underlying structure of tray's sides. A ruled surface was placed between the tubes (Figure 04), which was then developed with little deformation. The benefit of describing a surface in this manner is that, materially dependant, the surface can be then cut out of a flat sheet and rolled or offered up to position. (Fully developable surfaces are those which can be unrolled onto a plane without deformation, a cylinder being one of the easiest to visualise.) The steel hoops share the same principle but at each instantiation are unique. In this case a parametric feature was designed to regenerate itself for the varying conditions each time it was repeated. The hoops vary at increasing angles along the bridge length and are made from steel flats laser cut and fabricated into T-sections (Figure 05). However, the T-sections are not perpendicular, as the flange is always parallel to the polycarbonate (providing an even surface for fixing) while the web is in the plane of the rotating axis.

The guide for the hoops was the polycarbonate top which was defined in a manner not dissimilar to the tray, although without any explicit geometry. The centre line of the deck was found about which a 2700mm radius tube was extruded. The bi-tangency was then found between the outside tubes of the tray and the tube to establish the surface. Intersections with this top guiding surface were made with the ability to move up and down the bridge and vary in angle.

2.2 Variations and comparison

The constraints were tested and variations made to compare the parametric tray with the original Arup model. With the guiding curves constraining the model's design space, the main tube could be varied between 500mm in diameter up to 1750mm in diameter. Variations were then rapid prototyped in wax and comparatively measured; proportions of tube to plate and dimensional variation from the original (Figure 06). In fact, during the project supply was the most important issue, with the final tube switching from 1050mm diameter to 900mm due to unavailability of the larger size.

The parametric model was developed in Melbourne, with a physical model reviewed in London. Communication during this period was mainly asynchronous, textual via email and often supported with explanatory images. Models, drawings and sketches of details were exchanged, but the overall volume of such material was minimal. In fact the process of distilling written information was found to be invaluable in founding the declarative process which in turn was used to define the parametric schema.

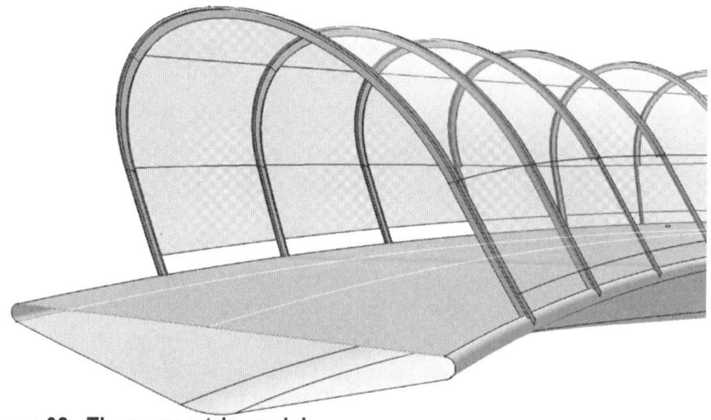

Figure 02. The parametric model.

Figure 03. Fabrication method. The bridge's tray in cross section showing tubes under construction. Photo: Ed Clarke (Arup)

3 Analysis

Speculation about the ability to leverage the finite element analysis and advanced meshing tools in CATIA for use in structural engineering led to an investigation of the single model concept, opening discipline-specific views to the parametric model. Finite element methods are computationally intensive and have only recently migrated to the desktop of engineers. In finite element analysis complex geometries are divided into small elements defined by geometric nodes that can be described mechanically by analytical equations. The equations are linked together in large matrices by the computer in order to describe the behaviour of the complete form. Used for many years in the aerospace industry, they are not commonly applied in structural engineering, as building structures tend to be broken down into two-dimensional planes where elements or sub assemblies can have the rules of statics applied. However, with more complex building forms finite element methods become a critical tool for locating critical stress concentrations.

3.1 Analysing the parametric bridge

In establishing a structural engineering view of the bridge's parametric model, our collaborative process began by passing a portable computer between engineer and architect, constructing a single digital space while sketching and writing ideas to convey each other's principles, toggling views of the model between analyses and geometry, and vice versa.

Arup's in-house structural analysis software is called GSA (General Structural Analysis), incidently an almost identical acronym to CATIA's (Generative Structural Analysis). For this purpose the paper refers to 'Arup GSA' and 'CATIA GSA' so as to distinguish between the two. Comparative results using finite element meshing and analysis require different methods to conventional structural engineering analysis. A one-dimensional beam (stick meshing), two-dimensional surface mesh, and three-dimensional volumetric mesh were used to first corroborate the results between both Arup GSA and CATIA GSA.

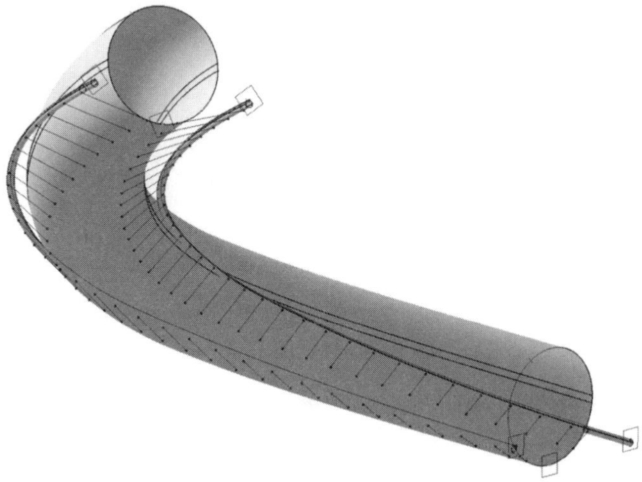

Figure 04. Bi-tangent lines between main and side tubes.

Figure 05. Variations from the same parametric parent.Developed T-Section flanges of the hoops.

For the purposes of the research, the tray and deck of the bridge were determined to be an acceptable approximation of the form for the structural analysis. The bridge's cable restraints were later added. A two-dimensional surface mesh was generated on the parametric model and a finite element analysis performed to determine the bridge's displacement and stress. Through the discipline specific view of the structural engineer, this operation involved the addition to the project of local axes and restraints at the ends of the bridge, linear loads, and the application of material qualities including thickness (Figure 07). A routine of meshing the parametric model and computing the result of the analysis in CATIA GSA then followed any modification of the bridge's design geometry.

3.2 Variations of the parametric bridge

Through the Product Engineering Optimiser, a *Knowledgeware* function in CATIA, parameters can be optimised to a target value, be it minimum, maximum, or given. Free parameters are then offered for variation and steps and ranges can be set. Two algorithms are used by CATIA, a localised Gradient "hill climbing" method or Simulated Annealing, which adds in some randomness to offer the potential to "jump" the hills and further explore a design.

Consideration was given at this point to the flexibility of the design space. The parametric model had been limited by the design curves, which were explicit and therefore without parametric variability. As already shown, iterating through the free parameters in the geometric model which were related to tube sizes had already mapped the potential variation. In seeking to extend the perimeters of the form and increase the parameters which affected it, the parametric model was rebuilt so the guiding curve for the main tube, the underside of the bridge, was defined by a combined curve (the result of the intersection of the extrusion of two curves). This process was also informed through reviewing the strategy with the architects. A vertical parameter controlled the depth of the bridge and when added with a horizontal parameter, the combined curve freed up the position of the model in space. This operation required carefully re-editing the parametric database to replace the explicit curve with a parametric curve. This was time consuming and is at the limits of redefining hierarchical parametric geometry.

Several scenarios were then designed for optimisation (Figures 08 to 10). Every iteration during optimisation requires the consistency of the model's database. In the bridge's case, this means adhering to its fabrication constraints. Each model outputted could therefore be identified as a tube deformed in two directions with bi-tangential sides of ruled surfaces. The values of each parameter used in the optimisation routine are recorded at each change in a spreadsheet (Table 1. provides an example), and the figuration at each iteration interpreted at a later stage. By simply resetting the parameter's values states can be selectively revisited if so desired.

The displacement analysis results generated from CATIA GSA were used as targets for the following constraint solving optimisation procedures using the engineering analysis to visually optimise the form. The process then, to understand the scope of what might influence a model's geometry and its potential design space, becomes increasingly important in a collaborative sense to all those taking part in the mediation of the artefact.

4 Collaboration

Today, the potential of finite element methods recalls an earlier enthusiasm for the graphic methods of statics, an engineering

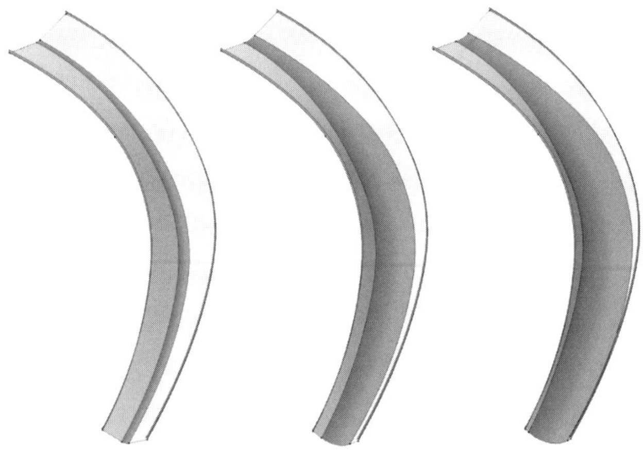

**Figure 06. Parametric comparisons.
L-R. 500mm, 1500mm, 1750mm radius main tube**

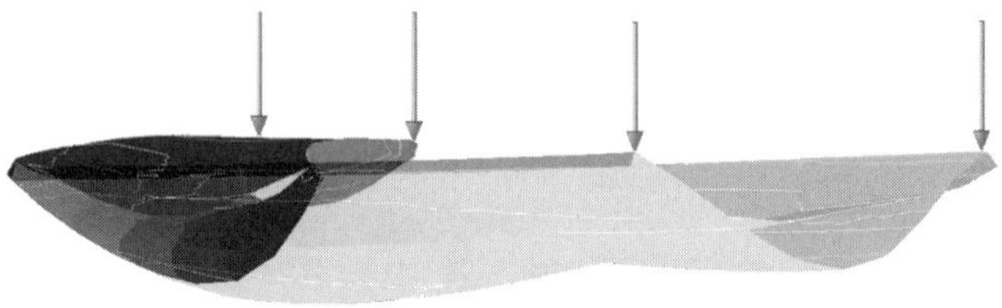

Figure 07. An analysis view of the bridge. Steps taken from a stress animation.

practice developed late in the 19th century. Structural analysis through graphic statics allowed the exploration of forms not easily analysed before its introduction. The funicular hanging models Antoni Gaudi used to arrive at his unique solutions were in fact three-dimensional graphic analyses. He first employed them on the Colonia Guell church (1898, 1908 - 1914), where a scaled model was hung in a workshop creating a dialogue between his assistants who would, upon instruction, shift the bags of lead about to vary the shape, which would then be photographed, turned upside down, and rendered to give effect to the form. This unique process was done with both the interior and exterior of the church (Figures 11 and 12). Not only did this funicular model provide a method of communication between Gaudi and his assistants, but as a structural analysis tool it also provided a forum for cross-disciplinary collaboration.

Proximity and face to face contact, it would seem, are still essential to seed collaborative processes. Two key meetings were held for this project when the authors were in London, one at its inception and one for review. These were followed by periods of research and reflection in Melbourne. Then a final intensive session of collaborative work on the single model was undertaken while collocated at Arup in London.

In our research project, we found that synchronous technologies, which generally mimic conventional communication, such as web chatting, internet meetings, and video links at best augment the design process. These essentially serve to perpetuate connectedness, and in doing so reinforce the absence of communication tools that support the heterogeneity of complex processes that inform the act designing.

Collaborating on a single digital model between two separate disciplines demands more than document workflow facilitation. A bi-directional flow of information not normally associated with communication between the disciplines is required. Our team extended beyond architects and engineers; in this project mathematicians and fabricators were also authoritative. A design structure which can be influenced by structural analysis and optimised to target a visual solution adopts and borrows techniques from both disciplines, and yet cannot be expected to be of either discipline. This certainly has implications for the adoption of traditional methods of communication when collaborating.

4.1 Extending the process

The research drawn from this project could be extended in two directions. Firstly, to what extent can the process be adopted to delimit the boundaries of a design space at the conceptual stage? Although the case for parametric design is well founded at a detailed design stage, how might this collaborative process be applied when dealing with the incomplete knowledge inherent at the beginning of a design project? Conceptual analysis tools such as the Evolutionary Structural Optimisation method (Xie 1997) might be useful in establishing a cross-disciplinary dialogue.

Secondly, automation techniques in fabrication could be investigated when linked to parametric databases. How might the intersections of bi-tangency be inscribed onto a tube or could the hoops be constrained to minimize wastage based on efficient cutting patterns?

5 Conclusion

Through the sponsorship of the parametric bridge project we have been able to explore the potential of a digital design model offering cross-disciplinary collaboration between architects and engineers. While parametric modelling might at first be regarded as another specialisation, here we have shown an approach or technique for possibly understanding equally well architecture and structural engineering.

This work involved considerable technology transfer, adopting methods from outside the fields of architecture and engineering, and challenging established techniques in each discipline. As the outcome of the research could be considered greater than the input of each contributor, it could be said to be a truly collaborative process.

Iteration	Maximum Displacement (mm)	Cable Restraint Location (mm)	Tube Vertical Location (mm)	Tube Horizontal Location (mm)
	23.4008	12798	1484.59	5745.23
	23.4008	14385.8	1466.18	5739.07
	23.4008	13228.7	1538.32	5787.56
	23.4008	12449.3	1441.57	5775.39
	23.4008	11784.1	1507.41	5824.81
	23.4008	12797.7	1484.57	5745.18
	23.4008	12141	1545.82	5645.9
	23.4008	10935.1	1515.71	5744.4
	23.4008	12797.7	1484.57	5745.01
	24.1539	13318.8	1482.65	5761.29
	24.1539	12567.7	1439.34	5741.03

Table 1: Example of changing parametric values during optimisation.

Scenarios with three or four free parameters were run for approximately seven hours at a time—not yet a real-time process, but indicative of the processing power required. The location of the bridge's restraining cable was iterated along the length of the deck, and the curve of the main tube was freed horizontally and vertically.

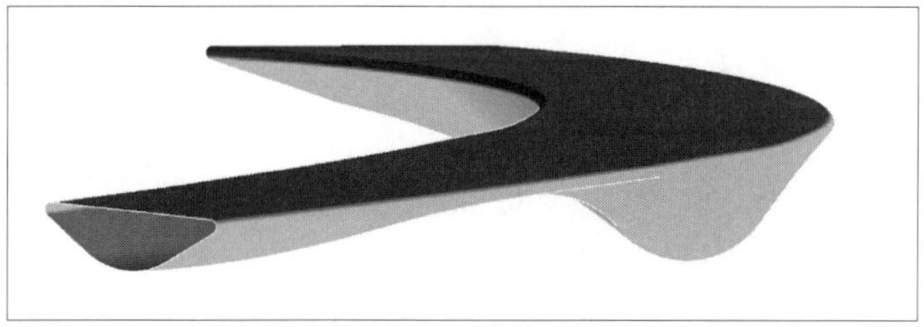

Figure 09. Vertical optimisation (Curve Depth) Geometrical view of the model.

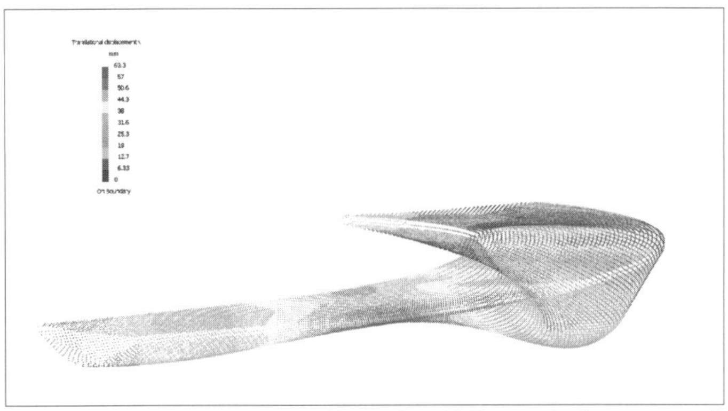

Figure 08. Vertical optimisation (Curve Depth) The vertical parameter of the tube's position optimised to minimise displacement. This generated a distinctly different shape, thinning at one end then swallowing to a much deeper point than the original point. Analysis view of the model.

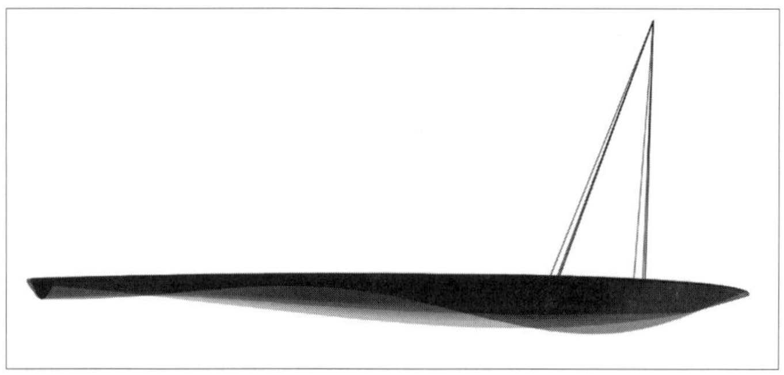

Figure 10. Combined bridge forms. Several iterations of optimised trays overlaid.

Figure 11. Gaudi's hanging model.

Figure 12. Inverted photographs used to render forms.

References

Burry, M. (1993). *Expiatory church of the sagrada familia*. London: Phaidon Press.

Burry, M. (1999). Paramorph: Anti-accident methodologies. In *Hypersurface architecture II*, edited by S. Perella. Chichester: Wiley.

Evans, R. (1995). *The projective cast: architecture and its three geometries*. Cambridge, Mass: MIT Press.

Gann, D. M., and A. J. Salter. (2000). Innovation in project-based, service-enhanced firms: the construction of complex products and systems. *Research Policy* 29(7-8): 955-972.

Glymph, J., D. Shelden, C. Ceccato, J. Mussel, and H. Schober. (2002). A parametric strategy for freeform glass structures using quadrilateral planar facets. In *The space between the physical and the virtual*, 303-321. Pomona (USA): The Association for Computer Aided Design In Architecture.

Klercker, J. (2002). Architect and structural engineer in interactive design. In *Connecting the real and the virtual*, 386-389.

Warsaw (Poland): Education and research in Computer Aided Architectural Design in Europe.

Kvan, T. (2000). Collaborative design: what is it? *Automation in construction* 9 (4):409-415.

Wittenoom, R. (1999). Automating realisation of integrated project models. *Automation in construction* 8(3): 249-267.

Xie, Y. M., and G. P. Steven. (1997). *Evolutionary structural optimization*. New York: Springer-Verlag.

Acknowledgements

The authors would like to thank Arup for this research opportunity and are grateful to the many people at Arup who have supported this research, contributing their time, expertise and knowledge.

Research Team

RMIT University's Spatial Information Architecture Laboratory: Professor Mark Burry and Andrew Maher

Arup: Jan-Peter Koppitz and Ed Clark (LG4), Alvise Simondetti and Dr. Kristina Shea (R&D)

Future Systems are the architects for the new Selfridges store in Birmingham

VIRTUreALITY Digital Urban Modelling as a Community Design Form*

Adrian Dobson, Peter Lancaric
University of Luton

Abstract

This paper describes a practice-led research project that investigates the application of digital modelling and communication technologies in urban and architectural design. The project is being carried out by our team with the collaboration of the architecture and planning departments at local borough council and local community participation. The main methodology for the project revolves around the evolution of an interactive three-dimensional digital urban model, which incorporates a variety of visual, graphic and numeric data. This digital model is utilised within a web site to help facilitate a participatory approach to the physical and social regeneration of an inner urban zone, in terms of both the built environment and the attempted creation of a virtual community.

*A Digital Work In Progress

VIRTUreALITY
Digital Urban Modelling as a Community Design Form

Adrian Dobson, Peter Lancaric
University of Luton

1 Context

The focus of this digitally mediated urban design project is the Plaiters Lea Conservation Area in Luton. Luton with its population of about 180,000 is a middle-size post-industrial satellite town of London. In terms of the national context, Luton benefits from its central location and function as an important transport node. Luton will continue to be a major employment centre in the south east of England. As the town has limited space for expansion, the planning priority is to enhance the quality and density of the existing urban environment, through sustainable economic development and regeneration. Luton has a major international airport, but unfortunately many of the airport users do not visit the town itself. This is not only due to the peripheral location of the airport, but also the apparent lack of any specific attractions in the town. This represents a missed economic opportunity. The town has a vibrant multi-cultural community, but suffers from a negative image in its more affluent hinterland.

2 Plaiters Lea Conservation Area

Plaiters Lea is an economically and socially marginalized inner urban area, with a transient residential population and a mixture of light industrial, commercial, retail and housing premises. Historically the area was the centre of Luton's hat making industry. The area developed as an industrial zone in the Victorian period, after construction of the Midland railway, being strategically positioned between the railway station and town centre. Plaiters Lea was designated as a Conservation Area in 1991. Many Victorian and early twentieth century buildings of high quality remain, but there are also many vacant sites and dilapidated premises. The existing buildings are mainly examples of the hat factories, which formed the original industrial activity of the Area; buildings of unique functional purpose and form. Post-war re-development, including the Arndale shopping centre, resulted in physical isolation of the area, which is bounded by railway lines, the bus station and the heavy mass of the central shopping mall. Nevertheless, the area is a key gateway to the town.

Today the area provides for a diversity of functions and populations. Entertainment facilities, accommodation for asylum seekers, student housing, hotels and light industries co-exist within Plaiters Lea. The physical regeneration and social enhancement of the area are the focus of this project. The aim of our urban proposal is to enhance and revitalise the Plaiters Lea Area, which, in spite of its significant location within the town's urban structure and history, has been neglected in the second half of the twentieth century. The intention of the interventions is to support small-scale commercial activities, to increase residential accommodation, to encourage greater leisure activity by day and night, and to strengthen the urban identity experienced by pedestrians. Apart from the potential of the existing built forms for redevelopment and adjustment to contemporary and future needs, there are several vacant sites suitable for new development. This is to be achieved through incremental, socially responsive development, rather than the large-scale urban re-development characteristic of post second world war re-construction. As society evolves and social taboos disappear under the influence of the media and cultural change, urban environments need to adapt to new realities. In terms of sustainability we need to consider the future social tendencies. The impact of economic liberalisation, loosening of social taboos, and increases in personal wealth are forming a new sociological context that is key to new urban development. The project recognises this by operating at the interface between urban policy, urban design and community debate.

3 Strategy

Plaiters Lea is a conservation area and contains several listed historic buildings. Therefore the new architectural inputs are considerably limited in their volumes and masses. Our strategy is to approach each vacant site individually as a fragment of urban structure, then to combine them into a mosaic of the whole. Each one reflects and represents a certain element of society present within the Plaiters Lea Area, and contributes to the specific identity of the place.

The proposal (Figure 1) will demonstrate unconventional approaches to new design interventions in historic areas. Though respecting all relevant conservation regulations, it will present a notion of how such an environment should reflect future economic demands and sociological trends.

As the architectural forms are more or less defined, the intention is to emphasize the new buildings by means of application of textures, fabrics and structures of surfaces. The proposals being developed include elements of architectural and urban design, landscape design and public art. Essentially, we are proposing and designing external walls rather than buildings – the surfaces, envelopes of the buildings. The buildings are being perceived by pedestrians as surfaces in a street elevation, and it is an issue of dealing with an environment experienced in this way. Could all the vacant spaces be built up to complete the urban form, or would this create inconvenient obstacles in the existing living environment? Can new urban surfaces appropriately supplement gaps without interfering with the mass structure?

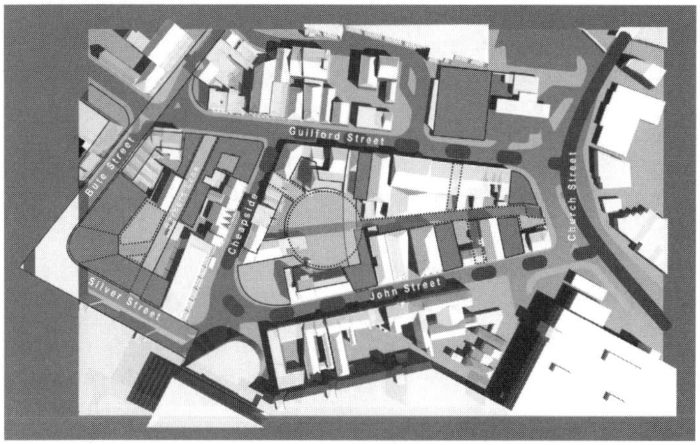

Figure 1. Urban Design Framework

The overlapping of urban and architectural design aspects and fine art is significant for this project. Analysing existing surfaces, proposed uses of new buildings, character and identity of the Area informs the development of new patterns of streets and squares. Texture in architecture begins in detail of a material surface, continues in the combination of different materials or repetition of elements, and then develops into a texture of the street frontage within the context of the urban structure. The new buildings are partly determined by the Area's character. Through applying various textures within an existing urban pattern we emphasise the new buildings and improve the Area's originality and attractiveness. Applied textures will be digitally generated from the visual elements taken from the Area. Usage of materials, colours and light enables variation in the appearance of the buildings and streets at various times of day and night.

Figure 2. The Interactive 3D Urban Model

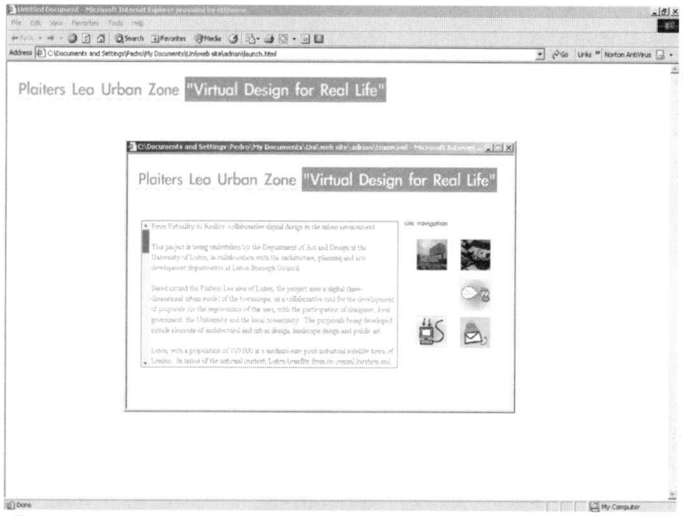

Figure 3. The web site home page

4 Methodology

The main methodology for the project revolves around the evolution of the interactive three-dimensional digital urban model (Figure 2), and the construction of the web site structure that enables the model to be used as a collaborative tool, which incorporates a variety of visual, text and numeric data (Figure 3). The location of the model within a website means that the various stakeholders can access it at any time through simple personal computing technologies.

Research by the Centre for Advanced Spatial Analysis at University College, London, in 2002, identified over 60 different digital models of urban centres throughout the world, demonstrating widespread international interest (Centre for Advanced Spatial Analysis 2002). The Architecture and Building Aids Computer Unit at the University of Strathclyde produced one of the first digital urban models in the UK, to illustrate development opportunities in the Edinburgh Old Town (Grant and Paterson 1994). In their article "Living with a Virtual City," Alan Day, Vassilis Bourdakis and Joe Robson, of the Centre for Advanced Studies in Architecture at the University of Bath, provide an analysis of the construction and application of digital urban models (Day, Bourdakis and Robson 1996). In addition to digital urban modelling techniques, the principles of virtual design studios have also informed this project. Researchers at the University of Sydney's Key Centre for Design Computing and Cognition have carried out extensive investigation of the virtual design studio concept, in which computer-aided design and internet communication technologies are used to support collaborative design (Simoff and Maher 2000). At our university, we have been working with colleagues at the university in Slovakia on virtual design studios that enable undergraduate students at the two institutions to collaborate on design projects. These earlier projects have utilised web site, email, videoconference and related technologies, and these experiences have been formative in the development of the methodology applied to the Plaiters Lea project.

The digital model produced for this project allows us to present the Area in various contexts and circumstances, to virtually simulate proposed schemes in the existing urban structure. Digital technology gives us an opportunity to combine unreal, i.e. virtual, with real. This leads to a situation where a non-built environment can be experienced as if it existed. As well as the simulation of the proposed urban scheme we are creating functional virtual space. In such cyberspace originates a new community with new means of communication. Virtual form can respond to change flexibly, but in our case we are still limited by the existing environment that we supplement. However, creativity and imagination are less limited by structural realities.

The web site is divided into two main sections: "Plaiters Lea Today" and "Plaiters Lea Tomorrow." The "Today" section provides text and visual information both on the area and the

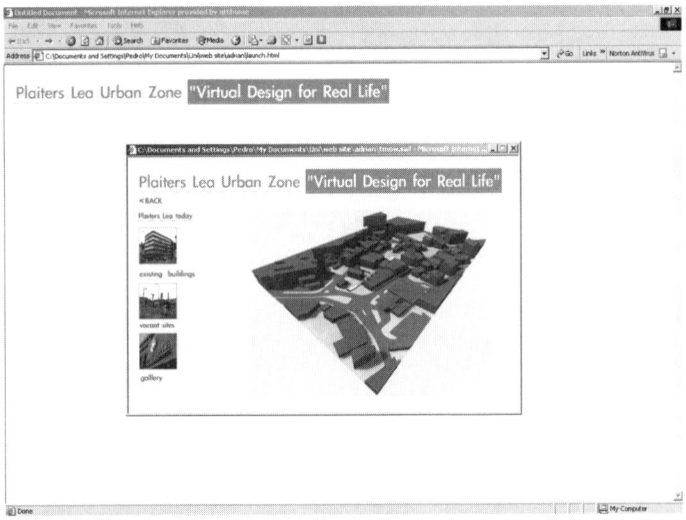

Figure 4. "Today" section of the web site

individual buildings (Figure 4). There is also an urban design framework to explain the urban design intentions.
A three-dimensional model of the existing urban environment is also available. Several shots in the "Photo Gallery" introduce the character and atmosphere of the Area.

The urban design framework is further developed in the "Tomorrow" section, where a general brief and detailed individual briefs for seven key vacant sites are provided. The briefs include textual guidance, general planning diagrams and rough massing studies (Figure 5). This section also contains the interactive three-dimensional model with a walkthrough mode. Within the browser environment visitors can watch the pre-set flythrough sequence, switch between seven proposed buildings and see them in their spatial context, or manually manipulate the camera to move through the model. Communication and collaboration are facilitated through email, discussion board, downloadable site models and design submission functions.

Such a medium has broad applications. First, we can see it being applied in a real context. Luton Borough Council wishes to prioritise the Area's enhancement. Our product can inform about

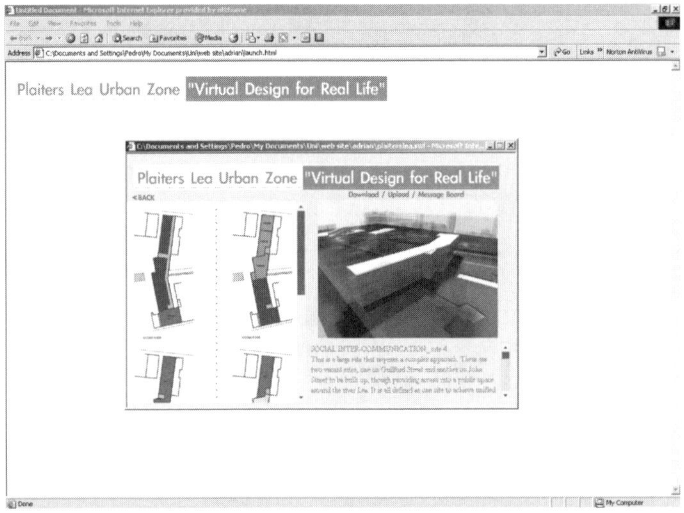

Figure 5. A site brief for one of the vacant sites.

future design intentions, provide the briefs for developers and architects interested in working on participatory projects, and give an opportunity for communication between the council, designers and public. Designers commissioned to work on a particular site can download all the necessary surveys and site information, as well as submit their proposals electronically. The submitted proposals can be presented for public comment. The Area's inhabitants have the opportunity to take greater control of proposed developments, and are given space to make remarks and express their opinions. In a similar way, such a principle can be applied in architectural competitions. Secondly, such a medium can be applied in architectural education, in particular for distance learning modes. Students can get to know the area, download the briefs for their assignments, communicate with their tutors, and submit their work to be presented within the web site. Thirdly, there is a potential purely virtual application. Here the real urban environment would be presented in a virtual way. On-line visitors could explore an area that exists for real from their homes. Via accessing the provided information they could become familiar with the existing buildings and functions. Additionally, there would be virtual buildings proposed for the vacant sites. In this case, the Area would have two kinds of inhabitants and visitors—real and virtual. It is a challenge to enable an interaction of these two communities. Optionally, by giving more solutions for each site, each virtual visitor could create their own environment. Naturally, the medium would have to be adjusted and tailored for a particular use, but also it could be applied for several purposes simultaneously.

Current technology makes it possible to visit a place without actually being present there. This is a stage where real and virtual overlap. The new proposed buildings do not necessarily need to be built in order to be visited and used. It is a creation of a virtual architecture based on real physical urban form. Does the architectural scheme need to be built to become a 'building'? In a virtual world we can go anywhere without leaving our desk or sofa. Geographical location loses its importance when we create a virtual space accessible from a computer located anywhere. The uses we propose for the vacant sites and existing buildings are inspired by the activities that can be also carried out in a virtual world, places of social interaction—library, gallery, workshops, playrooms, entertainment facilities, etc.

5 Conclusion

Computer-Aided Design and Digital Graphic Design are used not only to support the design, but also to present technology as a means of design and interpretation. The creative process will be illustrated in various stages.

The intention is to encourage a multiplicity of conversations about the future of Plaiters Lea. The urban design strategy utilises incremental development, working with the scale and grain of the townscape.

The completed interactive three-dimensional digital model and urban design framework have been incorporated within a prototype web site. The effectiveness of the browser environment for communication and collaboration is being tested through its use in an undergraduate design studio. The students are able to engage with digital technologies, and to contextualise their work within a social, political and economic reality; virtual design for real life. Initial experiences indicate that the ability to interact with the three-dimensional model within the browser environment enhances the accessibility of the project.

References

Centre for Advanced Spatial Analysis, 3D Cities Review, http://www.casa.ucl.ac.uk/research/3dcities.htm, (2000)

Day, A., V. Bourdakis, and J. Robson (1996). Living with a virtual city. In *Architectural research quarterly* 2(1):84-91

Dobson A.P.H., I. Kosco, and J. Tucny. (1998). Around the table on the net: Intranet and internet design studios and teaching. *Proceedings of the EAAE-ECAADE international workshop*. University of Leuven.

Grant, M.,and I. Paterson. (1994). Urban modelling. In *The virtual studio proceedings of the 12th european conference on education in computer aided architectural design*. University of Strathclyde, 7-10 September 1994, 135-139

Simoff, S., and M. L. Maher. (2000). Analysing participation in collaborative design environments. *Design Studies* 2

02 >> Connecting Digital Fabrication

Chairs: Branko Kolarevic, Marta Male-Alemany

Digital Fabrication: From Digital To Material

Branko Kolarevic

In the past, architects drew what they could build, and built what they could draw, as observed by Bill Mitchell. This reciprocity between the means of representation and production has not disappeared entirely in the digital age. Knowing the production capabilities and availability of particular digitally-driven fabrication equipment enables architects to design specifically for the capabilities of those machines. The consequence is that architects are becoming much more directly involved in the fabrication processes, as they create the information that is translated by fabricators directly into the control data that drives the digital fabrication equipment.

Some architects were quick to exploit the design and construction opportunities that were opened up by the newfound ability to digitally generate and supply the manufacturing information to fabricators and contractors, and, in turn, their ability to reciprocate by providing accurate material and cost estimates. In these newly discovered mutually-beneficial processes of direct information exchange, the digital design information became the construction information, and vice versa, without the intermediate time-consuming and error-prone steps of drawing production. These digital processes, pioneered by Frank Gehry's office, represent a radical departure from the normative practices – they eliminate, rather than automate, the production of various construction documents as paper drawings. The digital data are passed on directly, i.e. In paperless fashion, to fabricators for cost estimation and fabrication.

The ability to digitally generate and analyze the design information, and then use it to directly manufacture and construct buildings, fundamentally redefines the relationships between conception and production – it provides for an informational continuum from design to construction. New synergies in architecture, engineering and construction start to emerge because of the use of digital technologies across the boundaries of various professions. As communication among various parties increasingly involves the direct digital exchange of information, the legacy of the twentieth century in the form of drawing sets, shop drawings and specifications, will be inevitably relegated to the dustbin of history. The need to externalize representations of design, i.e. produce drawings, will lessen as a direct consequence of the new digital possibilities for producing and processing information.

In this scenario, the digital model becomes the single source of design and production information (the "holy grail" of the computer-aided design research community) that is generated, controlled and managed by the designer. It encodes all the information needed to manufacture and construct the building. Layers of information are added, abstracted and extracted as needed throughout the design and construction, as architects, engineers, contractors and fabricators work in a collaborative fashion using a single digital model from the earliest stages of design.

For Gehry's office, a digital model created in CATIA (Computer Aided Three-dimensional Interactive Application) – the design and manufacturing software used mainly in the aerospace industry – is the single source of design and construction information. In a remarkable departure from the current norms of practice, the three-dimensional digital model is actually a key part of the contract documents, from which all dimensional information is to be extracted during the fabrication and construction of the building. In other words, the digital model takes precedence over any other construction document, legally and in practice, on the construction site. This is a radical, revolutionary change in building practice, for which Gehry's office will probably be remembered in future history books (and not only for the sinuous, curving geometries of the Guggenheim Museum in Bilbao, Spain).

It is this newfound ability to generate construction information directly from design information, and not the complex curving forms, that defines the most profound aspect of much of the contemporary architecture. The close relationship that once existed between architecture and construction (what was once the very nature of architectural practice) could potentially reemerge as an unintended but fortunate outcome of the new digital processes of production. By integrating design, analysis, manufacture, and the assembly of buildings around digital technologies, architects, engineers and builders have an opportunity to fundamentally redefine the relationships between conception and production. The currently separate professional realms of architecture, engineering, and construction can be integrated into a relatively seamless digital collaborative enterprise, in which architects could play a central role as information master builders, the twenty-first century version of the architects' medieval predecessors.

Branko Kolarevic (Ddes, Mdess-Harvard, Dipl.Ing.Arh.-Belgrade) teaches design and digital media courses. Prior to joining Penn in 1999, he taught at several universities in North America and Asia. He has lectured worldwide on digital media in design, and has authored and edited several books. He is a former president of ACADIA.

Connecting Digital Fabrication

Marta Male-Alemany

We live a period where the digital revolution seems to reach a first stage of maturity. After new technologies introduced a higher degree of efficiency and versatility in traditional design processes, recent research focuses on the experimentation and application of specific potentialities of the digital for both the generation and material production of architecture.

The end of the century was the beginning of the integration of computer aided manufacturing (CAM) processes into architecture. Widely used in the industry, computer driven fabrication systems promised to develop building technologies in new directions. Today, this tendency is a widely spread reality, both in practice and architectural education.

Digital fabrication in architectural practice

As CAD-CAM technology becomes more affordable and available in the market, a number of contemporary large offices –which include Gehry Partners, Foster Associates, Grimshaw have used digital production technologies to resolve construction issues related with the execution of complex geometries and optimise the production of their building components.

At another level, an increasing array of smaller practices have instead incorporated CAD-CAM processes as part of their design agenda; architects like Bernhard Franken, Decoi, Garofalo Architects, William Massie, SHoP, or Kolatan & Mcdonald are exploring the conceptual and material opportunities that emerge from a simultaneous employment of digital design and manufacturing techniques. Furthermore, while design information now drives numerically controlled machines, research also goes on exploring an inversed interference: how fabrication data can affect creative processes at the level of design foundation.

Digital fabrication in architectural education

The same interest has grown in education. Envisioning emergent changes in the profession, many schools of architecture have started to integrate digital production equipment as part of their facilities.

The academic exploration on CAD-CAM processes stimulates the convergence of otherwise separated subjects (such as design and construction), setting up new conditions for teaching architecture in studio environments. While the computer has proven to be a suitable media for the development and communication of architectural projects, numerically driven machines stimulate testing design ideas in the physical world. The move from simulation/representation to realization/execution is strongly encouraged by the possibility to fabricate complex, non-standard forms with extreme precision and control. With the possibility to build parts at 1:1 scale, the design studio reaches out to the execution of actual buildings.

In fact, and no matter how expensive the investment, the implementation of CNC equipment is an important step for academic institutions to build and consolidate their vocation: the opportunity to play a central role in driving innovation.

Concluding notes

Today digital fabrication is a vibrating context for theoretical and applied research in architecture, which touches on almost all the dimensions of the discipline.

An overview of this context highlights changes in-progress and opens the perspective of others to come. When architecture becomes closer to the construction industry, these digital design and manufacturing technologies are indeed reconfiguring the role of the architect in the midst of building processes. Similarly, the convergence of several fields of expertise–as they come together in a continuous design-to-manufacturing processes- stimulate a new dimension of interdisciplinarity and collaboration.

No longer dependent on standardization paradigms, there are real conditions and possibilities for architecture to take advantage of mass-customization production processes with visible effects on the building environment. In this context - and given its potential for research & development- academia can strengthen the link with the reality of practice. By focusing on a theme that has important consequences in the building environment, architecture schools can create new conditions for education in design studio environments, and play an important role in driving innovation in the production processes architecture.

Marta Male-Alemany (B.A. ETSAV-UPC, Barcelona, MS.AAD Columbia University) has taught at UCLA and is currently with the design faculty at SCI-ARC and ESARQ-UIC. Parallel to her academic dedication, she works as an independent architect and digital production consultant. In her practice, she investigates both conceptual and material opportunities that emerge from the use of advanced CAD-CAM applications. Recent works on digital production include a bench structure for the Barcelona Forum 2004 and an installation at SCI-Arc Gallery. She has been writing and lecturing on the subject of digital fabrication.

Function Follows Form: 10 Sticks (and a Bench)

Mark Cabrinha
California State Polytechnic University, San Luis Obispo

Abstract

While the introduction of digital media in the design studio often emphasizes virtual realms, the effect of new fabrication technology on the architect brings the architect back to the realm of master-builder rather than distancing the architect from reality. While purely digital projects have pushed the development of form, they have also placed an emphasis on form over material. However, with the intention to physically build a project, the connections between process, form, and material become intertwined.

The inception of this project also served as a clear reminder that the tools we use affect the way we think. This project began as a simple idea: how a column becomes animated to form an arch over time. The digitization of this idea took literally minutes in Maya. It was exported and further modeled in AutoCAD, and then rendered and reanimated in 3D Studio-Viz.

This was a very brief, two-week introductory project, in a class on drafting and wood light-frame construction. It served to make a greater connection between digital media, the design process, analog drawing, and the role of craft and material.

"The idea becomes a machine that makes the art."
-Sol Lewitt

"There is a growing appreciation of new abstractions. Increasingly, computers let us treat abstract relations as visible, working things."
-Malcolm McCullough

Function Follows Form: 10 Sticks (and a Bench)

Mark Cabrinha

California State Polytechnic University, San Luis Obispo

1 Introduction

While the introduction of digital media in the design studio often emphasizes virtual realms, the affect of new fabrication technology on the architect brings the architect back to the realm of master-builder rather than distancing the architect from reality. While purely digital projects have pushed the development of form, they have also placed an emphasis on form over material. However, with the intention to physically build a project, the connections between process, form, and material become intertwined. As schools scramble to dedicate massive funding for specialized equipment for 3D Printers and CNC milling machines, this project presents an alternative. This project was a very brief, two-week introductory project, in a class on architectural practice dealing with drafting and wood light frame construction. While the class was typically based on an average suburban house, this project served to make a greater connection between digital media, the design process, analog drawing, and the role of craft and material.

The inception of this project also served as a clear reminder that the tools we use affect the way we think. Taking a clue from Sol Lewitt's statement that "the idea becomes a machine that makes the art," (Lewitt 369), this project began as a simple idea: how a column becomes animated to form an arch over time. Though simple, the conceptual idea took the longest to germinate, and would have been inconceivable to me without my prior experience with Maya. The digitization of this idea took literally minutes in Maya, was exported and further modeled in AutoCAD, and then rendered and reanimated in 3D Studio-Viz. The decision to build at full scale only emphasized that the design process and the fabrication process are inseparable, a conclusion that would not have been reached without actually building. The following account describes the connection between process, form, and material in the development of this simple project, and concludes with several significant, yet unexpected outcomes of this process.

2 Design Process – Digital Tools & Transferability

While the plausibility of such a simple idea came from Sol Lewitt, the potential value of the idea came from Malcolm McCullough: "computers let us treat abstract relations as visible, working things" (McCullough 28). In this case, the relationship is between the visible transformation from column to arch over time. In addition, the computer allows this visible relation to develop as a flexible system. Rather than approaching the computer as tool for production of a preexisting idea, digital media in this case can test an idea and develop a working system to fabricate that idea.

While AutoCAD was used to translate the conceptual line to a solid model of a stud, Maya was essential in laying the conceptual groundwork and exporting these results into AutoCAD. Due to the simplicity of this example, 3DS Viz was used only for rendering and reanimation. Without my basic understanding of Maya, I would neither have conceived nor been able to test the conceptual idea that this project was based on only emphasizing that the software we use affects our thinking.

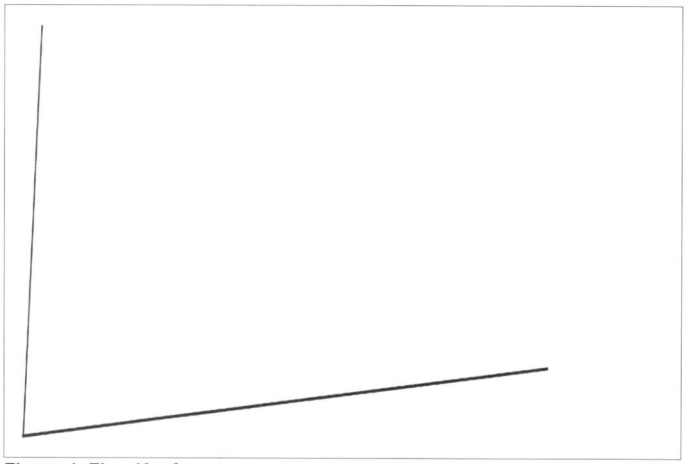

Figure 1. First Keyframe

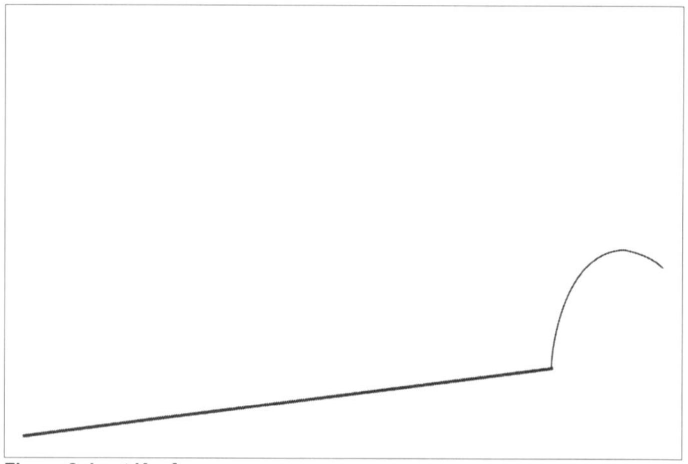

Figure 2. Last Keyframe

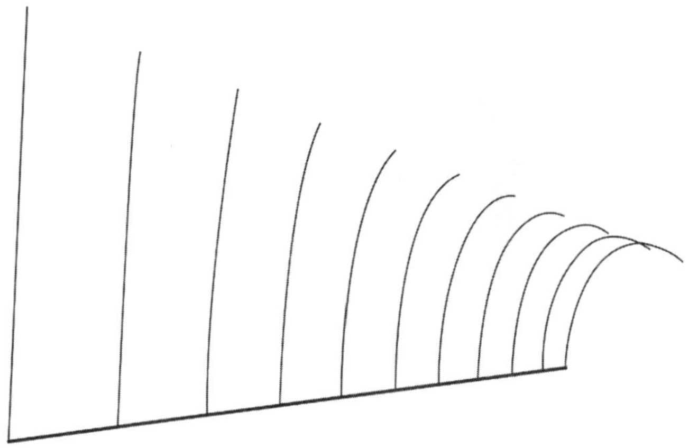

Figure 3. Animated Snapshot

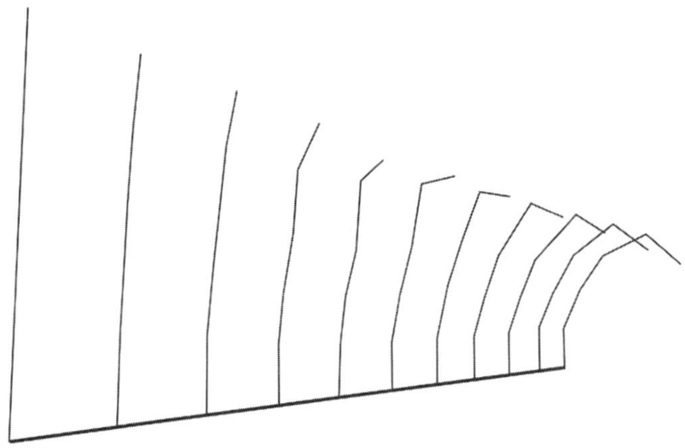

Figure 4. Rebuilt Snapshot

Figure 5. Spike Anchor Study

A rough draft was quickly developed testing the idea in Maya and then the process of transferability between Maya and AutoCAD. The idea was first tested with the most basic of animations – the first key frame with a vertical line and the last key frame with the modulation of that line into an arch (Figures 1 and 2).

An animated snapshot was created to fill the gaps between the first and last keyframe—a process commonly referred to as "tweening." While I could have continued to bring form to these lines in Maya, it was more efficient and accurate to export them into AutoCAD and give them volume there.

From this first draft of the process, two concerns came up: first, how many pieces are necessary to complete this idea, and second, what material would be used to fabricate this? In regard to the first concern, I knew I would have between 15-20 students, so I simply ran the animated snapshot twice, once with each student having his or her own stick, and once with one stick to two students. The number of sticks, about 10 or 20, did not affect the clarity of the idea, and therefore I decided that it was more appropriate to have each stick fabricated by a team of two as this would reduce cost and facilitate the fabrication process with one student on each end of the stick. As this was tested in a class on drafting and wood light frame construction, wood was the obvious material. The literal transcription of the idea from column to arch resulted in a series of free form curves that could have easily been fabricated in plywood with a CNC milling machine or full size template. However, there would have been a significant cost and waste of material associated with this literal transcription, nor did I have access to a CNC machine. Using a 2x4 would be far more cost effective and form a stronger tie to light frame construction, challenging the accepted uses of the ubiquitous 2x4 stud or "stick" found on every wood light frame construction site. With this choice to use a 2x4, the project took on added value in expressing how material affects the choice of form, but can still maintain the conceptual idea. In my view, this made the project more interesting, not less. It was at this point that I decided that this idea was worth pursuing as not simply an exercise in building form, but in how process, form and material can be manipulated to test an idea in full scale.

Following from the rough draft, the above process was then recreated with the introduction of scale into Maya. This was achieved simply in AutoCAD by drawing a 7'-6" line for the first stick, and an approximately 30'-0" line for the animated path, and then imported into Maya. The animation was re-created as above, including the animated snapshots. The next significant step in the design process was to manipulate these free form curves to be fabricated from a 2x4 (Figures 3 and 4).

One of the significant features of Maya is its ability to "rebuild" a curve or surface. Each animated snapshot could be rebuilt in Maya as a system of segmented lines, but what criteria would I use to rebuild this line? As I had decided above that a team of two would fabricate each stick, it became natural to then evenly distribute the pieces between each student. I tried a few variations between 4-8 pieces. However, once seeing these

Figure 6. Photomontage

results, I realized it was not the pieces themselves that were difficult to fabricate, but the connections between the pieces that were significant. Therefore, I decided that each stick would be composed of five pieces, with a total of four joints (two joints for each team member). While in word this may seem cumbersome, in actuality this was a five minute process with the conceptual model in Maya and only reiterates the connection between design material and fabrication. These rebuilt lines in Maya were again exported to AutoCAD and then scaled so that each stick was precisely 2'-0" on center. The lines were then offset, joined, and extruded to the precise dimension of a stud.

Concurrent with this digital process, a full size mock-up of the joint was developed to create a seamless connection to maintain the continuous appearance of a single stick. With the help of a tenoning-jig, a simple glued spline joint was able to make the connection without exposed fasteners and was unaffected by the multiple angles of each piece.

At this point, despite my emphasis on testing ideas, form, and material, I must admit I was aware of one major limitation but had not yet tested it: how would this thing stand? Concerned with deviating too far from the intentions of the class syllabus, I considered simply anchoring these pieces to the grass quad via foundation form spikes (Figure 5).

Yet, the reliance on another surface for stability seemed to weaken the simplicity of the idea, to say nothing of a statically problematic structure on public display. Naturally I was trying to find some integrated element that would make this structurally static and freestanding. The introduction of function, a bench, solved this problem and presented another unanticipated outcome: the reversal of the iconoclast belief that form follows function. In this case, literally, the function served to support the form. The bench was then simply and conventionally conceived and modeled in AutoCAD.

This 3D model was then imported into 3D Studio Viz and rendered with simple mapped materials and then imported into Photoshop for photomontages in situ (Figures 6 and 7).
A conventional animation was created in Viz to go full circle from conceptual animate form to an animation of the final product. This entire process from animated design concept, development, and final animation was combined as one brief animation and played on the first day of class as an introduction to the project.

3 Fabrication Process

On the second class period before the fabrication process began, we met at a local lumberyard. This was an opportunity to present the many different products in wood light frame construction, but moreover an opportunity for the students to select material free of defects and deformations. As their first

Figure 7. Photomontage

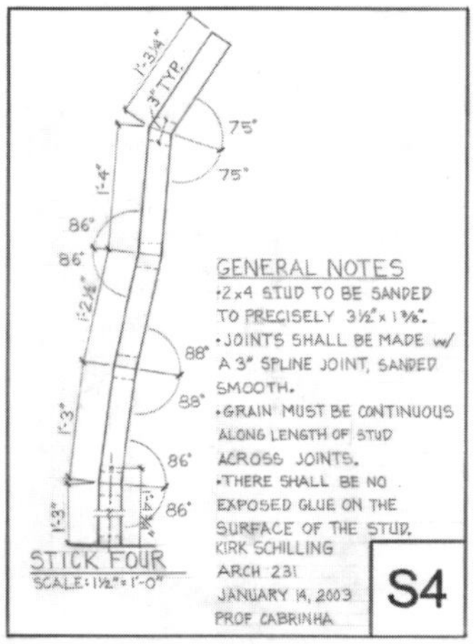

Figure 8. Student Drawing

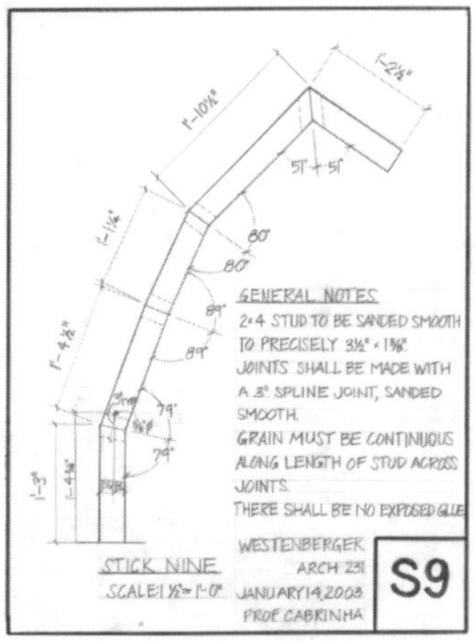

Figure 9. Student Drawing

step was to make drawings for fabrication, it also reminded them of the material that they were representing on paper. Fortunately, it also gave the lumber time to acclimate in the shop.

While the design process was purely digital, the fabrication process followed more traditional means. The first step in this process was developing what were effectively shop drawings. For many of these students, the lines drawn for this project were the first "hard lines" they have ever drawn. From an analog view, the fact that these drawings were in essence shop drawings emphasized that the lines we draw have a direct correlation to what gets built. It also addressed the issue of clarity and legibility through density of lines necessary for making multiple reproductions, particularly necessary to keep the original vellums out of the messy shop, all necessary skills to fulfill the drafting requirements of the syllabus.

Each team of two was given a line drawing from AutoCAD, which indicated the angles of each joint and was plotted to 1/4" scale. Considerable effort was placed to ensure a uniformity of appearance, a reproducible legibility, and certainly accuracy in these drawings. While craft in drawing was emphasized, craft in the fabrication of the parts was emphasized with four required "general notes." The 2x4 had to be planed to 3 3/8"x1 3/8", joints were to be made from a 3" spline joint sanded smooth, the grain must be continuous along the length of the stick, and finally there was to be no exposed glue on the surface of the stud (Figures 8 and 9).

While these steps may not seem relevant to a digital process, what did surprise me was that through the drawings students took ownership of their stick. Each team of two was very particular about their drawings, and it was very interesting to watch the perceived difficulty of the stick as it became more arch like, even though each stick had exactly the same criteria, only the angle and dimensions changed. Before we went to the shop, all of these drawings were pinned up in studio to see the progression of all the sticks, emphasizing collaboration and coordination.

The equipment used to fabricate this project can be found in any wood shop: a planer, a miter saw, and a table-saw with tenon jig. The planer was used to set the material to the precise dimensions. To ensure uniformity, all materials were planed at the same time to ensure consistency in dimension. There was some general confusion in cutting their first angle in the compound miter saw, but after that, the cuts were made easily (Figure 10).

The table saw was set-up with a dado blade to the precise depth and width of the spline joint, and a tenon jig was set to center the joint (Figure 11).

Finally, each team was given a set of 1/2" plywood splines, which were then glued into the joint, and cut to fit after the glue was dry (Figure 12).

As much as there was a transfer of ownership in the drawing of the stick, there was a much greater pride in the actual craft and fabrication of their stick. The finish criteria in the "general notes"

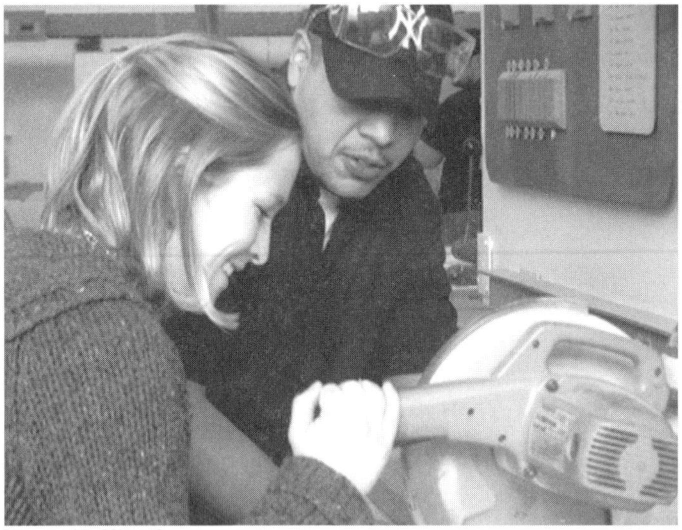

Figure 10. Miter Saw

Figure 11. Table Saw with Tenon Jig

Figure 12. Spline Joints

Figure 13. Finished Project

Figure 14. Finished Project

had the unexpected outcome of initiating an informal competition for the finest crafted stick. If there is any doubt as to the ownership these students placed on their sticks, it became clear at the end of the quarter when they decided to sign their sticks. While I had hoped we could fabricate all the pieces in one 3 1/2 hour lab period, it did in fact take two full periods. When we returned to studio with all of our fabricated pieces, all of the students wanted to see some of the pieces go together. To their amazement, the pieces came together in about a half hour to form the complete bench. The bench was moved in two pieces to a quad outside of our studio and placed in the public realm for one week. People were found staring at, sitting at it, and other planned activities took place around it—even one of my students, an avid surfer, realized that it also had unintentional symbolic form (Figures 13-16).

4 Conclusion

While I am aware of the irony involved in creating shop drawings for a process alluding to digital fabrications, the significance of this project is that in building accurately from the digital environment, the connection between process, form, and material becomes intertwined. The project was conceived to display the connection between digital media and craft. As a built thing, its roll of "display" in the public realm was significant on two fronts. For the students, it made a greater impression about the role of craft, and more broadly, emphasized the

Figure 16. Students on Installation Day

Figure 15. Playful Interpretation

connection between digital media and architecture to faculty and other students. The project also tested the transferability of digital information across several different programs through their ability to test ideas, transpose that idea to scale, and represent the idea before its actualization.

Sol Lewitt has remarked that the work of art can only be perceived after it is completed (Lewitt 372). While I am not suggesting this quick study is a work of art, the beauty of the experiment is in the many unexpected outcomes as a result of building at full scale. As has already been emphasized, this project emphasized the connection between process, form, and material. While in the digital virtual domain there has been an emphasis on form, with the integration of material in the process, an emphasis is placed on structure and connections. Quite by accident, this project questions the iconoclast relationship that form follows function. The result of this unintended polemical response is the necessity of a closer collaboration between form and function—in essence that form and function become one.

Above all, this project has illustrated the effect on the design process as a result of fabrication. While traditionally the use of digital media has emphasized form, the process of fabrication places emphasis on the tectonic qualities of architecture. Instead of fabrication being after the fact, the integration of digital media in design and fabrication develops a possibility for the return of the architect as master builder.

References

Garrels, G,, ed. (2000). *Sol Lewitt, A retrospective*. New Haven, Conn: Yale University Press.

McCullough, M. (1996). *Abstracting craft, the practiced digital hand*. Cambridge, Mass: The MIT Press.

Digital Architecture - What Would 6000 Points Turn Out To Be?

Naai-Jung Shih
National Taiwan University of Science and Technology

Abstract

This paper presents students' fulfillment of an assignment that explored the concepts of digital architecture using rapid prototyping (RP) process. A point cloud was given to students, and different representational data were substantiated as real 3D physical models. The presence of RP models and the sequential illustration of working steps in their reports revealed that the control of shapes often differed from what students perceived in VR worlds. The results thus confirm that physical models are useful for visualization as well as in design pedagogy.

Digital Architecture - What Would 6000 Points Turn Out To Be?

Naai-Jung Shih
National Taiwan University of Science and Technology

1 Introduction

A rapid prototyping (RP) machine can fabricate 3D models for visual inspection. Applications in architecture are made in the fabrication of building parts and design concepts (Krishnamurti & Earl 1992; Novitski 1999; Rotheroe 2000; Ryder, etc. 2002; Streich & Weisgerber 1996; Wang & Duarte 2002). RP in architecture is limited by the restrictions on size and time required to output a model. The footage of the model is another limit of an ordinary RP machine. A large model has to be separated into parts and assembled afterward. Another drawback is that the process is time-consuming. Normally, an RP production of industrial parts the size of a cell phone cover may take up to 10-20 hours. Ordinary RP materials like polymer can create a thin cover with the strength of plastic. Another drawback is that RP models are made in white or a plain color. Although color-keyed components have been created recently, so that a uniform color can be assigned to a part (Karapatis, etc. 1998; Ming & Gibson 1999; Pham & Gault 1998), still, the limited variety of colors cannot provide adequate surface attributes such as the texture that is needed in architecture visualization, whether it is procedure texture (texture allowing for parameter change) or direct image mapping (texture using a predefined image as content).

The data used for RP do not have to be the final results of visualization; instead, this stage of application can offer benefits in the early design stages (Simondetti 2002). Similar RP application in the field of art can be seen in the creation of cartoon characters and visual arts (Connolly 2001; Tome 2001). It seems RP has worked well with current modeling processes in a specific and purposely integrated manner. But how useful is it in architecture? It is still to be seen whether a direct connection with a modeling process can be established.

2 An Assignment

In a course entitled "Digital Architecture" offered by the author, an assignment was given to students to create forms based on any simulated behavior of objects. With the enlightenment of forms manipulated in digital designs, most of the students produced free forms (see Figure 1). These outcomes led to a second assignment for which works were to be created from an ill-defined structure of geometric data. Assignment 2 was designed to use smoke particles generated from Hazard II (a fire simulation program) as a raw data set of point clouds. Although each point represented a particle of fire or smoke, the attributes were removed and hidden from students for a pure geometric study of the potential development of forms. The point cloud and the instructor's illustrations of possible developments can be seen in Table 1.

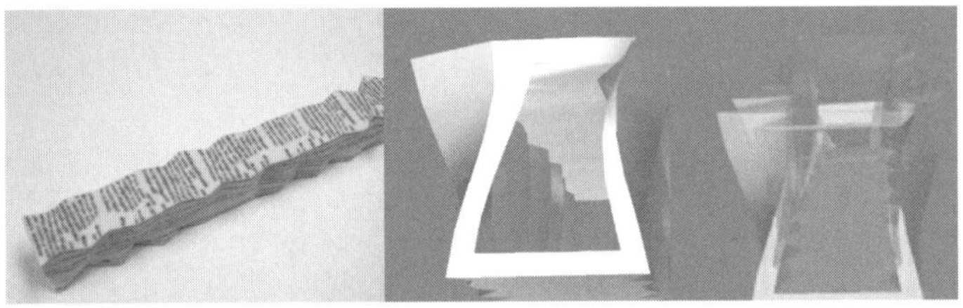

Figure 1. An RP exemplification from assignment 1 and its original digital form

3 Observation of student work

When the assignment was given to students, the instructor hypothesized that they had no preconceived notions of tools, data interpretation, and presentation. The kinds of titles students used for the second assignment were "6000 points," "Inside or outside!?," "Combination of three-way frames," etc. (see Table 2). Their reports showed they perceived that points were disoriented and not measurable by size. 6000 points were considered as a single entity as well as a group of multiple objects. For some students, points were static, so a "wrap" operation could be made. For other students, in contrast, points were dynamic, so the connections among them either showed the movement of parts or that their presence enabled turbulence made by other types of geometry. Points were the subjects that "interfere" with a plane in order to reveal their presence in a certain form.

A typical development of concept starts from a theme (which could be a metaphor), involves parts buildup, and ends with RP output (see Figure 2). In creating forms from a point cloud, the development of student concepts can be classified as using:

- Feature-oriented approaches: involving the boundary of a point cloud, the behavior within this cloud, or the roles of being active or passive in relation to intrigued points
- Application-oriented approaches: involving path extrusion, section sweeps, wraps, traces, and turbulence
- Methods of illustration: involving stepwise proof of rendering or screen captures

4 Discussion

Comments were given to students and RP outputs were displayed based on their input. A Z-406, also called a 3D printer,

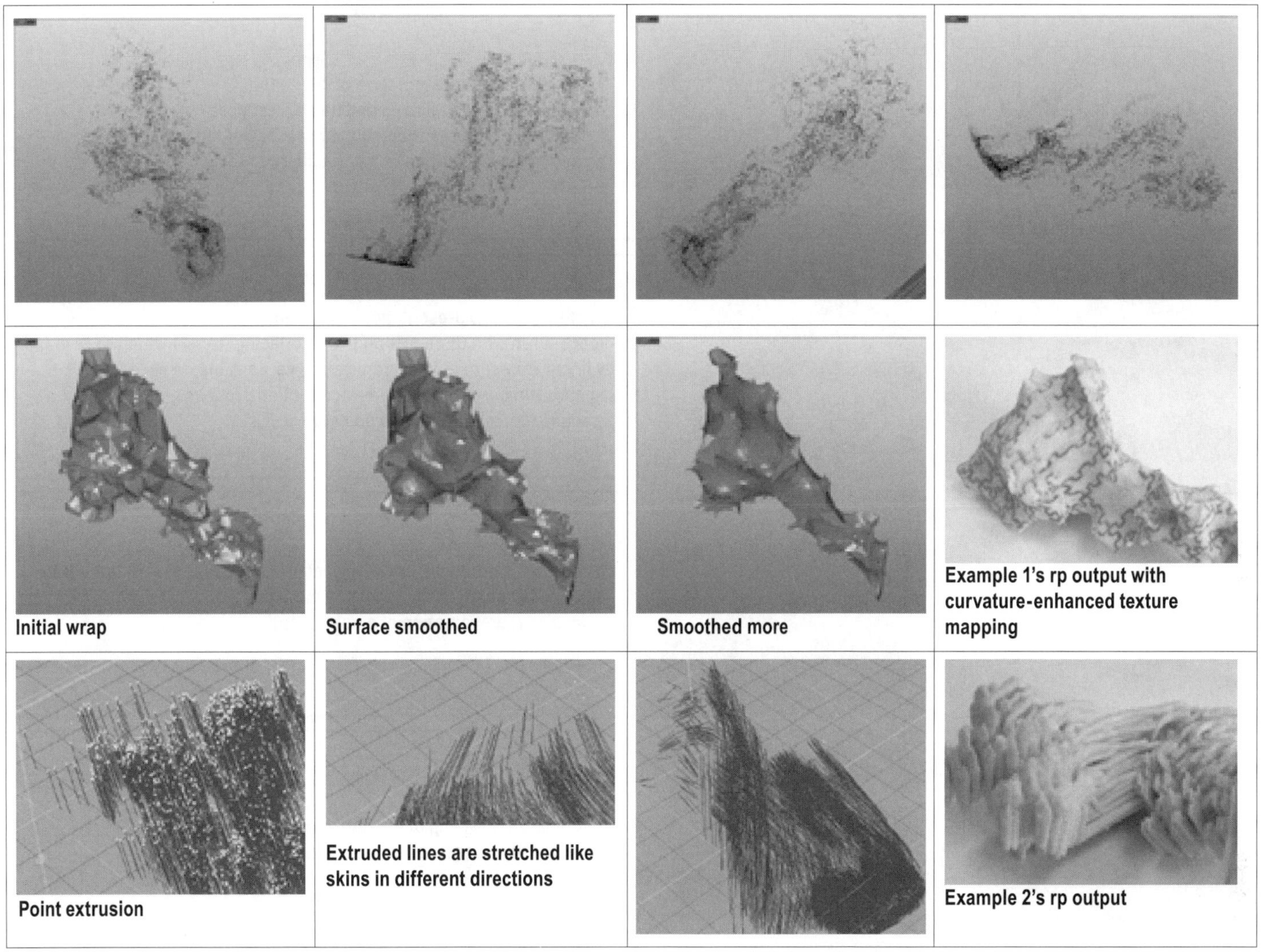

Table 1. Point cloud and the instructor's illustrations for assignment 2.

was used for layering type output of models. Students were asked for VRML model files to allow color textures to be added to output.

- Students developed a method to create forms out of a cluster of basic geometries. When elements were modeled one by one, the initial piece of the installation had a strong influence on the following pieces, as it changed the spatial relationship of the installation. The presence of sequences sometimes acted as a strong guide for the following installation. Since the number of points had increased to a level that, in one way, was difficult to control point by point, and in another way, made the distribution of points unable to lead to a clear distinction in density as a clue to develop forms, students were working on the development of orders to interpret these points from boundaries or from the inside. But most of the time, the more than expected number of points gave possibilities to fulfill the declaration of orders because there were always some points available. It turned out that a framework for geometric form emerged for each student to use to define forms.
- The development of order needs to be controlled by explicit procedures. So frames of the development process (see Figure 3) are shown not only for illustrating the requirements of the assignment, but also to act as tracing the previous steps in order to facilitate personal control over the following development of concepts. Frames of

		- a heterogeneous presentation of elements - space wrap-up with planes and tubes interlaced - a point–face, point–sweeping path process of modeling - an active representation of a point cloud
		-a heterogeneous presentation of elements -space fill-in with three orthogonal interlacing frames which were made by linear elements of inter-connecting vertices inside each frame -a point–three-way frame–inter-connecting process of modeling an active representation of a point cloud
		- a void space defined by multi-orientational tracing of a 3D boundary - a point–sweeping path process of modeling - a passive representation of a point cloud
		- a volumetric wrap-up of juxtaposing sets of point clouds - an active representation of a point cloud
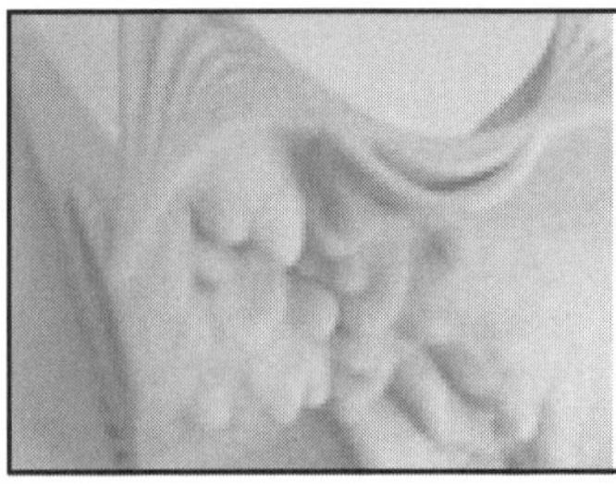		- a void space description made by a point cloud's interference to planes - a point-plane interaction process of modeling - a passive representation of a point cloud

Table 2. Exemplifications from assignment 2

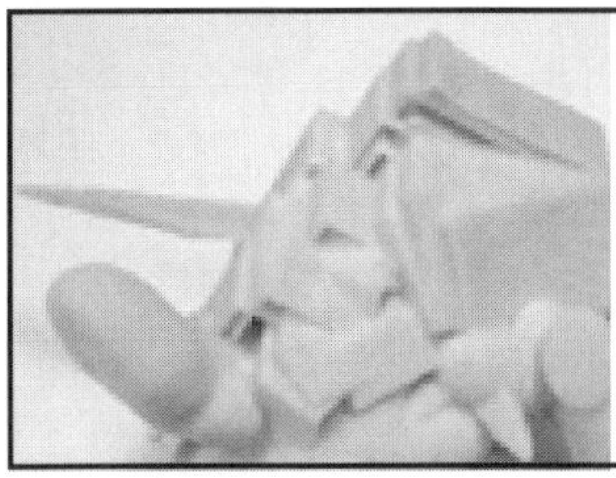	- space fill-in of three juxtaposing routes made by different configurations of a section - a point–path–extrusion process of modeling - an active representation of a point cloud
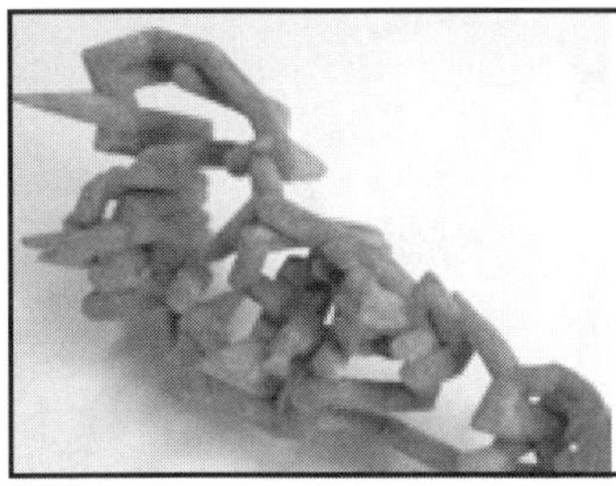	- space fill-in of paths made by tracing points with a point cloud - a point–line–face process of modeling
	Table 2. [continued]

views were used afterward to inspect the series of steps previously done for the instructor as well as for the students themselves. The sequence of views did not have to follow original process, but interpretation could be subject to it.

Figure 3. An example of frames of concept development

- A modeling process is also an interpretation management process of views and vocabulary. Almost all the students presented their works as frames of views or steps to enhance the concept delivery. A typical differentiation of views comes from default computer windows; despite that there are still many angles unseen. These discrete views are usually associated with an enriched vocabulary of description. For example, the third case from Table 2 was interpreted by the student as a baby lying down from a top view, as a stock chart from a front view, as a walking phantom from a left view, and as a high-heel shoe from a perspective.

Most of the responses to RP models from viewpoint-based illustration were complex. Just as it is confusing to merge the four characteristics together, it is difficult for the student initially to come up with a summarizing term for the RP model. Interestingly enough, the description, which used to be a kind of proof shortening the distance between a real world and a virtual world, becomes useless when the switch of views becomes so intuitive, continuous, and straightforward as it does with an RP model in hand. It seems a larger gap exists between before and after an RP model is made, along with the management process involved in point cloud interpretation.

- From the instructor's side, the output of the digital model did not come in plain colors. In order to enhance the order of forms, color texture was purposely mapped to models (see Figure 4). The content-explicit texture helped to identify collapsed parts and their relative positions to the original form. The texture also helped to enhance the curvature made by turbulence on a surface. In several cases, the instructor applied RP to enhance the configuration of shapes as a way to allow for better comprehension.

Figure 4. The "Dao" (left) and its detached parts printed with texture clues (right)

- Most of the students declared that the RP models helped them to identify parts of a model; i.e. the relative location of parts came with visual depth that could not be achieved in a VR environment without auto-stereographic display. For those students who had discussed their assignments beforehand, observations were threefold: the inspection of the RP model either 1) made some students doubtful of their original perceptions; 2) confirmed their expectations; or 3) shed light on other's deviations between original perception and outcome. The physical output helped students to critique each other's designs in a more substantial manner by allowing them to point to

Figure 2. Concept development from an image metaphor, to parts buildup, to RP output

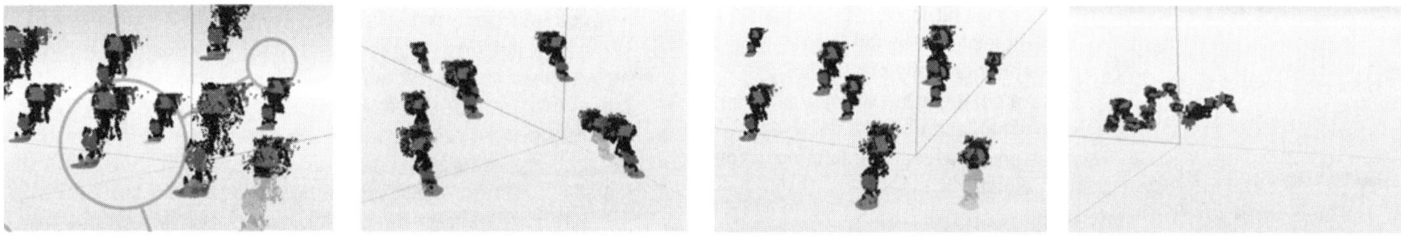

Figure 3. An example of frames of concept development

Figure 4. The "Dao" (left) and its detached parts printed with texture clues (right)

particular parts, locations, or relationships. When dealing with geometries alone, it seemed hard to tell whether students knew what they were doing. A VR world seemed not quite adequate enough for distinguishing an object's components under certain deformation circumstances. Responses showed that computers need more capability in real-time display of shaded forms with depth of field in true color. Unlike the continuous display that is possible when an RP model is held in hand, discrete displays cause a delay in the design response or an inactivation of an individual's sensitivity to forms.

5 Conclusion

A frozen state of particle movement is as enlightening as a particle's trails of movement. From assignment 1 to 2, it was shown that an un-preconceived operation could lead to many answers. Some of the forms under development were too abstract to be realized as output; otherwise, a frozen state would have been presented in the design process. The outcome of this assignment was a total surprise in that not only did students show personal styles of CAD tool application, but the development of concepts also led to diversified digital forms. When personal interpretation meets digital media, we found a VR world was not enough to state the actual appearance of artifacts. RP models helped by allowing for actual physical touch. The influence is not merely at the level of reality, but also one that gives students a sense of control over the forms being created.

References

Connolly. J. (2001). RP becomes an important tool for one artist's work. Magazine - TimeCompress.htm, Oct. 2001.

Karapatis, N.P., J.-P.S. van Griethuysen, and R. Glardon. (1998). Direct rapid tooling: a review of current research. *Rapid prototyping journal* 4(2):77-89.

Krishnamurti, R., and C. F. Earl. (1992). Shape recognition in three dimensions. In *Environment and planning: Planning and design* 19:595-603. London: Pion.

Ming, L. W., and I. Gibson. (2001). Specification of VRML in color rapid prototyping. *International journal of CAD/CAM* 1:1598-1800.

Novitski, B.J. Rapid prototyping. (1999). *Architecture record,* November 1999.

Pham, D. T., and R. S. Gault. (1998). A comparison of rapid prototyping technologies. *International journal of machine tools and manufacture* 38:1257-1287.

Rotheroe, K. C. (2000). Manufacturing freeform architecture. *ArchitectureWeek* – Tools 2000_0927.files, p T1.2, Sept. 27 2000.

Ryder, G., B. Ion, G. Green, D. Harrison, and B. Wood. (2002). Rapid design and manufacture tools in architecture. *Automation in construction* 11(3):279-290.

Simondetti, A. (2002). Computer-generated physical modelling in the early stages of the design process. *Automation in construction* 11(3):303-311.

Streich, B., and W. Weisgerber. (1996). *Computergestützter Architekturmodellbau.* Birkhauser.

Tome, C. (2001). Designers spice up a miniature set by using RP technology to generate physical pepper models. *Computer Graphics World* - graphics, 3d modeling, cad and visual computing.htm, *Computer graphics world,* June, 2001.

Wang, Y., and J. P. Duarte. (2002). Automatic generation and fabrication of designs, *Automation in Construction* 11(3):291-302.

Model credits

Figure 1: Jeh-Zen Hu
Figure 2: I-Don Shu
Figure 3, 4: Jan-Cha Chang
Table2: 1.:Ham-Gin Kan, 2:Bou-Yang Chang, 3:Der-Luan Huang, 4:Jan-Cha Chang, 5:I-Don Shu, 6:Chien-U Cheng, and 7:Jeh-Zen Hu.

Fabrication of Partially Double-Curved Surfaces out of Flat Sheet Material Through a 3D Puzzle Approach

Axel Kilian
Massachusetts Institute of Technology

Abstract

The topic of this paper is the connection of digital modeling with generative programming and rapid prototyping, to produce physical sketch surface models. The physical surface models are assembled out of developable strips connected through a puzzle-like detail. The use of programming as a design approach allows the generation of connection details that corresponds to the rules of flat sheet rapid prototyping techniques of laser cutting and water jet cutting. With numerically controlled cutting, there is no need to keep the joint detail related to manually achievable forms or to apply a standardized dimension. This paper demonstrates the possibilities of programming to generate cutting geometries that adapt to the local surface properties. The larger perspective of the research approach is the question of how to formulate and capture design intention through programming. What influence does the use of generative modeling in combination with rapid prototyping have on the design language of physical objects?

Fabrication of Partially Double-curved Surfaces out of Flat Sheet Material Through a 3D Puzzle Approach

Axel Kilian
Massachusetts Institute of Technology

1 Introduction

Rapid prototyping and CNC machining tools are increasingly making their way, not only into production, but also into design schools. The machines are posing new challenges, not so much in their ability to execute drawings done on a CAD system by a process very similar to drawing, but by their ability to cut any geometry within the limitations of the machine. The question is how to expand the use of such machines and explore their potential. Two possible approaches are:

- Extract the capabilities of the machine and embed them into a generative program that explores the possible forms and cuts within the limitations
- Design an object and adapt it to the machine's capabilities

There are always shapes for which a particular fabrication process works well and other shapes that need to be redesigned in order to be fabricated efficiently. As in conventional craft and manual production processes, there are "easy" and "hard" procedures in CNC. In this sense, CNC machines do not differ from the tools and processes involved in a conventional craft. What does differ is the potential for the creative reinvention of details originating in conventional craft in a CNC process. This can be accomplished through generative techniques where a customized solution for each detail is produced. However, few designers have explored these possibilities. _

2 Fabrication and language of details

The language of a detail results from the combination of material, required performance, design intentions and its manufacturing process. If any of these parameters change, there is potential for a new detail to emerge. So far, few specific details have

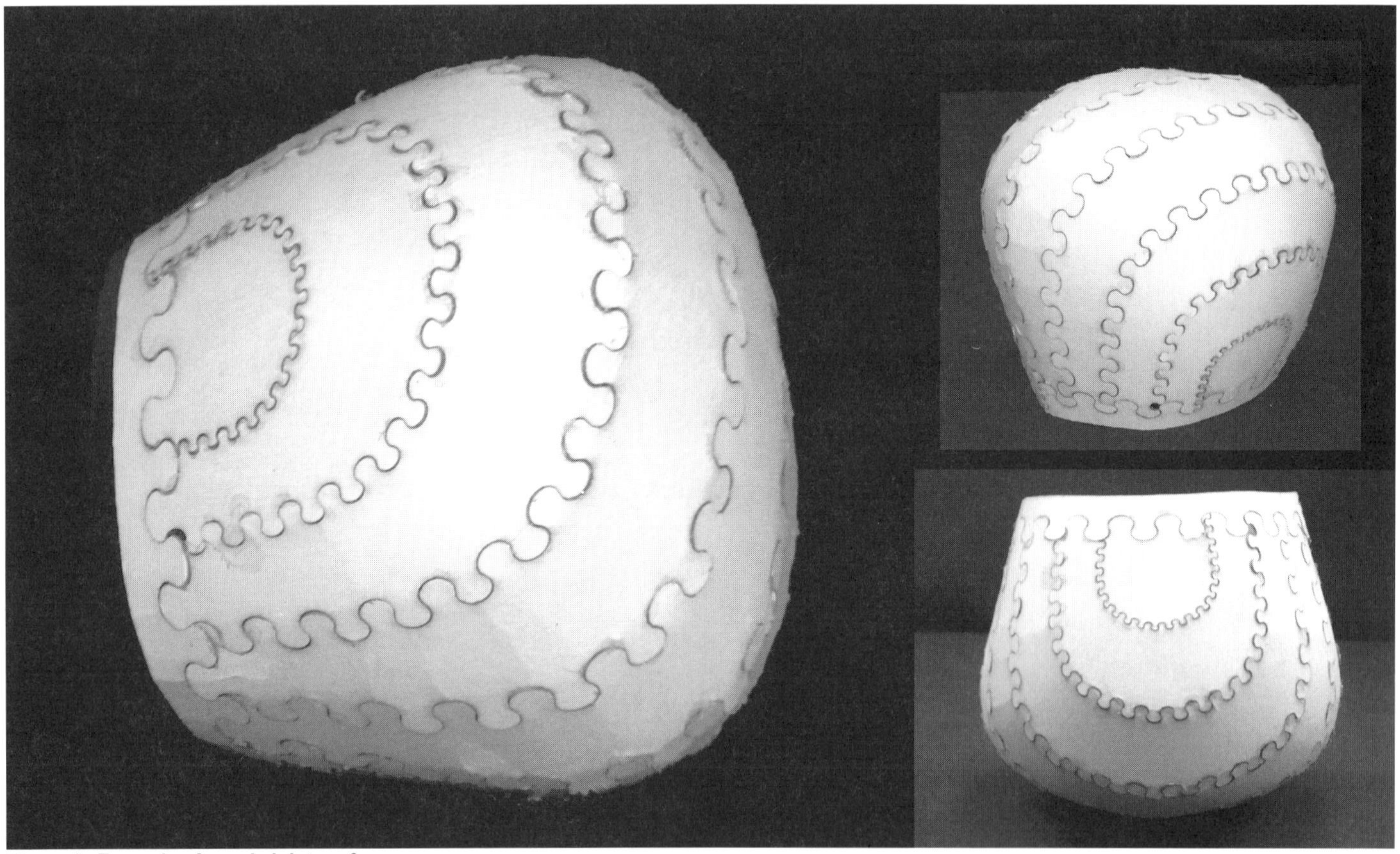

Figure 1. Example of puzzle joint surface

emerged from the use of computer controlled machining. This paper proposes an adaptable detail over a curved surface that would have been very hard to produce in any way other than through the combination of computer-controlled fabrication and generative modeling.

2.1 Tolerances, between pressure fit and constructability

The process of fabrication allows for the specification of very precise cutting dimensions. In the given example, the precision is crucial in order for the joint to be a pressure fit joint. But too high a precision in the fit will prevent the assembly of the joint: due to its spatial curvature, the continuous detail cannot be assembled all at once but only sequentially. The sequential assembly requires larger fitting tolerance to allow the pieces to move into place. The challenge is to find the right balance between a tight fit that would cause problems in the assembly, and a looser fit and that might cause the pressure fit joint to fail. Ideally this would have to be modeled into the geometry generation in the first place rather then to compensate for the variations through the cutting tolerances during fabrication.

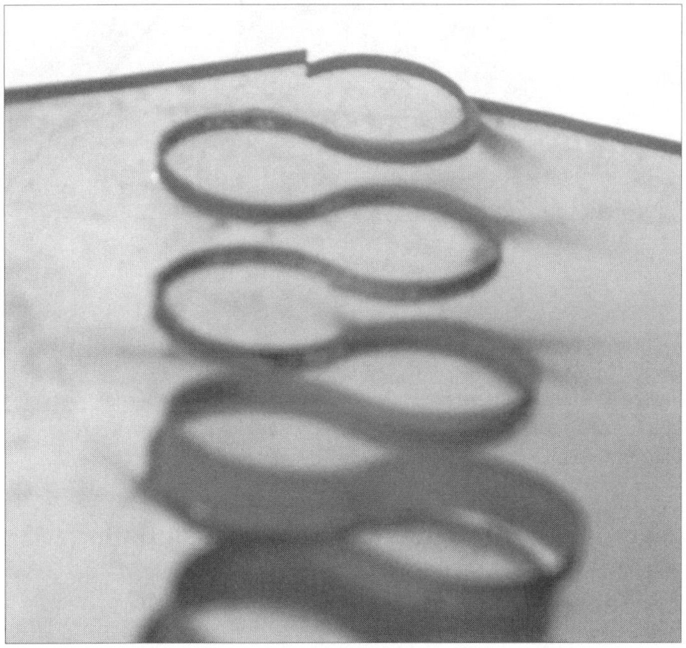

Figure 2. Balance between fitting tolerances and the constraints of assembly tolerances. The first nodes lock into place but prevent the following nodes to reach their position due to a fitting tolerance that is too tight.

2.2 Ability of details to adapt to their geometric context

A connection detail for a varying geometric context needs enough flexibility to work in the complete range of scenarios. Many experiments have been made, for instance in textile and membrane design, to come up with adaptable details to correspond to the geometric context. Assembly details in car design often depend on geometrically adaptable connections. For instance, a door seal follows the curved rail of the car body and the frame between the double-curved windshield and the car body describes a spatial curve. Such geometrically adaptable details are nothing new. What is novel though about the detail in this paper is that its geometric dimensions vary based on the context and are manufactured for that exact location. A further extension of this approach is to allow different variations of the detail during generation based on conditional checks of the local context. For instance if a curve becomes too extreme for one type of detail, a different type might be used.

2.3 Changes in standardization

Figure 3. Depending on local context the detail's scale and orientation changes.

With the generation of geometry through scripts that allow for parameter-based variations, the notion of standardization shifts from dimension based descriptions to a topologic system of relations. It is no longer necessary to fix a certain dimension at the interface between components, but the relationship of the two parts defines the shared dimension. The standard shifts to the description of the relationship. It is important to know how elements relate to each other, but it is not necessary to know their absolute dimensions. Parametric modeling has set the stage for the expression of elements as a set of relations that have variable dimensions. A non-dimensional based standard relies heavily on fabrication techniques that allow for the production of varying geometries based on a system, as in the example of the joint shown here. Generative approaches through programming allow the generation of complete systems out of a set of rules. Robert Aish, Director of Research at Bentley System, has developed a very promising approach to programming integrated into parametric modeling systems in the Custom Objects extension to Microstation.

2.4 Importance of material modeling in the design process

The example of the 3D puzzled surface shows the importance of material simulation for the design process. Material behavior should be captured in correspondence to the geometric distortions. In the example, the material is not simulated. The distortion of the strips causes the dimensions of the pieces to change, which affects the relationship of the parts to each other. This in turn affects the assembly process. Without simulation or anticipation of the material response any digital geometric model is just a representation of the desired form. It lacks the information how to manufacture it correctly. The shortcoming of the puzzle surface demonstrates that clearly. The majority of the geometries produced develop problems during the assembly process due to the lack of material simulation in the generation process. Simplified techniques of embedding material properties are for instance constraining models to planar or to developable surfaces. Dennis Shelden, Director of Computing at Frank Gehry's office, has developed different tools and techniques using this approach as well as the modeling of material properties of paper. "Parametric technology allows relationships among geometric elements to be encoded in the model as part of operations on these elements,"(Shelden 2002).

2.5 Self-registering geometries

When using manufacturing techniques that require post-fabrication assembly, it is very helpful to have self-registering geometries that allow for exact alignment of pieces in space. The puzzle joint is one approach to this problem. The continuous curvature of the joint provides a continuous fit between parts. In addition, it allows, in most cases, for only one, unique assembly of the pieces. In order for the pieces to snap together, they have to take on the desired three-dimensional shape. This ensures proper alignment of the pieces and the approximate three–dimensional shape of the overall form. However, inaccuracies result from the transformation of the digital geometry into the physical representation, as the current digital models do not take into account material properties, as for instance resistance to bending and material stiffness. When, in the case of the joint, one node forces a partial buckling of the surface, it affects the neighboring nodes as well. In the worst case, the propagation of these deformations renders the assembly of the pieces impossible.

2.6 Finite element analysis study of a joint sketch model

The author has done a draft analysis of the joint properties in the finite element analysis workbench of the CAD program CATIA. The results shown here are very preliminary and are shown only to illustrate the general properties of the joint behavior in terms of qualitative stress distribution and points of high and low friction. The friction distribution is particularly interesting, as friction is essential in making the joint work. The joint simulation was done with a 0.01 mm pressure fit overlap between the contact surfaces of the two test pieces. Friction is highest at the tips of the nodes, where the displacement tends to be the highest.

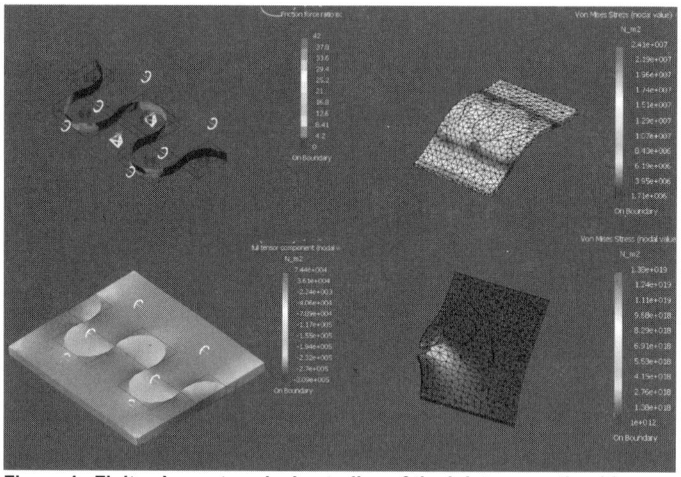

Figure 4. Finite element analysis studies of the joint properties (the studies are very preliminary and not representative of accurate force distributions.)

2.7 Extending the approach to 3D printing

The approach of writing code can be extended to other prototyping machines, such as 3D printers and milling machines. It is important to capture the machine's properties. The generating code for the fabrication process should make optimal use of the machine's properties, while staying as close as possible to the actual geometry of the piece. Each technique requires a particular type of detailing to respond to the requirements of the chosen techniques. For instance, material thickness does not scale well. A cardboard sheet cut at the correct model scale on a laser cutter might be too thin to work in a friction joint. Or a 3D print at the correct proportion might break due to the brittleness of the print material. The joint

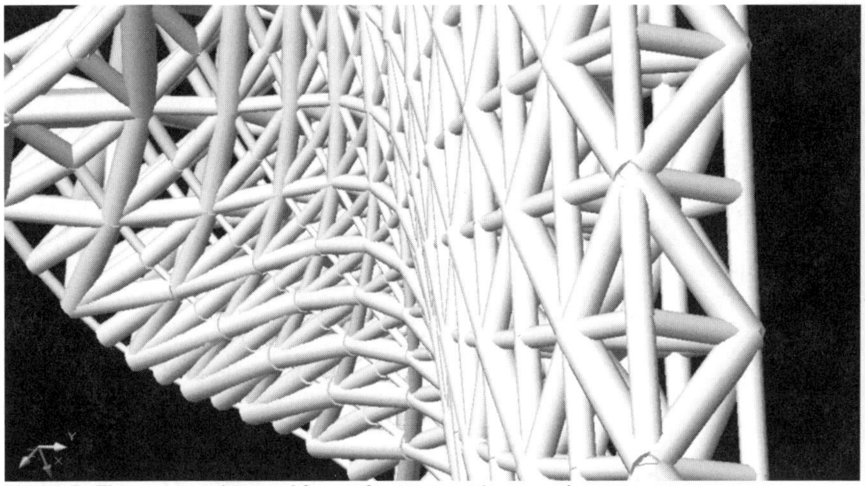

Figure 5. The same script used for surface generation can also generate a solid space frame over the spline surface that can be 3d printed on rapid prototyping machines.

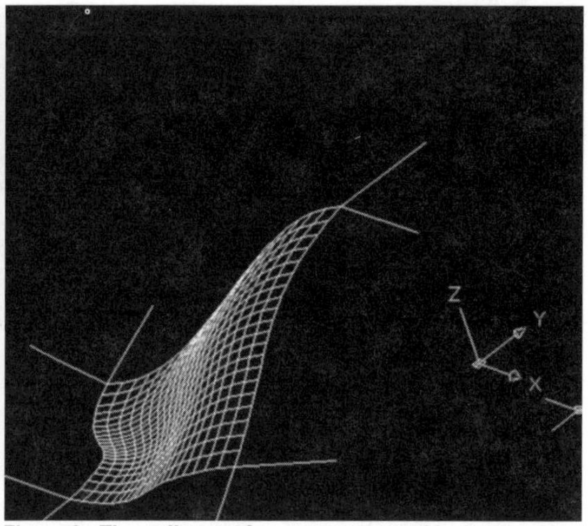

Figure 6. The spline surface, as generated in Autocad by the script. Its grid resolution is set to 20x20 cells.

example in this paper was initially developed in 1999 when the author witnessed the purchase of a laser cutter and attempted to explore the potential of computer-controlled cutting. The process was explicitly developed in response to the machine to provide for rapid production of physical sketch models from three-dimensional surface models. A similar approach was taken for the 3D printing process as illustrated with the space frame example. Recent work has explored the connection of scripting and 3D printing in depth. "This exploration has been guided by an intention to design physical objects through procedural programming"(Loukissas 2003).

2.8 Issues of scale

As rapid prototyping machines have limited bed sizes, the question of assembly is important, especially in an educational context. The ability to build larger, cheap prototypes out of pieces with a limited size requires connection joints that can be put together without additional hardware. The linear puzzle joints helps in connecting surface-based materials in a planar fashion. It establishes a tension and compression connection as long as the joint stays within the plane of the surface connection. This connection is achieved through pressure fitting the parts and does not require additional fasteners. Exceptions are materials where the material thickness is too thin to provide a pressure fit connection. For this condition a flexible rubber seal was used to allow for a continuous connection, for instance between aluminum sheets. This seal could also act as a preliminary water barrier in providing a continuous surface seal.

2.9 Shift of the design focus from geometry toward building systems expressed through generative or parametric systems

Increasingly, the introduction of digital-based modeling will shift the focus of design away from fixed geometry towards parametric or generative constructs capable of producing a variety of geometric output. The important difference is that parametric and generative models can be set up to contain fabrication constraints and material properties that allow for the exploration of form within these constraints.

3 Description of the process of fabrication

The following describes the process of producing a puzzle-jointed surface through an application written in Autolisp within AutoCAD. The process has been developed since spring 1999.

3.1 The surface

A surface is modeled with the help of a custom-written quadratic spline surface modeler in AutoCAD using an Autolisp script. The surface is defined through eight slopes, two each at the surface corner points. The slopes define the incoming and outgoing slope of the surface edges of the spline surface. The spline surface is adjustable in its grid cell resolution through a custom command. The grid cell resolution determines how close the surface approximates the numerical spline surface and is the basis for the generation of the puzzle joint detail as well.

3.2 The strips

Once the desired form and resolution is achieved one can use another custom command to develop the strips in one of the UV directions of the surface as strips onto the ground plane.

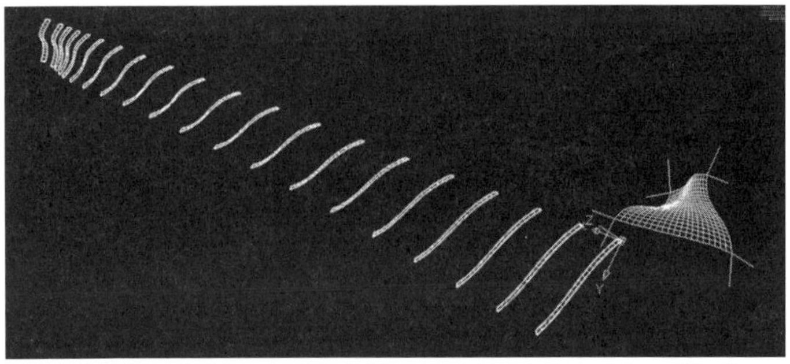

Figure 7. After running the fabrication script over the surface 20 strips are flattened out

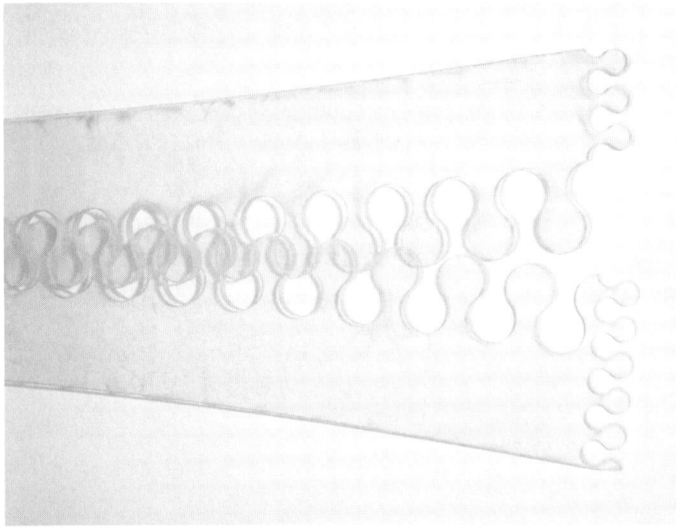

Figure 8. A testing strip made of polycarbonate clearly showing the joint properties

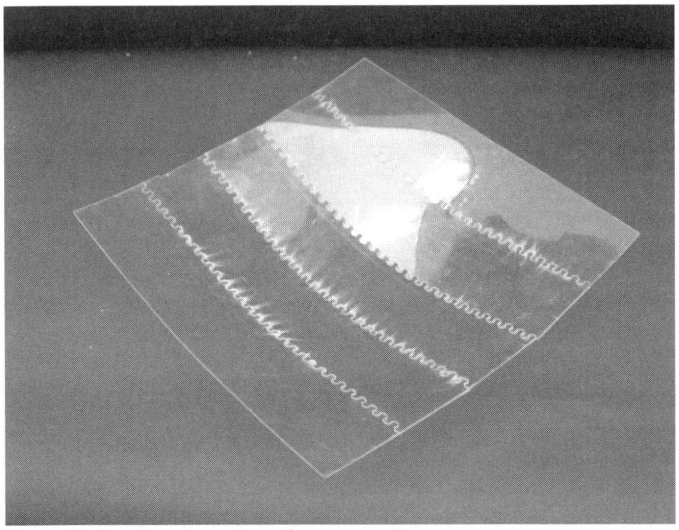

Figure 9. A polycarbonate surface example

The process uses a crude triangulation technique, but since the topology of the surface elements to be flattened is known and each strip has only one neighboring strip with one shared edge, this approximation is not a problem. The flattening technique also ensures that there are no overlaps between the parts when they are flattened. Once the parts are flattened, the joint detail is generated based on the resolution of the surface strip. The variation of the edge line spacing is based on the overall grid resolution of the initial surface.

3.3 The joint

Once the cutting line layout is generated, the testing begins to fine-tune the balance between cutting tolerance, material thickness, material stiffness, and the friction of the faces of the cut. This balance influences how well the joint will pressure fit. Since the pieces are curved, the assembly can only be done one joint at a time. The offset introduced through the curvature is much larger then in a planar configuration. The joint has to have enough play to be assembled. But if the tolerance is too great, the joint will not stay connected through the material friction. The actual joint geometry was born out of the quest for a geometry that would allow for fastener free surface connections, which would be able to transfer forces within the surface, both in tension and in compression.

3.4 The material

For various materials, iterations of test joints with different cutting tolerances were made. Tested materials were polycarbonate, aluminum, various cardboard types, wood and Plexiglas.

3.5 The cutting

Once the tolerances for the cutting process are established, the layout is cut either with a laser cutter or a water jet cutter, depending on the material. Most cardboard and wood materials could be cut with the laser cutter, whereas polycarbonate and aluminum were cut on the water jet cutter. Once the pieces are cut, they are assembled. Curvature is applied along the lines of ruling. A rubber hammer is used to pound the joints into places. This is necessary in order to overcome the friction in the joints that hold the pieces in place.

The polycarbonate piece has been the most successful in terms of assembly and strength after the assembly process. For the polycarbonate sheet, a special cutting technique was applied. Every other strip was mirrored before cutting, in order to use the valley shaped blasting crater of the water jet cutting process to the advantage of the joints. Through mirroring the cutting line of every other strip, the surfaces of the cutting edges lie parallel and greatly increase the friction between them.

3.6 Side effects of the puzzle joint

Since the puzzle joint does span over the edge-line of the

Figure 10. Cutting of the polycarbonate pieces in an OMAX™ water jet cutter

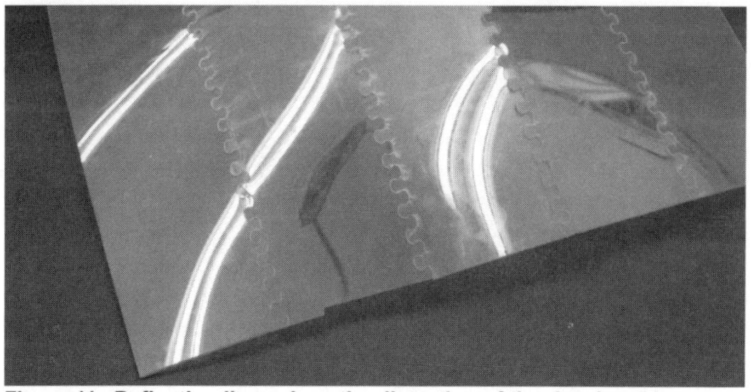

Figure 11. Reflection lines show the distortion of the developable strips into partial double curvature due to the joints bridging the ridge between the strips.

developable surface strip, it is geometrically not a clean component. It is attached to one strip with single curvature, but through the joint properties it is forced to lie within the surface of the neighboring strip, which does not share the same curvature. It therefore takes on a partial double curvature. This actually helps the pieces to approximate the numerically double curved surface the strip approximation is based on. But the process is very uncontrolled and hard to predict. In many cases it fails, and the bending force pulling the puzzle node out of its position is greater then the friction force keeping it in place. However, the process also has positive effects. The joints are pre-stressed which increases the friction in the joints through the increased forces acting on the joint seam.

3.7 Layout of the surface patches that use the puzzle joint

The basis for the puzzle joint is the geometry of the actual puzzle pieces. In the demonstrated approach, the chosen form is that of a developable surface strip. The spline surface is divided up based on the isopram UV lines at regular intervals. This guarantees a certain correspondence between surface properties and strip properties. But it does not take into account the difference in curvature between neighboring strips. A more promising approach would be the use of a tiling scheme that analyses the local curvature condition and orients the seams in the optimal orientation to the slope of the surface. A study was done by the author using Genetic Algorithms for the description of finite state automata that would walk across the surface reacting to the local curvature. It is a relatively complicated interconnected model that does not allow for very reliable results due to the number of parameters that can be adjusted. The main challenge is to define a reliable fitness function for selection of the FSA for the strip production that does allow for new patterns to emerge but does not limit the selection too closely.

4 Conclusions

The larger perspective of the research approach is the question how to formulate and capture design intention through programming, and what influence the use of generative modeling in combination with rapid prototyping has on the design language of physical objects. The author predicts changes in the language of details by generating details that adapt to local geometric and material properties through programming. The designer writes programs as part of the overall design. Code will be written that adapts a design for a particular fabrication method and incorporates machine-specific properties into the design. There is a general distinction between rapid prototyping for the means of production and large-scale fabrication, rapid prototyping for representational purposes for studying the form, and rapid prototyping as a design exploration tool. As a design exploration tool it allows the designer to generate large number of iterations of physical models that are representational, but are also studies of the assembly process, material properties and fabrication sequences.

The goal of this exercise in the long run, is the integration of the material properties as well as the methods of fabrication into the generation of geometric representation. In the best case an integrated design cycle takes full advantage of the possibilities of the digital medium and the computer controlled tools.

5 References

Aish, R. (2000). Custom objects: A model oriented end-user programming environment. Draft paper submitted to the Visual End User Workshop VL2000

Loukissas, Y. (2003). Rulebuilding, exploring design worlds through end-user programming. SMArchS thesis, Department of Architecture, Massachusetts Institute of Technology, Cambridge, MA.

Shelden, D. R.(2002). Digital surface representation and the constructibility of Gehry's architecture. Ph.D. thesis in Department of Architecture, Massachusetts Institute of Technology, Cambridge MA.

Using Actuated Tensegrity Structures to Produce a Responsive Architecture

Tristan d'Estrée Sterk
The School of The Art Institute of Chicago, USA

Abstract

The major theoretical roots of responsive architecture lie within the work of Nicholas Negroponte, and its most inspiring realization, to date, is found in the work of dECOi Architects. The work of NOX, and Diller & Scofidio provide two other built examples of responsive architectures. Each of these works is impressive within its own right. However, all of them have their shortcomings, suggesting that several possibilities for alternative visions still exist.

While Negroponte's work identifies the characteristics of a responsive architecture, it does not propose a model that is suitable for implementation. On the other hand, the work of dECOi architects does not address the technical needs of a building envelope designed for real world conditions of weather and structural load. Diller & Scofidio's work, also does not have a functional envelope, and NOX's work lacks physical responsiveness, favoring a palate of virtual responses instead. This paper, after examining the four specific precedents of Negroponte, dECOi, Diller & Scofidio, and NOX, will examine how a fifth precedent—that of Buckminster Fuller's model of tensegrity structures—may be applied. The paper will propose that by actuating a tensegrity structure a responsive architectural envelope that addresses real world weather and structural loading conditions becomes feasible.

Using Actuated Tensegrity Structures to Produce a Responsive Architecture:

Tristan d'Estrée Sterk
The School of The Art Institute of Chicago, USA

1 Introduction:

The common definition of responsive architecture, as described by many authors, is a class of architecture or building that demonstrates an ability to alter its form, to continually reflect the environmental conditions that surround it.

The term responsive architecture was given to us by Nicholas Negroponte, who first conceived of it during the late nineteen sixties when spatial design problems were being explored by applying cybernetics to architecture. Negroponte proposes that responsive architecture is the natural product of the integration of computing power into built spaces and structures, and that better performing, more rational buildings are the result (Negroponte 1975). Negroponte also extends this mixture to include the concepts of recognition, intention, contextual variation, and meaning into computing and its successful (ubiquitous) integration into architecture. This cross-fertilization of ideas lasted for about eight years. Several important theories resulted from these efforts, but today Nicholas Negroponte's contributions are the most obvious to architecture. His work moved the field of architecture in a technical, functional, and actuated direction. Since Negroponte's contribution, new works of responsive architecture have also emerged, but as aesthetic creations—rather than functional ones. The works of Diller & Scofidio (Blur), dECOi (Aegis Hypo-Surface), and NOX (the Freshwater Pavilion, NL); are all classifiable as types of responsive architecture (Diller & Scofidio 2002; Liu 2002; Lootsma and Spuybroek 1997). Each of these works monitors fluctuations with the environment and alters its form in response to these changes. The Blur project by Diller & Scofidio relies upon the responsive characteristics of a cloud to change its form while blowing in the wind. In the work of dECOi, responsiveness is enabled by a programmable façade, and finally in the work of NOX, a programmable audio–visual interior. All of these works depend upon the abilities of computers to continuously calculate and join programmable digital models to the real world and the events that shape it.

This paper proposes that from the general features of these works (their dependence upon computing, their connecting digital models of the world to the real world, and their desire to make continuously altering forms of architecture), two very simple categories of features are realizable. The categories of features are: 1) that responsive architectures must be able to cope with dynamic loading conditions that result from environmental changes; and 2) that the adjustments made in response to these changes must be controlled. To complement these categories a further category may arise if future responsive architectures are functional. This third category is, 3) that all responsive buildings must provide shelter from changing environmental conditions. By adopting the stance that responsive buildings provide a means of improving the functional abilities of architecture, this paper will focus upon those characteristics that arise from the first and third points. The paper will begin by describing four precedents, their features, and downfalls, then suggest how functional responsive architectures can be made by using actuated tensegrity structures.

2 Responsive Architecture's Built and Un-Built Precedents:

Understanding that responsive buildings belong to a type of architecture that is definable and that has three categories of features does not provide one with a sufficient understanding of the subject. Responses can be generated in many different ways and for different reasons, so it is advantageous to examine existing built and un-built precedents to gain an initial understanding about what variety of responses is possible—and the uses to which they have been put.

The precedents are few, and are deserving of a much deeper exploration than can be offered within this paper. Problems of performing research within this area should now be acknowledged. These are: 1) few precedents currently exist; 2) precedents that do exist are poorly documented; 3) precedents that do exist tend to focus upon aesthetic responses rather than functional responses; 4) until a built, functional responsive architecture exists, studies about efficiency, thermal performance, and social effects are impossible to perform with accuracy; 5) many of the reasons for producing a functional responsive architecture are hard to demonstrate without empirical data to back them up.

2.1 Diller & Scofidio's Blur:

The work of Diller & Scofidio, called Blur, was built by using a traditional (static) tensegrity structure to support an open deck. The structure, cloaked by a network of computer-controlled nozzles, was then shrouded by mist to produce a responsive building envelope that had the ability to change its shape whenever the wind blew. This technique allowed the size of the cloud, and therefore the size of the building envelope, to be directly related and responsive to the environmental conditions that surrounded the building. Only one changeable parameter controlled all of this—the density of the mist produced.

Sensors were placed to measure wind speed and the natural air humidity both within the building and along the shoreline in order to collect the environmental data used to control the rate of mist produced by the computer-controlled nozzles. A further level of control was then made possible by breaking the building down into several individually controllable zones that enabled portions of the building to be shrouded at different rates. The aim of controlling the building in this way was to produce enough mist to cover the entire structure while not allowing it to drift or stray too far from the building (Diller and Scofidio 2002).

While this work of architecture uses responsive technologies to control the size and shape of its envelope dynamically, the scope of control exerted over the building form is limited—although still sufficient to achieve a new design aesthetic. The architects of this building use the ability of a cloud to blow in the wind to evoke emotional responses from building users. They accept that a single parameter of control and the materials used do not produce a new type of architecture that is functional.

2.2 dECOi's Aegis Hypo-Surface:

By using very different techniques from those of Diller & Scofidio, the work of dECOi architects called "Aegis Hypo-Surface" was built upon a framework of pneumatic pistons, springs, and metal plates, all of which were used to deform a façade-like surface (Liu 2002). By reverse engineering the wall from sources of published information, a plausible picture of the inner working of the surface follows. Behind the façade's surface, many pneumatic pistons attach to metal plates that form the wall surface. Springs are then attached to both the pistons and the static structural frame, helping to control the location of each piston by providing it with a failsafe means of returning to a known starting point or resting state. By understanding the typical way pneumatic pistons are controlled, we can also understand how the wall is actuated by distributing air pressure between two different pneumatic chambers (within the body of a piston) in different combinations to allow the piston to extend, to contract, or alternatively jitter in a mode that enables it to extend and contract very rapidly. A computer was then programmed to fire each piston sequentially in order to produce a series of patterns that responded to environmental stimuli—sound being the particular stimuli used. A very traditional, static, frame supported all structural loads. Like the Blur project, dECOi's work does not attempt to provide functional solutions for a new type of architecture. The strategies used to produce the wall do not resolve or identify how architectural facades or weather resistant responsive building envelopes are made. It also does not provide a connection between dynamic building skins and the structures that support them. Thus a responsive architecture that consists of a functional building envelope which shelters people from environmental loads by addressing the principles of cold bridging, rain screens, and the dynamic transferring of structural loads still needs to be resolved.

2.3 NOX's Freshwater Pavilion:

NOX's Freshwater pavilion in Holland provides another powerful example of what the future of responsive architecture may hold. The Freshwater Pavilion has a responsive interior that uses the advantages offered by virtual environments to produce programmable spaces.

It accomplishes this by connecting a virtual representation of the world to the physical world through a vast array of blob trackers and light sensors connected to three different "interactive" systems that operate together (Lootsma and Spuybroek 1997). These three actuating systems drive 1) projected animations, 2) a lighting system, or 3) an audio system. Each of these three systems is placed throughout the building to make a rich, multimedia environment. At close range, blob-tracking sensors monitor environmental changes such as the movement of bodies in space (blob tracking demands video sensors). In the distance, changes in light levels (sensed either by video sensors or photo-resistor technologies) further control how environmental responses occur. Lars Spuybroek writes, "Every group of sensors is connected to a projector that shows a 'standard' wire frame grid which translates every action of a visitor into real-time movements of (virtual) water. The light sensors are connected to the 'wave'. Every time one walks through a beam of infra-red light one sees a wave going through the projected wire frames . . . visitors can create any kind of interference of these waves" (Lootsma and Spuybroek 1997).

Although not yet of a physical form of responsive architecture this work does suggest the possibility of producing spaces that are completely responsive. Furthermore, the work suggests that by layering a digital world model onto the real world the depth and complexity of responses produced within a space can be very rich—a point echoed by traditional models of artificial intelligence. Incidentally, the computational model of this environment is based upon embedded computation. This model, with some 190 lights, driven by 190 different distributed microprocessors, differs significantly from dECOi's model that uses one computer to drive several hundred actuators.

2.4 Negroponte's Model:

For Negroponte responsive architecture is a function of intelligence (Negroponte 1975). He believes that the integration of artificial intelligence into architectural environments is critical to producing a responsive architecture that is capable of performing adequately (the recognition of just how much intelligence is required to identify the context of an event and the appropriateness of a response is important to Negroponte). He also believes that responsiveness in architecture will manifest itself in two different forms—as informational responses that are not physical—and as responses that are overt, physical actions (Negroponte 1975). Negroponte calls each of these two forms of responsiveness, reflexive action, and simulated action, both of which are functional.

Citing a hypothetical example of a reflexive architectural

action, Negroponte quotes Avery Johnson's 1971 work called "The Three Little Pigs Revisited," and says "walls that move to the touch–relevant to the function of support or moving back in retreat–that change color and form: streamlining themselves to the wind or shrinking down when unoccupied, are all possible" (Negroponte 1975). Simulated actions, on the other hand, include a room that can emulate an environment to entertain users. Breaking these ideas down still further, Negroponte suggests that two different varieties of simulated or reflexive responses are possible and describes them as being either operational or informational (Negroponte 1975).

Operational responses include those that contribute to how a place functions (a robot that responds to clean a house is the particular example he gives). Informational responses are similar to operational responses but they specialize in the control and provision of information that is useful or desired by users within a space.

Summarizing all of these response types, Negroponte proceeds to describe the overall picture of a responsive architecture as being the production of a "dramatically different relationship between ourselves and our houses, one characterized by intimate interaction" (Negroponte 1975). He goes on to say that design processes within this type of architecture will change, one result of which may be the integration of design and building processes into a single, continually operational process. His work does not suggest how these architectures may actually be built—although he does favor the use of soft materials and structures (such as inflatable membranes) over hard materials and structures (no examples of hard materials are given) (Negroponte 1975).

3 Producing a Functional Responsive Architecture:

Against the criteria of function, the discussed precedents are not adequate. No built precedent provides for responsiveness in structure and shelter together. Negroponte's work, as an un-built precedent, does give us examples of what this architecture might look like and how it should function; however, it does not realize how it can be built. So, how can a functional responsive architecture be built? Are there any other precedents that can be used or modified to suit this cause?

The ideal version of a functional responsive architecture is one that can provide shelter against changing conditions, as well as calculate how these changes affect the type of shelter needed. It would also have the capability of calculating how dynamic and changing structural loads are distributed through the structure successfully. These loads come from two basic sources, those loads caused by the building's own responses (shifting walls, etc.), and those caused by external loads acting upon the structure such as wind, rain, or snow. To produce this type of architecture and ensure that it is functional, traditional principles of weather screening, cold bridging, and load transmission need to be observed.

The incorporation of these principles within a responsive architecture does provide a challenge for architects—many of whom turn to inflatable technologies or "soft" materials to solve perceived design problems. The following work results from the endeavors of this author to produce a responsive architecture from "harder" materials and structures. When modified, Buckminster Fuller's system of tensegrity provides one means of making a functional responsive architecture that meets the above criteria.

3.1 Using Tensegrity To Produce A Responsive Architectural Envelope:

In 1962, Fuller and Snelson patented Tensegrity (Oppenheim and Williams 1997). Tensegrity systems are those composed of two types of discrete members, tension members and compression members that form self-stressing structures. The type of tensegrity system proposed for use by this paper consists of a repeated module in which three compression members meet to form what can be simply described as a tripod whose legs are tethered by tension cables—as depicted in figure 1. Repeating this module in a regular pattern, results in the formation of two membranes that have variable and controllable rigidity—figure 2. In principle the act of controlling the rigidity of these two membranes results in the possibility of producing structures whose shapes can alter. Thus by actuating the structure, in the correct locations, a deformable, responsive, structure can be made.

Two important structural principles help us further understand this position; both are discussed in a book called *Smart Structures and Materials*, written by Brian Culshaw. Culshaw notes that restraints in load transmission must be met in all structures, whether or not they are responsive. Thus "the 75-kg weight lifter will make no progress on lifting his or her own weight unless the bench on which he or she stands is capable of surviving the 150-kg load regardless of how adaptive or intelligent the weight lifter may be" (Culshaw 1996). He also suggests that one of the key features to any responsive structure is its ability to alter its stiffness rather than strength. "In most cases the adjustable strength aspects of the structure will involve more material, more weight, and certainly more complexity than the more simple structure designed to operate under the full range of loading condition" (Culshaw 1996). His thesis turns to natural structures that employ variable stiffness to distribute loads dynamically through their bodies in order to overcome difficulties in load transmission.

3.2 The Location, Limits, and Role of Actuation:

Actuators are mechanical devices used to alter the state of a physical system or structure. Actuation refers to the application of a mechanical device to achieve a physical task. For this paper, actuation implies the use of mechanical devices to manipulate the rigidity of a structure.

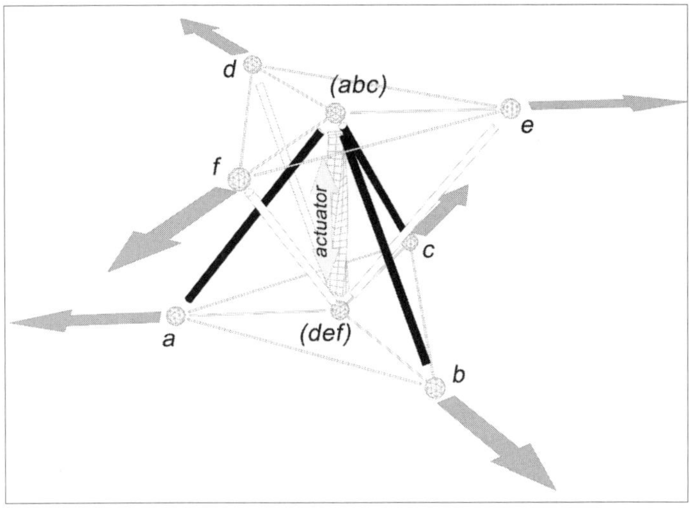

Figure 1. The simplest actuated unit of a tensegrity structure, made more rigid by pulling each apex towards its opposite, forcing each 'tripod' leg outward until the cables are tight.

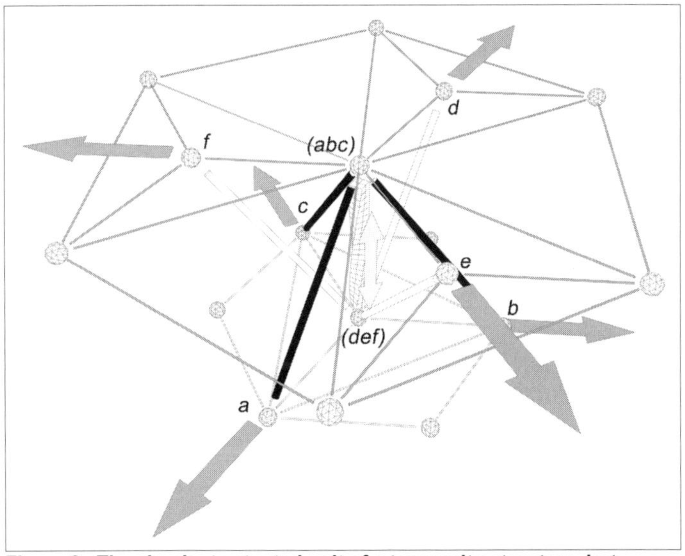

Figure 2. The simplest actuated unit of a tensegrity structure, but this time shown with a cable configuration that enables the unit to be multiplied out into a much larger structure.

Actuating a structure, however, is not enough to produce responsive architecture. Responsive architectures only come into being when actuators are coupled with other devices so that activities and changes within the real world can be interpreted, computed or processed, and then outputted back into the real world as an action or response. By tying these responses or actions to a structure and building envelope, responsive architecture becomes feasible.

The location or position of an actuator within a tensegrity structure is especially important and determined by two guiding principles, those being: 1) that cables can only be loaded in tension, and 2) that struts can only be loaded in compression. Culshaw's previous words dictate that actuation should also provide for the greatest amount of control over the structure's rigidity—this implies that the best location for actuation occurs at the apex of each structural unit, where the three compression members meet and where opposing structural apexes may be connected by an actuated component. Through the mechanical action of an actuator, force may be applied to each structural unit in combination, either pulling them towards each other to increase structural rigidity, or pushing them apart to decrease rigidity. Limits to the amount of applied force imposed by an actuator upon a structure are determined by examining the shape of a structure as well as the way in which a structure is required to operate (how much movement is desirable).

The manner in which a structure transfers its loads and the form (or shape) that a structure needs to adopt helps us know how much tension is required for the building to maintain or take a shape. With this in mind, the form of a tensegrity structure relates to both its physical design (the length of tension and compression members) as well as the ability for an actuator to apply forces to the structure and make it rigid. Accepting that the only readably changeable variable within a built structure is its rigidity further links building shape to actuated forces. Figure 3 describes this condition for the case of a parabolic vault like construction. In this particular example, the lower portion of the vault must remain rigid to maintain a vertical position, while the upper vault slackens to produce a curved surface. Removing tension from the lower region of the vault, by reducing forces applied by an actuator, allows deformation suggesting that the stiffness of this region may warrant a limit (to avoid possible structural collapse).

Actuators, when controlled by a computer, or several distributed computers, should be conceived of as programmable and thus as providing a means to connect computation to the physical control of a structure or building envelope. As a model, this opens the door to producing a responsive form of architecture that connects computation to a class of "harder" materials and structures that are capable of being responsive, and perhaps more suitable than structures made responsive through inflatable technologies. Responsive architecture demands that the role of actuation be linked to computation, no matter what its brand (be it analog computation or digital computation or a hybrid of both).

The methods I believe most suitable for establishing control and linking it to events within the real world will now be discussed in conjunction with issues of waterproofing, insulating, and future applications.

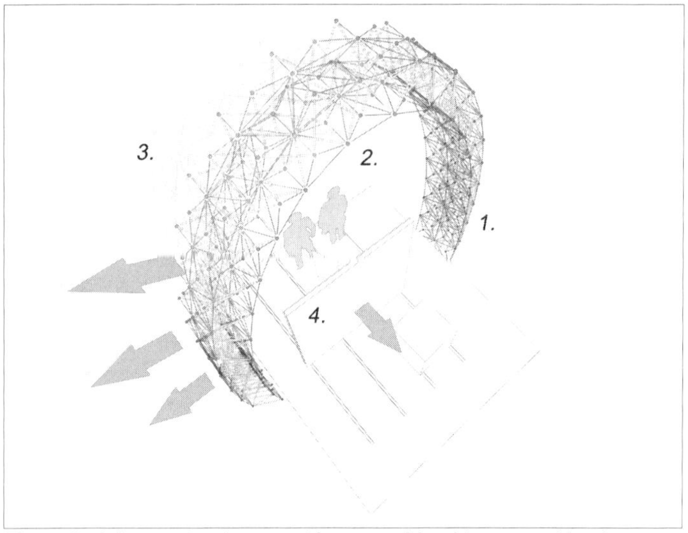

Figure 3. 1. lower structure must be more ridged to support loads without collapse. 2. upper structure can be less ridged. 3. by adjusting the tension and rigidity of the structure physical movements are enabled. 4. when coordinated with other responsive elements (ie. an internal partition) the functional abilities of buildings may be further extended.

3.3 Bringing It All Together:

To reiterate, all functional architectures must shelter people from environmental conditions as well as perform structurally. Responsive architectures must perform in a similar way if they aim to be functional.

The primary principle or method used to waterproof buildings today is the rain or weather screen. Rain screens work by separating building components that have different functions into two distinct layers of construction. One layer deals with insulating the building, and the other layer protects the building (and the insulating layer) from water. Each of these two layers is separated to allow for a natural airflow between the waterproof membrane and insulation. The function of this gap is: 1) to remove the chance of negative air pressures forming behind the waterproof membrane, thus stopping water from being sucked into the structure; and 2) to provide a draft that evaporates any moisture which collects upon the insulation, thus increasing its capacity to insulate. The layering required for producing a rain screen can easily be built into tensegrity structures because tensegrity structures also depend upon natural separations between three different functional layers—with two layers consisting of tension members between which a third layer of compression members is sandwiched. By cloaking one layer of tension members with a soft waterproof membrane, and the second layer of tension members with an insulating membrane it becomes possible to turn a tensegrity structure into a weather tight building envelope—Figure 4. By merging each discrete system, a responsive architecture that protects building users from environmental conditions becomes feasible.

To control the protective envelope a suitable strategy for integrating distributed computing into the structure becomes the next goal. After having previously identified the way in which the rigidity of a structural unit can be controlled, it is possible to realize that entire structures may be modularized and made controllable by distributed and embedded computing power. The simplest actuated control module thus consists of two opposing "tripods," an actuator (that connects the structural units together), a processor, a sensor, and power source, which may or may not be modularized. The resulting active structural unit can then be designed to collect information from the real world (via its sensor), calculate and process the collected data, and then adjust the actuator to tighten or loosen the structure thus affecting the rigidity of an architectural envelope. Within this configuration, a structure that consists of many hundreds or thousands of actuators produces a very robust building envelope that moves in an emergent way.

The system may be constructed differently still to produce more useful behaviors. For example by pooling sensor data together from several regions of a structure (by connecting many actuators, processors, and sensors together), the scale of a response can be increased to enable larger (less localized) structural responses to occur. Larger scale responses add functionality to a responsive structure and enable it to cope with loads that are exerted over larger areas, such as earthquake or wind loads. Responses that are still more useful are generated by further modifying the system to allow for the inclusion of higher levels of processing (for example reasoning processes generated by Bayesian networks or other forms of artificial intelligence), to motivate actual building responses. The complexity of this topic is beyond detailed resolution within this paper—a recent paper by this author, dealing with issues in controlling responsive architecture is located within the proceedings of the eCAADe conference, Graz Austria, September 2003.

4 Future Applications In Architecture & Its Practice:

Actuated tensegrity structures may make a functional responsive architecture, but are visions for the practical use of this type of architecture foreseeable?

Theatres that dance with performers, houses that shrink to reduce their surface area and heated volume in the dead of winter or that cover themselves in the glare of a summer's sun, and skyscrapers that alter their aerodynamic profile to reduce wind loads, provide three very different applications of this technology all of which are plausible and foreseeable. Further applications that deal with the networking of buildings to coordinate responses between many individual buildings and structures are also foreseeable. To envisage how a network of

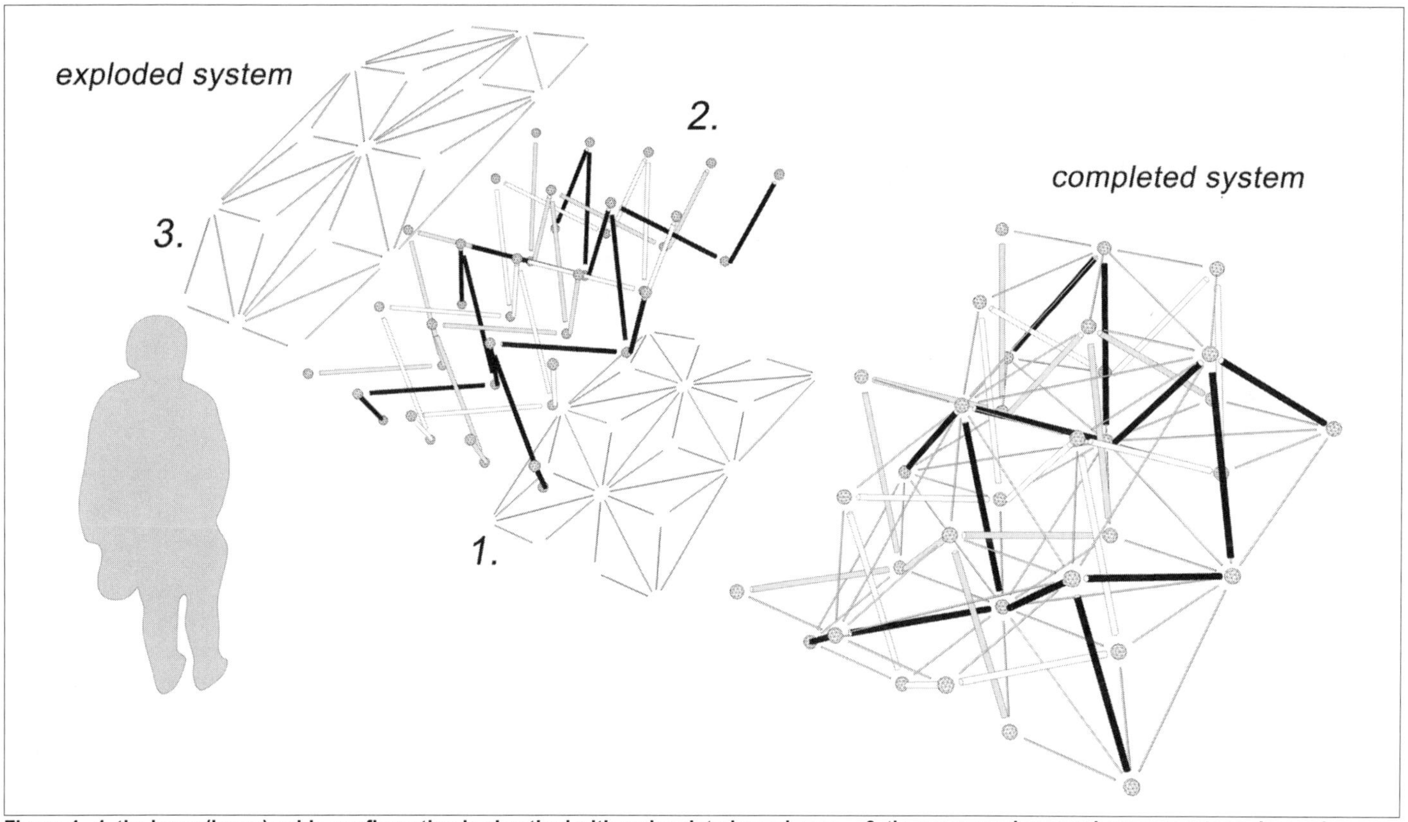

Figure 4. 1. the inner (lower) cable configuration is sheathed with an insulated membrane. 2. the compression members separate each membrane. 3. the outer (upper) cable configuration is sheathed with a waterproof membrane.

buildings can coordinate their actions to good effect, consider the following example. If a cluster of tall responsive buildings is exposed to wind, and one of those buildings changes its shape to reduce the wind load exerted upon itself, but in the process of doing so accidentally reflects wind onto a second structure, a situation may arise that harms the second building. The most elegant way of preventing this problem, or rapidly solving it when it arises, is to network buildings together so that the actions of one building and the consequences of that action (within a community) become associated, identified, and avoided (if the consequences are harmful). On the flipside of this same coin, it also becomes possible to envisage how the advantageous actions of a building can become more readily identifiable. For example, networks may allow a series of buildings to make unexpected discoveries when an action produced by one building enables other buildings to achieve a higher level of performance. Applications of this technology can occur within all types of building envelopes. They will occur whenever building envelopes need to demonstrate changes of function and use, or when responses help buildings become more sustainable. As a new type of architecture, it also offers the potential to challenge some of the conventional design methods and models used within architectural practice.

The aesthetic opportunities raised by a responsive building envelope make these technologies favorable for building types where the events that occur within a space should influence the shape of a building envelope. Familiar principles that generate this type of aesthetic come from some of the original arguments of modernism, as expressed by the notion of form following function, or the similar idea of having buildings reflect, and be the natural product of, truthful (or obvious) connections between the envelope of a space, its structure, and the events that fill it—all because responsive architectures have the ability to translate spatial activities into changing architectural form.

The sustainable opportunities of responsive building envelopes appear to be more promising still. The possibilities raised by an architecture that can respond to sunny, shady, hot, or cold conditions would suggest that responsive buildings possess the means to produce spaces that are informed by environmental conditions. As a by-product of this, it is entirely conceivable that actively changing spaces that monitor and adjust to suit surrounding environmental conditions will provide those who inhabit responsive buildings with new, active, relationships to the natural environment.

Other opportunities that responsive architectures raise are those that affect architectural practice. Responsive architectures, especially those based upon computational models that are heuristic, or artificially intelligent and self training, open architectural practice to the handing over of design activities to those who own or occupy space. Responsive architectures, are programmable by nature and as such offer any individual the chance to modify the way buildings behave. This change may result in an individual's ability to remove and replace the original architectural behavior of a design, with new, more appropriate, suitable, and useful building behaviors. One might conceive of this shift as being the "soft" equivalent of extending a house. However, as the earlier example of networking skyscrapers suggests, the ability to program a building to respond differently than intended may need to be limited. Reprogramming a skyscraper to purposefully deflect wind onto a neighbor might not be favorable—limits would have to apply.

Architectural practice is also likely to alter in a second, less anticipated way. It is very likely that the practice of architecture will change when the opportunity to access real world data collected by responsive buildings presents itself to the discipline. Architects who operate within this new environment, who have access to information about the performance of their buildings, would not just be bound to safeguard the privacy of a client but also use this data to improve future building designs.

5 Conclusion:

This paper outlines how actuating and applying rain screen principles to tensegrity structures produces a functional responsive architecture. It examines four precedents to understand the qualities of their manufacture, their functionality, and the intentions of their designers.

The ideas contained within this paper result from work carried out by the author to build a functional and responsive tensegrity structure (measuring 1.5 meters by 1 meter - flat), actuated by thermally sensitive memory metals. Each actuator is controlled through a mixture of distributed, embedded, digital, and analog circuitry.

I will soon be extending the work contained within this paper to produce a large-scale structure in the form of a parabolic vault (measuring 2.8 meters tall by 2 meters wide). The prototype will be built from aluminum, rubber, steel components, and controlled by a mixture of digital and analog technologies that are distributed through the structure. To further complement this work, a paper addressing control issues of responsive architectures has been written for the September 2003, eCAADe conference, in Graz Austria.

References

Culshaw, B. (1996). *Smart structures and materials*. Boston, MA: Artech.

Diller, E., and R. Scofidio. (2002). *Blur: The making of nothing*. New York: Harry N. Abrams, Inc.

Liu, Y. (2002). *Defining digital architecture, 2001 FEIDAD award*. Berlin: Birkhauser.

M. Goulthorpe, M. Burry, and G. Dunlop. (2001). Aegis hyposurface: The bordering of university and practice. *Proceedings of ACADIA 2001*, 334-349.

Lootsma, B., and L. Spuybroek. (1997). Aquatic pavilion and interactive installation Neeltje Jans, Holland. In *Domus: Architecture, design, art, communication* 796:28-33.

Negroponte, N. (1975). *Soft Architecture Machines*. Cambridge, MA: MIT Press.

Oppenheim, I., and W. Williams. (1997). Mechanics of tensegrity prisms. *Proceedings of the 14th international symposium on automation & robotics in construction*.

03a>>Connecting Digital Pedagogy

Chairs: Thomas Seebohm, Aron Temkin, George Proctor

Connected Courses: Methods Of Network Communications

Thomas Seebohm, Aron Temkin

Where are we now?

In the recent NJIT survey of digital media in the design schools twenty-eight out of twenty-nine architecture schools reported to have networked design studios (NJIT, 2003). This would seem to indicate a ubiquity of digital media tools. While the use of these tools is still often limited to design presentation (computer aided drawing and modeling) rather than design generation, the studio is historically a place of discovery and experimentation: with computers so available in this fertile environment we are poised to evolve the medium forward towards improved design development.

This evolution is initially apparent in the way presentation methods and presentation processes are shifting. Not only are students becoming increasingly digital in their approach to design, but methods of working and presentation are also changing.

Virtual distance studios (also referred to as virtual design studios) pioneered by Jerzy Wojtowicz and colleagues in 1994 (Wojtowicz, 1994) capitalized on the newly available capacities of the internet and related software (white board, image-sharing, video conferencing) to link design studios in disparate locations and time zones. This opened the door to synchronous or asynchronous collaboration on designs and sharing of design reviews. Studios have evolved from this initial step to share information using internet databases, bulletin boards, dedicated chat rooms, and even shared design projects – with students collaborating from several locations (Johnson et. al., 1998). While as a means of expanding the dialog of a design studio beyond a particular place and time, this has also prompted the question, "how can we create better virtual places for the interaction to occur (Engeli, 1999). One the most sophisticated of these web-based environments is the ETH world project, a merger of communications and information infrastructure (Carrard and Engeli, 2001). Herein, the school of architecture has set up, arc-line, perhaps the most sophisticated web-based infrastructure for allowing collaboration, project submission, viewing, reviewing design projects and access to design resources. Arc-line has been used effectively by up to 170 students at a time (Angeli, 2000).

Connectivity, therefore, has already changed the way architecture is taught in some schools with a new emphasis on collaboration and on seeking the virtual environments that encourage (and facilitate) these new methods of exchange. In non-studio courses changes are also occurring whereby web-based infrastructure supports the lectures, facilitates the handing in of assignments and encourages discussion outside the classroom. With wireless networking it is possible for students to bring their laptops to every class and to follow the lecture material simultaneously in the classroom and on their individual screens. Another expanding use of network technology is facilitating distributed design reviews where a critic or peer group is remotely but visually connected to a presentation through collaborative software (such as Microsoft Windows Messenger and Netmeeting). Presumably the current generation of architecture students will be well versed to work in digital environments where collaboration with other offices, locally or internationally is becoming routine. Most noted for such collaboration is the office of Norman Foster and partners where the use of extranets (really just a private portion of the internet with secure access available only to collaborators) has been pioneered to link distant offices. Concurrently, with networked studio environments comes the responsibility to provide adequate computing resources. This includes computers for students, output devices such as printers and plotters, projectors and display screens. Should schools provide computers for the students or should students be asked to supply their own? Should the computers be laptops or desktops? It raises issues about how much students should be expected to pay for their education.

Where are we going?

The internet bubble, for everything it was not, was nonetheless a remarkable moment in the history of communication and media. Despite the short-lived success of many e-commerce sites this explosion was a very powerful illustration of how new methods of connectivity can (and have, and should), expand the ways that we work, communicate, and teach.

In the architecture schools we are facing our own bubble: we are evolving the way we implement media, facilitate access to computers, and confront barriers of distance. As we get past these barriers of logistics and infrastructure we are free to revisit the questions:

- How does the way we work affect what we make?
- How should the ways we communicate affect the way we work?
- How can these tools of communication evolve the way we dialog (beyond the issues of who, where, and when)?
- Ultimately, what can we achieve that we could not realize before?

Perhaps a dialog regarding connectivity should distinguish a network as a delivery system versus a network as a web. Using a network as a delivery system, when dialogs occur back and forth connecting individual points (such as using email or a messenger interface), what we gain is accessibility. Using email I can reach someone in an office in Europe as easily as in the office next door. While this has obvious advantages over written mail, the nature of the dialog is still not far removed from a phone call or conversation. We expand this condition once we begin to email a list of people, and further still when using a chat room, the typed equivalent of a conference call. All of these methods permit a dialog with fewer boundaries – whether these boundaries are of distance or of time.

A web, on the other hand, if we follow the metaphor prescribed by a spider, is no longer limited to a linear dialog between two participants (or two participants at any one time). A web of information, in its most ideal form, is best considered as threads of an idea linked together at several points. The Wikipedia (www.Wikipedia.Com) is a great example of this model, while you can use it to link to a traditional reference source, the interconnectedness encouraged by the 'Wiki' culture and interface permits a path of discovery that is not longer limited to a single path of inquiry (or a single path of response).

We might go as far as to suggest that delivery networks are for seeking answers while web networks are best suited to seeking questions. When we ask a question in a linear dialog system we are not looking for an alternate view as much as we are looking for progress towards a destination. When we brainstorm (something of a real-time web) we allow ourselves to be usefully distracted by an alternative view or direction of inquiry.

With a web based dialog a thread may be conceived as either a beginning or an end. We put ideas (conceived as drawing as easily as words) out into a public (or semi-public) realm, opening the work up for discussion and response where we can just as easily use a single intervention to raise larger issues of design. For instance, we can go beyond asking, "is this library design effective?" And open a discussion up to, "what should a library become?"

Research is already asking these bigger questions. One early example asked, "how can we evolve the way we search for precedent? In shape based reminding as an aid for creative design, Ellen Do and Mark Gross described 'reminding software' designed to link freehand sketches to an index of precedents. (Do and Gross, 1995). With a typical web search we must know what we are looking for: a student is limited by their foreknowledge of formal paradigms or their ability to translate a formal condition into a written description. With digital shape recognition a student's search is connected to the act (and product) of drawing.

What other connections can we make? Where the pursuit of connectivity begins at the physical level of computers, ethernet cables, T1 lines, and wall-ports, if we are going to justify the expense of these resources, of this infrastructure, then we must pursue the evolution of design process and design quality.

References

Angeli, M.,et al. (2000)Arc-line:architecture on-line, Swiss Federal Institute of Technology, Department of Architecture, See also http://www.Ethworld.Ethz.Ch/nw/projects/details/22

Carrard, P. and Engeli, M. (Eds.) Conceptual competition ETH world: virtual and physical presence, GTA Verlag, 2001

Do, Ellen Yi-luen, and Mark D. Gross.(1995) "Shape based reminding as an aid to creative design". Sixth international conference on computer-aided design futures. Pp. 79-89.

Engeli, M and A.Mueller,(1999) " Digital environments for learning and collaboration, architecture, communication, and creativity". Acadia '99, Ataman and Bermudez eds., Pp. 40-52

Johnson, B., Kurmann, D., Kolarevic, B., Schmitt, G., Hirshberg, U., "*An experiment in design collaboration: Digital design studios, Do computers make a difference?,* Acadia '98, Seebohm and Van Wyk eds., October 1998, pp.90-99.

Wojtowicz J. (ed.) *Virtual design studio*, Hong Kong university press. 1994.

Thomas Seebohm is a registered architect and an associate professor of architecture in the school of architecture of the University of Waterloo, in Waterloo, Ontario, Canada. He specializes in digital design technologies and is currently focusing on these areas: digital design pedagogy; rule-based generative design and expert systems; double shell tensegrity structures, digital lighting design; and interactive, real-time, 3D architectural and urban modeling in stereo.

Aron Temkin is an Assistant Professor at Florida Atlantic University where he coordinates the junior phase and digital media components of the Architecture School curriculum. He received his Master of Architecture from the Cranbrook Academy of Art in 1997 and his Bachelor of Architecture with University

Honors from Carnegie Mellon University in 1992. His research explores digital modeling as a device for design refinement and animation as a device for temporal analysis of space. His professional practice includes graphic design, master planning, and architecture with an emphasis on sustainable place making. Through his built work he aspires to reconnect people to the variable conditions of their surroundings.

Digital Pedagogy: A- Digital Foundations: Building A Base For Digital Futures

George Proctor

Has "the digital" been absorbed by the discipline or has "the digital" absorbed the discipline? Depending on your perspective, architecture either continues to disintegrate or has reformed around a new definition of "the master builder." Digital technology has opened a variety of new career opportunities for the graduates of a digitally advanced architectural education. Some depictions of this trend have the discipline of architecture continuing to fragment into specialties. However, software has established platforms from which the activity surrounding a design project can be directed, managed, and built. But, does the capacity of software to re-center what is required to make a built environment mean that the design and making of such will fall to the historic notion of "master builder" or "the architect"?

Much of what applies to the general education of an architect can also be said for the digital portion of architectural curricula. Some students come to the university with digital media skills, some are autodidactic, a large number are waiting to be taught, and some either struggle to absorb digital skills or probably do not fit a life in architecture. In the midst of this new landscape, sketching and drawing freehand has become more important and necessary. Ironically, less time is provided to build these "old" skills because more time goes to learning a variety of digital skills. Synthesizing digital media training and tool use into an already demanding professional curriculum along with the financial demands of upgrading and absorbing changes is overwhelming for students, faculty, pedagogy, and the institution. In light of criteria for connected courses, NAAB requirements may need to be reorganized to accommodate this paradigm shift.

George Proctor directs the digital media curriculum at Cal Poly, Pomona. He has taught digital media courses and design studios in digital design methods since 1993. His writings are in the area of digital tool use in studio and design education. Proctor chaired the 2002 ACADIA conference at Cal Poly Pomona.

Requirements for an Effective Distributed Design Review

Wassim Jabi, Glenn Goldman
New Jersey Institute of Technology
Brian Johnson, University of Washington

Abstract

With the wider availability of high-bandwidth communication networks and the maturity of commercial collaboration software, schools of architecture are experimenting with computer-aided distributed design reviews. A distributed design review enables geographically-distant participants to discuss a common design project using computer-supported collaborative technologies such as videoconferencing, voice over IP, and shared applications. While potentially beneficial to students, and attractive to teachers, there are a number of challenges facing the integration of synchronous distributed design reviews into the design studio by technically inexperienced faculty without significant technical support. This paper seeks to make it easier for faculty to make routine utilization of such reviews by examining our own experiences with a number of such reviews, in a variety of contexts, distilling out a set of guidelines for future reviews.

Requirements for an Effective Distributed Design Review

Wassim Jabi, Glenn Goldman
New Jersey Institute of Technology
Brian Johnson, University of Washington

1 Background and Motivation

Design education relies heavily on various types of conversation between design students and their instructors or mentors, including lectures, small group discussion, and design reviews. Design reviews are one of the most important forms of pedagogical communication between design instructors and students (Cuff 1993). These conversations between the designer and one or more reviewers fall into two broad categories: desk crits and formal reviews. Desk crits are informal (but not necessarily casual) exchanges, usually held on a regular basis, where the studio instructor examines the student's recent work and discusses strategies, plans, and challenges. It is commonly held at the student's desk. The conversation is primarily between these two principals, but may expand to include others. That is, while nominally private, eavesdropping is encouraged.

In contrast to desk crits, reviews are formal events, generally held at important project development milestones (including end of term). They often take place in special review rooms or areas and involve formal (stand-up) presentations that each individual or group has worked hard to prepare. The principals include the presenting student(s) and a group of invited guests (the jury). Conversation sometimes strays from consideration of the current project, involving give and take between guest critics. Classmates of the presenting student(s) are expected to pay active attention to the discussion.

Both types of design review are collaborative conversations. That is, they involve the input of and communication between at least two individuals: the student and the instructor, with appropriate turn-taking, both verbally and graphically. In fact, justification for the design studio teaching strategy often relies on the aggregate studio culture created by successive shared and overlapping design conversations.

Studio instructors occasionally travel or support practices in two cities, taking them out of town on a weekly basis. They might well wish to follow and review their students' work from afar, rather than compressing or eliminating studio hours. Conducting some or all of the normal desk crits via Internet connection would be a great boon to these faculty and their students.

Formal reviews benefit tremendously from guests who bring with them informed and articulate alternative views. These special viewpoints may be essential to all phases of the design development for a community-based project or a design for a different culture. However, financial and logistical difficulties, which are common enough when trying to invite local jurors to one's design review, are often insurmountable when the potential jurors are at any distance. The ability to use the Internet to involve remote expertise at a minimum cost would significantly expand the pool of candidate reviewers.

With the wider availability of high-bandwidth communication networks and the maturity of commercial collaboration software, schools of architecture are experimenting with computer-aided distributed design reviews. A distributed design review enables geographically distant participants to discuss a common design project using computer-supported collaborative technologies such as videoconferencing, voice over IP, and shared applications.

While potentially beneficial to students and attractive to teachers, there are a number of challenges facing the integration of synchronous distributed design reviews into the design studio by technically inexperienced faculty without significant technical support. This paper seeks to make it easier for faculty to routinely utilize such reviews by examining our own experiences with a number of such reviews, in a variety of contexts, distilling out a set of guidelines for future reviews.

The use of distributed design reviews also introduces students to an environment which challenges them to construct effective and communicative presentations consistent with likely future professional requirements, but quite different from traditional, paper-based presentations. Donald Schön has identified talking and drawing as the two most fundamental components of what he termed a language of design (Schön 1983). A distributed design review provides a means to study the interconnectivity of talking and drawing and to compare it to what usually happens in traditional design settings. This paper concentrates on these two activities as they occur during distributed design review sessions.

2 Related Work

In this project, we are interested in two main issues: 1) Making optimum use of the Internet to link remote jurors to a formal review by identifying the most important features of their interaction, and 2) Simplifying and rendering more natural the process of turn taking in both the verbal and graphical exchanges during reviews, minimizing the attention required by the interface. This work builds on that of a number of other researchers.

While this paper concentrates on design reviews, a narrow and well-defined activity within the design studio, the work is part of a larger interest in researching the requirements for an effective distributed collaborative design studio–or what William J. Mitchell referred to in 1992 as the *Virtual Design Studio – or VDS for short* (Wojtowicz, Davidson and Mitchell 1992). The general requirements for an effective computer-supported cooperative design system have been outlined by several researchers (Tang and Leiffer, 1988; Jabi, 1996; Turner and Cross, 2000). The VDS oeuvre has described many of the opportunities and pitfalls of Internet-based collaboration. In the first VDS experiment, students at two different institutions were asked to co-design a project, review and exchange comments using e-mail, and conduct an electronic, long-distance design review. The authors viewed asynchronous digital correspondence as vital to the collaborative process but de-emphasized the use of synchronous tools. This may have been due to the duration of the project, the difference in time zones as well as the relative immaturity of real-time synchronous tools at the time the experiment was conducted. In 1994, a year after the completion of the first VDS studio, a second VDS studio included students and tutors from six different institutions and five different time zones (Wojtowicz 1995). VDS 94 clearly illustrates the use of synchronous videoconferencing as an effective tool for collaboration. Yet, asynchronous communication remained an important tool for the VDS project. Wojtowicz said it simply and clearly: “E-mail exchanges were the life-blood of the Virtual Design Studio.” Later researchers have pursued various aspects of design collaboration, including comprehensive collaboration and review environments that have been created to support VDS projects (Wenz and Hirschberg 1997; Kolarevic et al. 1998; McCall et al. 1998; Maher and Simoff, 2000).

While our small-scale project concentrated on more traditional presentation techniques (still and video images using Microsoft PowerPoint and simple web pages), others have described the potential and pitfalls of multi-modal, 2D and 3D immersive techniques. For example, Daily et al. describe in their paper an integrated immersive virtual reality environment that supports multi-site connections using avatars, high-fidelity audio, and shared artifact manipulation. They conclude in their research that while it is possible to communicate design concepts and ideas with a natural, intuitive interface over great distances, a key future goal would be to overcome the widely disparate interface modalities they encountered (Daily et al., 2000). Gross and Do have described a number of shared drawing (Qian and Gross 1999) and design annotation systems (Jung et al., 2002), while Johnson has described a formal review tool used in online competitions (Johnson 1999). Kalisperis et al. also report that Virtual Reality (VR) setups can be affordably constructed and implemented in the initial phases of the design process (Kalisperis et al., 2002). Their research intersects ours in that we are both interested in an immersive and natural environment for design presentation. We both believe that the technology belongs in the studio and should be made available to students throughout the design process. However, their work concentrates on the visualization of design, rather than the conversation of the remote reviews. Rather, we have researched several commercial interactive screen technologies which we will report on below.

3 Setup

We looked for affordable, off-the-shelf, collaboration software that allowed shared audio and video, and shared network sketching. Within the presentation space, we made use of a large interactive whiteboard (Smart Technologies, Inc. SmartBoard 580) as the display surface (Figure 1). The SmartBoard enabled the students to interact directly with the large projected image, without requiring use of a mouse or keyboard.

The review events involved about 15 students, two or three co-located jurors, and one remote juror. Since our aim in this experiment was to concentrate on inexpensive software and hardware, we selected essentially free, off-the-shelf, collaboration software from Microsoft Corporation (Windows Messenger and NetMeeting). The Windows Messenger software allows participants to share almost any Windows-compatible application, which in our case was Microsoft PowerPoint, which the students used to assemble their presentations. Sharing simply means that the remote participant can view and optionally control a single graphical user interface, visible in both locations. Effectively, the remote participant can follow a presentation as it progresses, can see the marks and annotations being made and can (optionally) take control of the presentation and create his own marks. The software also provides an audio channel both ways. We connected the computer to speakers so students could hear the remote participant’s voice, and used a microphone to transmit our voices. After experimenting with a shared microphone as well as multiple microphones, we concluded that one high-quality, omni-directional microphone is sufficient to capture all voices within a medium-sized room (approximately a 12-foot radius). Since the software also provides a separate video channel, we experimented with the use of video through webcams, but found it to be of little use other than to initially introduce the participants to each other. As Donald Schön predicted, all that was needed was the combination of talking and sketching. Coupled with voice, this technique was effective in carrying out a fluid design discussion.

In order to engage the local jurors and audience, we increased the size of the presentation through projection. This also mimicked traditional stand-up presentations in which the presenter stands in front of and points to the presentation board. The SmartBoard provides a projection surface. It also acts as a large digitizing tablet. The software creates a virtual transparent layer on top of the projected image, on which one may mark using one of three color-coded inkless pens. The software recognizes, through a sensor built into the board, what pen is being used and creates marks on the screen of the correct color. An *eraser* works in a similar, but reverse fashion. The fact that the marks are projected back onto the screen and spatially aligned gives the illusion that the user is sketching *in situ* with virtual ink. Alternatively, if the user presses with his/her finger instead of a pen, the SmartBoard simply passes it through to the operating system, which treats the action as a mouse click or drag and responds accordingly. The resulting effect is a flat

2-dimensional version of a hybrid physical-virtual environment–a cybrid (Anders 1998).

The remote juror is not required to have a comparable setup. At a minimum, a standard Windows desktop PC with a mouse and keyboard is required. If available, the juror would benefit from the use of a small digital drawing tablet (e.g. Wacom) which provides a much more natural interface for the juror to annotate and sketch over the drawings.

Figure 1. Design review setup using an interactive SmartBoard with projected image.

4 Case Study

As discussed above, design reviews tend to vary along two dimensions. The first dimension indicates the degree of formality while the other dimension indicates the geographic location of the participants. These two dimensions yield four possible design review settings as illustrated below (Figure 2). The setup described above has been used and documented via still photography and digital video for one semester in third year studio in three different settings. The SmartBoard was made available in studio for weekly informal use for desk crits. It was also used in studio for more formal design reviews that did not include a remote juror. Finally, the setup was moved twice to a review room to be used for a formal design review that included three or four invited jurors–one being a remote juror. The fourth alternative, informal distributed desk crits, was not evaluated in this sequence. It is expected to be the subject of future research.

4.1 Informal Local Desk Crits

In studio, the SmartBoard was used occasionally as a replacement for trace paper and pens. Although no remote capabilities were utilized, the studio instructor and student would stand in front of the board, discuss and sketch over the drawings. This proved to be an effective method in discussing the project at hand and did not require a lot of preparation. The media used included static images stored in folders, PowerPoint Slides, AutoCAD drawings, 3D Studio MAX models, AVI animations, and Spherical Panoramas. Control of the interface, while involving new paradigms, proved to be intuitive, and the ability to non-destructively sketch over any image or model proved to be useful. All students positively mentioned the use of the SmartBoard in their end-of-term evaluation form.

	Informal	Formal
Local	Desk crits Layered Sketching, Talking Design History	Design Review Pre-made Presentation Turn-taking Gestural Sketches Pointing Talking
Distributed	Virtual Desk crits Virtual Sketching, Voice over IP Online Design History Threaded Discussion	Distributed Design Review Pre-made Online Presentation Turn-taking Gestural Sketches Pointing Voice over IP, Video, Application Sharing and Control

Figure 2. A matrix of possible design review settings.

4.2 Local Formal Design Reviews

In studio, the SmartBoard was used occasionally for design presentations. The students prepared PowerPoint slides and used the board mainly as a projection screen. Again, the added ability to non-destructively sketch over the drawings in a natural manner enabled a more fluid presentation. The ergonomics were improved since the student did not have to fiddle with a mouse and keyboard and could stand in front of the screen and face the audience in a natural position.

4.3 Distributed Formal Design Reviews

As mentioned above, the SmartBoard and collaboration software setup was used twice during the term to conduct formal reviews. The first session (mid-term) was conducted with a remote juror in the same country, but with a 3-hour difference in time zones. The second review session (conducted at the end of the term) involved a remote juror who resides in a different country with a 7-hour difference in time zones. In both cases, the remote reviewer was connected via voice and application sharing. Below are some brief observations on those two sessions:

A slight operating system incompatibility necessitated the use of an older version of the collaboration software to initiate the review session. While workable, this solution was not immediately obvious and probably represents a weak point for the less technically experienced. We are also concerned that Netmeeting/Messenger is platform-specific, but find such software to be more integrated and functional than available platform-agnostic counterparts.

Initially, the remote reviewer had microphone problems. This was resolved through the use of a mobile phone, but the lack of projected audio transformed the review into a one-on-one desk crit because the audience could not hear what the remote reviewer was saying. This was so unsatisfactory that we suspended the remote review, resuming it after the remote juror located and connected another microphone to his computer. There is a lag inherent in voice-over-IP technology. In addition, the remote microphone may pick up some of the audio signal and play it back to the speaker. Due to the lag, it arrives back at the speaker's end 1.5 to 2 seconds later. Initially, this caused critics and students to speak much more slowly and deliberately –artificially slow. Adjusting the volume and exercising the ability to mute the microphone when not speaking solved that problem. While testing prior to the second review session, we discovered that network security implementations (firewall) prevented the collaboration software from functioning properly. Network administrators could not solve the problem in time. However, we were able to address the problem by issuing the remote reviewer a temporary password, allowing him to establish a Virtual Private Network (VPN) connection that allowed his computer to behave as if it was placed on our local network behind the firewall. In session #2, the remote juror felt it necessary to speak faster, keep comments short and to the point, ask permission to start speaking and clearly indicate that he was done speaking. However, the exchange did become more fluid towards the end of the review with natural interruptions, juror-juror comments and jokes.

In session #2, the local jurors almost never went up to the board to sketch and/or gesture. Instead, they either used the shadow of their hand in front of the projector or a laser pointer. Obviously, these gestures are not transmittable. Thus, the remote juror could not easily follow what parts of the drawing the local jurors were commenting on. This indicates that we need to find a way to remotely, wirelessly, and easily enable local participants to affect the screen. To compensate, the manager of the review tried as much as possible to follow the laser point with the cursor icon. In contrast, the student presenters used the SmartBoard to its full potential with sketching and interactive mouse clicks. Animations embedded in PowerPoint caused a major delay and breakdown. However, we shared the AVI files separately, and the remote juror reported that they worked reasonably well although a bit choppy on his side.

Video (headshot) was tested and worked, but found to be unnecessary for an effective review. It consumed too much bandwidth, and voice was enough to convey meaning. Video was mainly used to introduce the remote juror and give the audience a view of who he is (to become more real to them).

Students and faculty informally reported that the whole process, while a bit strange due to its newness (e.g. one juror referred to the remote juror as "the voice"), was useful and informative. The remote juror did not clearly know who was speaking so, he referred to that person as "the critic who last spoke, or I agree with the comment made..." It might be helpful to have individual microphone channels that, when activated, display the speaker's identity on the screen.

One juror complained about the glare coming from the hotspot generated by the projector. We are hoping a rear-projection system, as illustrated below, will solve that problem along with the shadow problem commonly associated with front-projections (Figure 3).

5 The Ten Commandments

Figure 3. Rear Projection SMART Board 3000i (left, photo courtesy of Smart Technologies, Inc.) and An *RPS/Complete* Rear-Projection System (right, photo courtesy of Draper, Inc.)

Based on our experience with design reviews, we have derived Ten Commandments that we believe can help avoid some of the most common pitfalls associated with conducting distributed design reviews and make them productive conversations:

1) Start early (plan ahead): While it may take only a matter of minutes to establish the review connection in the end, it may take several days, or even weeks, to verify the preconditions for the review (room reservation, camera function, software, microphones, speakers, etc.). Similarly, it is necessary to get placed on the remote reviewers' calendar early, to make sure that they have allowed adequate time with a minimum of distractions.
2) Test. Test. Test: Complex modern systems of software and hardware often involve many layers of data exchange

and encoding, plus filtering by internet routers and firewalls. They are also a moving target as university staff work to control hacking, or software piracy, and vendors sometimes rush products to market before they are ready. While it has become significantly easier to get/make viable connections in the real world, including those between heterogeneous systems, each component should be adequately tested to assure run-time viability for the review. An OS update may leave you unable to use your camera driver, or you may have to establish how to get NetMeeting and Messenger to talk to each other.

3) Know thy neighbor: In the normal course of a face-to-face review, presenters and reviewers each have a part to play and each knows their part. Nonetheless, a significant amount of adjustment may take place due to the exchange of social cues. Remote reviewers may not be familiar with the local "scene." It may be necessary to address some of these issues in advance, in an explicit form, or protocol which sets out the timing of the review, the order of the students, the amount of time each has "center stage", the biases or "spins" being supplied by the studio mentor(s), and so on. These help set the stage for responding to the student work.

4) Use back-channel diplomacy: During the review event it may become necessary for a remote reviewer to communicate with the host about the review. While it may be necessary to break in on the presentation or conversation then underway, it is quite disruptive to do so. Having an alternative "back-channel" communications means (email, un-projected chat window, phone, etc.) provides for this kind of communication.

5) Adjust expectations: Remote reviews take longer than their face-to-face counterparts. In the face-to-face review process, each student receives the focused attention of the reviewers for a period of time, but it is still possible to handle three to four reviews an hour. During remote reviews, you should expect to do two or three in an hour, rather than three or four.

6) Keep it cozy: These technologies are not well suited to large-scale reviews. In particular, reviews involving multiple remote reviewers are ill-advised because the social cueing that is necessary for a smooth conversation is disrupted by the time-lag found in voice-over-IP. For one remote reviewer it is likely that an informal "wait" protocol will evolve–analogous to that seen on TV when a reporter is half-way around the world–using long silences to signal conversational turn-taking. With two or more remote reviewers, there is no good means of cueing turn-taking between the remote end-points, with the result that the reviewers will often collide with and talk over each other.

7) Know thy software: In an environment as dependent on technology as a remote design review, it is important that all participants have experience with the software and the specific way it will be used during the review. Each student, supporting faculty and the remote reviewer should practice with the software prior to the review. During this time it is possible to discover "glitches" (playing movies in PowerPoint, etc.) which profoundly affect the presenter's plan.

8) Encourage symmetry: One-way mirrors may connect two occupied spaces, but they don't provide both occupants with the same sense of social presence. It is important that the tools be set up and configured in such a way that every participant feels they are part of the exchange.

9) Use big pipes: While viable reviews can certainly be completed using slower speed or even asynchronous review protocols, additional bandwidth provides the flexibility to conduct a review without carrying quite the same cognitive load that slower-speed connections require. At the same time, almost any connectivity speed can be overwhelmed by an overly ambitious project (e.g. 1024x768x30fps animation).

10) Have a plan B. . .and C (a.k.a graceful degradation): You should expect one or more aspects of your setup to fail. To the extent that it is possible, have backup plans in place for continuing the review (placing PPT files on the web, with telephonic, chat or email reviews, having a reserve of redundant equipment, etc).

6 Concluding Remarks

Despite the inherent technical difficulties associated with introducing new technologies and processes, we firmly believe that the ability to regularly conduct distributed design reviews is an invaluable opportunity for both faculty and students –if implemented with care. One fundamental challenge is to understand the degree to which a distributed design review is, or is not, similar to a traditional face-to-face studio review. For example, one may find fault in the apparent linearity of online presentations. Yet, business presentations and lectures are generally linear as are most, written works. The ability to move laterally between images and components can be improved by running multiple types of software in parallel and by displaying the slide sorter screen to which critics may refer. While face-to-face reviews and many distributed reviews occur at the same time (synchronously), asynchronous web-based design reviews have also been gaining popularity as a way to continue design work outside normal studio hours and at a distance, include a larger set of viewpoints, compensate for time-zone differences, and acknowledge varying connection speeds.
Yet, one of the described case studies points to a benefit to conducting synchronous design reviews across different time zones. Specifically, the use of multiple time zones may actually facilitate synchronous reviews because a critic may be available at a time when he/she might otherwise be teaching a class. As most design studios require consecutive large blocks of time

(generally three to five hours), this would then overlap available time slots when working with critics in other time zones. So this process may actually expand the pool of available critics, all without significant time spent on travel to and from remote locations. As we conduct more review sessions, we will continue to develop, refine, and report our findings such that we may benefit others when setting up and utilizing such environments.

References

Anders, P. (1998). *Envisioning cyberspace: Designing 3D electronic spaces*, New York: McGraw-Hill.

Cuff, D. (1993). *Architecture: The story of practice*. Cambridge, MA: MIT Press.

Hirschberg, U. and F. Wenz (1997). Phase(x) memetic engineering for architecture. In *Automation in construction*, Elsevier, 9(1):387-392

Johnson, B, and B. Kolarevic (1999). EVAL: A web-based design review system. *Media and design process, Proceedings of the 1999 annual conference of the association for computer-aided design in architecture (ACADIA)*, eds. Attaman and Bermúdez,30-39.

Kalisperis, K. et al. (2002). An affordable immersive environment in beginning design studio education. *Thresholds,proceedings of the 2002 annual conference of the association for computer-aided design in architecture (ACADIA)*, ed. G. Proctor, 49-56.

Jabi, W. (1996). An outline of the requirements for a computer-supported collaborative design system. In *Open house international*, 21(1):22-30.

Jung, T., M. Gross and E. Do (2002). Sketching annotations in a 3D web environment. *Proceedings of the ACM conference on human factors and computing systems* (CHI), 618-619, ACM Press.

Kolarevic, B., G. Schmitt, U. Hirschberg, D. Kurmann and B. Johnson. (1998). An experiment in design collaboration. *Proceedings of the 1998 annual conference of the association for computer-aided design In architecture* (ACADIA), eds. T. Seebohm and S. van Wyk, 90-99.

Maher, M.L, and S.J. Simoff. (2000). Collaboratively designing within the design. *Collaborative design, Proceedings of codesigning 2000*, eds. S. A. R. Scrivener, L. Ball and A. Woodcock, 391-400. London: Springer-Verlag.

McCall, R., S. Holmes, J. Voeller, and E. Johnson (1998). World wide presentation and critique of design proposals with web-PHIDIAS. Digital design studios: Do computers make a difference? *Proceedings of the 1998 annual conference of the association for computer-aided design in architecture (ACADIA*), eds. T. Seebohm and S. van Wyk, 254-265.

Qian, D. and M. Gross (1999). Collaborative design with NetDraw. *Computers in building, Proceedings of CAAD futures 1999 conference*, G. Augenbroe and C. Eastman,eds. 213-226.

Schön, D. (1983). *The reflective practitioner: how professionals think in action*, New York: Basic Books.

Tang, J. and L. Leiffer (1988). A framework for understanding the workspace activity of design teams. *Proceedings of the second conference on computer-supported cooperative work*, ed. I. Greif, 244-249.

Turner, S. and N.Cross. (2000). Small group design activity and requirments on collaborative technologies. *Collaborative design, Proceedings of codesigning 2000.* S. A. R. Scrivener, L. Ball and A. Woodcock,eds, 253-260 London: Springer-Verlag.

Wojtowicz, W., J. Davidson and W. Mitchell (1992). Design as digital correspondence. Computer supported design in architecture. *Mission, method, madness, Proceedings of the annual conference of the association for computer-aided design in architecture*, eds. K. Kensek and D. Noble, 89-95.

Case Study of Tacit Knowledge Sharing in a Distributed Design Studio

Jeong-Han Woo, Mark Clayton, Robert Johnson,
and Benito Flores
Texas A&M University

Abstract

This paper demonstrates the effects of experts' tacit knowledge on improving architectural students' design artifacts in a distributed design studio. In geographically distributed design environments, the Internet is an important medium by which architects can share tacit knowledge in the form of dialogue via online communication technologies, such as online chat and Instant Messaging (IM). In spring 2003, the National Aeronautics and Space Administration (NASA) and 8 schools conducted a collaborative design studio to develop a crew restraint system for space flights. Online chat software was used as a primary communication channel. Throughout the entire design studio, NASA professionals served as knowledge holders while undergraduate students participated as knowledge seekers. An interpretive content analysis and case study methodology were used in this study. We qualitatively observed the interactions between NASA and the students based upon two aspects: knowledge reflection and design improvement. Data were collected using document analysis of all knowledge sources and students' design artifacts. The findings of this study indicate that the online chat system is useful in sharing tacit knowledge for the early part of design processes in a distributed design environment. Experts' tacit knowledge appears to not only influence how students understand problems, but how they initiate conceptual design. This study provides empirical evidence regarding tacit knowledge sharing, and strengthens Schon's (1983) claim about knowledge reflection in design studio. Furthermore, this study introduces architectural practitioners to the practical necessity of tacit knowledge sharing. This study is significant because its findings indicate the appropriate knowledge management strategy for architectural practitioners.

Case Study of Tacit Knowledge Sharing In a Distributed Design Studio

Jeong-Han Woo, Mark Clayton, Robert Johnson, and Benito Flores

Texas A&M University

1 INTRODUCTION

Human knowledge can be simply classified into two types: tacit and explicit. According to several literatures, tacit knowledge is highly personal (Polanyi 1966), implicit (Reber 1991), context-specific (Sternberg 1994) knowledge housed in the human brain, such as expertise, skill, understanding, or professional insight formed as a result of experience. Tacit knowledge has tremendous value when made available to the right people at the right time.

However, several researchers point out that tacit knowledge is hard to formalize, write down, and communicate (Nonaka 1995) because it is deeply embedded in employees or organizations. However, there is a range of different degrees of tacit knowledge as shown in Figure 1. Ambrosini and Bowman (2001) point out that deeply ingrained tacit knowledge (Type A) is not accessible by the use of languages or codes. Highly tacit knowledge could be only accessed using physical meeting, demonstration, or learn-by-doing (Schon 1983), strategies requiring the physical presence of knowledge holders. In this study, tacit knowledge sharing is subsequently limited to Type B Knowledge (imperfectly articulated tacit skills) and Type C Knowledge (articulated tacit skills) (see Figure 1).

In geographically distributed virtual design environments, the Internet provides an important

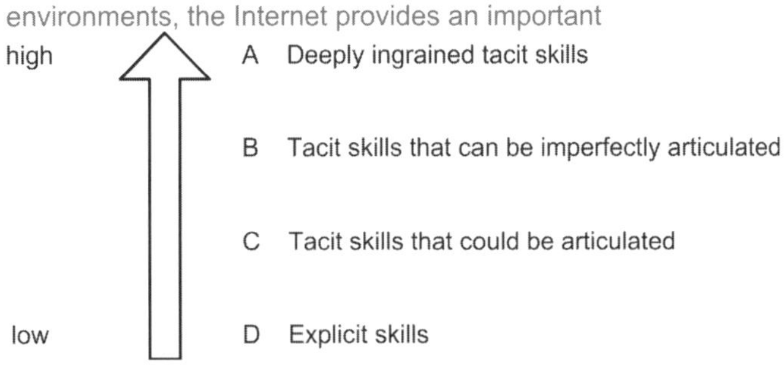

Figure 1. Degree of Tacit Knowledge (Ambrosini and Bowman 2001)

medium by which architects can share their tacit knowledge in the form of dialogue. The primary communication channels for online tacit knowledge sharing are typically an online chat system or instant messaging (Ribak 2002). Although the functionality of these two tools is widely adopted for entertainment purposes, several articles (Isaacs et al. 2002, Ribak 2002) report cases where these tools successfully support knowledge sharing and informal communications in a large firm.

Novice architects gain tacit knowledge through real experience or receiving instructions, and begin to extend the web of knowledge in the architectural domain. Although Donald Schon (1983) convincingly demonstrated that experts' tacit knowledge is a significant resource in the architectural profession, architectural practitioners continue to concentrate on explicit knowledge management, driven by exponential advances in Information Technology (IT) solutions, which make knowledge explicit and store it as computer software and databases. Although tacit knowledge is important to success, architects grant little recognition to it. The literature (Hansen et al. 1999, Johannessen et al. 2001) indicates that IT-based solutions only allow people to search for and retrieve only explicit knowledge. Therefore, the emphasis on IT may reduce the attention to tacit knowledge; consequently, experts' tacit knowledge could be wasted and ignored.

Several researchers in the field of architecture have emphasized the importance of tacit knowledge sharing in architectural design environments. Schon (1983) explored the traditions of the architectural studio to investigate how architectural students learn from instructors in a design studio. He observed the learning process of architectural design in a studio setting from the beginning of the semester to the final review. Through in-depth description, he found two forms of the learning process: learn-by-doing and reflection-in-action. In a design studio setting, instructors usually tell and demonstrate what they want to show, and students listen and imitate that. As a result, Schon points out that tacit knowledge is the primary mechanism for sharing expertise from the experienced designer. In addition, Cross (1995) concludes that the collaborative process significantly influences the quality of design.

Huang (1999) also studied knowledge sharing in distributed design environments. Throughout 60 interviews and observations of designers involved in collaborative efforts, he analyzed the collaboration patterns among design participants and derived how these patterns change with the introduction of new collaborative media. One of the significant findings from his research is the relationship between knowledge sharing and innovative design. Consequently, he insists that knowledge required to make sound design decisions should be distributed and leveraged within organizational boundaries. He concludes that such sharing contributes to innovative design solutions, and the actions of participants are more transparent and shared, while the systems may reduce the costs of knowledge transfer. A distributed design studio initiated by NASA led us to conduct this study based on the same research inquiry of the studies noted above. Several design studies have been conducted

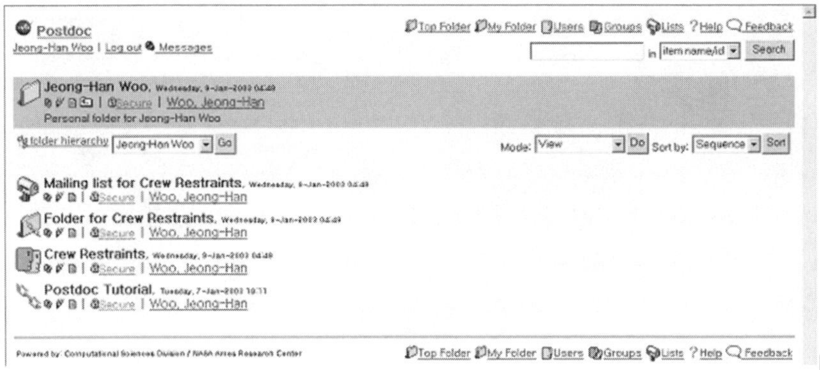

Figure 2. Screen Shot of PostDoc Main Page

concerning collaborative media in the architectural profession. However, these studies rarely focus on the impact of tacit knowledge on the design artifact. This unexplored topic of the design studio enabled us to clearly observe the effect of knowledge reflections on the students' design artifacts. We qualitatively observed the improvements of students' design performance in a design studio setting based upon two aspects: knowledge reflection and design improvement. The qualitative content analysis was conducted on all dialogue records, documentations provided by NASA and students' design artifacts. This study is significant because its findings guide the development of an appropriate knowledge management strategy for architectural practitioners.

2 METHODS

2.1 Distributed Design Studio with NASA Context

The design studio was conducted during the 2003 spring semester. NASA initiated a distributed design studio to develop requirements, guidelines, and conceptual designs for an ergonomic crew restraint system. The agency is interested in benefiting from the creativity and ingenuity of undergraduate students while providing them with a challenging subject for a class project. NASA final deliverables include:

- Development of functional requirements
- Design concept prototype development
- Computer modeling evaluations of concepts
- Microgravity evaluation
- Implementation plan.

Participant

The design studio was led by four NASA design professionals. Approximately seventy undergraduate students and ten faculty members from eight schools were invited to this design studio. All undergraduate students are naïve designers in terms of design experiences, representing multiple design disciplines and approaches such as architecture, mechanical engineering, industrial engineering, and human engineering. However, it does not matter how the students design, so long as they concentrate on all design activities in producing the final description of the proposed work according to the instructions from NASA.

Knowledge Sharing

Since no school has experience in crew restraint systems design, NASA staff members exclusively provided knowledge resources about these systems. At the beginning of the studio, the agency provided a set of documentations containing extensive data, information and knowledge about crew restraint systems in the form of video, written document and photographs. As explicit knowledge, the documents provide details of the requirements already developed, lessons learned, and information about existing designs. The documentation was previously used to develop preliminary operational and functional design requirements for a multi-purpose crew restraint system. Additional documentation was provided upon request. Students used the documents as the manual for proposed design concepts. The documents were posted and accessible through the password-protected web site called PostDoc (https://postdoc.arc.nasa.gov) as shown in Figure 2. While all knowledge resources were posted on PostDoc, each school held physical face-to-face meetings with their course instructors.
In addition to the accessible documentation, three NASA professionals shared their tacit knowledge by actively communicating with students using an online chat system (http://www.nsbri.org/Chat/hhfo/). Throughout chat sessions, students held reflective conversations with NASA staff, who scheduled the chat sessions. The first chat session was conducted from 2:00 P.M. to 5:00 P.M.on February 5, 2003: seventeen people from five different schools and NASA participated, generating 170 messages. The second chat session was conducted from 2:00 P.M. to 4:00 P.M. on February 6, 2003: thirteen people from four different schools and NASA participated, and 107 messages were generated. All dialogue was captured and posted on PostDoc.

Online Chat

The chat system used was typical chat software providing login awareness of the system users, and supporting one-to-one communication. All dialogues were saved as natural conversations and made accessible for students to review for sharing ideas and expertise in the dialogue. The chat sessions opened with a brief welcome from NASA staff. Students then asked questions about crew restraints system. Each message varied in length. Since the chat sessions were held exclusively for the project, all messages related to the restraint design. Some messages contained relatively long explanations of the situations with the international space shuttle. Since only three NASA professionals answered all questions from the students, the answers were often delayed.

Overall Design Processes

The design studio was initiated with a telephone conference between NASA and all school participants at the beginning of the 2003 spring semester. NASA staff and studio participants held numerous online chat sessions and telephone meetings throughout the project. At the end of the semester, the students submitted their final design presentations.

After sharing extensive knowledge, the students developed their preliminary conceptual designs for a critique, utilizing a video conference.To refine their designs for the next step, students received consultations from NASA staff via chat sessions and from their own instructors in the local design studio. After getting the correct design directions, the students conducted the remainder of thier project primarily with the instructors.

NASA staff reviewed the final designs and ranked them within each university, evaluating whether or not each project met enough of the requirements and showed enough feasibility to pursue. After posting the final project on the Web site, the design studio was completed.

3 Data Collection

Data sources include knowledge resources provided by NASA and students' design artifacts. Data for this study were downloaded from the PostDoc website hosted by NASA.

3.1 Tacit Knowledge Sources

NASA provided six different tacit knowledge resources via the Web site as shown in Figure 3. The primary tacit knowledge resources were chat transcripts captured by NASA staff and posted on PostDoc. "Preliminary Focus Group Findings" refers to the summary of a series of meetings held to discuss lessons learned from "Restraints and Mobility Aids" (R&MA) and solicit ideas and concepts for restraints. Other tacit knowledge resources were the summary of comments from design professionals.

File Name	Format	Description
Preliminary Focus Group Findings	MS Word	Preliminary Focus Groups Meetings were held and findings were summarized.
Chat sessions	MS Word	Compiled questions and answers.
LSG Question and Answer	MS Word	Life Science Glove box Question and Answers dealing with hardware details of configurations.
Compiled Crew Restraint Comments	MS Word	Database of Crew Debrief comments on individual restraints (pros/cons).
Restraint Summit Comments	MS Word	Restraint Summit Meeting Summary Notes were compiled with crew comments of restraint systems currently on ISS.
Question and Answer Session Feb 21	MS PowerPoint	Presentation covering all the questions posed by participating universities.

Figure 3. Tacit Knowledge Sources

3.2 Explicit Knowledge Resources

Explicit knowledge resources were also posted on PostDoc, as shown in Figure 5. The contents of explicit knowledge resources mostly cover all disciplines and guidelines of restraint systems design. Conversely, the contents of tacit knowledge resources and supplement explicit knowledge were exclusively based on expertise.

4 Data Analysis

Ethnographical study conducted by Schon (1985) and Cross (2001) is most relevant to the data analysis of this study. Their studies show that detailed observation enables systematic descriptions of designers' improvement followed by experts' instruction. Likewise, the main task of data analysis is to qualitatively observe the improvements of students' design performance as "reflection-in-action" (Schon 1983) in a design studio setting. While thoroughly searching for students' knowledge reflection, this research qualitatively describes the improvements of students' design performance.

The first step entailed reading the online chat transcripts. Those for one-to-one conversations were not included in this study, since the majority of the contents were simple clarifications of the discussion. To investigate what people discussed in the chat sessions, we conducted qualitative content analysis on the two chat session transcripts.The content of online dialogue comprises messages between NASA professionals and groups of students and faculty. The dialogue occurred as students' questioned NASA staff about problems, and presented ideas for resolving the problems. During the reading, the problems were unsystematically grouped into categories as follows:

- Comfort/Injury
- Foot Restraints
- Body Restraints
- Handrails
- Maintenance

There were no restrictions about what might count as a problem category. We simply summarized themes that emerged with repeated reading. Next, the students' design artifacts were thoroughly investigated.

5 Findings

Cross (2000) introduces French's (1985) model of the design process based on the following activities: analysis of problem,conceptual design, embodiment of schemes,detailing. Qualitative analysis of dialogues and design artifacts resulted in observations about knowledge reflection in design artifacts in the following aspects:

- Tacit knowledge sharing
- Analysis of problem
- Conceptual design
- Feedback
- Works from non-participants

5.1 Tacit knowledge sharing

Three NASA staff members actively participated as knowledge holders in the online chat sessions. Their previous experience with restraint systems design made it possible for students to identify a problem about which only an expert might be aware. Furthermore, this process helped students comprehend the significance of tacit knowledge sharing, in addition to the understanding of how dialogues during the early stages of design can assist NASA staff and the students themselves. There were several dialogues such as:

<Student 1>	*Are these chat sessions set up for the various schools to share ideas as well?*
<NASA 1>	*Certainly, you can use these sessions to share ideas as well.*
<Student 2>	*Will the chat session be held routinely?*
<NASA 2>	*In regards to CHAT session times, we will try to hold them routinely if necessary. But for this week it will only be today (now until 5 pm Central) and tomorrow 2 - 4 central time.*

The participants definitely wanted to talk with other team members via chat sessions to share ideas and experiences. A complex and unique project like this, amplifies the importance of tacit knowledge sharing. Increasingly, the students expected to face situations in which their previous knowledge would no longer be sufficient to complete a good design project, since the knowledge needs in this studio are dynamic and complicated. Therefore, experts' tacit knowledge should be shared to achieve better quality on design projects.

<Student 3>	*Any chance of getting complete transcripts of both chat sessions, say, on post-doc?*
< NASA 1>	*Yes, we will be sending out the complete transcripts of both chat sessions.*
< Student 4>	*The summary of chat session yesterday organized by topic was really useful. Thanks.*
< Student 3>	*Thank you so much, Rosie and Mihriban! Super-helpful chat.*
< NASA 1>	*I believe there is another Chat at 4 pm Central. I think this is our cue.*

This series of dialogue indicates the successful conversion of tacit knowledge to explicit knowledge. In this dialogue, the participants definitely shared significant tacit knowledge about the project. NASA professionals offered numerous professional recommendations, intuitive expectations, and their experiences on other crew restraint design projects. The students knew that they could not receive such advice from explicit knowledge sources currently in existence. Because of past experiences, NASA professionals can share what must be undertaken at any given point. However, conventional tacit knowledge sharing requires physical face-to-face meeting (Nonaka 1995).

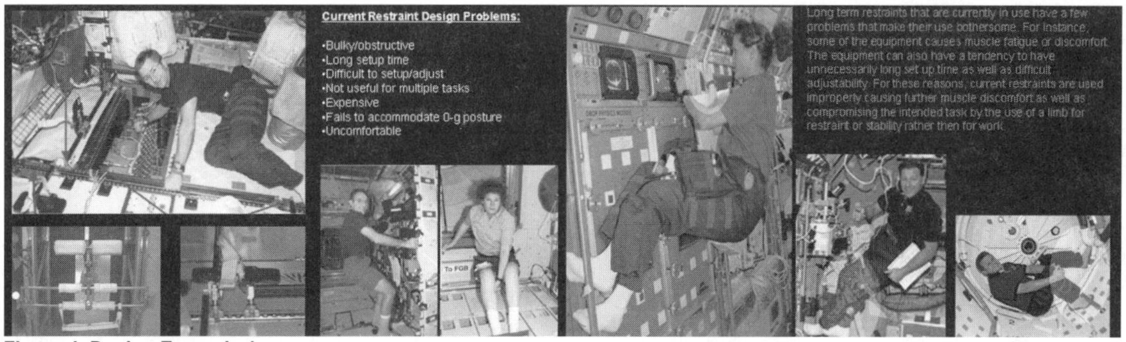

Figure 4. Design Example 1

In a distributed design studio, the need exists to share tacit knowledge at remote locations, such as different buildings or different offices, and receive immediate help. The online discussions addressed the same topics that could be discussed in the meeting room. It is less dynamic than face-to-face meetings, yet more dynamic than written messages alone.

5.2 Analysis of Problem

The findings of this study show that for analysis of problem experts' tacit knowledge is more informative than explicit knowledge. At the first stage of the design studio, all students thoroughly studied provided documentation broadly covering all aspects of crew restraints design, including design guidelines, manuals, technical specifications, and graphic samples. However, those materials were limited in use for the analysis of problem. Therefore, through the chat sessions, the students asked about problems they encountered. Cross (2000) says "the very first conceptualizations and representations of problem and solution are critical to the kinds of searches and other procedures that will follow, and so to the final solution that will be designed." A significant portion of the online chats was devoted to the clarification or explanation of real problems, and the majority of the problems were identified in the chat sessions. The discussions focused on important questions such as:

- Have existing restraint systems caused muscle injuries?
- Have the foot loops been useful in any particular task?
- Do the LSG arm holes restrain the upper body?
- Do astronauts want their feet restrained completely, or would they prefer more flexibility?

NASA answers for these questions formed the most concrete evidence of the problem and were part of the problem statement of each design project. Quickly, the students identified particular problems that would influence their approach to developing a conceptual design. Many problems were also clarified through the online chat sessions. The students could easily catch a well-defined problem, and then focus their work on one of those problems.

During online chat dialogues, one student opened up a new question about discomfort caused from current restraints. The following dialogue examples demonstrate typical conversations influencing the design. NASA staff was also able to provide information from previous experience.

<Student 5> *Have there been muscle injuries due to existing restraint systems?*

<NASA 1> *We didn't have any serious muscle issues but some discomfort reported. Use of handrails as a foot restraint caused some discomfort on the toe knuckles.*

The first problem the students encountered was the use of handrails as a foot restraint. Based on this problem, some of the students offered proposals to handle this problem as shown in Figure 4.

The second problem students encountered was complaints about the foot loops.

<Student 6> *There have been numerous complaints about the foot loops. Have the foot loops been useful in any particular task?*

<NASA 1> *Foot Loops - 1. Adjustment mechanism is not effective and comes loose 2. Collapsible so not easy to get in 3. Footplate is slippery with socks so they curl toes to restrain*

<Student 7> *Can any spring loaded mechanisms be utilized in the restraint designs?*

<NASA 1> *As long as it is simple, spring loaded mechanisms can be utilized. Based on above dialogue, a student generated the following design proposal (See Figure 5):*

The third problem was storing and maintaining the restraint systems.

<Student 8> How much space is devoted to storing restraints on-board the ISS?

<NASA>

<NASA> *Long term and temporary stowage config. for restraint are critical. There isn't any set dimensions. However, for temp. stowage, the config should be out of the aisle as much as possible with minimal interference with its surroundings. Also, it should be easily temp stowed. We can provide dimensions for the stowage containers.*

<Student 9> *Are current RMAs considered adequate for multiple rack translation and maintenance, including the tilt-out procedure?*

<NASA> *In regards to your question of current RMAs for multiple rack translation and maintenance.....Crew can do the work but is not sufficient for safety and not ideal. Current RMAs do not completely assist adequately for all tasks. Did I answer your question?*

The fourth problem is long set-up time and difficult adjustability. A student writes a problem statement as follows (See Figure 6):

"Long term restraints that are currently in use have a few problems that make their use bothersome. For instance, some of the equipment causes muscle fatigue or discomfort. The equipment can also have a tendency to have unnecessarily long set up time as well as difficult adjustability. For these reasons, current restraints are used improperly causing further muscle discomfort as well as compromising the intended task by the use of a limb for restraint or stability rather then for work."
In the dialogue, NASA staff said that the handrails are the most effective system onboard ISS. A NASA staff member said:

"To add on to it, the only one that has been reported to be the most effective one onboard ISS thus far is the handrails. Quick note that there are plenty of them onboard thus they don't need to move or remove it."

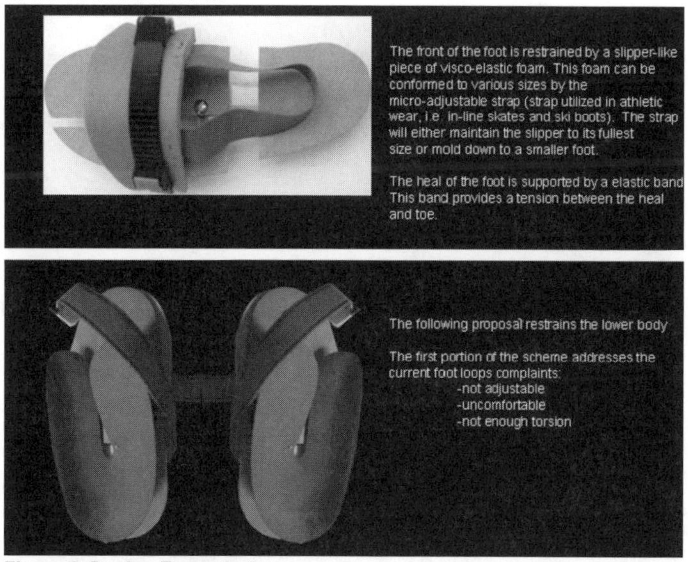

Figure 5. Design Example 2

<Student 10> *What are the size/weight constraints and envelope dimensions of the crew restraint?*

<NASA> *There isn't any specified in any documentation. But, due to the upmess, both size and weight should be minimized as much as possible.*

< Student 11> *Is there an IVA specific document for design requirements, as in NASA STD-3000?*

< NASA> *Yes, SSP 50005 is for the vehicle human factors requirements and SSP 57000 is for the payloads human factors requirements. We can try to have them available on postDoc (at least the relevant sections),*

<Student 12> *Rosie - referring to the anthropometrics data, we wanted to know if there is a required range of height, weight, and size for an astronaut?*

<Student 13> *Check the NASA "how to become an astronaut" page on spaceflight.nasa.gov for height requirements*

< NASA> *The SSP 50005 reference document will have that anthropometrics information (at least it will be one of the relevant chapters we will include).*

< Student 1> *Thank you Mihriban.*

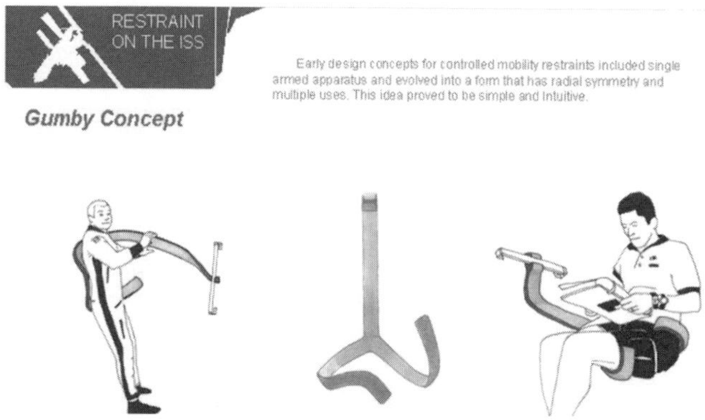

Figure 6. Design Example 3

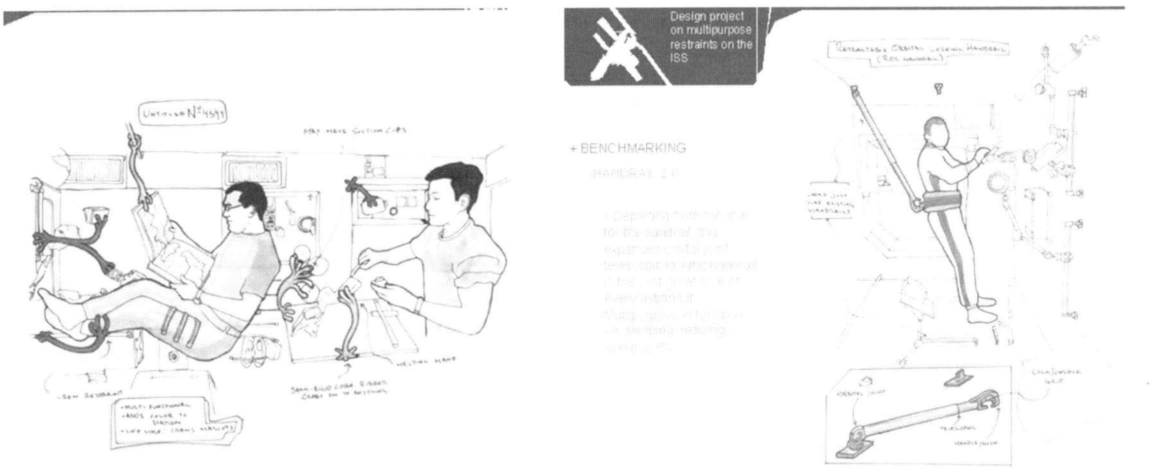

Figure 7. Design Example 4

The scientific approaches from engineering backgrounds appear to be too realistic to develop a creative and innovative design. So, NASA staff suggested that students ignore engineering data and concentrate on issues of stability, comfort, ease of use, and ease of installation.

<Student 14> *Are the handrail and seat track a vendor item? Can we obtain samples or detailed engineering drawings of these parts? Is seat track still to spec MS33601?*

<NASA> *Jason--yes, the seat track that we use is made primarily by Boeing (although some international partners get seat track elsewhere). I do not know of a capability to get a sample.*

<NASA> *I'm not familiar with MS33601....is this a military spec? For the purpose of this project, we are looking for CONCEPTUAL designs, so the details of the seat track are not particularly critical*

<Student 14> *Thanks Susan*

<Student 15> *I know there is a Generic Design Requirements Document (GDRD) for EVA, is there one for IVA?*

<NASA> *I believe there is a requirement document for IVA equipment design, but for the purpose of this project it is not necessary for CONCEPTUAL designs. Does this answer your question?*

<Student 15> *Yes, thank you*

<Student 16> *Astronaut Anthropometrics Data - Yes there is data available. For this project it*

<NASA> *will not be crucial to concept design....*

Are there any significant material constraints, i.e. plastics, composites,

<Student 17> *etc.??*

<NASA> *We are not too concentrating on material constraints or exact measurements of restraint system but of concepts ideas that address issues of stability, comfort, ease of use, ease of installation.*

5.3 Works from non-participant schools

Only one school did not participate in the online chat sessions. Its students' approaches to recognizing problems, formulating concepts, and developing designs are markedly different from those of the other schools. The students from the non-participant school initiated their project by performing an extensive literature search and review. While the literature provides an impressive amount of information, there are limitations for understanding real problems for the crew restraints system. Design artifacts reflecting tacit knowledge are more likely to be complete, and thus more credible.

5.4 Feedback

The chat scripts are especially useful when they remind the participants of the topics discussed. Because of the volume of material, students might have difficulty in recalling all the conversations. If students have access to repositories containing such conversations, their works reflects experts' knowledge to a greater extent, and is more fruitful and competitive. To this end, a method for capturing knowledge should be developed. When professionals handle information of high value, they intuitively want to capture it, but they cannot spend time to capture and store in an appropriate place. When professionals leave an organization, knowledge also leaves. Therefore, systems should extract, reflect and retain experts' tacit knowledge within organizational boundaries before they leave. Processes to develop these systems in a working organization are heavily dependent upon the manager's business strategy. What is required is a manager who can imagine a more desirable future and invent ways of reaching it.

The final step of the study was to present its findings from this study to NASA professional staff members. Since this study included their dialogues, they could check the reliability of the data, as well as validate the instuctors' findings. The students did not participate in the validation process.

6 Conclusion

This study demonstrates the applicability of tacit knowledge sharing in a distributed design studio. We conducted a content analysis on three different types of media: tacit knowledge resources, explicit knowledge resources and students' design artifacts. It is difficult to separate the impact of tacit knowledge only and to determine which type of knowledge is more effective, since students typically develop projects based on both types of knowledge. However, we find that online chat dialogues contain exclusive tacit knowledge provided by NASA. Since NASA staff holds exclusive tacit knowledge of crew restraint systems, their answers or comments about the design work contained critical suggestions. The findings of this study show that students' design artifacts are practically improved by tacit knowledge sharing. Expert designers therefore appear to be a richer source of new ideas and alternative perspectives.

We have seen that the online chat system is useful in sharing tacit knowledge for the early part of design processes in a distributed design environment. It is apparent that tacit knowledge sharing generates a well-defined problem. The participants share their knowledge and reflect the solutions in action. Experts' tacit knowledge appears to not only influence how students understand problems, but how they start conceptual design. We believe this study provides empirical evidence regarding tacit knowledge sharing, and strengthens Schon's (1983) claim about knowledge reflection in design studio. Furthermore, the significance of this study introduces architectural practitioners to the practical necessity of tacit knowledge sharing. They must develop more effective ways to share employee's various levels of tacit knowledge. While deeply ingrained tacit knowledge may only be shared through learning by doing (Schon 1983), lower levels of tacit knowledge can be effectively articulated and shared by using Internet technology.

The essence of tacit knowledge sharing is a collaborative attitude and a willingness to collectively accomplish work and to jointly discover and develop the best solutions. This study suggests that a distributed design studio should be implemented based on the collaborative culture. A distributed design studio should consider cultural factors influencing knowledge sharing, trust and collaboration. Improving collaboration and cultural trust is one of the major tasks for effective knowledge management.

7 Future Study

This study was limited to qualitative research methods. To quantitatively analyze the impact of tacit knowledge on design artifacts, a questionnaire will be distributed to the participating students in the future. The final deliverable required by NASA was the conceptual designs. So, the results of this study are limited to partially showing the impact of tacit knowledge. In a future study, we will observe the impact of tacit knowledge on the entire design process.

Acknowledgement

The research reported here was made possible through the help and assistance of the National Aeronautics and Space Administration staff in the Usability Testing and Analysis Facility. We gratefully acknowledge their support. Susan Baggerman helped me obtain the necessary data. Dr. Mihriban Whitmore gave considerable time and energy for knowledge sharing. Finally, the Department of Architecture at Texas A&M University provided funding for this research though The William W. Caudill Research Fellowship.

Reference:

Ambrosini, V., and C.Bowman, (2001). Tacit Knowledge: Some Suggestions for Operationalization, *Journal of management studies* 38(6): 811-829.

Cross, N., and A.C.Cross, (1995). Observations of teamwork and social processes in design, Design studies. 16:143-170.

Cross, N. (2000). *Engineering design methods*: *Strategies for product design*. 3rd ed. Wiley & Sons, UK.

Davenport, T., and L. Prusak, (1998). *Working knowledge: How organizations manage what they know*. Boston: Harvard Business School Press.

Dorst, K., and N.Cross, (2001). Creativity in the design process: Co-evolution of problem-solution. *Design studies.* 22(5):425-437.

Gero, J. S., and T.McNeill, (1998). An approach to the analysis of design protocols. Design studies, 19:21-61.

Hansen, M., N.Nohria, and T.Tierney, (1999). What is your strategy for managing knowledge? *Harvard business review*, 77(2): 106-18.

Huang, J. (1999). Knowledge haring and innovation in distributed design: Implications of internet-based media on design collaboration. *International journal for design computing*, DCNet '99.

Isaacs, E., A.Walendowski, S.Whittaker, D.Schiano, and C.Kamm, (2002). The character, functions, and styles of instant messaging in the workplace. *Proceedings of the CSCW'02,* 126-135. New Orleans, Louisiana.

Johannessen, J.A., J.Olaisen, & B.Olsen, (2001). Mismanagement of tacit knowledge: The importance of tacit knowledge, the danger of information technology, and what to do about it. *International journal of information management*, 21:3-20.

Nonaka, I., & H.Takeuchi, (1995). The *knowledge creating company.* New York: Oxford University Press.

Polanyi, M. (1966). *The tacit dimension*. Garden City: Doubleday.

Ribak, A., M.Jacovi, and V.Soraka, (2002). Ask before you search Peer Support and community building with ReachOut. *Proceedings of the CSCW'02*,126-135. New Orleans, Louisiana.

Reber, A. S. (1993). *Implicit learning and tacit knowledge: An essay on the cognitive unconscious*. New York: Oxford University Press.

Schon, D. (1983). *The reflective practitioner: How professionals think in action*. Basic Books, USA.

Schon, D. (1985). *Design studio*, London: RIBA Publications.

Sternberg, R. J., G.B.Forsythe,J.Hedlund, J.A.Horvath, R.K.Wagner, W.M. Williams, S.A. Snook, & E.L. Grigorenko, (2000). *Practical intelligence in everyday life.* New York: Cambridge University Press.

Appropriate Levels of Access: An Empirical Study on the Availability of Computers in Studio*

Matthew Bernhardt and Beth Blostein
the Ohio State University

Abstract

One of the most significant technological challenges facing architecture schools today is how to provide an appropriate level of access to computing resources. As the computer has become a significant tool in the study and practice of architecture, students need to have access to that tool in order to further their studies. But in facing this question of access, what is "appropriate"? Is there such a thing as too much access? Is 1:1 access—a computer for every student—the minimum level of access that schools and students should accept? Or is there a point beyond which more resources just means more waste; computers sitting idle and unused, or students using the computer for unproductive ends? These questions were the subject of an experimental series of studios in the spring of 2002, wherein three studios were given varying numbers of computers for a term. The use of these computers was then tracked, and compared with previous terms. In tandem, the quality of work produced by these three studios was compared. While additional experiments are most likely needed to draw firm conclusions, the results of this experiment seem to support defining "an appropriate level of access" at less than 1:1.

*A Digital *Work In Progress*

Appropriate Levels of Access: An Empirical Study on the Availability of Computers in Studio

Matthew Bernhardt and Beth Blostein
the Ohio State University

1 Introduction

Over the past decades, the computer has assumed a position of increasing importance in architectural education. What was first considered a novelty with dubious relevance is now seen as an extremely useful, even necessary, tool for learning the theory and practice of architecture. Yet for all its usefulness, schools face considerable hurdles in their attempt to provide this resource to their students. The cost of purchasing and maintaining a reasonable amount of computer resources can be prohibitive. Naturally, schools want to ensure that those resources which they do purchase will be used effectively—rather than either sitting idle or being misused for non-productive ends. This paper describes one attempt to mediate these potentially conflicting desires, and help schools establish appropriate goals for student access to computing resources.

2 Background

Our school is comprised of roughly 500 students in 3 different sections. The architecture section is made up of graduate and undergraduate programs, and has approximately 270 enrolled students. All student activities are housed in one building, although faculty offices and school administration are in a separate location. In the next few years the school will be opening a brand new building that will house all aspects of the school. It has been determined that, as we move through this transition, the method we use to provide digital resources will change. We will move away from our current computer lab model toward a model where computers are integrated into the studio environment. The specifics of this integration and the method of providing computer resources are still under discussion.

Traditionally, computing resources have been provided via dedicated labs of desktop computers. While these labs have grown in number over the past decade, over the past 5 years there have consistently been 5 labs of approximately 100 computers. The resources in these labs are funded by a combination of student technology fees and matching funds provided by the college. The computers in these labs are from 1-3 years old at any given time, with computers distributed among the labs as evenly as possible.

In anticipation of our move into a new building, over the past 4 years we have begun placing desktop computers directly within design studios. These computers once resided in the labs; each computer is initially installed in one of the labs and then moved out to the studios after a year for the rest of the warranty period. The distribution of computers among the studios privileges higher-rank students, because these students tend to be best able to take advantage of them. However, each studio is given a mix of computers of varying ages, so even the sophomore and first-year graduate studios have some younger computers—if fewer of them. The distribution for the 2001/02 school year is listed in Table 1.

Year	Level	Students	Computers	Ratio
Second	UG	84	12	7.00 : 1
Third	UG	75	12	6.25 : 1
Fourth	UG	70	12	5.83 : 1
Three-Plus	G	12	2	6.00 : 1
Fifth	G	24	5	4.80 : 1
Sixth	G	22	8	2.75 : 1

Table 1. 2001/02 Computer distribution

Our philosophy when it comes to information technology has been to inconvenience the students as little as possible. Put into practice, this means that we maintain software licenses to meet the greatest conceivable demand—and when we encounter a shortage, we buy more licenses rather than accept that there will be times when students will have to wait to use a program. We maintain 17 printers and plotters for student use, realizing that at times some of these printers will sit idle. There are times, however, when every printer and plotter on the network is working simultaneously. During those periods of high demand, we do not want students to wait any more than absolutely necessary.

The other side of this philosophy, however, is when we encounter a resource that is barely used at all, or that duplicates one already available. Over the past several years we have faced several of these situations and removed the resource in question. In the case of software packages such as After Effects, or 2D CAD digitizing tablets, they were simply not used to any appreciable extent. On the other hand, we have eliminated Macintosh computers and programs such as Bryce or Minitab because they are duplicated by more popular resources (Form*Z, SYSTAT, and PCs respectively). In these scenarios, the money and time necessary to support these less necessary resources would be better spent addressing areas where students are encountering more serious shortages.

3 The Experiment

In light of the forthcoming building, coupled with the need to maximize student access with limited financial resources, during the 2001/02 school year we explored how student computer use patterns change in response to different levels of access to computers.

We selected 4 studios for participation in this study. All were vertical studios, comprised of students in their 3rd or 4th year of undergraduate education. Three of the studios had 10 students, while the fourth had 12. The details of the 4 studios are given in Table 2. The projects assigned to each studio were similar, although not identical.

3.1 The 1:1 Studio

Studio	Students	Computers	Studio in Separate Room?
1:1 Studio	10	10	Yes
2:1 Studio	12	6	No
Control A	10	5*	No
Control B	10	3	Yes

Table 2. Comparison of 4 experimental studios

The principal studio being studied was designated as the "1:1 Studio," and every student in the studio was provided with a desktop computer. These computers were the same as those provided to the other design studios—ranging from 2-4 years old, with identical operating systems and applications. These computers were arranged in the studio so that each student had two adjacent work desks—one for drafting and modeling, and one for computer use.

The project assigned to this studio was an "Institute for Food Engineering Research." This project was consistent in site and scale with the other studios in this study, although the specific program was different for each studio. While the studio instructor has an interest in digital technologies applied to architectural design, no device or tool was required to be utilized by the students in the production of their work.

The students in the studio completed a site analysis during the first week of the quarter. They then proceeded to design a full-scale cavity wall, accommodating needed water, air, chemicals, and heat/cooling to support a family of genetically modified corn. Digital fabrication tools were introduced at this point as well. Eight of the ten students worked in pairs, with the final two students working alone. Three of the pairs and one individual made use of this equipment, while the other students also used computer models to varying degrees. This phase of the studio concluded in the 4th week, and ended with a midterm review.

The remaining 6 weeks of the term were spent designing the Institute itself, and concluded with a final review. Progress meetings were conducted individually with the instructor, or as small group presentations. Each group determined the manner and media in which it worked independent of instructor feedback. One group and one individual student produced digital work almost entirely, while another group and two individuals split their work evenly between digital and manual production. The final group and one individual tended to eschew the computer in favor of manual production.

3.2 The 2:1 Studio

Another studio was designated as the "2:1 Studio," and the studio was given a computer for every two students. These computers were also identical to those given to all other studios. The computers were arranged in pairs, and distributed as evenly as possible in the studio in an attempt to provide all students equal access—but we did not specifically assign any computers to any students.

3.3 The Control Studios

The final two studios were designated as control studios, and were given computers using the same principles as every other studio in the school. The computers in these studios were placed in a single location within each studio, and no computers were specifically assigned to any students.

In this study we attempted to vary only the level of access that the students in each studio had. Students were also able to use any of the computers in the labs, and like all students in the school they were discouraged from using the machines assigned to any other studio.

3.4 Our Hypotheses

In conducting this experiment, we hoped to test the validity of two hypotheses. The first was that while use levels between the differing studios were expected to vary according to each studio's level of access to computers, those differences were not expected to be significant enough to justify the expense of providing 1:1 computing throughout the school. This hypothesis would be evaluated quantitatively, by using the use logs generated by a utility already in use in the school. The second hypothesis was that increased access to computers should result in a higher quality of work, because the tool would be readily available at all times—allowing the student to be simultaneously working on the computer as well as on a physical model or hand drawings. The second hypothesis would be evaluated qualitatively by the studio instructor in light of her experience leading previous studios.

It was necessary to test both of these hypotheses together because any attempt to verify either hypothesis alone could yield a misleading conclusion. Computer use is not an end in itself, so it is not enough to only induce students to use computers more often; the use must positively impact the process of studying architecture. On the other hand, increased computer use is certainly the goal of providing more computers; so there does need to be some form of quantitative element to verify that use is actually increasing.

3.5 Methods of Evaluation

In order to evaluate the first hypothesis, we utilized the computer use logs generated by Sassafras Software's KeyServer. This program is used by the school to ensure that the number of copies of a program running at any given point does not exceed the number of licenses which have been purchased. In performing this task, KeyServer logs who is using what software packages, during what times, and on what computers. By analyzing these logs we would be able to determine how much use each studio was generating, and thus test the validity of our hypothesis. More information about KeyServer, including a list of programs under its control, can be found in the Appendix.

We used these logs to construct two general comparisons. The first comparison is between the 4 studios in this experiment, specifically during the quarter of the study. The second comparison focuses on the 1:1 Studio and one of the Control studios, and compares their use between the quarter of the study and the 5 previous quarters. For both comparisons, we look at the same set of 3 variables:

1) The average time that the students in the studio used a computer.
2) The average time that the students used 4 specific software packages.
3) The average session length as the students used those 4 specific software packages.

Similar qualitative comparisons were made by the 1:1 Studio instructor, based on her experience of leading design studios for several years.

4 The Results

Before discussing the results of this study, it is important to describe some complicating factors which arose during the course of the quarter. The first and most significant is the theft of 3 computers from the 2:1 Studio approximately halfway through the term. The stolen computers were replaced, but not until after several days had passed. The loss of half of the computers dedicated to this studio, even for several days, potentially changed the students' use habits significantly enough that any conclusions drawn from the 2:1 Studio data set must be viewed skeptically. It is for this reason that this paper talks primarily about the experience of the 1:1 Studio.

The second complicating factor stems from the physical layout of some of the studios in this study. While the 1:1 Studio and one Control Studio were taught in their own room, the 2:1 Studio, the other Control Studio, and 2 unrelated studios were all taught in one large room. The layout of this room for the term had two banks of computers—the computers given specifically to the 2:1 Studio, and a separate bank of 5 computers that were provided for the 3 other studios in the room—one of which had been designated as a Control Studio. Perhaps because of the aforementioned thefts, and also because of the ambiguous "ownership" relationship in that room to begin with, the students of the 2:1 Studio used all 11 computers in the room to fairly significant extents—while the students of the other 3 studios used only the 5 computers provided to them. It is for this reason that the results of the Control Studios are broken down into Control A and Control B. Control B is the studio that had the dedicated room with no outside competition for computers, while Control A faced such outside competition regularly. It is our position that this competition does not invalidate the results of the Control A studio, but that it is something to take into account when considering the results of this study.

With those caveats having been addressed, here are the results of the two different comparisons described above.

4.1 Latitudinal Comparison

This comparison looks at the differences in use between the 4 studios in this study for the quarter during which the experiment took place. The results of this comparison are displayed in Table 3.

Studio	General Use (days)	Core Use (days)	Average Duration (hours)
1:1 Studio	60.46	58.12	12.31
2:1 Studio	8.75	6.20	1.58
Control Average	5.15	4.54	1.76
Control A	(4.09)	(3.65)	(1.14)
Control B	(6.22)	(5.44)	(2.39)

Table 3. Latitudinal comparison results

The average student in the 1:1 Studio used a computer for just over 60 days and 11 hours during this quarter. That figure represents a 1,074% increase over the average student in one of the Control Studios, who used the computers for about 5 days and 3 and a half hours. This is also 591% more than the average student in the 2:1 Studio. The students of the 2:1 Studio, meanwhile, used computers 70% more than the students in the Control Studio. These relationships are illustrated in Figure 1.

Of the more than 30 software packages that students could use during this quarter, 4 programs accounted for 72% of the software used. Those four packages were Adobe Photoshop, Autodesk AutoCAD, Auto*des*sys Form*Z, and Macromedia FreeHand. This is in line with previous quarters, as these packages have accounted for 70-90% of software use for the past 2 years. These programs tend to be used more because the students are actively instructed in their use via a series of classes in the sophomore year. Other programs, such as Creative Labs Poser or Macromedia Dreamweaver, are taught only sporadically, or spread through word of mouth among the student body. In order to control for this haphazard method of instruction, we next compared the amount of use for only these 4 programs. Those results are illustrated in Figure 2, and fairly closely resemble the findings in Figure 1.

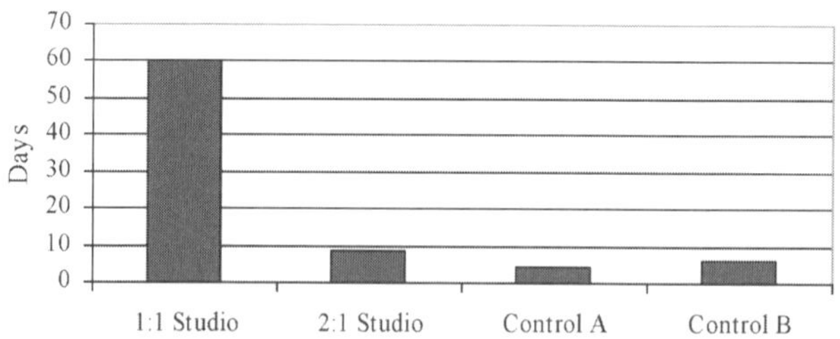

Figure 1. Average computer use per student

The students of the 1:1 Studio used the 4 core programs 1,179% more than the two Control Studios, and 837% more than the students of the 2:1 Studio. Comparing the first two variables, it seems that the students of the 1:1 Studio emphasized the 4 core programs more heavily—spending 96% of their computing time in one of those 4 applications. By contrast, the 2:1 Studio generated 71% of their use in the core programs, while the Control Studios spent 89% of their time using the core programs.

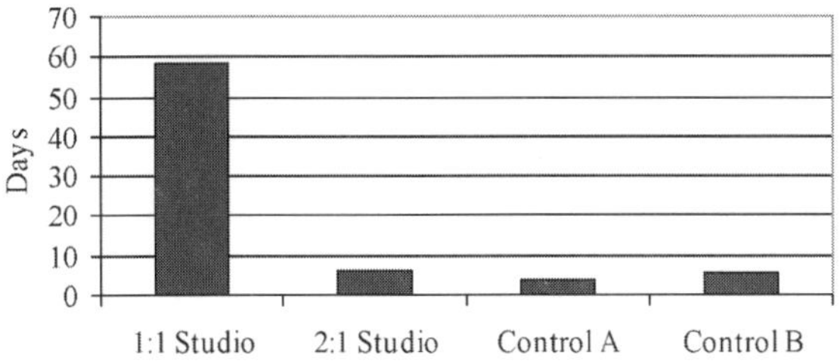

Figure 2. Average core software use per student

With this drastic difference in use one must ask whether the students of the 1:1 Studio were doing anything else differently, beyond just using computers more frequently. One answer can be found by examining the average length of time that each application was open. The average session duration is the final component of the latitudinal comparison, and is the subject of Figure 3.

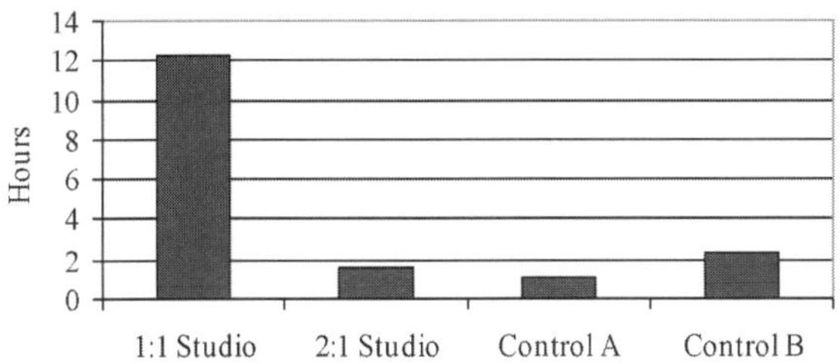

Figure 3. Average session duration

The average application session for the 1:1 Studio lasted almost 12 hours and 20 minutes— 599% longer than those for the Control Studios, which were just over 1 hour and 45 minutes long. They were also 679% longer than the average session length for the 2:1 Studio—which lasted about an hour and 35 minutes.

Looking at these results, it is highly doubtful that any group of students would be productive for an average of 12 hours at a time over the course of a quarter. The 12:20 average session duration leads us to suspect that the students of the 1:1 Studio were in the habit of leaving their computers running even when they were not working. This possibility is problematic; it suggests that for some portion of the quarter even though the computers were in use, they were not actively being used. The longer that an application session lasts, the greater the likelihood that it includes a portion of idle use. A session that lasts 2 hours is more likely to be entirely productive, while a session that lasts 24 hours probably contains a large amount of inactive time.

To explore this situation in more detail, we have regenerated the chart from Figure 1, focusing on sessions of specific lengths. Figure 4 shows these results. There are four series of data in this figure. The first includes all sessions and is identical to Figure 1. The second includes only those application sessions that were shorter than 24 hours in length. The third includes only those sessions under 16 hours in length. The last includes only those sessions under 8 hours in length.

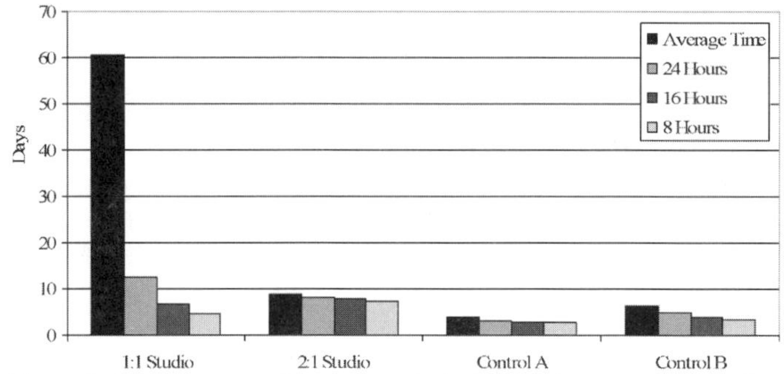

Figure 4. Average computer use per student, focusing on sessions of varying lengths

When sessions of extraordinary length are excluded from the sample, the use levels for the 1:1 Studio are reduced to a range similar to those produced by the other 3 studios. For sessions under 24 hours in length, the 1:1 Studio used computers 215% more than the control studios, and 50% more than the 2:1 Studio. When the data are restricted to sessions under 16 hours in length, the 1:1 Studio used computers 97% more than the control studios, and 16% less than the 2:1 Studio. Overall, 79% of the computer use observed from the 1:1 Studio came in sessions that lasted longer than 24 hours. This is in contrast to 5% of use by the 2:1 Studio and 23% for the Control Studios. It is risky to proceed too far down this path, however. While it is true that the great majority of use generated by the 1:1 Studio was from sessions over 24 hours in length, it is inaccurate to assume that none of that time was actually spent productively. It may be outside the capabilities of this analysis technique to accurately determine how much use was productive in nature as opposed to time the computers spent idly running the software. This is an area that should be investigated further, perhaps with a different set of monitoring tools.

In conclusion, the latitudinal comparison of these four studios indicates that our first hypothesis is accurate, to some extent. Students with greater access to computers will tend to use those computers more often. Conversely, our hypothesis was less accurate with regards to the extent to which those use levels increased. When students were given their own computers, they used those computers 1,000% more. By contrast, when students were given 2:1 access to the computers, they used those computers 70% more. While there are indications in the data that much of this increase is due to idle use, more analysis is necessary to evaluate that possibility.

4.2 Longitudinal Comparison

One possibility that must be examined is whether the students of the 1:1 Studio were predisposed to use computers more or less frequently than the average students. Such a condition would distort the results of this study, making evaluation of the first hypothesis more difficult. We have attempted to control for this effect in two ways. First, the students were not informed of the differing levels of computer access among the 4 studios before they signed up for their chosen studio. This prevented students from self-selecting into any particular study group. Second, we have conducted a time-based comparison—comparing how the students in the 1:1 Studio used computers in this quarter to how those same students had used computers in the previous 2 years. This longitudinal comparison looks at the same 3 variables as the first comparison. For the sake of contextualizing these results, we have also conducted this comparison for the students in the Control B studio. The results of these comparisons are displayed in Tables 4 and 5.

Quarter	General Use (days)	Core Use (days)	Average Duration (hours)
Spring 2002	60.46	58.12	12.31
Winter 2002	3.10	2.88	1.48
Autumn 2001	No reliable data available		
Spring 2001	4.34	3.97	0.80
Winter 2001	2.41	2.39	0.67
Autumn 2000	0.21	0.19	0.36

Table 4. Longitudinal comparison results for the 1:1 Studio

Quarter	General Use (days)	Core Use (days)	Average Duration (hours)
Spring 2002	7.37	5.44	2.39
Winter 2002	3.54	2.80	1.41
Autumn 2001	No reliable data available		
Spring 2001	5.76	5.40	0.93
Winter 2001	2.27	2.20	0.71
Autumn 2000	0.22	0.19	0.45

Table 5. Longitudinal comparison results for the Control B Studio

One difficulty that we had in completing this comparison is the fact that we have no reliable data for the autumn quarter of the 2001/2002 school year. During that quarter, it was discovered that a configuration error was preventing KeyServer from completely recording all network activity due to software on the computers being incorrectly configured. As a result of this error, much of the network was not reporting any use data whatsoever. The problem was fixed shortly after it was discovered, but the result is that there are no reliable data for the first half of the quarter. Rather than attempt to extrapolate from the data for the second half of the quarter, we have elected to omit this quarter's data entirely.

It should be noted that although this problem did occur, there is no reason to believe that the KeyServer system was incorrectly configured for any other quarter. We can say this with surety because the type of configuration problem observed in the autumn quarter will completely eliminate any use data being submitted for a specific computer and application. For the other 5 quarters examined in this study, no such far-reaching lack of data is evident. All programs submit at least some data from each computer at least once in the quarter, indicating that any lack of reported use stems from an actual lack of use, rather than the actual use not being reported.

The first variable in the comparison is the total amount of time that the average student in each studio used the computers. This relationship is expressed in Figure 5 for both the 1:1 Studio as well as the Control B Studio.

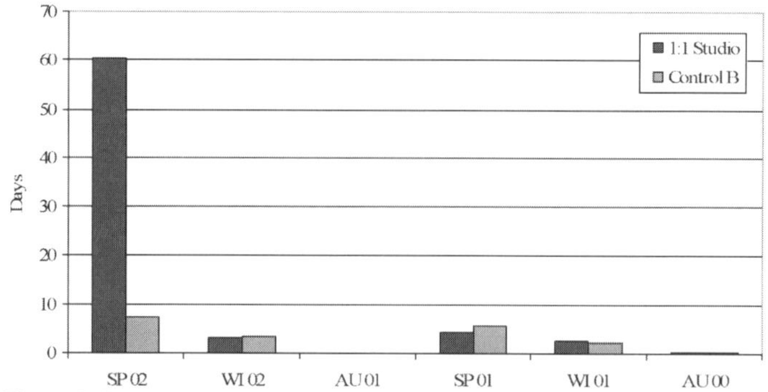

Figure 5. Average computer use per student, over 6 quarters

Before the beginning of this study, the students of the 1:1 Studio used computers roughly as much as the students of the Control B Studio. This similarity ended for the quarter of our study, as the use levels for the students of the 1:1 Studio increased by 1,852% over the previous quarter, and 1,294% over the previous spring quarter. The students of the Control B Studio, meanwhile, used computers 109% more than the previous quarter, and 28% more than the same quarter the previous year. Because of this, it seems that the increase in use is directly related to the level of access provided to the students, rather than any previously existing patterns of computer use.

The second step of this comparison is to focus only on the 4 core programs of the school. In addition to controlling for disorganized methods of software instruction, this step also controls for the changes in supported software that existed between the 2000/01 school year and the 2001/02 school year. This variable is expressed in Figure 6.

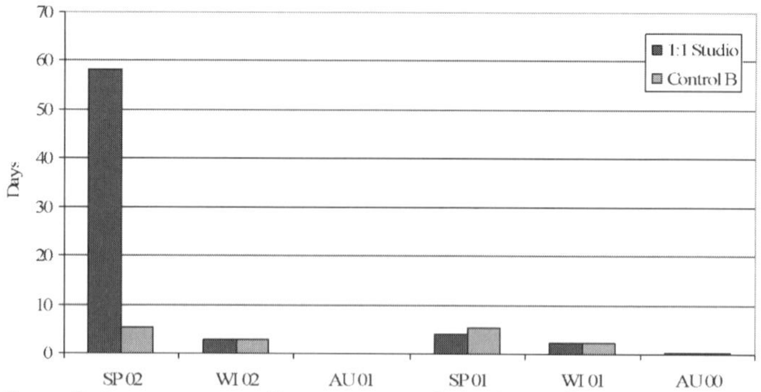

Figure 6. Average core software use per student, over 6 quarters

These results mirror those presented by the first variable in this comparison, which is that before this study the students in the 1:1 Studio did not use computers significantly more than their counterparts in the Control B studio. It is only when they were provided a dedicated computer that their patterns of use changed, even among the 4 core programs.

The final step in this comparison, then, is to examine how

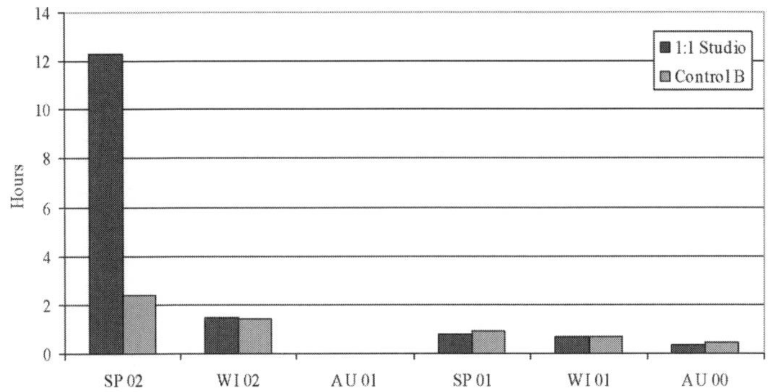

Figure 7. Average session duration, over 6 quarters

application session lengths changed over the past 6 quarters. This variable seems to confirm the same results that were previously hinted at—that the use patterns of the students of the 1:1 Studio were not initially different than the students in the other studios. In the quarters leading up to this study, the students of the 1:1 Studio and the Control B Studio tended to use the 4 core programs for approximately the same length of time per session—differing at most by 18%. Those session times increased drastically, however, when the 1:1 Studio was given greater access to computers. Session lengths for the 1:1 Studio were 317% longer than those for the Control B Studio, 737% longer than the quarter preceding this study, and 1,477% longer than the same quarter a year ago.

This comparison indicates that, before this study began, there were no significant differences between the use habits of the 1:1 Studio and the other studios. It is then reasonable to conclude that the differences observed during this study were caused by the differing levels of access between the studios, rather than any pre-existing differences in work habits.

4.3 Qualitative Comparison

Turning our attention to the second hypothesis, that increased access to computers should result in a higher quality of work, it is our observation that while the data indicates significant utilization of design software within the 1:1 Studio, there was incongruency between this use data and the observed data which warrants speculation. According to the instructor of the 1:1 Studio, the quantity of work (i.e. the number of drawings, images, etc.) actually presented during an average studio day was similar to that of other studios taught by the same instructor. This suggests that the increase in use resulted from activity other than the productive development of the project at hand. This could include the production of work the student deemed unsuccessful or inappropriate for presentation, or time spent grappling with software functionality. This brings to question whether or not students have the techniques and skills needed to effectively use the computer as a tool for architectural development. The quality of the work that was presented and level of architectural investigation was also not markedly different than other studios, as the grade spread for this quarter directly matched that of other studios taught by the same instructor (A- through B-).

It is also significant that even with individual "ownership" of a computer in the design studio, 8 of 10 projects heavily utilized hand production methods. This suggests that only in very rare circumstances would every computer within the studio be active. Thus, a 1:1 computer-to-student ratio would not be warranted.

5 The Conclusions

This study was undertaken to test two hypotheses. The first was that students with greater access to computers tend to use computers more heavily, but not heavily enough to justify providing a computer for every student. The second hypothesis was that increased access to computers should result in a higher quality of work. We believe that although a first reading of the results indicates that both hypotheses have been disproved, there are details in the results which strongly indicate otherwise.

After observing the use patterns of one studio of students who were each given a computer to use exclusively, it was initially observed that the students used the computers far more often than they had in the past, and far more often than other students in similar studios. However, there is reason to doubt these initial observations, as a large majority of the observed use came in continuous blocks that lasted for longer than 24 hours. This indicates that what appears as use was actually computers sitting idle, running software with no one at the keyboard.

When those extraordinarily long sessions are filtered out, use patterns fall back to levels comparable to the other studios of this experiment. If this alternate reading is valid, it would verify our first hypothesis—that levels of use do not increase significantly enough to justify the expense of providing 1:1 access.

If we accept the observed levels of use at face value, the second hypothesis was also refuted—despite such a drastic increase in use, the quality of work produced by the students did not increase. If we instead accept the alternate reading, that productive use did not increase significantly, it is difficult to evaluate this hypothesis at all as it was predicated on an increase of computer use.

It is our position that the alternative reading is correct, that productive use did not increase significantly enough to justify the effort of providing 1:1 computing, and that the second hypothesis cannot be fully evaluated. Although we believe that the results of this experiment are significant and valid, more study of this issue is clearly warranted. Repeating this experiment, perhaps with changes to the technologies used to monitor computer use, will help indicate whether our alternate reading of the data is valid. Further study can also help explore issues that were not considered in this experiment, such as whether students use laptops differently than they use desktops, or how a studio might be structured to help students take advantage of the resources available to them. Continuing to explore these issues will become more important as schools continue to face the problem of allocating limited resources to providing appropriate levels of access to computers.

Appendix

Sassafras Software's KeyServer monitors only those programs which are placed under its control. Because of this, we do not monitor programs like Minesweeper, Internet Explorer, or any email programs. This setup keeps our records free of activity such as web browsing, email, or game playing.
Another aspect of how KeyServer works is that all use times are calculated based on *program* use, not *computer* use. If a student has two programs open simultaneously for an hour each, it shows up in the logs as 2 hours of use. Time that a student is logged in, but not using any controlled programs is not counted at all.

Software that was controlled during the spring 2002 quarter is listed below:

- Adaptec EasyCD Creator
- Adobe InDesign
- Adobe Photoshop
- Adobe Premiere
- Alias|Wavefront Maya
- Architectural Graphics Standards
- ArcInfo
- ArcView GIS
- Autodesk AutoCAD
- Auto*des*sys Form*Z
- Bentley MicroStation
- Curious Labs Poser
- Energy Scheming
- Extensis Portfolio
- GAMS
- GTK Build
- GTK Radiant
- IDRISI
- Limdep
- Macromedia Dreamweaver
- Macromedia Fireworks
- Macromedia Flash
- Macromedia Freehand
- MS Access
- MS Excel
- MS PowerPoint
- MS Word
- PCSWMM
- QTVR Authoring Studio
- Quake III Arena
- Rhinoceros
- SAS
- Stella
- SYSTAT

03b>>Connecting Digital Pedagogy

Gregory A. Luhan, Nancy Yen-wen Cheng

Digital Curricula: Effective Integration of Digital Courses

Stitched-spaces and Digital Permutations

Gregory A. Luhan

Digital strategies and tactics

If, "the purpose of art is to awaken reality" as Paul Klee writes, what then, is the generative purpose of the digital as it relates to architecture? By uniting the traditional ways of knowing with the more contemporary and technologically advanced ways of knowing, the architect then would be able to develop the capacity to visualize and to understand unseen spatial relationships and exploit their latent characteristics. The computer consequently allows a direct synthesis to occur between the original idea and its formal application, in a sense providing new questions to old answers.

There is little debate that new technologies associated with digital media are valuable to architects and designers. Yet, how and when a faculty introduces students to the field of computing in architecture is still at question. I would posit an early integration of computers into the architecture curriculum that moves beyond the checklist of merely learning the tools of software through tutorials. As architects, we must approach the digital at the conceptual level where a framework exists. We must combine skill and intellect to allow for a new type of architectural assemblage – one that informs, as well as represents. The digital is not just a tool for documenting what one believes a building or product to look like. The device of digital drawing brings the energy of architectural intention into an operative presence. It is a medium with which to express the release of the idea from the mind.

A curriculum for architecture that vacillates between computation and representation will undoubtedly create a valuable place where operations like games have important meaning. It is not enough to play. It is more important to narrow the boundaries between meaning and making so that practiced application, independent assessment, and professional ability result. The union of the digital with the strategies of game has the ability to establish permutations in terms of pedagogy, knowledge, and composition. If more fully developed, this amalgamation could provide an intriguing path towards better understanding the role of the computer in architectural education.

Games and discovery

A fundamental aspect of architectural education lies in the ability to think and to demonstrate three-dimensionally. Architects articulate their imagination by drawing three-dimensional ideas in two-dimensional representations and then translate them further into three-dimensional form. As professors we provide a unique opportunity for our students to play in innovative ways – not only outside of the box, but in directing the seeing of the inside of the box in new ways. Architecture students, in particular, link the elastic qualities of the imagination to understanding precedent, exploring analytical methods, and deploying design methodology. The hope of this process is for students to develop their own philosophy upon which to base a design. If the context of game were of value to architectural education, then the strategies of those games would be just as plastic.

The struggle to find a starting point often leads architects outside of the realm of architecture. The accepted papers for the topic node digital curriculums: effective integration of digital courses, present an interesting outside insertion into the realm of architecture – using 'games' within the context of the traditional design studio. As presented, the use of games in architecture is relatively straightforward. Like most games, there are rules, desired outcomes, strategies, and tactics. The authors present a series of actions that address the individual student, the collective studio, and the role that pedagogy plays in understanding the assessments of such a deployment. Without exception, the major void left in this process is that the student/author/participant has no way of fully understanding the ideas behind the game, that is to say, the techniques required to create a truly meaningful result and the implications of their design decisions in real or virtual space.

Permutations

In extreme cases, games without space beyond the extents of the boardscape become generic, homogenous, and two-dimensional. While digital making is a necessary process of the game's strategy, it is limited to merely use the digital to make what could have otherwise been made without the digital. Since the game's objective might not solely be inhabitable space, the intention of the game should align with more augmentation, innovation, and experimentation than with replacement as currently presented. The true use of a game in the context of architecture would exploit the seams of the rules, use the digital in imaginative ways, and have assessable consequences and time would have a definable role. The intersection of computer space with architectural space, I believe, would result in active and adaptable spaces that challenge our thinking about observation and perception and enhance our comprehension of the unique relationship between participation, experience, and built form. These in-between seam spaces or stitched-spaces would therefore begin to define an environment within which all students could discover something for themselves and in turn challenge the practice of architecture in the future.

Gregory A. Luhan is an Assistant Professor of Architecture at the University of Kentucky, College of Design. He practiced architecture in New York City at Eisenman Architects after he graduated from Princeton University (M. Arch) and Virginia Polytechnic Institute (B. Arch). He has written articles relating to the Synthetic Landscapes of Digital Architectures as well as the Porosity of the Urban Environment as depicted through his digital models of Venice, Italy; Shanghai, China; Louisville, Kentucky; and New York City. Professor Luhan teaches a digital studio and seminars on design theory and computing. He is currently completing a book manuscript on modern architecture in Louisville.

Digital Curricula: Effective Integration Of Digital Courses - A Delicate Balance

Nancy Yen-wen Cheng

One of the challenges faced by digital design teachers is how to fit our piece into the larger puzzle of architectural education. How can we make computing support architecture's varied endeavors and thinking modes? Students must be able to explore and communicate design ideas fluidly using digital or traditional media, as suitable to specific queries. We need to expose students to a palette of current and emerging techniques and help them develop a personal set of media skills.

Resolving tensions in curricular planning

What's the best way to do it? In planning what to teach, we face lots of decisions: architectural problems or artsy multimedia? Descriptive case studies or generative design exercises? Last year's topics or the next big thing? The apparent dualities in curricular planning can be resolved by prioritizing and timing. Rather than choosing one over another, it's a matter of figuring out how and when it fits into a student's education.

I follow Howard Gardner, who advocates different kinds of training for different times in a child's development. In To Open Minds, he looked at methods of teaching music and art in China and America – marveling at the contrast between the rigidly structured Chinese lessons and more exuberant American approaches for teaching elementary students. Consequently, he believes in early free expression followed by several years of apprentice-like training to encourage disciplined, structured learning for pre-teens and young teens. As teens methodically acquire skills, they can gradually move beyond classical exercises and find new modes of expression.

So, in introductory classes, we encourage students to experiment and create 2D and 3D compositions that can incorporate happy accidents. As they get to know applications better, we balance expressive creative projects with descriptive ones that require more understanding of subtle controls. Through projects using architectural precedents or prescribed generative functions, they learn skills that are then applied to developing design studio projects. As students are more aware of the need to present their ideas rather than develop them through media, much of the learning needs to occur in a design context. We want our students fluent and empowered to experiment and discover new design ideas. To check this competency, we can screen portfolios or use timed exercises.

Amid the machines and software, design must remain central. We cultivate visual judgment by starting the palette small and the problems simple but open-ended. In teaching 3D applications, we introduce view navigation and rendering early so that students can bring graphic appeal to even the simplest cubes. As technology is a necessary evil to many design students, I concentrate on strategies for approaching new technology and talk about technical concepts in support of design tasks. Reinforcing technical ideas works best on a need to know basis, with help available on demand.

Today vs. Tomorrow

A big question is how to keep our courses timely and fresh without pushing the latest thing because the teachers benefit rather than the students. We need to find a kind of dynamic equilibrium: moving forward while keeping in balance.
For example, it is important our students understand that architectural CAD programs can quickly generate 3D buildings from simple 2D drawings and that they have the database

structures to link all sorts of building information for cost estimation, structure, etc. into the same model. Yet many of us feel it is more appropriate to start design students on generic form-makers that are not architectural because of the inherent bias for traditional (yawn!) forms that the architectural software contains. We show them the more advanced automated programs only after they understand generic operations. We need to expose the students to the advantages and disadvantages of each approach even if there is not enough time for them to master both.

In our quest to be cutting-edge, we have to make sure that technology doesn't get in the way of education. In pursuing the latest and greatest, driven by our curiosity and our need to publish, we may be pushing new gizmos for which students are not ready, or are not ready to disseminate. Whether it is multimedia, nurbs modeling, generative design, virtual reality, rapid-prototyping, or tangible computing, it can take a lot of patient tinkering to pioneer technical pathways and generate rich examples.

In looking at how to push a research agenda within a professional program, I've found it most rewarding to start with top students in independent studies and research seminars, and then gradually introduce the technology to an advanced class that can generate assistants to teach methods in required courses. With the advanced students, we can test out ways to introduce material and get articulate feedback. Advanced students can create examples for beginning students and act as their coaches.

Cultivating change

Rather than choosing the most technically-savvy as teaching fellows, I look for a combination of articulate charisma, design talent and technical know-how. I need at least one glamorous assistant to help make digital look cool because, to reach fruition, a digital design sensibility must pervade the whole school culture. It is too hard to figure out computers alone: faculty, staff and students need to share ideas and reach outside of the school to other resources. We need full-time faculty with broad knowledge as well as expert adjunct application specialists. A diverse learning community is crucial to making a digital curriculum effective in architectural education

References

Gardner, H. (1989). To open minds: Chinese clues to the dilemma of contemporary education. New York: Basic Books. Basic books paperback with new introduction, 1991.

Nancy Yen-Wen Cheng (B.A. Yale, M.Arch. Harvard) researches how digital media can enrich the architectural design process at the University of Oregon. She currently investigates mobile tools for capturing places. She is active in the AIA Technology in Architectural Practice group, the International Journal of Architectural Computing, and ACADIA.

Collaborative Design Process Simulation Game

Yehuda E. Kalay and Yongwook Jeong
University of California, Berkeley

Abstract

Collaboration is an important aspect of the architect's education. However, it is not amenable to the traditional project-based learning pedagogy that works so well for developing form-making skills. Being a process, rather than a product, it cannot be revealed by judging the results alone, which is often how form-making skills are taught and judged. Rather, the process of collaboration is only evident when the number of the participants exceeds a certain threshold, and when actions taken by other participants affect an individual's on-going design decisions. The advent of on-line, multi-player simulation games provides an analogy and an opportunity to explore interactive collaborative design pedagogies. Their abstract nature helps focus attention on the core issues of the simulated phenomenon, while the playful nature of a game, as opposed to "work," encourages immersion and role playing that contribute to the learning process. This paper describes an on-line game for simulating the design collaboration process. It espouses to simulate, exercise, and provide a feel for the social dimension of collaboration, by embedding mutual dependencies that encourage players to engage each other—in adversarial or collaborative manners—to accomplish their goals. Specifically, it is intended to help students understand what collaboration is, why it is necessary, and how it is done. The game is modeled after popular board games like Scrabble and Monopoly: players build "houses" made of colored cubes on a site shared with other players. Actions taken by one player immediately affect his/her neighbors. A carefully constructed set of rules awards or deducts points for every action taken by a player and by his/her neighbors. The rules were constructed in such a manner that players who collaborate (in a variety of ways) stand to gain more points than those who do not. The player with the most points "wins."

Collaborative Design Process Simulation Game

Yehuda E. Kalay and Yongwook Jeong
University of California, Berkeley

1 Introduction

Collaboration is an aspect of the architect's education that is often neglected in favor of developing form-making skills. As a result, when they choose to study architecture many students envision the misleading image of Howard Roark, the fictional hero architect in Ayn Rand's 1943 novel *The Fountainhead:* a professional who is in complete command of his/her destiny and the project. It is not until they graduate that students confront the socially complex reality of architects as agents in a collaborative enterprise, subject to a multitude of rules, regulations, economic realities, speculation and negotiations that constrain and direct their own professional contributions.

Moreover, collaboration is not amenable to the project-based learning pedagogy that works so well for developing form-making skills. Being a process, rather than a product, it cannot be revealed by judging the results alone, which is often how form-making skills are taught and judged. Rather, the process of collaboration is only evident when the number of the participants exceeds a certain threshold, and when actions taken by other participants affect an individual's on-going design decisions. For the same reason it is also not amenable to lecture or seminar-style teaching, whose abstract nature allows students to comprehend the social dimension of the process only intellectually, without actually experiencing it.

Attempts to introduce UC Berkeley students to the collaborative dimension of the architectural design process began in the late 1970s, through a comprehensive design exercise given to third year students directed by Architecture Professor Marc Treib (Figure 1). It was intended to teach them, among other things, how to deal with the creation of places as a collaborative form-making enterprise, rather than as an individualized effort. The exercise involved the design and physical construction of a cardboard "city" in a pre-designed "urban landscape."

Students were assigned 3'x3' plots in the yard, and instructed to design a "defined place for sitting." Although the project was assigned as an individual design task, students were required to make an effort to conform their designs to the designs of their neighbors, or come to some common agreement on the vocabulary of form. As in real life, they soon found out that meeting this requirement often entailed endless discussions and political power plays, turning the Cardboard City project into an exercise in collaboration, as much as it was an exercise in physical design. Students learned the importance of politics in design, the destructive force of obstructionists, and the impact decisions made by others had on their own designs. It became the "right of passage" exercise to upper-level studios, and a source of pride to the students who participated in it. But the creation of a large-scale cardboard city by 75 students also inflicted so much damage on the studio facilities - in terms of cardboard mess, gauged tables, floor tiles, and any other surface the students could use for cutting - that the exercise was discontinued.

The advent of computing technology, in particular the Internet, allowed us to resurrect the Cardboard City exercise in the late 1990s, using computer visualization in lieu of cardboard (Figure 2). Archville, as the new exercise was called, was pedagogically similar to the Cardboard City exercise (Peri 2001). As in the original exercise, each student was given a plot in an urban landscape. However instead of a physical space, Archville used a computer model of a hypothetical city. Instead of reduced-scale 3'x3' physical plots, students were assigned "life-sized" virtual plots. Instead of designing a "defined place for sitting," students designed houses or other structures. As in the Cardboard City exercise, students were asked to design their houses in agreement with their neighbors. Specifically, they were required to establish and agree upon some common design elements, such as style or color. Using VRML, Archville allowed students to virtual "walk" through the "city." Each student's work was always visible to other students, eliminating the problem of making design decisions based on obsolete information. Students could also see each other walking though the environment, in the form of avatars, and communicate with fellow students by chat and e-mail. Work done in previous semesters was not "taken down" at the end of the exercise, as in physical design studios. Rather, it was left on the site, creating a sense of history and a city that grew and evolved over the semesters. When more space was needed, more landscaping was added to the computer model. Paradoxically, Archville's advantages have also been its limitations: students put most of their effort into creating their individual buildings—a time-consuming activity accomplished through commercial CAD tools like 3DStudioMax, FormZ, and VRML—leaving little time for exercising the social dimensions of the project. Our attempts to extend the exercise to include such dimensions as economics, negotiations, and tradeoffs failed to dislodge the students' preoccupation with form-making.

A similar tendency to focus on form-making, rather than the collaborative aspects of the architectural design process, was exhibited when the virtual environment was substituted by a physical scale model of a city. Called CADville, this exercise combined computer-aided design and physical scale modeling to create 80-100 houses located on scaled city plots. The students were asked to respect (actual) local zoning laws, existing

Figure 1. Cardboard City (c. 1980).

structures and morphologies, and coordinate their designs with other students in their immediate vicinity (Figure 3).

The result was a scaled-down city center, which generated much excitement for one afternoon every semester. But the students' preoccupation with their own designs, their reckless disregard of fellow students' designs, and the difficulty of (manually) enforcing collaboration, resulted in architectural chaos. While this outcome was appreciated by the students, and served to underscore the need for collaboration, it did little to help them actually experience it.

To overcome the students' natural tendency to focus on form-making, and to concentrate their efforts on the collaborative aspects of the design process, we have been developing a simulation game that provides a simplified framework within which a large number of students can experience the process of collaboration. In essence, it replaces complex form-making with simple colored cube-shaped "rooms," which the players must "buy" or "trade" with each other. Instead of intricately-crafted buildings, the game emphasizes the impact of actions taken

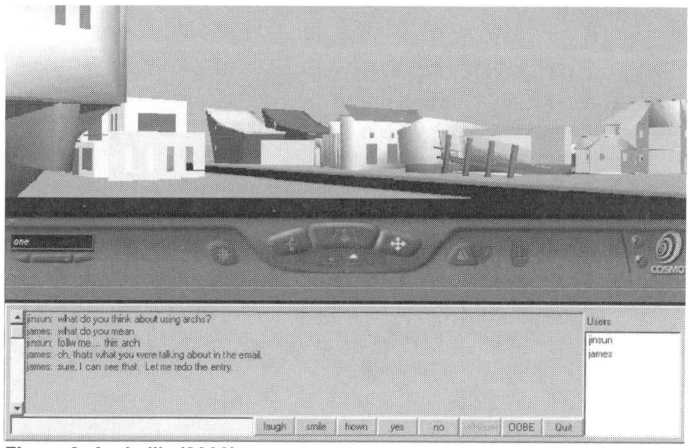

Figure 2. Archville (2000).

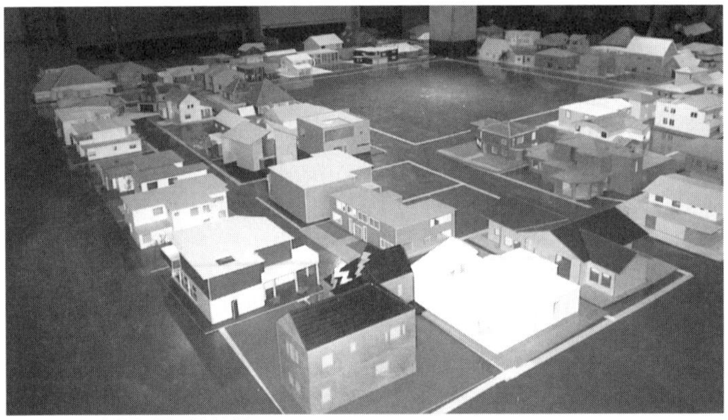

Figure 3. CADville (2002).

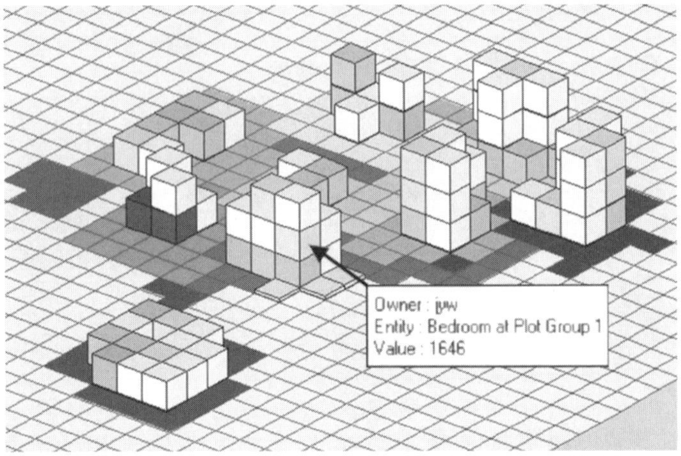

Figure 4. The collaborative design process simulation game (2003).

by fellow "designers" and the opportunistic nature of forming collaborations on the individual students' ability to accomplish their own goals.

2 Simulation games

The use of game-like strategies to benefit learning processes is well-known in education, where knowledge acquisition is often achieved through the medium of games (Dewey 1957). Their potential to enhance architectural education has been suggested by several researchers (Hubbard 1980; Woodbury 2001; Scriver & Wyeld 2001). By simplifying complex phenomena, games put players in an un-encumbered learning mood. By using abstractions and well-defined (if not always explicit) rules, games focus on the core issues of the simulated phenomena. Players are introduced to the simulated principles in an active, playful manner, as opposed to formal lectures or course projects. Abstraction prescribes a limited solution space of possibilities, framed by a mutually respected set of rules. The playful nature of a game, as opposed to "work," encourages immersion and role-playing that contribute to the learning process.

Of particular interest to this project and to the pedagogy it espouses is the social dimension of games: to accomplish their goals players must engage each other—in adversarial or collaborative manners. This can be done by embedding mutual dependencies within the game, which help to elucidate the social, collaborative nature of the process. The robustness of the game as a structure of design-thinking, and its ability to elicit playful yet critical inquiry, further enhance the appeal of using the gaming analogy to learn about the social nature of architectural design. However, the same properties that make simulation games an attractive pedagogical tool also complicate their development: the thin line separating the retained principles of the simulated phenomena from the discarded ones, establishes the game as a pedagogical tool, compared to entertaining but intellectually trivial pastime.

3 The collaborative design simulation game

To exercise and provide a feel for inter-dependent decision making, albeit in a highly abstracted form, we have developed a collaborative on-line design simulation game. Unlike other networked collaboration exercises (discussed in the Conclusion section of this paper) which focus on the results of the collaboration, our Game is intended to help students understand the process of collaboration, by providing positive reasons to collaborate (to achieve more than can be done alone), and illustrating the negative effects insufficient collaboration (e.g., interference with one's ability to accomplish his/her goals). The vehicle we chose for implementing these objectives is building a "house" made of colored cubes, on a site shared with other students who build, their own houses (Figure 4). A carefully constructed set of rules awards or deducts points for every action taken by a player or by his/her neighbors. Players who collaborate (in a variety of ways) stand to gain more points than those who do not. The player with the most points "wins."

3.1 Method

The game is modeled after popular board games like Scrabble and Monopoly, though without "turns" (players do not have to wait for others to complete their transactions to make their move). Players build "houses" like words in Scrabble: using individual cubes on a griddled site. Individual cubes represent a different types of "room," each with a certain point value. Adjacency rules restrict the placement of cubes (which color cubes must be adjacent to other cubes, and which cubes must not touch one another). Additionally, a complete "house," much like an acceptable word in Scrabble, must include a certain number of cubes of certain types (the equivalent of having a bathroom, a kitchen, a bedroom, etc.). The value of a house depends on its number and types of rooms (i.e., a small house may have only a kitchen, one bedroom and one bathroom, whereas a large house may have a kitchen, five bedrooms and three bathrooms), and on the values of the neighboring houses.

3.2 The "economic" model

Collaboration, like other human activities, requires motivation. To encourage and measure collaboration, a point system indicates the value of each player's house. This value is not only a function of the value inherent in the cubes that make up a player's own house, but also a function of improvements other players make to neighboring plots. Thus, a house that neighbors large houses has more value than a similar house that neighbors small houses or un-developed plots. The economic model underlying the game is thus based on real-estate "speculation": players gain points through growth in the property value, due to the development of their own plot and owned by other players. Since improving one's own property also increases adjacent property values, it is in the players' best interest, to help their neighbors improve their properties.

Property is defined as a contiguous set of squares belonging to the same player (a player may own more than one property). Its value is calculated according to the following formula:

$$V_p = \sum S_{i,p} * I_p * \prod N_{j,p}$$

where $\sum S_{i,p}$ is the sum of the values of all the squares from which property P is made; I_p is the overall improvement factor; and $\prod N_{j,p}$ is a 'neighbors factor' multiplier.

The value of each square $S_{i,p}$ is calculated as follows (Figure 5):

1) Original value of the square (as determined by the site).
2) The value added by each room associated with this square (stacked vertically).

The "improvement factor" I_p is calculated as follows:

- 0.9 – if the property is not owned by any player (it belongs to the "bank")
- 1.0 – if the property is owned by a player who made no improvements to it (i.e., no rooms, no landscaping)
- 1.1 – if the player has purchased some rooms, but they don't yet add up to a "house"
- 1.2 – if the player has built a small "house" (kitchen, one bathroom, and one bedroom)
- 1.3 – if the player has built a medium 'house' (entrance, kitchen, two bathrooms and three bedrooms)
- 1.4 – if the player has built a large "house"(entrance, kitchen, three bathrooms and five bedrooms)

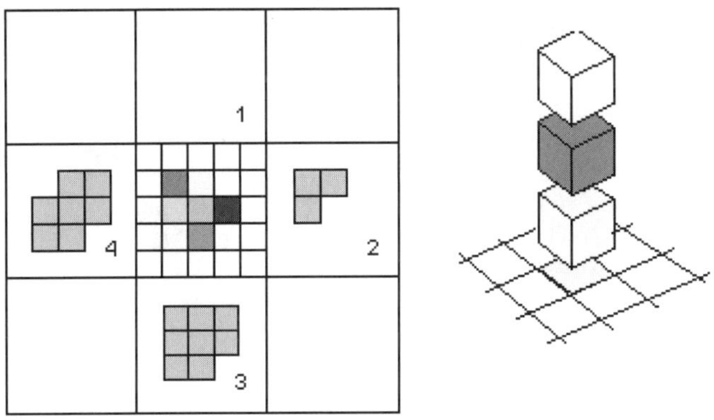

Figure 5. Calculating the value of Ip as the sum of the values of the plot and the cubes stacked vertically on that square.

The "neighbors factor" $N_{j,p}$ is the product of each neighbor's property value index, calculated according to the following algorithm:

a. set $N_{j,p} = 1$
b. for each neighbor j calculate its own Improvement Factor I_j
c. for each neighbor j of P: $N_{j,p}$ □ $N_{j,p} * I_j$

A 'neighbor' is defined as an adjacent property that shares n squares with the evaluated property.

For example, the house depicted in Figure 5 would have the following value:

$$V_p = \sum S_{i,p} * I_p * \prod N_{j,p} = 450 * 1.3 * 2.002 = 1{,}171.17$$

calculated as:

$\sum S_{i,p}$ = values of all squares + improvements = 450
I_p = 1.3 (medium house)
$N_{1,p}$= 1.0 (owned by a player, but no improvements)
$N_{2,p}$= 1.1 (not yet a house)
$N_{3,p}$= 1.3 (medium house)
$N_{4,p}$= 1.4 (large house)
$\prod N_{j,p} = 1.0 * 1.1 * 1.3 * 1.4 = 2.002$

Note the dramatic effect of the neighbors' houses: although the player's investment in the property amounts only 450 points, its value—according to this example—is over 1,171 points. If all neighbors had built large houses, its value would rise to more than 2,247 points. This dramatic effect should be enough to encourage players to help each other improve their properties (in later versions of the game we allowed players to use this "equity" to purchase and develop additional properties, thereby allowing them to further capitalize on their investments).

3.3 Implementation

The game has been programmed in Java3D, as a web-accessible, multi-user domain (MUD). It allows for accommodating a large number of players, administering the rules and calculating point values. Players log-on to the game web site, where they are able to see what other players have been doing, and communicate with each other through chats and e-mail.

In addition to tools that allow players to add, remove, and re-locate cubes, and change the view parameters (zoom, rotate, etc.), several tools allow players to gain information about the status of their own and other players' buildings. One tool, called "property" (Figure 6a), lets players see what types of rooms they have acquired, and check the state of their resources. Another tool, called "consol" (Figure 6b), allows them to study in detail how the value of every players' property has been calculated at any given time. Together, these tools provide real-time, immediate and total transparency to all players, who can use the information to determine where improvements may be made, either to one's own property or to his/her neighbors. Total transparency and real-time evidence are key elements in collaborative processes, although they can be used for individual gains as well.

Entity	S1	S2	S3	S4	S5	Total	Property
EN	1	.	.	.	.	1	20
KT	.	.	.	.	.	.	.
LV	1	.	.	.	.	1	20
DN	1	.	.	.	.	1	20
BD	3	.	.	.	.	3	30
BT	.	.	.	.	.	.	.
GA	.	.	.	.	.	.	.
RD	.	.	.	.	.	.	.
TR	.	.	.	.	.	.	.
ST	22	.	.	.	.	22	266/500

```
Calculating site's value at jyw's group 1
1. My House
-> 1st Floor's adjacency test = true
-> 2nd Floor's adjacency test = false
-> 3rd Floor's adjacency test = true
-> My house's level : N/A
-> My house's improvement factor : 1.0
-> My house's property only : 447
2. My Neighbors
-> gg's improvement : 1.1
-> yk's improvement : 1.1
-> jaylee's improvement : 1.3
-> swkim's improvement : 1.3
-> Non improvement : 0.9
-> April's improvement : 1.4
-> arch2's improvement : 1.3
-> arch1's improvement : 1.1
-> My neighbors' improvement factor : 3.6845007
3. The result
-> My house improvement factor(A) = 1.0
-> My property only value(B) = 447
-> My neighbors' improvement factors(C) = 3.6845007
-> A * B * C = 1646
```

Figure 6. (a) the property inspection tool allows players to see the status of their resources; (b) the Consol tool allows them to find out how the value of their own and other players properties have been calculated.

4 Collaboration strategies

At the start of the game players are assigned a given sum of "money," in the form of points, which they can use to "buy" cubes and plots. Much of the game's strategy, however, is in the types of agreements the players make among themselves, which lead to association, teamwork, and even creative *collaborations*:

3) Association occurs when players organize into groups for joint purchases of plots, thereby avoiding the speculative, inflationary effects of development: since the value of a property depends on the state of improvements of its neighboring properties, it is less expensive to buy a plot neighboring undeveloped plots, rather than to buy into an already developed neighborhood.

4) Teamwork occurs when a player purchases a large number of cubes ("rooms") of a particular type and sells or "rents" them to others. Since the number of rooms of any given type is finite, owning many rooms of a particular type is a kind of franchising, and a source of additional revenue (and competition) among players. "Renting," in the context of this game, means that the original player retains "ownership" of the cube, even though they are used in constructing other players' houses. The owner is "paid" in points proportional to the value of his/her rented room within the context of someone else's house. Thus, franchising and renting represent specialization of individual players, who choose to "invest" in one type of cubes. Players may even choose not to build a house of their own at all, only sell or rent their cubes to other players.

5) Creative collaboration occurs when two or more players decide to share their resources and combine their talents in pursuit of more expensive plots or more elaborate houses. In this case, the rewards are also shared.

Despite the simplicity of the game, the flexibility afforded by the cubes, plots, and rules provides a rich gaming environment, which can be tested and changed subject to mutual consent of the players. Concepts borrowed from the business world allow participants to test different methods of contracting, including multi-player secondary and tertiary agreements that may be needed to complete a "deal."

5 Results

In a course on collaboration several different versions of the Game were used. The simplification of the "buildings" to colored cubes had the desired effect of focusing students' attention on collaboration strategies, rather than on building beautiful houses. This, in turn, proved successful, though not always in the manner intended by the instructor.

The first implementation of the game allowed players to purchase individual "squares" for their building site. Students quickly discovered that the most profitable strategy does not require collaboration, only maximizing the number of neighbors. This could be accomplished by purchasing squares that made for highly irregular plots, with "tentacles" reaching the sites of as many other players as geometry allowed (see Figure 4). A side effect of this strategy has been "choking off" other players, by surrounding their site with a single row of squares.

To counter this strategy, the game was modified to consist of pre-defined plots, much like a housing development. Players could only purchase entire lots, rather than single squares. This restricted their neighbors to a fixed number, and put the emphasis on collaboration (Figure 7). Active e-mail, chat, even phone calls were used to nudge and encourage neighbors to take action they might not have intended. Quid pro quo bartering occurred, even acts of philanthropy where students helped neighbors who ran out of money to buy more rooms, so the value of their property would rise. Still, scheming and strategizing were in evidence, each student trying to maximize his/her own equity value. This became even more apparent when equity could be used to purchase additional plots, making some students very "rich." It leads us to believe that the game engine might lend itself to exercising other subject matters and pedagogies. For example, it could be used to teach different business models, economic models, social models, and political models. Clearly, the kinds

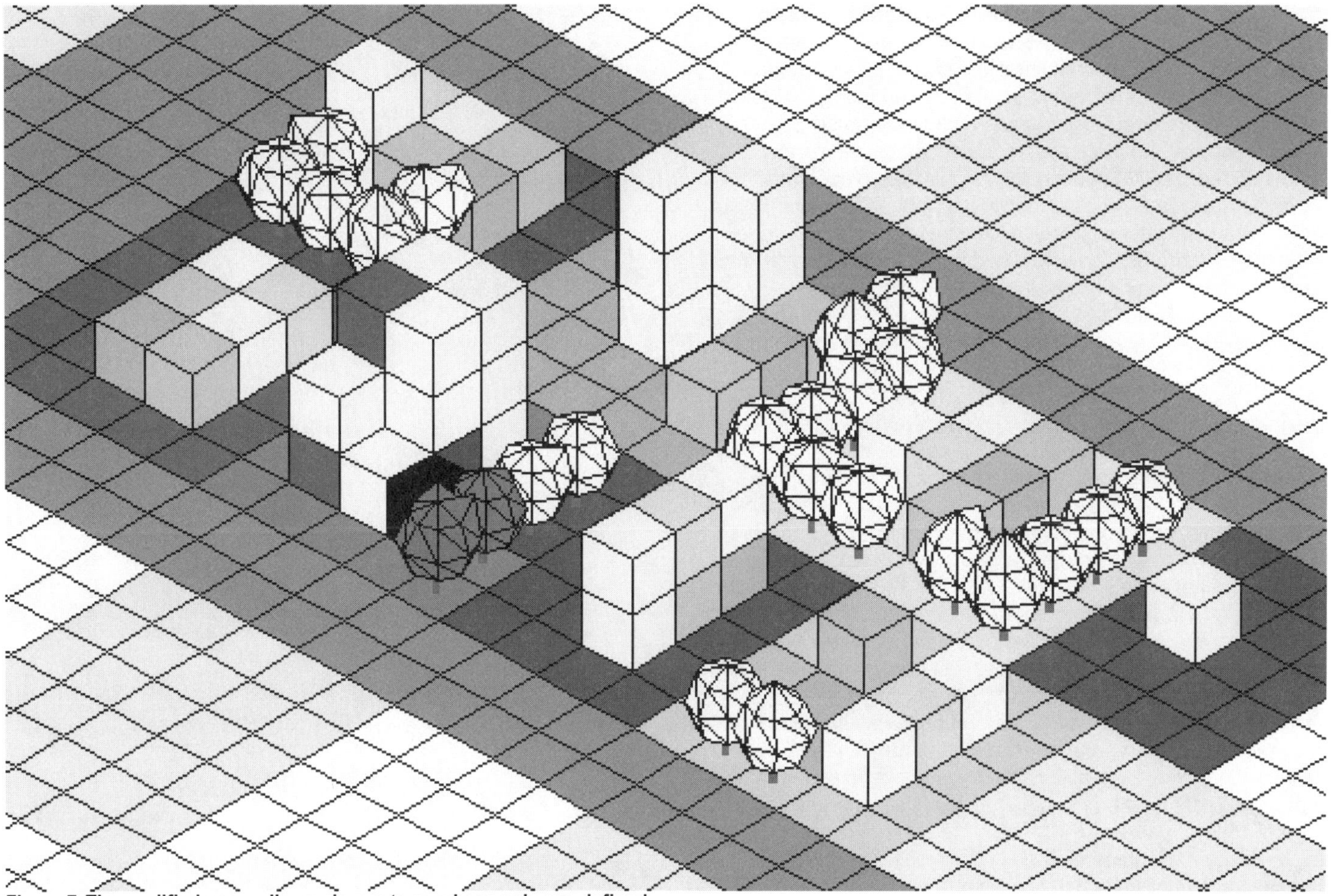

Figure 7. The modified game allows players to purchase only pre-defined plots, thereby engendering a more collaborative gaming strategy.

of rules needed to support such pedagogies must be carefully considered, a task that can only be done when the game is available for testing them.

By observing the students while they were playing the Game (through their actions and chat), and from their comments, it is clear that the Game helped them understand the dynamics of collaborative action. It was also clear that their collaboration was motivated by their desire to “win” the Game, through gaining as many points as possible. This led to carefully choosing plots with many neighbors, examining each other’s designs to discover how they could be improved, and making suggestions to that effect. Although the Game is designed to be asynchronous—players do not have to be logged in at the same time—students made arrangements to do so, for on-line chats. The students also made many suggestions to improve the game, which were implemented, as much as possible, during the semester, resulting in improved versions of the game.

6 Conclusions

The notion of digital collaborative design exercises is not new. At Stanford University, Fruchter and her colleagues have been engaged in digitally-enhanced collaborative A/E/C research and education for over a decade (Fruchter 1998). At the ETH in Zurich, Schmitt and his colleagues have been experimenting with different networked design collaboration tools (Engeli & Mueller 1999). And digital collaborative design studios have been popular, for a while, in many parts of the world (Hirschberg et al. 1999, Wojtowicz et al. 1993).

Yet, the overt goal of these experiments has been to foster the production of one or more architectural (and other) designs that reflect the collective wisdom and creative talent of many individuals. That was not our goal. Rather, this particular collaboration game has been designed to introduce students to the essence of the collaborative process itself. Hence, the results of their collaboration - actual "houses"- have been intentionally made abstract, and of no architectural value. Instead, their "value" has been explicitly defined in a quantitative, measurable way which, like a thermometer, is used only to judge the success or failure of the process itself. It has no intrinsic value of its own. In fact, a "house" can be small, or a plot can be completely un-developed, yet it may have a high point value due to the improvements made by its neighbors. In terms of our Game, such a plot will be considered more successful and have higher point value than a large house surrounded by un-developed properties (an evidence of non-collaboration).

Moreover, most, if not all, exercises cited above tended to partition the design process spatially, temporally, or by disciplinary contributions. Thus, for example, in the ETH's phase(x) project, "collaboration" is understood to be the disjointed, temporally-distinct continued development of another designer's product (Hirschberg 1997). Its Information Landscape project partitions the design spatially: each team of designers is responsible for one tile in the overall information landscape. While students were encouraged to match their contributions to those of others, they were not likely to suffer adverse effects had they chosen not to do so (Engeli & Mueller 1999). And Stanford's Computer Integrated Architecture, Engineering and Construction project follows the traditional division of labor (and expertise) of the A/E/C industry, which enshrines, rather than overcomes, the travails of collaboration (Fruchter 1998).

In contrast, the goal of our Collaboration Game has been to engender a contemporaneous, highly-dependent type of collaboration, where the actions of one student immediately and explicitly affect the efforts of other students. Agreements among the players are a necessary condition to achieve success. The motivation for collaboration is clear (if simplistic), as are the means to accomplish it: they are not subject to personal taste or interpretation. As such, the product may not qualify as particularly aesthetically pleasing, or even innovative. Instead, the exercise clearly focuses on the role, value, and pitfalls of the collaborative process itself: the fact that collaboration can lead, in some cases, to inferior products is a valuable lesson in and of itself.

7 Acknowledgements

The authors wish to thank Christopher Peri, who developed Archville and shared his experience and thoughts in developing this game. We also wish to thank the students who played the game and whose comments helped revise and refine it. Finally, the reviewers deserve much credit for helping focus the paper and clearly differentiate the goals of the Game.

References

Dewey J. (1957). *Experience and education.* New York: MacMillan.

Engeli M, and A. Mueller. (1999). Digital environments for learning and collaboration, architecture, communication, and creativity. *ACADIA 1999*, O. Ataman & J. Bermudez, eds.Salt Lake City, UT.

Fruchter, R. (1998). Internet-based web-mediated collaborative design and learning environment. *AI in structural engineering,* 133-145.

Hirschberg U. (1997). Phase(x) – memetic engineering for architecture. *Proceedings of 15th eCAADe Conference* ed, B.Martens,Vienna.

Hirschberg U., G. Schmitt, D. Kurmann, B. Kolarevic, B.R. Johnson, and D. Donath. (1999). The 24 hour design cycle: An experiment in design collaboration over the internet. *CAADRIA 1999*, Shanghai, China.

Peri C. (2000). Archville: A distributed VR environment for teaching real-time design collaboration. *ACADIA 2000* M.J. Clayton & G.P. Vasquez De Velasco, eds, Washington, DC.

Scriver P, and T.G. Wyeld.(2001). Exploring contemporary architectural history and theory through games of form and discourse. Playful design learning Forum 2001, Adelaide University, South Australia.

Wojtowicz J., J. Fargas, P. Papazian, J.N. Davidson, and N. Cheng. (1993). Asynchronous architecture, *ACADIA 1993,* F. Morgan & R. Pohlman, eds, College Station, TX.

Woodbury R.F., S.J. Shannon, and T.D. Sterk. (2001). What works in a design game? Supported by student reactions to being made to play.*CAADRIA 2001* S. Chase and M. Rosenman, eds, Sydney, Australia, 411-420.

Exploring Playful and Effective Digital Design Process with Games: A Framework for Digital Design Studio Teaching and Learning

Pei-Ling Wu
National Chiao Tung University

Abstract

The idea of developing a framework, to integrate design studios and computer graphics, is derived from the nature of architectural design, which has always combined creativity and technology. Furthermore, as computers are being increasingly used in design studios, a systematic digital pedagogy, which can take advantage of the strengths of computers in all stages of design, should be developed simultaneously to facilitate learning.

This paper attempts to propose a playful and effective digital design process that can be flexibly applied to computer-based design studios and design-based computer graphics courses. The pedagogical framework is based on a set of digital design games that follows a general design process presented by the author. First, the components of digital design games will be defined and the relations of those game components will be clearly depicted. Then, a framework will be proposed, followed by the use of an example demonstrating applications of the framework.

Continual advancements in digital technology have created generation gaps among teachers at architectural schools. A structured digital design process can help teachers, with varying levels of computer-capabilities know what, when, and how, adjustments should be made to achieve the goal of digital design education.

Keywords: digital design process, playful and effective, digital design games

Exploring Playful and Effective Digital Design Process with Games: A Framework for Digital Design Studio Teaching and Learning

Pei-Ling Wu
National Chiao Tung University

1 Introduction

The scope of computing in Architecture has broadened tremendously since the introduction of *Computer Aided Architectural Design* written by William J. Mitchell in 1977. The development of digital media not only provides new production methods such as computer rendering and modeling, but expands our abilities to create, see, express, compose, and understand design in new ways (Neiman and Do 1999). Architectural schools have increasingly incorporated computer-aided design into design studio over the past twenty years. Although a greater number of teachers are now skilled at applying digital media to design, rapid integration of computing technology has created communication and generation gaps within the profession (Loy 2001). It is difficult for experienced studio instructors with limited computer capabilities to take advantage of digital media. "As the software embodying knowledge becomes more user-friendly, it will give architects new power to bring together a multitude of issues in a holistic way without themselves being specialists" (Seebohm 2001). This is certainly a wonderful idea, which I look forward to, as this ideal software should empower the design potential. However, before it is realized, how can instructors with limited computer capabilities bring together issues of a digital design process? The structurized format of digital design process and the pedagogical model presented in this paper will attempt to clarify and systematize a digital design process so that instructors have a clear idea of how it works. Consequently, even inexperienced computer-capable instructors should be able to include digital media in the design process by incorporating technical teaching assistants in collaboration with other computer-based courses. The integration of a design studio with computer graphics would allow computers to explore new architectural design possibilities rather than leaving students themselves to bring coherence to the two fields (Wu 2002).

In conventional computer graphics courses for entry-level students, a great deal of attention is placed on acquiring software skills. However, working too much on the level of operating technological skills in an instrumental way tends to be boring and ineffective. So, how can beginners of architecture learn technological skills playfully and effectively? The approach proposed here is to learn computer skills through the process of operating a series of digital design games, which, at the same time, can be a potential new means of understanding aspects of design and digital technologies. Therefore, creating games that are intrinsically interesting and relevant to learning about design is one of the purposes this paper tries to achieve.

2 Analytical Review

2.1 Design Metaphors

Game, play and puzzle are three powerful metaphors to interpret the nature of design. Archea (1987) suggested that the best description for architects' uncommon mode of action is puzzle-making. *Puzzle* aligns itself with experimentation, testing of procedures, and challenging representation or abstractions. *Play* and design are both states of being absorbed in action for its own sake. Woodbury (2001) proposed that putting play and design into metaphorical relation, lets each inform the other. Play is often aligned with phrases like playing around, speculation, ability, and performance. Play is generally an open-ended activity with unique and ephemeral results.

Game possesses many different characteristics that can be classified in numerous ways. Whether it be a bet, lottery, roulette or baccarat, players' attitudes remain the same. They do nothing but await the outcomes. On the other hand, a boxer, runner, and chess player, must work as hard as they can in order to win (Caillois 1961). However, Game is not always associated with winning or losing. The essence of a game lies in a person's immersion in the process, subject to rules, and immersion implies a complete absorption in the activity (Radford 1997). Game is aligned with strategies and tactics or procedures with potential, known, or desired outcomes. Games have a predicable outcome because they involve well-defined systems, and they also capture attention by providing an unfolding understanding of the rules of a system (Cheng 1999).

One reason that this paper uses a system's rules *game* as the analogy to design is that game has a predicable outcome and well-defined systems. For architectural students just entering this complicated domain, a more systematic pedagogy with less serious atmosphere can better help them to acquire design knowledge and skills. Psychologists have confirmed that a playful attitude gives a person the chance to experiment by reducing associated penalties (Lieberman 1977). Moreover, a well-defined system provides studio instructors with limited computer abilities the opportunity to plan out necessary technical assistances in advance and incorporate digital technologies in their design studios.

2.2 Design Methods

The pedagogical doctrines evolved in the studios of the Ecole des *Beaux-Arts* in Paris during the 18th and 19th centuries have a rigidly formalized staging of work process (Carlhian 1979; Egber 1980; Middleton 1982). Sequential teaching phases were directed toward elaboration and detailed presentation in plan, section, and elevation. Throughout each stage, the activity was carefully monitored (Rowe 1987). The first American professional school of Architecture was founded at MIT in 1865. Beaux-Arts and Gothic revival approaches dominated American schools for their first half-century. Beaux-Arts education stressed ornamental details, specific proportions, and the composite settings (Wright and Parks 1990). The systematic approach to design and its veneration of the classical tradition implied the tendency of more hierarchical teaching methods.

A number of significant contributions during the late 1950s and 1960s, regarded design as a series of stages characterized by dominant forms of activity, such as the phases of analysis and synthesis in *Notes on the Synthesis of Form* written by Christopher Alexander in 1964. Besides, Asimow (1962) distinguished two structures in the design process: a vertical structure involving a sequential phasing of activities from a definition of need through feasibility study, preliminary design, detailed design production planning and production itself; and a horizontal structure in the form of a decision-making cycle from analysis to synthesis, evaluation and communication. Other celebrated methods include Jones' (1970) factors, Archer's sub-problems, Cross' (1977) automated architect, and Rittle's (1972) issue-based information systems. However, only a few design methods theories retreated to a small number of courses in architectural schools, and were survived to become the foundation for some of the first commercial CAD (computer-aided design) systems.

The preferred media underwent a change through time from delicate watercolors and metal-point pencil to photographs, quick sketches with a soft #2 pencil (Wright and Parks 1990) and then digital media today. Computers have the potential to radically change three fundamental ingredients in the classroom: students, instructions, and instructors. Changes of this kind obviouly spell out a commensurate change in design pedagogy (Akin 1990).

For the past twenty years, the application of computers has changed the design method (Liu 2001). Many famous architects such as, Frank Gehry, Peter Eisenman, Daniel Libeskind, Greg Lynn, Tom Mayne, and Eric Owen Moss and so on, have created amazing spaces through the assistance of computer technology. Those methods are changing the way that buildings will be designed in the future.

To sum up, although design methods might be changed through time, media trends, and designer's personal perspective towards the project, the dominant design thinking underneath can be integrated into the sequence of analysis and synthesis. Therefore, I propose a general and fixed design process for the discussion in this paper: information collection, data analysis, concept generation, design development, detail design and design representation.

3 Digital Design Process

3.1 The Components of Digital Design Games

Game and design can be put into analogies in many ways as stated above. The study here has analyzed and characterized six elements that are derived from both game and design. At the same time, it has the potential to encourage students to become more creative and imaginative by studying the components of the game.

The most important criterion is that the game must be relevant to learning about design using digital media. The content of the game can be changeable according to the course objectives, but the components of the game should be fixed by the following six elements: context, digital tools, clues, exploration, interaction and reward.

- Context: theme of the game relates to learning about design.
- Digital Tools: various kinds of digital media that can be used in different stages of the game, including both

Figure 1. Images of Concept Generation Stage Using Different Media (from the Left to right: 3d Max, Photoshop, and Digital Camera)

hardware and software. For example, in the concept generation stage of a course titled Digital Design Studio instructed by the author, students are encouraged to engage in all kinds of digital media that can best inspire and represent their ideas, as shown on figure 1.

- Clues: instructions, hints or rules of the game.
- Exploration: possible paths of the game that need to be traced out.
- Interaction: a platform or forum for multiple players to receive and make comments and communicate with colleagues and juries to improve their performances.
- Reward: the self-fulfilling intrinsic playfulness derived from the game.

3.2 The Relations of Components

The six components of digital design games are all related. However, according to their individual characteristics some of them are more relevant than others. I propose to organize them into two groups: game-creating and game-playing.

To apply the game-creating and game-playing process, instructors should be as much involved as students, but in different ways. Instructors are the main game-creators and partial game-players, while students are the main game-players and partial game-creators.

3.3 The Framework of Digital Design Process with Games

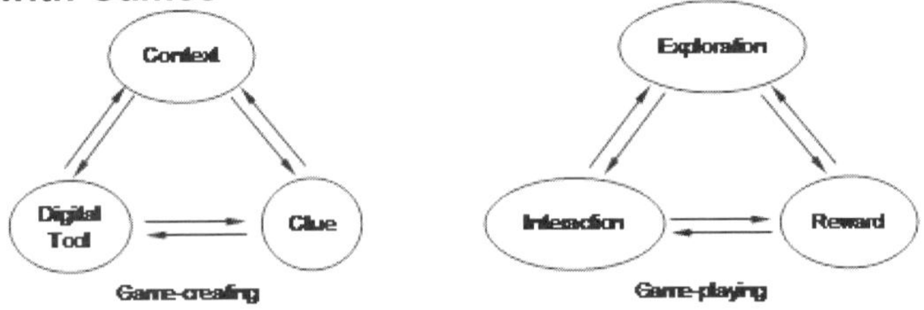

Figure 2. Relations of Digital Design Game Components

The digital design games proposed in this paper are embedded in general design process to provide an understanding of design operations. To implement the essence of game-creating and game-playing, the general design process and game components are combined and developed into six packages of digital design games. Game components (context, digital tool, clue, exploration, interaction and reward) and design process which are (information collection, data analysis, concept generation, design development, detail design and design representation), are both fixed. Digital design games form the horizontal structure of the framework, and the general design process defines the vertical structure sequentially.

3.4 Process of Game-creating and Game-

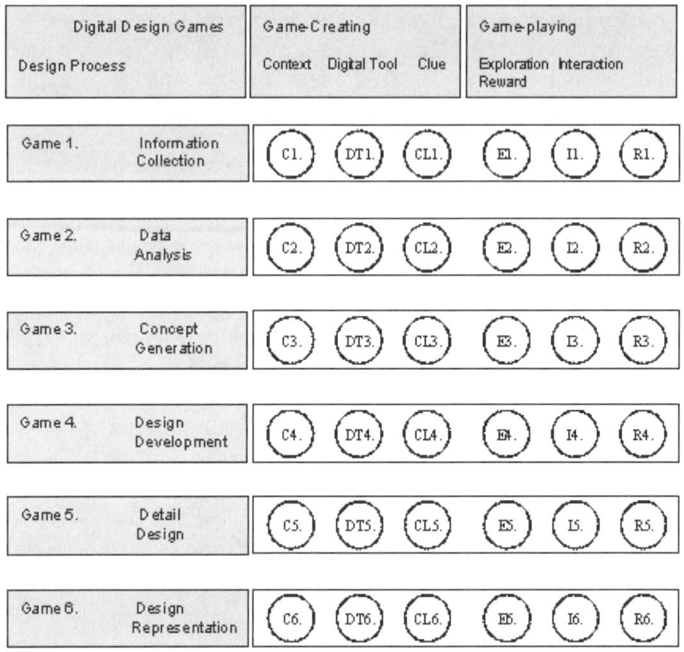

C: Context R: Reward CL: Clue

E: Exploration I: Interaction DT: Digital Tool

Figure 3. Framework of Digital Design Process with Games.

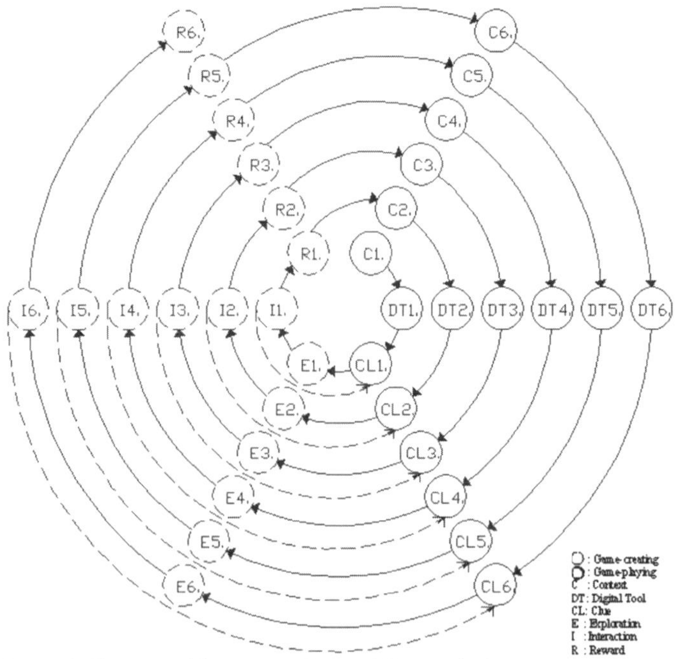

Figure 4. Process of Game-creating and Game-playing.

playing

Each of the game packages is sequential. Participants must play the games one after another. Instructors and students create and play games under a pedagogical structure, which will direct all players to achieve the end of the game.

To further clarify the use of this framework, I would like to further emphasize more on how instructors create the games and when students are supposed to join the games. In addition, further explanations will be given for how to run the six packages of the games.

Before the digital design games start, instructors must have the game-creating components ready, which means that the theme of the design, the digital tools that can be applied to the design process, and the game's instructions are made available to all students. However, one of the components of game-playing - interaction - should also be prepared beforehand. Because interaction of the game-playing means a virtual or physical platform and may allow players to communicate with colleagues and juries, the preparation for setting up hardware and software may be time-consuming. Students are asked to follow the clues to explore possible paths using digital tools. The time limit for each game is restricted. Students have to complete the exploration and interaction of the current stage before advancing to the next game. If any of them fail, they must spend extra time going over the clues of the stage and study further instructions given by the instructor until they have successfully completed the stage. Players should be aware of the deadline of each game, as the starting point of each game is the same for everyone.

It is important to remember that the reward of the game is the self-fulfilling and intrinsic playfulness of the game itself. While the game is still in progress no player will be asked to terminate the game for any reason. After completing the game, students will each have their own individual interpretations of reward.

4 Example: Application of the Digital Design Framework

The digital design framework is developed for integrating design studios and computer graphics courses. The objectives of the framework are as follows:

- To use digital media to collect information, to analyze data, to generate concept, to develop design, to design details and to represent design.
- To understand the design process.
- To have playful learning experiences.

A number of design subjects can be explored through the game-creating and game-playing process described in this paper. Based on the digital design framework, many kinds of digital design curricula can be developed. A course titled Digital Design Studio instructed by the author is an example of the application of the framework. Originally, there are three topics in the course, and the digital design framework is only applied to the last section called "Playing with Forms in Eisenman's Language", which runs for about six weeks.

All the teaching material and information are placed on a class website before the game-playing starts. The course participants are asked to submit their work on-line to a shared folder on the server. Whenever students feel that they have done enough exploration or need advice and comments from others, they are encouraged to post their work on a platform called *Playground* on the class website. Otherwise, there are explicit deadlines by which all participants must post the results of their exploration on *Playground* to share with the whole class. The following table shows the gaming-creating work prearranged tby the instructor .

Digital Design Process	Context	Digital Tool	Clue
1. Information Collection	Meeting Digital Eisenman	Going online is definitely the most convenient means to gather information.	Make a list of websites related to architects, especially those who have used digital technologies to create amazing spaces. Other manual and notes will be given according to the feedback and interaction with students.
2. Data Analysis	Interpreting Eisenman's Language	Use digital photo processing techniques to decompose images and compose collage.	
3. Concept Generation	Transforming Eisenman's Language	Continue to use digital photo processing techniques and other digital tools such as digital camera, scanner, and so on.	
4. Design Development	Sculpting Your House with the Transformed Language	Experiment with manipulating tools provided by Form Z, 3d Max, Maya or other 3d modeling tools.	
5. Detail Design	Designing the House	Manipulate the model more and apply color, light and texture to it.	
6. Design Representation	Visualizing the Aesthetics	Integrate the design to sophisticated digital presentation including static images and dynamic animations.	

Table 1: Example of Game-creating.

5 Conclusions

The applied example provided in this paper is not a thorough experiment designed to verify the framework. It is mainly used to further explain the framework. The Digital Design Studio stated above is a pilot study conducted by the author, and some phenomena that emerged from it will be foundations for future experiments.

Due to the premises of the framework, all participants achieve the goal in the end of the semester, and have their own individual interpretations of rewards after completing the games. This is crucial to the entry-level students because this learning framework has given them the confidence to continue and the competence to perform. Effective learning has much to do with taking risks (Lieberman 1977). This paper hypothesizes that the engagement of game elements in digital design processes will not only help students to learn effectively, but also enjoy the playfulness derived from it, particularly when instructors and students are both absorbed in the game-creating and game-playing process. Even the inviting atmosphere can increase students' learning competence.

Furthermore, the framework of digital design process presented in this paper clarifies and systematizes a digital design process so that even inexperienced computer-capable instructors are able to incorporate digital media in the design of curricula, while taking advantage of the great potency of digital technologies.

For further studies, besides the experiment that should be conducted to examine the framework, the performance of each component of the digital design games has not been fully developed. Especially when it comes to the interaction of game-playing, it should be more than just Web-based communications and comments from colleagues and juries. More interactive activities and evaluation systems can be achieved by technical advances.

References

Akin, O. (1990). Computational design instruction: Toward a pedagogy. *In The electronic design studio: Architectural knowledge and media in the computer era*. McCullough, M., W.J Mitchell. and P.Percell. eds, Cambridge, MA: The MIT Press.

Archea, J. (1987). Puzzle-making: What architects do when no one is looking. In *Principles of computer-aided design. computability of design*, ed. Y. Kalay,37-52. New York: John-Wiley & Sons.

Asimow, M. (1962). *Introduction to design*. New Jersey: Prentice-Hall.

Caillois, R. (1961). *Man, play and games*. New York: The Free Press of Glencoe, Inc.

Chang, T. W. (2003). Class discussion of independent study, National Chiao Tung University, Taiwan.

Cheng, N. (1999). Playing with digital media: Enlivening computer graphics teaching. *In Proceedings of Acadia '99*, eds. O. Ataman and J. Bermudez, 96-109.

Cross, N. (1977). *The automated architect*. London: Pion Limited.

Egber, D. D. (1980). *The beaux-arts tradition in French architecture.* Princeton, New Jersey: Princeton University Press.

Lieberman, N. (1977). *Playfulness: the relationship to Imagination and creativity*. New York: Academic Press.

Liu, Y. T., ed. (2001). Defining digital architecture: 2001Feidad Award. Basel: Birkhauser.

Loy, H. A. (2001). Foundation for a thorough CAAD education. In *Proceedings of Ecaade '01*, 301-308.

Mitchell, W. J. (1977). *Computer aided architectural design*. London: MIT Press.

Neiman, B. R. and Do, Y. L. (1999). Digital media and the language of vision. I*n Proceedings of Acadia '99*, eds. O. Ataman and J. Bermudez.

Radford, A. (1997). Games and learning about form in architecture. *In Proceedings of Ecaade '97*. (cdrom; unnumbered pages).

Rowe, P. G. (1987). *Design thinking*, London: MIT Press.

Seebohm, T. (2001). The ideal digital design curriculumn: Its bases and its content. *In Proceedings of Ecaade '01*, 180-185.
Woodbury, R., S. Shannon and A. Radford. (2001). Games in early design education. In *Proceedings of Caad Futures '01*.

G.Wright, and J.Parks, (1990). Introduction. In T*he history of history in American schools of architecture 1865-1975*, Wright, G. and Parks, J. eds., 7-12. New York: The Temple Hoyne Buell Center for the Study of American Architecture and Princeton Architectural Press.

Wu, P. L. (2002). *Experience the fun of creating digital spaces.* Taipei: Lamper.

An Inductive Approach to Digital Modeling Instruction

Kyle Talbott
University of Wisconsin - Milwaukee

Abstract

An argument is presented for respecting the student's process of inductive reasoning in introductory digital modeling instruction. The inductive education methods of Montessori and VanDamme are reviewed, and relevant portions are applied to the problem of digital modeling instruction. Two primary concerns are presented: 1) the need to systematically reorient the student from the physical world to the digital world and 2) the need to sequence the presentation of introductory concepts according to logical dependencies inherent in these concepts. Five principles of inductive digital modeling instruction are established, which could act as the basis for a teaching method that reduces alienation among apprehensive students, eases the transition from traditional media for veteran designers, and speeds comprehension of core concepts of digital making.

An Inductive Approach to Digital Modeling Instruction

Kyle Talbott
University of Wisconsin - Milwaukee

1 Introduction

As practicing architects recognize the power of digital modeling, its applications expand beyond the production of presentation renderings into the realm of design. What was previously the province of CAD technicians is now becoming a general architectural skill. This invigorated interest has created a surge of introductory digital modeling instruction both in academic institutions and especially among professional "CAD trainers." As the focus of instruction shifts away from digital drawing to digital modeling, and as the digital modeling system becomes the tool of choice among practicing architects, better methods of modeling instruction are in demand.

Under pressure from this demand, academic and professional educators often build instructional methods on-the-fly, racing to meet the needs of a hungry population rather than developing a systematic approach based on sound educational theory. This paper argues that such grounding is important to effective introductory digital modeling education, and in particular, inductive reasoning theory provides the needed instructional foundation.

Regarding the research method of the paper, it is worth mentioning that no attempt is made here to validate conclusions through empirical experiment. While experimental verification is a worthy goal, the method used here is philosophical. Rather than test a hypothesis, the paper establishes a set of premises validated through common human experience or occasionally by reference to prior empirical studies. Conclusions are then drawn from these premises through the application of logic. In other words, what is presented here is an argument – specifically an epistemological argument – not the results of an experiment. The goal of the argument is not to validate a particular educational technique, but to establish a set of principles that could guide the development of a valid technique. Since Maria Montessori's method is discussed later at some length, it is also worth noting that she too pursued an epistemological validation of her method, not a scientific one. Although she embraced the early twentieth-century fervor for scientific pedagogy, she believed the scientific method alone failed to provide sufficient guiding vision. In her words, "We start essentially from a method, and it is probable that psychology will be able to draw its conclusions from pedagogy so understood, and not *vice versa*" (Montessori 1964). Although the Montessori Method does include elements of technique, it is at root a philosophy of education – a precondition for the development of verifiable technique. While the scope of Montessori's work is broad and ambitious, the present paper seeks to address a single issue in the philosophy of education and establish its relationship to digital pedagogy.

2 Background

According to the inductive theory of knowledge, all knowledge begins with sensory experience of the physical world. As children we form our first concepts directly from sensory experience of physical entities, and as our repertoire of sensory-level concepts grows, we integrate them to form higher-level concepts, which enable us to achieve greater degrees of abstraction from our sensory starting point. "Chair," "table," "bed," and "dresser" are examples of sensory-level concepts. These concepts refer directly to something we can point at. The concept "furniture", on the other hand, is a higher-level abstraction formed by identifying a similarity among chairs, tables, beds and other items. The even wider abstraction "tool" subsumes not only furniture, but a host of other useful things. Later generalizations such as "furniture" and "tool" follow from and are based upon earlier ones, creating a dependency among concepts. This means a higher-level concept cannot be grasped if the necessary lower-level component concepts have not yet been formed. The theory of inductive reasoning holds that concept formation progresses in stages from sense perception to less abstract concepts and finally to broader abstractions drawn from earlier concepts (Piekoff 1991).

This premise creates a pedagogical imperative. If there is a necessary order in the formation of concepts, then there is a necessary order in the presentation of concepts, which the teacher must not violate (VanDamme 2002). When a teacher presents a new concept before the student grasps underlying concepts, the student lacks the foundation needed for real understanding. The new concept can be described as "empty" or "floating" in the mind of the student. Left in such a state, the student can only memorize the new concept as a word without connection to other concepts or to sensory experience. An anecdotal but illuminating account of the undermining effect of "empty" concepts in childhood development is described by Feynman (Feynman 1999).

I first became aware of the need to follow a particular order in the presentation of digital modeling concepts by observing recurring points of confusion among students. I noticed that such confusion occurred at consistent points in my presentation. For example, after explaining the concept of the Working Plane and Object Snaps, many students continued to struggle when locating a desired point in space. The students seemed to regard as mysterious guesswork something they surely could (and needed to) anticipate with certainty. At first I could not understand the source of this confusion. In the context of the modeling environment used in this instruction, the Working Plane and Object Snaps were the only factors effecting point selection, and after interrogating the students, they seemed to understand both mechanisms.

Eventually I discovered the cause of the confusion. While the students understood both mechanisms in themselves, they did not understand their relationship. In terms of the inductive reasoning process described above, I had left out a crucial step in the chain of concept formation necessary to understand how to select a point in digital space. I had neglected to explain how the Working Plane and Object Snaps work together to determine the point. There are of course circumstances where these two mechanisms contradict each other. If the Working Plane is located far behind a cube and the student snaps to the corner of the cube, the selected point could occur at the corner of the cube, or it could be projected onto the Working Plane beyond. It depends on which of the two mechanisms is dominant, and most modeling systems allow the operator to control this. After explaining the concept of a dominant point selection mechanism, and explaining how the student controls which is dominant, the confusion vanished.

Despite my good intention to guide students to real understanding, I sometimes skipped crucial concepts or introduced and relied on a concept before I had properly introduced it.

There are surely options in the order a mind can form concepts, and there is a vast collection of physical entities that provide the ultimate sensory basis for concepts. Consequently, there is a whole family of varied instructional sequences that respect the nature and requirements of inductive reasoning. However, as described in the example above, some approaches violate these requirements. The following argument establishes some principles to help instructors recognize such errors, and to shape a systematic method of instruction that respects the requirements of inductive reasoning.

3 Reorienting to the Digital World

3.1 Inductive Education Applied to Physical Laws

Many teachers recognize the need to present concepts in an order that facilitates inductive reasoning, but they resort to trial and error to find such an order. As I described in my experience with the Working Plane and Object Snaps, many teachers filter out errors by closely observing students and compensating when confusion arises. While such teachers implicitly accept an inductive method, there are explicit theories of inductive education. Maria Montessori's approach to teaching children age three to six is one of the earliest examples of formalized inductive reasoning in an educational setting. She referred to this component of her method as the "Education of the Senses" (Montessori 1964). Montessori works from the premise that a child's progress in forming sensory-level concepts of material properties such as color, hardness and weight is substantially enhanced by filtering and systematizing the child's exposure to objects possessing these properties. The earlier prevailing attitude was that formation of such basic concepts in the child's mind happens *automatically,* just by virtue of perceiving the physical world. A similar strain of educators today believe a student "picks up" digital understanding just by virtue of exposure to digital tools (Nicol 1990). In this view, if we just give students the tools, they will figure it out on their own. Montessori discovered that this is not true in the physical world, and as we shall see, it is not likely true in the digital world either.

A more recent innovator in inductive education Lisa VanDamme of the VanDamme Academy in Laguna Hills, California, is developing an inductive education curriculum for fourth through seventh grade. Her method builds on the foundation of sensory-level concepts attainable with Montessori's Education of the Senses, and extends beyond these concepts to higher-level concepts of gravity, friction, mechanical advantage, air pressure and so forth (VanDamme 2002).

Both Montessori and VanDamme emphasize the need to isolate and reduce to direct perception each material property or natural law. The student does not just read about the force of friction and how it produces heat as a byproduct, nor does he merely learn to manipulate an equation that calculates the amount of heat produced. The teacher never asks the student to accept any behavior of nature on his authority. Instead, the student directly witnesses and measures the phenomenon.

The mechanism by which this happens is an educational experiment. In the Education of the Senses, Montessori uses a "didactic object" to isolate a material property for study. In one experiment the child is confronted with a peg board containing holes of graduated diameter, and a scattered collection of pegs with equivalent graduated diameters. The child solves the problem of matching peg diameter to hole diameter. In another peg board experiment, the board contains holes of equal diameter but varying depth. The pegs have a corresponding graduated set of lengths (Montessori 1964). Van Damme uses a similar series of experiments, though more elaborate, to isolate and study the behavior of physical laws. Other test experiments, require the student to evoke already formed concepts to explain a newly encountered phenomenon. For example, at the conclusion of two separate series of experiments on friction and air pressure, the teacher wets the rim of a plunger, pushes it against the top of a stool, and then lifts the stool into the air using the handle of the plunger. This is followed by the question, "Why did this happen?" Although the students have not previously seen the experiment, some offer sophisticated explanations that integrate the concepts of friction (as viscosity) and air pressure (VanDamme 2002), and without prompting from the teacher.

3.2 Inductive Education Applied to Digital Laws

Most of us learn digital modeling in the context of architectural design only after reaching adulthood. And many veteran architects are still acquiring this skill later in life. This means the student of digital modeling has a fundamentally different context of knowledge from that of a child. He has already formed many high-level concepts of the physical world and its behavior. But in another sense, the student of digital modeling is not so different from a child. A child must learn the fundamental concepts of the physical world, and the student of digital modeling must learn the fundamental concepts of a digital world. Since a digital world operates according to its own rules, which do not necessarily correspond to the laws of nature, the student of digital modeling is set again in the state of a child experiencing a world anew. He must build an understanding of digital laws in the same way he did of physical laws, starting with fundamentals and building upon them gradually through a process of inductive reasoning, ultimately tied to direct sensory experience.

Yet digital modeling instruction cannot proceed as if the student is a child. The student has a vast experience of the physical world that is not forgotten when he enters the digital realm. For this reason the process of inductive reasoning undertaken by a student of digital modeling is more difficult than that of a child experiencing nature. Not only must the student acquire digital concepts in a proper sequence, but he must also integrate digital concepts into an existing body of knowledge based on his experience of nature. If digital concepts are not related back to what is already known and familiar in the physical world, these new concepts remain alien for a long time and undermine the student's chances for educational success. Yet, if a mental connection can be made between newly encountered digital laws and familiar physical laws, alienation quickly diminishes (Erickson 1990).

It is instructive at this point to introduce some examples of differences between physical laws and digital laws, in order to illustrate how these differences influence the student. My examples are drawn from the capabilities of Bentley Systems MicroStation, which is the modeler I use in introductory instruction. However, the issues discussed here apply to most or all mainstream modeling systems.

The first example is gravity. Gravity does not exist in MicroStation, nor is it simulated in any mainstream modeling system available today. Yet gravity is deeply connected to the human way of grasping spatial orientation and the relationships among objects in the physical world (Templeton 1973). The student must understand the consequences of operating in a gravity-free environment, and why an alternative means of spatial orientation is needed. The student has lived his whole life relying on gravity to assist spatial understanding; hence the absence of gravity in the digital realm fundamentally undermines his ability to comprehend digital space. However, we do use other means to achieve spatial orientation in the physical realm. The most important of these is visual perception of horizontal and vertical (Prinzmetal and Beck 2001). Establishing this visual frame of reference again makes basic orientation concepts such as "up" and "down" meaningful. In digital space, a horizontal and vertical reference, because it can be depicted visually, is easier to achieve with current technology than simulated gravity, and this visual reference is the main way spatial orientation happens in digital space. Because it functions alone, the horizontal-vertical reference is crucial, and if a student does not understand how to find and use this reference, much of what happens in digital space remains unintelligible. Thus, the student must adjust his habitual orientation paradigm to remove the reliance on gravity and replace it with a heightened awareness of the horizontal-vertical visual frame of reference. This adjustment is not automatic. It requires explanation and practice in the form of focused exercises.

A second example is our tactile sense. The highly developed sense of touch in the human hand is highly developed and provides precise feedback about the surface qualities of objects (Derevensky 1979). Using the hand in combination with the eye, we gain even greater precision, identifying the location of minute deviations on a surface or shape (Klatzky and Lederman 1987). We learn the feel of an object edge versus an object face, and by adulthood this means interaction is thoroughly integrated into our spatial paradigm. Yet this basic means of interacting with objects is stripped from us in the digital realm. As in the physical world, we must "touch" digital objects often in the process of building a model. We select objects and we locate precise edge and corner conditions. In current mainstream computer hardware, since tactile feedback is more difficult to implement than visual feedback, the student is asked to make a crucial substitution. His tactile sense is replaced by graphic feedback such as object highlighting (for selecting) and cursor events (for locating precise geometric conditions such as corners or edges – i.e., snapping). This substitution is no less fundamental than the gravity substitution described above, and the student must adjust his basic spatial paradigm accordingly. This adjustment is not automatic. It requires explanation and practice in the form of focused exercises.

It is important to note that these examples might not always be relevant. It is reasonable to project a future where computer hardware and modeling software simulate gravity, touch, and a host of other physical properties and laws. A more thorough simulation of nature might be a hindrance, though, since it could undermine the potential of digital modeling to surpass the limitations of the physical world. New and radically different digital worlds become increasingly possible, and such worlds might open exciting creative possibilities.

The point here is pedagogical, not technological. Until we have holographic chambers in the spirit of *Start Trek*, or brain links into virtual worlds in the spirit of *The Matrix*, there remain differences between the laws of the digital world and those of nature. (In fact, this is true even in *Star Trek* and *The Matrix*.) And to the extent these differences exist, the inductive starting point for digital modeling education must be to bridge this divide – to provide a way for the student to systematically adapt his habitual physical world paradigm to one appropriate to the digital world of his choosing.

Notice that inductive education is vital to the development of radically different digital worlds. If advances in computer technology serve the goal of natural simulation, then eventually inductive education, at least in its role described here, becomes obsolete. Yet when a student is confronted with a radical departure from nature, an inductive approach is crucial. For it is here that a digital world is most alien, and the student is most in need of the teacher's assistance bridging the conceptual differences, thus enabling his knowledge of a new digital world to integrate with an existing body of physical world knowledge. In other words, the more a digital world differs from nature, the more important it is for the teacher to explain the differences. Only this can make the digital intelligible.

The increasing attraction of spatial computer games among the young erases some aspects of this divide by the time such youngsters reach adulthood and begin design education. Particularly at the level of basic digital perception, early exposure to digital worlds could ease the adult's transition into a design system. In fact, because of the age of its customer, the computer game industry is more sensitive to the issue of digital reorientation than most developers of mainstream design systems. This heightened sensitivity reinforces the point that regardless of where the reorientation happens – in the games of childhood or in the design systems of adulthood – the reorientation must happen. And despite some useful similarities between games and design systems, it is unlikely that the former will become a complete tutorial for the later. The designer generally requires a more sophisticated control over digital space and its objects than a child enjoying a digital adventure.

4 Respecting the Conceptual Hierarchy

After the student has adjusted his habitual means of interaction to accommodate the unique laws of the digital world, he is prepared to learn about the many capacities of this new world, gradually expanding his digital knowledge. Here the process of inductive reasoning is equally important. The central concern for the teacher is the order of concept presentation, which must respect the logical hierarchy inherent in any body of knowledge. In the following section an argument is made for a particular order of presentation, emphasizing its logical necessity and noting some common problematic deviations.

The subtly different capabilities in mainstream modeling software result in possible variations in the sequence of presentation. What is described here is a wider conceptual framework that applies more broadly. It establishes a standard of evaluation that can be used to identify an inductively valid presentation order, or to identify induction errors in an existing presentation order.

The first concept in the framework is *Perception*. Before we can take any purposeful action in the digital realm, we must know that the realm exists and we must know at least something of its nature. We must establish contact with the digital world through some type of conscious awareness. This awareness can take any form, from pressure-controlled gloves to audible tones produced by a microphone, but it must take *some* form. Without a way to perceive what is happening in digital space, we cannot act purposefully. The most common means of perceiving digital space in mainstream hardware and software is of course the graphical display, which combines the computer screen with the concepts of Window, Viewpoint and Camera. We see a representation of digital space through a Window, which always inhabits the plane of the screen. The particular portion of digital space displayed defines our Viewpoint, and we control our Viewpoint within the Window by means of a Camera (or Eye Point) location. Unlike the Window, the Camera inhabits digital space.

The order of presenting the concepts of Window, Viewpoint and Camera might be optional, and in fact, these concepts might eventually become obsolete, but some means of perceiving digital space is necessary, and the student must understand what his means of perception is and how to control it. Before any other meaningful digital actions are possible, he must first open his digital eyes and look around.

The second concept in the framework is *Position.* Establishing a position in digital space is a second precursor to purposeful action, since a modeling action is not purposeful if it occurs at an arbitrary location. Positioning is the process of identifying a desired point in space. It requires a means of transposing a point selected on a flat screen with a pointer to some position within the volume of digital space. Two mechanisms used to accomplish this in mainstream software are the Working Plane and the Object Snap. A Working Plane allows access to the depth of space by transforming the plane of the screen to a location in space, which then allows a screen point to be projected onto the plane. Object Snaps allow a screen point to be projected onto identifiable parts of an object's geometry, such as corners and edges.

The order of presenting the concepts of Working Plane and Object Snap might be optional, and surely other means of spatial positioning will be invented, but whatever the means of positioning, it must be presented *after* the means of Perception described above. A position is only meaningful to the extent one is aware of it. Providing a student with a means to determine a spatial position without first establishing the means by which that position can be understood and verified through perception makes the act of positioning unintelligible.

The third concept in the framework is *Transposition.* This is the act of moving, rotating or otherwise altering the position of a digital object. Transposition involves a number of sub-concepts such as Direction and Distance. In order to move an object, for instance, one must determine which direction to move it and how far. This might involve any combination of reorienting or repositioning the Working Plane, Snapping to various points on objects, or keying in numbers. Regardless of the mechanism used, a Transposition requires the identification of two points in space, a start position and an end position. These two positions constrain both the direction and distance of the Transposition action. And thus, Transposition relies on the concept of Position. Without first knowing how to locate one position in space, a student cannot comprehend how to locate two positions. Even a simple alteration of the Working Plane – moving it from one location to another – presupposes the concept of Position.

The first three concepts in the framework might seem self-evident. These three stages of digital understanding are so fundamental that deviating from the order described above is often catastrophic. The common teaching error made in these early stages is the omission of concepts, rather than an inversion of sequence. Those who teach digital modeling are often advanced practitioners, and they take for granted many of these early steps in the learning process. They have long forgotten their own experience learning these things, and they come to believe such concepts are obvious. Yet such fundamentals are only obvious to the expert after study, practice and habit formation. Especially with Perception and Position, it is common practice among professional CAD trainers to race through these concepts as though it is a review of something already known, and students proceed from the beginning with an incomplete foundation upon which to build.

The fourth concept in the framework is *Creation.* This is the act of making a new object out of nothing. The most basic way this happens is by generating a primitive geometry such as a cubic solid, sphere or cylinder. Creating a primitive requires an understanding of the geometric nature of each primitive, and the kind of information needed by the modeling system to define it. For example, a cubic solid usually requires the student to designate four points in space, one defining its general position, which acts as the start point for creation, and then three more points to define height, width and depth. A cylinder, by contrast, can be defined with three points – start position, radius and height.

It is easy enough to see how Creation presupposes Perception and Position. A student cannot comprehend object Creation without first being able to perceive objects and locate the points in space required to define a new object's position and extents. The fact that Creation also presupposes Transposition is not obvious, and this is a point in the inductive chain often breached. Many fail to recognize that Creation is almost always a two step process. In its most basic form it is as follows. First, move the Working Plane to the location where the new object will be made, and then second, make the object. This process requires the student to already understand the process of Transposition as applied to the Working Plane. An alternative method is to first make the object at any convenient location, then as a second step, move it to where it belongs. This method is necessary because it is often difficult to position a new object directly as desired during the process of defining geometric extents. This second method, too, relies on an existing understanding of Transpostion, since the object must be moved into place after Creation. Without understanding the relationship of Creation to Transposition, purposeful Creation is undermined.

The tendency is to place Creation too early in the instructional sequence, sometimes even before Perception and Position. The usual thinking is that one must first create something before one can learn how to view it, to locate positions on it, or to move it. The decision to place Creation first follows directly from the way one uses most mainstream software – first one makes a new file, which is empty, and then one makes an object in the file. However, the order of operations used in software to perform work is not always commensurate with the order of concept presentation needed to grasp the nature of the work. The indiscriminate alignment of learning procedure with software procedure in this way undermines inductive learning.

In response to the Argument for Creation First – i.e., that objects must be created before Perception, Positon and Transpositon are possible – I would answer as follows. Objects must exist, but the objects used to demonstrate these earlier concepts *do not need to be created by the student.* One implication of the framework defined here is that in the early stages of learning a student should never encounter empty digital space. When learning to perceive the digital world it must be richly populated with things to perceive. When learning concepts of Transpositon, there must be a dense field of existing objects for the student to "play with." Consider Montessori's peg board experiments. The child is given a provocative set of objects as a starting point. If Montessori had expected the child to make the pegs himself before learning basic concepts of size and shape, the inductive chain would be inverted and the child would be dumbfounded. How can the child make pegs of incremented lengths before he grasps the concept of length? Expecting a student to learn the process of object Creation before Perception, Positon and Transpositon is equally devastating to effective learning.

The student should never confront the disorienting void of unpopulated digital space until he masters all the basic concepts described here. Even when learning the process of Creation, the student should always make new objects in the context of a provocative digital environment inhabited by other objects, which is pre-established by the teacher.

5 Conclusion

In summary, we may distill from the above argument the following five principles, which support inductive digital modeling instruction.

- The first task is to reorient the student from the physical world to the digital, by showing the differences in world behavior. The more a digital world differs from nature, the more important it is for the teacher to explain the differences explicitly and systematically, and to allow the student to experience the differences directly through practice. Only this can make the digital world intelligible to a being that inhabits the physical world and necessarily uses it as context.

- Each concept must be isolated for study and practice by a precisely constructed educational experiment that allows the student to perceive the referents of the concept directly.
- The student should be given ample time to adjust (through focused practice) his physical world habits to account for the different characteristics and behaviors of the digital world. This process is often slow and difficult for the student, despite often seeming self-evident to the expert.
- After the student has successfully adjusted his orientation and interaction habits to the requirements of digital life, the central concern of inductive digital modeling instruction is the order of concept presentation, which must respect the logical hierarchy inherent in any body of knowledge. Respect the general order of Perception, Position, Transposition, and Creation. Resist the tendency to place Creation too early in the presentation sequence.
- The student should never confront the disorienting void of unpopulated digital space until he has mastered Perception, Position, Transposition and Creation. Instead, he should always encounter a pre-populated world of compelling objects, just as a child does in his first experiences of nature.

References

J.Derevensky, (1979). Relative contributions of active and passive touch to a child's knowledge of physical objects. *Perceptual and motor skills*. 48:1331-1346.

Erickson, D. (1990). Working with interface metaphors. In *The art of human-computer interface design*, Brenda Laurel ed., 65 – 73. New York: Addison-Wesley Publishing Company.

Feynman, P. (1999). *The pleasure of finding things out,* 3 – 8. Cambridge, Mass.: Perseus Publishing.

Klatzky, Roberta L. and Lederman, J. (1987). The intelligent hand. *The psychology of learning and motivation*, 21:121-51.

Montessori, M.(1964). Education of the senses. In *The Montessori method*, 167 – 223. New York: Schocken Books.

Nicol, Anne (1990). Interfaces for learning: What do good teachers know that we don't? In *The art of human-computer interface design*, B Laurel ed., 113 – 130. New York: Addison-Wesley Publishing Company.

Peikoff, L(1991). Knowledge as hierarchical. In *Objectivism: The philosophy of Ayn Rand,* 129 – 141. New York: Dutton.

Prinzmetal, W. and D.M Beck(2001). The Tilt-constancy theory of visual illusions. *Journal of experimental psychology: human perception and performance*. 27(1): 206-217.

Templeton, W. B. (1973). The role of gravitational cues in the judgment of visual orientation. *Perception & psychophysics,* 14(3):451-57.

VanDamme, L (2002). *Role of hierarchy in education.* Gaylordsville, CT: Second Renaissance.

04 >> Connecting Digital Practices

Chairs: John Marx, Raffi Tomassian

Digital Practice

John Marx, Raffi Tomassian

Technical competence in computer technology has become a conditio sine qua non of landing a job at a respectable architectural practice. By itself, though, this does not imply that all architectural practices are now doing their work in a revolutionary way. In their overwhelming majority they have been forced into the digital domain by the ubiquity of technology itself. The digital file has replaced the drawing as the information backbone in building profession. However, the common convertible currency of this information down the construction process is still lines on paper, albeit physically produced by incredibly sophisticated devices.

A few practices are looking beyond the drafting and visualization solutions offered by digital technology and finding themselves reshaped in the course of this interaction. The problems that those practices solve today are less related to design than to organization and project management. This reflects the uniqueness of practice among the other architecturally related endeavors, such as theory or education.

Technology has a revolutionary potential in architectural practice, but an ingrained psychological stigma needs to be abolished first. A torrent of energy will be unleashed when the legal framework of the industry stretches to accommodate the digital model as a legitimate appendix to or replacement of the traditional bid documents. Until the profession finds a non-mediated route between digital design and digital fabrication, the changes in the practice will be more cosmetic than internal.

John Marx, AIA is a design principal and partner at, San Francisco based, Form4 Architecture. He has designed over 150 buildings in 11 different countries. Mr. Marx has lectured around the world on “digital practice”, including Kyonggi University, Seoul; the Technion; Israel, UC Berkeley, and the University of Sydney.

Raffi Tomassian, UBA, is an architectural designer at Cincinnati based Glaserworks. He has won awards at two international competitions. His work on the Cincinnati Zoo Kids' shop received the Cincinnati AIA chapter honor design award and has been featured in several publications. He is a frequently invited critic of academic assignments.

Towards Comprehensive Space: A context for the programming/ design of cybrids

Peter Anders
CAiiA-STAR, University of Plymouth

Abstract

Cybrids have been presented as mixed realities: spatial, architectural compositions comprised of physical and cyberspaces (Anders 1997). In order to create a rigorous approach to the design of architectural cybrids, this paper offers a model for programming their spaces. Other than accepting cyberspaces as part of architecture's domain, this approach is not radical. Indeed, many parts of program development resemble those of conventional practice. However, the proposition that cyberspaces should be integrated with material structures requires that their relationship be developed from the outset of a project. Hence, this paper provides a method for their integration from the project's earliest stages, the establishment of its program. This study for an actual project, the Planetary Collegium, describes a distributed campus comprising buildings and cyberspaces in various locales across the globe. The programming for these cybrids merges them within a comprehensive space consisting not only of the physical and cyberspaces, but also in the cognitive spaces of its designers and users.

Towards Comprehensive Space: A context for the programming/design of cybrids

Peter Anders
CAiiA-STAR, University of Plymouth

1 Background

This paper uses the term Comprehensive Space to denote the polyvalent empirical space of cybrid projects. Cybrid denotes architectural, spatial compositions that integrate physical and cyberspaces (Anders 1997, 1998). As proposed, cybrids produce a holistic effect that merges simulated and material elements within phenomenologically coherent spaces. We propose that Comprehensive Space comprises cyberspaces and material environments of cybrids as well as the designer/observer's mental space of cognition and memory. In the following pages we will see the effects of this concept upon the programming of an educational institution called the Planetary Collegium. This project was undertaken as part of the author's research into architectural mixed realities as a demonstration of the cybrid hypothesis. The project merges physical and cyberspaces in the design of a cybrid, an integration that affects all stages of the project from the program statement to the design product itself. We will here limit our discussion to the project's programmatic definition.

2 Project Description

The project presents a new form of learning institution, one distributed globally, yet unified through electronic networks and periodic meetings. This institution–the Planetary Collegium–is the vision of Roy Ascott, an internationally recognized leader in the field of interactive media arts and founder/director of the CaiiA-STAR center. Unlike CaiiA-STAR, the Planetary Collegium will be independent of any host institution. It resembles its predecessor in its mission: the exploration of human possibility through new integrations of arts, science and technology. The Collegium aims to embody the future in its operation, community, and public presence. The Planetary Collegium will closely resemble the current CaiiA-STAR model in operation. As before, it will couple face-to-face interdisciplinary dialog with the decentralized, nomadic affordances of an Internetworked community. Despite the decentralization of its nodes, the Collegium will act as an organic whole. While the nodes would be scattered, the whole of the Collegium would be centered in cyberspace. This centering is experienced in time (the system is always "on") and as a spatial/empirical continuum, a refined blend of physical and telematic presences. Within one node, we would effectively be in the presence of all nodes. Engagement with a part means engagement within the cybrid whole.

Each node of the Planetary Collegium serves as a hub of activity and as an iconic presence within its host community. The nodes will be purpose-built, residential seminar centers, and their architecture will address the needs of an ecologically, technologically informed social environment. As proposed by Ascott, the nodes will "be embodied in an architecture of unique distinction while contributing to a planetary infrastructure of extreme sophistication and subtlety" (Ascott 1994). This infrastructure is represented locally as an immediately recognizable, iconic building, and globally as a networked communications environment.

3 Comprehensive Space

We may imagine our project occupying a conceptual space whose contents are vaguely defined. We know, however, that although they will serve one institution, they are physically situated in several locations worldwide. They are dispersed yet in constant contact through networked, electronic media. Also they will house a number of residents for several days at a time. Although no part of the project presently exists, it occupies this conceptual space. While some parts of it are propositional –verbal descriptions shared by readers–others exist in an evolving project space of the mind. This space–the designer's comprehensive space–is informed by memory, experience and by the artifacts of production itself. The space exists prior to, during and after the project (Anders 2001). It exists prior as concept/design artifacts to guide construction. It exists during as a supportive, operational infrastructure for maintenance, security and communications. And it exists after as a digital archive or domain that survives the building itself.

A network of artifacts forms the project space's mnemonic structure for the user. These artifacts may be material –notes, sketches, drawings, models–or, increasingly, digital and interactive. Some may be placed on a tabletop, others conveyed only by images on computers. All these artifacts, including the final building itself, disclose the project's general, collective space, for each is a unique window onto the project. The relationship between these artifacts, at first, is determined by their role in the planning process. In conventional practice, sketches lead to more refined drawings, drawings then inform specifications, etc. Later, however, these expressions take a different role. Record drawings become reference documents for repair and modifications after the project is occupied. The actual built project and its planning drawings offer distinct yet coherent views for directing new work. This consistency is readily attained with digital technologies. CAD sketches may be easily turned into technical drawings and 3D models, for unlike conventional design on paper, the vectors of sketches simply merge into the

next stage of design. The vectors used to denote construction may be reused in perspectives and animations. They may have simultaneous applications ranging from lush renderings to abstracted contract documents. CAD files are a living, spatial archive of the project's development. They form an increasingly important part of the project space, its cyberspace.
The products of CAD in architecture can be opportunistically employed to other ends than construction. The spatial configuration of the project's cyberspace offers several benefits. For instance, 1) it can help in creating an on-line community for the project owner. 2) The conceptual framework for construction can become a context for external telecommunications. 3) Internally, abstract information workspaces may be affixed to the framework, extending the project beyond its physical scope. This surprising resolution of spatial/informational needs is a by-product of the design process. As the demand for high-bandwidth, image-intensive communications increases, so too will the need to organize its content and orient its users. Designers can exploit the subtle connections between physical surroundings, digital technology and memory to unforeseen ends. For example, telepresence– a technology that conveys the visual and acoustic likeness of callers –is implicitly spatial. In some cases the transmitted presence is so realistic that it allows the sender to make eye contact with those on the receiving end. This requires orientation both with the receiving space (an office) and with the conversational partner. Such is the level of realism that it evokes a social/spatial response otherwise only found in physical interaction (Lanier 2001). As telepresence technology develops beyond screen-based communication, the spatial framing of interaction will become increasingly important. Presences observed via head-mounted displays or projection in virtual/augmented realities will need to be appropriately situated in the receiving physical space. This orientation can be more easily managed in an environment that has a digital double with appropriate sensing and display technology. What holds true for people also applies to objects in telepresence. Artifacts form an important part of any project's development. This applies not only to design professions, but any other productive collaboration. We use artifacts–objects, documents, displays–to convey our intentions and pursue goals. Telepresence entails their negotiation and exchange.

4 Establishing the Planetary Collegium Program

The Planetary Collegium program's development consists of five steps: 1) defining a project space conceptual structure, 2) distinguishing activities within the project space, 3) determining the degree of abstraction of these activities, 4) establishing the need for physical or cyberspatial support for each activity, and 5) integrating the physical and cyberspatial infrastructure within the cybrid whole. This will result in a program for the Collegium and its nodes.

4.1 Project Space Conceptual Structure

In order to avoid biasing the program toward material construction, we will re-state the project as a site of human and institutional activities, stressing verbs over nouns. Material building is not a foregone conclusion, for each activity requires infrastructural support that may or may not be built. We anticipate that portions of the project may resolve themselves instead as relays and displays of information–with only their interfaces rendered spatially.

4.2 Activities within the Project Space

Re-stating the project in this way also helps identify activities within each hub and the Collegium as a whole. This will distinguish activities according to their global/local nature and the role they play in the institution. Finally, categorizing these activities will give us a framework for developing and spatializing the program.

4.3 Degree of Abstraction of Activities

Identifying the abstractness of an activity suggests the degree to which it may be mediated electronically or otherwise (Anders 2000). Determining abstractness can be difficult since each activity may have within it several levels of abstraction. For example, a face-to-face meeting may, in addition to its highly concrete elements, have abstract artifacts such as text, graphics, and projections. These latter artifacts lack the richness of physical presence but serve the propositional nature of formal dialog. In their abstraction they appeal to specific modalities, and are increasingly susceptible to mediation through digital networks and electronic displays.

Activities, like artifacts, have concrete and abstract qualities. The verb build, for instance, connotes physical materials and effort –attributes of our sensory world. However, build also implies configuration, coordination, and goals that are more abstract than concrete. *Build* is more or less abstract depending on the way we look at it. Many verbs are not absolutely abstract or concrete; rather they exist on a continuum somewhere between. The abstractness of a verb also depends on the measuring stick we use. The labels we assign to the extremes of our scale affect the verb's status. These labels are the polar ends of a category and demonstrate the contrast between concrete and abstract. For instance, within the category "Nature of Activity" we might assign the terms material and symbolic to the poles. Or, in the category "Temporal Participation within Activity" we could label the extremes synchronous and asynchronous. Each category reveals something different about the verb. We can observe the abstractness of an activity by subjecting it to different categories of abstraction.

Example:
Let's view meeting, in this case of the Collegium's board members, from the standpoint of the "nature of the activity" ranging from symbolic to material. We could argue that it is symbolic because of the dialog, but it is also somewhat material in the physical/spatial gathering of participants. Since the (abstract) dialog is often the purpose of meeting, we might say that meeting weighs more heavily on the abstract/symbolic end of our scale. On our scale of abstraction, we could map meeting with the "weight" of the verb tipping slightly toward the symbolic. In the diagram below, the shaded area indicates the spread occupied by the verb between material and symbolic extremes:

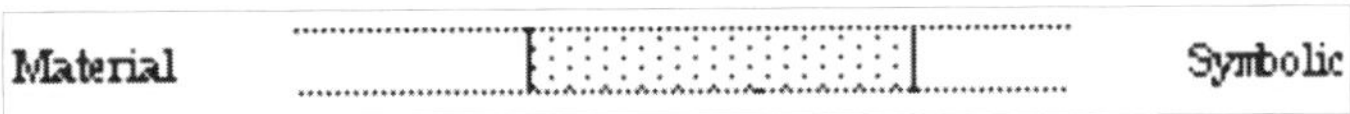

On the other hand, if we view meeting with respect to duration–with the concrete and abstract poles occupied by permanent and temporary–we would find that its location on the scale changes. Since meeting is usually a scheduled, temporary activity, we'd expect it to be nearer the abstract end of our scale. Compared with our previous diagram it might look like this:

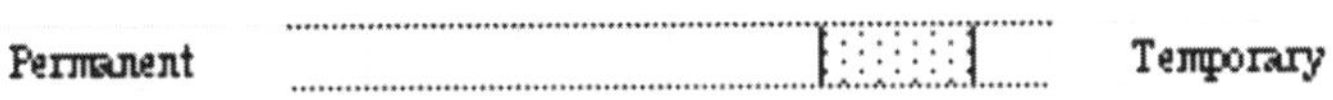

This method is admittedly subjective as it relies on individual judgment to set the levels of abstraction. However, we are not relying on the scale to pinpoint values but, instead, to give us a qualitative sense of how abstract the activity is. We do this by subjecting each activity to analysis according to several categories. To get a greater accuracy–or relevance–of the data, we can increase the sample by having several subjects evaluate the verbs. Such an evaluation could be played like a game with a number of participants–ideally the prospective users of a facility.

To create the program for the Planetary Collegium, we used these scales of abstraction to allocate material and informational resources. Each activity was mapped onto scales of abstraction in seven categories. These categories contrast the activities' levels of abstraction, but also to help distinguish simulated entities (abstract) from those that require material fabrication (concrete). The seven categories–with their polar pairs–include the following:

1. Nature of activity	Material	Symbolic
2. Appeal of activity to participant	Sensory	Conceptual
3. Site of activity	Local	Distributed
4. Likelihood of activity	Consistent	Contingent
5. Duration of activity	Permanent	Temporary
6. Temporal participation in activity	Synchronous	Asynchronous
7. Regularity of activity	Cyclical	Spontaneous

The scales' categories, particularly their extremes, were determined by their relevance to digital media. For this reason we find *symbolic, temporary, asynchronous* at the abstract end of the scale, and their opposites at the concrete end. While there is nothing necessarily abstract about *distributed*, the term is associated more readily with computer networks than its opposite, *concentrated*; thus we find *distributed* at the more abstract end of the scale. A similar logic applies to placing *symbolic, conceptual, contingent, temporary, asynchronous* and *spontaneous* nearer the abstract limit.

Example:
Returning to our examination of *meeting,* we can map the verb's abstraction within the seven categories described above. With reference to our list of categories, one such mapping results in the following scalar diagram:

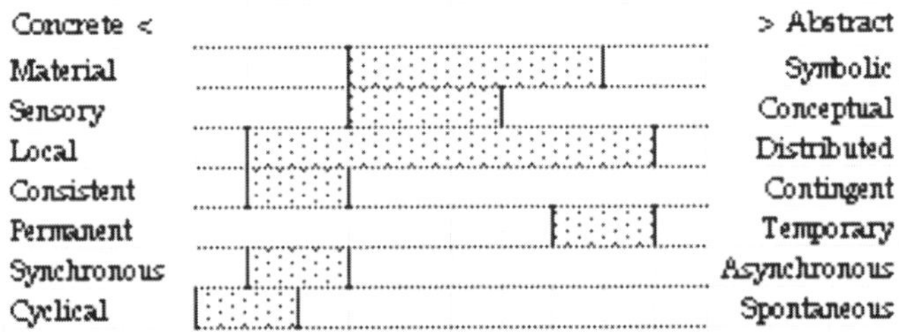

The diagram can be debated. In this case we assumed that meeting referred to Planetary Collegium activity, but the verb would map differently if we were describing a nightclub or church function. The method is also relative to its users since even among the Collegium's staff, an administrator may interpret the activity differently from, say, a researcher. All those who will occupy or use the project should, ideally, map their activities in this way during the design process. Planners could then prepare an aggregate diagram for program development.

Scalar diagrams that weigh toward the abstract end of the scale conduce to digital technology resolutions. Those weighing more toward the concrete are best resolved with material spaces and construction. But in our example the overall tendency is unclear; *meeting* seems to be poised between extremes. Fortunately, the diagram comprises several smaller scales for each topic: Nature of Activity, Appeal of Activity, Site, etc. Each of these sub-scales may be verbally translated to describe *meeting* in the context of the Planetary Collegium.

For instance, the fourth scale offered by the diagram, *Likelihood of Activity*, ranges from Consistent to Contingent. Since our shaded selection area weighs heavily toward the Consistent extreme, we could say that meetings at the Collegium are fairly regular. With verification from the client, we could say the scale describes "Regular meetings several times a year." Similarly, the fifth scale describing *Duration of Activity* indicates that the meetings are of short duration: "Meetings [of the Board Members] have a duration of a few days." In discussion with the client, the sixth scale, which describes *Temporal Participation*, may be translated to say "Co-local discussion is concurrent and

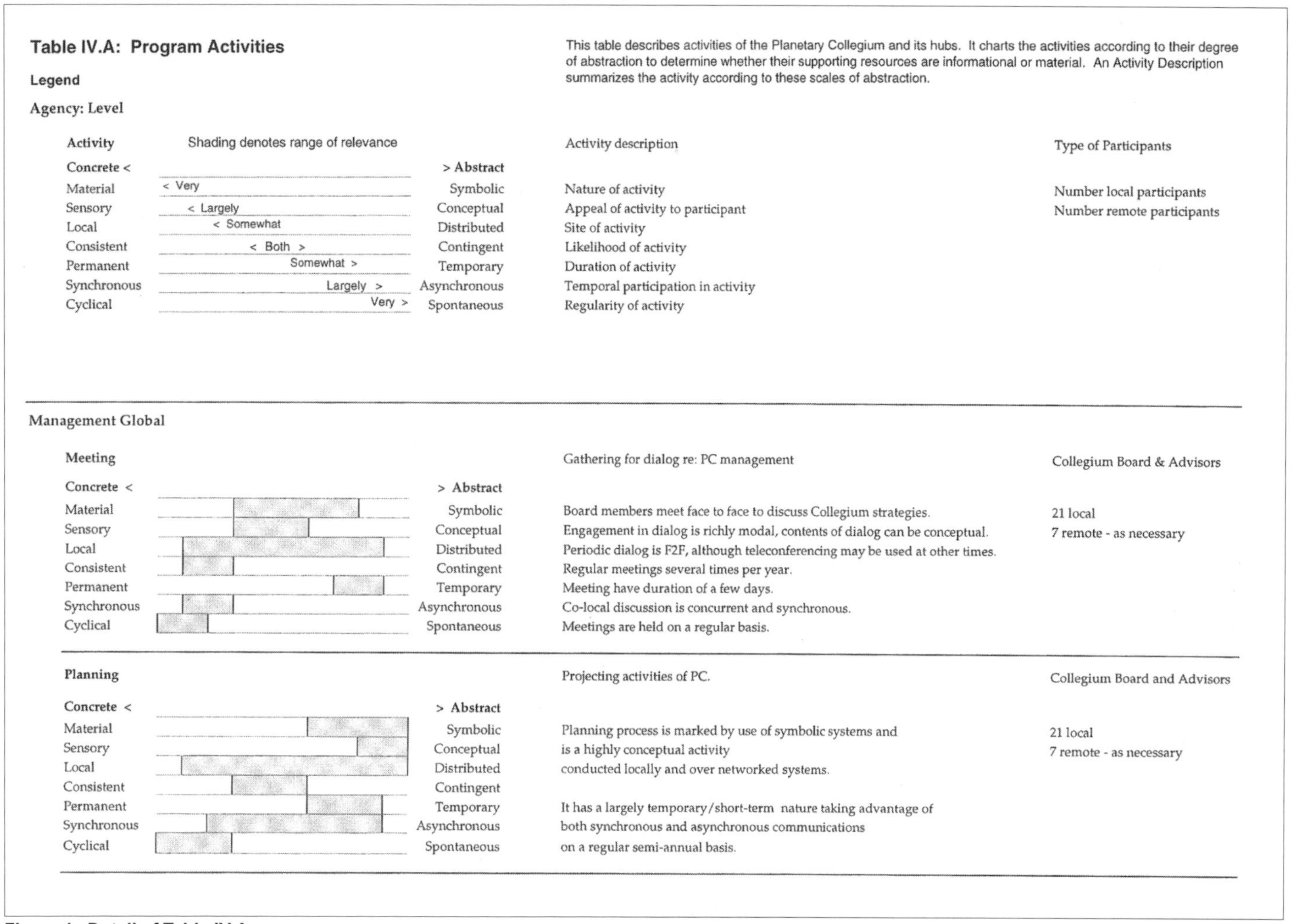

Figure 1. Detail of Table IV.A.

synchronous." And from the seventh scale, "Meetings are held on a regular basis." In this rote, line-by-line fashion we can write a short paragraph describing Board meetings within the Collegium. Enhanced by client discussion, one such paragraph may read:

> Board members meet face-to-face (F2F) to discuss Collegium strategies.
> Engagement in dialog is richly modal and contents of dialog can be conceptual.
> Periodic dialog is F2F, although teleconferencing may be used at other times.
> Regular meetings occur several times per year.
> Meetings have a duration of a few days.
> Co-local discussion is concurrent and synchronous.
> Meetings are held on a regular basis.

Note the importance of client/designer discussion in interpreting the scales. The scalar diagram is an armature for developing the project's description and program, only a starting point. Its interpretation is subject to dialog between consultants, designer and owner, even those who separately developed diagrams for the same activity. Ultimately, a statement describing Board meetings is agreed to, and the designer and client determine the support for the activity, be it physical or otherwise.

4.4 Assigning Support for Activities

With reference to the preceding analysis we can estimate the resources and support required for each activity. This support may be physical–a building or room–or as abstract as a Web site or digital archive. If the activity requires a mix of physical and cyber amenities, the support itself may become a cybrid. Table IV.B tabulates the activities and their support requirements according to the resources' informational, cybrid or physical nature. (For the sake of brevity we have only included the first pages of this and ensuing tables to suggest the strategy employed.) As in the foregoing analysis, Table IV.B assesses activities according to their role within the Collegium. These include the following:

1. Management/Global
2. Management/Local: Academic
3. Management/Local: Facility
4. Operational/Global
5. Operational/Local: Academic
6. Operational/Local: Facility
7. Public Presence: Global
8. Public Presence: Local.

Some miscellaneous local support–circulation, parking, mechanical/electrical spaces–is also accounted for at the end of the table.

We assigned a set of resources to each activity according to its description in Table IV.A. The elements of each set may be unique to that activity or, more likely, be shared with others. For this reason we find that *Archive Space* is required for a variety of activities–among them *Meeting, Planning, Sharing, Advising*–on both Global and Local scales. Users may share amenities by time-sharing. The same auditorium may serve several activities within a week, for instance. Sharing may also occur concurrently within physical or simulated environments. A library might serve research, teaching and social functions simultaneously. Or several visitors can concurrently use a digital resource, like a Web site, for a variety of purposes. Additional spatial or temporal overlaps would be likely in cybrid resources such as teleconferencing facilities or a media resource center. Table IV.B includes quantitative information – number, population, area – that further defines each resource with a separate *comments* column for additional clarification. Readers will note the resemblance of this table to conventional functional analyses by architects. The primary difference between Table IV.B and those of traditional practice is that simulations and cybrids are among the resources supporting client's activities. These resources' further resolution as spaces is the subject of Table IV.C.

Having assigned support to each of the activities, it is now possible to determine the kinds of spaces and resources that the Planetary Collegium requires. Table IV.C is a reinterpretation of

Table IV.B: Program Activities & Support

This table assigns resources to activities of the Planetary Collegium. It lists these resources according to the degree to which they are informational, material, or mixed.

Legend

Activity	Resource & Ontology	Quantity	Population	Area (sm)	Use Duration	Comments
	o informational, emulated ª mixed, cybrid • physical, material	AN: as needed NA: not applic.	NA: not applic.	Area (sm) NA: not applic.	# uses/yr FT: full time PT: part time AN: as needed	
Management Global						
Meeting						
	o Meeting space	1	for 7	20	<1x/yr.	Emulate room of 20 s.m.
	o Archive space	1	NA	varies	<1x/yr.	Variable size emulation - may be reconfigured by user/use.
	ª Access to home workplace	21+	varies	varies	<1x/yr.	Emulation varies according to size or use of home space.
	ª Teleconference facility	1	for 21+	50	<1x/yr.	Include area for media support.
	ª Meeting room	1	for 21+	50	<1x/yr.	May be part of or same as teleconferencing facility.
	• Access to room & board	21	AN	varies	<1x/yr.	Room and board may be on or off premises as needed.
	• Food service	1	for 21+	varies	<1x/yr.	Food service may be on or off premises as needed, see Café
Planning						
	o Planning space	1	for 7	20	<1x/yr.	Emulate room of 20 s.m. - may be part of or same as meeting space.
	o Archive space	1	NA	varies	<1x/yr.	Variable size emulation - may be reconfigured by user/use.
	ª Teleconference facility	1	for 21+	50	<1x/yr.	Include area for media support.
	ª Access to home workplace	21+	varies	varies	<1x/yr.	Emulation varies according to size or use of home space.
	ª Meeting room	1	for 21+	50	<1x/yr.	May be part of or same as teleconferencing facility.
	• Access to room & board	21	AN	varies	<1x/yr.	Room and board may be on or off premises as needed.
	• Food service	1	for 21+	varies	<1x/yr.	Food service may be on or off premises as needed, see Café
Conversing						
	ª Access to home workplace	21+	for 21+	varies	<1x/yr.	Emulation varies according to size or use of home space.
	ª Teleconference facility	1	for 21+	50	<1x/yr.	Include area for media support.
	ª Changes of venue	varies	for 21+	varies	<1x/yr.	Inclusive of all varied spaces used for congregation and dialog. Indoor and outdoor.
	• Food service	1	for 21+	varies	<1x/yr.	Food service may be on or off premises as needed, see Café

Figure 2. Detail of Table IV.B.

the previous table that delineates the resources/spaces required for the project. The table lists these resources/spaces according to their increasingly physical nature. For instance, we find the Web site and digital Archive Space at the top of the list, while Janitorial support and Mechanical Rooms are at its conclusion. The listing of spaces in this way–from informational resources at the top to material resources below–implicitly merges the "upper" realm of abstraction with the "lower" physical world. This metaphorical strategy will help spatialize the project and will be used again later in the project's development. Table IV.C also vertically separates the resource/spaces into informational/digital, mixed/cybrid, or material categories. This distinction of resource type is also evident also in the table's initial columns, which further define the types as material spaces, simulations, services and/or systems.

As we may note from the table's legend, the columns to the right of *Resource Types* recapitulate much of Table IV.B and are arranged according to the degree that the activity categories are private to the Planetary Collegium. For example, Public Presence: Global is the first of these column categories while Management: Global is the last. The vertical and horizontal axes of the table help distinguish physical from digital resources/spaces as well as their public or private natures. While it is only two-dimensional, this table is a first step in spatializing the Planetary Collegium's program, a process we will pursue in following tables.

5 Localizing Space and Resources

As its vertical and horizontal ordinates indicate,Table IV.D derives directly from Table IV.C . Unlike the previous table, however, Table IV.D shows the degree to which a resource is

Table IV.C: Program Spaces and Resources

This table shows the spaces and resources required to meet the program needs. It arrays the data so that as one reads left to right the resources become increasingly private to the Planetary Collegium. As one descends the chart, the resources become increasingly concrete.

Legend: • Appropriate; 1 Quantity; 21 **Area**/pop.; PT Duration. PT Part time; FT Full time; # Times/yr.; NA Not applic.; AN As necess.

Increasingly Private to Planetary Collegium >

v Increasingly Concrete

Resources/Spaces	Resource Type	Space	Emulation	Service	System	Public Presence: Global	Coordinating	Conferencing	Public Presence: Local	Conferencing	Hosting	Management Local: Academic	Advising	Management Local: Facility	Administering	Operational Local: Academic	Conferring	Researching	Presenting	Communing	Additional Support: Local	Resources/Spaces	
Information Spaces																							
o Archive space			•		•								• 1 21 FT		• 1 3 FT			• 1 21 FT	• 1 21 FT				
o Web site			•	•	•		• 1 NA FT			• 1 FT FT	• 1 FT FT												
o Cyberreal model of facility			•								• AN AN AN												
o Planning space			•		•																		
o Meeting space			•		•		• 1 AN AN	• 1 AN AN		• 1 AN AN	• AN AN AN												
Mixed/Cybrid Resources																							
Internet access/extranet			•		•		• 1 AN AN	• 1 AN AN		• 1 AN AN	• 1 FT AN							• 1 21 FT					
IT network/infranet			•		•						• 1 FT AN							• 1 21 FT					
Phone network					•																		
Media support			•		•														• 1 21 AN				
Access to home workplace		•	•				• 21 NA AN						• 21 NA AN										
Data garden		•	•															• 1 21 FT		• 1 AN AN			

Resources/Spaces	Operational Local: Facility	Administering Hospitality	Sheltering	Boarding	Retreating	Communicating	Leasing	Monitoring	Controlling	Operational Global	Conferencing	Sharing	Coordinating	Archiving	Management Global	Meeting	Planning	Conversing	Presenting	Sharing	Comments
Information Spaces																					
o Archive space		• 1 NA FT			• 1 21 AN	• 1 21 FT					• 1 21 FT	• 1 21 FT		• 1 21 FT		• 1 NA <1	• 1 Bd. FT		• 1 21 FT	• 1 21 FT	
o Web site						• 1 ? FT	• 1 NA FT					• 1 NA FT	• 1 NA FT							• 1 NA FT	
o Cyberreal model of facility								• 1 AN FT	• 1 AN FT												Transcends entire scope of project.
o Planning space																	• 1 7 <1				
o Meeting space						• 1 21 AN										• 1 7 <1					
Mixed/Cybrid Resources																					
Internet access/extranet		• 1 3 FT				• 1 21 AN	• 1 3 FT	• 1 3 AN	• 1 3 AN			• 1 3 AN	• 1 3 AN	• 1 NA FT						• 1 AN AN	General to Project.
IT network/infranet		• 1 3 FT				• 1 21 AN	• 1 3 FT	• 1 3 AN	• 1 3 AN			• 1 3 AN		• 1 NA FT						• 1 AN AN	General to Project.
Phone network						• 1 21 FT															General to Project.
Media support								• 1 3 FT	• 1 3 AN										• 1 AN AN		
Access to home workplace			• 21 NA 3X								• 3 NA AN					• 21 NA <1	• 21 NA <1	• 21 NA <1			As necessary.
Data garden					• 1 AN AN																

Figure 3. Detail of Table IV.C.

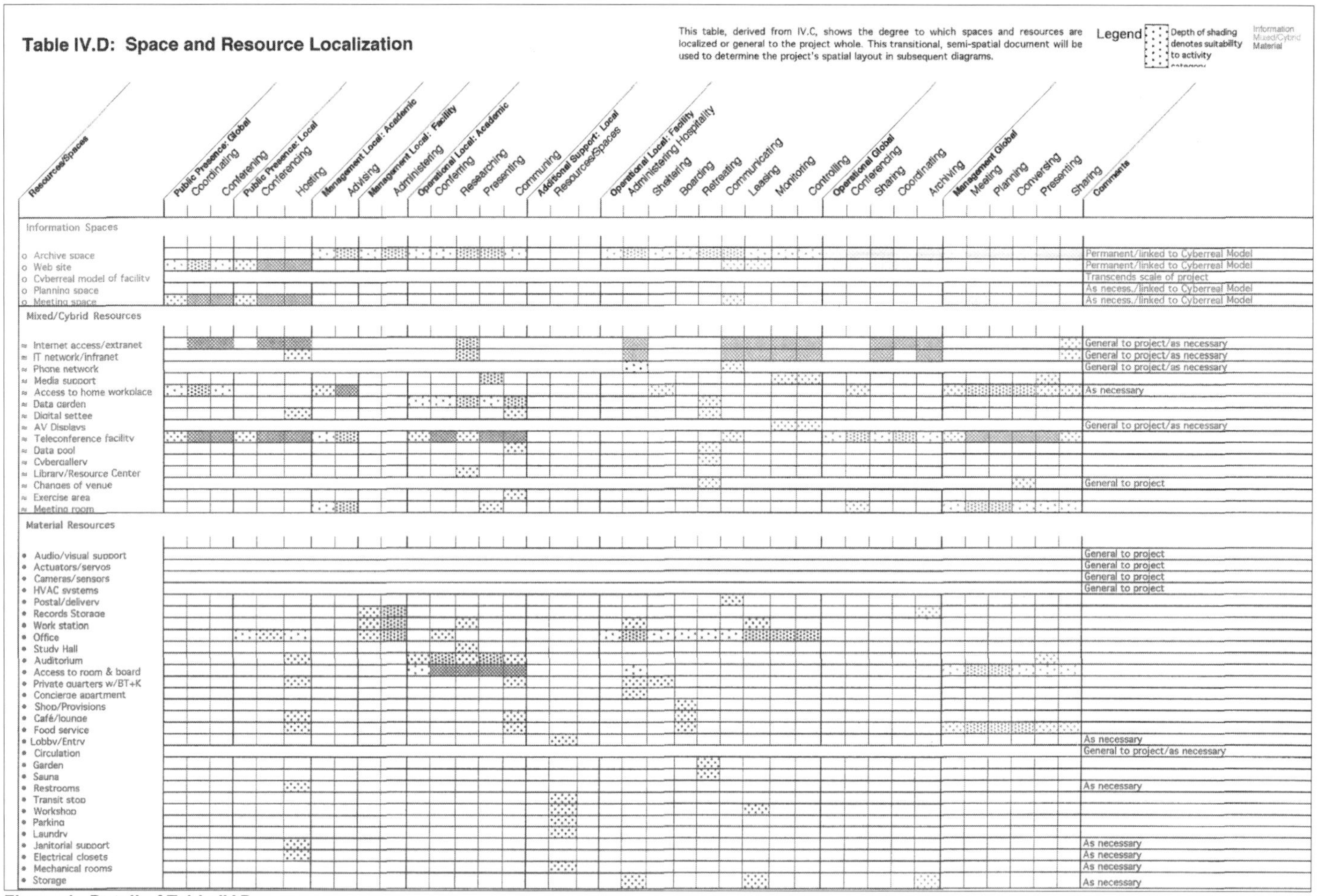

Figure 4. Detail of Table IV.D.

located specifically or distributed generally throughout the project. The intensity of color in each cell denotes a resource's suitability of a resource to a specific activity. As indicated in the table's legend, the color–yellow, green, blue–depends on whether the resource/space is informational, cybrid, or material. This table is tributary to the spatialization diagrams found in Tables IV.E1, E2, and E3.

The diagrams in Table IV.E1, E2, and E3 (only E1 is shown here) individually lay out the resource/space rows of Table IV.D. A loose bubble is drawn around the activity cells with the greatest intensity of color. The diameter of the bubble is roughly related to the color intensity and the concentration of colored cells. While this process is somewhat subjective it quickly shows the degree to which a resource is distributed or local. In some cases, such as the facility's phone network or HVAC support - the resource is general to the entire project. In others, bubbles show where the resources may be most concentrated. Table IV.F1, F2, and F3 (not shown here) are identical to the Table IV.E series except that the underlying cells have been removed. Finally, Table IV.G concatenates the Table IV.F series into a single diagram. Table IV.G is entitled *Programmatic Section Diagram* as it will be used to develop the sectional design of the Collegium.

In order to consolidate a schedule of program spaces and winnow out redundancies we created Table IV.H (not shown) to illustrate the various versions of all resources/spaces described in Table IV.B. The winnowing process is best explained by example. Table IV.B contained several listings for *Archive Space,* each with its own requirements. Table IV.H shows these redundant listings and indicates the one with the most demanding specification. This specification will be part of the final program space area for the resource/space. This process is carried out for all resource spaces. Table IV.H concludes with a summation of areas required for the project. A feature unique to this analysis is its assignment of area, volume, and location to non-physical resources. Quantities for area and volume in cyberspace have no conventional meaning besides the creation of an icon, metaphor or other symbol within the space of the cybrid composition. Such resources/spaces may take the form

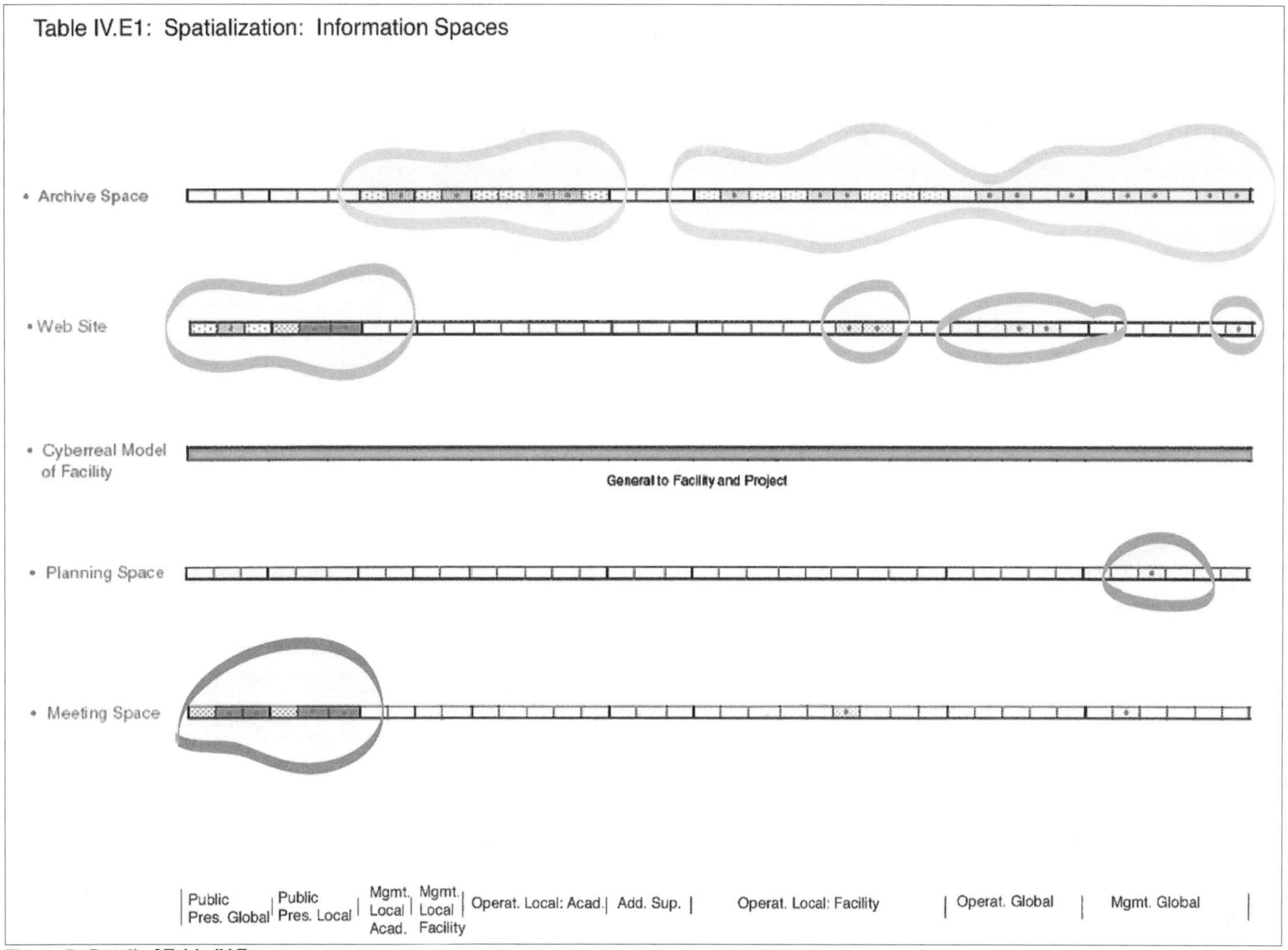

Figure 5. Detail of Table IV.E.

of Web sites, digital worlds or other cyberspaces. Regardless of their informational nature, they have a place and presence different from–but analogous to–material components of the project. This situates the element for the end user, giving it identity and presence despite its abstraction. Such reification is a natural –and useful–feature of planning a cybrid.

A final analysis for spatializing the Collegium program is familiar to architects and planners: a proximity schedule. This schedule, Table IV.I, relates the spaces defined in Table IV.H to one another to determine their need for adjacency. For example, one would expect the café and food service areas to be close to each other, as indicated by dark shading of the appropriate cell in the diagram. Light shading or no shading at all here means that proximity is not a great concern. Once again this analysis differs from conventional proximity charts in its inclusion of information cyberspaces. Since the focus of Table IV.I is to relate spaces, any cyberspaces so linked to a physical amenity effectively render it to be a "second-order" cybrid. That is, the cyber and physical spaces are contiguous but not integral to each other.

6 Preparing for Conceptual Design

We can now use the information generated in these tables to design the Collegium. Some of these tables/diagrams will directly influence the form, while others will help in refining the project. We have to this point stressed the relationship of physical and cyberspaces in the project in response to the program requirements. However, aside from functional/utilitarian aspects of the project, we have yet to address the end users and their cognitive role in completing the project. We anticipate the need to create a mnemonic context, or frame, whereby the user can understand the project. Consequently, in addition to our

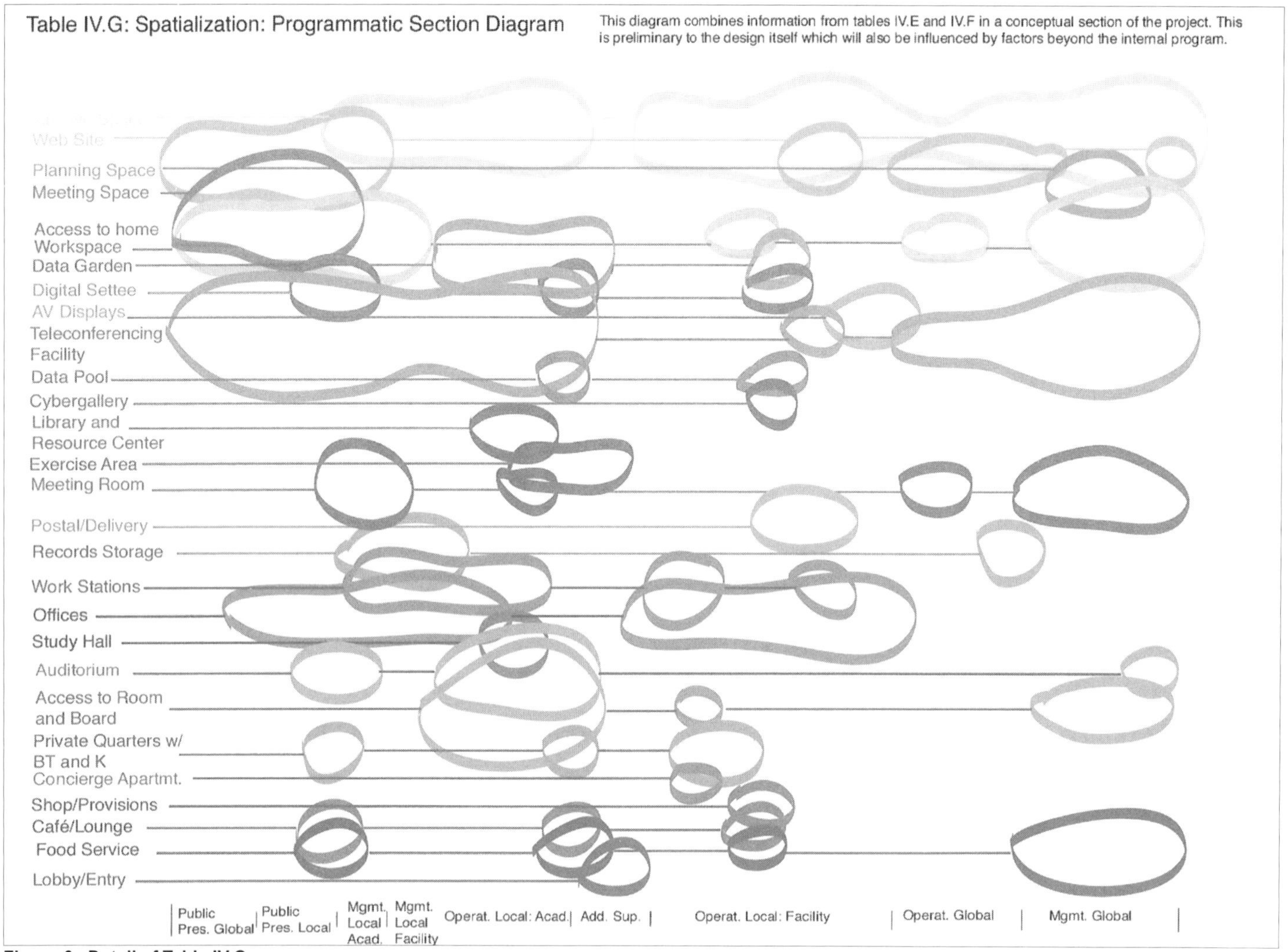

Figure 6. Detail of Table IV.G.

analyses, we will need to employ metaphor, myth and narrative in generating the Collegium's design. In effect, these create a sustaining schemata for the project–one that employs the user's memory/cognition in the project's completion and use.

7 Conclusions

We have suggested that the concept of comprehensive space–a space that includes mental, physical and cyberspaces–may be an important tool in developing cybrids. Using the principles of cybrid design outlined at the beginning of the paper, we have begun designing projects to demonstrate their use and the application of comprehensive space to the early stages of design. This space was useful in distinguishing physical from informational activities in the Planetary Collegium. This had a subsequent effect on the program of the project and its ensuing design resolution. Next steps in the project entail the design development of the project and its manifestation as a cybrid entity. Importantly, the comprehensive space of the project already exists in the minds of the designer and the present reader and will last long after resulting buildings and cyberspaces are gone.

References

Anders, P. (2002) Comprehensive space: Harnessing consciousness in architecture and design. Paper presented at 4th International CaiiA-STAR Research Conference, Consciousness Reframed 2002: Non-local, non-linear, non-ordinary. Curtin University, Perth, Australia. August 2-4 2002.

Anders, P.(2001a) Anthropic cyberspace. *Leonardo* 34(5): 409-416.

Anders, P. (2001b) Domains of body and mind. *Convergence: The journal of research into new media technologies* 7(2): 90-100.

Anders, P. (2000) Places of mind: Implications of narrative space for the architecture of information environments," presented at Consciousness Reframed 3, August 23-26, 2000. Paper also presented and published in proceedings at ACADIA 2000 conference in Washington D.C. October 19-22, 2000.

Anders, P. (1999) *Envisioning cyberspace*. New York: McGraw-Hill.

Anders, P. (1998) Cybrids: Integrating cognitive and physical space in architecture.*Convergence magazine* 4(1):85-105.

Anders, P. (1997) Cybrids: Integrating cognitive and physical space in architecture. In *Representation and design, Proceedings of ACADIA conference*, Cincinnati, Ohio, 3-5 October, ed. J.P. Jordan, B. Mehnert, A. Harfmann,17-34.

Ascott, R.(1994) Planetary collegium. *ISEA '94, Catalogue and proceedings of the symposium*. Helsinki: UIAH.

The Level of Knowledge of CAD Objects within the Building Information Model

Magdy Ibrahim, Robert Krawczyk
Illinois Institute of Technology

Abstract

The first generation of CAD software depended on entity objects that were manipulated and interpreted by the user as meaningful graphics symbols. These entities only represented the geometrical properties of the architectural elements. With the present emerging generation of CAD systems, a new concept shifts a drawing-based model into a Building Information Model with the potential of modeling true architectural objects. Theoretically, these CAD objects will provide all related data to the designer describing the geometry, as well as any related data associated with how the object is actually used.

The knowledge required to support an object should have structure to it. Different levels of knowledge need to be included, such as the geometrical information, which should be flexible enough to accommodate any type of shape and modification while keeping the object's integrity as a unit and maintaining its relations to other objects.

The CAD object concept, as remarkable as it is, might also have potential problems. It has some implications over the design process, as well as the architectural profession itself.

The Level of Knowledge of CAD Objects within the Building Information Model

Magdy Ibrahim, Robert Krawczyk
Illinois Institute of Technology

The New CAD Concept: BIM

BIM stands for Building Information Model. In fact, the idea of BIM-based CAD is not new: it has always been foreseen as the ideal way to represent buildings digitally, but it has never been mainstream for commercial products until recently, mainly due to the increased capacity of personal computers. Graphisoft ArchiCAD Virtual Building concept may have been the first commercially available package that utilized the building model; now more and more CAD software is being built around this new concept. Object oriented programming is not new. All applications written in C++ are object-oriented, but it took the CAD industry some time to apply this software concept to the building elements themselves.

The building industry has traditionally communicated building construction information through drawings with notes and specifications. CAD technology automated that process, and object-oriented CAD extended the idea of adding information to graphics. The result of earlier manual drafting and CAD systems were identical, creating graphic abstractions of the intended building design. Intended for building graphics and generating two-dimensional printed/plotted drawings, these systems were capable of handling and managing information about a building only on a limited basis. Other industries, such as manufacturing, have realized great benefit from non-graphical, parametric information technology tools. The BIM-based generation of CAD systems, designed with current technology, is required to fully realize the benefits of object-oriented CAD. This next generation of information-centric software provides building information modeling instead of building graphic modeling.

Building information modeling operates on digital databases. By storing and managing building information as databases, BIM systems can capture, manage, and present data in ways that are appropriate and customary for a particular designer, contractor, vendor or client. Such applications start with capturing and managing information about the building, and then present that information back as conventional drawings view or in any other appropriate way such as tables or perspective views, and make it available for use and reuse at every phase in the project (AutoDesk 2002).

With the arrival of the BIM-based CAD, came new concept of objects.These objects are not only programming objects, but they have specific meaning to the architect. They have an equivalent physical meaning to real world objects, and provide an abstract computer representation of the physical world that is convenient for architects (Ruppel, Meissner, and Bernd, M, 1993). A wall as an object in the CAD system represents an actual wall in the physical world, and a door as an object represents a real door. With objects, all the standard object-oriented programming concepts apply. Objects have properties, methods, and events. The advantage of the object model is that it allows for the extension of the properties or attributes, not to be confused with the block attributes as found in AutoCAD.

Entities vs. Objects

An *object* from a computer science point of view is an independent procedure that contains both the instructions and data to perform some task, and the programming code necessary to handle various messages that it may receive (Morris 1999).

Both industry and academia have devoted countless hours of research and development to the problem of describing geometry digitally so it can be stored, presented and manipulated on a computer and a plotter. The "geometry engines" resulting from these efforts were, and remain, the core technology in today's products (Revit White Paper 1998).

AutoCAD is an example of a C++ written, object-oriented program which used a general concept of objects to create the "drafting elements" or "drawing primitives" such as lines and arcs. This is where the confusion begins.

While AutoCAD itself is an object-oriented program, the objects it provided were only graphical objects or "entities." Although such objects had all the concepts of programming objects, they were used mainly to draw a representation of well-understood drawings of highly symbolic information about the building. The architect must interpret the meanings of what has been drawn, in the exact same way as with physical drawings. Using the same drawing legacy, a replica of what could have been drawn by hand was created using the computer as a drafting system. Even the creation of a symbols library, blocks in AutoCAD, is very dependant on the previous knowledge of the symbols used by the profession and to some extent equals the use of drafting templates. The architect could have named the symbol any name and still can be able to use it the correct way, because the interpretation relies on how the designer uses it.

These drawing entities only include geometrical aspects of the real objects that they represent, and never had knowledge of what they are, or how to behave or interact with each other. With the exception of Blocks with Attributes and their equivalent in other CAD packages, which to some extent had included more information about themselves, all entities were just a collection of basic drawing primitives.

With the BIM generation of CAD systems, embedded information can describe the geometry, as well as materials, specifications, code requirements, assembly procedures, prices, manufacturers, vendors and any other related data associated with how the object is actually used. Mechanical CAD already has many of these features. A door as a smart object that understands its relationship to a wall and reacts accordingly should be a great help to the designer. The potential of using CAD smart objects is very appealing in the production phase of a project. Although the architect is not obliged to give full information about the object he is using, that object has blank attributes waiting for such input. As a result, in the schematic design phase an object could even be represented symbolically to the architect, a wall could be a line, and a door could be two simple lines indicating the door opening. As the architect advances to the design phases, these semi-defined objects should become better defined and takes more decisions about the building. Adding information will always be the architect's responsibility.

In the production phase, objects are in full throttle, as generating the bill of materials is a matter of a button click, and consequently the cost estimation is easily achievable. Any changes done to the building database will simultaneously be reflected in the entire set of documents the architect is responsible for: plans, elevations, sections, schedules, and bill of materials.

For a design firm utilizing BIM technology this means savings in time and resources needed to coordinate changes. Even with advanced current CAD methods, like external references and writing routines to automate drawing production, this would have not been achievable with the ease and accuracy a BIM-based CAD could deliver.

This can lead to a problem where the customization of CAD packages may not be possible. Technical support teams in most firms now can easily automate repetitive tasks, and develop even more intuitive tools to help in their production. With the new breed of CAD that depends on smart objects, the customization capabilities of the older and simpler entity-based systems might be in question. It can be foreseen that the same need for customization will take place no matter how sophisticated the software becomes, but the inherent complexity in the new systems may make it more difficult.

To be Smart, Objects Must Have Knowledge

Constraints and parametric variation, which BIM CAD is built around, have been active areas of investigation in computer-aided architectural design for over fifteen years (Eggink, Gross, and Do 2001). Parametric design relies on the ability to change an object's properties numerically without the need to redraw it. The CAD system takes care of the redrawing part of the parametric object, but the parameters themselves must be previously assigned to the object.

A "door" object has a finite set of parameters that dictate its shape. The coding of the door object has to include these parameters, and this requires previous knowledge of the parameters involved in the creation of a door (Figure 1). The very basic parameters of a door object are the geometrical

Parameter	Value
Thickness	50.8
Assembly Code	C1020
Door Material	Door - Panel
Frame Material	Door - Frame
Height	2032
Rail Width-Center	101.6
Top Panel	914.4
Trim Projection Ext	25.4
Trim Projection Int	25.4
Trim Width	76.2
Wall Closure	By host
Width	1727.2
Model	
Manufacturer	
Type Comments	
URL	
Description	
Assembly Description	Interior Doors
Type Mark	24
Rough Width	
Rough Height	
Construction Type	
Fire Rating	
Cost	

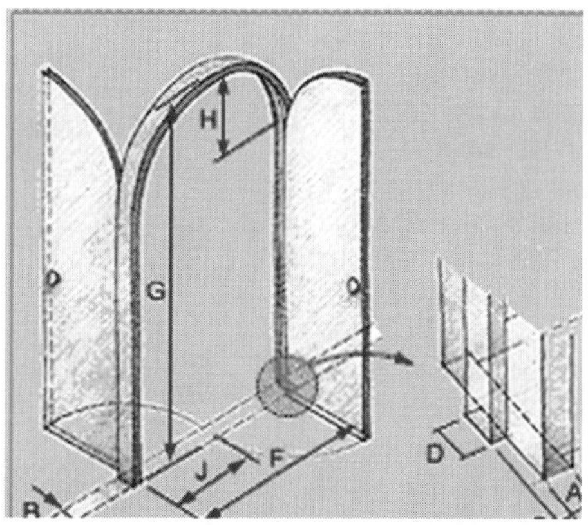

Figure 1. A "Door" object as it appears in the properties dialogue box in AutoDesk Revit 5.0 (left) and the different parameters connected to a "Door" object as it appears in AutoDesk Architectural Desktop 3.0 (right).

information, such as width, height, sill-height and frame dimensions. Parameters are always a predefined list of properties that the user has to select from, or abide by their rules for the manipulation or creation of a new object.

The necessary information for the set of parameters of a door object makes up architectural knowledge. The object will not be useful without the knowledge used to build it. But the problem is that the object is as good as the knowledge behind it.

Adding more information to that object becomes a question because the way the code is written may make it hard for an average user to manipulate. The object itself may become a prisoner of the predefined parameters, giving little chance for changing its character unless an entirely new object is defined. The knowledge required to support an object should have a certain structure to it, as the concept of the smartness will depend on how complete and how smartly the embedded information reacts to other objects. Different levels of knowledge need to be included, such as:

1) Geometrical information:
It should be flexible enough to accommodate any type of shape and modification to it while keeping the integrity of the object as a unit and maintaining its relations to other objects.

2) Non-geometrical information:
Materials, codes and assembly requirements should also feed back to the geometry of the shape by setting the limits of the possibilities the form may take.

Online Knowledge

The architectural profession relies on vendors and manufacturers' catalogs for specifications. For example, doors are rarely a custom design. Architects depend on a pre-designed unit selected from catalogs, which include the knowledge needed for the creation of the object inside the CAD system. For example, if an object could extract the needed information from a web page catalog written in XML, and change its parameters accordingly, then all the knowledge at the manufacturer side has been transferred to the object provided by that that object is coded to handle that kind of information. This will be accomplished if the main players in the industry agree on making it happen. In the production phase of a project, correctly and automatically adding all the specification related to an item will be a great benefit to the architect.

Some issues can be concluded here:

1) Objects should allow the designers the flexibility to design what they think without being limited by what is implemented.
2) Objects are like catalog items: they must be well connected with real vendors' catalogs to access their necessary parameters.
3) Vendors must agree on a standard for specifying parameters that is compatible with different CAD packages.
4) Objects should be flexible enough to adapt with the accumulation of information attached to them, throughout the design process.

How will this Change the Profession?

As remarkable as it is, the current development of the smart CAD concept might have a set of negative implications.

The Master Apprentice Relationship and CAD

CAD objects enable embedded information to be the primary reference for an architect, placing less emphasis on the master apprentice model that has developed in architectural practice. Young architects will not need technical support from their seniors as long as the computer provides this feed back. Will this lead to a new kind of draftsperson, who might not require much help and will complete a task with relatively fewer mistakes? How will this affect the development of problem solving skills, the professional education of an architect, and the master apprentice relationship in the workplace?

(Eggink, Gross, and Do 2001) presented a model for smart objects that would change its parameters depending on its boundary conditions; a beam-as-an-object should set its depth according to the span it covers, and change accordingly as the span changes. Another example, a door object should automatically set its fire rating according to the room where it belongs, depending on its knowledge of the room's function and code requirements. Theoretically, this can be achieved, and should enhance quality control in drawings. Although such intelligent behavior has not yet been implemented in current CAD programs, it is this kind of development that will be expected in the future development.

Evolution of Objects

How are objects represented during different phases of the design process? From the schematic design to design development, objects should have empty properties that might be added while the design is being developed. Can these properties/attributes be added dynamically as needed? It is possible to make objects dynamic enough to expand their knowledge as needed, like containers which will keep filling up with information during the different design phases. This should not be limited to a previously determined set of parameters, but to the possibility of easily adding more parameters as needed.The architect should be able to add more specifications to the object as parameters not just as textual description. There is no indication that current developers have addressed this issue.

Innovation and Creativity

Should smart objects allow for nonstandard uses? The smart object concept may not allow the architect to combine non-compatible components. How might this affect innovation? Pre-defined rectangular shape of a door opening from an object is normal, but what about the other door shapes? Unless supported by the vendor the current software does not allow architects to create their own non-orthodox objects.

What will the support group within a design firm need to know about software to change its parameter to support more nontraditional concepts? The architectural student might need to be trained differently to cope with this kind of change in the tools, understanding the potentials and limitations of the tools, and above all having a good understanding of the theories behind these tools. As future architects and IT support those students will constitute the users for such systems. The worst case changes will not be allowed.

Dependability on The Software Industry

If firms cannot easily add new objects, must they wait until the next version of the package comes to market? The obvious answer is yes. This is what is happening now, waiting for a curtain-wall tool in AutoDesk ADT, while other companies race to provide the same feature remain competitive. This kind of healthy competition benefits end users, but they must wait for a tool to be implemented. Consequently, architects will invest more money to obtain new features through upgrading.These systems might eventually become comprehensive enough for most users, but there will always be some special needs not foreseen.

Conclusion

It is very important to define the potentials of the building information model, and the implementation of objects in architectural CAD. The benefits of such systems will depend on better understanding of architects' needs in the office. Paying attention to the potential problems might make these systems more successful in the future.

References

Alshawia, M., and J. Underwood. (1996) Applying object-oriented analysis to the integration of design and construction. *Automation in construction*, 5(2):105-121.

AutoDesk, white paper, Building Information Modeling, *Autodesk building industry solutions(2002)* San Rafael, CA: Autodesk,Inc.

Autodesk Revit. White paper. The parametric building modeler: Answers to technical questions.

Beucke, K., and D.Rang Lack, (1993). Computing with objects: What does industry hope to gain from it. *Computing in civil and building engineering: Proceedings of the Fifth International Conference (V-ICCCBE)*, Louis F. Cohn. Anaheim, California, the American Society of Civil Engineers.

Eggink, D., M.D. Gross, and E. Do. Smart objects: Constraints and behaviors in a 3D design environment. *Architectural information management: 19th eCAADe conference proceedings*, Hannu Penttil,460-65 Helsinki,Finland,Helsinki University of Technology (HUT), 29-31 August 2001.

Fischer, T., M. Burry, and R. Woodbury. (2000) Object-oriented modeling using XML In *Computer-aided-architectural and educational Cad. CAADRIA 2000, Proceedings of the Fifth Conference on Computer Aided Architectural Design Research in Asia*,145-155, Singapore, 18-19 May.

Henkemans, D. and M. Lee. (2001). *C++ programming for the absolute beginner*. Premier Press.

Rozmanith M. Product management, autodesk revit. White paper. The parametric building modeler: Answers to technical questions.

Revit. White Paper. The Aec technology platform question.

Revit. White Paper. An introduction to revit.

Reymendt, J. and J. Wörner. (1993). Object-oriented modeling for concrete structures. *Computing in civil and building engineering: Proceedings of the Fifth International Conference (V-ICCCBE)*, Louis F. Cohn. Anaheim, California, The American Society of Civil Engineers. June.

Rudolph, D. (1999). *Mastering AutoCAD 2000 objects*. Alameda, Calif: Sybex, December.

Stephen M., *Object-oriented programming for Windows 95 and NT*. Digital Press, 1999.

Ruppel U., U. Meissner, and M.Bernd.(1993).Object-oriented data exchange for the integration of design processes in structural engineering," *Computing in civil and building engineering: Proceedings of the fifth international conference (V-ICCCBE)*, Louis F. Cohn. Anaheim, California, The American Society of Civil Engineers.

Weisfeld, M. A. (2000). *The object-oriented thought process*. Indianapolis, Ind.

Digital Innovation and Organizational Change in Design Practice

Robert E. Johnson, Eberhard S. Laepple
Texas A&M University

Abstract

The real estate and construction industry is among the largest industries in the world. It also is one of the most fragmented industries, with few economies of scale and historically low productivity. Recent technological advances in the use of information and communication technology have the potential for dramatically improving construction productivity. But substantial organizational barriers exist that inhibit the effective adoption of these technologies.

This research project (in progress) examines the practices of selected, innovative firms in order to develop an in-depth understanding of the factors that have influenced the effective adoption of information and communications technology in the design and construction industry, and, potentially, provide examples that may provide prototype models for an alternative, future organization of the AEC industry.

Digital Innovation and Organizational Change in Design Practice

Robert E. Johnson, Eberhard S. Laepple
Texas A&M University

1 Introduction

In our previous research (Johnson et al. 2002), we have argued that there is an interrelationship between business goals, work processes, and the adoption of information technology. That is, changes in business goals generally require revising work processes which can be enhanced further by the introduction of information technology. But we also recognized that innovations in information technology create possibilities for new work processes that can, in turn, alter business goals (see Figure 1). In order to understand how information technology influences architectural practice it is important to understand all three of these interrelated elements.

Figure1. Business Goals and Information Technology.

This model seems to be useful to understand the role of technology in other industries. History has demonstrated that the introduction of new technology into an industry often results in dramatic changes in that industry. For example, the industrial revolution had significant and long-lasting impacts on many industries, such as the transportation industry. Automobiles are now produced in a manner that fully integrates design, engineering, and manufacturing. Additionally, many virtual organizations have emerged that could not have been imagined before the introduction of the Internet.

In contrast, the practices of architecture and construction have not changed very much despite the introduction of the Internet and, earlier, computer aided design. The reasons for this are varied and complex. We suspect that the fragmented nature of the building design and construction industry has been an inhibiting factor. Furthermore, technologies such as CAD (Computer-Aided Design or Computer-Aided Drafting?) and project management systems can be used without any major organizational changes. More significant integration in the industry is inhibited by designers, developers, contractors, and construction managers all of whom tend to focus on their own areas of expertise and protect their own interests in the building process (Henderson 2002). It is unlikely that major innovation in the building industry will take place without a change in the rules that promote fragmentation

There are a number of technological innovations emerging that may help to change some of the rules. The changes we are most interested in are those that have been in development over many years though the efforts of many academics too numerous to mention; cooperative organizations, such as the International Alliance for Interoperability; software developers, especially the relatively recent agreement regarding the terminology of the building information modeling (BIM); and users of organizations in the design and construction industry. Much of this research is reported in Eastman's book on Building Product Models (Eastman 1999). Building Information Modeling (BIM) refers to an agreement among major design software developers about the terminology, originally adopted by Autodesk, describing the use of object-oriented, parametric solid-modeling systems (see especially issues 15, 16, 17 and 18 of the Laiserin Letter, www.laiserin.com, for a discussion of this agreement).

The purpose of the research now underway and reported in this short paper is to understand how leading, innovative companies are adopting these technological innovations. This research project examines the practices of these firms in order to develop an in-depth understanding of the factors that have influenced the effective adoption of these technological innovations in the design and construction industry and, potentially, provides examples that may describe quite a different future for the AEC industry.

2 Research Methods

The exploratory nature of this research suggested the use of a case study for these investigations. Half-day site visits are being conducted with approximately 6-12 firms from various sectors in the AEC/FM industry in the United States. These firms are being selected primarily from referrals and industry publications. For each site visit we first develop an overall understanding of the organizational structure of the company and obtain a description of any long-term relationships with other companies (e.g., alliances). When possible, information is gathered prior to the visit and may include a description of the history, organizational structure, current business context (including mission statements), and future business trends of the company. A fundamental part of each site visit is to determine the degree that information and communication technology solutions have been used to help improve the delivery of design and construction projects. This part of the site visit will provide a description of the decision-making process used to determine the need for information technology solutions.

At this point in our research we have completed one site visit. Others are in progress. The case study was written and submitted for review by the company we visited. The entire case study is reproduced below. Due to the requirements of the

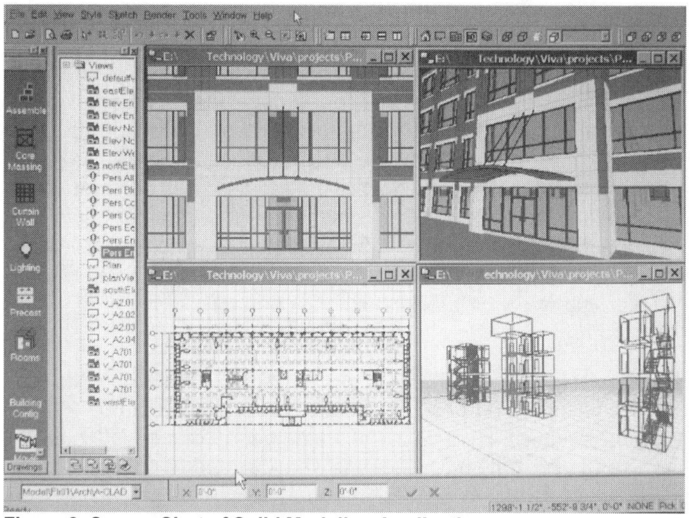

Figure 2. Screen Shot of Solid Modeling Application

human subject review process, all references to the company or individuals who we met during our site visit remain confidential.

3 Case Study: Achieving Integrated Project Delivery

The following case study is an example of the result of our research. It describes how the legal rights to a Building Information Modeling system were purchased by an integrated architecture, real estate, and construction company and later used, together with significant organizational changes, to achieve what they have called "Integrated Project Delivery."

The organization described in this case began as a 90-year old, established, family-owned construction company. There are more than 600 employees, distributed among 10 offices nationwide and internationally. Their 70-80 percent repeat rate with customers shows they have been successful.

The company determined that the construction business was becoming increasingly competitive. Average profit margins for constructors had been reduced from 5 percent to about 2.5 or 3 percent. They believed that continuing to do business the traditional way was fruitless.

Rather than continue their traditional construction business, they decided to take the lead and help reinvent the industry. This meant developing a totally integrated approach to building. The goal of this organization was to reduce both the cost and time of construction by removing the "pain" in the construction process on a project-by-project basis.

The company has made many, permanent changes to achieve its goal of integration. Several years ago, it merged completely with an architecture firm and added to its staff experts in real estate development. It has also formed formal alliance agreements with manufacturers and suppliers and invested heavily in software development. Changes made in the company, culture, and work processes are:

3.1 Acquisition of architecture and real estate expertise

The company recognized the need to systematically include other disciplines into their internal work processes. Therefore, in 1999 the company merged with a 45-person architectural firm. Previously, real estate development experts had also been added. This additional organizational capability provided the foundation for an integrated approach to design and construction, and provided the basis for internal organizational learning.

3.2 Changes in company leadership and culture

Over a period of several years, the board of directors changed from those with an all-construction background to directors with a wide range of backgrounds. The 10-member board of directors now includes representatives from architecture, real estate, and financial management as well as construction. At the operational level, interdisciplinary project teams were also established. The architecture and construction groups initially maintained separate offices. Recently, the lease and renovation of additional space has allowed these project teams to become fully integrated groupings of estimators, architects and constructors.

3.3 R&D software investment

As the organization was changing, the leadership of the company strongly believed that "technology tools dictate the way we work." Thus, the company began searching for software to facilitate the integration of design and construction information. They were unable to find an "off-the-shelf" software solution. After some research and experimentation the company bought the rights to a parametric, object-oriented, solid modeling software package, Reflex, and hired in-house software developers (see Figure 2). This software initiative began in 1996, but it has only been within the past 18 months that it has been used on projects by this company.

The software can best be described as providing value engineering at very early stages in the building design process. It incorporates a great deal of specific information, such as building codes for specific locations, costs provided by specific suppliers, and engineering calculations for systems such as the building structure and energy analysis. It also contains construction rules so that the concrete pours can be calculated. Structurally, the system can perform detailed calculations down to the level of determining rebar and mesh sizes.

The outputs of the program consist of detailed cost estimates, architectural details, outline specifications (in Microsoft Word format), and a construction schedule (in Microsoft Project format). The level of detail provided by the program is very extensive. It will soon be able to produce cut ticket details for manufacturers and suppliers. Due to the user interface, significant training is required before a user can become proficient. At present, the program models about 70 percent of a building, mainly the core and shell.

To date, this software has mostly been used as a cost estimating and planning tool at very early design stages. One of the first integrated projects to be modeled with this software was a 200,000 sq. ft. office building. Using this software and working as an integrated team the company was able to obtain a cost savings of about 18 percent and a reduction in delivery time of 30 percent.

3.4 Work process changes

This company believes that subcontractors possess most of the knowledge in construction. Gaining access to this knowledge and integrating it into the work process is fundamental to developing an integrated delivery system. By developing on-going relationships with subcontractors, suppliers and manufacturers, it was possible to identify redundancies, inefficiencies and time-consuming tasks that increase costs. The key to making these improvements in the work process is a separate, customized alliance contract with each subcontractor. The goal for every alliance contract is to reduce delivery time, get a better price, and improve methods of working together.

Each alliance agreement is different because each supplier is different. Typically, suppliers successfully bid only a fraction of their jobs. This results in significant unnecessary work and increases supplier costs. The alliance contract guarantees that there will be no bidding and that suppliers will participate during design and disclose their pricing information. Obviously, this requires both trust and appropriate incentives. The incentive for suppliers is the “no bid” guarantee.

3.5 New Marketing Approaches

When selling this integrated delivery process, their reputation as a very good “traditional” contractor is not an advantage. An integrated construction process is significantly different. This has required the company to communicate the benefits of the new process not only to owners, but also to employees who have been involved in their traditional construction business. The integrated delivery process is becoming accepted: 40-50 percent of the remainder of the jobs for the current year is integrated projects.

3.6 Summary and Discussion

Throughout its history this company had developed a reputation as a quality, traditional construction company. In the last few years, it has radically reinvented itself in response to a changing business environment. It has heavily invested in a process and supporting software that is only just beginning to show positive results.

The technology highlighted in this case study was the use of Building Information Modeling together with other organizational changes to achieve a level of vertical integration and efficiency that is unusual in the building and construction industry. The use of a single building model is not a new idea. In an article by (Novitski 2000), Robert Aish explained how Alias Sonata, a single building model system, was introduced to the U.S. only to fail, at least in part, because it required detailed input by architects for the benefit of “downstream” contractors and engineers. The extra effort of the architects was not rewarded by extra compensation. In this case, the incentive issue was either handled internally or through alliance contracts.

4 Very Preliminary Conclusions

For this research purpose, it was our intent to seek out only those companies who are at the leading edge of innovating with the use of information technology. The knowledge obtained from the case study above cannot be generalized to all practices. The AEC industry is very diverse with a wide range of sizes and types of firms. Each time we complete a case study we are presented with ideas worth pursuing instead of conclusions. Here are several ideas that might be worth pursuing.

1) Information technology. This case-study company made a substantial investment to acquire the rights to an object-oriented, parametric modeling system. This indicates the importance of this decision to achieving their vision of integrated project delivery. However, they also realized that this technology alone would not be sufficient. At this point in their evolution, the case-study organization has concluded that successful, integrated projects are due 80% to the changes in work process and only 20% to the software technology.

2) Work Process and Collaboration. Work group productivity and process improvement are two areas that are heavily influenced by information technology. However, this case study points out that the technology may need to be augmented by other work process issues. Internally, the case-study company reformed all of its work processes into multidisciplinary teams that were previously co-located. Furthermore, various organizations in the design and building process have a tendency to protect their own interests. Sharing competitive information is not the norm in this industry. The alliance contracts with external suppliers were the mechanism used to overcome this potentially significant obstacle. The building information modeling that was done on each project using internal software was the key to facilitate the integration of information.

3) Cost and schedule reductions. In our case study, the company’s main business goals were reductions in cost and schedule. Merging multiple organizations under the

umbrella of a single company can eliminate some scheduling problems and reduce costs. As indicated by one author (Coase 1937), transaction costs that occur within a firm are lower than transactions costs using the market. He also determined that the cost of constantly developing new contracts with outside firms can be higher "relative to those of signing a long-term contract with an employee who agrees to carry out the commands of the employer."

4) Incentives. The numbers of external subcontractors on even medium sized-projects are too numerous and diverse to merge into a single company. The ability to achieve significant collaboration in this case study was may be addressed by improving incentives through specific alliance contracts with each external subcontractor and supplier. Trust was maintained by a specific guarantee that the subcontractor would not be asked to submit bids to be considered on projects. This case study suggested that the lack of appropriate incentives may be an important reason why collaborative design tools do not achieve their full promise.

The purpose of this on-going study is to identify innovative approaches to the delivery of design and construction projects that rely heavily on the use of digital processes for their effectiveness. While we do not expect to be able to generalize the findings, we anticipate that these examples may provide interesting prototype models that may point the way to the future of the design and construction industry.

During the site visit our informants said they had participated in a seminar conduced by Clayton Christensen (Christensen 1997), whose book, *The Innovator's Dilemma*, raised some interesting questions and potentials for their company. Christensen argued that major innovations are not likely to be developed by large, established companies. His research suggested that truly revolutionary innovations—those that could change industries—are most likely to come from small companies who do not have an established market with established customer expectations. It will be interesting to see if the company reported in this case study will achieve its goal of reinventing the design and construction industry.

We plan to conduct additional site visits to innovative firms that explore various parts of the design and construction industry. Among the types of organizations that we plan to contact are: 1) one of the "virtual" architectural practices that have formed out of several smaller firms in separate geographical locations, 2) an innovative supplier or manufacturer, 3) a large owner, and 4) other firms offering integrated services under one roof.

References

Christensen, C. M. (1997). *The innovator's dilemma.* New York: Harper Business.

Coase, R. (1937). The nature of the firm. *Economica* (November 1937):386-405.

Eastman, C. (1999). *Building product models: computer environments supporting design and construction.* CRC Press.

Henderson, L. (2002). Paths to collaboration. Artifice, Inc. Available from: http://architectureweek.com/2002/0522/tools_1-1.html

Johnson, R., M. Clayton, G. Xia, J.-H. Woo, and Y. Song. (2002). The strategic implications of e-commerce for the design and construction industry. *Engineering, construction and architectural management* 9(2):241-248.

Novitski, B. J. (2000). Turning today's research into tomorrow's software. Artifice, Inc. Available from: http://www.architectureweek.com/2000/0705/tools_3-1.html

Form Follows Software

Pierluigi Serriano
University of California, Berkeley

Abstract

Software selection affects design outcome. Computer applications externalize in their graphical interface and in their internal logic a set of assumptions about how objects are constructed and space is represented. Accessibility of tools is in direct correlation with their rate of use. Depending on how user-friendly particular functions are, their use will appear with higher frequency than those foreign to the technological frames of the user groups for which software is designed. As each software is geared towards the needs of specific communities, it replicates in digital fashion those disciplinary practices already present in the analog world. However, modeling results are bracketed at its inception the very moment a particular 3D package is chosen from a diverse array of digital offerings. If the application adopted is designed to appeal to the computer animation industry, the modeling results will bear the imprint of those organic qualities: buildings will appear character-like. Since computer programs have built-in slant meant to aid disciplinary specific users, they yield families of designs with formal commonalities. Unquestionably, proficiency of software use also broadens inventiveness of design. Nevertheless some applications make particular transformations harder to achieve, and as a result will be likely to exclude those modeling options from architects' imaginary world.

Keywords: modeling options, built-in slants, form-making, technology of orders.

Form Follows Software

Pierluigi Serriano
University of California, Berkeley

1 Introduction

In the bestseller *The Tipping Point*, *Washington Post* reporter Malcom Gladwell gives a provocative account of how ideas and trends snowball from being the prerogative of a narrow group of acolytes to becoming object of collective attention in global communities. He argues that there is a moment in the history of any macro scale social phenomenon when a ripple effect kicks in, its rate of diffusion escalating exponentially to peaks unimaginable in the early stage of its growth. The sudden rise of sales of Hush Puppies—fashionable shoes in the American market—and the inexplicable change of crime rates in New York City neighborhoods of Brownsville and East New York are two manifestations of tipping points. The author proposes to think of these rapid developments and spreads of social events as epidemics in order to understand processes of reciprocal influences and behavioral fluctuations in groups (Gladwell 2002).

Digital Design had its tipping point in the mid-nineties, but traces of its up-and-coming pervasiveness are distributed in the history of modernity. The twentieth century was the stage for the celebration of scientific knowledge. Disciplinary domains underwent a process of scientification that recast the expectations and hopes of what had then become the knowledge society (Böhme and Stehr 1986). Computer technology matured under the pressure of defense priorities, but spilled over to non-military purposes in the fifties. In the realm of computer visualization, Sketchpad made its entrance in 1962 giving birth to the field of computer graphics through the effort of Ivan Sutherland (Gere 2002). A computer-generated mesh, flying in an imaginary non-place, first appeared in the January1965 issue of Architectural Record. The article titled "Will the Computer Change the Practice of Architecture?" reported on the future avenues of Computer Aided Design. A great many of these unprecedented resources were discussed at a conference at the Boston Architectural Center held on December 5th, 1964, in the presence, among others, of Serge Chermayeff and Walter Gropius. As the readership was being coaxed into the magic of fluid forms, machine-generated aesthetics, and tales of liberation from the dictatorship of the glass box, architecture was officially registering the introduction of computers in its horizon.

2 Methods

The argument of this paper is constructed using qualitative research methods to identify modes of use of computer applications in architectural practices, whose members have diverse hands-on expertise with the software. "If you want to understand what a science is . . . you should look at what practitioners do" (Geertz 1973). The implementation of qualitative methods through interviews and non-participant observation is designed to retrieve what the anthropologist Clifford Geertz calls "thick description." This notion shapes a methodological approach that factors in the socio-cultural environment in which human actions take place. In the context of this paper, using computer technology is enmeshed in the subculture of the workplace and the personal trajectories of its community members (Forsythe 2001).

Two levels of analysis inform the paper:
First, a comparative approach between three modeling programs adopted in diverse architectural practices and of appeal to signature architects. Literature review and usability testing will help to stake out the organizational properties of each graphical interface. This will cast light on ease of use and attitudes toward the extent to which computers can formally generate design outside of the broader set of concerns—social, cultural, technical, structural, and so on—in which architecture is customarily practiced.

Second, six case-studies are used to gain an insider's perspective on the adoption of 3D Modeling packages in the design process. Unstructured interviews were conducted to retrieve data on behavioral patterns in sequencing computational functions to monitor the incremental refinements of design ideas. Although the focus of the paper is to establish a correlation—and possible causation—between commands and digital forms, narratives of team members interaction, and profiles of personal and professional backgrounds of the parties involved will be variably inserted into the text.

3 The Precedents

While in the '60s only a few architectural firms were already adopting CAD software for production aims, it took twenty more years for this technology to gain broader exposure and leave an imprint on the imagination of architects. Those familiar with the early stage of rendering algorithms will remember the iconic computer image of the Museum of Contemporary Art in Los Angeles by Arata Isozaki at the beginning of the eighties, maybe the first digital eye stopper in architectural memory. Reminiscent of the early paintings of the Italian painter Giorgio De Chirico, the solitude of that suspended landscape, with primary shapes arranged on an evenly lit ground plane, epitomized the start of a new era in architectural culture. Ever since, Computer Aided Design has transitioned from being the monopoly of competence of professional elites to being routine expertise in the contemporary design office. Twenty years later, Digital Design is a collector of widespread media attention and an uncontested object of professional interests.

The ever increasing level of computer literacy in the architectural workplace has swiftly permeated every aspect of the practice of architectural design. It is widely accepted to argue that the adoption of digital technology in professional practice streamlines the production process, empowers the design team, and multiplies exponentially the exploration of alternative schemes. As of 2003, the sight of a drafting board in an office is often interpreted either as the tangible remainder of an obsolete mode of production or a nostalgic holding on to a bygone approach to the making of architecture. In the analog age, a case among others, those conversant with Descriptive Geometry had obvious advantages in form-making compared to others who had less developed modeling skills. Comparatively speaking, to draw by hand a three point perspective was for many an intimidating, complicated, and labor intensive effort than crafting a single point perspective. It would take days and a much higher level of skills to deliver comfortably seductive bird-eye views: that was the prerogative of those few designers who were fully conversant with the complexities of descriptive geometry. The result was the abundance of single point perspectives in the representation of architectural designs, also as a byproduct of its being simpler to construct than multiple-point perspective. Nevertheless the rectilinear quality of many of those visions had its roots in the glorification of the rational and the efficient. The historically unprecedented possibility to represent the infinite through a dot (the vanishing point), gave rise to iconic images charged with highly symbolic value, among them The Last Supper by Leonardo and View of an Ideal City by unknown. But even more importantly the profile of those shapes was scripted in the very tools adopted to draw. Factual limits in the repertoire of forms were set by the very use of T-squares, the triangles, and compass to externalize arrangements existing in the mind.

4 The Hypothesis

It is my contention that the current 3D software packages follow the same logic of their analog counterpart. Morphological manipulations and their resulting forms can hardly be separated from the software that defined them. The construction of the graphical interface, the arrangement of the modeling and rendering icons, and the organization of the interrelated menus structure the task environment and the input of the topological data. As a result, their digital outcomes are bracketed in geometrically identifiable limits and bring about strongly patterned sets of architectural propositions. It follows that the choice of software is a primary, if not the utmost variable, bearing heavily on digital design. “Technological innovations open up new fields of possibility, which society either ignores completely or embraces without the assumption of any mechanical predetermination” (Lévy 1997). In the context of this paper the notion of form is extended to include not only shapes, outlines, or configuration of anything, but also the broader capabilities of software to generate formal outcomes in space. This entails looking beyond the focus on objecthood and assessing how mental processes find their digital correlatives in a modeling program.

If it is common sense today to use computers in the conception and execution of design, that common sense is not innocent. This paper presents a set of critical questions raised through a cursory analysis of three widely used modelers—Form*Z, 3DS Max, and Maya. These will be concisely analyzed in their graphical interfaces and compared in the modeling results that they yield. The thesis is that there exists a “Form*Zness,” a “3 DSMaxness,” and a “Mayaness”—if you will—built into the code that either enhances or hinders the exploration of three-dimensional alternatives in the design process other than those readily available in the defaults of each software. Tool is here defined as a combinatory procedure granting either interactively or through numeric input the generation of form. The ease—or difficulty—of use of each tool is in direct correlation with the frequency of use of that tool in the course of the modeling progression. If that procedure is scripted so that it can be grasped relatively easily by non-expert users, groupings of those shapes will populate the design. The number of iterations of that particular procedure will produce a distinct volumetric hallmark belonging to a family of identifiable forms; the more user-friendly the modeling tools, the higher the occurrence of those predetermined shapes will be in the formal outcome. A concrete and ubiquitous manifestation of this logic is the current proliferation of blob architecture.

5 Software Selection

Choosing a software is making a commitment to a world view. In basic programming practices, when the task to be accomplished is complex, pseudo code is used as the intermediary language to specify a sequence of actions to achieve a set of quantifiable goals (Grillmeyer 1998). In plain English, the software developer states a plan in linear fashion of how to accomplish the intended result. That pseudo code bounds the action domain, encapsulating the realm of possibilities end-users will have to come to terms with when implementing their design intentions. “The programmer designs the language that creates the world in which the user operates” (Winograd and Flores 1987).

It is widely known that computer applications in the private sectors target communities of potential users, and embed their practice into the code, in order to transform them into loyal buyers. Market demands are paramount forces in dictating the expansion of capabilities and the future directions of applications. Since a computer program stands for the computational arrangement of assumptions about how work is performed and how the process can be carried out, it follows that we shape software just as software shapes us. We could write a paper in Form*Z, and draw a plan in Microsoft Word, but we customarily choose not to do that, or at least this is not the first use that comes to mind. Form*Z is for modeling, whereas Microsoft Word is for writing. We operate according to our technological frames

(Orlikowski 1993), i.e. mental models or frame of references structuring our understanding of the environment around us and the technology that supports it. These cognitive elements are shared via similarities in educational and professional background as well as social interactions: they are the tissue allowing us to make sense of the world.

"Technologies are ways of building orders in the world" (Langdon, in MacKenzie and Wacjman 1995). The notion of value-free technology is untenable. For each technology, there is a conscious plan to structure human activity narrowing the array of effective courses of action available to the user. Technology is intentional just as design is. Today multiple metaphors guide the interpretative process of current digital design, particularly when it comes to arguing for what is known as blob design, the lure of the informal. Clay has now become digital to sculpt imaginary spaces and virtual worlds that we can see, yet can't quite grasp in their tectonics. The rhetoric of the polished renderings invariably touches the slick visions of positive architectural realities. Computer applications are partial accomplices in the fabrication of these fantasies. From our experience in the real world, we know that it is virtually impossible to have a perfectly flat surface using physical clay, and equally unattainable to draw organic forms using the straight edge, triangles and protractors. Each instrument embodies a range of possible uses, not all of them.

"When a work of architecture departs from culturally established patterns, it always requires a collective effort of clarification" (Bonta 1979). Kostas Terzidis ventures in outlining a taxonomy of the clichés, morphological common places, and formal strategies defining classes of digital designs (Terzidis forthcoming 2003). Caricature Form (Deformation), (Un)Folding Form, Hybrid Form (Morphing), Kinetic Form (Motion), Warped Eye, and Algorithmic Form are the classificatory categories used to comprehend the singularities of forms unimaginable a decade earlier. Drawing upon aspects of human perception problematized throughout cultural history, Terzidis offers a post-rationalized reading of geometrical bundles. But where is the software in all this? The following is a cursory review of the modeling programs, their menus, their defaults, and their digital underpinnings. Most of the remarks will attempt in a necessarily incomplete form to outline some of the basic principles of the software and its mode of use.

6 Form*Z

Form*Z is a general purpose modeler conceived and designed by architect Chris Yessios and a team, for his fellow architectural colleagues. Despite its initial focus on modeling for architects, Form*Z has progressively widened its scope to accommodate trans-disciplinary modeling needs. Officially released in 1991, this software has gained increased recognition among an architectural elite of signature designers such as Morphosis, and Coop Himmelblau, among the most notable. Yessios maintains that the underlying mathematical geometry technique of the program is Void Modeling (Serraino 2002). "Void modeling offers the means to deal with architectural design during its soft and dynamically tentative states, while a design solution is still unknown and under exploration" (Yessios 1987). Drawing from the notion that certain classes of objects are containers of fluids, a digital object in Void Modeling comprises of a container and a contained part. The former is an envelope of 0 width on which different attributes can be assigned; the latter is responsive to modeling transformations on objects so that they yield satisfactory results (Yiessios 1987).

As a default, the graphical interface displays a single viewport containing a ground plane in a 30x60 axonometric view. Multiple windows can be opened to model objects saved on the same file. Extrusion is a key modeling principle for object formation. Broadly speaking, massing is built by outlining an open or closed 2D shape on the ground plane and extruding the resulting shape either to an infinite vanishing point (box-like) or to a finite point (cone and pyramid-like). From these entities, multiple entities can be generated through the derivative tools, giving a wide spectrum of modeling capabilities. Meshes and C-Meshes (Controlled Meshes), among others tools, add further capabilities to modeling, but even in those cases extrusion of those outlines gives massing to otherwise two-dimensional objects. Coordinates can be accurately typed when needed, yet precision is at the discretion of its users. According to the case studies here introduced, Form*Z tends to be an excellent tool to take the temperature—so to speak—of a design under formation.

Although rendering and animation are available, the strength of the program rests on its modeling capabilities. Within the architectural world, Form*Z is intuitive enough to be picked up by architects, as it replicates in the digital realm what they are accustomed doing the most: physical modeling. This has made the application very popular in the Anglo-Saxon world, with peaks of users in Asia, and Europe as well. Ever since the launch of Form*Z 4.0, a new modular structure has been introduced to give users the option to be more selective in the modeling tools they want readily available according to their disciplinary domains. Additional plug-ins and the possibility to run scripts have further broadened the modeling capacity of the program.

7 3DS max

Former 3D Studio Max, 3DS MAX 5 is a solid modeler with extensive use in design visualization, animation, and rendering for film, televisions, and game developments. Most of its acclaim in the digital community is based on its ever-increasing potential to produce quasi photographic images and its flexibility in generating accurate animations. This polygon-based software offers extensive capabilities to achieve unprecedented realism through a distinctive graphical interface. In order to accomplish these results, a steep learning curve faces users due to the layout of the menus and the logic behind the modeling procedures.

Five different areas construct the interface of the application. The 3DS MAX default layout displays at the center of the interface a view port configuration with four distinct views which provide navigation in the virtual space. Similar to the orthogonal projections of Monge, from the top left going clockwise there is a top, front, perspective, and left view. Surrounding the edges of the view, a series of tabs gives access to tens of thousands of commands (Metossian 2001). Drop-down menus, context-sensitive menus, rollouts, flyouts, floaters, and floating and docking toolbars are some of the ways in which the user can access the software power. Although the interface appears tightly structured, way-finding can be a daunting task. Commands are layered to the extent that it requires context-based extensive practice to take full advantage of the digital resources of the application. Modeling allows for the construction of parametric as well as non-parametric objects on ground planes. Generally speaking, outlines are drawn on a ground plan, then extruded, and further modified. Foundation of object creation to generate basic geometric forms are the cone, the cube, the cylinder, the sphere (Metossian 2001). These premade geometry sets are the stepping stone for assembling more complicated scenes. Additional levels of sophistication in the modeling process are available through the Create tab with extra options to include extended primitives, meshes, NURBS, patches, and more. However, modeling transformations can take numerous steps what the results they are supposed to yield. To perform a Boolean subtraction on compound object, for instance, takes six steps, as opposed to the same operation done in Form*Z, which requires only two steps once digital objects overlap.

Rendering and animation are two main winning points of the software. As opposed to Form*Z, whose primary focus is modeling, 3DS MAX offers a full array of possibilities to create scenes and add life to them. Texture mapping, the available material library, and lighting options provide wide range of choices to detail the model and add a high degree of realism to its virtual worlds. Import and Export procedures are available to take advantage of the strengths of other programs making the software either the environment where the model is fully assembled and rendered or a transitional program for its rendering capabilities. In the course of the proposed case studies, it will show that 3DS MAX is precisely used in the latter fashion. MAX scripts are also available to supply users with additional modeling choices.

8 Maya

MAYA is a node based program (Riddel 2003). This means that objects are represented through numerous nodes each editable interactively or mathematically. It is a rather resource-intensive application requiring a substantial amount of RAM and processor power, and a three-button mouse. Some of its features are: polygon-modeling tools, advanced character-animation tools, dynamics (particle simulations to reproduce real-word forces following the laws of physics), effects, Sub-division surfaces, Matchmoving, and more. These digital capabilities endow users with great control over the behavior and look of the form generated and its subsequent editing. Similar to the 3DS MAX, the MAYA interface captures in a rather condensed form menu sets all amounting to countless commands. The default layout displays four views, called panes: Front, Side, Top, and Perspective. The menu sets are available on the top left corner of the interface in the Status line, which holds selection functions. Directly below is the Shelf Menu displaying the most often-used tools. In each pane, the user can access additional menus. Commands and menus, just like much software, can be reached in many different ways.

A powerful built-in feature of MAYA is the Construction History. In the progressive refinement of a model, the discrete steps are digitally memorized. Should the starting point for the modeling change, the software applies all the transformations entered to that point. NURBS, polygons, and subdivisions are the primary primitives of MAYA. NURBS (NonUniform Rational Basis Spline) are equations defining curves or surfaces. Instead of tracing a curve through a set of points, the B-spline defines a curve sensitive to the position of the defining vertex points. The software capability to create smooth surfaces is a point of appeal to those designers interested in fluid forms. Once objects are generated, they undergo surgical transformations to accommodate interdisciplinary design intent. In addition, MAYA allows to run scripts to further extend its capabilities.

The primary user groups are film and video artists, computer game developers, and design professionals who use it to construct sophisticated digital imagery, animation, and visual effects. The program is designed largely for character and organic modeling. In architecture, a younger generation of designers—with either formal or informal associations with the architecture program of Columbia University in New York City—is at the forefront of MAYA users to identify alternative approaches to form making. However, due to the system requirements and its associated costs this software is used by a rather restricted group when compared to Form*Z and 3DS MAX. Nonetheless, the introduction of MAYA in the kit of digital tools is central for architectural discourse. Designs engaging the capabilities of MAYA have triggered debates in the specialized community and the general audience about form and its ramifications in the tectonics of artifact as well as its yet to be determined civic signification.

9 Six Case Studies

The proposed examples present similarities in how the adoption of computer technology has informed and influenced design decisions. In all cases design ideas were already formed prior to implementation of digital technology, yet software was pivotal in giving final formal expression to those visions. Here architects capitalize on computer visualization and modeling capabilities with a broad spectrum of attitudes concerning the release of control to the machine for the generation of forms. Although these six professional practices are different in scale of projects undertaken, design attitude, and office organization, the adoption of computer technology has broadened the opportunities to explore design themes which are the hallmark of their individual signatures. Three case studies are based on Form*Z, one is a combination of 3D Studio Max and Form*Z, one shows a project modeled with Maya, and the last one presents an unconventional use of AutoCAD.

1 Wes Jones

In the personal trajectory of Wes Jones, former founding partner of the now dissolved firm Holt, Hinshaw, Pfau, Jones, the transition from hand drawing to digital output occurred in 1994. As he was shopping around for CAD programs on display at MACWORLD in San Francisco, Jones picked Form*Z. "We detected a congruence between our practice and the software assumptions," he recalls in a phone interview. The imaginary world informing Jones's architectural visions was pre-digital, without the computer being necessarily part of its formation. His fascination with mechanical parts, joinery, and the aesthetic of the machine constructed the rhetoric of his drawings and renderings and concocted a distinguished mechanical formalism (Figure 1).

Looking at the materials of that world was the motivating source of his designs. A comparison between the pre and post-digital portfolio exhibits consistencies of tectonic references, yet with one distinct characteristic: increased detailing (Figure 2). "For us there has been little if any change that could be ascribed to the software, so maybe it is just a happy accident that we chose a software right away that so perfectly fit our needs . . . Form*Z was designed as a solid modeler for architects, and this is how we had always thought about design, i.e. stuff that could be modeled with chipboard and styrene and plex, so Form*Z has always been obvious to us in the same way—only difference is the added possibility for detail" (Wes Jones, e-mail message. 04 May 2003) (Figures 3 and 4).

Jones is himself an accomplished Form*Z user. His first hand exposure to computers goes back to his involvement in the military, where he became quite conversant using Fortran. During his graduate days at Harvard—he used Modelshop, a CAD package which is no longer supported. As physical model making was where he invested time in design investigation, the logic of Form*Z turned out to be a good fit with his way of working out designs. However, none of the parametric capabilities available today in Form*Z feed Jones's work. He admits that he uses the Mesh Tool, occasionally, but modeling options such as the Metaformz primitives and editing are never implemented. As far as modeling is concerned the commands available in the earlier versions of the application were sufficient enough to assemble his digital landscapes. It follows that although the application has grown to incorporate more and more organic modeling commands with the purpose of conquering wider market sectors, the architect shows no interest in that direction. His work builds primarily on the notion of extrusion. Objects are first built as 2D shapes on the reference planes and extruded according to the available Object Types. Then the Derivatives palette supplies the architect with the necessary tools for the geometry he is keen on. Jones laments the limited benefits of the current ray tracing algorithm. As soon as the scene has some advanced level of details, he maintains, Form*Z fails to deliver in that capacity. For Jones, architecture is an activity that goes far beyond simple form-making. It certainly is disposition of objects in space, but this is only one side of the story. In his view, architects have to come to terms with the public nature of artifacts. Computers—therefore—are not generative, but powerful companion to an articulate, precise, and already fully pre-determined vision of the world. However, computers also brought new challenges: the fast-pace of computer development triggers anxiety in users, who are constantly panting behind the latest in software and hardware development, hardly ever fully investigating the power of those tools. To echo some of the most recent words of renowned New York Times critic, Herbert Muschamp, "Architecture is not just sculpture blown up to urban scale. It is a social art, and for many, it will operate as a symbol of unwanted change" (Muschamp May 18, 2003). That is why Jones expresses no interests in programs like MAYA, which he feels are tools for the production of self-indulgent forms.

2 Thom Faulders: Beige Design

Thom Faulders is the sole principal of a small architectural firm called Beige Design based in Berkeley, California. Recipient of numerous design awards, Faulders undertakes the question of digital form and its physical construction. The use of computers comes in after well defined initial concepts have been formed. Three-dimensional exploration of those ideas is carried out through physical and digital models. For Faulders Form*Z offers a visualization technique, a way of testing a notion that precedes the engagement of computer technology. Yet, although substantial portions of the design are formally done directly on the computer, the design forms remain pictorial. "It is a bit like designing in perspective," he says (interview with Thom Faulders 25 June, 2003). The transition from the pictorial to working drawings is still intensely problematic. Once a form has been produced, being able to make exact determinations regarding the dimensions of individual pieces is rather complicated.

The designer has some first-hand knowledge of Form*Z, however he relies on those working with him to implement ideas through the application. Having limited expertise with the general purpose modeler, he believes, might actually help to dodge some of its most obvious uses. This means stretching and bending part of the assumptions on how to construct shapes in Form*Z, to the point of defying codified uses or modes of streamlining the modeling process. Often this comes with the undertaking of supremely long tasks to carve broader digital scenarios. Faulders's main quest is to develop complexity out of regularity. To account for the need of the construction industry to standardize building components, the architect investigates the intersection of unconventional forms and their factual feasibility. Here the software is not generative of form per se, yet it influences form, because it allows intentions to be tested. How

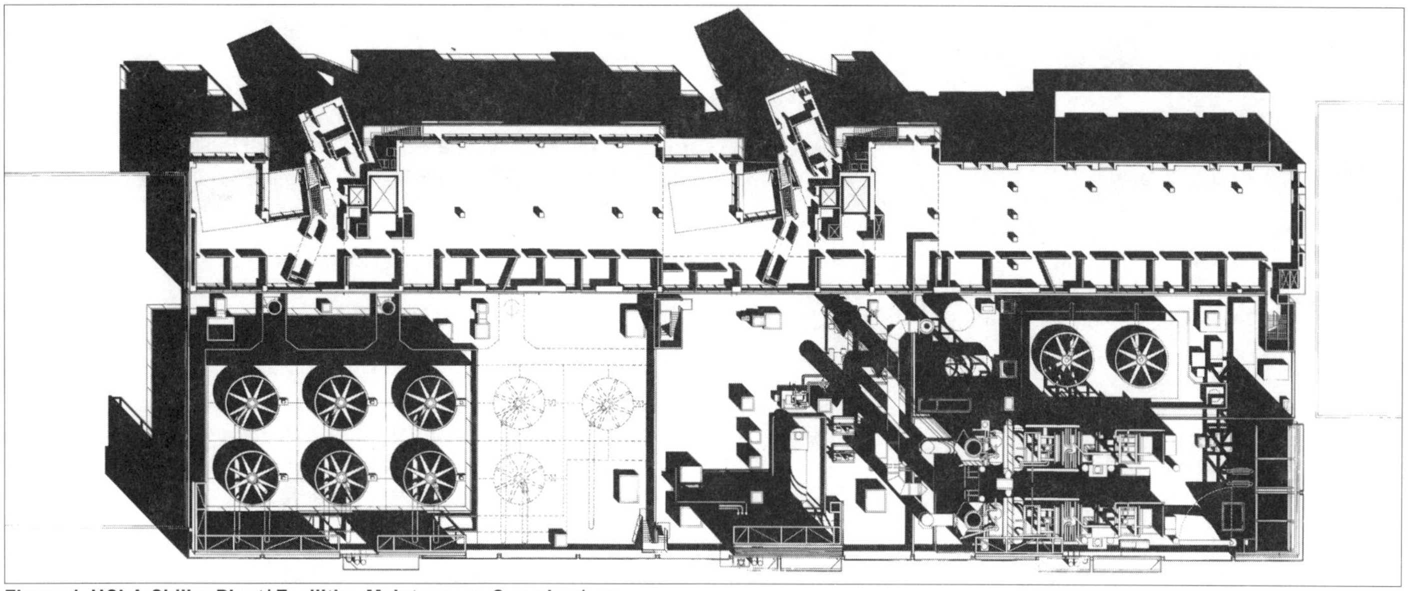

Figure 1. UCLA Chiller Plant/ Facilities Maintenance Complex (pre-computer)

Figure 2. Exterior of Sub-'burb, House of the Future (post-computer)

Figure 3. Close-up of Sub-'burb, House of the Future (post-computer)

does Form*Z play out in this design itinerary?

Three small-scale schemes address the notion of establishing micro modeling units, which produce elaborate spatial proposition through incremental changes and multiplications. Monolithic in their material expressions, they all carry the idea of cloning form out of digital cells. Faulders operates surgically on the individual components and its points of connection to sculpt fluid massing and evocative movements. Of these three laboratory moments, the first is a competition entry for the redesign of a parking lot, the second is an installation, and the third is a volumetric sign for the entry of a subspace within the California College of Arts and Crafts. Although Form*Z was not the starting point, the final three-dimensional outcome in all instances comes from the formal negotiation between the initial design idea and the available modeling tools. Volumes could be distorted to create effects, Faulders adds, yet it was impossible to do it in a measureable way. The constant negotiation between extreme economy of means and the determination to build forms foreign to everyday architectural vocabulary without the costly technology of CAD/CAM brought about a hybrid design-build process.

Figure 4. Interior of Sub-'burb, House of the Future (post-computer)

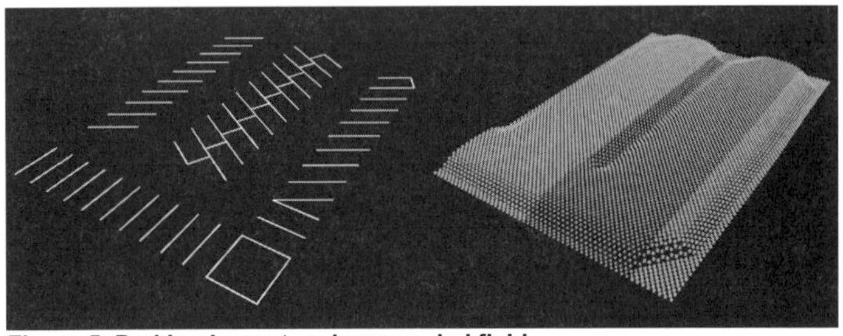

Figure 5. Parking Layout and suspended field

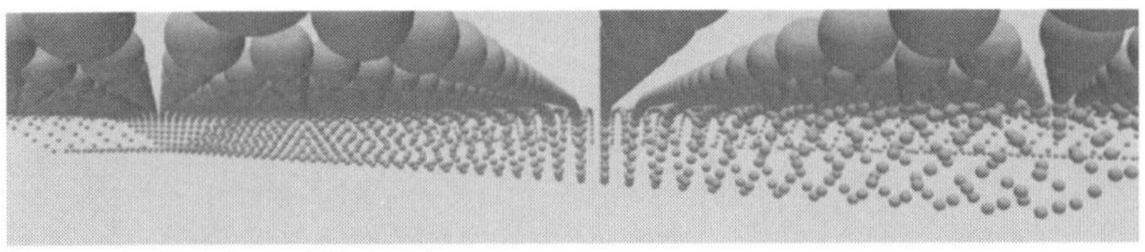

Figure 6. Inside and Outside

Figure 7. Parallax views

Suspended Field is the proposed vision for a parking lot intervention in Cincinnati, Ohio. A veil of plotted points floats on a parking layout to map different conditions of use. Lightweight balls held through cables determine cognitive moments, which help to navigate the space and by virtue of their mutual position effect multiple visual experiences. Multiple sections were drawn to determine a mesh on whose vertexes the balls were individually placed (figures 5, 6, 7).

Particle Reflex is an installation for the San Francisco Museum of Modern Art commissioned in 2001. Here, Faulders confronted the constructability of a fluid form. Repeatable panels and adjusted increments were the ingredients of a strategy designed to make a commitment to the tectonics of this unique shape. Once the volumes have been modeled in Form*Z using meshes, the designer gets into the specific of each panel and adjusts it individually to assemble the conceptual surface (figure 8, 9, 10). Wattis Entry reflects a further refinement in generating atypical planes through stitching construction units each customized differently from its adjacent ones. Form*Z proved to be ineffective in manipulating surfaces in a controlled fashion. After several attempts, Faulders drew the individual sections according to a predetermined design idea. He then transitioned to the digital by precisely drafting the specific outlines and transfer them in an orderly arrangement into the Form*Z environment. From there, he skinned the sections to have a smooth shell. This allowed him to determine the exact size of the discrete elements. In this case the application was stretched to do what was a rather specific mental process, yet not immediately feasible using the conventional tools of Form*Z (figures 11, 12, 13, 14).

3 Tom Leader Studio

A former partner of Peter Walker and Partners, landscape architect Tom Leader embarked in a new professional venture with Phillippe Coignet in 2001. The distinguishing theme of their practice is the examination of site-specific resources and their stratification through time. Leader's biological reading of Rome in 1999 is the starting point for design ideas feeding his later work. In this provocative approach, the landscape architect looks holistically at the transformation of the ecosystem of Rome through the centuries in the course of 3300 years. By slicing time every 200 years and juxtaposing over a dozen of historical transparent plates, Leader generates an analytical artifact of unparalleled critical clarity to grasp in one moment centuries of earth development and land use.

Navigating space through time and mapping the site components via situated readings of the land underpin the current portfolio of the studio. Form*Z is the vehicle for this journey of historical investigation, where these temporal sections are modeled. Each element is assigned a surface style with distinctive color and transparency to make this information readable, a digital see-through to gain insights on its stratified formation. In plotting and superimposing the geological and human-made stratifications determining the current state of a site, Leader defines a new approach toward land use and

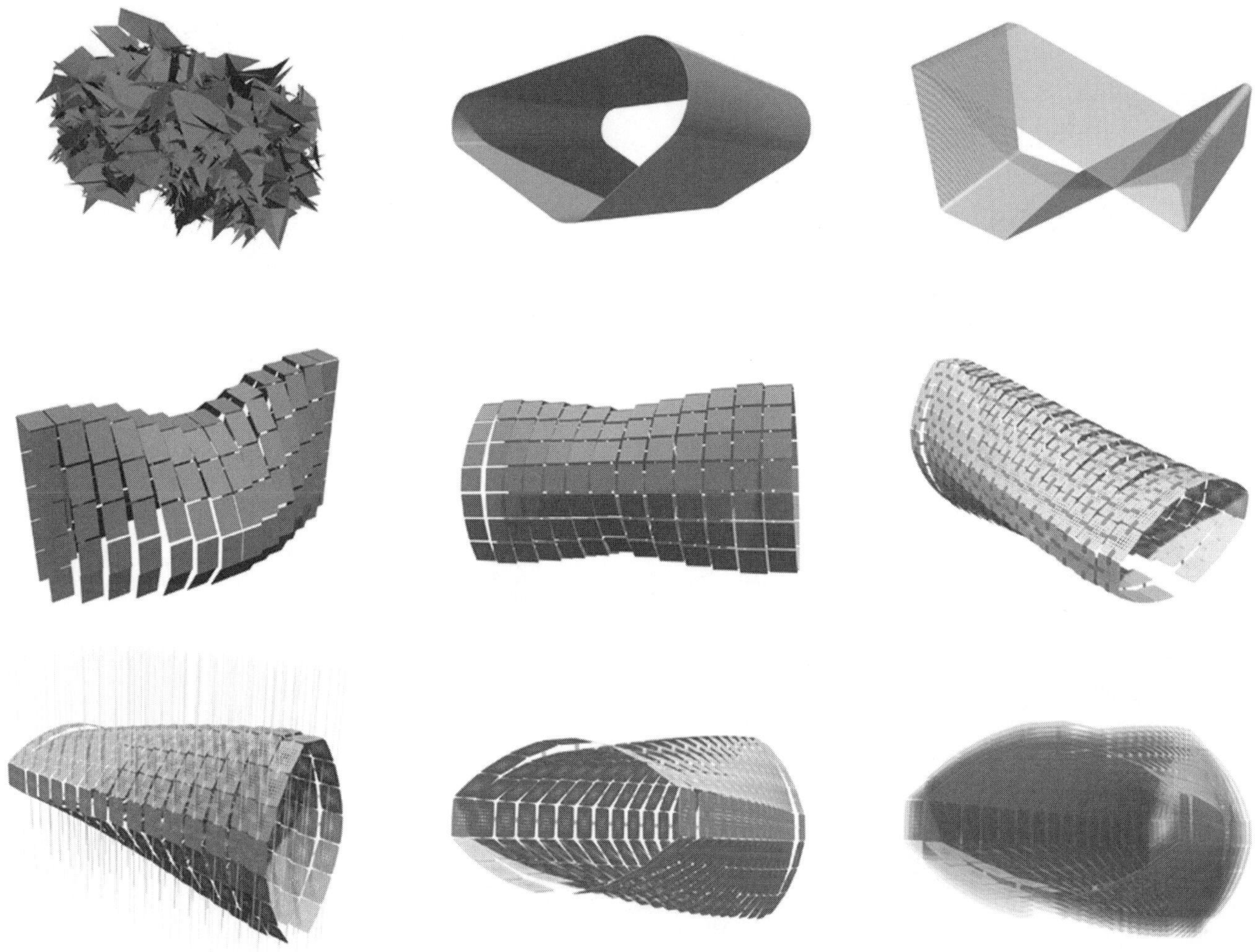

Figure 8. Digital Diagrams

an instrument of civic awareness regarding the environment. Coignet admits that, like Faulders, it is rather hard to manipulate precisely the model in Form*Z to produce accurate and measured transformation, especially when the topological elements are being moved parallel to the reference planes. Vertical changes, instead, are a bit easier to implement.

The competition entry for the Fresh Kills Landfill in Staten Island, New York, makes manifest the notion of sectioning the site through time. The competition was launched to rethink the role of one of the greatest plots of land for the collection of garbage in the New York City area. As the competition was taking place, the terrorist attack of 9/11 struck the World Trade Center. The debris was collected in the Fresh Kills Landfill, giving the site a unique symbolic dimension in American history. Leader's scheme brackets a 150 year-time period: 100 years to the present belonging to the past of Fresh Kills, the remaining projecting layered tendencies into the future. Rather than choosing a prescriptive strategy, the team conceived of a framework, where diverse possibilities of use can take place still within the identity of the site (figures 15, 16,17, 18,19, 20). Form*Z comes into play as a way of testing the spatial implications of overlapping sequential maps of the site, an unexplored form of cartography to bring to the fore the dynamics that make the place what it is today. Layering becomes a mechanism to achieve new consciousness of how functional transformations can unfold within a coherent development of

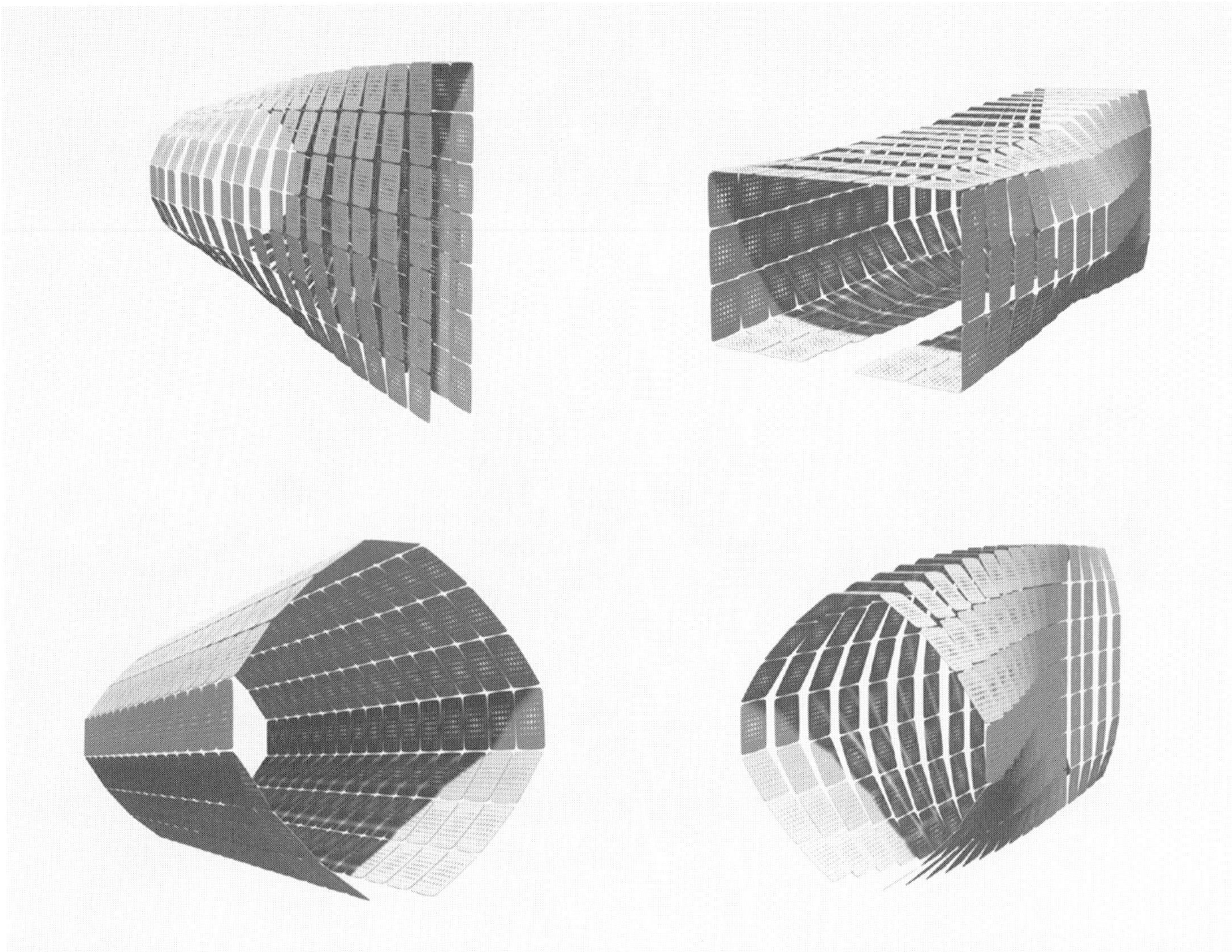

Figure 9. Flex Diagram

diversity. Mapping the local ecosystem, urban debris and its impact on the site's surface, its transportation system, its physical edges, and the composition of the garbage come together in a composite image. Fly-thru animations grant the studio vantage points to assess the dynamic reading of the site, which through public participation would determine the future development of its destiny. This case study presents a rather uncommon approach to mainstream use of the software, yet it offers a critical attitude toward modeling as an opportunity to visualize the socio-cultural and geological forces that make any place the physical reality that it is.

Figure 10. Front View of Installation

Figure 11. Sequence 1

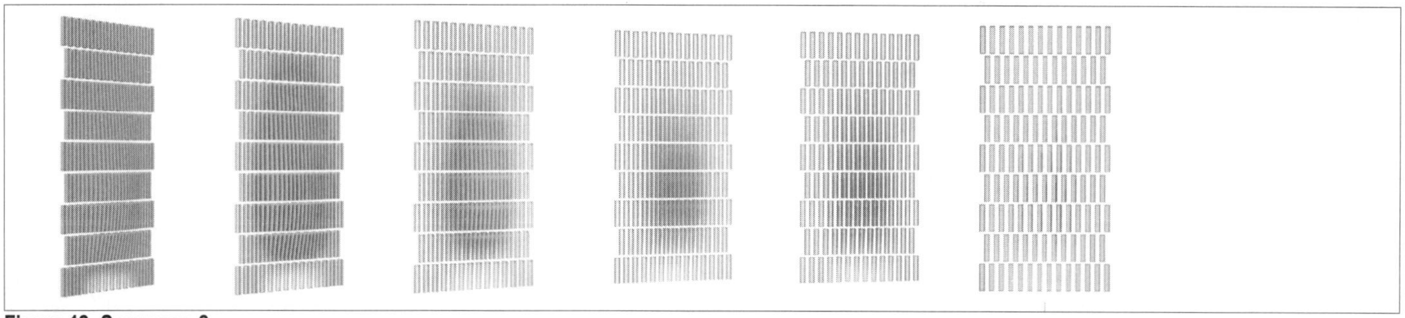

Figure 12. Sequence 2

Figure 13. Final Layout)

Figure 14. Side View of Wattis Entry

Figure 15. Sequence 1

Figure 16. Sequence 2

Figure 17. Sequence 3

Figure 18. Sequence 4

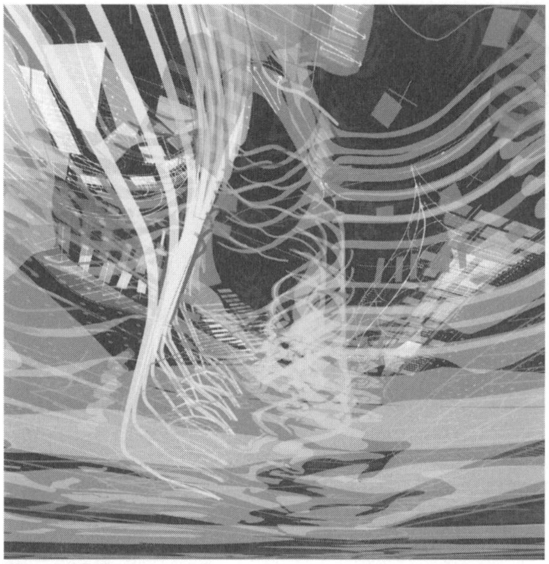

Figure 19. Sequence 5

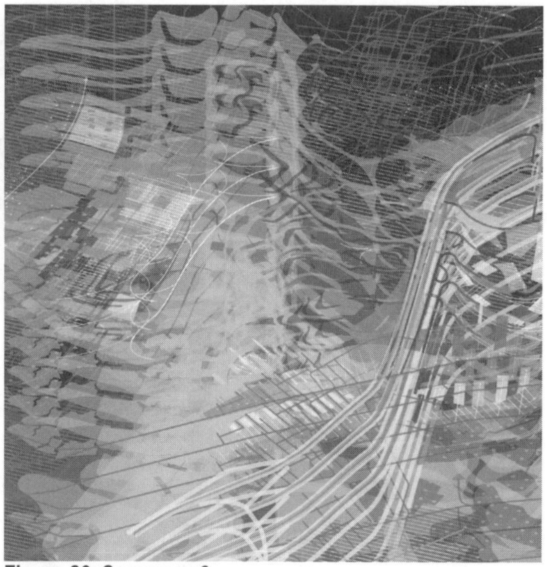

Figure 20. Sequence 6

Figure 21. Changi Airport. Canopies Detail

Figure 22. Changi Airport. Interior Detail

4 Gensler, San Francisco

For Benjamin Ward, a Gensler associate, 3D Studio Max is a powerful rendering program. Modeling, however, presents procedural complexities that in his opinion are absent in Form*Z. "It takes more steps to perform a Boolean operation in 3DS Max than in Form*Z". Despite his expertise in both, Ward deems 3D Studio cumbersome in its modeling capacities due to the organization of the interface, its hidden palettes, and how deep the user has to go to get tools than are critical since the inception of digital modeling. High detailing in 3DS MAX comes with large investment of modeling time. For the Changi Airport scheme in Singapore, Ward used a combination of Form*Z, 3D Studio, and AutoCAD to transition from modeling, to rendering, to measured drawings. Each view was modeled separately to endow the scene with high level of details without encumbering the entire model with unnecessary polygons. Quick studies were done in Form*Z since its internal logic allows designers to explore forms without any significant commitment of dimensions, yet in a rather efficient fashion. Ward initially attempted the same in 3DS MAX, but that proved to be harder than initially estimated.

Great attention was paid in the modeling of the canopies, which was achieved through axial sweeps along one path. Derivatives and Boolean operations were critical to develop the imagery for the skylights (figures 21, 22, 23).

But when it came to study the material quality of its surfaces, their reflections, and the lighting, 3DS MAX demonstrated its power. The Form*Z model was imported in 3DS MAX, materials were assigned, and different light sources were positioned. Lighting studies helped to make further determination on the overall architectural effects and materials to be used. Accuracy

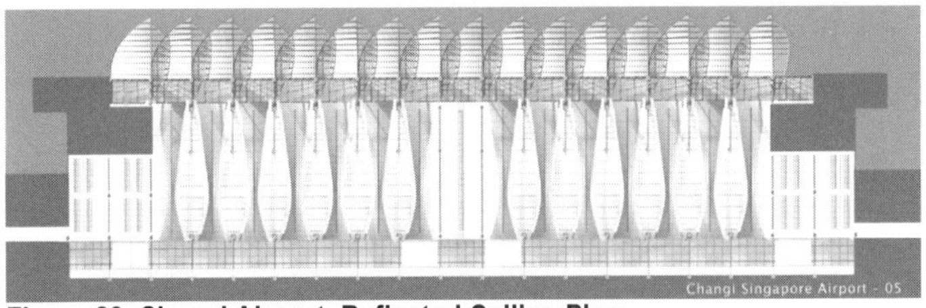

Figure 23. Changi Airport. Reflected Ceiling Plan

Figure 24. Changi Airport. Canopies Detail using Vray

Figure 25. Changi Airport. Detail of Skylights

Figure 26. Changi Airport. Interior

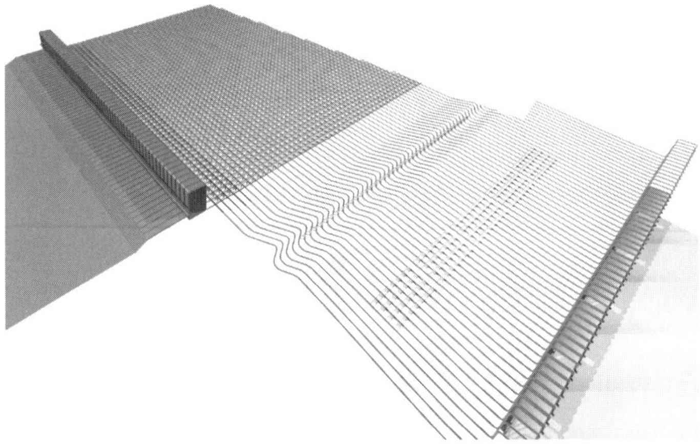
Figure 27. Framework of lines for the lower level

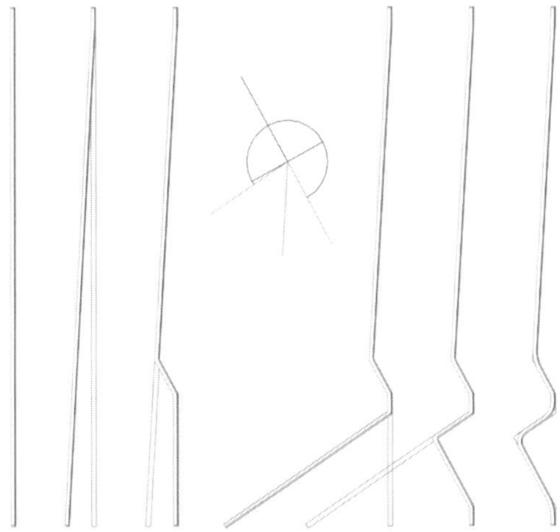
Figure 28. Framework of lines for the lower level

Figure 29. Mapping the victims

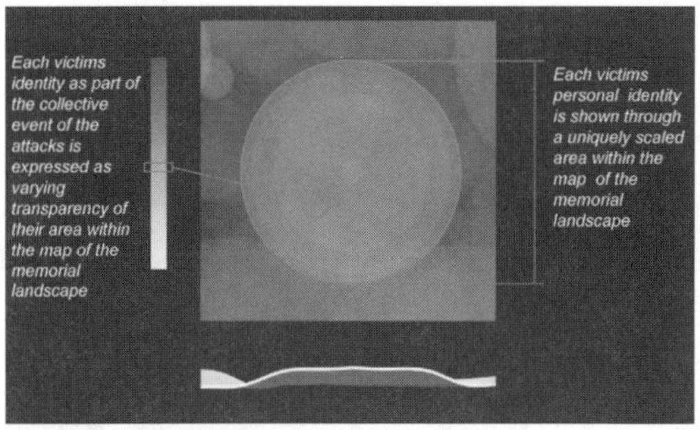

Figure 30. Mapping rules

in lighting simulations were pivotal in the final arrangement of the ceiling structure. In particular, Vray, a plug-in for 3DS MAX, yielded impressive results in the shading of the building components. Global illumination alone generated an image virtually indistinguishable from a physical model (figures 24, 25, 26).

Hopping from one application to the next is customary practice at Gensler, where software is used for what can bring the fastest results with the highest level of accuracy. The world of forms available in Form*Z seems enough to model some of the design choices at Gensler. However, only a few individuals are fully proficient with 3D-modeling. Once the massing is established, it is 3DS MAX that takes the lead in software use and informs the design choices of the office.

5 Cory Clarke and Jason Vigneri-Beane

Cory Clarke is a designer and an instructor of Advanced Digital Design courses at Columbia University in New York City. His proficiency in MAYA and Form*Z (he is co-author of one of the first popular Form*Z tutorials), is a critical vehicle for making informed decisions about software use and design scope. Being aware of the pros and cons of each application, Clarke and Vigneri-Beane adopted a combined approach in modeling by using both MAYA and Form*Z for different portions of their competition entry for the World Trade Center Memorial Competition held in May 2003 to honor the memory of those who perished in the 9/11 attack.

The choice of adopting both programs is directly correlated with the perceived capability to control object formation in each software. The central idea of the scheme is to map on the site the individual trajectories of the victims and their common fate. Personal information of each casualty provides the raw data for the construction of a continuous hardscape. For every life lost in that tragedy, an area with specific physical properties is identified and stitched to adjacent parcels representing other individuals. Once common rules have been established, the resulting landscape gives scale and identity to a global loss of human life. The memorial turns into a site for participatory mourning as well as a space for the experience of private pain. The proposal is articulated into two layers. Memorial markers standing for the silent symbols of the individual deaths dot the lower level. Each marker's position establishes a correlation between the victim and the location of his or her death. Directly above is the undulating public park, a place for gathering and spiritual renewal (figures 27, 28, 29, 30).

To give tangible form to this tragedy was the challenge that the designers undertook using tools that could precisely translate tables of personal data of the victims into a physical artifact. Cory Clarke states: "The reasons why we choose MAYA over any other software are because of (1) MEL, the MAYA embedded language, (2) it is a procedural modeler, and (3) it is a NURBs surface modeler" (Cory Clarke e-mail message, 2 July 2003). The first capability made it possible to convert the database of the victims' profiles into a two-dimensional map through custom made scripts. The next step was the extrapolation of the floating landscape out of the map using NURBs. What makes MAYA so powerful compared to other programs offering NURBs is the creation of seamless fluid objects out of discrete pieces of information in a controlled, editable fashion. As a procedural modeler, the user enters a set of instructions generating previously undetermined form. As the commands are entered, they are remembered in the machine, building up the construction history palette. Once a sequence of commands has been processed, it is possible to go back into that linear path and change the specific instructions. All subsequent modifications would be traced down to its final form. This feature allows for an iterative process, trial and errors, to reach a satisfactory form for the design intent.

For the landscape portion of the project, the process was converting data into a map through MEL and then the map into a surface through NURBs. MAYA granted critical flexibility to achieve desired results about the character of the floating surface. The lower layer comprising the matrix of lines and the memorial markers was modeled in Form*Z. The section of the WTC Memotial designed in Form*Z was then exported in MAYA and then rendered to its final stage. For more basic shapes, ironically MAYA performs less competitively than the general purposed modeler. It follows that choosing MAYA as modeler brings about a set of forms influenced by NURBs. Fluid, pliable shapes are relatively easy to achieve, but modeling and editing primary shapes, according to Clarke, can be more problematic. Designs generated in MAYA will likely exhibit geometrical traits veering away from assembling known sets of Platonic shapes: it will feel more organic (figures 31, 32, 33, 34).

6 Skidmore, Owings & Merrill LLP (SOM), New York

High-rise design is a forte in the design competence of SOM. From the heyday of the mid-century classic Lever House on Park Avenue in New York to the more recent accomplishments disseminated throughout the globe, SOM continues to explore this building type, adding to the skylines of the built environment. Skin and massing are two central concerns in the urban characters of a great many of these vertical statements and constant objects of design explorations. CAD programs were already implemented in the SOM practice of the early seventies.

Figure 31.The two layers of the Memorial

Figure 32. View from the lower layer

Figure 33. Inside the lower level

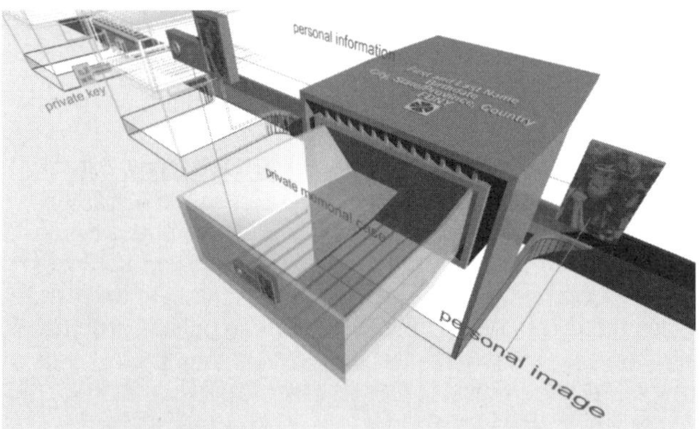

Figure 34. Memorial marker

Specifically the firm had developed a proprietary drafting program called "Draft." Later in a collaboration with IBM, the application changed its name to "AES" (Architecture and Engineering Series). In more recent years the office has switched to AutoCAD. Used often as production tools connected through intranets that allow file sharing by design teams and as marketing devices to attract increasingly demanding clientele, computers in the SOM working routine have recently come to cover a more central role in determining architectural images as well.
A case in point is the competition entry for the Central Bank of Kuwait (CBK) Tower in Kuwait City designed in May 2003. "Local environmental influences is a central principle of this design" states Anthony Feldman, SOM Associate Partner in charge of this project. The architectural interpretation of site identity

Figure 35. CBK against the skyline of Kuwait City

Figure 36. Nighttime View of CBK in Kuwait City

and cultural context provide the design guidelines to establish the final form. The result is an inside-out skyscraper carrying a unique interpretation of a traditional Middle Eastern courtyard (Figure 40, 41).

On a square plot measuring 45m x45 m, the designers extrude a 185-meter tall tower with a 20m x 20m inner courtyard whose walls are plumb from the top to the lower most levels. The glazing system stands for only 10% of the outer wall to protect the environmental quality of the indoor space. A script run in AutoCAD 2002 generated the apparent randomness of the lighting pattern of the outer wall according to five rules:

- Each window could be placed at one of four elevations within the typical 5-foot by 14-foot "unit": at floor-level, seated eye-level, stganding eye-level, or ceiling-level. (All openings were placed to avoid conflict with the floor "sandwich".)
- Two windows must occur in each "unit."
- Six horizontal units are then grouped into 30-foot wide "panels," constituting the structural pre-cast construction module); two out of six units within each panel must remain devoid of windows to allow for vertical transfer of the structural load.
- Five total panel types are repeated throughout the tower wall to create economy within a seemingly "random" system.
- No more than three same-elevation windows could be placed adjacent to one another for structural considerations (figure 37).

What distinguishes this project from mainstream high-rise building design is the unconventional use of AutoCAD to generate the fenestration pattern of the exterior envelope. The formal reference is the Mashrabiya, a distinctive type of wood carving particular to the Arab East mainly used for windows, which allowed cool breezes to enter homes in the heat of summer. To capture the mood of that regional motif, the designers turned to the computer for the iterative process

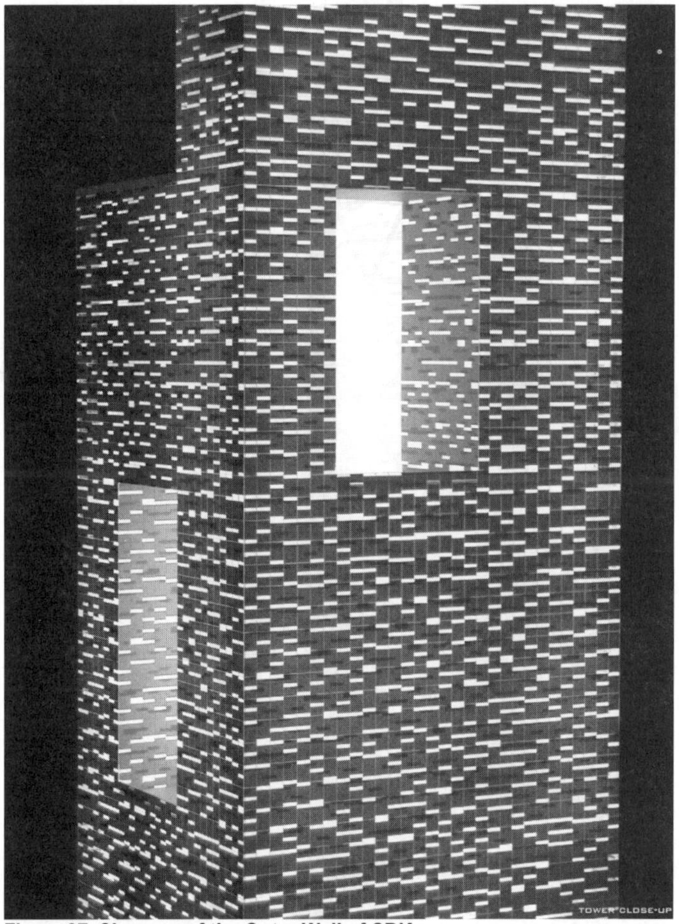

Figure 37. Close-up of the Outer Wall of CBK

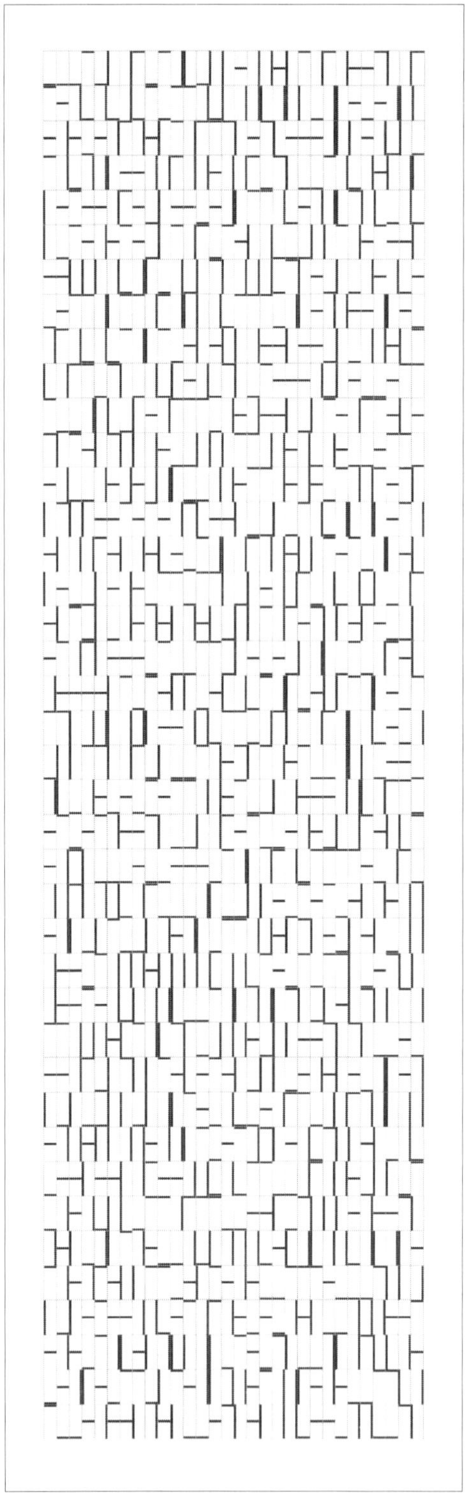

Figure 38. Sequence 1

Figure 39. Sequence 2

Figure 40. Sequence 3

Figure 41. Sequence 4

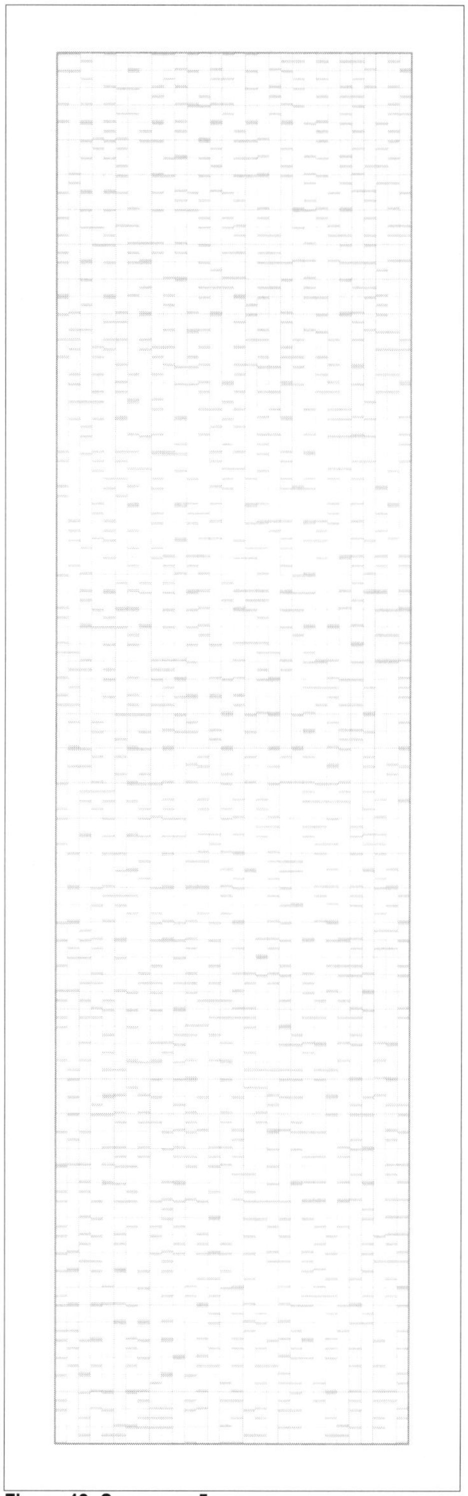

Figure 42. Sequence 5

(Figure 43. Interior View of CBK)

of finding a systematic approach in punching the windows on the buildings skins. Feldman came up with the idea of using computers to generate those iterations and established the formal rules for the arrangements of the windows. Neil Katz, an in-house expert in computer graphics within the SOM design department, wrote the code in AutoLISP.

Katz recalls: "Anthony approached me with a problem I found extremely interesting—developing an elevation based on certain criteria: a random appearance; relatively small openings (based on the climate in which the building is located); and modularity. Anthony and I worked together to develop the modules: squarish bays, with a band of window either horizontal or vertical, and located either at the center of the bay or at one of the edges: for the 'vertical' bays the window can be at the left side, in the center, or at the right side of the bay; for the 'horizontal' bays the window can be at the top, in the center, or at the bottom of the bay" (Neil Katz e-mail message, 25 June 2003).

The following is the pseudo-code use to determine computer-generated randomness:

```
-----
create List-Of-Bays: 1:VerticalLeft 2:VerticalCenter 3:
VerticalRight 4:HorizontalTop 5:HorizontalCenter 6:
HorizontalBottom

loop:for each floor
loop:for each bay
get-random(1 to 6)
place-bay
next bay
next floor
-----
```

Through progressive stages of refinement and post-rationalization for constructability purposes and economic considerations, the elevation achieved its final form (figures 38, 39, 40, 41, 42).

Directly mapped onto the outer walls, the computer generated distribution of these formal rules is converted into an architectural chart guiding the punching of the windows. Although software-driven, the resulting tapestry of lights is evocative of the glittering glamour of New York City skyscrapers, yet responsive to site specificity: a felicitous tangible intersection of ingrained design practices and computer aided design (figure 43).

10. Conclusion

Practicing architectural design with any three-dimensional modeling software is partaking in a technology of spatial ordering put into effect by the software developer. If these built-in slants are ignored, embracing technology for its own sake could lead to an uncritical stance both on the behalf of the users as well as on the critical assessment of those designs. The celebration of particular propositions in the press and in educational environments customarily groups propositions of very disparate architectural intentions under the general umbrella of digital design. But since architecture is a human activity that engages collectively many destinies propelled by hybrid interests, it might be worthwhile to go beyond the fact that whimsical forms can be built and raise the critical bar of what civic identity entails for the urban communities of the twenty-first century. As applications come and go, design obsolescence goes hand in hand with how fashionable morphological manipulations are. Additional case studies and quantitative tests are needed and quantitative tests to measure the rate of frequency of form elements yielded by specific software designed to further corroborate the statement that as of today form follows software.

References:

Bonta, J. P. (1979). *Architecture and its interpretation: A study of expressive systems in architecture.* London : Lund Humphries.

Böhme, G., and N. Stehr, editors. (1986). *The knowledge society: The growing impact of scientific knowledge on social relations.* Dordrecht ; Boston : D. Reidel; Norwell, MA. Series title: Sociology of the sciences: a yearbook ; v. 10.

Forsythe, D. (2001). *Studying those who study us: An anthropologist in the world of artificial intelligence.* Edited, with an introduction, by D. J. Hess. Stanford, Calif: Stanford University Press.

Geertz, C. (1973). Thick description: Toward an interpretative theory of culture. In *The interpretation of cultures; selected essays.* New York: Basic Books.

Gere, C. (2002). *Digital culture.* London: Reaktion.

Gladwell, M. (2002). *The tipping point: How little things can make a big difference.* 1st Back Bay pbk. ed. Boston: Little, Brown.

Grillmeyer, O. (1998). *Exploring computer science with scheme,* New York: Springer.

Lévy, P. (1997). *Collective intelligence: Mankind's emerging world in cyberspace,* New York: Plenum Trade.

Muschamp, H. (May 18, 2003). Who gets it? In The *New York Times Magazine,* 13-14.

Metossian, M. (2001). *Visual Quickstart guide: 3DS MAX for Windows*, Berkeley: Peachpit Press.

Orlikowski, W. J. (1993). Learning from notes: Organizational issues in groupware implementation. In *The information society* 9:237-250.

Preece, J., ed. (1993). *A guide to usability: human factors in computing.* [written by] David Benyon [et al.] Wokingham, England; Reading, Mass: Addison-Wesley.

Riddell D. (2003). Visual Quickstart guide: Maya for Windows & Macintosh. Berkeley: Peach Pit Press.

Schamber, Linda. (1994). Relevance and information behavior. In *Annual review of information science and technology* (ARIST) 29:3-48, Martha E. Williams, editor.

Serraino, P. (2002). *History of Form* *Z. Basel: Birkhäuser.

Terzidis, K. (2003 forthcoming). *Expressive forms: A conceptual approach to computational design.* London: SPON Press.

Winner, L. (1999). Do artifacts have politics? In *The social shaping of technology* 2nd ed., eds. D. MacKenzie and J. Wajcman, 28-39. Buckingham [Eng.]; Philadelphia: Open University Press.

Winograd, T., and F. Flores. (1987). *Understanding computers and cognition: A new foundation for design.* Reading, Mass: Addison-Wesley.

Yessios, C. I. (1987). The computability of void architectural modeling. In *Computability of design,* ed. Y. E. Kalay, 141-172. New York: Wiley.

Project Credits:

UCLA Chiller Plant/ Facilities Maintenance Complex. Wes Jones, Jane Cee, Rich Curl, David Gadarian, Lourdes Garcia, Marc Hinshaw, Paul Holt, Jeff Logan, James McKissick, Jim Park, Peter Pfau, Scott. Laidlaw, Craig Schultz, Dave Willet, Robert Yue

Sub-'burb, House of the Future. Wes Jones, Doug Jackson, Jim Rhee, George Tolosa, Arlene Lee, Kaoru Murayama, Jean Young-Jones

Particle Reflex, San Francisco, 2001. Thom Faulders, designer. Assistant Designer/Rendering: Hajime Masubuchi.

Suspended Field, Cincinnati, Ohio, 2000. Thom Faulders, designer. Project Assistants: Hajime Masubuchi, Niro Stern. CCAC Wattis Institute Entry, San Francisco, 2003. Thom Faulders, designer.

Fresh Kills Landfill, Staten Island, New York, 2001. Tom Leader Studio: Tom Leader, Principal Phillippe Coignet, Associate - A collaborative competition proposal with Mathur/Da Cunha, Urban Studio, Ove Arup, Applied Ecological Services and Leah Levy

World Trade Center Memorial Competition, New York, 2003. Cory Clarke and Jason Vigneri-Beane

Central Bank of Kuwait. SOM NY, 2003: Gary Haney, Design Partner, Stephen Apking, Interiors Partner, Imad Ghantous, Project Manager, Anthony Fieldman, Senior Designer, Aybars Asci, Neil Katz (author of the pseudo-code), Gaw Devakul, Verena Haller-Kuhnert, Donald Holt, Nestor Santacruz, project team, Guy Nordensen, structural engineer

Development of a Knowledge-Rich CAD System for the North American Precast Concrete Industry

Charles Eastman, Ghang Lee
Georgia Institute of Technology

Rafael Sacks
Israel Institute of Technology

Abstract

The downstream production sectors of the construction industry are developing powerful parametric modeling design and engineering tools for fabrication modeling. This paper reports an effort by the North American precast concrete industry toward developing such tools. Some implications for architectural design and practice are outlined.

Development of a Knowledge-Rich CAD System for the North American Precast Concrete Industry

Charles Eastman, Ghang Lee
Georgia Institute of Technology

Rafael Sacks
Israel Institute of Technology

1 Introduction

A significant revolution is taking place in the production of buildings. After years ignoring the development of digital modeling methods in manufacturing and electronics, the construction industry is beginning to adopt these methods. Journals and AEC software firms have adopted the term "Building Information Model" (BIM) to refer to this new technology (Laizerin 2003). BIM assumes that a fully detailed 3D model is the base representation for building projects, used by architect, contractor, sub-contractors and as required for design, production and erection. Drawings are semi-automatically produced as reports from the building model, as are bills of material and production plans such as 4D simulation (Koo & Fischer 2000). Subcontractors, such as those for steel structures, precast concrete and cast-in-place concrete, façade, and curtainwall fabricators, would all use the Building Information Model for detailing and shop production, with the general contractor using the various BIM models to coordinate all specialties.

While it was originally expected that architects would lead this transition, they have not done so. A construction level 3D model, with fully attributed objects, involves more information than is currently provided in drawings. With tight, fixed fee structures, there is little incentive to provide more information for downstream users without additional compensation. Justification for additional compensation for 3D modeling has not been forthcoming.

More fundamentally, software tools to model contract-drawing-level definition of whole buildings, beyond the scale of a single-family residence, have not been readily available. Few systems have been able to support interactive modeling of more than a few thousand parts, while a medium sized building may have millions. While the potential of such capabilities has been promoted since the 1970s, the knowledge to realize them, the hardware technology, and the software have not been widely available. The CAD literature is filled with firms formed by young innovators promoting these changes—Calma, GDS, Reflex, RUCAPS, Sonata, TriCad and more.

Part of the reason that this transition may occur (this time) is that other parts of the construction industry have already begun to make the transition. Structural steel is largely designed, analyzed, detailed, fabricated, and erected using integrated 3D modeling systems (using such programs as Xsteel, SDS/2, 3D+, StruCad and others). The precast concrete industry is currently developing similar capabilities. These sectors of the construction industry have recognized that 3D modeling is not a religious belief, but rather a practical business decision. Even starting with architect's drawings and building their own 3D models, they gain major benefits, including: faster design, detailing and production, improved support for automation, and reduced errors due to internal coordination (Sacks et al. 2003b).

These activities involve technologies that architects may eventually utilize, or with which they will need to exchange data. Some of the technology challenges in these industry sectors resolve issues also encountered in architectural design. There have been concerns expressed that architects have become too separate from the methods of construction (Cooke 2000). Yet active involvement in the development of IT in these other sectors of construction gives architects a leading role in guiding and directing future practices in their industry. The technologies are leading to re-structuring of the construction industry, affecting the possible roles that architects may play.

The authors are the technical consultants to a non-profit consortium, called the Precast Concrete Software Consortium, which consisted of 23 precast concrete producers. The purpose for forming this consortium was to develop a strong business plan for advancing IT application in the precast concrete industry of North America. The consortium shared in the cost of developing a plan for bringing advanced information technology capabilities to the precast concrete industry and then funded its realization. The authors prepared the business plan and are now coordinating its implementation. This paper gives a short review of the precast concrete industry, then reviews the project as undertaken, and lastly describes some of the implications of the project for architectural design and practice.

2 An Industry Led Consortium to Develop Advanced IT

While the Romans were the first to precast concrete, it was first introduced into North America in the 1920s; then it became more widespread during the 1950s with increased use of prestressing (PCI 1999). It is a significant contributor in many building types, including office buildings (whole buildings or facades), sports stadiums, and parking garages. The precast concrete industry's share of the construction market in general is small in comparison with other industrialized regions (Sacks et al. 2003a), the total being 1.2%. The largest single market is that for parking deck structures, with $1,010M, representing 13% of the market. In contrast, in Finland, 25% of all structural slabs and 11% of all building facades are precast (FCIA 2000; RTT 2001). In contrast to wood and steel, few standard stock items of precast can be bought "off-the-shelf." Only hollow-core floor slabs are of this character. Tees, spandrels, beams, and double tees are custom designed for span and loading, as are all wall panels. Most external panels have custom surface finishes. Connections must be custom designed for their conditions, including loading and appearance. In contrast to steel, a single precast concrete piece may involve a hundred or more individual component parts that must all be defined and fabricated. Almost all precast pieces are designed and engineered to-order, and many of their component elements are also custom fabricated from library designs.

While most precast concrete companies operate as subcontractors to a general contractor in the traditional manner, several highly successful precast firms also provide design-build services. These provide complete services for the design and construction of largely precast structures, especially parking garages. A few also offer design-build services for office buildings.

A variety of production innovations are being explored by precast fabricators, including styrofoam molds for architectural faced panels that are easily produced from 3D models (Columbia 2000), automated rebar and reinforcing, mesh bending and placement (Dunston & Bernhold 1993), and automatic pouring and curing assembly lines.

The competitors of precast are cast-in-place reinforced concrete (CIP) and steel construction. Their relative shares of the market for building structures in 1997 were: CIP concrete: 69%, Structural Steel: 21%, and Precast: 10% (PCI 2001; Economic Census 2000; Economic Census 2001). (Some of these figures are difficult to compare; some deal with building construction, while the earlier ones deal with all construction.)

2.1 An IT Plan for Precast Concrete

This precast concrete IT project arose because of parallel activities in other competing industry sectors and on the recognition that future detail design and construction in the precast concrete industry could be greatly enhanced through automated 3D modeling.

While the precast industry had adopted several automation tools, for both engineering design and fabrication, almost all firms relied on 2D drafting software such as AutoCAD and Microstation. Thus any automation tools had to rely on separate input and output translation. They also had the standard construction errors caused by inconsistencies between drawings (Sacks et al. 2003b). The consortium members also had extensive experience in developing custom software and add-ons, either internally by their firms, or through contracting with software firms. At least one firm had gone through three generations of such efforts. These inevitably led to continuing maintenance costs and eventual obsolescence. They expressed desire for development of a commercial product by an established CAD company. They wanted a product that could support the whole precast concrete industry, in North America and possibly the world. They hired (the authors) to generate a white paper (8 week effort) for a plan for precast IT development (Eastman & Augenbroe 2000).

The resulting plan included:

1. elicitation and compilation of detailed process models of how each firm contracts, designs, produces, and erects precast concrete structures (whether as complete buildings, as facades or other components of an overall structure, or as individual pieces), to identify key business process, bottlenecks and cost items;
2. development of a detailed specification describing the functionality required for next generation parametric modeling CAD design and engineering software, to provide the design and engineering data to be used by all other processes;
3. distribution of the specification to potentially interested software companies, evaluation of the alternative proposals and selection of the software development team with which to work;
4. technical coordination to develop a detailed specification, jointly developed by the consortium and the selected software company, with review and assessment of the software, as it becomes available,
5. development of a building data model to integrate the engineering and design functions of the specified software with other company software.

The process modeling exercise led to the recognition that traditional process modeling efforts were weakly effective, which in turn led to the development of a new process modeling method and process modeling tool. These efforts were directed at eliciting stronger input information for capturing information flows within a process to support the development of improved tools and backend data model (Lee et al. 2003).

Step (2) included development of an 88 page specification that relied on the collected process modeling information. It described parametric 3D modeling technology that would allow significant re-engineering of precast concrete design, engineering, and production. The software would have to support automated engineering and semi-automated production of drawings. The specification and its implications are reviewed further in the next section. Step (3) involved discussions with 26 companies, with development proposals received from 13 business groups. Through multiple levels of review, these were reduced to 5, then 2, then the selection of the winner, Tekla Corporation, a large software firm from Finland that already has steel detailing applications. We are currently involved in steps (4 & 5), developing a detail specification and reviewing and assessing the software as it reaches beta production. The consortium will begin study of the product model in the Fall of 2003.

This effort allowed the authors to review the current state of parametric CAD. It also allowed us to specify an advanced design and engineering CAD system that took full advantage of newly available parametric capabilities. The effort also required gaining a thorough understanding of the engineering, design, and production expertise that goes into a precast concrete product. For more detail, see (Sacks et al. 2003c).

3 Overall System Architecture Specification

The parametric CAD platform had to respond to a wide range of requirements. This included different businesses, where some precast fabricators contracted for, designed, and produced whole buildings, while others produced a system such as a floor structure or façade panels as a sub-contractor. The consortium included members from Canada and Mexico, as well as the USA; they rely on a variety of building and structural codes and standards. At the same time, many firms had special connections and piece designs they liked or were specialists at producing.

3.1 Process Model

The overall domain of functionality of the precast design software was derived from the different process models acquired from the precast companies. It is summarized in Figure 1. The software had to support different starting points: (1) importing a 3D model from the architect and contractor; (2) acquiring digital drawings from the contractor or architect and constructing a 3D model from them; (3) building a 3D model of selected assemblies when whole systems are not required, and design of individual pieces

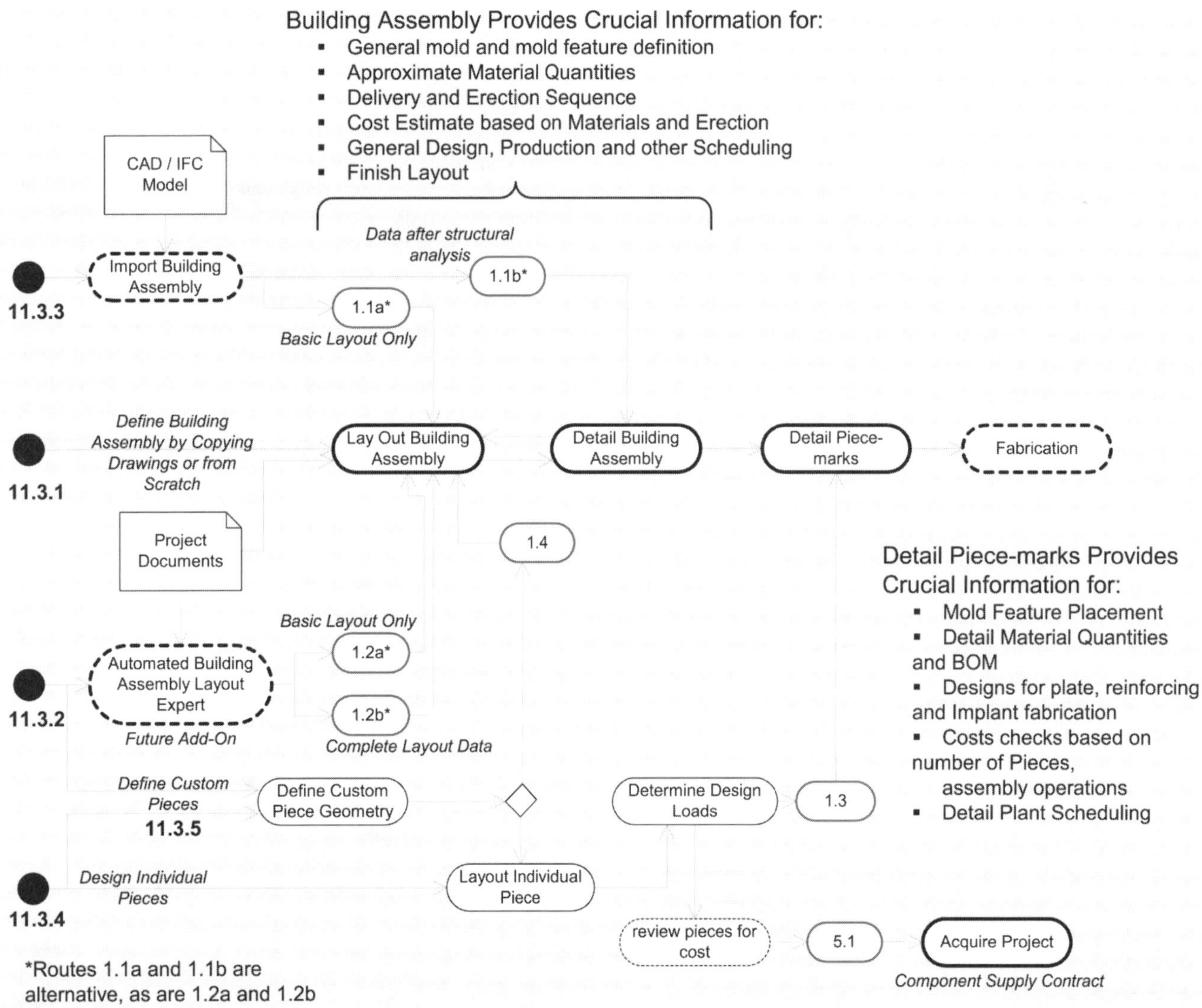

Figure 1. – A high-level process plan of the functional role of the precast concrete design and engineering application described in this article.

when assemblies are not required. The process followed is top-down, with the overall building assembly being designed first, with detailing of the assembly to deal with connection locations, coordinated surface treatments and finish layouts, assembly level definition of reveals, bull noses, and other architectural shapes. The building assembly is also analyzed structurally to determine the loads and reactions applied to individual pieces.

The individual pieces are then detailed, within the context defined by the overall building. Each piece is designed in response to spatial and aesthetic issues, then engineered to behave correctly, given its loads and reactions. It has its connections defined according to the types and arrangements determined at the building assembly. The fabrication of each part is planned in terms of its geometry, component parts, materials, embeds, finishes, and so forth.

3.2 System Architecture

The widely varying functional and engineering capabilities that the precast concrete design and engineering package had to provide led to a somewhat elaborate system architecture, shown in Figure Two. This industry alone was not likely to be able to support its own geometric modeling platform, and there are a rich set of such platforms existing already. However, a general-purpose 3D parametric modeling system, such as Autodesk Inventor or Solidworks was not sufficient either. What was needed was the development of a *precast concrete platform*, consisting of effective interactive procedures to define any type of precast concrete piece, lay out any pattern of reinforcing and pre- or post-tensioning, layout and detailing of finishes and 3D architectural detailing, and definition of all embedded components for connections. In addition, to support parametric design, these components had to be defined generically, so they could take any form, but have automatic updating behavior, so that, for example:

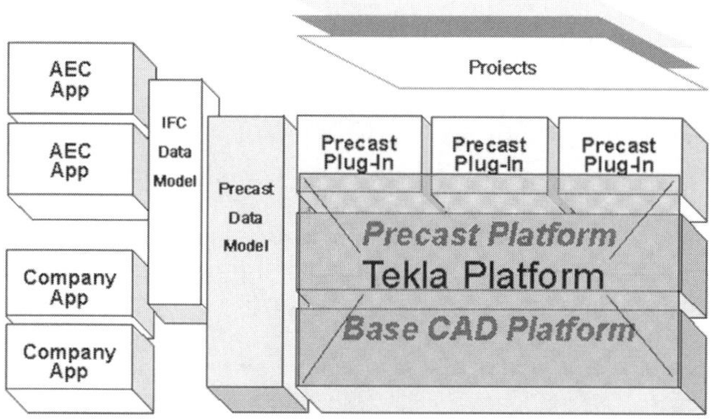

Figure 2. – System architecture for the PCSC Precast Software; Tekla proposed a system that incorporates a base CAD platform, a precast platform, and several automated design and engineering functions.

- connections move and automatically redefine themselves as the pieces they connect are modified;
- floor layout systems update themselves when their boundaries change;
- or façade layouts update themselves when the panel partitions or fenestration patterns are modified.

These behaviors have been worked out carefully to work within the context of the Tekla software. In some cases, however, expansion of the parametric modeling platform capabilities was required and these are included in the detailed specifications. Because of the wide range of building types, earthquake zones, and company practices, it was recognized that a wide and open range of customization would be required. Plug-in development, using an open Application Programming Interface (API) was specified, incorporating Common Object Model (COM) and VBA (Visual Basic for Applications) scripting. Some of these applications, developed by third parties, have already been prototyped. The most immediate requirement is for automated engineering and layout of precast piece reinforcing and the development of building system structural analysis. Other plug-in applications proposed include those for bridge girders and for automated design and detailing of parking garages.

Because the specified application would generate all the geometry and design data, it needs to interact with a range of other applications. These include (of course) coordination with 3D models of all the other systems. While for complex integration it has been assumed that the precast model may also model some critical systems it interacts with (structure, electrical conduits), the main expected interface will be with the Industry Foundation Class (IFC) building exchange model, developed by the IAI (IAI 2003). A Precast Concrete Building Model is planned. It will provide the IFC interface, those with general-purpose structural analysis applications, with CNC code generators (if needed) and bill of materials, scheduling, material resource, and Enterprise Resource Planning (ERP) systems.

In the competition resulting from the Request for Proposal for this system (Eastman et al. 2001); (in early 2002) twelve submitters proposed to develop systems based on this architecture. These included AutoCAD developers, who generated three proposals (that were eliminated because the AutoCAD platform lacked parametric modeling capabilities). Others included Bentley Triforma, Nemetschek Allplan, two Solidworks developers, Tekla, and Unigraphics from EDS-PLM. Benchmarks and technical development were assessed, as well as business practices and levels of expected support. The mixture of criteria for: strong parametric modeling, ability to interactively model at least 250,000 elements, easy extensibility and customization, and an open architecture to support the whole industry, resulted in there being only a few companies that could contend. This situation has not changed much today, though we expect significant changes in the next two or so years. Finally, Tekla's Xengineer was selected, with significant additional required enhancement. Their product and proposal provided for the CAD platform, the Precast CAD platform, and some level of plug-in level automation, as an integrated package (as shown in Figure 2).

The detailed specification of the system, based on this architecture, is well along. Partial implementations are being continuously evaluated and some pilot testing on full buildings is scheduled for the summer of 2003. The full product release of the software, with all enhancements, is scheduled for October, 2004. Many aspects of this effort offer insights into efforts that might be taken in other realms in construction, including architectural practice. Two aspects are reviewed in more detail below.

4 Automated Engineering

Buildings are complex structures that involve significant knowledge and decisions regarding layout and detailing at every level of design, from schematic design to detailing. Automation is being applied to all levels of design and engineering of precast concrete.

4.1 Structural Stability

While precast structures must respond to a variety of requirements, including thermal and acoustic, the most universal functional requirement of precast structures is structural stability. Satisfying the structural requirements for precast involves two levels of design: at the building and at the piece level. At a high level, the building system must be analyzed according to the various loading requirements required by different regions of the country (or world). For low-rise buildings, most precast firms rely on formula-based analyses, based on the PCI Design code (PCI 1999). For medium and high-rise construction, analysis is done using general-purpose finite element modeling systems. The first capability will be supported through development of plug-in applications. General-purpose structural modeling systems are expected to be supported through the Precast Concrete Data Model, similar to the interfaces already provided by the CIMsteel model for structural steel (Crowley and Watson 2000). Given the results of the analysis at this level, which usually requires multiple iterations, and making assumptions regarding piece-level design, a working solution is found. These results are then used to drive two more detailed designs: of the individual pieces, and of the connections between the pieces.

The piece level detailing involves automatic layout of the reinforcing and prestress cables of a given member shape to satisfy the loads imposed by the overall structure. The plug-in applications will provide these services, based on the varied codes applied in different regions of North America. They define the longitudinal and cross-sectional reinforcing responding to the varied loading conditions throughout the length of the piece and must take into account the possibility of a changing profile along the piece's length, as well as holes and other irregularities within the piece.

In design, a connection is a logical entity whose main role is to modify the two pieces being connected. Precast connections are highly varied, ranging from the ledge on an inverted tee, to pockets that might be used on a thick column, to corbels that protrude from a piece to carry another member. These may be selected interactively or assigned automatically, based on local conditions. In either case, their detailing will be driven by the loads they are determined to be carrying in the building level analysis. Because of the local loads on a connection, which will vary by type, they also carry local reinforcing.

There is not a clear dependency relation in the order in which piece reinforcing and connection detailing are to be undertaken. In some cases, it makes sense to do the connection design first, in others, the piece reinforcing. However, in the end, they must both work together, with no spatial conflicts, with some lapping of reinforcing, and other criteria. It has been specified that reinforcing and embed clash checking be included, and that this capability can be embedded in higher level checking routines. This example of automated engineering design, with the limits of what can be automated and what cannot, shows both how great improvements are possible and, at the same time, that there is still need for additional research for further improvements in the future.

4.2 Detailed Assembly Layout

The primary method of embedding engineering and construction practices into a design with CAD drafting technology is the copying and adjusting of detail sections. Typical sections are provided by window, curtainwall, door, fixture, exterior material, and other material suppliers. However, these cut-and-paste operations often lead to inconsistencies with the actual context where they are specified or to details that are inappropriate for the condition to which they are applied, leading to leaks, wear, and poor installation and operation.

In the precast concrete software, every piece is defined with its spacing tolerances, with cover requirements for concrete (for embeds), and its shape relationships with other pieces (such as a corbel connection on a column). See Figure 3. Thus the form of the detail is not stored, but rather the rules for generating the appropriate form in various conditions are. As specifiers of the system, we play the game of asking how a piece should behave when changed in unusual ways. We try to cover them all. The proposed revisions are reviewed by a technical committee who together have hundreds of years of experience making such design decisions. The end result is that we will have embedded a significant portion of the design and engineering practices into this new system. Will it be infallible? No. But it will go a very long way in automating the everyday engineering and design practice of this industry. Will it prohibit unusual designs? That it does not has been a strong and continuing requirement. It must be possible to override every aspect of the design so that users are not limited by the system. If a better way is found for a connection, or seam between pieces, then it should be easily

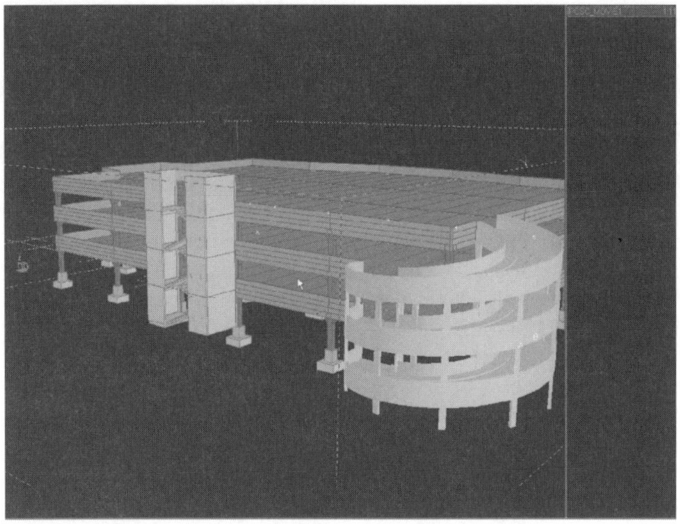

Figure 3. A Common precast building – a parking garage.

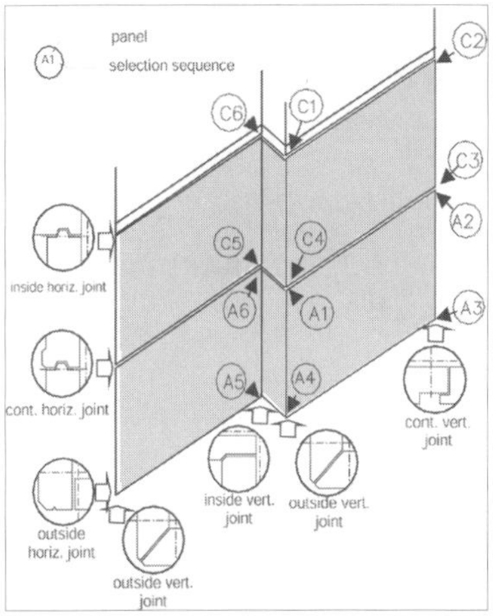

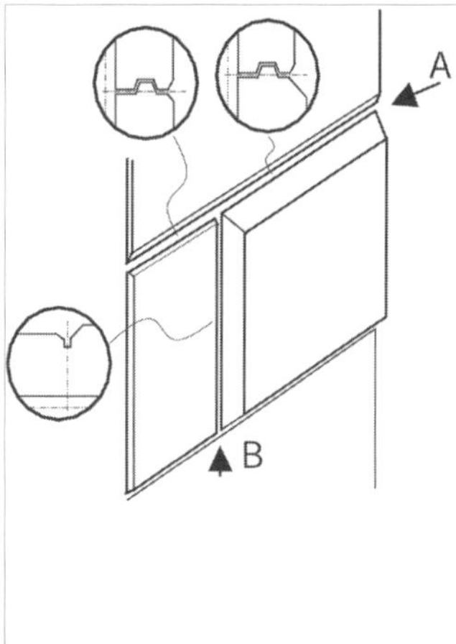

Figure 4 (a) **Figure 4 (b)**

Façade panels are identified by selecting their joint boundaries, in order. Joints may be one or two-sided. Rules have been defined for dealing with two joints that join on a joint tine.

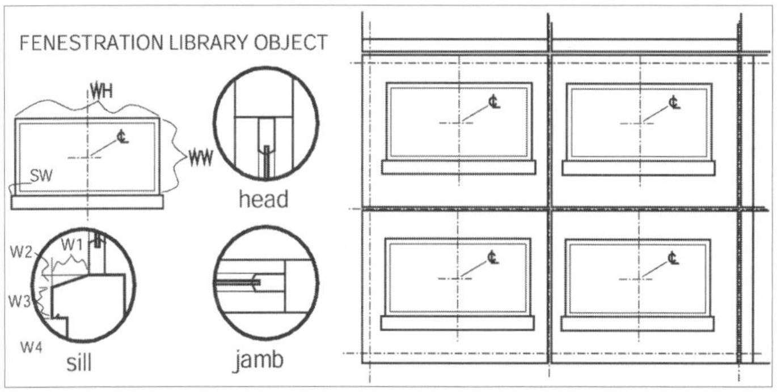

Figure 5. A fenestration library is defined for a project. It includes the panel features that are located with the opening.

automated, so that it can be used with the same efficiency as previously automated features.

5 Façade Detailing

An important large assembly for some precast firms is a precast facade. An architectural precast facade is composed of a possibly complex surface partitioned into a set of panels separated by joints between them, with associated regions with different materials, thickness, and finishes, with fenestration at some specified layout, with a possibly complex pattern of reveals, bull noses, sills, and surface treatments. The façade must include potentially complex joints with other facades, including non-precast elements. On the back side, the façade must carry the necessary supporting connections, indents for columns, be adequately reinforced, and carry specified insulation, embeds for electrical and other utilities. Facades are complex assemblies, currently sometimes taking more than a day per panel to draw using AutoCAD.

The PCSC precast application specification addresses most of these requirements. It allows the layout of a façade as a whole, where a façade is one or more planes of the building exterior. The façade layout design consists of parametric positioning of joint lines that might be irregular. Panels are defined by specifying the joints that bound them. Joint details are selected from a predefined library, or one composed for the project. Two figures from the proposed specification are shown in Figure 4(a) and (b). The joint geometries are automatically applied to the panels, creating 3D solids. The joint information also includes bills of material data, allowing these to be accurately derived. Window assemblies are predefined in a company library, then customized as needed for each project. They are embedded as predefined fenestration assemblies, as shown in Figure 5. The sill, arch, or other header and jamb conditions are specified so that they are automatically aligned with the window. If the window moves, they all do. Like the joints, they modify the 3D model of each precast panel. The precast design components of bills of material for the window assembly are included.

Other capabilities provide means to deal with surface treatments, including brick coursework, tiling, reveals, bullnoses, and other patterns. Other capabilities include the assignment and detailing of connections, with any subtraction of material required on the inside surface due to structure. See Figure 6. These capabilities are not only layout operations, but rather automatically update themselves as other parts of the design change. It is expected that these capabilities will tremendously facilitate the definition and layout of precast concrete facades and allow more complex facades to be developed.

From these layouts of a façade assembly, the 3D assembly model is defined, including 3D models of each façade panel. Later, reinforcing, joints for connecting the façade to the structure, insulation panels and conduit, if needed, are added. From the 3D model, piece drawings of each panel are automatically generated, including all of the detail dimensioning, placement of embedded elements and other details needed

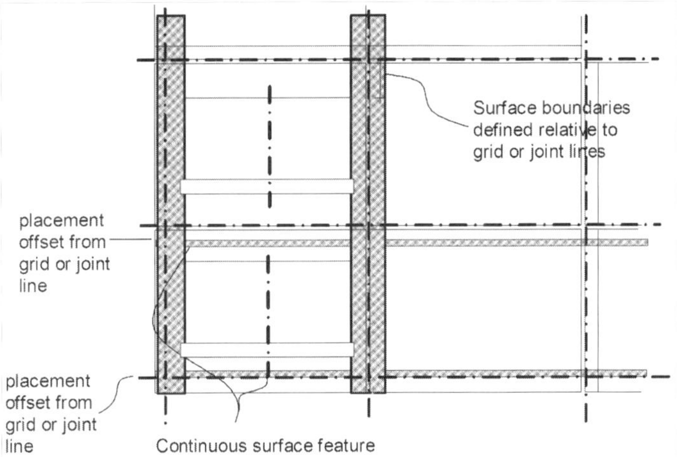

Figure 6. Surface treatment layout is defined parametrically so that it can be easily adjusted.

Figure 7. Example architectural façades, models of those to be generated by the Façade Assembly capabilities described (figures courtesy of Concrete Technologies International).

for fabrication, along with the piece-level bill of materials. If a custom mold is required for the part, a plug-in is envisioned that will support mold definition. Two example facades are shown in Figure Seven.

This façade layout and behavior definition is only one example of over twenty areas of specification now defined in detail for the first production release of the precast software.

6 Implications for Architecture

This type of technology effectively addresses custom facilities based on standard construction technologies. It appears that more innovative construction technologies, such as those incorporated into the buildings of Frank Gehry, are based even more strongly on computer technology. From these examples, it appears that future construction expertise will become more and more embedded in knowledge-based building information systems.

As this technology matures, the roles of designer, draftsmen, and engineers will significantly change, as engineering and drafting are automated. While precast concrete and other building producers are moving strongly into 3D modeling for production purposes, they clearly see the potential of this technology to change the scope of their businesses. Some are planning to use this technology at the early sales stage, allowing potential clients to see and walk through a building, while at the same time getting strong cost estimates and production schedules. A few general contractors have already begun doing the same (MIT 2001). Alternatively, there is interest by Consortium members to see architects adopt this technology, to speed construction and reduce costs. There is likely to be increasing competition with players competing at the boundaries of traditional services. Architecture, which at one time aspired to be responsible for the full scope of construction (a la the “master builder”) has in fact traditionally reduced its scope to address ever fewer technical and social aspects of building, leaving these for others. This has been especially true in the schools. However, new construction-level technologies, if strongly adopted by architects, provide the option for architects to regain an active role in downstream construction-level aspects of building. One can also envision a number of parallel systems being developed for specialized architectural practices where at the design-level detailed knowledge and expertise are important. These might include, for example: libraries and hospitals, airports, and other transport facilities.

Note: The work reported here has been undertaken with the support of the Precast Concrete Software Consortium, and has been published with their permission. The authors also acknowledge the Tekla Corporation for their support in this undertaking.

References

Columbia University. (2000). Concrete Materials Research at Columbia University Prof. C. Meyer, Dept. Of Civil Engineering. Mail Code 4709, Columbia University, New York, NY 10027-6699.

Cooke, A. (2000). The business of complex curves. *Architecture*, (December 2000): 54,124.

Crowley, A., and A. Watson. (2000). *CIMsteel integration standards*. Release two, 5 volumes, Steel Construction Institute and Leeds University.

Dunston, Ph.S., and L. E. Bernold. (1993). Intelligent control for robotic rebar bending. In *Proceedings of the tenth international symposium on automation and robotics in construction*, Houston, TX, May 24-26,101-108.

Eastman, C. M., and G. Augenbroe. (2000). *PCI study: Design computing research report.* Atlanta, GA: Georgia Institute of Technology.

Eastman C. M., R. Sacks, and G. Lee. (2001). *Software specification for a precast concrete design and engineering software platform.* Atlanta, GA: Georgia Institute of Technology.

Economic Census. (2000). Industry Summary, 1997 Economic Census, Document EC97C23-IS, U.S. Dept. of Commerce, Economics and Statistics Division.

Economic Census. (2001). Manufacturing subject series for 1997, Doc. # EC97M31S-PS, U.S. Dept. of Commerce, Economics and Statistics Division.

FCIA . (2000). *Internal report, Finnish concrete Industry Association*. Helsinki, Finland.

IAI. (2003). see http://www.iai-international.org/iai_international

Koo, B., and M. Fischer. (2000). Feasibility study of 4D CAD in commercial construction. *Journal of construction engineering and management* ASCE 126(4):251-260.

Laiserin, J. organizer. (2003). Autodesk and Bentley debate building information modeling. Leading design software executives in face-to-face webcast recorded on April 3, 2003, also in *Laiserin Newsletter*, July 1, 2003.

Lee G, C. M. Eastman, and R. Sacks. (2003). Eliciting information for product modeling using process modeling. *Data and knowledge engineering* (in review).

MIT. (2001). The Beck group, Bringing DESTINI to market: Revolutionizing the industry case study: E-Commerce and the internet in real estate and construction, construction engineering and management, center for real estate, at: www.beckgroup.com/whitepaper/casestudyformit.pdf

PCI. (1999). *PCI design handbook.* Chicago: Precast/Prestressed Concrete Institute.

PCI. (2001). *Annual financial and cost data survey, Fiscal 2000.* Chicago: PCI Precast/Prestressed Concrete Institute, 1-69.

RTT. (2001). *Yearbook - economic outlook – 2000.* RTT Helsinki, Finland: Finnish Association of Construction Product Industries.

Sacks R., C. M. Eastman, and G. Lee. (2003a). Process model perspectives on management and engineering procedures in the North American precast/prestressed concrete industry. ASCE *journal of construction engineering and management* (forthcoming).

Sacks, R., C. M. Eastman, and G. Lee. (2003b). Process improvements in precast concrete construction using top-down parametric 3-D computer-modeling, *Journal of the precast/prestressed concrete institute* 48(3):46-55.

Sacks, R., C. M. Eastman, and G. Lee. (2003c). Parametric 3D modeling in building construction with examples from precast concrete. *Automation in construction* (forthcoming).

05 >> Connecting Digital Representation

Chairs: Lisa Tilder, Frederick Stacy Norman

New Media

Lisa Tilder, Frederick Stacy Norman

Architecture, technology and representation
How do architectural representation paradigms shift in an increasingly digital age?

As digital technologies and connective systems begin to redefine traditional notions of place, space and time, how might architecture itself transform? Over the past century, extreme conceptual and spatial transformations have come about in relation to the introduction of mechanical reproduction, computer graphics and redundant systems, however architecture and representation have remained somewhat constant. This is evident in the continuity of traditional architectural representation methods that draw primarily from renaissance models - though the original impetus from which such projection methods evolved no longer bear the same significance to culture.

In a cultural landscape in which newly defined models of transience, connectivity, and place offer up new paradigms for exploration, how might architectural representation change? How do contemporary models of communication, mass production, distribution and imaging influence the conception and production of architecture? How might hybrid models influence architectural production, from pre-manufactured housing to consumer products, brand identity to mass-market advertising? How might raster and vector models inscribe paradigms for popular culture? Below are three aspects of contemporary representation that explore emerging connections between architecture, media, representation and culture: Drawing, Modeling + Fabrication, Graphics + New Media >>

Drawing
Whether handcrafted, computer-translated or computer-generated, drawing provides us with abstraction capable of communicating architectural design ideas. With the increase in digital media and availability of computer graphics applications and hardware, the medium of the drawing is changing. With a change in mediums analog to digital, should that impose a change in how we draw, what we draw and the intended use of a drawing? Will the two-dimensional flattened image give way to intelligent three-dimensional digital models for construction?

Modeling + fabrication
Digital media is providing an opportunity to return a sense of materiality to an immaterial realm. The relationship between architectural design and production are brought closer together given the fluidity and accuracy of digital tools. Computer-aided design and computer-aided fabrication processes provide the means for architects to create new forms of architectural practice and challenge traditional methods of project delivery.

Presentation graphics + new media
As computing technologies have begun to be absorbed into the popular realm, the general public has become acclimated to an inundation of media. Relationships between architect/client may be facilitated by the use of popular or experimental media such as television, computer games, and the web. Architects might look to popular media for techniques of communication to the general public – the AIA advertises through television commercials, the U.S. Army via computer games, for example.

As methods of representation change, architecture's definitive boundaries transform. Relationships between disciplines may join more readily, forging collaborative partnerships. Students now enter architectural education and the profession from a technologized generation: as students become more facile and familiar with digital tools and environments, they begin to effect representational changes in both education and the profession from the bottom up. How might all of these changes underway impact the profession and education?

Lisa Tilder is an Assistant Professor of Architecture at the Ohio State University Knowlton School of Architecture, where she teaches architectural design, computer graphics and seminars that address the relationship of technology, design and representation. As an educator and architect, Tilder's work pursues the critical relationship of technology to architecture and culture through various means: web-based projects, interactive constructions and installations, competitions and building projects.

Frederick Stacy Norman is an Assistant Professor of Architecture at Ball State University. He is the site chair for the ACADIA22 Conference2003 in Indianapolis. Frederick was also co-chair of the 2002 digital design exhibition: http://www.Bsu.Edu/dde. Professor Norman is the recipient of the 2003/4 Paul Rudolph Visiting Assistant Professor, Auburn University, School of Architecture.

To Proceed Analysis of Dynamic Virtual Environment by Using Physical Model as a Protagonist

Chien-Hung Shih
National Chao-Tung University

Abstract

This paper intends to combine architecture with state-of-the-art software technologies and operational methods of other domains to free architectural rendering from the restrictions of cold, still graphics or unrealistic computer pictures. The author transforms physical models into digital models through industrial design software, and synthesizes these digital models into motion pictures of the environment via film production software. This way, a designer can effectively turn the ideas of his mind into rough handmade models, instead of spending enormous amounts of time building computer models, and viewers will be able to quickly grasp the conditions of the site through the motion pictures.

To Proceed Analysis of Dynamic Virtual Environment by Using Physical Model as a Protagonist

Chien-Hung Shih
National Chao-Tung University

1 Introduction

Vision simulation always possesses a dominant influence on the development of environment analysis and the design process (Fukuda 2002). As a result, before construction designers are used to synthesize their design works with the environment photos in order provide samples of future images (Liu 2001).
In the domain of industrial design, using techniques in reverse engineering to transfer hand-made physical models automatically to digital models helps avoid obstacle and practice in the software. On the other hand, in the domain of popular art, designers in the movie industry use dynamic Camera-matching techniques originating from 20 years ago to gather information from other realms and keep on updating new devices combined by hardware and software. Nowadays with the devices and more powerful digital tools, we could build a virtual space in which an audience cannot distinguish reality from modeling (CG 2001).

With progress in software technology and hardware computation performance, the industrial design sector and filmmaking industry have begun to utilize automatic high-speed tools to enhance efficiency (Paul 1996). In the area of architectural and environmental design, however, designers are still relying on the still photomontage technique of the over ten year old programs such as Photoshop. So the ambition of this paper is to shorten the distance between designers and digital development: to utilize the advantages from the movie industry, including digital techniques, precision, velocity, and low-price in order to efficiently observe the physical model on the real site and present a more high quality, dynamically synthesized film.

2 Camera-Tracking Software

In 1975, George Lucas formed ILM (Industry Light Magic) Studio for his movie, Star Wars, where he tried to repeat the camera path for composition of flying scene of spaceships mechanically. These scenes have shaped the camera-matching technology, and the digitally controlled camera path has become the mainstream of the filming industry for the past 20 years, along with advancement in software and hardware technology.

With the renewal of computation methods and program language, it has become a trend to use camera-tracking software and automatic computation cameras to replace huge mechanical devices. The change results in significant cost savings and a wider application of camera-matching techniques due to a lowered threshold (Figure 1). Using the dynamic synthesizing software 2d3 Boujou--which was awarded in Ammy Engineering Technology Award 2002 for example (Boujou 2001)--designers now only have to input the film into the software and Boujou will automatically grab trackers such as the specific positions of the signboard and cornice. Through sequence frames computation, Boujou will automatically produce information concerning the movement and rotation of the camera during the filming and allow designers to freely apply the data. For a film of 10 seconds, the automatic computation only takes 30 minutes.

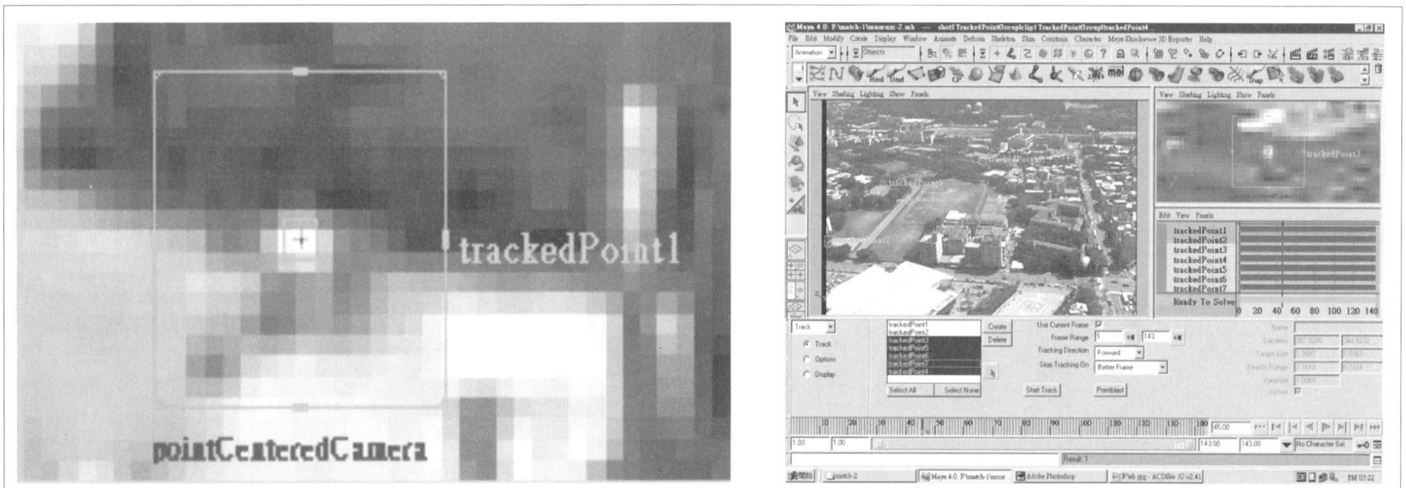

Figure 1. Camera-tracking software

3 Silhouette Modeling

In the field of industrial design, due to the limit of 3-D modeling it is very difficult for designers to turn the design in their minds into digital models if they have not been through long-term training. As a result, reverse engineers utilize contact, photoelectric or photographic 3-D scanning techniques to save time and to automatically and accurately transform design concepts into computer model through manual production of simple models (Edward 2001).

Silhouette modeling is a new approach that employs reverse engineering. The only device it requires is a rotating plate at the numbered point. Quality models can be quickly and efficiently produced this way, and there will be no ill combination between polygons breach of the model. Silhouette Modeling takes a 3-D cylinder or cube, and according to the 16 Silhouette Lines of the object, it conducts 16 times of subtractions in Boolean to obtain a digital model that simulates the physical model (Figure 2). After the pictures taken from various angles are merged into a UV picture, we can produce a texured model that contains up to 10,000 faces.

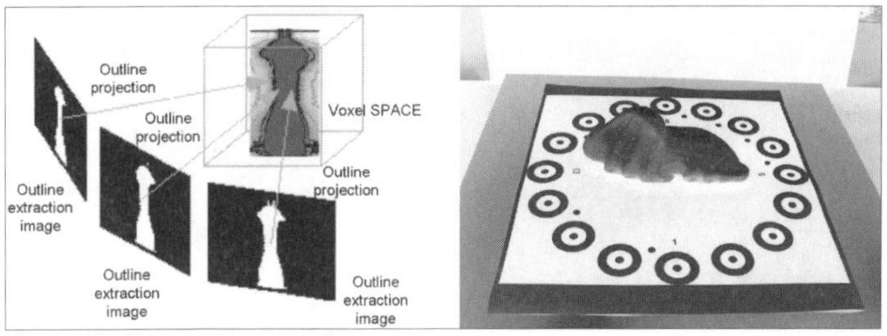

Figure 2. Silhouette modeling

4 Exploration

After reviewing the newest development of other domains, if the presentation of architecture designers is to reach the quality of dynamic environment animation technique with the same quality as a movie, then the huge size of the camera-matching tool, the expensive budget, and the limitation of the software remain unsolved questions. Applying these to the architecture domain is not economical at all. Therefore in the domain of environment and architecture design, we still use static photomontage software such as Adobe Photoshop to simulate reality. However, the effects and sensation of still images are much inferior to dynamic camera-matching motion picture. It naturally becomes a goal for the environmental engineer to pursue how to insert accurately a hand-made model for effective study in the dynamic virtual environment. Hence, the objective of this research is a study of how to apply cutting-edge software and techniques of industrial design and the movie industry to the environmental analysis in order to reach a high level of dynamic motion simulation. The hope is to enable designers using simple workflow to observe the relations between their design works and the whole environment on the concept of animate timeline, and at the end, to present the synthesis film with movie quality.

5 Media Steps

This research is focused on applied media. The hardware used is only a specific rotating plate that is marked with numbers for D-sculptor (D-sculptor 2002). The software used is 2d3 Boujou and d-vw D-sculptor which comes from other professional domains. The 3D Studio Max is utilized as post-production software to render synthesized film.

5.1 Automatic Generation of Digital Model

Place the manually made physical model on the rotating plate that is marked with numbers and position points. Take a series of pictures of this model with each position point as center. Then through the Alpha Channel of Adobe Photoshop transform the silhouette of the object mask (Figure 3). Following the input of D-sculptor, utilize the Boolean Subtraction mentioned in Media Review to speedily produce 3-D models and mapping texture for later matching. Currently, the only matured D-Sculpture technique in the market is produced by D-vw.

Filming Plan and Trackers

With the digital model in place, designers shall plan the range of the site for the model and the shot range to facilitate the actual filming in the future (Figure 4). In addition, as explained in Media Review, Boujou needs a lot of trackers to help with the computation. So after the filming range is determined, designers shall set up trackers on the site before filming, e.g., placing A4 papers on the ground.

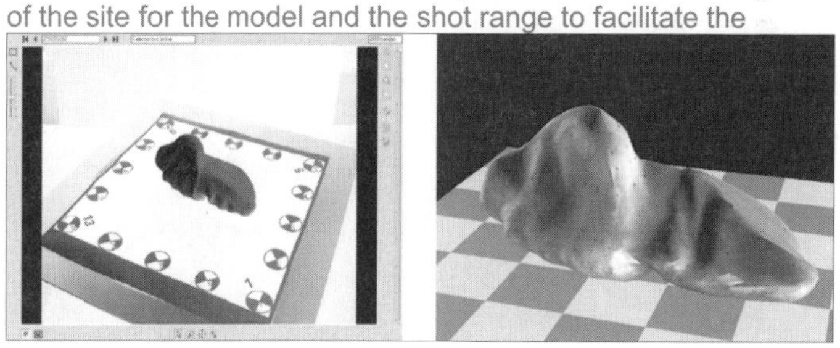

Figure 3. Generate physical model to digital one

5.2 Utilize Boujou to compile

Input the film from Step.2 into Boujou. The software will automatically grab trackers for each frame and through the positioning data of several trackers determine the movement of the 3-D camera. With tracks of movement in place, designers shall delete the trackers that Boujou has automatically grabbed for each frame (Figure 5), leaving only the previously set up trackers on the site to cut down the time needed for inputting the synthetic software to look for positions.

5.3 Synthetic Output of Animated Picture

Synthetic Output of Animated Picture: Input the movement data of the camera into the 3-D Studio MAX and switch the animate background to actual filming. Select Camera01, and the trackers

Figure 4. Filming plan

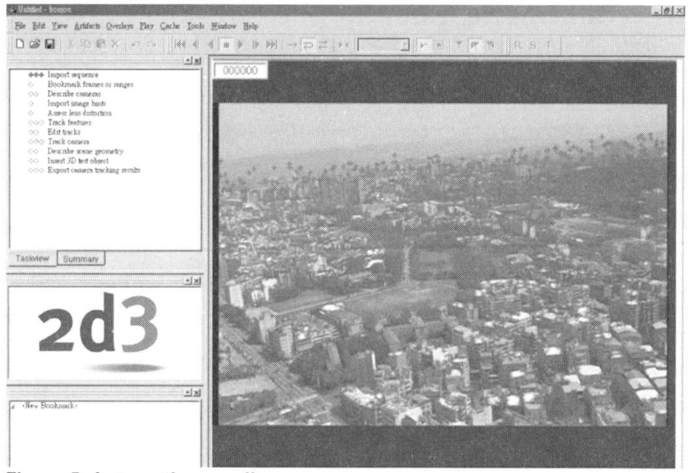

Figure 5. Automatic compile

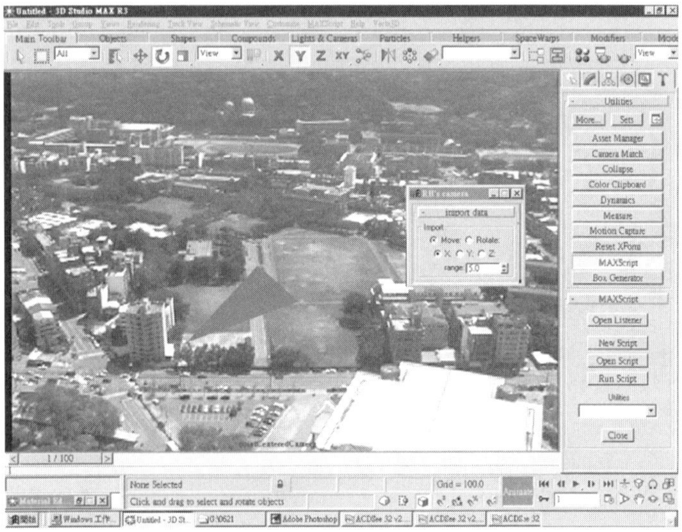

Figure 6. Reference plan

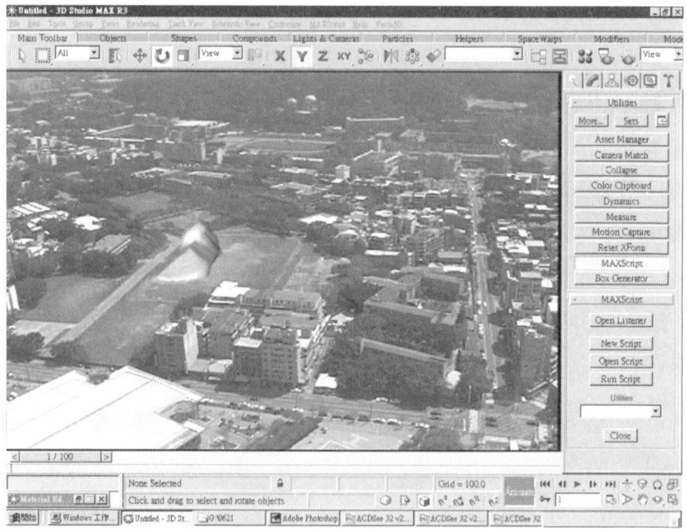

Figure 7. Synthesize model

steps	software	significance	Key point	Running time
Automatic Generate of Digital Model	D-sculptor	Physical to virtual	Modeling	1.5 hr
Filming Plan and Trackers	X	Position of trackers	Trackers	1 hr
Utilize Boujou to compile	boujou	Automatic compile	Path of camera	1 hr
Synthetic Output of Animated Picture	3D studio Max	Render to animation	synthesis	1 hr

Table 1: The compare of Media steps.

previously set up on the site will show the background picture with the sequence frames focused on the background. At this moment, designers can set up a reference plane by using several trackers and incorporating the digital models established in Step 1 into this reference plane, adjusting the proportion and rotation angle (Figure 6). After this is completed, when the designer scrolls the timeline of the animated picture, the model will stick to the site in the background film (Figure 7). When this is verified in the test run, the animated background and the model can be rendered together as a synthesized film through the 3-D Studio MAX (Table 1).

6 Project: ITRiS 2010

The author quickly applied the media steps to an actual project. ITRIS 2010 is a project that constructs the freeform model of digital architecture on the actual site. Due to the fact that the construction of a freeform digital model on the computer is quite difficult, the author pulled out several desired shapes from the clay and through D-Sculptor turned these shapes into digital files and utilized the software to finish the detail. Then via Boujou and 3D Studio Max, the author incorporated these models into films shot from different angles, such as the overall environment, portrayal of the entrance, and view of the pedestrians. Lights and materials were adjusted through MAX to match the conditions of the site. For example, 3 coarse models and 3 background films of the site can be quickly merged into 9 different environmental simulation films of different time and angles. The position of the coarse models can be easily adjusted to match the site for studies and for editing the multimedia film of ITRIS 2010. In ITRIS 2010, these synthesized films show the relations between design works and site dynamically producing lifelike simulation effect (Figure 8). These also demonstrate that the research and methods are reachable, producing a high quality presentation film that designers have never seen (Tang 2002).

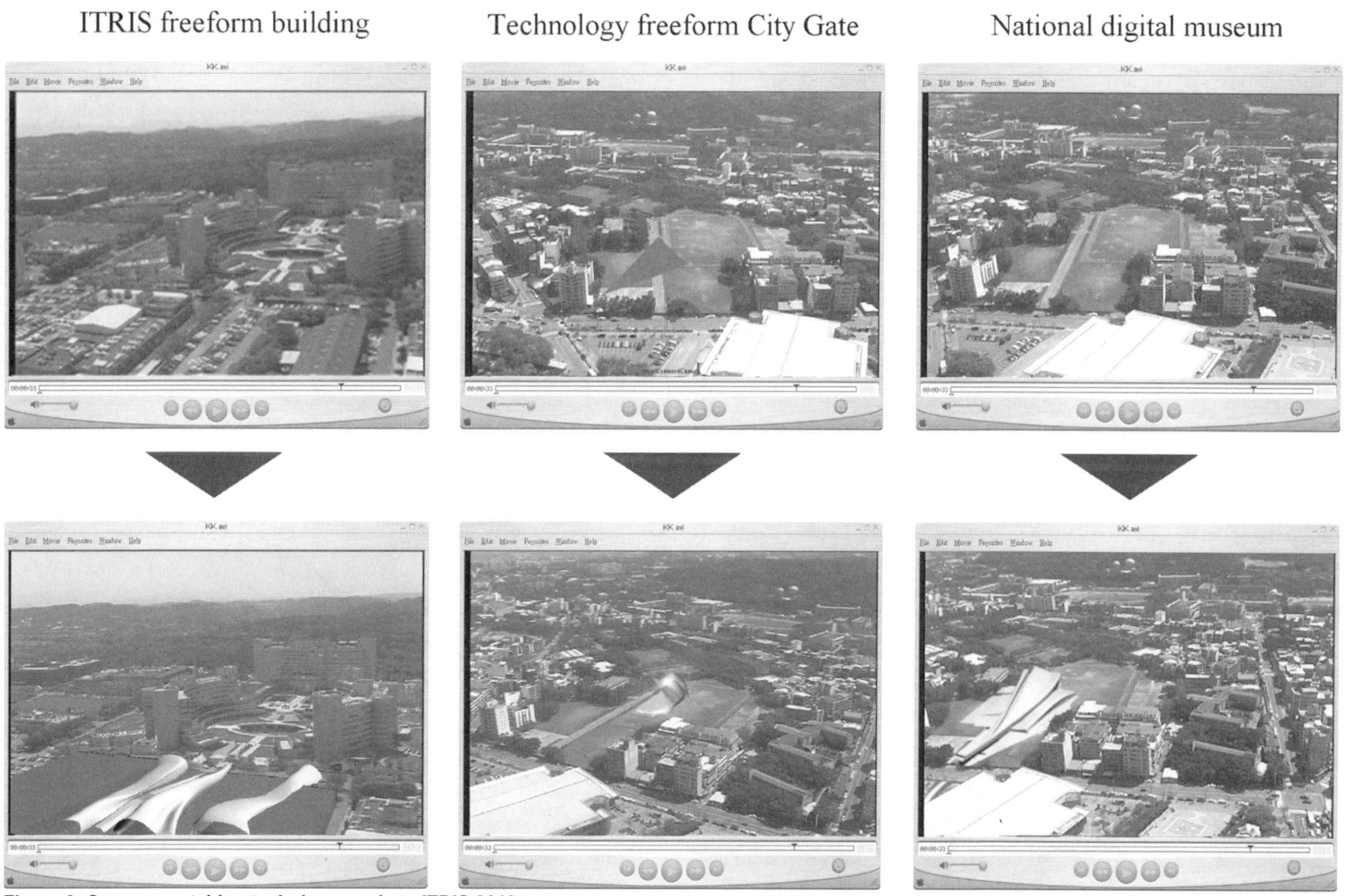

Figure 8. Camera-matching technique apply to ITRIS 2010

7 Application

As the outcome of the project indicates, this media research intends to incorporate recent technologies of the other domains to enable designers to effectively study their ideas within a short period of time and render presentations that are as good as commercial films. Due to the fact that the simple procedures proposed in this research, as well as the automatic software it recommends, will greatly reduce the threshold of applying technologies of other fields to architectural design, small-to-medium-size architectural firms will be freed from the restrictions of budget and facility and will be able to swiftly demonstrate design concepts and how the model fits into its site through synthesized films of various angles.

There are two restrictions to be resolved: The Boolean subtraction of D-Sculptor is unable to effectively render the dent faces of the model, and as a result there are flaws in the pasting process. In addition, currently Boujou is still not capable of performing automatic computation for the zooming shot of the camera. Pictures can only be taken through fixed focus, and the variety of shots is consequently reduced. Further study could orient to developing real-time synthesize technique of interactive panorama environment (Scenewe@ver 2001) to lead the standstill situation of environment simulation in the design domain forward to the much more lifelike reality and rituality combination standard (Lou 2002).

8 Reference

2d3 Group. (2001). The Manual of Boujou 1.3.http:/www.2d3.com

CG designer. (2001). Camera-matching. In *CG world 21*(2001). H.K: CG World.

D-VW Inc. (2002). The manual of d-sculptor.http://www.dvw.com

Edward, M. (2001). *Introduction: Modern photography*. New Jersey: John Wesley & Sons.

Fukuda, T. (2002). Collaboration support system for city plans or community designs based on VR/ CG technology. In *CAADRIA 2002*, 257-264. Kuala Lumpur: Computer Aided Architectural Design Research In Asia.

Liu, Y.T. (2001). The Hsinchu experience: a computerized procedure for visual impact analysis and assessment. In *Automation in construction* 10(3):337-343. Amsterdam: Elsevier.

Lou,C.A.,A. Kaga, and T.Sasada.(2002). Environmental design with huge landscape in real-time simulation system. In *CAADRIA 2002*, 265-272. Kuala Lumpur: Computer Aided Architectural Design Research In Asia.

Paul, E. (1996). Modeling and rendering architecture from photographs. In *Siggraph* 96, 11-30. New York: The Association for Computing Machinery, Inc.

RealViz Inc. (2001). The Manual of Scenewe@ver. http://www.realviz.com

Tang, S.K. (2002). A digital reconstruction procedure for a disappeared city space and its activities. In *ECAADE 2002,* 598-603. Poland: Education in Computer Aided Architectural Design in Europe.

Seeing Architecture with a Filmmaker's Eyes

Aron Temkin
Florida Atlantic University

Abstract

Where do the methods of architectural communication cross over to other disciplines? As digital tools provide greater opportunities to communicate pre-built design in both space and time, in motion and in video, how should our methods of presentation (and therefore our method of seeing) evolve to meet this need? While filmmaking is a much younger art form than architecture, it is already much wiser with regard to motion-based presentation. If we are to evolve beyond the unsophisticated motion of the average fly-through animation, we need to develop a process of seeing and composing in time that better relates to the way we perceive temporal space. A well-edited film detaches us from the confines of the medium: we do not think about how many cameras are used in a scene if it is filmed (and edited) in a manner that is natural to the way we see and perceive.
Where can the filmmaker's art inform an architecture student's processes of presentation and design? This paper will discuss ways that filmmaking can be used to inform the process of architectural design and animation with specific examples from the work of our advanced digital media course.

Seeing Architecture with a Filmmaker's Eyes

Aron Temkin

Florida Atlantic University

1 Introduction

Even the least sophisticated animation offers a remarkable opportunity to communicate the dynamic conditions of movement through space. Animation creates new and exciting opportunities for presentation. We can illustrate not only space, but also the dynamic condition of movement through space. The typical fly-through is composed as a single line of motion; the line of sight is perpendicular to the path of travel: the pace of motion is artificially constant. This methodology reflects architects' naivety with motion-based presentation tools. If we cannot look within to resolve these issues where should we seek wisdom?

In film, the term "scene" refers to the context of a situation. Any one scene may contain several camera views, depending on the dialogue of actors or vantages (objects of interest). In our advanced digital media class we are attempting to evolve student methods of architectural presentation in motion to accommodate a process of architectural filmmaking that de-emphasizes a line of motion in favor of a line of perception. When we turn to look from one side of a room to another, we do not pay equal attention to everything in our field of vision, but rather move from one point of interest to another. Our eyes may see everything between these two conditions, but it is these nodes that define the emphases of our attention. The discipline of filmmaking already recognizes this characteristic of perception. The beauty of filmmaking is that if done well, the motion looks natural. We take for granted that what we see is what we are supposed to see.

2 Dynamic Design Methods 2

The student work illustrated in this paper is primarily representative of *Dynamic Design Methods 2,* an advanced elective emphasizing 3D modeling, digital video, and interface design. Most of the course projects center around the presentation and description of a building: either a previous studio project or a significant contemporary building. Students spend the first half of the semester developing the model and the latter half of the term developing a film (using Adobe Premiere), an interface application (using Macromedia Director), and a website (using Macromedia Dreamweaver) dedicated to the presentation of the project.

The students have already taken *Dynamic Design Methods 1*, where they have learned Form•Z and previously developed a small but complex building design. The course is open to architecture students from junior year forward, but most students wait until their senior or thesis year to take the class. The course group is small, up to fifteen students, as limited by the advanced teaching lab facilities. The class meets for only three hours a week, and this time is usually divided between an hour dedicated to the review of current work and two hours dedicated to the introduction of software, concepts and examples.

The students' first submission is a short, live-action video that they design and develop in groups. Usually, the intense schedule of the course motivates the students to maintain these sub-groups for informal discussions and review in between class sessions.

Two stages of development are critical to the success of their film project. First, students must move past thinking of animation as a single camera path and must begin thinking of animation as a sequence of planned vignettes. Second, students must begin thinking of the construct of components requiring direction, structure, and rhythm. This is then further developed by the addition of sound. Some of the most creative solutions have come from students who use sound to give their modeled buildings an indication of context.

3 Watching Movies: A critical method of seeing

At the beginning of the process students are taught how to view a movie (rather than watch a movie), documenting camera changes, recording the focus of the shot, and paying special attention to motion and light. We play each short segment several times over; the first time students watch the movie following the storyline as intended. The subsequent times students are asked to examine the construction of the movie noting specific conditions:

- How is the path of view divided between camera segments?
- How many different camera angles were used in the sequence?
- How did the editor transition between clips of film?
- Where is the subject of the video located within the field of view?
- What is the darkest or lightest place within the field of view?
- How does the soundtrack coincide or contradict the visual condition?
- Where does the director want us to focus our attention?

These clips are taken from both short film media and major motion pictures. Some of the best examples come from movies like *Gattaca* (Niccol 2001) where the lighting and scale of powerful buildings contributes to the ambiance of the movie. This has been particularly effective in nurturing a reconsideration of the potential connectivity between architecture and film.

3.1 Optics: What's automatic and what's expected?

After watching several film segments students become aware of issues like depth of field and the distortion of wide-angle lenses. While the student projects are mostly animated it is still important to discuss these and other optical effects. There are several things that are natural to the way we have been taught to see, like depth of field which affects how much of the background is in focus, that are a product of recording through a lens. Depth of field is not automatic when recording digital animation, although like most optical effects it can be simulated. Lens flare is another example: this is a very natural effect when shooting with a lens, but does not occur with a virtual camera. The issue is that sometimes these conditions are natural to the way we *expect* things to appear. Several animated films, like *A Bug's Life* (Lasseter and Stanton 2000), are entirely digital but include a lens flare whenever the camera moves in front of the sun because it appears more natural.

3.2 Resources

Atom Films (www.atomfilms.com) offers great opportunities for the students to view short films illustrating varying styles and camera techniques. This website features short animated and live action films. The DVD series *SHORT*, a DVD magazine, is another useful resources. The film *Blue City* (Birdsell 1999) from the sixth volume *SHORT 6 - Insanity* (*SHORT 6* 1999) was used as a case study in the spring 2003 term. This film was produced early in the morning with a very small cast, so the nature of space, of sound, and light, each have an easily identifiable role in creating the resulting environment.

DVDs have been a useful teaching aid since many discs now contain bonus tracks with additional production information. The *Fight Club* DVD (Fincher 2000) has several tracks of film where complex scenes are broken down to show all of the camera angles required to record the shot. The disc from the animated movie *Shrek* (Adamson and Jenson 2001) has several useful segments for illustrating the storyboard process. In the tracks, *Storyboard Pitch of Deleted Scenes*, the lead animators are pitching their storyboard sequences with dialogue and sound effects: their storyboard drawings are shown frame by frame during the presentation.

4 Learning Digital Video

Because the *Dynamic Design 2* students are expected to learn the digital video software at the same time that they are composing the model for the final film project, the students were assigned a shorter film project. Using the School's mini-DV camera the students were to record and compose a short video about the School, its people, and surroundings. Students develop this project in four topic groups: the people, the place, the work, and titles/credits. Each group composes its segment individually with a separate soundtrack. The only exchange between the groups occurs during in-class reviews of the work. The group responsible for titles and credits does not have to acquire film content like the other groups, but it ends up with the responsibility of trying to combine the dissimilar parts into some coherent whole.

Since the content is mostly digital stills and digital video the students can spend most of their time on this project learning how to compose and edit the pieces. Typically, one of the three segments is strong and the other two are weaker. Over the last two years the strong groups have finished earliest, giving their classmates a chance to see their work with time to make revisions. Typically, the urge to compete that develops between the groups makes the whole project more effective.

4.1 NTSC and Widescreen– Designing within a module

Digital video, unlike digital still photography, requires a much more consistent approach to frame size. A digital camera can be turned ninety degrees for a vertical composition, but video does not permit the same flexibility. This is particularly true with live action video since the camera one is using prescribes content format. The standard for North American televisions and video cameras is NTSC, or a 4:3 proportion frame. Many digital modeling programs, like Form•Z, have an option to render animation in a standard NTSC window, but one benefit of digital animation is that the designer is not bound to any camera's proportion system. An animated film can be just as easily composed and rendered in a widescreen frame (16:9) or even in a wider panoramic view (see Figure 1). While Premiere and Final Cut Pro both have workspace settings for the standard video modules you can compose video to a custom size as well. In completing the School video students get a sense of how binding the video frame can be.

4.2 Editing the Clips

Students are shown how to adjust the in-point and out-point of each segment so dead space in a clip need not be contained in the film. They can also use these tools to sub-divide a single animation sequence into a series of individual film captions. This way, for instance, if an animated procession moves through a wall the part before and after the collision can be used without having to view the error in the middle.

4.3 Transitions

We have been teaching students to compose and edit in a two-track (A/B) environment. This arrangement is typically easier for novice users. Video segments are inserted into either the A-track (above) or the B-track (below) with a separate track for transitions

Figure 1. Animated progressive section of a rammed-earth house by Todd Evans composed using a widescreen frame.

in between. The two-track layout helps students understand how video segments can be made to flow from one to the next with varying levels of continuity. Where a traditional flythrough is composed of camera moves in a continuous sequence, using a video editor there is the opportunity for blended transitions in concurrence with changes of view angle or subject of focus (Figure 3).

Premiere includes a large selection of transition types. Most of these transitions are very graphic and initially students are overzealous about using these very direct and very graphic flourishes. We go over several in class, but the dialogue of discussion is particularly with regard to where a transition is supposed to make a break between dissimilar parts versus a transition that is intended to weave segments together. Another incidental benefit of the group video project is that students get most of the special effects transitions out of their system.

4.4 Panning and Still Images

Still images can be added to the video tracks as easily as a video segment. The only difference is that a still image has no innate duration. Students are encouraged to include still images in their films. Still images can help slow down the pace of the video composition and emphasize key views or spaces. Often, details of material such as brick coursing, or a detailed texture are not clear in a segment of motion video. These conditions only show up clearly through stills or *very* slow animation sequences. Another advantage of still images is that they render much more quickly. Still images are useful for filling in segments where an animated sequence may not be complete. They can also be used as placeholders while the movie is being composed.

A dynamic way to use a still image is to pan across a long view. Horizontally, the effect is like scanning across the horizon; only a portion of the whole image is seen at one time. Students are very taken with this tool since it gives a still image the effect of motion.

4.5 Adding Sound

Students learn how to add a music track, typically an mp3 file, to their film. Since there is usually no dialogue in these projects the soundtrack has a significant impact on the rhythm, pace, and transitions of the film. Premiere can accommodate several sound tracks, but most students do not use more than two. Students learn to fade sound in and out: the soundtrack should not start or end too abruptly, or it sounds like an editing mistake.

4.6 Adjusting Speed and Duration

Students have a lot of flexibility as per the speed of individual film segments as the animation segments are not populated. Students are encouraged to align the visual transitions (variable) with the audio transitions (fixed). Despite the use of storyboards the animation sequences are usually not executed specifically for a certain place in the soundtrack. Students are recommended to animate at thirty frames per second: with so many frames a slowed-down sequence can still appear smooth in the final film.

5 Storyboarding – Ordered Strategy

Like drawing the cartoon set of a final presentation, storyboarding is an annotated outline of a time-based composition. While storyboards can be entirely drawn, the students are encouraged to use a drawing with annotation format so they can make notes about the lighting requirements, camera angles, or transition styles to be used along with the sketch of each camera angle.

The storyboard can be used either to document the project camera move by camera move, or scene by scene. We have had the most success introducing students to this process initially as a scene-by-scene (space-by-space) record of where they are going and in what order. This model is very useful with regard to Director applications and web design. In these contexts the storyboard is used to document the relationship between the home page condition and the subsequent chapters or sub-pages of an interface design.

One of the primary lessons when we begin interface design is about creating some consistent organization from one page to another so that the user can follow the navigation system from one page to the next. Storyboarding provides an effective means of helping students to map out both the variable elements of each page (content) versus the constant elements of each page (navigation tools).

With the film projects students begin by developing scene-by-scene storyboards and then, after the basic order is resolved, are asked to break each scene into a series of camera moves. So far we have not had enough time in the project sequence to have students consistently document the camera changes. This more exhaustive method of notation can assist the author in isolating the key vignettes within a progression. Used correctly, students should be less inclined to render long sweeping motions where shorter faded transitions would be more natural. This is also more efficient for production: when they execute their animations

Figure 2. One segment of a fly-around depicting Richard Meier's Giovannitti House in a film by Erik Garcia.

Figure 3. Flash transition used to segue between a distant and near view of Steven Holl's Y-House in a film by Jaime Calabrese.

this way the rendering time is usually faster since they are rendering shorter four-second to eight-second segments.

5.1 Planning the Model

While many of the students have already applied Form•Z in their studio work, most have not developed a methodology appropriate to a more detailed presentation of a building. Just as traditional rendering requires forethought as to which areas of the building are to be shown and what level of detail to apply to foreground and background elements of a view, so too detailed modeling should ideally be founded upon a plan of priorities and emphases. The students cannot realistically model the entire building at an equal level of detail. The objective of this planning stage is to determine (as possible):

- What parts of the building are most important and therefore most likely to be shown?
- Where will the building be seen up close and therefore in more detail?
- Where will the building be seen at a scale where textures or material joints are going to be apparent?
- What will only be seen from a middle distance?
- What will only be seen only from a far distance?
- How much of the context is important for understanding the building?
- How abstract or realistic is the model going to be?
- How should the level of realism/abstraction of the model impact the level of realism/abstraction of the context?
- What can be reasonably achieved in the time allotted to the project?
- What is not going to be seen and therefore can be omitted from the model?

If we are modeling in a thoughtful manner the process should permit an opportunity for discovery – for realizing some unseen quality of place that was not apparent via other means. This said, the animator should not preclude the possibility of discovery and therefore adaptation within the scope of the project. On the other hand, without a plan of attack a detailed modeling project can be difficult to fathom and harder to finish.

6 Making the Movies

6.1 Capturing Movement

After documenting the composition of several short films students have begun to see just how short a single camera move can be. Initially they resist this with great effort, composing thirty-five and forty-five second animations that sweep around their buildings at high speed. We critique these in class several times during the term. It only takes one member of the class to catch on, then seeing the effect in one of their own projects, the others begin to follow suit. The work becomes much more sophisticated once they can conceive movement up a flight of stairs or around a corner less as an extended line of motion and more as a series of single movements stitched together with transitions. The fourth frame of the image sequence below (Figure 4) illustrates a change between two camera movements into Louis Kahn's Exeter Library.

Since the emphasis of the filmmaking process is to create a more natural experience of occupancy, the students are encouraged to place the most emphasis on views that are natural to the inhabitants of the space. More artificial views are expected to serve a specific end, expanding the viewer's perception of the work. A good example of this is shown below in Figure 5: the student used an unnatural camera angle to illustrate the details of a complex roof system from one of Renzo Piano's buildings.

Figure 4. Camera switch moving into the center of Kahn's Exeter Library in a film by Scott Maggart.

Figure 5. Camera sequence moving inside the roof system of Renzo Piano's Cy Twombly Gallery in a film by Landry Starling.

Figure 6. A short camera sequence of Tadao Ando's Water Temple is enhanced by the reflected sunlight in a film by Morr Yeashoua.

6.2 Light

Adequate lighting is essential to the success of the animations. The students spend most of their time on lighting interior spaces. Beyond simply providing enough light, some directionality (i.e. gradient) in the lighting scheme is necessary for surface and depth changes to read properly. This can be more difficult with dark and patterned surfaces. Most students render their final projects in Form•Z. Once they are comfortable with custom lights they use these more frequently. The custom light settings allow for a more directional distribution of light to be defined. These can be less direction than a cone light without being as uniform as a spot light.

In the analysis phase of the course students are asked to look at the color of the light and how this color indicates the difference between natural light and artificial light, or morning versus mid-day light. The students who are most sensitive to these conditions show a much broader range of color in the lighting of their film. A good tool to this effect is Graphisoft Artlantis. Form•Z will write an Artlantis native file. In Artlantis students can create solar studies of their models. These models beautifully represent the movement of the sun along the floor or wall of an interior space. Even more importantly, a morning to evening sun study simulates both the sun's direction and the sun's chromatic shift. Even if the students do not elect to use this for their final rendering, witnessing the color change in the short animations appears to inform the range of light colors used in the films.

7 Conclusions

In learning the process and methods of digital filmmaking students discover a valuable tool for both delineating and testing designed space. While we watch the film projects develop in class, the evolution of the students' thinking is apparent in the evolution of their work. They evolve from composing a path to composing a procession. Moving through these virtual buildings they become more sensitive to how the architecture defines a specific path through a space.

The time they invest building the model is a strong motivation toward lighting the work effectively. Students become more comfortable with the tools, and they recognize light as a device for communicating change – inside to outside, morning to evening. The students show a greater facility for lighting after this project that seems to permeate their subsequent studio work. Students think more specifically about the pace of movement and about ambient sounds in the space while learning to add sound to the projects. The soundtracks change and evolve along with the project reflecting changes in the students' understanding of how these places can be experienced. The most effective movies usually use jazz, ambient, or classical music behind the imagery. Backed by rock music the films typically move too fast and the end result is often disconnected. If a student does not learn this lesson through their own work they usually reach this conclusion after watching the more successful work of their classmates.

The process of animation presents powerful tools for the presentation and critique of architecture; that this should have a transformative affect on the discipline is clear. A critical dialogue regarding the success and application of this media would be well served by acknowledging the filmmaker's insight into human perception and the choreography of movement. To be effective with this media we must be willing to acknowledge that the context of architectural movies does not in itself change how people perceive space and motion. By seeking insight from the discipline of filmmaking, we can aspire to a more natural and informed delineation of movement and occupancy in digital space.

References

Adamson, A., V. Jenson, dir. (2001). *Shrek*. (DVD). Redwood City: Dreamworks Skg.

Birdsell, D., dir.(1999) "Blue city." (1999). In *Short 6 – Insanity*. (DVD). Hollywood: Warner Studios.

Fincher, David, dir. (2000). *Fight Club*. (DVD). Century City: 20th Century Fox.

Lasseter, J., A. Stanton, dir. (2000). *A Bug's Life*. (DVD). Burbank: Disney/Pixar.

Niccol, A., dir. (2001). *Gattaca*. (DVD). Hollywood: Columbia/Tristar Studios.

SHORT 6- Insanity. (1999). (DVD). Hollywood: Warner Studios.

Digital Exploration of Unbuilt Architecture: A Non-Photorealistic Approach

Daniela Sirbu
University of Lethbridge

Abstract

This paper presents a new approach to the digital investigation of unbuilt architecture. A navigable world, emulating the architect's graphic style, is built as a 3D non-photorealistic reconstruction of the unbuilt project. A cinematic journey through this world intermediates the exploration of the architect's possible mental visualizations during the creative stages. The goals of the proposed approach are: to open new avenues for investigating the conception of architecture, to help architectural students visualize and experience important unbuilt projects that have shaped the practice of architecture, and to popularize lesser-known architects to the general public. The approach stems from the idea that architectural drawings are the artifacts reflecting most accurately the architect's creative and thinking processes. Anchored in the concept of multi-dimensional space developed by the author, the proposed method uses the original drawing of the artist as the main artifact on which the reconstruction process is based. The present paper concentrates on those aspects related to extracting information from the architect's drawing and embedding historic knowledge in the 3D reconstruction of the unbuilt project. It calls to attention the idea that technological progress creates tools that the Architect uses to operate with the fundamental concepts of place, space, and time.

Digital Exploration of Unbuilt Architecture: A Non-Photorealistic Approach

Daniela Sirbu
University of Lethbridge

1 Introduction

3D reconstructions of unbuilt architectural projects have been tried before. An impressive collection of 3D reconstructions including many unbuilt projects by Frank Lloyd Wright, Antonio Sant'Elia, and others, was put together by B.J. Novitski (Novitski 1998). Probably the most successful 3D reconstructions of unbuilt architectural projects to date were proposed by Kent Larson (Scully 1993) for some of the most influential projects of Louis Khan.

The approach taken in this paper diverges from the current trend in the area of computer reconstruction of unbuilt architecture. It does not try to provide realistic or "hyper-realistic" (Ojeda and Guerra 1996) reconstructions based on the utilization of natural textures. Kent Larson's reconstructions were aimed to offer highly realistic visualizations of Kahn's unbuilt projects. His approach attempts to facilitate the investigation of the unbuilt by taking, in the virtual world, the next logical steps in the life of the architectural project and to represent the building as it may have appeared if constructed in the real world (Larson 2000).

This paper advocates a completely different approach. While the architect's drawings continue to represent the starting point for the research, the main objective of the reconstruction is not to complete the unfinished project. Instead, the computer reconstruction goes in the opposite direction. It tries to recreate the steps taken by the architect during the conceptual phases, to investigate the creative process itself, and to explore the possible sources of inspiration. The architect's 2D renderings and conceptual sketches are translated into digital 3D spaces. These are meant to assist the investigation of the project conception in various design stages. The proposed approach differs from the current trends in terms of the main objectives of the research, the research methodology, and the employed digital reconstruction techniques.

The central characteristic of the proposed approach is the translation of the architect's drawing into a 3D navigable medium while concomitantly aiming to preserve the architect's graphic style. The available 3D software packages are generally optimized to create realistic representations. Although results have been obtained in the area of digital non-photorealistic representation (Gooch and Gooch 1998; Strothotte and Schlechtweg 2002), these are not flexible enough to recreate a specific graphic style of an artist, but rather focus on emulating traditional media in general. As a result, non-standard techniques were devised to achieve the goal of recreating the graphic style of the architect in the 3D environment. Custom collections of textures were extracted from the architect's drawings and were processed to allow the creation of complex materials required to build the 3D environment. As in art restoration, the process aims to digitally emulate the architect's specific graphic treatment, including the representation of depth and lighting in interaction with the architectural volumes.

A cinematic exploration of the virtual architecture facilitates experiencing the architect's concept of dynamic space as it can be understood from his drawing. Unlike Cameron McNall who uses Canalleto's drawing only in the opening sequence to create atmosphere (McNall 2000a), the proposed approach maintains a consistent look and feel suggested by the architect's drawing during the whole movie. Another difference in approach is that unlike McNall who uses the Microscribe digitizer (McNall 2000b), the elements used in the present project were modeled directly using 3D Studio Max.

2 Related Works and Methodology

Two categories of problems are raised by the present paper. One refers to the approach proposed for the investigation of conception rather than perception of architecture through the reconstruction of unbuilt. The second refers to reconstruction techniques that allow the transposition of the graphic style of the drawing into the 3D navigable space. Numerous works have approached both problems before.

2.1 Artistic Restoration or Automated Reconstruction?

The latest trends in the domain of non-photorealistic rendering show the emergence of a large spectrum of algorithms aiming to digitally simulate traditional media. Two main sets of techniques were used in reconstructing artistic textures. In the first set, the simulation results mainly from mechanically applying sets of procedures to the final image (pixel algorithms). In the second set, procedural algorithms are applied to the three dimensional geometry with visible results at render time.

Recently, due to the general interest in the domain of knowledge management, some interesting projects have tried to apply the progress in this domain to knowledge-based architectural CAD. Prototype knowledge based architectural modelers were developed and applied by Chassagnou and his team for reconstructing Gothic vaults (Chassagnou et al. 1998), or Boucard and his team for columns (Boucard et al. 2002). Another promising direction is represented by the development of a system for sketching in 3D. This attempts to preserve

the "degree of expression, imagination, and simplicity of use achieved by 2D drawings" (Bourguignon et al. 2001).
All these methods allow working with simple architectural elements. While their evolution could provide in time an aid for those involved in the artistic 3D reconstruction (restoration) of the unbuilt projects, no techniques could replace the creativity and the insights of an artist or architect.

The proposed approach stems from the idea that remediating (Bolton and Grusin 1999) the architectural drawing from one medium to another is a process demanding artistic abilities similar to those required for restoring original artworks. The human intervention could not be replaced in this process. Apart from preserving the artist's graphic style, it also helps to maintain the integrity of the architect's concept on the project and explore the emotional, metaphoric, and symbolic content of the work.
A multi-dimensional virtual reconstruction aims to create a digital solution space allowing the exploration of the architect's possible visualizations during the conception stages. Translating the architect's graphic style in the 3D space is not a purpose in itself. It represents the means to expand the drawing into a navigable virtual space that is as close as possible to the original artifact (the drawing), the direct result of the creative process. While transposing the architect's graphic style from a 2D drawing to a 3D space is challenging from a computational point of view, it is even more difficult to expand the experience of navigating the virtual environment into a journey in the architect's conceptual space. That goes beyond the mechanical reproduction of style and the automated navigation of an artificial environment. It is here that human intervention and specialized art skills are necessary to make the sensible connection between style and content throughout navigation in the virtual space.

2.2 Methodology

The proposed non-photorealistic approach to the digital reconstruction of unbuilt is centered on using human artistic abilities and expertise with new media technology to translate a 2D architectural drawing into a 3D anthropomorphic space. This approach aims to facilitate access to abstract concepts drawing on human experience gained through interaction with the natural environment (Anders 1999). In terms of preserving the graphic style and content integrity, the process is similar to the restoration of original artwork. Simultaneously, the method facilitates the exploration of hypothetic creative spaces anchored in historic research. The proposed solution is divergent from the mathematical/algorithmic non-photorealistic approach to the digital simulation of traditional media.

The overall process incorporates two major phases. The first phase investigates the direct and contextual information regarding the project. The second phase represents the digital reconstruction process.

The purpose of the first phase is to provide the necessary data for the transposition of the unbuilt architecture into an expanded 3D representation. Knowledge management packages could facilitate this phase. These can assist the artist/architect in selecting the significant dimensions from multiple available solutions for a specific instantiation.

The second phase uses the information generated in the first phase as foundation data for the digital reconstruction. Any such reconstruction is the result of a bounded creative process. The artist/architect needs and handles all the available knowledge. Different artists/architects could interpret differently the body of knowledge accumulated by historians. Because new data may become available later due to the research process, the final result is only a materialized instance of the multi-dimensional space defining the solution. Unlike in the restoration process, the virtual reconstruction does not interfere with the preserved artifact and the solution could reflect different schools of thought, different inferences, and different positions. It produces an artistic interpretation of the unbuilt project which can be used as a milestone reflecting the current accumulated knowledge.

3 3D Reconstruction Project

To exemplify the proposed approach, a digital reconstruction has been developed around the unbuilt project "Pont destiné à réunir la France a l'Italie" (1829) of the nineteenth century French architect Henri Labrouste (Levine 1982). The reconstruction is based on Neil Levine's photographs of the original drawings (Figure 1). A wireframe view and a full perspective view of the 3D rendering are provided in Figure 2 and Figure 3.

3.1 Digital Reconstruction Process

The purpose of the digital reconstruction is to make possible the experience of passing over the bridge following the dynamics of the original graphical composition and synthesizing the spirit of that experiment as expressed by Labrouste. The filmic mode of investigation is preferred over interactive exploration due to the coherent exposition of information.

The first step is to provide a computer version of the perspective drawing (Figure 3). Different angles of view demonstrate the consistency of graphic style between the 3D architectural representations and the original drawings (Figures 4, 5, 6, 7, 8). Ensuring the visual continuity of transitions between different viewpoints is a first step toward a natural dynamics of the virtual exploration.

The digital movement is designed to convey real movement. Where the investigation of the virtual architecture assumes impossible standpoints for the human viewer, the digital camera motion is based on established representation conventions used by the film industry. These are already natural to the viewer and allow her to concentrate on the space exploration while the computer medium becomes an invisible agent to support the experience. Preserving the integrity of the graphic style in the 3D representation makes the investigation of the virtual space a permanent visual citation of Labrouste's drawings. Natural shifts from views staged to remind of Labrouste's frontal, section, and elevation drawings smoothly introduce angles of view never shown directly by the architect.

3.2 Depth

The suggestion of the third dimension by means of linear perspective is mathematically resolved through computer calculation. The accuracy of the automated process eliminates the approximations resulting from manual manipulation. The automated solution implicitly resolves some other depth cues as overlapping planes and relative size of objects. Therefore, these are also interpreted as the result of automated computing. The representation is highly objective.

Elements contributing to the suggestion of aerial perspective require more interpretation and decision-making. These assume a great number of manual parameters selections for both setting up and fine tuning the digital camera, colors and materials, various atmospheric effects, and particle systems. The results are then evaluated through qualitative changes in the rendered two-dimensional output. The process of digital reconstruction in the 3D medium emulates a combination of real life processes of building, film production, and traditional painting. The subjective character of the 3D field structuring is alleviated by the technical data provided in Labrouste's drawings. The bridge has a well-defined 3D composition, and the digital depth is developed around the predefined spatial structure of the bridge. In the digital representation, the background closely replicates the drawings. The choices regarding the middle ground and foreground planes do not involve the restructuring of the spatial relationships between objects, as both their size and placement are pre-determined. This allows for a very limited modulation of negative and positive volumes in conveying depth. A specific spatial suggestion can eventually be emphasized by an optimal selection of the key viewpoints.

3.3 Texture

Texture is an essential factor in translating the pictorial quality of the traditional rendering into the digital medium. Apart from this role, textures have been used for compositional purposes and for space articulation in ways trying to emulate Labrouste's solutions for resolving the same problems.

The best textures for realistic architectural modeling are based on digitally adjusted photographic material taken from real buildings. The modifications applied to photographs consist in eliminating any cast shadows, important differences in the lighting of the surface, obvious accidents in the surface due to mechanical actions, and in adjusting the perspective to obtain the texture represented in full frontal view. These digitally adjusted textures are then applied to the geometric model and the stretching of the texture around geometry is ensured through various texture mapping techniques. Numerous settings allow the fine control of the way in which textures are applied onto the digital surface.

These procedures have been adapted to the special purpose of the bridge model. The basic photographic textures have been replaced with textures extracted from Labrouste's photographed drawings. The extracted textures in raw form are represented in perspective. The most dramatic modification applied to these first forms of the textures consists in digitally repainting them in order to recreate them in full frontal view. Each painted stroke has been created by cloning portions from some other parts of Labrouste's drawings and merging these gradually over a transparent grid, which helped matching the proportions of the new texture with the existing one. Modifications at pixel level followed most of these changes, and they derived from the need to preserve Labrouste's line continuity and style, which suffered deformations

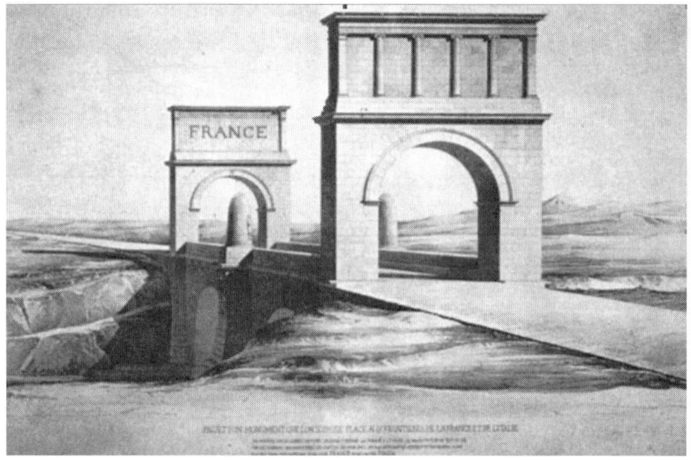

Figure 1. Labrouste: Perspective drawing

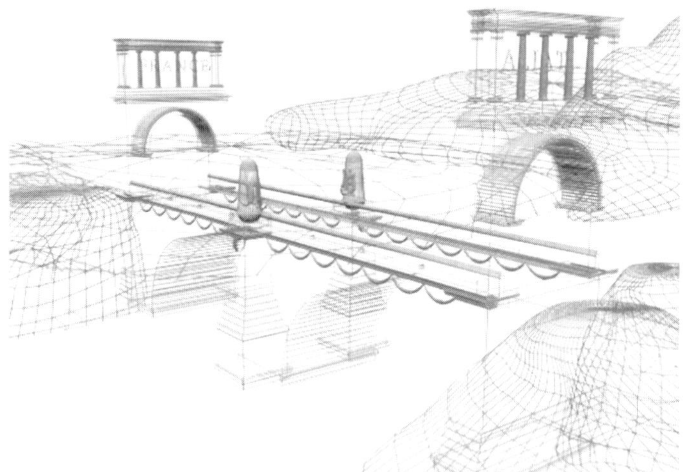

Figure 2. Wireframe view of perspective drawing

Figure 3. Reconstruction of final drawing: View 1.

Figure 4. Reconstruction of final drawing: View 2

Figure 5. Reconstruction of final drawing: View 3.

Figure 6. Reconstruction of final drawing: View 4

Figure 7. Reconstruction of final drawing: View 5.

Figure 8. Reconstruction of final drawing: View 6.

during the first raw adjustments.

A library of Labrouste-textures has been created for the specific purpose of the digital reconstruction. The hand-made quality of the textures was an important factor in conveying the traditional medium in the digital surface rendering. The texture library is organized in two dedicated collections, one for the landscape part of the model and one for the bridge. This organization is due to the way in which textures have been used in the computer model and the slightly different digital adjustments applied to them.

In Labrouste's drawings, the surface definition is subordinated to the volumetric quality of the architectural forms. The direct illumination of the frontal face of the gate emphasizes the clarity of the plane surface, the roundness of the arch, and the rectangular character of the gate's enframent. Labrouste rendered the stone block texture with elaborated accuracy to suggest the material but subordinate it to the overall geometrical character of the volume. The suggestion of a natural surface results from the manner in which the mathematical alignment of the stone blocks is combined with the illusion of slight imperfections in the surface. This is achieved through subtle modulation in the treatment of the overall surface suggesting the natural non-uniformity of materials and the uneven response to erosion. The overall feeling conveyed is that of a life-like uniformity of the surface, with subtle variation and randomness in the repeating details.

The traditional architectural rendering, even when various mechanical instruments like rulers, compasses, etc. have been used, remains very different from the rendered 3D image due to the manual quality of the contours. Various techniques offered by the digital medium for suggesting aerial perspective alleviates much of this problem especially for the representation of objects which are fading in the distance. For anything situated in the close area of view, the treatment of the contours was solved by applying more complex texturing techniques or by manipulating the geometric model based on raising the mesh resolution.

In the particular case of the bridge model, this problem was addressed by using complex composite materials with multiple texture layering. These softened the artificial perfection and sharpness of the outlines. In general, the base material used is a standard material with the diffuse channel based on one of the digitally processed textures from Labrouste-textures library. The supplementary layers may add some random imperfections to the base material. This helped to exaggerate the cast shadows effect along some of the margins of the object's surface, and was instrumental in altering the artificial sharpness of the edges. The last effect is mainly based on the use of transparency maps in the opacity channel of the base material. These maps are digitally created and are based on gradients from black or a selected grey to white. The lightest margin is placed along the contours that have to be softened by merging in a controlled degree with the other materials from the composite and with the background image. Additional slight imperfections can be added on different levels of the component materials. While the resulting contour is closely, but not entirely, matching Labrouste's line, the overall feeling conveyed in the digital rendering is that of manual manipulation of the contours. These effects combined with the use of Labrouste-textures produce the desired effect of realistic rendering in the traditional medium.

The treatment of the landscape texture mapping is different from that applied to the bridge in a number of ways. A separate collection of Labrouste's landscape textures was created. The need to obtain an accurate frontal view representation of the texture is not as strict as it is in the case of the architectural surfaces. Representing landscape in the 3D medium requires high-resolution meshes. The realistic representation of the landscape in Labrouste's drawings ensures good suggestions of volume in almost all of the landscape textures. This helped to convey terrain with lower polygon geometry, based on Labrouste's textures. For the terrain in the close area of view it was necessary to pay more attention to the contour treatment. The applied materials have been maintained as simple standard materials, and the irregularity of the terrain volumes was handled directly from the geometry of the 3D model by slightly increasing the mesh resolution. The irregularities are not shown in close detail, and a few accidents in the terrain forms ensured the necessary feeling of randomness and variation while still using low polygon geometry.

In Labrouste's drawings, texturing plays an important role in the graphical composition and in creating the suggestion of aerial perspective. The shadowed texture on the ground in the fore plane has an important visual weight. The texturing of the architectural forms is subordinated to their volumetric character, and emphasizes their almost purely geometric definition. The relationship between the detailed shadowed foreground textures and the faded textures in the middle and background planes has an important contribution in the articulation of space.

In the 3D medium, the compositional texture contrast between the ground in the front plane and the bridge automatically results from the application of adequate textures on the geometry and from the interaction with the digital lighting, coloring, and various other atmospheric and combustion effects. The texture mapping applied to both the landscape and bridge geometry uses the same maps numerous times in both close and far distance. These are automatically modified for representation in linear perspective. The modifications suggesting aerial perspective result from the interaction of the textured surface with light and other atmospheric effects which are set by manual manipulation of given parameters.

3.4 Light

The problem of using digital light is in many respects similar to the use of light in real life. 3D lights are manipulated by applying film and television production techniques, and the results are evaluated in the rendered output as a pictorial composition. Thus, the 3D light was applied through the metaphor of light in real settings, but was conceptualized as a brush with the capability of changing the perception of the objects' color, volume, and position representation in the final flat image.

The lights have been manipulated as light objects, with clearly defined positions in the 3D world, and with adjustment parameters emulating the operation of lights in the real world (light intensity, color, shadow, transparency and softness, size of the light cone and falloff area) plus other parameters which are more specific to the computer medium. However, the digital lights are in many ways different from real lights allowing, for example, the control of the cast shadows' color and way of blending with the environment. In order to emulate the graphic reality of the drawing, the capabilities offered by the digital lights must be used as painting tools for the purpose of the final two-dimensional representation. For this reason, manual manipulation of light parameters was the preferred choice over automated lighting solutions like radiosity and raytracing. This allowed greater flexibility in the process of digital painting.

A global illumination system has been defined manually. The direct illumination is organized in the form of a ring array of omni lights of variable low intensity with a central key light, which has the highest intensity and is elevated by approximately 30 degrees from the plane defined by the ring array. The color of the key light varies from yellowish-orange to a slightly yellowish tint emulating lighting conditions at the end of the morning and before noon. The lights in the array are non shadow casting and suggest the skylight contribution. Those placed in the semicircle opposing the key light have a color tint complementary to the key light, covering a range of blues. Those placed on the semicircle behind the key light in relation to the position of the bridge, have neutral white colors, with a very slight yellowish tint. The light-bouncing phenomenon is simulated with local lights and it is more accurate in relation to the architectural forms of the bridge, and more economic and loose in relation the landscape. A great amount of fine-tuning of the local lights has been done in order to render the pictorial effects from Labrouste's drawings. In spite of the emulation of photographic and film lighting techniques, the process can be resumed as one of digital painting with light.

3.5 Time

In the digital space, time and movement coexist intimately interwoven. The feeling of time in the 3D medium is related to the way in which motion is perceived. In real life, while one is static, time can be experienced in various objective and subjective ways. In the digital medium, as soon as the movement ceases, the computer representation loses dynamics and becomes a still picture. The illusion of life is lost and with it, the temporal dimension of the digital space.

The main object of the exploration, the bridge, is a still element. All the primary motion comes from the environment: water, clouds, cast shadows, mist. The movement of the water, clouds, and fog happens in objective time. The accelerated movement of the cast shadows sublimates the objective time, and leads observers to qualitatively different experiences, in a subjective time and space. The movements of the shadows create directional forces around which the bridge investigation is structured in a symbolic time.

Camera movement is instrumental for creating meaning. Often, it offers a subjective angle of view. It takes the viewer inside the digital time and space. It takes the viewer from the objective time of the physical simulation of the bridge into the subjective time of a transcending experience toward another space of existence.

3.6 Movement

The exploration in the multi-dimensional space is organized around the main compositional lines of force from the perspective drawing. The goal is to follow the path of movement and capture the dynamics of the architectural space as suggested in the original design.

The graphical composition in the perspective drawing indicates a passage over the bridge from east to west with an evident discontinuity related to the cippi. The core of the symbolic meaning comes from the experience provided by this interruption in the action of passage.

Another avenue of movement is suggested in the lateral view. The symmetrical arrangement of the architectural forms defines the cippi as the central element of a symbolic motion of passage from the earth to the sky. As this motion is centered on the cippi both as a boundary stone and a symbolic container of meaning, the symbolic vertical movement becomes tied to myth motifs: beginning and end, death and rebirth, and cycle (Figures 9, 10, 11, and 12).

The dynamics of the cinematic exploration is centered on these two passages: one following the natural direction indicated by the architecture of passage, and the second following a vertical direction suggested by the symbolic components in the bridge architecture, the cippi. The two passages are discontinuous and overlap, while their dynamics help the viewer perceive the sacral connotations of the interior space of the bridge.

The exploration of the architectural forms is mediated by their interaction with the natural environment and interferes with the sacral dimension assigned to the bridge. This gives intensity and a dramatic quality to the experiment emulating the feeling raised by a possible transcendence from the human world to another incomprehensible world. Crossing the bridge becomes a "rite of passage" related to the bridge as a temple.

3.7 Color

The material artifact that provides the basis for the multi-dimensional space reconstruction consists in black and white photographs from original drawings. In general, Labrouste used a restricted, low-energy color scheme based on a dominant pale yellowish-ochre. Both the ornaments and the use of color are austere and subordinated to the architectural forms, leaving the major compositional role to the interplay of volumes. The lighting used by Labrouste is important in supporting this approach.

The color dimension of the digital reconstruction was developed based on Labrouste's specific color range and lighting scheme giving the bridge an evocative character. The ineffable value of the digital exploration comes from the feeling that we enter an intangible world of the past.

3.8 Digital reconstruction of sketches

Other sets of reconstructions developed include 3D visualization of earlier stages of Labrouste's design process and cinematic interpretations of the bridge's symbolism. Renderings and movies were generated based on Labrouste's sketches (Figures 13, 14, 15, and 16).

4 Conclusion

New computer tools, new approaches, and ultimately new philosophies facilitate new ways of manipulating space during the architect's creative process. As Louis Kahn wrote "Architecture is the thoughtful making of spaces. The continual renewal of architecture comes from changing concepts of space" (Kahn 1957). While Architecture moves rapidly toward the paperless office (Norman 2001) and regardless of the techniques used it remains obvious what Fredrick Norman pointed out: "digital media is a tool for design." Architecture has been and will be about the traditional notions of place, space, and time. The architect's traditional forms of representation will continue to evolve. While New Media may remediate paper, clay, or wood, in the architect's studio, line, shape, texture, transparency, volume, time, movement, and light will remain the real objects manipulated by the architect. New equipments and software solutions will be successful only if these are developed to help the architect in this process.

The present paper is an attempt to answer the question: "how artificial worlds and new technologies begin to reconstruct ideas of place?" (Tilder 1998) It proposes the use of the architect's drawing as the basis for the digital re-creation of unbuilt architectural projects promoting the research of the architect's vision. It introduces a new approach to the reconstruction of the unbuilt architectural projects rooted in the known truth that architecture is mainly in the realm of concepts, ideas, and propositions, and not necessarily in concretized forms of expression. Unbuilt projects allowed architects to advance impressive analytical, descriptive, and experiential scenarios. This paper looks towards this rich world and proposes the creation of parallel multi-dimensional worlds on the basis of the architect's drawing. This could allow the "graphic reality" of the architect's representation to be transformed into a digital navigable environment adding new opportunities for critical thinking besides the traditional architectural walk-through.

5 Acknowledgements

I would like to thank Professor Greg Andonian from the School of Architecture, Carleton University, Ottawa, for the constructive discussions on the topic of new media and architecture and for his suggestions which resulted in a more rigorous methodological approach to the present research. I would like to thank Professor Martin Bressani from the School of Architecture, McGill University, Montréal, for opening my interest for the Nineteenth Century French Architecture and for bringing to my attention the work of Henri Labrouste. Professor Bressani has emphasized the importance of symbolic meaning in Labrouste's work and called to my attention the Janus motifs in the bridge project. Some of these ideas have been seminal during the development of the digital cinematic investigation of the project. Finally I would like to thank BMG for allowing me to build the movie around Sir James Galway's expressive rendition of Claude Debussy's 'La plus que lente.'

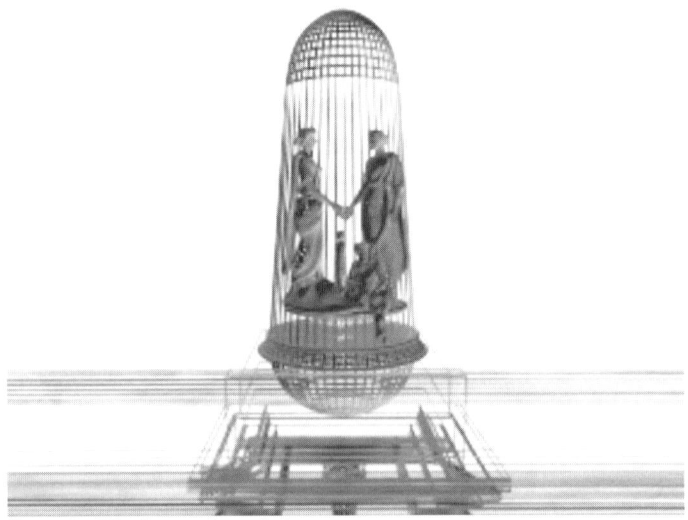

Figure 9. Wireframe view of cippus.

Figure 10. Rendering of detail: cippi

Figure 11. Rendering of detail: cippi.

Figure 12. Rendering of the cippi group.

Figure 13. Labrouste: Sketch.

Figure 14. 3D reconstruction of sketch Version 1.

Figure 15. 3D reconstruction of sketch Version 2. View 1.

Figure 16. 3D reconstruction of sketch Version 2. View 2.

References

Anders, P. (1999). *Envisioning cyberspace: Designing 3D electronic spaces*. New York: McGraw-Hills Companies Inc.

Bolton, J. D., and R. Grusin. (1999). *Remediation: Understanding new media*. Cambridge, Mass.: MIT Press.

Boucard D, S. Huot, Ch. Colin, G. Hegron, and D. Siret. (2002). An Image based and knowledge based system for efficient architectural and urban modeling. In *Thresholds design, research, education and practice, in The space between the physical and the virtual, ACADIA 2002 Conference Proceedings*.ed. G. Proctor, 231-240.Panoma, CA USA, October 2002.

Bourguignon, D., M-P. Cani, and G. Drettakis. (2001). Drawing for illustration and annotation in 3D. In *Eurographics 2001: Computer graphics forum,* vol. 20, eds. A. Chalmers and T.-M. Rhyne, C114-C122.

Chassagnou A.,F. Guena , M. Maille, and L.P. Untersteller. (1988). Modelisation and calculation of gothic or ogive vaults. Presented at the First European Congress on Restoration of Gothic Cathedrals. May 1988.

Debussy, C., *"La plus que lente,"* from Dances for Flute. (1993). (BMG Classics). Flute: Sir James Galway.

Gooch, B., and A. Gooch. (2001). *Non-photorealistic rendering.* Natick, Mass.: A. K. Peters Ltd.

Larson, K. (2000). *Louis Khan: Unbuilt masterworks.* New York: Monacelli Press.

Levine, N.A. (1975). *Architectural reasoning in the age of positivism: The neo-grec idea of Henri Labrouste's bibliothèque Sainte-Genevieve*. Ph.D. Thesis. Yale University.

Levine, N.A. (1982). The competition for the grand prix in 1824. In *The Beaux-Arts and nineteenth-century French architecture*, ed. R. D. Middleton, 66-123. Cambridge: MIT Press, 1982.

Kahn, L.I. (1957). Architecture is the thoughtful making of spaces. The continual renewal of architecture comes from changing concepts of space. In *Perspecta, The Yale architectural* journal, (IV, 1957):23.

McNall, C., director and animator. (2000a). T*he Last Drawing of Canaletto,* movie presented at SIGRAPH 2000.http://www.siggraph.org/s2000/media/facts/et.html

McNall, C. (2000b). *Digitizing with a MicroScribe digitizer: tutorial*. In 3D Gate, May 22, 2000.http://www.3dgate.com/techniques/000522/0522microscribe.html

Norman, F. S., Towards a Paperless Studio, Presented at the ARCC Spring Research Conference at Virginia Tech, April 2001, 85-91.

Novitski, B.J., (1988). *Rendering real and imagined buildings: The art of computer modeling from the palace of Kublai Khan to Le Corbusier's villas.* Rockport, Mass.: Rockport Publishers Inc.

Ojeda, O. R., and L. H. Guerra. (1996). *Hyper-realistic computer generated architectural renderings.* Rockport, Mass.: Rockport Publishers, Inc.

Scully, V. (1993). A virtual landmark, Hurva Synagogue. In *Progressive architecture* 9 (1993):81-88.

Strothotte T., and S. Schlechtweg. (2002). *Non-photorealistic computer graphics: Modeling, rendering and animation.* San Francisco, CA: Morgan Kaufmann Publishers.

Tilder, L. (1998). A temporary building in wall street: Architecture and representation in a digital age. In The *architectonics and aesthetics of artificial worlds conference,* Brandenburgische Technische Universitat, Cottbus, Germany. http://www.theo.tu-cottbus.de/wolke/eng/Subjects/981/Tilder/tilder_t.html

Architectural Design and Digital Paradigm: from Renaissance Models to Digital Architecture*

Paolo Fiamma
Università di Pisa

Abstract

Means of expression have always affected our ways of thinking. Designers, who have to interpret signs, languages, and evolution in order to translate into an organised "form" the recurring problems and values of mankind, have left thoughts, projects and wishes to the study of representational techniques. In this way, they have also disclosed a unique view of reality and at the same time a "way of being" towards the meaning of design itself. In the relationship between architecture and representational techniques, Brunelleschi said that "perspicere" was no longer just the science of optics, but also the science that contained the lines of research on geometry and shape that he was the first to exploit in design. Centuries later, in the axonometric representation advocated by De Stijl and intended for factories and industries, the object, shown in all its parts, easy to reconstruct even in the space to which it referred, revealed with extreme clarity the mass-production building and assembly materials and systems. Digital representational media make a great entrance in the heuristic process, invalidate all signs, and promote its quality. The result is an ever-changing, computerised architecture, dominated by curvilinear, wavy shapes that flow from a generative process made of the deformations, additions, and interference of different volumes.

*A Digital *Work In Progress*

Architectural Design and Digital Paradigm: from Renaissance Models to Digital Architecture

Paolo Fiamma
Università di Pisa

1 Digital Architecture

Today, the new representational technology affects the way designers work, in terms of speed, as well as promoting the use of static elements (paper, plastics), of such notions as time, motion, flow, through to the generation of simulations that can be used to work differently, to imagine space, and to relate to it in a new way.

The new technology is dramatically changing our approach to design; it also allows us to work with a vector geometry which marks the end of the rule of the Euclidean geometry. This breaking off involves our conceptual and designing potentials as much as their implementation. We could say that, somehow, this also increases our designing abstraction skills.

Increased production, reduced designing costs, improved communication of the executive building choices, and a new conception of the architectural space are just some of the major consequences of the use of new technology in architectural design.

The contribution given today by digital technology to the development of modern buildings is undeniable, as shown by the latest Venice Biennale.

The computer paradigm, that goes so far as to propose coatings that turn into screens on which pictures flicker (a blend of architecture and media), also delves into the classic, the so-called Euclidean forms: it disjoints them, runs through them with planes, and overlaps, making them iridescent and sometimes even dynamic. This change is revealed, for instance, by the change in the architectural "shells."

The dynamism of architectural space and the envelope as its expression appear to have reached a current statute of feasibility thanks to the achievements of modern instruments of computation and virtual simulation, message of a design concept and of constructive techniques that declare expressed today, following digital models, that verification which in the past was implicit in the rules of the art set by tradition.

The electronic and digital management of the design allows competing that envelops fresh and complex articulation, three-dimensional synthesis of experiments on the dynamism of space, whose processing and visual restitution is no longer consigned to traditional graphic representation systems, and on the nonlinearity of performance requirements, paradigm of a new digital message that comes to assume theoretical bases of fractal computation, beyond the concept of the Euclidean principles, towards the complexity of the nonlinear dynamics generated by the meeting of forces and resistances—inside the matter of constructive components—with the flow of climatic factors coming from the outside (Figure 1. Foster & P., Swiss Re Building, London).

Figure 1. Foster & P., Swiss Re Building, London.

The envelope is broken down and recomposed in three-dimensional space; it is framed by a fresh variety of viewpoints; it is dematerialised by plastic and curvilinear shapes, by the subtraction of parts, by an almost evanescent transparency that invites experimentation in crossing it; it is brought to the most contemporary fluid deformations of the architectural material until the expression of an almost vital dynamism.

The envelope can be read as a dynamic field where its constructive components push and broaden until the static and thermophysical paradox. An extensive diagram in which vectorial signs and systematic lines of force can be reduced to synthesis, which allows controlling the manipulation of the shapes under light, the increases in scale, the combination of viewpoints, the movement and the stagnation.

It is the metaphor of a new information landscape, magically unstable and dynamic, which proclaims in the envelope the symbolic passage from the building as machine to the building as computer. A new "science" of architecture and its vanguard must decide what cultural position to take with respect to the permanence of shapes, to the search for tradition and memory, to the spirit of place, to the value of history.

The plan "City of Culture" in Santiago de Compostela—Peter Eisenman—is an example of the relationship between topological surface and historical-cultural heritage (figure 2).

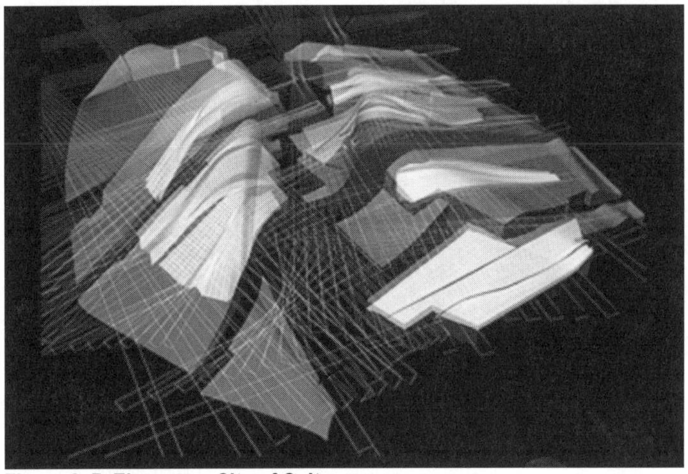

Figure 2. P. Eisenman, City of Culture.

The design develops from the overlapping of three sets of faces: the plan of the old city centre, the Cartesian grid of Mediaeval streets, the topography of the hill that disrupts the two plane geometries by creating a topological surface (neither figure nor land) that superimposes and mixes the old and the new. A designing and cultural transformation process: we can think of a relationship between "the software" and "the Genius of the Place" (E-topia, William J. Mitchell).

Traditionally, architecture has always been regarded as a semiotic system that expresses a well-defined expansion of the matter. Today, the saturation of communication technology contributes to create a phase of implosion and social reversal. This implosion marks the passage from a semiotic culture obsessed with representation—with an excess of information—to another post-semiotic sensitivity.

In it, weak meanings and symbols, that belong in a fading imagination, give up to traces and signals that produce an alternative condition of the figure and the land.

2 Dynamic representation

One can even redefine the acquired terms of representation as well as the size, the space, and the structures, or "invent" new ones, more suitable for expressing such changes. We no longer work within a limited 3D system, but within a media hyperspace (more cultural than technical) which reopens the question of space in the way we are used to perceiving and conceiving of it. Currently, the representation of the project has a new dimension (the video) that was not available in the past.

Thinking, for instance, of the potentials of virtual navigation within the designed spaces, one can see that this increases, improves the process of knowledge (knowability and creativity, and therefore also design) to such extent as to allow the cognitive processes themselves to move from a symbolic-reconstructive value to a perceptive-motor value.

This interaction between the object (the project) and the subject (the author of the project) is only believed but not made concrete. The modality of animation and introspection across virtual paths allow this. Animation techniques turn movement more into a force than into a sequence of pictures.

More than a handy tool for viewing and controlling designs, we could say that animation becomes a designing tool. It is not about designing buildings whose appearance recalls motion; this would be like referring back to what the modern movement produced when inspired by boats or other industrial products. This is about having design take place in a dynamic environment of forces, in which form and matter can even be replaced by digital information and mass communication.

In architecture, changing the environment where design takes place involves a dramatic change in the way the architectural space is conceived of and designed.

Shape becomes information, information as a set of ever-moving, ever-changing data. Information turns time into a spatial parameter. Once able to move, space and time become inseparable. While architecture has always been compared to the study of the inert, of everything "static," the coming of IT technology brings this assumption to an end.

There is a connection between representation—the approach to the real (and therefore to design)—and culture. In the Renaissance, representation was conditional on the philosophy of anthropomorphism. The vision of reality expressed by the Renaissance box into which one looks is static (the Arnolfini family, by Van Eyck). Perspective is man-sized: the onlooker's eye is the human eye, and builds a world in which architecture is its background. Later on, the Cartesian model becomes a way to represent the architectural space, which is the symbol of a new society. The position of the object can be known: its distance from the subject becomes zero (the approach to the real is conditional on positivism).

By the late eighteenth century, the need was felt to represent a reality that was to be used for the technical reproducibility of those products that would respond to those same needs. Since the nineteenth century, representation has had to be able to reproduce the architectural object: no longer as just a unique, unrepeatable "model," but often as a serial piece. At the beginning of the twentieth century, the viewpoint aims at infinity; one wants to portray the whole of things, not just part of them. In its meanings, representation suits the new meanings underlying design. Nowadays, the digital tool is so successful also because it is an "answer": an answer to what a new architecture asks for, to represent itself in a society that is more and more complex, heterogeneous, dynamic and relational.

There are two main aspects: First, there is the theoretical side, about the possibility of discovering a kind of visualization of our *mental space*. Secondly, there is the technical side, about the possibility of rendering some portions of space visible that would otherwise usually lie beyond our perception.
Today, the new representational technology allows the conception of a variable architecture, capable of representing not only finished shapes but the very conditions of formalization (e.g. the design by algorithm of Marcos Novak: in fact the algorithm expresses a system of relations, an "order" which binds variable elements to each other).

And the digital tool is also an answer to the more and more complex needs of today's design. The digital tool certainly contributes to the concept of "formal complexity," but also to that of the "exhaustiveness of design" by enabling design to become more and more integrated. This contribution affects not only the design concept but also its verification and the semantics of the design specifications, targeted to all the professionals involved in the designing and building process.

3 3D model: the form and the technique

With regard to the development of the project, an observation should be considered: a tri-dimesional model of a building may be modelled substatially in two different ways: with a generic shape or with constructive components. In the former case, the function of generic modelling propopsed by the CAD system. Conversely, in the latter case, when the building model has to be developed by constructuve components it is necessary to consider softwares (A.E.C.) that are dedicated to architectonic projects.

This methodology works similarly to a simulator, in a unique larger logical, physical and functional model, that is a prototype of the manufacture, then the pictures, the reports, and computations, etc.

For the techniques of creating projects in the fields of engineering and architecture, it seems that the contribution offered by the use of dedicated software solutions for the creation of three dimensional models is becoming increasingly important. The possibility of creating a complete functional-logical model of the projected structure is closely linked to the development of specific object oriented caad, which re-propose, in the construction of the three dimensional model itself, the logic which will govern the construction of the actual building. It becomes, therefore, necessary to be able to create a virtual model using elements of construction such as pillars, beams, bricks, and fixtures, and at the same time calculate, for example, the cost, the resistance characteristics, the thermo-physical properties, etc. This will favour the on-going process of a project in independent steps, allowing the recovery of its meaning as an expression of a single and simultaneous concept of all the aspects involved (structural, economical, functional, etc.)
The contribution given by the possibility of quickly changing the solutions adopted, as provided by the introduction of digital modelling, highlights the need to regard the project as a "verified concept" through an interactive process running across different disciplines and iterative between the time of the ideational expression and the time of its verification, now based on a wide-ranging concept of numeric modelling which underlies the digital 3D models.

In this respect, it is increasingly important to focus the efforts of research on thinking about the great innovation introduced by digital 3D modelling in the housing sector, not only in the merits but also in the methods of the designing conception.
Thinking of an object-orientated constructive 3D model does not merely mean to represent it, but also to conceive it, by generating it within an *existing* although virtual space.
This encourages one to focus not only on the formal and compositive side, but also on the technical and technological side of the future building, whose constructive components are brought in, arranged, and above all *connected* within the virtual building, as will happen in the practice of building, according to the building rules.

Specific A.E.C. software solutions for the building sector need the users to enter accurate constructive details for each component through dedicated graphic interfaces. The object is built in a virtual space, a preview or an extension of the real one, to which it will be given back later on, in the building to come.

4 Digital tools and digital method

To make the most of the possibility to develop an integrated virtual model, the design concept needs to be integrated at an early stage. The development of this virtual plastic model, which establishes relations among aesthetics, materials, costs, structural resistance, and overall energy efficiency, all *at the same time,* seems to articulate, in a topical manner, the directions given by the masters of the Renaissance on the need of constructive models for designed works. In this sense, the digital tool (A.E.C. technology), is certainly a tool but looks increasingly set to offer *a method*, an approach to design which is new, but ancient at the same time.

The relationship with traditional design seems convincingly related to integrating the ancient process based on the experimentation of design perceptions, corroborated by an empirical tradition, where the current expectations can be tested with "a priori" models before the work is developed.

The digital tri-dimensional model permits to obtain in an

unicum, not only the possibility to present a project, to study the different phases of construction, to produce explanatory graphics for the building yard, to explore the object in movement, to simulate the light and the shadow, and the thermic loss or the structures, but allows the generation of all these elements *in a combined manner*. (The Renaissance model, did not have this feature).

The data included in the electronic images of a project are not more rigid (like in the traditional computer support programs), but they are easily modified. To modify the thickness of a wall in an electronic model involves the simultaneous assessment of the cost of the thermic values regarding the light penetration on the internal or external images because the parameter thickness could be interactively linked with many others. (We should go so far as to assume that the construction of digital 3D building models may play a "regulatory" role as part of the design approval procedures, thus becoming an integral and no longer an integrable part of it).

The research, aimed at filling the gap between the design and the model and at the same time between the model and the product, can eventually provide an important contribution to the future development of digital designing techniques, that will allow this type of modelling to be more and more substantially used in building engineering.

Digital culture across...

5.1 The past . . .

The need to investigate the relationship between the most innovative digital representation technology and the historical-cultural heritage and the meaning of such relationship is extremely topical. A case-study concerns the relationship between tradition and innovation in the representation techniques: the plan of restructure of an ancient castle in one Island in Tuscany, Italy (figure 3), in two closely related phases, the reading of the built structures and the outlining of a work plan.

Figure 3. The ancient Castle

Paper documents on the most significant building stages in the development of the castle were very poor and partly missing; the possibility to gain an insight of the current state of the castle was partly limited by its peculiar location: the place is impassable; some ridges are inaccessible and dangerous, and often swept by strong winds; even inside, some significant areas are covered with a thick, all-invading vegetation which could not be removed. The method chosen was to synthesise both the historical reconstruction and the on-spot survey into a 3D digital model (for the moment, a geometrical one) that could also be used as a basis for outlining the potential work plan (to be therefore completed by adding constructive components).

The progress of the extensions and alterations that have taken place over the centuries and therefore the *room* occupied by the castle as it extended *over time* was examined through a 3D model which blended these two dimensions into a virtual dimension: this resulted at first in a chronological journey that was used, later on, to simulate a contemporaneity of moments that are remote in time: from the past to today and beyond, through to the future work plans. This directly affected the possibility to gain an insight into the construction, its liveability, its "ambience." The virtual decomposition and re-composition of the fortified construction highlighted constructive problems that could be open to uncertain readings.

Through the dynamic method, we could experiment with constructive conditions that are typical of the building process and which otherwise would have been purely imaginable (because of collapses or restrictions), thereby reconstructing the accessibility and usability that would have been reconsidered at the design stage. Digital simulation was key to another two aspects: the designing and the informative one. The works, based on utmost feasibility and compatibility criteria, even in the choice of materials, had to be prefigured in the way they would fit in with the context (including some provisional devices).

5.2 . . . and the present

The digital tool has potentials that are unexplored because it frequently reduces its expression to just images. It is a rapid, dynamic, pure, and amazing electronic image that changes continuously and disappears; therefore, it seems unable to leave a permanent trace (it is not a statue). But this is only a general definition, an apparent contribution. However, at a deeper level there is another definition that is often forgotten, in particular, regarding architecture.

Digital technology offers a new possibility to architecture. The potential of artificial tools is not only a mere artifact. You can get an image from a picture; the image is bi-dimensional. A three-dimensional model is not an image; it is not only a representation, it is an object: it means the transformation from a "dual" reality to a reality.

One often thinks that the virtual is in contrast with the real or, vice versa, that the virtual is a continuation, an extension of the real: I think that the virtual is a dual existence, compared to the real. To understand this "dual" reality concept, just think of the dual gender of some European languages. Dual: it exists in its own right, but in a form other than the one we usually attach to the existence of things. There is a harmonic development, for example, between the virtual dimension and the real dimension, which now needs to become more and more fitting. An example is the "capturing-processing-plotting" process, that can be obtained through the latest 3D scanners (combining laser and optic components): the real object is captured and immediately modelled in the virtual space, where its design is altered; then it is embodied again in man's physical space by the printers, also 3D printers, used in quick prototyping.

However the idea of space is changing due to influences that stem from temporal contractions and the new dimensions of interventions produced by the media, with which architecture enters in an always intensifying dialogue. The media bring "dominants" (a concept of European formalism from the early twentieth century) into architecture: i.e. "factors borrowed from other arts, able to rewrite the interpretative codes and affect the different components of a work."

Mass communication must be straightforward, clear, simple, to put across one's message in a concise way and establish a relationship with the receiver: to create correspondence straightaway. Digital media help this form of communication. Digital architecture is often the architecture of relation: it does not keep its distance from the onlooker; it asks the onlooker to enter the building.

Architecture is no longer defined by the space it offers, but also by the number and features of the services it supplies—its ability to change as quickly as possible, to be open to anything without contradictions. The building becomes, in itself, a service whose value is related to its ability to fulfil a given number of requirements.

This is a cultural model of "relation". But one should consider that extreme communication speed and profusion of information risk making everything look like everything else, making everything relative, a loss of accurate points of reference.
A shallow communication, that tends to impress at first but leaves no marks isn't deep (because it must leave the floor to the next piece of information, which is coming up). This leads to fragmentation, segmentation, and division. This may be the case of an architecture in which the form of the building stands out, prevails over its function, on the consistency of the constructive decisions—a way to design to become independent. Locally, this produces buildings that after some time are unliveable. Thus, even digital architecture can risk reducing its message to pure form, a magnificent but empty shell. The risk could be a fashion leaning towards aestheticism, that makes the representation ("marketability") prevail over "the fact" it refers to (the correctness and operation of the architectural design).
Digital media can help shape surfaces that flow so well they fly away. They impress, they attract at first, but they leave no marks; they don't turn into experience, reflection, critical awareness. This produces a shallow architecture: the metaphor of a lack of depth as is often stated by postmodernist culture.

The opposite also applies. I think that at the bottom of the need of interrelations, which is typical of today's communication, prominence should be given to the wish to create a bond between the person and the surroundings and "within the person": among all the needs it is made of. The possibility to tend to express oneself as a unity is a culturally strong position. Perhaps this can be compared to digital media (and digital architecture) if used to prefigure an architecture "of depth" where all the sides involved are holistically looked at through a constructive 3D model: we overcome the concept of images as "mere artifacts."

References

Baborsky M. S. (2001). XX Secolo- architettura, Milano.

Dringoli M. (1997), La frontiera, la campagna, il mare, Pacini Editore.

Eloueini A. Architettura virtuale: nuova frontiera dello spazio e Architettura e macchine astratte (Internet).

Heinsen G. L. (1995). Appunti della lezione sul disegno in Architettura, La Editrice Artistica Bassanese e la Scuola Remondini. Bassano del Grappa.

Mitchell William J. (1999) *E-topia*. The Mit Press.

Nantois F. Lo stile informazionale in architettura (Internet).

Uddin M.S. (1999). *Digital architecture,* Mc Graw-Hill.

Next 8^ Mostra Internazionale di architettura (2002) Marsilio Editore.

06 >> Connecting Digital Thinking

Chairs: Mahesh Senagala, Cristiano Ceccato

Digital Theory

Mahesh Senagala

The computer has gone from being an isolated box to become part of a gigantic digital network of networks that shapes our collective future. The way and pace at which we connect, communicate, memorize, imagine and control the flows of valuable information have changed forever. There are at least six digital phenomena that directly affect the architectural world: miniaturization (of all that can be shrunk), ubiquity (being everywhere, global), realtime (communing globally in realtime, which is 1/10th of a second), noospherization (networking every-thing), virtuality (all that is solid melts into knowledge), and anamnesia (inability to forget). Temporal contiguity and temporal connectivity have taken precedence over spatial and geographical contiguity. The strands that animate our life today emanate from spatially distant but temporally contiguous/connected places. These phenomena have squeezed, stretched, restructured, reconfigured, and redistributed most major human institutions. Consequently, the built world's role, importance and nature have changed. Architecture as traditionally understood has become more marginalized than before. Many practices, however, have been repositioning themselves to take advantage of the new opportunities beyond the bounds of traditional architectural practice. Design, practice, fabrication and construction are increasingly becoming networked affairs. The new measures of architecture are connectivity and speed. The architecture of a new world needs to recognize these transformations and think differently.

Mahesh Senagala is an Assistant Professor of Architecture at the University of Texas, San Antonio and runs an international practice. His areas of expertise include systems theory, cybernetics, sustainability and design computing. He has written and lectured extensively about digital culture, thinking and architecture.

From Emergence of Form to the Forming of Logic

Cristiano Ceccato

Driven by digital design tools and production methods, the interplay of theory and practice in architecture is converging on the notion of *process*. Process definition and process tools are now an essential part of design, design development, fabrication and construction. The word *process* itself can be interpreted in different ways, as being deterministic or non-deterministic.

Computer programming can be understood as a design process and a structuring mechanism. Rather than making finite designs (products), architects are beginning to understand their roles as *toolmakers*, developing algorithmic processes that incorporate constraints and intents into software / procedures / programming. New methodologies such as parametric-associative design hierarchies are a clear example of semantic design structuring (a form of grammatical ordering); the creation of hierarchical parametric models can be understood as a form of visual programming. In a deterministic sense, it can be argued that if a process is correct and critical, then by definition so will be the product.

Non-deterministic usage of computation differs in its goal to search for solutions rather than generate them through finite generation algorithms. Examples include evolutionary design, neural networks for pattern and form recognition, and decentralized cellular design systems. All these can be explained as types of design-structural data-mining that yield solutions that were not determinable before the application of a particular form-searching (as opposed to form-generating) process.

The question, then, must be: what are the implications of this for practice? Practice here must be understood beyond the experimental fashioning of rapid-prototyped test forms, though these may aide in gaining an understanding of the geometric constructability of materials. Rather, we must understand practice in the sense of actual construction of complete projects, with all the limitations, constructability requirements, legal complexities and particularly the serendipitous events that mark the uncertainty that is the production of buildings.

Norman Foster's office employs a sophisticated set of techniques that utilize structured hierarchies of geometric mechanisms to achieve complex form constructs through clearly discernible sequences of computational procedures. Complexity, in this case, arises from the systematic overlay and feedback of geometric information, while constructability is addressed and maintained by incorporating form restrictions and geometric limitations of components. Frank Gehry's methodology, by contrast, is the inverse, conceptually oriented towards what John Frazer has termed a *post-digital* process. Here, the architect does not deterministically control technology for finding form, but rather is liberated from technology by technology itself: the cogent application of computational post-rationalization of form allows us to explore a design process without having to first explicitly encode rules of formal structuring or computational morphogenetic processes.

Architects operating within the realms of theory-driven conceptual projects find they are required to rapidly produce workable schematic designs that embody their ideas. Nowadays, there is an expectation of everyone to 'put their model where their mind is,' in the sense that purely abstract discourses no longer find enough traction to substantiate a theoretical claim– they have to be tangibly demonstrated in practice.

The question that follows this, then, must be: how would a *post-computational* design process be structured, meaning how can forms be explored computationally without having to resort to preset rules or geometric hierarchies? How can a logical substructure of form be found without having to first describe it through literal geometric relationships or the [grammatical] programming of information? And, how can such a design process still be rigorous and rational enough to ensure constructability, capitalizing on the efficiencies of modern fabrication techniques, mass-customized industrial methods and a post-fordist economy?

Transcending the restrictions imposed on architects by current technological paradigms and the structuralism of form-finding algorithms is a logical progression in the development of design computation. Current tools are focused either on the generation of complex-form geometry, or its optimization for material behavior and componentized constructability, or both. The challenge will lie in moving beyond the implicit structuring imposed by the grammar of programming, the relationships of objects and object hierarchies which are used to describe discernible form topologies. Beyond the emergence of structured form, we can explore the emergence of structural topologies and form typologies from unstructured information – the *forming* of structured logic.

Cristiano Ceccato is an architect and computer scientist, specializing in the development of computationally driven architectural design tools and associated fabrication methods. He has conducted extensive research and development at Gehry Partners, where he is responsible for the development and application of parametric design tools and integrated modeling principles, and associated digital construction methods. He is also a director in a new subsidiary company, Gehry Technolgies, where he is responsible for technology transfer and pilot projects, developing design tools based on Gehry's 3D computational building construction methodologies. Ceccato has practiced architecture in Europe, Asia and the US. He has lectured widely on the subject of computational rule-based design systems and parametric form finding in digital building processes. He has held academic faculty positions in London, Milan and Hong Kong.
he received his diploma in architecture from the Architectural Association (1996), an MS in Computer Science from the ImperialCollege of Science and Technology in London (1997).

Deep-Time Probe Investigations in Light Architecture

Gregory A. Luhan, Suketu Bhavsar, Bruce L. Walcott
University of Kentucky

Abstract

This paper presentation presents an interdisciplinary research project conducted by a design team comprised of faculty from the Colleges of Architecture, Engineering, and Astrophysics. The title of the project, Deep-Time Probe, Investigations in Light-Architecture, explores the use of an optically active-SETI experiment that centers on the thematic of time, vision, and movement through space. The realm of architecture was the digital glue that united the varied disciplines.

The core of the project is broken down into three intrinsically linked components—data representation—collection, storage, and modulation; the Project Mission Wall; and the resultant Light Architecture or Deep-Time Probe.

A small team of architecture students under the direction of one architecture faculty member designed the Mission Wall while the Robotics Department provided CNC machinery to digitally mill and fabricate its components. This same team assembled the 40'x60'x15' structure in one day. The site of the launch created an adequate interface for the public art structure at the scale of an urban park. The scale of the Mission Wall addressed a variety of places, paces, and scales that mediated between the laser, the context of the surrounding plaza, and pedestrian and vehicular circulation, all while concealing the laser from direct view. The Mission Wall served three functions. It provided a housing for the Deep-Time Probe laser. It created windows and scaffolding for lighting. Moreover, it established a series of "View Corridors" that provided the onlooker with multiple vantage points and thus multiple-readings of information as architecture.

Nearly fifty "Time Probe Reporters" gathered information through oral interviews. In addition to messages linked to the interviews, the Deep-Time Probe contained verbal and graphic information, images depicting the design and fabrication processes. At the time of the launch, the design team digitized, specially formatted, converted, and modulated the data into a special high-powered laser that was "launched" into space. An advanced civilization in the universe could theoretically receive and decode this information.

The Deep-Time Probe project visualized the strengths of each profession, fostered the creative aspects of each team member, and resulted in a unique and dynamic experience. The deep time probe is right now passing through the Oort Cloud, the debris left over from the formation of our Sun and planets, present as a halo surrounding our solar system . . . a distance of nearly 1.5 trillion miles.

Keywords: Interdisciplinary Design Research, Information Visualization, and Fabrication

Deep-Time Probe Investigations in Light Architecture

Gregory A. Luhan, Suketu Bhavsar, Bruce L. Walcott
University of Kentucky

1 Introduction

In June 2002, the University of Kentucky received a $5 million grant to create an innovative and interdisciplinary Center for Visualization within the College of Engineering. The following project is applied research addressing both built form and the fragments of information used to create inhabitable space. As the first step in linking Architecture with Engineering, Astronomy, and Physics, the design centers on data representation and modulation using light as the occupied conduit for communicating relationships between time, vision, and movement.

1.1 Center for Visualization

The title of the project, *Deep-Time Probe, Investigations in Light-Architecture,* explores the use of an optically active-SETI experiment that centers on the thematic of time, vision, and movement through space. The realm of architecture was the digital glue that united the varied disciplines. The deep space time probe is just one of many exciting events occurring on our campus. Our campus is also involved in a "New Economy" initiative, which hopes to bring state government, the private sector, and the university community closer together to work as partners in spurring knowledge-based economic development. The key to this successful "New Economy" partnership is to identify emerging areas of mutual interest to both the private sector and academic researchers.

One emerging area which will enable new science and discovery in a number of cross-disciplinary research areas is visualization. What is visualization? In layman's terms, visualization is defined as the methodology of using high performance computers to generate visual representation of complex data or virtual environments. This broad definition covers the two main areas of visualization research: data or scientific visualization and rendering of virtual environments. Clearly, the concept of a deep space LASER time probe with its representation of abstract data is an ideal candidate for visualization as the probe passes through our solar system and beyond.

Investment from "New Economy" funds, together with strategic federal and private partnerships, has enabled the formation a new Center for Visualization. A list of the projects the new Visualization Center is enabling includes math education, 21st century manufacturing, minimally invasive surgery, and novel display methodologies. One of the key partnerships in the new Visualization Center concerns the use of novel polygon rendering techniques to reduce the computational requirements of high-resolution architectural rendering. With core visualization competencies in computer science, engineering, and architecture, this partnership hopes to continue to flourish and spawn further creative cross-disciplinary research.

2 The Idea Festival

On 18-21 September 2002 over 5000 authors, artists, scientists, idea enthusiasts, and students converged on the city of Lexington, Kentucky, to discuss and present ideas at an Idea Festival whose theme centered on "A Matter of Time." Brian Greene, a Columbia University Professor of Physics, Mathematics, and the author of the *Elegant Universe,* set the

Figure 01. Deep-Time Probe Advertisement.

tone for the Festival by challenging all participants to think beyond the box in regards to time, memory, and movement. The next day Leonard Shlain, a San Francisco surgeon and author of *Art and Physics: Parallel Visions in Space, Time and Light*, presented an overview of the integral relationship between art, the physical world, and technology. Less then 100 yards from these two pivotal presentations, the Deep-Time Probe (Figure 01) and Mission Wall lay dormant waiting for night to fall.

2.1 The Collaboration Process

The intersection of the Deep-Time Probe with the Idea Festival started as a challenge from Kris Kimel, the President of the Kentucky Science and Technology Corporation (KSTC), to design a "clock" for the Festival. The multidisciplinary nature of the project dictated that it was best to work in collaborative teams. During the course of the ensuing conversations, it became clear that three of us were in accord. The "clock team" comprises three faculty, Assistant Professor Gregory A. Luhan of the College of Design, School of Architecture; Associate Dean Bruce L. Walcott of the College of Engineering, Electrical Engineering; and Dr. Suketu Bhavsar of the Department of Physics and Astronomy.

Our first meeting together was more like a jam session on time rather than a discussion about "what is clock?" It became obvious that the issue of time and time travel was more fascinating to us then the marking of time. Nevertheless, was there a method of working that could give KSTC their clock and allow each of us to define an adequate place of abstraction that would be interesting to us individually? Our search for inspiration narrowed the boundaries between thinking, meaning, and making. In doing so, the traditional registers of architecture—most notably through writing, drawing, modeling, and building—became active. This project laid the framework for activating the gravity-less space of the computer as a viable place to literally make something from nothing.

2.2 Making Something from Nothing

Between the real and the perceived lies the process of discovery. However, where do ideas come from? The struggle to find a starting point often leads architects outside of the realm of

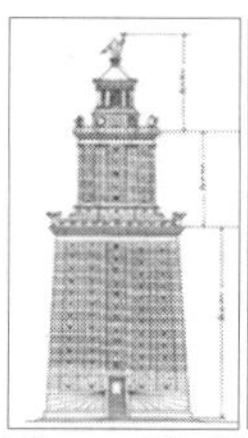
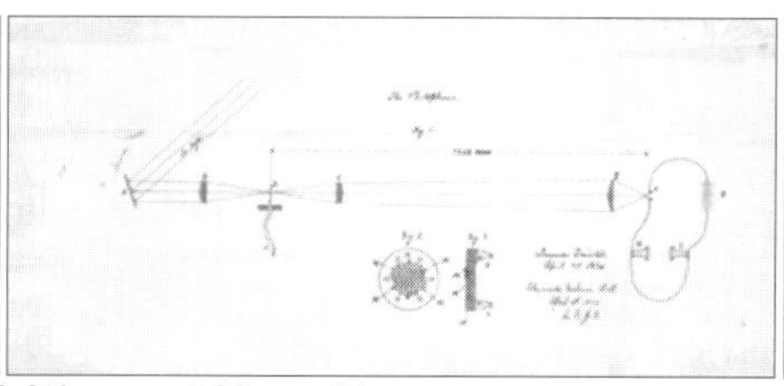
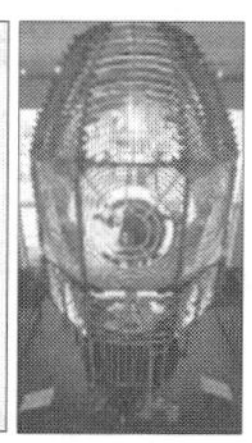

Figure 02. Lighthouse at Alexandria.

Figure 03. Alexander Graham Bell, Photophone Invention.

Figure 04. Fresnel Lens designed by Augustin Jean Fresnel, 1822.

Figures 05 and 06. Theodore Harold Maiman, 1960 visible light experiments; Laser Communication hypothesis.

architecture. As professors we provide a unique opportunity for our students to play in innovative ways—not only outside of the box, but in directing the seeing of the inside of the box in new ways. Architecture students, in particular, link the elastic qualities of the imagination to understanding precedent, exploring analytical methods, and deploying design methodology. The hope of this process is for students to develop their own philosophy upon which to base a design.

It became apparent that we needed to design an infrastructure framework that addressed security, liability, siting, scale, and material selection. By addressing these issues upfront, it would allow the students to hone rather than limit their investigation. The first task was to clearly define guidelines for putting three faculty together. It was agreed by the three faculty that we would take a lead role in each one of these categories and present the core ideas and issues in the form of daily seminars. This would therefore allow the design studio to be a dynamic place of interaction, deliberation, and conversation.

The nucleus of the project contains three intrinsically linked components. The components align with each of the three disciplines: Engineering, Architecture and Astronomy/Physics. [Engineering] data representation—collection, storage, communication, and modulation—information that is encoded and transformed from audio and graphics and uses light as the conduit for exchange; [Architecture] the Project Mission Wall—schematic, site, materials, and public art; and [Astronomy/Physics] the resultant Light Architecture or Deep-Time Probe—fragments of information.

2.3 Terrestrial Optical Communication

Communication is a fundamental component of any civilization-terrestrial or extraterrestrial. Using light and digital modulation to communicate is not unique to the modern world. In fact, communication via light can be traced back to the dawn of civilization. The seventh wonder of the ancient world was the lighthouse at Alexandria (Figure 02), whose mirrored light source could be seen from 35 miles off shore.

The roots of today's extensive optical communication networks can be traced to Alexander Graham Bell. While renown for his telephone patents, Bell received four of his eighteen U.S. Patents for the photophone. The photophone (Figure 03) was similar to his telephone with the notable exception that the device used sunlight in lieu of electrical current to transmit information. While

Bell did not adequately insulate the device from changes in ambient lighting, the photophone is considered the forerunner of today's fiber optical communication network. Current estimates list the amount of traffic over these networks at over 10% of the world's messages, and this number is increasing.

2.4 Light Amplification

Critical to communicating via light over long distances are practical methods to amplify light. For over 2000 years, glass has been used to bend and magnify light. The famous "Lanyard Lens" dates to 700 years BC. However, it was not until the 1600s that multiple glass lenses were used in tandem to create optical instruments such as the telescope and the microscope.

Of course, the optical telescope is still used as a means to amplify a received terrestrial or extraterrestrial light. But, what about advancements in ways to amplify light transmission? In 1822, a frail French mathematician named Augustin Jean Fresnel fashioned a lens from a series of stacked prisms. The resulting "Fresnel" lens (Figure 04) could focus and retain 83% of a given light source and enabled ships to navigate treacherous straits and rocky harbors. Nearly a century and a half later in 1960, Theodore Harold Maiman built the first visible light laser (Figures 05, 06) building upon the theory of photons as espoused by Einstein. The acronym, L.A.S.E.R., stands for Light Amplification by Stimulated Emission of Radiation.

2.5 Optical SETI

Simultaneous to Maiman's invention, Frank Drake—today's Chairman of the Board of the SETI Institute—conducted the first search for extraterrestrial intelligence. Drake used an 85-foot radio telescope (or antenna) to detect radio waves at a frequency of1420 MHz from alien civilizations. A year after Drake's experiment, Robert Schwartz and Charles Townes proved that LASERS could be used for interstellar communication and the debate between the optimal means to detect extraterrestrial intelligence ensued. Proponents of Radio SETI argue that the presence of alien life can be detected from radio transmissions not necessarily aimed into space such as our radio and television broadcast signals. Communication via LASERS from extraterrestrial civilizations would have to be intentional. Analogous to a message in a bottle, aliens would aim LASERS toward stars and clusters believed to have a high probability of intelligent life.

While the above argument seems to favor radio detection as the better means of detection, if one considers power and density variables, optical SETI has a clear advantage. The fundamental unit of either radio or optical transmission is the photon. The energy associated with a photon is inversely proportional to the wavelength of the electromagnetic transmission. Thus, the photons of the green light used in the Deep Space Time Probe launch have nearly half a million more times the energy than that of a typical radio wave. There is also a great deal of background noise or static in the universe as well as man-made and natural static in radio frequencies. Interstellar communication via optical frequencies has no such problem.

Another argument in favor of LASER communication is the amount of information that could be carried in such a signal. Literally, the entire library of congress could be sent to other civilizations via LASER communication. Perhaps the most compelling argument in favor of searching the heavens for signs of optical communication is the fact that two of the U.S. most prestigious universities, Berkley and Harvard, have now started research programs in Optical SETI.

2.6 Data Representation – Collection, Storage, Communication, and Modulation

After designing the framework for our discussions, nearly fifty "Time Probe Reporters" from elementary schools in Fayette County and its three surrounding counties gathered information through oral interviews of University faculty, local and state politicians, local entrepreneurs, and fellow students. Each reporter asked the same question: "If you could communicate with another intelligent life form, what would you say and what would you want them to know about our civilization"? In addition to messages linked to the interviews, the Deep-Time Probe contained verbal and graphic information, images depicting the design and fabrication processes, and seminar presentations. The College of Engineering then modulated this information in both real-time and analog.

3 Light Architecture or Deep-Time Probe

Our universe is a space-time continuum. Events happen in space-time. Each event has three spatial coordinates and one time coordinate, thus a four dimensional continuum. It is impossible to imagine four dimensions. Let us visualize space-time in two dimensions. We will use a representation where one axis of our coordinate system (say x) measures length and the other (y) measures intervals (or time). Therefore, a diagonal line in the x-t plane would represent moving from A to B along a line in a few seconds.

An example of a three dimensional representation is the orbit of the earth around the sun, which is planar, an ellipse, nearly a circle. Suppose we define the spatial plane of earth's orbit by the x-y plane and plot the position of the earth at different times along the z time axis. We get a spiral describing the motion of the Earth around the Sun. This is the earth's world line. This spiral shaped world line of our home planet formed a basis for the idea of the structure. The resulting form blends the relationship between landscape and architecture—between structure, surface, and contour (Figures 07, 08, 09).

Figures 07, 08, and 09. Project Mission Wall Component Assemblage, 2002.

3.1 Project Mission Wall

> Machines in the modern age showed that a "well stated problem" always met its solution as in the car or the airplane, but that the "problem" of the dwelling went far beyond utility. Clean lines, sharp light, and fresh air were to nourish the mind and the body of the modern citizen, and no doubt, to foster the same clarity of thought that Le Corbusier found endemic among engineers and so foreign to architects. All the same, satisfaction of the intellect was not enough, and the architect had to prove himself a plastic artist and no "mere engineer" by his mastery of profile and contour, through which measure alone architecture could touch the heart. (Hogben 1991)

The Circuit and District Courthouses constructed in 1998 in downtown Lexington left an open green plaza at the heart of the city. The plaza was the site of an International Design Competition in 2000, but two years later, it remains a blank site. The Idea Festival events surrounded the plaza or were along Main Street, so it made sense that the plaza would be the site for the Project Mission Wall (Figure 10). However, determining a scale for the project within this 128' wide x 224' deep plaza that has a grade change of 10' from north to south became a central issue, as did finding a way to construct the Mission Wall on the plaza without being on site everyday, as well as general concerns about liability and site security. The site of the launch created an adequate interface for the public art structure at the scale of an urban park. The scale of the Mission Wall (Figures 11 – 14) addressed a variety of places, paces, and scales that mediated between the laser, the context of the surrounding plaza, the monument of the eternal flame located in Phoenix Park across Main Street, and pedestrian and vehicular circulation, all while concealing the laser from direct view.

We challenged the students to open up the plastic possibilities of digital abstraction. We asked each individual student not to abandon what he or she knew, rather to augment their familiar ways of looking at things so that they could see the "problem" of design in new ways. Simply put, the studio provided a unique environment of place of abstraction where students could create a critical distance between their ideas and the making of those ideas.

A team of ten architecture students, under the direction of Professor Luhan, designed the Project Mission Wall. For ease of fabrication, part of the infrastructure framework called for all components to be the same length and bolted together. (I had hoped to use aluminum for the skeletal frame, but time constraints and generous donation of materials dictated the use of wood). By using standard materials in non-standard ways, the resulting project embedded the spirit of invention.

Students designed their own prototype. The faculty design team and Prototyping Specialists from the University of Kentucky Manufacturing Center Product Development Division (CRMS), then evaluated each prototype for structural integrity and buildability. It became apparent that there were two types of projects—objects and landscapes. To integrate rather than negate each student option, it was determined that both object and landscape schemas would be incorporated into the final design proposal (Figure 15). The final project is essentially one large 60' long, 40' wide truss that rises from 0" to a height 15'-0" off the ground. The ends of the truss are anchored 3' into the ground and tied together at the "basket" at its core. We designed the structure to negotiate the 10' differential in slope and withstand 75 mph wind loading. Once the final scheme was designed and stereo-lithographic, rapid-prototype models built, the project went before the Lexington-Fayette Urban County Government and Architecture Review Board. The project was unanimously approved.

The Robotics Department at the College of Engineering provided CNC machinery to digitally mill and fabricate the components. The components that could not be fabricated at CRMS were milled in the Furniture Design Studio Woodshop at the College of Design in Pence Hall. The studio received material donations for the project from local manufacturers and merchants. The design, fabrication, and sealing processes took two weeks. The design team then assembled the 40'x60'x15' structure in one day.

3.2 The Event – Earth Date 20.09.2002

The Mission Wall served three functions. It provided a housing for the Deep-Time Probe laser. It created windows and scaffolding for lighting. Moreover, it established a series of "View Corridors" that provided the onlooker with multiple vantage points and thus multiple-readings of information as architecture. It was determined that a light structural diaphragm that enclosed, but did not bound space would be the preferred method of construction. Depending upon the viewer's location, view corridors either open or close deep or direct views into the space (Figures 16 – 19). The plan of the structure, the accompanying information wall, and the overall siting of the exhibit were designed to structure the physical and psychological experience of the visitors and include them as part of the spectacle.

Figures 10. Lexington-Fayette County Courthouse Lawn.

Figures 11 – 14. Night and Day images of the Project Mission Wall on the night of the Deep-Time Probe Launch, 20 September 2002.

Figures 15. 1/8" = 1'-0" Basswood Scale of the Final Design Solution.

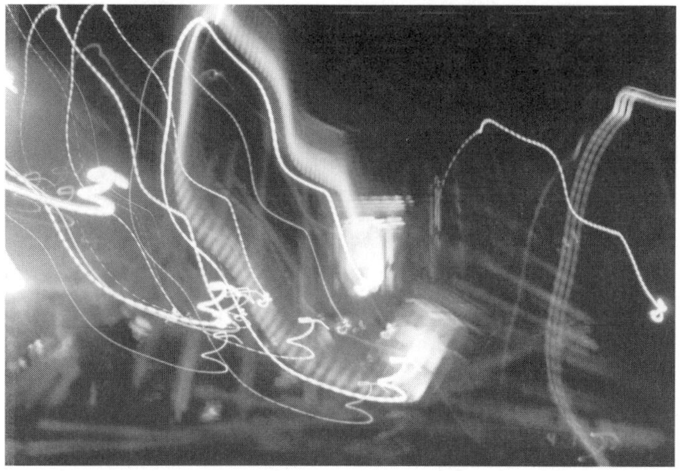

Figures 16 – 19. Images of the launch taken from four different "View Corridors".

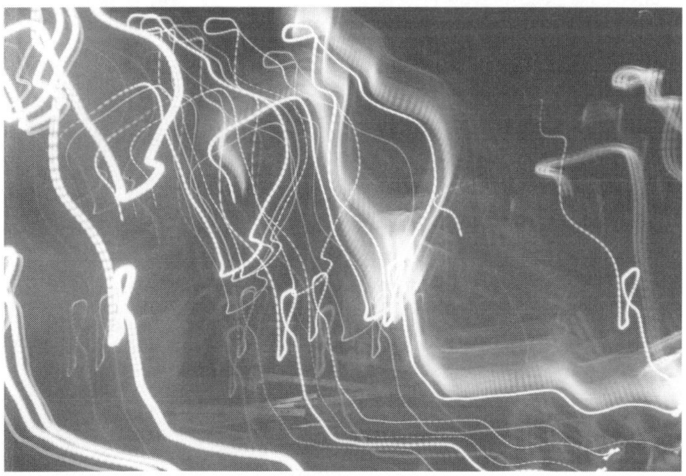

Figure 20. Photograph of the Launch of the Deep-Time Probe, 20 September 2002.

In order to shoot the laser we had to work directly with the FAA to shut down the flight patterns over Lexington during the event. We had a 45-minute window with which to launch the laser. The trajectory, calibration, and target selected by the Department of Astronomy and Physics was the event horizon of the closest known black hole to Earth (4000 light-years away). It was our intent to aim the laser to hit the event horizon of the black hole and have the DataStream ellipse back towards earth, theoretically returning to Lexington in the year 10002. In order to aim and direct a laser of this magnitude the laser was mounted on a Global Positioning System that adjusted to the rotation of the earth over time and held focus on the proposed target. Without this device, the DataStream would be sprayed along an arc in space and miss its mark. At the time of the launch, the design team digitized, specially formatted, converted, and modulated the data into a special high-powered laser that was "launched" into space.

> Modern science is still working to unlock the secrets of time travel, but the crowd downtown Friday night got a possible preview with the launch of the Deep Time Probe. A small but powerful green laser (Figure 20) launched from the Fayette County Circuit Courthouse lawn shot across the inky night sky. Inventors, artists, and performers stood watching the spectacle. They gazed at the green beam, six inches in diameter that was packed with digitally modulated information ready to be read by a civilization light years from Earth. (Lannen 2002).

4 Beyond the Event – Public Reaction

Artist Pat Gerhard commented about the project:

> It is obvious that Lexington is ready for such a site. The recent Idea Festival erected a wonderful deep space probe (Figures 21 – 25) that might be a work of scientific intent but looks almost like public art. This project shows how a large open space can immediately be adapted by our imaginations and put to creative use. (Feedback 2002).

A typical design studio at the University of Kentucky is fifteen weeks in duration. This project, with all of its collaborative components and civic involvement, was designed, fabricated, installed, and launched within four weeks. The pace of the delivery of information was fast. One student commented, "Complacency in this studio is not tolerated. The compaction in time, made for a completely different type of design studio, one where each student had to play a critical role in the built form." I would argue that this type of collaboration is necessary to the architecture design curriculum. It is important for students to realize that their ideas have actualizable consequences and that by including outside of the box critique forces the architect to look inside of the box in new ways.

Figures 21 – 24. Photographs of Project Mission Wall; Joinery Details, Light Basket, Rib-like Structure, and juxtaposition to the Courthouse entry volume, 2002.

Figure 26. Project Design Team, 2002. (From Front to Back) Sarah Reed, Nick Dobson, Travis Roberts, Daniel Everhart, Tien-Li Cheng, Jennifer Anderson, Chris Keelsing, Professor Gregory A. Luhan, Craig Jacobs, and Nathan Speck.

5 Conclusion

Most art is a representation in space. Any particular piece "moves" through time, as a whole unchanging. The spiral in the time probe project represents space and time. The laser, which is coherent, amplified light, is not confined by space or time. According to Einstein, space is infinitely contracted and time infinitely dilated for light.

With the act of the laser launch, we projected knowledge—both information and image—into space and theoretically into the future. An advanced civilization in the universe that has within its technological tool kit the ability to travel through time could theoretically receive and decode this information.

The structure remained in place for four months. Following the launch of the Deep-Time Space Probe, the laser was removed and replaced with mirrors that reflected the sun's rays back into the sky. In December 2002, the studio donated the structure to Artcroft, Inc., a 450-acre sculpture park and retreat for artists. It is in Kentucky, yet is similar to Storm King in New York State. In Summer 2003, we will reassemble and permanently install the structure at the entrance to Artcroft. This structure will be used for other interdisciplinary experiments between the Colleges of Architecture, Engineering, and Chemistry/Physics. Meanwhile, the last encounter of the Deep-Time Probe has been with the Oort Cloud that is more than three (3) light months from the Earth . . . a distance of nearly 1.5 trillion miles.

Acknowledgements

This is a collaborative project between the College of Design – School of Architecture, College of Engineering and the College of Chemistry and Physics – Department of Physics and Astronomy as fabricated by Fourth- and Fifth-year students in Professor Gregory A. Luhan's Virtual Design Studio. The design students include Jennifer Anderson (4th Year), Tien-Li Cheng (5th Year), Nicholas Dobson (4th Year), Daniel Everhart (5th Year), Craig Jacobs (5th Year), Chris Keesling (5th Year), Sarah Reed (5th Year), Travis Roberts (5th Year), and Nathan Speck (4th Year) (Figure 26).

I would like to acknowledge the following individuals for their time and leadership lent to this project:

Kris Kimel, Joanne Lange and Barbara Flexter of the Kentucky Science and Technology Corporation;
Susan Hill of Tate, Hill, Jacobs, Architects
Mayor Pam Miller, Charlie Milward, Bob Drakeford, D.L. Wilson, and Mary Wathen of the Lexington-Fayette Urban County Government;
Harold Tate of the Downtown Development Authority;
Ken Ross, Chuck Little, and Darryl Hager of the Parks Department;
RJ Robinson and Charles Arvin, Prototyping Specialists of the University of Kentucky Manufacturing Center Product Development Division (CRMS);
Chuck Heydinger, Mitchell Alonzo, and Carl Mudd of the University of Kentucky College of Design – School of Architecture Woodshop;
John Grossman and George Mears of Rhyno Productions, and my fellow colleagues Dr. Bruce L. Walcott, Associate Dean of the College of Engineering and Suketu Bhavsar of the Depart of Astronomy and Physics; Michael Jacobs (OMNI Architects), Len Wujcik, and Peyman Jahed at the University of Kentucky, College of Design – School of Architecture who offered critiques and structural analysis so that we could actualize this project.

This project has been made possible through the generous support of the Lexington community. I would to express sincere gratitude to the following donors for their continued support: Congleton Lumber Company, Home Depot – Turfland Mall, General Rubber and Plastics, Jiffy Fastening Systems, Porter Paints – Main Street, Lynn Imaging, Tate Hill Jacobs Architects, EOP Architects, and Ms. Louise Bast Stokes.

References:

Feedback: Panel, designer gave plaza a lot of thought. *Lexington-Herald Leader*, Monday 07 October 2002, Section A:10.

G. Hogben. (1991). Life in the Machine. *Progressive Architecture* (July 1991): 79.

S. Lannen. Is there anybody out there? Laser carries message into space. *Lexington-Herald Leader*, Sunday, 22 September 2002, Section B:1.

Representing Architectural Design Using a Connections-Based Paradigm

Ganapathy Mahalingam, Ph.D.
North Dakota State University

Abstract

Any making, including a work of architecture, is synthetic in nature and is made by making connections. To base the core of a computational representation of architectural design on connections is to base it on the very core of making. The articulation of the core of architecture, its architectonics, should be based on articulating its connections. This paper probes how connections can serve to represent architectural design. A paradigm consists of a core cluster of concepts that, for a time period, provides a framework to articulate the issues and problems facing a field and to generate solutions. This paper offers a connections-based paradigm to represent architectural design computationally. A number of connections-based strategies for the representation of architectural design have emerged. Modeling frameworks that have been identified include dendograms, bipartite graphs, adjacency graphs, plan graphs, planar graphs, Hasse diagrams, Boolean lattices, and Bayesian networks. These modeling frameworks have enabled the representation of many aspects of architectural design. Is it possible to extract a uniform modeling framework from all these frameworks that enables the computation of architectural design in all its aspects? Using biological analogies, will an integration of these modeling frameworks provide the 'molecular' structure of a 'DNA' that makes up the architectural 'genome'? This paper will attempt to answer these questions.

Representing Architectural Design Using a Connections-based Paradigm

Ganapathy Mahalingam, Ph.D.
North Dakota State University

1 Introduction

Resolving the computability of design has been a longstanding quest among researchers in computer-aided architectural design. One does not question whether design, as a cognitive activity, is possible, but one does question whether design is computable. Remarkable advances are being made in cognitive modeling using computer-based systems. The key to making design truly computable may lie in these advances in cognitive modeling. Researchers, who conclude that design is not computable, or is not computable in its creative aspect, invariably point out a computer-based system's inability to generate radically new forms. When you carefully examine what constitutes a radically new form, the answer that emerges is new connections at various topological levels.

Articulating the synthesis of forms or the generation of spatial organization has a long tradition spanning four decades. Beginning with Christopher Alexander's *Notes on the Synthesis of Form* (1964), the design profession has wrestled with the articulation of architecture. Lionel March and Philip Steadman's pioneering work on the geometry of the environment (March & Steadman 1971), followed by Lionel March's work on the architecture of form (March 1976) set the precedent decades ago for what may now form the core for representing architectural design. Articulating spatial organization found new energy in Hillier and Hanson's work on the social logic of space (Hillier & Hanson 1984). Hillier and his team have recently expanded their research to the broader framework of space as a machine (Hillier 1996). In doing so, they have begun to make the case for a non-discursive, analytical theory of architecture based on "configurations."

In his seminal work from the early '60s, Alexander attempted to get at the core process in the synthesis of forms, an issue central to architecture. In the preface to a later edition of his book on the subject (Alexander 1964), he carefully articulated his quest and its significance. He wrote:

> In this book I presented the diagrams as the end results of a long process; I put the accent on the process, and gave the diagrams themselves only a few pages of discussion. But once the book was finished, and I began to explore the process which I had described, I found that the diagrams themselves had immense power, and that, in fact, most of the power of what I had written lay in the power of these diagrams. The idea of a diagram, or pattern, is very simple. It is an abstract pattern of physical relationships which resolves a small system of interacting and conflicting forces, and is independent of all other forces, and of all other possible diagrams. The idea that it is possible to create such abstract relationships one at a time, and to create designs which are whole by fusing these relationships—this amazingly simple idea is, for me, the most important discovery of the book.

This book led to the widespread use of diagrams or patterns as the basis for designs, especially architectural designs. The subsequent search for diagrams and patterns extended the scale attempted by Alexander in his book, the scale of a village in India. The thought that diagrams could form the basis of designs took firm root. This paper is about an attempt to extend the tradition that began with Alexander's work into a new realm made possible by advanced computing techniques.

2 Connections-based Representations

A connections-based representation is quite simply one that uses connections as an organizing framework for the representation. In this paper, the term "connections-based" is deliberately used rather than "connectionist," which has its own connotations. The connectionist model is a subset of the broader category of connections-based representations.

The term "connectionist" is widely used to describe a computational technique used to model the human brain, especially its neural network. A connectionist model is made up of a network of many simple processing units that act in parallel to produce "emergent" behavior. These simple processing units have been described as intuitive, sub conceptual and sub symbolic entities that are linked in a dynamic system that does not allow a precise conceptual level description. There is a healthy and ongoing debate about the effectiveness of the "connectionist" model to represent the working of the human brain.

A connections-based representation, on the other hand, is a diagram made up of multiple nodes that are linked in various ways. The word "diagram" is based on its Greek roots *dia* and *graphein*, which mean "through" and "write" respectively. The Greek verb *diagraphein* means to "mark out by lines" from which the noun *diagramma* is derived. Originally the word diagram referred to a geometrical figure, and for a brief period even to a written list or register, which is very curious. Based on its etymology, the word "diagram" refers to an intrinsic structure, something that is drawn "through" an entity, like a skeletal framework. When coupled with the etymology of the word "understanding," diagrams provide intrinsic knowledge of entities. One of the goals of connections-based representations is to help acquire this intrinsic knowledge of architecture. Architecture, like connections, must be made and is not given (Rajchman 2000). The primary architectural act can be considered as the linking of two nodes. This is the beginning of synthesis and a plurality. Starting with this primary connection-based representation (Figure 1), a hierarchy of connections-based representations can be articulated. Connections-based representations that have emerged in research can be organized based on increasing complexity. Some of the representations that have emerged include the ones described in the following sections.

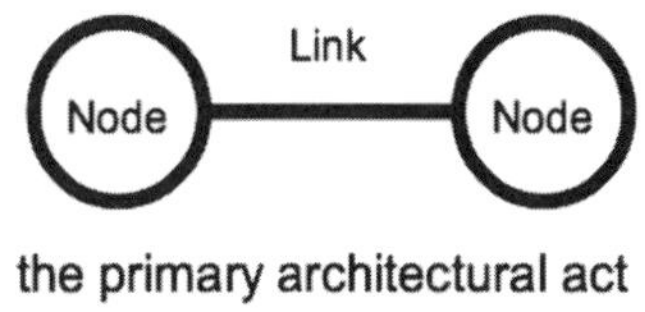

Figure 1. The architecture of connections.

2.1 Dendograms

A dendogram is a diagram that has a branch-like structure (Figure 2). Starting from a single node, branches or links lead to successive nodes. Examples of dendograms are parse trees, decision trees, and binary trees. Each terminal node of a 'tree' representation is appropriately called a leaf. In representations such as decision trees, the leaves represent outcomes that are a result of decisions made at the nodes. Parse trees can be used to verify if a particular architectural composition has been created using a particular architectural language. Decision trees can be used to represent a design process as a hierarchical sequence of design decisions, where each design decision leads to subsequent design decisions. Because of their architecture, dendograms are useful in representing hierarchical procedures or processes. A dendogram or tree of (n) nodes has (n-1) links. Figure 3 illustrates this rule.

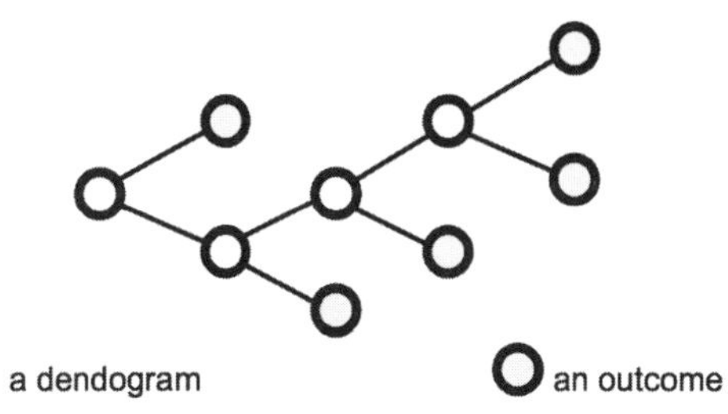

Figure 2. A dendogram.

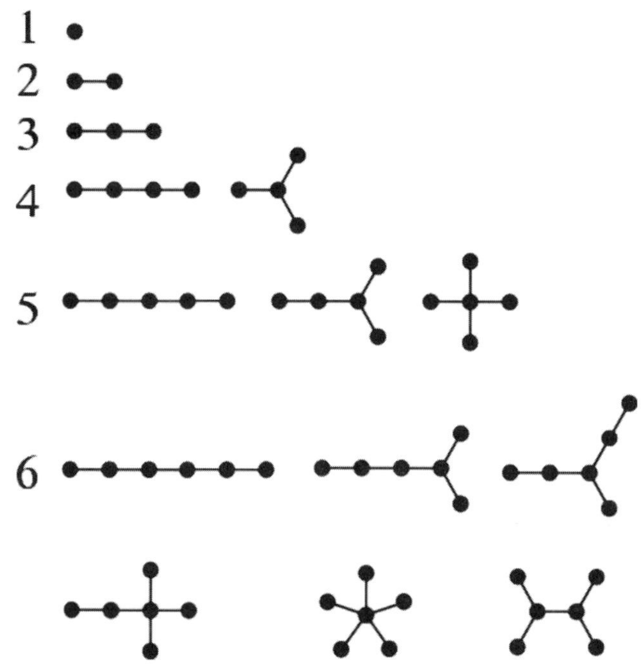

Figure 3. Dendograms of increasing order, i.e., number of nodes (image courtesy Weisstein, 1999-2003).

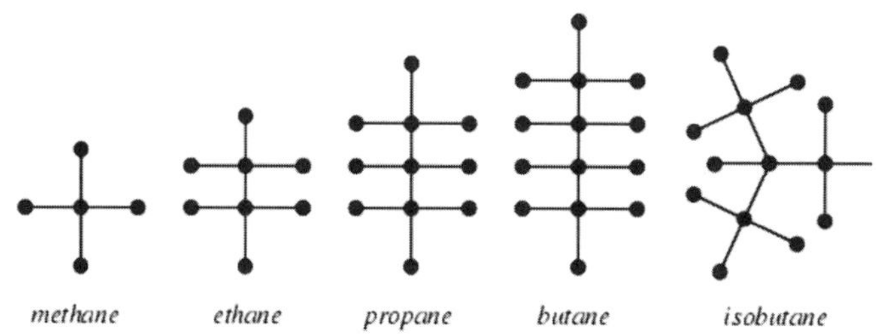

Figure 4. Molecular structures as dendograms (image courtesy Weisstein, 1999-2003).

Dendograms are especially useful in the modeling of molecular structures (Figure 4) and by analogy the relationships between spaces in a building. When the nodes of the dendogram are used as the insertion points or instantiation points of polyhedra representing spaces, dendograms can form the skeletal generating framework of the complex spatial form of a building. Dendograms can also be used to model the load-transfer action in structural assemblies. Each node represents a structural component and each link a load transfer path.
When dendograms are used to represent design processes, they

become the representation of time. In this case, the dendogram is used as a state-transition graph. Each node of the dendogram represents the state of a design at a particular time. Though the state-transition graph extends in space, the spatial boundaries of the entity whose evolution is being described by the state–transition graph can be fixed. When used as a decision tree, dendograms become design decision paths in action space that are traversed in time.

A more general case of the dendogram, which is not a hierarchical tree, called a permeability map, was developed by Hillier and Hanson (1984) to represent the privacy gradient in a set of spaces.

2.2 Bipartite Graphs

A bipartite graph is a connections-based representation whose nodes can be partitioned into two sets such that no two nodes in any set are adjacent (Figure 5). In a complete bipartite graph, in addition, every node in one set is connected to every node in the other set. A tree is also a bipartite graph. Bipartite graphs are useful when the representation has two distinct set of elements that are related to each other but not amongst themselves. Bipartite graphs are also used to model a type of representation called a Petri Net, especially the channel-agency form of the Petri Net. Petri Nets are used to model hardware devices, communication protocols, parallel programs, and distributed databases.

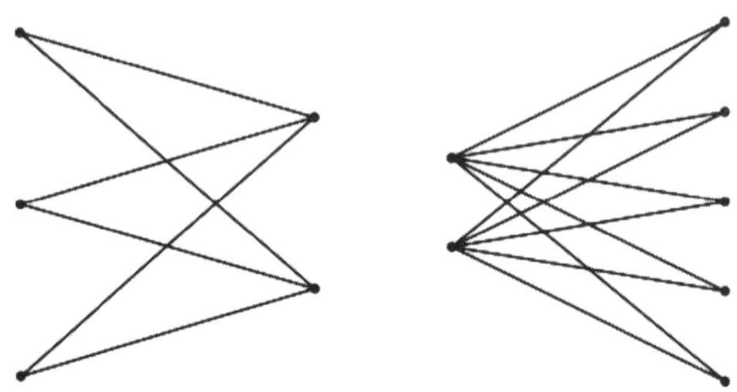

Figure 5. Bipartite graphs $K_{3,2}$ and $K_{2,5}$ (image courtesy Weisstein, 1999-2003).

The bipartite graph can be used to model a situation where a set of environmental sensors interacts with a set of architectural elements. A complete bipartite graph exhausts all the relations between the components in such as system.

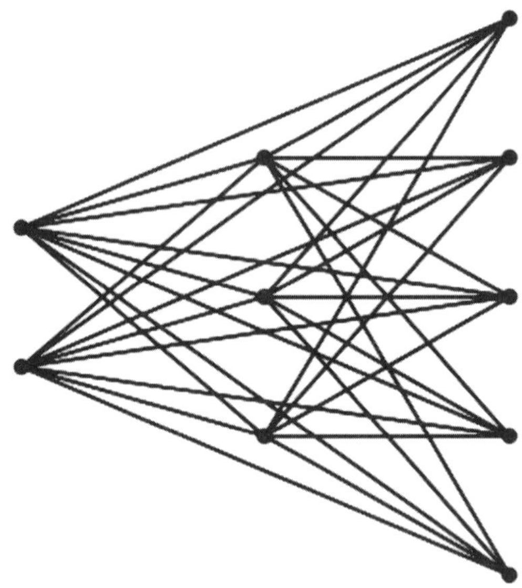

Figure 6. A 3-partite graph $K_{2,3,5}$ - an example of a k-partite graph (image courtesy Weisstein, 1999-2003).

The model of the environmental performance of an architectural space where there is a set of sources that generate environmental performance criteria, a set of receivers, that is, inhabitants who experience these environmental performance criteria, and a set of architectural elements, can be represented by a complete 3-partite graph (Figure 6) that exhausts all the relations between the various components.

Bipartite graphs can also be used as armatures for architectural designs. A notable example of the use of bipartite graphs in the arts is the use of a $K_{18,18}$ bipartite graph (Figure 7) in Umberto Eco's *Foucault's Pendulum*.

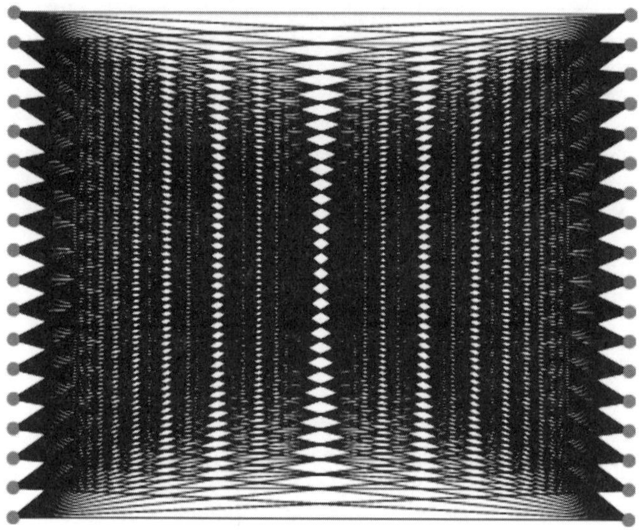

Figure 7. Umberto Eco's K $_{18,18}$ bipartite graph armature in *Foucault's Pendulum* (image courtesy Weisstein, 1999-2003).

2.3 Adjacency Graphs

In an adjacency graph, each separate space is represented as a node. Spaces that are in contact with another, that is, they are adjacent, are connected by links. In this representation, spaces that are connected only at corner points are not considered adjacent. The general exterior space is also represented as a node. All the 'interior' nodes connect to this general 'exterior' node. Adjacency graphs and their alternate form of representation, adjacency matrices, have been used in architectural design to establish proximal relations between spaces. When the duals of planar adjacency graphs are drawn, the 'wireframe' plan of a set of spaces can be generated. In a recent project (Hwang & Choi 2002), adjacency graphs were used as metadata for information retrieval in a spatial information storage system.

In an interesting analysis performed by Steadman (March & Steadman 1971), different designs by the architect Frank Lloyd Wright for different clients and sites were shown to have the same adjacency graph as the basis for the organization of spaces.

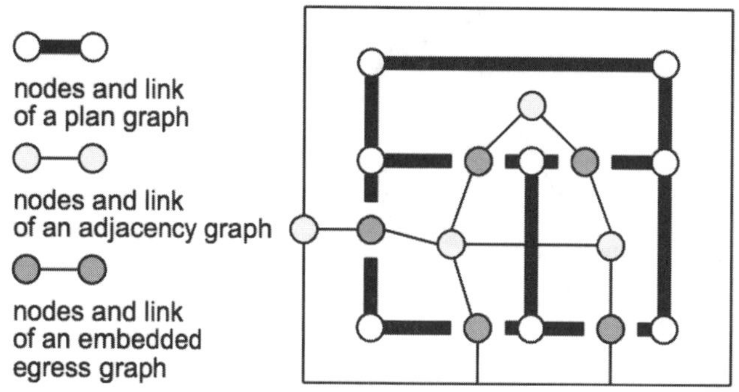

Figure 8. Plan graphs, adjacency graphs and embedded graphs.

2.4 Plan Graphs and Planar Graphs

In a plan graph (Figure 8), the junctions between walls in an architectural plan are represented as nodes and the walls themselves are represented as links. In this representation, the representation of "walls" is not restricted to physical barriers alone, but includes other divisions of space as well. A plan graph of a set of spaces is related to its adjacency graph. One is called the dual of the other.

A planar graph (Figure 8) is quite distinct from a plan graph, and it is easy to be confused by the similar sounding terms. A planar graph is a graph that can be drawn on a plane without any of the links crossing each other. A completely connected planar graph (Figure 9), that is, a graph in which each node is connected to every other node, cannot have more than 4 nodes. This implies that to maintain a complete set of relations between more than four components in a connections-based representation requires three-dimensional spatial thought.

Because of the way in which a plan graph is constructed, it is always planar. Plan graphs and adjacency graphs can be integrated with other graphs, which can be embedded in them. The example shown in Figure 8 represents the modeling of an egress pattern in the floor plan of a building. Each egress element, a door or a window, is represented as a node. This node is embedded in the link between nodes that represent spaces in an adjacency graph of the plan. The egress node is also embedded in the plan graph of the floor plan. If this representation is used to simulate egress from a building during an emergency such as a fire, then traversing the graph can establish whether there is a safe egress path to the exterior of the building.

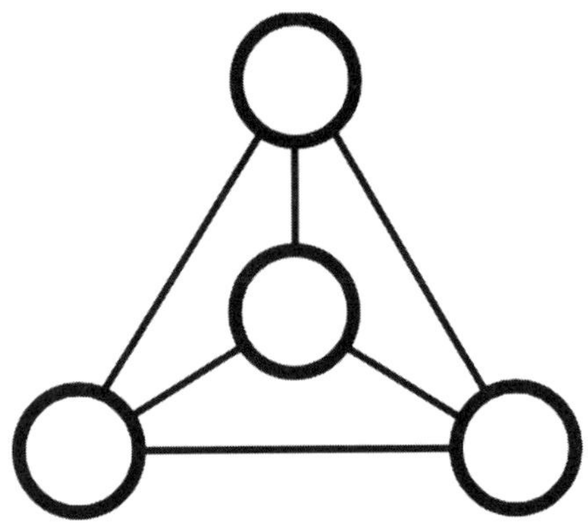

Figure 9. A completely connected planar graph.

2.5 Hasse Diagrams

According to March (1976), a Hasse diagram (Figure 10) is a diagram of connected nodes such that you can move from one node to another through a set of one or more "upward" links. As such it can be used to model "directional" synthesis of any set of entities. The Hasse diagram defines a progression from a null set to a full set of entities, where each intermediate set is a cover (a mathematical relation) of the immediately preceding set or sets. The directional buildup of an architectural design or a conceptual map that defines an architectural design as it evolves incrementally can be represented by a Hasse diagram.

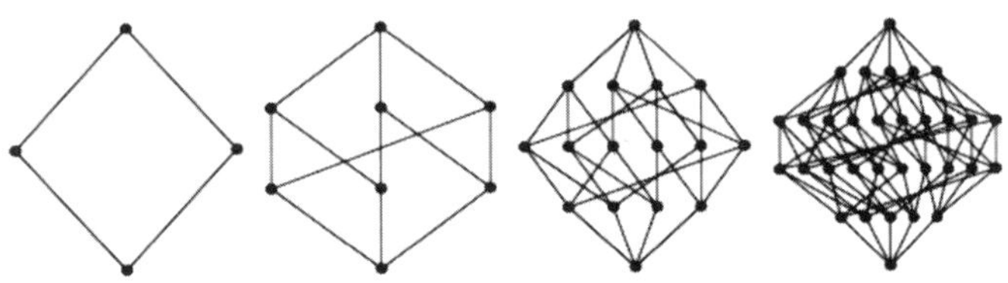

Figure 10. Hasse diagrams of sets with 2, 3, 4 and 5 entities (image courtesy Weisstein, 1999-2003).

2.6 Boolean Lattice

According to March (1976), a Boolean lattice is a representation of Boolean algebra as a complemented, distributive lattice. A Boolean algebra b(A) of a set A is the subsets of A that can be obtained by a finite number of the set theoretic operations of OR (union), AND (intersection) and NOT (complementation). Each element of b(A) is called a Boolean function. The number of Boolean functions of a set of 2 entities (say 1 and 0 as in a binary system) is 16. Computing circuitry is based on a Boolean algebra of 2 entities. The abstract structure of the Boolean algebra is isomorphic to specific algebras used in set theory, the algebra of events, symbolic logic, switching algebra, and automated process control. If the sequence of design operations that generates an architectural design can be represented by Boolean lattice, then it can be automated.

2.7 Bayesian Networks

A Bayesian network (Figure 11) has been described as a "belief" network. Each node in a Bayesian network represents the probability of a variable (a Bayesian variable) in a system. Nodes are linked to each other based on conditional dependence. The network is based on a probability model and distribution. The connections are causal connections and are directional. The direction is always from cause to effect. The dependent node is called a "child" and the influencing node is called the "parent." Time is also introduced into the model as a parent is the temporal antecedent of a child. In a complex Bayesian network, many cycles of dependencies can be set up. Once a Bayesian network has been set up, a variable is given a value based on observation. Calculations are then performed to find the values of all other variables based on their probability of occurring. Once all variables are established, the network defines the probable state of the system.

A Bayesian network can be used to create a predictive model of environmental performance criteria in the design of an architectural space. Such environmental performance criteria can include temperature, illumination, and sound intensity.

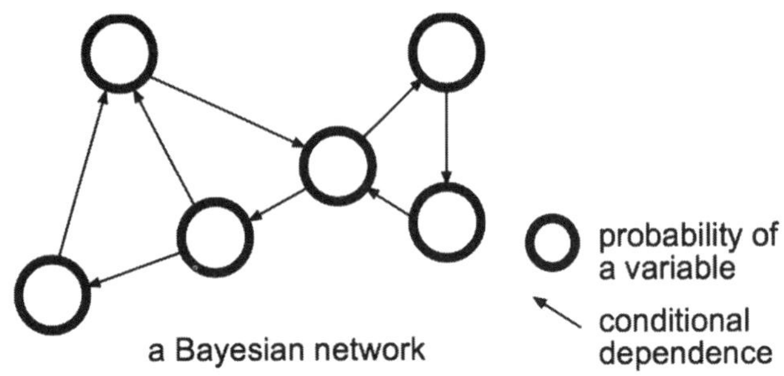

Figure 11. A Bayesian network.

Connections-based Representation	Architectural Representation
Dendogram	Relationship of spaces, Load-transfer in structures
Bipartite Graph	Environmental control using sensors, Modeling of environmental performance
Adjacency Graph	Relationship of spaces, Relationship of surfaces in a space
Plan/Planar Graph	Architectural floor plans, Surface distribution in spaces
Hasse Diagram	Architectural design generation using a kit of parts
Boolean Lattice	Automated architectural design generation
Bayesian Network	Prediction models for environmental performance

Table 1: Connections-based representations and their use in the representation of architectural design

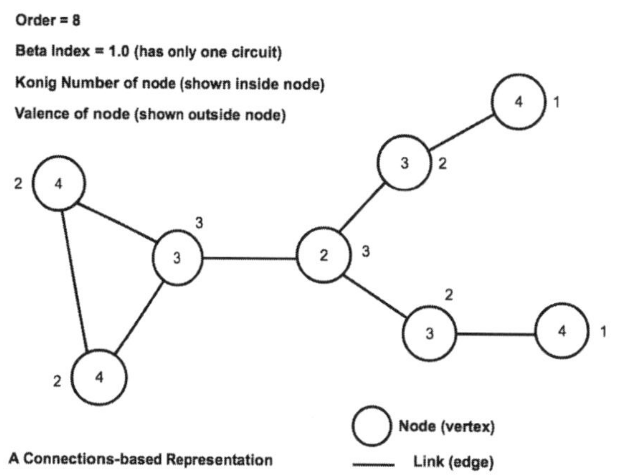

Figure 12. Properties of networks.

3 Modeling Architectural Design Using Networks

In the past, the computational representation of architecture, both as a product and as a process, has utilized a wide range of representational frameworks. Architecture has been represented as data structures, databases, procedures, algorithms, and virtual computers. A connections-based representational framework now extends this range of representations to include networks (Table 1).

3.1 Elements of a Network

A network has only two basic elements, nodes and links. The complexity of networks is based on the number of nodes and their interconnections or links. When used as a representational framework, networks provide the following opportunities:

- Nodes: the representation of state (properties, variables, parameters, probability elements)
- Links: the representation of relations (constraints, semantics, physical connections, causal connections, transformations, transfer functions, dependencies)
- Networks: the representation of state, the representation of a process, the representation of probabilities of outcomes
- Network of networks: the representation of complex spatial systems

3.2 Properties of a Network

The various properties of networks (Figure 12) lend themselves to various representations of architecture. Some of the properties include:

Hamilton Path/Hamiltoninan Cycle or Circuit: A path in a network that starts at a starting node, goes through each node only once, is not obligated to traverse each link, and ends at the starting node. It describes a circuit (Figure 13).

Euler Path/Eulerian Cycle or Circuit: A path that traverses each link of the network once, with no restrictions on the number of times it goes through a node. An Euler path is possible in a network only if the network is connected and no more than two nodes have an odd valence.

Order of the Network: The order of a network is the total number of nodes in the network.

Valence: The number of separate links to a node.

Konig Number of a Node: It is the maximum number of links in the shortest path to connect a particular node in the network to any other node in the network. The Konig number is used to establish the 'centrality' of node in a network.

Beta Index: It is a measure derived by dividing the number of links in a network by the number of nodes in the network. A network with a *beta* index of less than 1.0 is a tree, a network with a *beta* index of 1.0 has only one circuit, and a network with a *beta* index of greater than 1.0 is a complex network.

4 Advantages of a Connections-based Representation of Architecture

The proposal for a non-discursive, analytical theory of architecture (Hillier 1996), may on the surface look like an erosion of a much-fought-for-and-gained political freedom in architectural expression, but in the end, may turn out to be more liberating than political freedom.

The single major advantage of using connections-based representations is the potential for distributed representation. Artificial intelligence researchers modeling the working of the brain distinguish between two kinds of representations, symbolic representations and distributed representations.

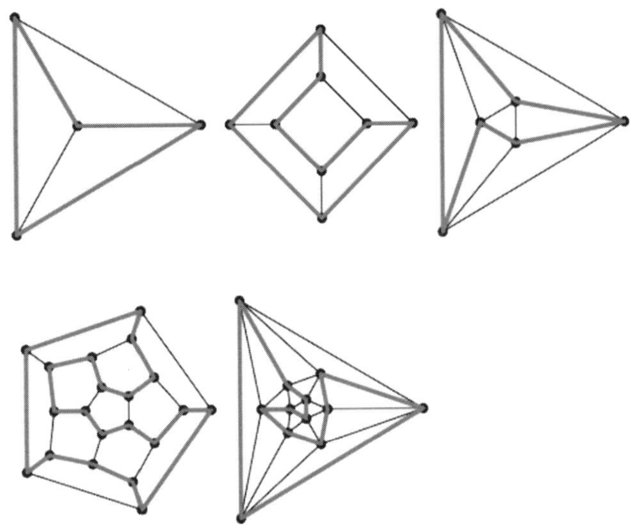

Figure 13. Hamiltonian circuits in graphs of Platonic solids (image courtesy Weisstein, 1999-2003).

Symbolic representations use symbols such as words and numbers. These symbolic units have meanings associated with them. These units are combined into propositions in a language using the grammar(s) of that language. For example, words are combined into sentences (propositions) using the grammar of the English language. Similarly, numbers can be combined into mathematical propositions using a mathematical grammar. The main disadvantages of symbolic representations are that they are language-based and propositional; they are "brittle" and not fault-tolerant. Symbolic representations are considered "brittle" because symbolic units either exist or do not. A word is there in a sentence or it is not. Symbolic representations are not considered fault-tolerant because minor damage to a symbolic conceptual structure can cause the loss of the entire concept.

Distributed representations are ones in which meaning is not captured in a single symbolic unit, but arises from the interaction of a network of units. The common example that is given to illustrate this is that the concept "grandmother" is not stored in a single "grandmother cell" in the brain, but in a pattern or network of interacting neurons (brain cells). Distributed representations now provide the foundation for realistic computational models of human cognition related to visual, olfactory, auditory, and tactile perception. Connections-based representations combine the features of symbolic representations (their structural sensitiveness) and distributed representations (their sensitiveness to statistical distributions of low-level perceptions) making them the ideal representational framework.

5 The Future of the Paradigm

The future of this paradigm lies in its ability to uncover the core of architecture, its architectonics. The architectonics of architecture may well be the architectonics of human thought. Rather than architecture being a theater of memory, through this paradigm architecture stands to be revealed as the theater of thought.

Stephen Grand OBE, a researcher from the UK and the developer of the computer game *Creatures,* has been developing an intelligent robot called Lucy. His goal is to ensure that Lucy graduates from nursery school. Based on his research, Grand believes that the crucial element for intelligence is a particular circuit of neurons in the cerebral cortex of the brain that enables learning. Grand's goal is to unravel this circuit and use it to create an alternative to the digital computer that is similar to a living system. Since architecture is created by some of the most exacting neural processing known to humans, the key to this neural circuit could conceivably lie in a work of architecture. A connections-based coding, hence understanding, of this work of architecture, can lead to the discovery of this "learning" circuit. On the other hand, Douglas Hofstadter, in his seminal book, *Gödel Escher Bach*, points out that the neural substrate of humans may pose barriers to certain processes of thought. He describes the problem encountered when someone tries to make "sense" of the Epimenides paradox thus:

> Now my feeling is that the Tarski transformation of the Epimenides paradox teaches us to look for a substrate in the English-language version. In the arithmetical version, the upper level of meaning is supported by the lower arithmetical level. Perhaps analogously, the self-referential sentence which we perceive ("This sentence is false") is only the top level of a dual-level entity. What would be the lower level, then? Well, what is the mechanism that language rides on? The brain. Therefore one ought to look for a neural substrate to the Epimenides paradox—a lower level of physical events which clash with each other. That is, two events which by their nature cannot occur simultaneously. If this physical substrate exists, then the reason we cannot make heads or tails of the Epimenides sentence is that our brains are trying to do an impossible task.

Hoftstadter proposes that when confronted with a situation such as making "sense" of the Epimenides paradox, the brain encodes the paradox in the neural substrate using "symbols" and processes it using "symbolic processing." He writes:

> Now what would be the nature of the conflicting physical events? Presumably when you hear the Epimenides sentence, your brain sets up some "coding" of the sentence—an internal configuration of interacting symbols. Then it tries to classify the sentence as "true" or "false". This classifying act must involve an attempt to force several symbols to interact in a particular way. (Presumably this happens when any sentence is processed.) Now if it happens that the act of classification would physically disrupt the coding of the sentence—something which

> would ordinarily never happen—then one is in trouble, for it is tantamount to trying to force a record player to play its self-breaking record. We have described the conflict in physical terms, but not in neural terms. If this analysis is right so far, then presumably the rest of the discussion could be carried on when we know something about the constitution of the "symbols" in the brain out of neurons and their firings, as well as about the way that sentences become converted into "codings."

Such limits in neural processing may be why architecture is intrinsically homeostatic, that is, it does not change in its inherent structure. It may also be why all works of architecture can be created with a simple programming language. This paradigm will reveal such limitations in architecture, if they exist. Though this sounds pessimistic, there is hope for this paradigm as revealed by Alexander. In describing the creative potential of abstract diagrams, Alexander points out that these diagrams can evolve:

> I have discovered, since, that these abstract diagrams not only allow you to create a single whole from them, by fusion, but also have other even more important powers. Because the diagrams are independent of one another, you can study them and improve them one at a time, so that their evolution can be gradual and cumulative. More important still, because they are abstract and independent, you can use them to create not just one design, but an infinite variety of designs, all of them free combinations of the same set of patterns.

Rather than use traditional genetic algorithms (Holland 1975) for the evolution of forms, which are used to transform one population of genetic characteristics (chromosomes) into another through processes of crossover (recombination), mutation and inversion, connections-based representation lend themselves to modeling based on biological analogies such as protein synthesis and morphogenesis (from developmental biology). Just as the molecular structure of DNA "instructs" protein synthesis, connections-based representations "instruct" the creation of works of architecture. A collection of connections-based representations (architectural DNA molecules—see analogy in Figure 4) then defines the "genome" of the field of architecture. Classifying this collection of connections-based representations, thereby defining the architectural genome, is a work on the scale of Durand's *Précis.* Unlike the process followed by Durand, who focused on lines and delineation, mapping the architectural genome will focus on the underlying structure or architectonics of architecture. These underlying connections-based representations are distinguished by the fact that they do not belong to the measurement-based "metric" space of architectural modulation and variation but the "invariant" space of relationships.

6 Conclusions

One can conclude with a quote from Alexander that captures the spirit of a connections-based representation of design:

> The shapes of mathematics are abstract, of course, and the shapes of architecture concrete and human. But that difference is inessential. The crucial quality of shape, no matter of what kind, lies in its organization, and when we think of it this way we call it form. Man's feeling for mathematical form was able to develop only from his feeling for the processes of proof. I believe that our feeling for architectural form can never reach a comparable order of development, until we too have first learned a comparable feeling for the process of design.

This paper offers *making connections* as a process of design which will allow that comparable order of development. The computational representation of architecture started with the representation of architectural entities as data structures and architectural design processes as procedures. It evolved into the representation of architectural entities and processes as virtual computers. The next stage in the evolution of the computational representation of architecture is the representation of architectural entities and processes as networks of virtual computers or computational entities. The examples of connections-based representations presented in this paper suggest that various aspects of architectural design from spatial synthesis to environmental performance control can be successfully represented using the techniques. Recent work by Wolfram (Wolfram, 2002) suggests that it is possible to go even further and model the evolution of networks, which can then be used as an overarching representational framework.

References

Alexander, C. (1964). *Notes on the synthesis of form.* Cambridge: Harvard University Press.

Durand, J. N. L. (1802) *Précis des leçons d'architecture.* Paris: Ecole Polytechnique.

Hillier, B., and J. Hanson. (1984). *The social logic of space.* Cambridge University Press.

Hillier, B. (1996). *Space is the machine: A configurational theory of architecture.* Cambridge University Press.

Hofstadter, D. (1980). *Gödel Escher Bach.* Vintage Books Edition.

Holland, J. (1975). *Adaptation in natural and artificial systems.* Ann Arbor: University of Michigan Press.

Hwang, J., and J. Choi. (2002). SpaceCore: Metadata for retrieving spatial information in architecture. In *Proceedings of the ACADIA 2002 conference*, pp. 199 - 217.

March, L., Editor. (1976). *The architecture of form.* Cambridge University Press.

March, L., and P. Steadman. (1971). *The geometry of environment: An introduction to spatial organization in design.* RIBA Publications Ltd.

Rajchman, J. (2000). *The Deleuze connections.* MIT Press.
Skiena, S. (1990). Implementing discrete mathematics: Combinatorics and graph theory with mathematica. Reading, Massachusetts: Addison Wesley.

Weisstein, E. W. (1999-2003). Eric Weisstein's world of mathematics (MathWorldTM) http://mathworld.wolfram.com/

Wolfram, S. (2002). A new kind of science. Champaign, Illinois: Wolfram Media, Inc.

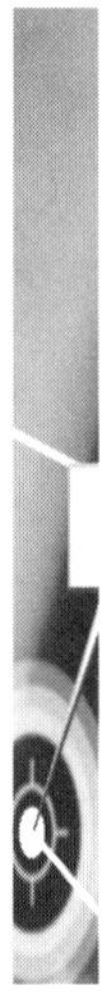

On the Limitations of Shape Grammars: Comments on Aaron Fleisher's Article "Grammatical Architecture?"

J. Michael Gerzso
Independent Researcher, Boulder, Colorado

Abstract

Shape grammars were introduced by Gips and Stiny in 1972. Since then, there have been many articles and books written by them and their associates. In 1992, Aaron Fleisher, a professor at the School of Planning, MIT, wrote a critique of their work in an article titled "Grammatical Architecture?" published in the journal *Environment and Planning B*. According to him, Gips, Stiny and later Mitchell, propose a hypothesis that states that shape grammars are presumed to represent knowledge of architectural form, that grammars are "formable," and that there is a visual correspondence to verbal grammar. The strong version of "the hypothesis requires that an architectural form be equivalent to a grammar." Fleisher considers these hypotheses unsustainable, and argues his case by analyzing the differences between language, and architecture, and by dealing with the concepts of lexicons, syntax and semantics. He concludes by stating that architectural design is negotiated in two modalities: the verbal and the visual, and that equivalences are not at issue; they do not exist. If there is such thing as a language for design, it would provide the means to maintain a discussion of the consequences in one mode, of the state and conditions of the other. Fleisher's observations serve as the basis of this paper, a tribute to him, and also an opportunity to present an outline to an alternate approach or hypothesis to shape grammars, which is "nonlinguistic" but "generative," in the sense that it uses production rules. A basic aspect of this hypothesis is that the only similarity between syntactic rules in language and some rules in architecture is that they are recursive.

On the Limitations of Shape Grammars: Comments on Aaron Fleisher's Article "Grammatical Architecture?"

J. Michael Gerzso
Independent Researcher, Boulder, Colorado

1 Introduction

Shape grammars were introduced by Gips and Stiny in 1972 (Gips and Stiny 1972). Since then, there have been many articles and books by them and their associates. In 1992, Aaron Fleisher, a professor at the School of Planning, MIT, wrote a critique of their work (Fleisher 1992). However, despite the fact that it was published over ten years ago, the community of architectural researchers remains unaware of its existence, as evidenced by the papers presented at ACADIA during the last seven conferences. This may be understandable given the fact that Fleisher's article is somewhat inaccessible by the way it is written. Nevertheless, it is very convincing by its thoroughness. It is really an abstract for a book or a series of articles. It would be very interesting if Fleisher wrote such a book considering the breadth and depth of his knowledge.

However, given that this is not the case, I have attempted to explain why Fleisher's criticism is important, why it can serve as a basis for a next step in the enterprise of representing architectural design rules as syntax production rules. This "next step" would be the subject of another article. This one focuses on what he has to say.

2 Research Methods in Architecture

Fleisher´s article points out many problems with the shape grammar approach. But, these problems are not only the result of the technical limitations of the appoach itself, but also of the underlying assumptions concerning research in architecture. It would be a mistake not to take these assumptions into account. Without them, it is much more difficult to understand Fleisher´s criticisms as well as the field of shape grammars. Fleisher assumes that inquiry or research should follow the procedure of proposing a hypothesis, testing it, and vigorously debating its merits or shortcomings in the widest possible forum. In contrast, the shape grammar approach assumes almost the opposite by using the following precepts (Gips, Stiny, Mitchell, Knight, et. al.), which–as it turns out–are common in many areas of architectural research:

1) It is important to be aligned with a "new" fashionable theory or movement, and most important, at the height of its popularity. The theories favored are those in linguistics, philosophy, science or mathematics. The more abstract and recondite they are, the better.
2) The new theory is argued to be relevant to architecture.
3) The new theory as applied to architecture must have its own jargon which includes terms borrowed from other fields. The jargon can be used in a loose and casual manner.
4) The architectural version of the new theory is to redefine how architecture is viewed and/or thought about, designed and evaluated. It attempts to legitimize new approaches to design and frequently invalidates old ones.
5) The articles or books on this new theory rarely contain extensive bibliography of the field being borrowed from. If they do, they cite one or two major unapproachable works, such as *Being and Time* by Heidegger. The references that do appear are usually of colleagues who are also promoting the new architectural theory.
6) There is little mastery of the concepts or techniques borrowed from the other fields, which are grafted onto architecture by following all the apparent precepts and forms of theory making.

A possible explanation for why these precepts exist may have to do with LeCorbusier, Mies and Gropius, the founders of modern architecture. They borrowed heavily from industrial engineering, naval architecture, and aviation engineering (Banham 1960,1969). By following all the apparent precepts and forms of theory making, contemporary architectural researchers hope that they will have the same impact on architecture as did Le Corbusier et al. did. It may also be the result of the perception that the most interesting intellectual and technical developments occur outside of architecture. However, since 1960, in academia, the trend is to only borrow from other academic areas.

3 Research Methods as a Variation of "Cargo Cult Science"

The way that shape grammar researchers follow all of the apparent precepts and forms of theory making suggests Richard Feynman's "cargo cult science," which was inspired by the cargo cult of the South Sea islands during the second world war (Hutchings 1997). The cult wanted to reproduce the arrival of transport aircraft containing supplies for the US armed forces. They arranged runways, fires along the runways, control towers, rigged a man with wooden headphones, and bamboo antennas. Even though they followed all of the apparent rituals of the US airman, no planes arrived.

He mentions the cult in his autobiography, "*Surely You're Joking Mr. Feynman!*," in relation to the lack understanding of the scientific endeavor of some physicists who think it is sufficient to "follow all the apparent precepts and forms of scientific investigation, but they're missing something essential, because " . . . it doesn't work" (p. 340, Hutchings 1997). The something "essential" is a "kind of scientific integrity, a principle of scientific thought that corresponds to a kind of utter honesty—a kind of leaning over backwards. For example, if you're doing an experiment, you should report everything that you think might make it invalid—not only what you think is right about it: other cases that could possibly explain your results; and things you thought of that you've eliminated by some other experiment, and how they worked—to make sure the other fellow can tell they have been eliminated" (p. 341). *"If you make a theory, for example, and advertise it, or put it out, then you must also put down all the facts that disagree with it, as well as those that agree with it"* [my italics] (p. 341).

In borrowing from linguistics and mathematics, have proponents of the shape grammar theory leaned over backwards by listing the facts that disagree them? Have they ever acknowledged competing theories? Have they ever explained why their theory accounts for things nonarchitectural, such as, for example, that the Le Corbusier spiral grammar also describes sea shells (p. 148, Mitchell 1990)? The answer is "no."

Therefore, from this point of view, it is fair to argue that shape grammar approach is a type of cargo cult research by grafting linguistic theories onto architecture. This point is not superfluous because it is fundamental in understanding Fleisher's article. As the south sea islanders were impressed by the logistics of military air cargo–as well as having access to some of the cargo–so too are the shape grammar researchers very impressed by the Chomsky school of linguistics of the 1960s and 1970s. In the same way that south sea islanders attempted to invoke the arrival of cargo planes, so do the shape grammar reseachers attempt to create a grammatical theory of architectural form, that is, by following all the apparent precepts and forms of theory making. Writers on shape grammars show little indication of a profound grasp of linguistic works. They tend only to refer to themselves. However, in his criticism of the shape grammar approach, Fleisher purposely takes seriously what it asserts. He takes for granted the "utter honesty" to which Feynman refers. This may be a rhetorical device in his article. However, he is utterly serious about attaining new knowledge about architecture and design whether it be by grammatical form rules, or anything else. For this reason, he is interested in what they have to say. Or better yet, as he says, is what they have to say interesting?

4 Claims Advertised by the Shape Grammar Field

To some readers, Fleisher's argument can be confusing. For example, during several seminars, I have become aware that some tend to misunderstand Fleisher's approach and conclude that his criticism is unfounded (Sundance Lab Seminars 1997). It has to do with his statement that the shape grammar enterprise is flawed because it is attempting to represent the visual—e.g. architecture—with the verbal—e.g. rules of string grammars. They say that Fleisher is wrong because the shape grammar approach is not seriously proposing a visual/verbal relationship, even though it states it explicitly and implicitly.

Agreeing or disagreeing with Fleisher depends on the research game one wants to play. If one adheres to the approach of cargo cult researchers, then indeed Fleisher is wrong. In this game it is acceptable to be loose and casual with terms such as "grammar," and go through the motions of constructing a production rule system that looks like a Chomsky grammar except that shapes are used instead of characters. Then by one or two carefully selected examples, it is "proved" that the grammar works by deriving layouts. The layouts that do not work are never mentioned (see examples of Le Corbusier spiral museum and Palladio buildings in Mitchell 1990, Stiny 1980, Stiny and Mitchell 1980).

On the other hand, if one does not accept the cargo cult approach, then Fleisher must be reckoned with. He first focuses on their claims or "advertisements" as Feynman would say, and then argues in a complicated but compelling manner that such claims are not entirely justifiable.

First the explicit claims:

1) Shape grammars promise "to provide the basis for describing, classifying, manipulating, extending, exploring, architectural form."
2) Expressions ("sentences") in the grammar "would describe consistent shapes, and therefore families of designs."
3) "Visual and verbal categories become equivalently expressive." That is, categories of shapes represented visually have some strict correspondence to a categories of shapes represented verbally.
4) (Architectural) "Style can be parsed, thereby parsimoniously explained, exhibited, referenced, compared."
5) "Architectural intent is considered merely a matter of assigning purpose to each rule of the grammar" (p. 221, Fleisher 1992).

These claims cannot escape the fact that they are a hypothesis about architectural design, "about designing, about the description, representation, and manipulation of architectural knowledge" (p. 221, Fleisher 1992). The hypothesis states that:

6) "Shape grammars are presumed to represent knowledge of architectural form."
7) That grammars are "formable," that there is a visual correspondence to verbal grammar.
8) The strong version of "the hypothesis requires that an architectural form be equivalent to a grammar" (p 221-222, Fleisher 1992).

5 How These Claims Hold Up According to Fleisher

Before we embark on the detailed version of Fleisher's argument as to why this hypothesis is not justifiable, let us consider his criticisms:

1) The shape grammar approach does not focus on the right question. It is not "about the rules of grammars. Those are just tactics." The fact that we can derive a layout of some building using a shape grammar only tells us that such a thing is possible for that particular layout. It "merely merits notice."

2) It avoids the real question, which is "the substance of the rule," that is, the hypothesis that is represented in a proposed rule.

An example of avoiding "the substance of the rule" can be seen in a paper presented at Acadia 2002, California State Polytechnic University, Pomona, by Liew (Liew 2002). A Palladio layout is generated from the bottom center to the top center, and by adding some squares around the periphery which are later deleted in order to attain the final layout. The fact that this layout can be generated this way is "worth noting," but in and of itself, explains little. What are the rules trying to say: that Palladio designed this way? Off hand, one would think that architectural designers would proceed differently. They would probably start by the central horizontal and vertical axis and work out. They probably would not add squares only to delete them later. Neither Liew's paper or the other shape grammar papers deal with this discrepancy. If we are stating that architectural designers use these rules deep down in their brains, then Liew is obligated to give some evidence that this is the case. Otherwise, we are left with the fact that for this particular type of layout, human designers will probably do it one way–or many ways–and that an algorithm can do another way. What does this mean? What do we know now that we did not know before?

3) Just because we can propose a hypothesis does not mean we should commit to it, or "hug it" as Fleisher says. We can hypothesize that aliens will take over the world through viral infections, but without hard evidence, it will not be considered interesting. And there are those hypotheses worth hugging, such as the geometry of circles representing round things. For shape grammars, "a case for hugging has yet to be made."

4) The question, "how can we represent architectural knowledge grammatically?" may not be a very interesting. "A CAD program would do as well, enlighten as much, provide freer dalliance and closer control" (p. 221, Fleisher 1992).

6 Fleisher's Argument

Fleisher's discussion goes through iterations of analyzing language, and architecture, by dealing with the concepts of lexicons, syntax and semantics.

6.1 Round 1:

Linguists and Language

What do linguists do? They develop a linguistic theory by means of a grammar that assigns a structure to sentences that are correct. They do not generate sentences. A correct sentence does not matter per se. All of us speak correctly. However, it is the grammar that is on trial by how it parses a correct sentence, and by how it helps us understand language.

The Shape Grammar Approach and the Languages of Shapes

What is an important objective of the shape grammar approach? It is the generation of structures or shapes. The grammar is judged by whether or not a shape fails visual sensibility. The shape is not assumed to be correct. The grammar is judged for the wrong reason. In contrast to language, shape grammar generation and parsing do not stand together.

6.2 Round 2:

Vocabularies in Language

A language grammar is a set of re-write or production rules on a differentiated vocabulary. The structure of sentences is given by its syntax. The words constitute a dictionary (lexicon).

Vocabulary in Architecture

Architectural "vocabulary" is not differentiated as in a language. "I am (not) sure that the vocabulary of architecture is equivalently differentiated" (p. 223, Fleisher 1992). There is an added complication though: architectural graphics (drawings) can be richly ambiguous, in contrast to a dictionary of words.

> *For example, a shape of a circle in an architectural drawing can be part of a sign indicating "north," a round stool in plan, a manhole cover, a lighting fixture, a decorative pattern as used Frank Lloyd Wright, and so on.*

Vocabularies in Shape Grammars.

Mere shapes are not differentiated enough for a vocabulary.

6.3 Round 3:

Syntax in Language

The rules contain terminals and nonterminals. Terminals include words in a vocabulary. Nonterminals represent the phrase structure of a sentence. Production rules only operate on nonterminals. The process of applying rules, whether in parsing or generation, is finished when no nonterminals remain.

Syntax in Architecture

Just as there is no equivalently differentiated vocabulary in architecture, Fleisher also states that "I am not sure that the differentiations are equivalently syntactical" (p 223, Fleisher

1992). This means that even though there are syntactical rules in architecture, they are not the same as syntactic rules in language.

According to the *Oxford English Dictionary*, the **first** definition of "Syntax" means "1.a. Orderly or systematic arrangement of parts or elements; constitution (of body); a connected order or system of things." The **second** definition has to do with grammar: "2. Gram.,etc. A. The arrangement of words (in their appropriate forms) by which their connexion and relation in a sentence are shown" (p. 487, *Oxford English Dictionary* 1989).

I think that Fleisher is using the first definition of "syntax" in his phrase "equivalently syntactical." By this, he means that the "Orderly or systematic arrangement of parts or elements" are not equivalent in language and in architecture. That is, for every way that elements are ordered in language, there is not an equivalent ordering in architecture.

At the same time, he is stating that shape grammars are described in terms the second definition of "syntax." As we shall see in the next section, he has a case because shape grammars are defined as string grammars in disguise.

Syntax in Architecture According to the Shape Grammar Approach

While linguists distinguish between terminals and nonterminals and maintain such distinction in dealing with their grammars, shape grammars are defined by making the distinction and then ignoring it. "Their rules much more usually match on markers (on figures) than figures or structures. Generation proceeds by subdivision or agglutination. Markers are the only control devices explicitly described." "Shapes have no formal finish or internal structure syntactically derived" (p. 223, Fleisher 1992).

Fleisher's comments imply that the definition and application of shape grammars are consistent. But this is not the case. Although, his analysis shows that their methods are flawed, they are actually worse than he describes. In reviewing the articles on shape grammars, I concluded the following (Gerzso 2000):

> Comparing shape grammars with standard context-free grammars is not straightforward because the definitions of shape grammars are not always consistent. According to Gips, a shape grammar is defined using string grammar terminology. He replaces words with shapes. He defines terminals as shapes, nonterminals as markers that are associated with shapes, and production rules as rewriting rules of shapes (p. 5 and p. 10, Gips 1974). Most of his grammars contain only one nonterminal. He shows how shape grammars can produce embedded or inscribed squares, arrays, snowflakes, and Hilbert curves.
>
> In one of the subsequent definitions of shape grammars, the explicit specification of terminals and nonterminals is dropped (p. 347, Stiny 1980). The grammars are cast as sets of lines. In this guise, they seem to be a variation of graphs. An interesting conjecture is that shape grammars are a subclass of graph grammars (Rozenberg 1997). In his explanation of his definitions, Stiny seems to be saying that terminals are shapes and that nonterminals are labeled shapes. A marker in the Gips sense is a type of labeled shape. Terminals and nonterminals exist albeit implicitly. In another version (p. 143, p. 147, and p. 148, Mitchell 1990), the definitions include once again the explicit notion of terminals, but nonterminals remain implicit as markers.
>
> The presentations of the definitions of shape grammars usually include only one marker or nonterminal. What does this mean? One could argue that a shape grammar with one nonterminal is like defining a string grammar in which the syntax only permits concatenating one type of word, such as nouns. This may be interesting in studying algorithms, but not in studying architecture or languages–natural or artificial.
>
> In applying shape grammars to specific architectural examples, the shape grammar formalism changes once again. Stiny presents the idea of applying shape production rules in two or more stages so as to be able to produce Mughul gardens (Stiny 1980) and Palladio villas (Mitchell 1990). For each stage, there is a set of rules to be applied. However, taken as a whole, shape grammars are no longer grammars in the CFG (context free grammars) sense.
>
> The rules in the first stage are CFG's, but the rules of the remaining phases are related to Chomsky transformation rules: (p. 89, Smith and Wilson 1979).

The structure of the shape grammar rules bolsters Fleisher's claim that they express a hypothesis that the rules about architectural form are equivalent to a grammar. He says "I do not know whether it was also noticed that the production is still a string: that the dimensionality of the shape resides entirely in the figures that are strung: that these productions cannot distinguish, do not understand top, bottom, back, front, within, or without of either figure or shape; . . ." (p. 222, Fleisher 1992).

In other words, shape grammars look like they are graphical representations of form, but upon close inspection, they are not. Consider the rules for a half-hexagon table, a simple grammar with scaling, and the Le Corbuiser spiral museum (p. 143, p. 147, Mitchell, 1990). They are string grammars in disguise. The linearity of string grammars is camouflaged in terms of a sequence of shapes which are generated in a linear manner with one marker. There is a string version for each one of these examples. We could easily write a string generator, produce a string, then run it through a computer program which will draw the shape or design. In computer science, these strings are commonly known as graphical languages (Foley and Van Dam 1982). The interpreters for these languages are ubiquitous. They reside in laser printers, plotters, ink jet printers, and video cards, to name a few. They are cousins of picture grammars (Shaw 1970). Despite this, the field of shape grammars has rarely acknowledged or taken advantage of these techniques.

However, Fleisher is not completely correct with regard to the

Palladio grammar (p. 155, Mitchell). In this case, the rules have more than one label or marker. The generation of a layout is no longer linear as in a string, which gives rise to an additional complication. Specifically, at the the fifth step of the derivation, it is possible to apply a rule on either the right side or left side of a square with markers. This means that a Palladio layout can be generated in more than one way, that is, it is not deterministic. In string grammars, this is also possible, but it is avoided like the plague because it makes parsing unmanageable. These types of grammars are known as ambiguous grammars (Aho and Ullman 1972).

It is tempting to use the Palladio grammars as a way to rebut Fleisher's claim that shape grammars represent an attempt to make "an architectural form be equivalent to a grammar." But the cure is worse than the disease. Nondeterministic layout generation is one reason, among many other ones that will not be considered here.

6.4 Round 4:

Semantics in Language

A lexicon supplies meaning to words (for example, the word "cat" refers to a four legged furry domestic animal, as well as possibly, three other meanings). Semantics supplies meanings to sentences. Semantic analyzers are applied to units of syntax. There exists a principle of compositionality. "The meaning of a sentence is composed of the meanings of these units, . . . [These] meanings do not change as the composition accumulates" (p. 224, Fleisher 1992).

Semantics in Architecture

The principle of compositionality in architecture is debatable. In contrast to reading, seeing is an act of renewable and revisable organization. "To look is to reason" (p 224, Fleisher 1992). The meaning of a shape cannot always be the accumulation of the meanings of sub-shapes.

Semantics in Architecture According to the Shape Grammar Approach

Shape grammars are purported to produce emergent forms. That is, figures can be distinguished in a serendipitous and unanticipated manner as a result of the combinations of other figures. This is a deadly mistake. It violates the principle of compositionality. The consequence is that the meaning of each shape in an aggregation of shapes will change as new shapes are added.

> *In order to understand this, consider the following hypothetical generation of a layout: a shape that represents a bathroom at one stage, but as a result of adding a shape that means "closet," the bathroom shape now means "basement," and with the addition of another shape that means "garage," the combined shapes "basement" and "closet" mean "heliport." This violates a lexical unit and semantical unit: "bathroom," "basement," and "closet."*

6.5 Round 5:

Semantics in Language

A lexicon (dictionary) is strongly fixed. Languages are redundant, but the order of words are spoken never varies. Therefore, the principle of compositionality is sufficiently reliable and frequent enough to transmit the meaning.

Semantics in Architecture

Visual lexicons are weakly fixed, if fixed at all. Graphic glossaries are common (such as Alexander's pattern language). Graphical dictionaries do not exist. Part of a picture reappears. It is frequent to have optical illusions. The order of "seeing" or scanning of a picture is never fixed.

Problems that the Shape Grammar Approach Has in Dealing with Semantics in Architecture

"Patterns of verbal semantics do not accommodate visual semantics comfortably" (p. 224, Fleisher 1992). This is an evident mismatch.

In languages, grammars lay structure on sentences in order to account for language capacity. This world is a given.
During the design process, architects invent structure and meaning simultaneously. Their world is under construction. Neither words or meanings exist prior to making shapes. Words and meanings are assigned on trial–as we go along, to see if it works–locally and globally, and also discarded. No order and no units can be prescribed or anticipated.
Architects like to do this.

7 "Whatever is a language for design?"

Whatever is the language for design is (or languages of designs), it is not what the field of shape grammars proposes, that is, the syntactical equivalence of natural language and architecture. If not, then what is? Or what must it take into account?

"However equivocal, designing is deliberate. Articulate drawings carry the architectural argument." " . . . [D]esigning is engaged as much in setting specifications as in searching solutions." But, "one would search, not thrash." "Searching must be constrained." "However, exhaustive examination, especially early in designing, is a doubtful tactic." "One would like a simple answer to a modest question: is there a good place to search?" "This generator is the language at issue" (p. 225 Fleisher 1992). "The language is for saying and seeing. Architecture is negotiated in two modalities. Equivalences are not at issue; they do not exist. The language would provide the means to maintain a discussion of the consequences in one mode, of the state and conditions of the other" (p. 225, Fleisher 1992).

Finally: "It may be that geometry is the only part of the architectural argument that is computable" (p. 225, Fleisher 1992).

Language	Architecture
there is an agreement as to what the units of a sentence are and what constitutes a sentence.	there is an agreement as to what the units of a building are and what constitutes a building
most of the time, there is an agreement as to what a sentence means.	in the everyday sense, a building has "meaning," but **not** in the same way a sentences does.
groups of sentences have recurrent syntactic patterns described by a grammar. A group is referred to as a language.	**some but not all** groups of buildings have recurrent spatial patterns. **Sometimes**, there is an agreement that certain groups comprise an architecture or style, such as "Greek architecture".

Table 1: Similarities between language and architecture.

Language	Architecture
sentences have no dimensions except for a linear sequence of characters or words	buildings have dimensions in three dimensional space.
sentences are not physical; they are not made of any materials.	in the everyday sense, buildings critically depend on building technology
other than their position in the sentence, the connectivity of sentence elements is not an issue.	all rooms in a building must have a direct or indirect connection to an outside access of the lot.
it is not common practice to permit the meaning of a sentence to change radically over time.	the "meaning" of a building can change radically: a factory becomes an apartment building, etc.
a sentence may be recorded, remembered, and reproduced many times. it can exist in several places at once.	a building comes into existence once and has a unique place in space and time.
sentences are "experienced" by thinking, uttering, hearing or reading them and during a short period of time (seconds, minutes). The sequence of sentence units is always the same.	buildings are experienced by moving around and through them. The sequence may vary constantly, which is considered an important aspect of architecture. Unlike sentences, the sequence can occur over long periods of time (hours, days, years).
to understand a sentence, it must be "experienced" in its entirety.	buildings may be experienced partially.

Table 2: Differences between language and architecture.

	Language	Architecture
	languages have recurrent patterns in their syntax.	**some** groups of buildings in an architecture have recurrent spatial patterns.
Math: Post production rules.	string production rules can be fashioned to account for patterns in syntax: Chomsky grammars.	diagrammatic/spatial rules can be fashioned to account for syntaxes of joined spaces, eg. spatial production rules SPR's (Gerzso 1978, 2000).
	these grammars are recursive	SPR's are recursive.
	Part of this hypothesis is that the <u>only</u> similarity between syntactic rules in language and <u>some</u> rules in architecture is that they are recursive. (Note: the formal mathematical definition of recursion is not being used here.)	

Table 3: The "deep" similarity between language and architecture: recursion.

An example of representing the visual—e.g. architecture—with the verbal—e.g. rules of string grammars—is the string version of an SPR of an instrustrialized housing system by Jorn Utzon (Gerzso 2001). For every layout of a house, there is at least one string of the SPR language. The strings can be shown to be grammatically correct. By analyzing the grammar, the strings for each layout, it becomes clear that this approach is a very limited and problematic as a design tool (Gerzso 1978).

8 Which Hypothesis to Hug? An Outline of a Proposal

Fleisher's argument is convincing, so much so that one is tempted to abandon the production rule approach all together. But before we surrender and cut our losses, let's start again and see what can be salvaged. We take Fleisher's article to help to restate the question. This is the basis for making a new proposal.

The first thing is to review what similarities exist between language and architecture. Some of them have already been dealt with previously (Table 1).
The second thing to do is to identify what additional basic differences exist between language and architecture that Fleisher did not mention (Table 2).
With this, we have a specification of what production rules must take into account:

1) Physical objects (buildings) occupy three dimensional space.
2) They are constrained by the limits of a site or lot.
3) Buildings that have space occupied by material, and inhabitable space.
4) The materials have been selected for their properties: structure, spatial delimitation, decoration etc. (Frampton 1995).
5) The inhabitable space must be connected directly or indirectly to the access of the lot.
6) The inhabitable spaces are designated for one or more uses or functions, which are usually constant over a period of years.

In order that we may hug the production rule hypothesis, how must these rules be fashioned? A first take on parts of the hypothesis (Gerzso 1978, 2000):

7) Some layouts can be accounted for with production rules. Which ones are those? They are SAR housing design method (Habraken 1976), Trulli (Allen 1969), Utzon (Weston 2002), and San Francisco Victorian houses (Vernez Moudon 1986), among others.
8) The form of the rules are divisionary: given a lot, architects divide space up.
9) The rules contain diagrams for representing chunks of space that contain materials, or are inhabitable space. They are nonstring rules called Spatial Production Rules (SPR's).
10) The form of the rules assure connectivity of each space to outside of lot. Examples: SPR's.
11) The form of the rules depends on the building technology: one rule based on stone masonry will be different from the one based on steel curtain wall.

As a result, hypothesis about the similarity between language and architecture begins to take form (Table 3).
This is weird, subtle, and possibly interesting.

9 Conclusions: The New Hypothesis and Shape Grammars

The approach presented above is different from that of shape grammars, which asserts that architectural spatial syntax rules are grammars because they are recursive, or can be modeled by recursive rules that are a type of language grammar. That is, because recursive spatial rules look like grammars, they must be a type of grammar. It fails to take into account that production rules are a way of modeling grammars in language, but they can also be refashioned or modified to model architecture, or something else, such as graphs. They are tools, such as a hammer, which is good for pounding nails. It turns out that there are nails to be pounded in linguistics and also in architecture. The fact that this is the case does not mean we are constructing identical structures of inquiry.

The shape grammar field fails to make this distinction. It could have remedied the discrepancy by taking into account Emil Post's work, the inventor of production rules (Davis 1994, Minsky 1967). He applied them to deal with issues of logic. He was not interested in accounting for syntax of words in a natural language, but he was interested in sentences in mathematical logic. As a result, more nails need pounding, but in a different structure.

It is also true that while considering how to construct such structures, there are other tools and fasteners available, such as screws, bolts, and the like. These options are analogous to the CAD programs that Fleisher refers to, which "enlighten as much, provide freer dalliance and closer control." By selecting a fastener, we must weigh the costs and the benefits. "Every process, or method, or tool carries a surcharge" (p. 221, Fleisher 1992).

Casting the shape grammar work as cargo cult research may strike some readers as extreme, unfair, and even biased. After all, the articles accepted for publications in *Envrironment and Planning B*, ACADIA, and other conferences, as well as the books, would seem to attest to their value. However, it is precisely these publications that are the basis of the criticism in this paper, as well as Fleisher's. Except for Mitchell (Mitchell 1990), articles on shape grammars tend to only refer to other articles in their own field, and fail to convincingly relate their work to the vast literature on grammars and graph theory in linguistics, computer science and mathematics, or even architectural history. Hersey and Freedman write, "It is curious that the two groups, those who study proportions (in architectural history) and those who study shape grammars, seem so little aware of each other's work" (p. 3 Hersey and Freedman 1992). Not only that, a small proportion of their publications are dedicated to reporting the testing of their hypothesis in terms of computer programs or design studio sessions (Chase 1999, Liew 2002). As far as I know, there are no widely used shape grammar generators downloadable from the Web.

Nevertheless: "We are indebted to the shape grammarians for pressing the argument that form can also be verbally explored. It is fundamental to the computability of architectural design." "It is awfully ingenious of the person who noticed that productions generating strings could be turned to generating shapes merely by substituting figures for the symbols in the database" (p. 222, Fleisher 1992).

Acknowledgements

I would like to thank Aaron Fleisher for sending me his article in the first place, and for being willing to discuss these issues along with Ray McCall, J.P. Protzen, Shane Rymer, and Anne Vernez.

References

Aho, A., and J. Ullman. (1972). *The theory of parsing translation and compiling, vol. 1, Parsing.* Englewood Cliffs, N.J.: Prentice Hall.

Aho, A., and J. Ullman. (1977). *Principles of compiler design.* Reading Mass: Addison-Wesley Publishing Co.

Banham, R. (1960). *Theory and design in the first machine age.* New York: Praeger.

Banham, R. (1969). *The architecture of the well-tempered environment.* London: Architectural Press.

Chase, S. C. (1999). Grammar based design: Issues for User Interaction models. *Media and design process. Proceedings of the 1999 Annual Conference of ACADIA,* eds. O. Ataman and J. Bermudez, 198-210. Salt Lake City.

Davis, M. ed. (1994). *Solvability, provability, definability: The collected works of Emil L. Post (contemporary mathematicians).* Boston, Basel, Berlin: Birkhauser.

Fleisher, A. (1992). Grammatical architecture. *Environment and Planning B*, 8:221-226.

Foley, J.D., and A. Van Dam. (1982). *Fundamentals of interactive computer graphics.* Reading, Mass: Addison-Wesely.

Frampton, K. (1995). *Studies in tectonic culture: The poetics of construction in the nineteenth and twentieth century architecture.* Cambridge, Mass: MIT Press.

Gerzso, J.M. (1978). *A descriptive theory of architectural built form and its applications.* Ph.D. Dissertation, University Microfilms.

Gerzso, J.M. (2000). Generating trullo Italian vernacular architecture with production rules and executable drawings. *Proceedings of the millennial open symposium on the arts and interdisciplinary computing,* eds. D. Salesin and C. Sequin. Seattle, WA: University of Washington.

Gerzso, J.M. (2001). Automatic generation of layouts of an utzon housing system via the internet. *Reinventing the discourse. Proceedings of the 2001 annual conference of ACADIA,* ed. W. Jabi. State University of New York at Buffalo. Buffalo: New York.

Gips, J. (1974). *Shape grammars and their uses*, Memo AIM 231, Palo Alto, CA: Stanford Artificial Intelligence Laboratory, Computer Science Dept., Stanford University.

Habraken, J. (1976). *Variations: The systematic design of supports.* Cambridge, MA: MIT Press.

Hersey, G., and R. Freedman. (1992). *Possible Palladian villas (plus a few instructively impossible ones).* Cambridge, Mass: MIT Press.

Hutchings, E., et al. (1997, reprint). *"Surely you're joking, Mr. Feynman!": Adventures of a curious character.* New York, London: W.W. Norton.

Liew, H. (2002). Descriptive conventions for shape grammars. *ACADIA 2002: thresholds. Proceedings of the 2002 annual conference of ACADIA,* ed. G. Proctor, 369-382. Pamona, CA., Dept. Architecture, College of Environmental Design, California State Polytechnic University.

Minsky, M. (1967). *Computation: Infinite and finite machines.* Englewood Cliffs, N.J.: Prentice Hall.

Mitchell, W. (1990). *Logic of architecture.* Cambridge, Mass: MIT Press.

The Oxford English dictionary. Second Edition (1989). Oxford: Clarendon Press.

Rozenberg, G., et al. (1997). *Handbook of graph grammars and computing by graph transformations: Concurrency, parallelism, and distribution.* World Scientific Pub. Co.

Shaw, A. (1970). Parsing of graph-representable pictures, *Journal of the ACM* 17(2).

Smith, N., and D. Wilson. (1979). *Modern linguistics, the results of Chomsky's revolution.* Bloomington, IN: IU Press.

Stiny, G., and J. Gips. (1972). Shape grammars and the generative specification of painting and sculpture. *Proceedings of IFIP congress 71.* Amsterdam: North Holland Publishing Co.; also in O. Petrocelli (ed.), *The best computer papers of 1971.* Auerbach, Inc.

Stiny, G. (1980). Introduction to shape grammars. *Environment and Planning B*, vol. 7.

Stiny, G., and W. Mitchell. (1980). The grammar of paradise: On the generation of mughul gardens. *Environment and Planning B* vol. 7.

Sundance Lab Seminars. (1997). Discussions during lunch seminars organized at the sundance lab by Mark Gross, College of Architecture and Planning, University of Colorado, Denver.

Verznez Moudon, A. (1986). *Built for change, neighborhood architecture in San Francisco.* Cambridge, Mass: MIT Press.

Weston, R. (2002). *Utzon,- inspiration – vision – architecture.* Hellerup, Denmark: Edition Blndal.

Cynergies: Technologies that Hybridize Physical and Cyberspaces

Peter Anders,
CAiiA-STAR, MindSpace.net

Abstract

This paper presents ways in which cybrids depend for their technology upon three existing models of architectural hybrid: display space, environmental computing, and augmented/mixed reality. Cybrids bring these techniques together into a synergistic whole that depends as much on the observer for its consistency as it does on its comprising technologies. This synergy is a product of corroborative behavior between different modes, which provide cybrid users with a coherent social/spatial experience. The paper notes cybrids' similarity to theater, not only for their technological dependency, but also for the tacit yet vital role of the observer in their effect.

Cynergies: Technologies that Hybridize Physical and Cyberspaces

Peter Anders,
CAiiA-STAR, MindSpace.net

1 Background

Cybrids are architectural, spatial compositions comprised of physical and cyberspaces (Anders 1998). This paper discusses three technologies that conduce to the creation of cybrids: display space, environmental computing, and mixed or augmented reality. These technologies, which hybridize physical buildings and electronic techniques, each bear values that support or vie with the phenomenological premises of cybrids and must be accounted for in their design. For example two of the technologies—display space and environmental computing—depend heavily on the integration of physical information technologies with the building fabric. Augmented or mixed reality technologies instead depend on the observer's ability to conflate simulated entities with the physical environment. Mixed reality, unlike the other two hybrids, is based on a psychological, phenomenological model of the observer. We argue that the other two are comparatively materialist in nature, requiring physical intervention for their effect on the environment and subsequently the observer.

Despite their overt differences, however, the technologies are not mutually exclusive. In the literature of Cooperative Building, for instance, the devices of display space are found among the varied components of environmental computing systems. Augmented reality, too, makes use of display systems and computer networks. Our thesis here is that the product of such technologies may be composed to a greater holistic effect: that of a merged reality that blends simulation with material fact (Johnson 2002). In the following pages we will see the role that these technologies may play in the development of cybrids.

2 Display Space

Among the popular motifs of contemporary architecture are images of buildings whose walls and surfaces are animated by large-format screens. Such designs are emblematic of technology's invasion of the environment—a fact readily observed on Times Square and in Las Vegas—and have been used to illustrate the integration of information technology with the material environment. However, the displacement of walls with screens becomes problematic when considering its effect on spatial experience and architecture itself. The notion that architecture becomes a substrate for arbitrary display underlies film theorist Lev Manovich's pessimism about the discipline's future. He notes that projected images overwhelm the presence of the physical, thereby devolving it into a mute background for effects.

"...architecture is becoming simply a support for computer generated images. Virtual space created by these images replaces the physical space of architecture . . . the image terminates the space. The role of architecture becomes purely utilitarian: to be a shelter for the image, not unlike a TV set, a billboard, a cinema hall, turned inside-out." (Manovich 1993)[1]

Along similar if more optimistic lines, theorist Peter Lunenfeld believes that the future of architecture lies in combining the hardscape of building with the imagescape of new technology. Imagescape, for Lunenfeld, comprises "electronic facades, linings, and elements on, in and throughout [the] hardscape" of buildings and cities (Lunenfeld 1997). In principle this proposal resembles those of architects in the 1960s. It recalls the work of Archigram, Cedric Price, 9999, Haus-Rucker, PULSA, Coop-Himmelblau, and other visionaries who set forth technologically advanced, image-saturated environments.

The concept of Lunenfeld's imagescape is implicit in Le Corbusier's Brussels Pavillion, Piano and Rogers' Centre Pompidou, and EAT's (Experiments in Arts and Technology) Pepsi Pavillion. Architects Robert Venturi and Denise Scott-Brown's designs also employed film/video displays. Examples include their concept of the decorated shed and their 1968 National Football Hall of Fame buildingboard project. Their analysis, in 1972, of Las Vegas' media-ridden environments pointed to a future (now present) proliferation of imaging technologies in architecture (Venturi, Scott-Brown, Izenour 1972). Today several designers pursue the display space approach in which architecture becomes a screen for the projection of images. The projected image here plays the role of surface ornament, its contents disjoint spatially and thematically from the receiving surface. The image space is incidental to the space of the architecture that, like its display technology, remains physical.

We see Display Space's latent materialism reflected in Jeffrey Shaw's inflatable cinema, Herzog and Meuron's Kramlich Residence, Kas Oosterhuis' Space Station Module and Transports projects, Frank Gehry's Rock and Roll museum, Diller and Scofidio's United Artists Complex Theater, and Rem Koolhaas' proposal for the ZKM among other projects. These hybrids imbed display systems into their material environment. Often only the effects, not the subjects, of the displays are considered in the project design. The result is thereby a collage of unrelated display and built fabric—like television sets in a living room.

Figure 1. Proposal for a building employing Display Space technology. Image by Peter Marshall

Figure 2. Images from Kas Oosterhuis' Saltwater Pavilion. Note the projections on interior surfaces. Images from Hybrid Spaces, by Peter Zellner.

3 Cybrids and Display Space

The virtues of display space include easy viewing of information by multiple participants, and freedom from the constraints of headsets and sensors. Cost benefits over head-mounted displays would be harder to assess—especially in the long run—since large displays are often expensive. This obtains whether the display is a fixed, flat-panel screen, or a laser projection system. Conceivably, relatively inexpensive electronic paper displays may evolve that could enhance Display Space's prospects, but the technology for such displays is still in development. We have already noted some of Display Space's drawbacks. The space of its images is rarely related to its surroundings in any way other than residing on the thin phosphor of the screen. By definition superficial, its spatial illusion is destroyed by the viewer's movement and changes in parallax. By moving from the ideal viewpoint, the viewer re-affirms the materiality of the display. A cybrid strategy integrating illusory and actual spaces would appear to founder on this limitation. But there are ways around this.

The trompe-l'oile evocation of deep space is an architectural technique that pre-dates the Renaissance. One could overcome Display Space's limitations by increasing the distance between the display and the viewer. In this way a moving viewer's parallax changes little with respect to the display's distance. This would cause the remote image space—on a suitably large screen—to merge with the space around it. Subtle tracking of the viewer with consequent adjustments to the display perspective could enhance the effect.[2] Similar principles apply to stationary viewing. Plastic depth, best perceived as the distance between viewer and object, approaches that of the space between the viewer's eyes. The mental reconciliation of disparate images plus the adjustment of eye muscles brings the subject into focus as a three-dimensional presence. Nearer external displays, then, would require each eye to receive unique images adjusted for perceived distance.

It is possible to do this without resorting to head-mounted displays or user tracking. Display systems are in development for providing three-dimensional effects, although few if any are available commercially. One promising technology uses diffraction grating filters applied to screen surfaces. Diffraction gratings are common in toys and novelty cards, providing illusions of movement or depth by deflecting different images to each of the viewer's eyes. The display technique requires that the underlying image be parsed into vertical strips, alternating the image from one to the next. The binocular effect can approach holographic quality (Zucker 1997). This approach requires no tracking of observers to maintain its illusion, although the viewing angle of the 3D image is restricted. The anticipated use of diffraction displays lies presently in gaming and specialty applications. Large screen displays are unlikely to emerge from their development.

Another option takes advantage of the materiality of the display. Distributing the displays within an existing space and conforming the screens to their content offers compelling opportunities. For example, one could place displays around a conference table, such that each screen presents a different remote participant (Negroponte 1995). This effectively brings the remote participants together, although the illusion of a combined virtual/physical space is limited to those at the table. The contrivance falls apart quickly once a visitor's face leaves its screen.[3]

Architectural cybrids' social use favors larger, environmental displays. However, the fixity of such displays constrains their use to specific sites, limiting the cybrid experience to discrete, non-immersive events. Head-mounted augmented reality displays might span the gaps between external displays, provided the designers correlate the different display modes for continuity. This coordination would also be required if several HMD users were to share an experience. Conjoining such displays with the virtual environment requires sophisticated sensing and display technologies. These might be worn or—equally likely—embedded in the material environment with wireless support for mobile displays (Wren et al. 1999).

4 Environmental Computing

Environmental Computing, also known as ubiquitous or distributed computing, proposes physical environments saturated with information devices. Its proponents hold that by linking the microchips embedded in our appliances, pocket computers, automobiles and work environments new, otherwise impossible, opportunities arise. This linkage would be sustained by a network of computers and processors. Ancillary appliances may be fixed, like the screens and speakers of Display Space. Or they may be mobile, connected to the network through wireless technologies.

Environmental Computing and Display Space are not mutually exclusive, for displays are only one of many devices used in Environmental Computing. Their chief difference lies in the former's coherent integration of devices, and the creation of systemic behaviors through artificial agents and networks. Unlike Display Space, this integration extends beyond displays to servo-motors, embedded and mobile appliances, even to external networks. Nevertheless, like Display Space, Environmental Computing is a material hybrid of environment and technology. Media content, space, and supporting system are conceived separately and often remain operationally distinct from one another.

Research on environmental computing centers on the supporting systems that enable communication between appliances. Its hybridization with the mundane is a result of embedding these appliances into the walls and surfaces of our surroundings. In this sense Environmental Computing differs little from prevalent concepts of Intelligent Building, aspects of Gelernter's Mirror Worlds, and William Mitchell's Recombinant Architecture.

Figure 3 and 4. Building systems are increasingly networked and controlled by computers. Image taken from Siemens brochure promoting building system monitoring technologies.

Environmental computing research also asserts the creation of "intelligent" devices that are systematically and behaviorally compatible. Their compatibility is key to providing consistency for its users. It makes possible a simple dialog between machines—say, having one's computer "recognize" and adjust to a new printer—or an elaborate and extended community of appliances that collectively give the impression of intelligence.

William Mitchell, Dean of MIT's School of Architecture, has written extensively on the effects of distributed computing on architecture. In City of Bits he carefully delineates the pressures of technology on building use and typology. If, he reasons, an ATM bank machine functionally stands in for the huge banking halls of the past, what becomes of the material architecture of banks? Moreover, as ATMs pervade public places, they change the use of the spaces they inhabit. The function of an airport terminal or regional mall now includes banking as well as travel or shopping. In what Mitchell calls Recombinant Architecture, buildings and cities become physical hybrids comprising networks, information appliances, and the brute materials of construction (Mitchell 1995). The reasoning emerges from the instrumental, even positivist, values underlying distributed computing. Simply put, machines provide services that affect the use and form of their environment. In this view—consistent with that of materialist practice—the user's experience is a mere consequence of the material surroundings. This reinforces a materialist view prevalent in architecture and obtains regardless of whether the environment is augmented with information technology.

5 Cybrids and Environmental Computing

Cybrids will certainly require some degree of embedded, environmental computing to ensure the coherent merger of physical and cyberspaces. Computational support for disclosing such linkage is typically housed in the surrounding architecture. While wireless networks allow mobility for digital devices, these appliances usually rely on fixed support: network connections, modems, servers, and transmitters. Although environmental computing implies uniform distribution of sensors and actuators in the material environment, its intended effect is local to individual users. Lights turn on in occupied rooms, doors open for users, calls travel to the phone nearest to intended recipients. These effects require an embedded system that responds to user position and—at times—orientation. Similar systems could apply also to generating electronic simulations since they would have to be "aware" of the location and vantage of users to create suitable effects (Pentland 1999; Ishii 1999). Such monitoring and display would have to accommodate a number of occupants both physically present and telepresent. Environmental computing does not preclude either display space or, as we shall see, augmented reality. Embedded sensor systems can support augmented reality just as built-in monitors serve display space. They are all compatible within an appropriate hierarchy of use.

6 Augmented/Mixed Reality

The overlay of simulations onto physical objects and surroundings has been variously referred to as augmented reality (AR) and mixed reality (MR). These technologies have emerged from those used in virtual reality, and many of the softwares and devices are similar. AR and MR have great implications for cybrid architectures. In the eyes of several AR developers the construction industry is a potential market for the technology. Their reasoning is straightforward: AR, like virtual reality, deals with spatial and symbolic phenomena in ways useful to architects, builders, and facility managers. These industries' increasing familiarity with—and reliance upon—computers makes them well suited for mixed reality technologies.

However, as with virtual reality before it, the success of such forecasts hinges on a variety of issues. Some of these lie outside the domain of technologists: compatibility and reliability of equipment, flexibility, purchase costs, training, and upkeep. Not least important is the degree to which AR systems serve the needs and values of architects. For if we use the history of virtual reality to guide us, AR's best prospects may not be in architecture at all. Many of the VR and imaging technologies developed for architects found more lucrative markets in computer games and Hollywood's special effects industry. Still, despite these reservations, a review of AR's recent development suggests many architectural applications. For, unlike VR before it, augmented reality keeps one foot in the material world, and so may serve both physical and symbolic activities of design.

6.1 Guiding construction

The overlay of spatial computer models onto buildings has uses in many stages of the building's life. A project's database can facilitate a building's design, construction, and maintenance. German researcher Gudrun Klinker proposes that a project's mixed reality would attend all stages of development, from the earliest siting of a building to its subsequent occupation. In a paper written on uses of augmented reality models on construction sites, Klinker and her colleagues speculate on AR's use in the building's life cycle.

> With AR, . . . virtual geometric objects can be integrated into the real environment during all phases of the life cycle of the building. Before the construction project is started, AR can support marketing and design activities to help the customer visualize the new object in the environment. . . . During construction, AR can help evaluate whether the building is constructed according to its design...After construction is completed, maintenance and repair tasks benefit from seeing hidden structures in or behind walls (Klinker, Didier, Reiners 1998).

This bears directly on the life-cycle management of the project, although it stresses the digital model's role in constructing and serving a building. The use of virtual models as annotation and guides for construction and manufacture is prevalent in AR literature. Indeed, among the earliest uses for AR was in overlaying instruction manuals onto the viewing field of factory workers at Boeing. Subsequent work by Stephen Feiner, Blair McIntyre and others illustrates the use of AR for the maintenance of copy machines and other equipment (Feiner, McIntyre Höllerer 1999; Reiners et al. 1999).

6.2 Seeing the invisible

Among other virtues of mixed reality is the ability of its users to perceive invisible aspects of their surroundings. Grant Foster and his colleagues at the University of Reading have described the uses of a simulation overlaid onto a building (Foster, Wenn,

Figures 5 and 6. An artist's rendition of an augmented reality, figure 5 shows the ovelap of virtual graphics and the actual objects that they attend. This technology would employ head-mounted displays linked to global positioning satellites for orientation. The present technology for such outdoor augmented reality is fairly encumbering as seen in figure 6. However, the decreasing size and cost of similar devices may make them more accessible to the public in coming years.

Harwin 1998). They have developed DAMOCLES, a system that enables vision or hearing impaired users to navigate a building by aural and visual cues. While this may also be used for guiding maintenance robots through corridors, Foster also believes that such AR systems can also let users see the invisible. Equipment that generates heat, for instance, can be visually keyed to keep operators from harm. Such thinking lies behind similar proposals for visualizing the invisible. Professor Anthony Webster while at Columbia University also explored the use of AR in architecture—particularly in the field of construction. With aforementioned colleagues Feiner and McIntyre, he was able to reveal the hidden reinforcing rods in a concrete column using a head-mounted display (Feiner et al. 1995). The ability to see through obstacles, such as concrete, murky water, or human flesh is a constant theme in AR's development.

7 Cybrids and Mixed Reality

Cybrids are augmented/mixed reality compositions—spaces, objects, or other entities—designed to be so from the start. For this reason, the simulation-to-construction methodology of architecture is well suited to cybrid strategies since the digital simulation and building are related throughout the process. However, in the case of cybrids such an overlap of physical and cyberspaces is not necessarily as congruent as it would be in a conventional architectural plan. There is rarely redundancy between physical artifacts and simulations in Mixed Reality. Most experiments in Mixed Reality place simulations into an existing, unrepresented physical space. Architectural cybrids avail themselves of this option while maintaining the direct, process-based correspondence between the built and unbuilt artifacts.

Despite occasional exceptions, much of AR and mixed reality is still a private experience. As in virtual reality the simulation is still enjoyed by the individual with the helmet, leaving others to wonder what he's seeing. Since architecture provides spaces for social interaction, it seems reasonable that architectural cybrids would serve a similar purpose. In the case of head-mounted AR, however, a shared, consensual hallucination for a cybrid's occupants would require head-mounted displays for each user. While this may be possible with fast, inexpensive future technologies, it is also prudent to consider larger, fixed displays of Display Space.[4]

8 Cybrid Synergy

The case for cybrids takes selectively from existing architectural hybrids, with full awareness of their biases and limitations. We have seen the limitations of each hybrid overcome by another. AR's bias toward private experience is countered by Display Space's public nature. The challenge of Display Space's fragmentation is met by the subtle coordination of Environmental Computing. And, finally, AR and Mixed Reality's cognitive model of the user offsets the materialist focus of both Display Space and Environmental Computing. Within these three types of

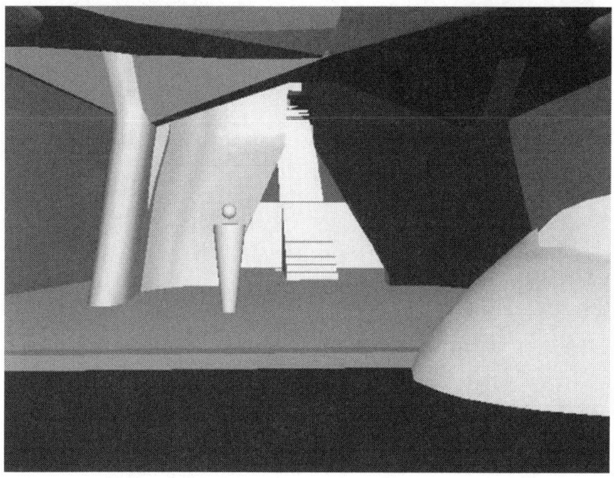

Figures 7 and 8. The author's virtual model of a building set upon a desktop using augmented reality. The model may be entered and experienced through scale and position changes of the viewer. At its larger scale, shown in figure 8, the model becomes a conventional virtual reality. The technology for this AR was co-developed with Mark Billinghurst by Hirokazu Kato. Kato has provided these images.

architectural hybrid we find the technology of cybrids.

Architectural cybrids are implicit in any projects whose development involves a database. Cybridity is a matter of how information is managed within the database—whether through initial drawing or modeling, or via live sensing/monitoring systems. Previously we have noted the informational aspects of designed artifacts and the process that generates them (Anders 2001). The extent to which the link between artifacts and their database is "live" determines—on a mechanistic level—the cybrid nature of the project.

Beyond our provisional definition of cybrid we can now outline, even elaborate, its technical behavior. A cybrid is a composition of interdependent material construction and electronic simulation. The simulation—a product of a managed database—precedes, attends, and succeeds any material manifestation of the project. It precedes manifestation as does any specification for construction. It attends a project by assisting the monitoring and management of the physical plant. It is also succeeds the manifestations by persisting—in its database—after their demolition.[5]

The simulation would also be the locus of any mode of information provided to the user: telecommunications; telepresence; simulation; or annotations/diagrams within the environment. Most importantly, all modes by which the user experiences the cybrid's cyberspace are mutually reinforced. Visual displays, spatial environments, sound, screen and head-mounted displays corroborate one another to reinforce the coherent, non-physical space of the cybrid. This space situates the images/avatars/environments conveyed from remote sites, as well as those emulations local to the project. Conversely, this space provides a consistent experience to both local and remote users. It forms the phenomenological backdrop of the project and its occupants.

9 The Domain of the Observer

Seen in this way cybrid becomes a theater for social, symbolic interaction. As in theater, fictional entities merge with the physical reality: facades recede within the faux space of the stage; real actors play fantasy roles; material props stand for their magical counterparts. The history of theater is filled with examples of how materiality and fantasy converge on the stage. We will not elaborate here except to say that theater depends on the observer's imagination for its effect. Trapdoors, greasepaint, scrims, mirrors, smoke are the theater's material attributes. But narrative coherence, magic of transformation, and spatial extension beyond the limits of the stage are all in the domain of the observer.

The crucial difference between cybrids and conventional theater is the apparent lack of a proscenium. The classical proscenium is a window onto the world of the play. It is a paradoxical boundary that exists simultaneously in both the material world of the audience and the fiction of the stage. It separates—yet links—the dark material space of the seats and the bright fantasy of the play. Cybrids diverge from the spatial juxtaposition of the proscenium theater, and are more closely allied with the montage of cinema. Montage seamlessly overlaps disparate scenes—worldviews—into one image. The effect of this overlap depends upon to a great degree upon the viewer's interpretation. Cybrids expand this cinematic notion to include the material ambience of the user as well as the simulated space and objects with which it exists.

Conclusions

We have here discussed ways in which cybrids depend for their technology upon three existing models of architectural hybrid: display space, environmental computing, and augmented/mixed reality. Cybrids bring these techniques together into a synergistic whole that depends as much on the observer for its consistency as it does on its comprising technologies. This synergy is a product of corroborative behavior between different modes, which provide cybrid users with a coherent social/spatial experience. We have noted cybrids' similarity to theater, not only for their technological dependency, but also for the tacit yet vital role of the observer in their effect.

References

Anders, P. (2001). Domains of body and mind. *Convergence: The journal of research into new media technologies* 7(2): 90-100.

Anders, P. (1999). Envisioning cyberspace. New York: McGraw-Hill.

Anders, Peter. 1997. Cybrids: Integrating cognitive and physical space in architecture. In *Representation and design. Proceedings of ACADIA conference,* Cincinnati, Ohio, 3-5 October, eds J.P. Jordan, B. Mehnert, and A. Harfmann, 17-34.

Feiner, S., B. MacIntyre, and T. Höllerer. (1999). Wearing it out: First steps toward mobile augmented reality systems. *In Mixed reality: Merging real and virtual worlds,* eds. Y. Ohta and H. Tamura, 363-375. New York: Springer-Verlag.

Foster, G. T., D. E. N. Wenn, and W. S. Harwin. (1998). Generating virtual environments to allow increased access to the built environment. *International journal of virtual reality,* 3(4): 12-19.

Gelernter, D. (1991). *Mirror worlds: Or the day software puts the universe in a shoebox: How it will happen and what it will mean*. New York: Oxford University Press.

Ishii, H. (1999). Tangible bits: Coupling physicality and virtual reality through tangible user interfaces. In *Mixed reality: Merging real and virtual worlds*, eds. Y. Ohta and H. Tamura, 229-245. New York: Springer-Verlag.

Johnson, B. (2002). Virtuality and place. In *Thresholds. Proceedings of ACADIA conference,* ed. G. Proctor, 79-86. Pomona, California.

Klinker, G., D. Stricker, and D. Reiners, (1998). The use of reality models in augmented reality applications. In *3D structure from multiple images of large-scale environments: European workshop, SMILE '98,* eds. R. Koch and L. Van Gool, 281-283. Berlin: Springer.

Lunenfeld, P. (1997). Hybrid architectures and the paradox of unfolding. In *Intelligent environments: Spatial aspects of the information revolution,* ed. P. Droege, 439-449. Amsterdam: Elsevier Science B. V.

Manovich, L. (1993). Avant garde, cyberspace, and architecture of a future. Paper presented at the Fourth International Symposium on Electronic Art (FISEA), Minneapolis, Minn., November 5.

Mitchell, W. (1995). *City of Bits*. Cambridge, Mass.: The MIT Press.

Negroponte, N. (1995). *Being digital*. New York: Alfred A. Knopf.

Pentland, A. (1999). Perceptual intelligence. In *Proceedings of ACM multimedia 99*, eds. D. Bulterman, K. Jeffay, and H. Zhang, 74-87. New York: ACM Publications.

Reiners, D., D. Stricker, G. Klinker, and S. Müller. (1999). Augmented reality for construction tasks: Doorlock assembly. In *Augmented reality: Placing artificial objects in real scenes,* eds. R. Behringer, G. Klinker, and D. Mizell, 31-44. Natick, Mass: A. K. Peters.

Venturi, R., D. Scott-Brown, and S. Izenour. (1972). *Learning from Las Vegas.* Cambridge, Mass: MIT Press.

Wren, C. R., S. Basu, F. Sparacino, and A. P. Pentland. (1999). Combining audio and video in perceptive spaces. In *Managing interactions in smart environments,* eds. P. Nixon, S. Dobson, and G. Lacey, 44-55. Berlin: Springer-Verlag.

Zucker, R. S. (1997). An architecture for a virtual environment using multiple video streams. Master's thesis, Department of Computer Science, University of California Irvine.

(Endnotes)
Notes

[1] Architecture as a material presence may be reduced, but, Manovich argues elsewhere, the discipline it employs may be used in the design of navigable, spatially complex digital environments. Here he cites the work of Malevich, Le Corbusier, Wright and Bernard Tschumi. Manovich, Lev. 2001. The language of new media. Cambridge, Mass: MIT Press. p. 264.

[2] Such tracking of course would imply that the display would work best for an individual viewer, thereby undercutting a cybrid's social function.

[3] In his book, Being Digital, Nicholas Negroponte writes of the projection of facial images onto phosphorescent screens shaped in the form of a head. Although originally intended for military briefing, this technology has since found its way into exhibits at Disneyworld, notably the Haunted House and Buzz Lightyear rides.

[4] In public displays of VR technology viewers can often see what the participant sees by means of large screens attending the exhibit. However, only the wearer of the helmet enjoys immersive interaction with the scene. CAVEs allow viewers and participants to share the experience more convincingly.

[5] We must here distinguish between the simulation, or better, emulation, and its supportive data base. The emulation is a presentation of the database formatted for the user. This may take the form of plans, images, sounds, behaviors, etc. As we use the term in this discussion, emulations are spatial representations of data contingent on the material components of the cybrid. Ideally the converse is also true: the material components are contingent on the emulations as well.

07 >> Connecting Digital Tools

Chairs: Ganapathy Mahalingam, Mark J. Clayton

Return To Roots: Computational Modeling as a Tool For Architecture

Ganapathy Mahalingam

In the early stages of their engagement of computer technology, architects approached the technology as an assistive technology that would enhance the practice of architecture. The scope of the engagement was captured in the phrase 'computer-aided architectural design.' In the four decades since, the role of computer technology in architecture has gained a marked significance. The scope has now been extended for architects to contemplate 'totally computer-mediated architectural design.' The key in the development of digital tools to enhance the practice of architecture has been the facility with which the various tasks involved in the practice of architecture have been represented, enabled or enhanced using computer technology. Tools have always been created for their instrumentality, that is, their ability to assist in performing desired tasks. Given the scope of the engagement of computer technology by architects in the early phases, the assistive nature of tools formed the focus of researchers. The focus on this assistive nature has continued to remain in the minds of researchers who see assistance as the proper role of computer technology in architecture.

Papers submitted in this category reflect the range of assistive tools that are currently being developed by researchers. These papers include descriptions of a computational tool to design and visualize a vaulted tensegrity structure, a tool to review lighting simulations for lighting quality based on cluster analysis, a tool to visualize the solar access envelope on complex sites, a tool to create spatial form by sketching, design tools for architectural form generation that utilize the features of complex adaptive systems, a tool to explore shape grammars and shape computation, a tool to utilize gestures in a pen-based interface to design systems and a tool to link spatial character in spatial planning.

These digital representations of architectural entities and the digital manipulation of those entities suggest alternate means to produce architecture. Very few aspects of architectural design are now outside the scope of computer-based representation and manipulation. Drawing, modeling, performance simulation, design collaboration, construction management and building fabrication are now routinely performed using computer-based technology because of the development of a wide range of tools. It is now possible to proceed from the conception of a design to its fabrication and construction in a computer-mediated environment. This success has revealed the untapped potential of the computational representation of architecture.

Advances in computing based on the study of natural processes such as neural processing, genetic evolution and emergence now suggest that the elusive nature of creative architectural thought can be articulated enough to be applied in a technologically-mediated environment. Digital tools may finally reveal what other architectural tools have hitherto concealed – the architectonics of architecture. Therein lays the promise. The future of digital tools rests on the extent to which architects can accept that exemplary architectural designs can be created in a computer-mediated environment and that digital thinking is indeed architectural thinking.

Ganapathy Mahalingam is currently the president of the Association for Computer-Aided Design in Architecture (ACADIA). He is also an Associate Professor of Architecture and Architecture Program Director in the Department of Architecture and Landscape Architecture at North Dakota State University in the United States of America. He holds a Ph.D. Architecture. Professor Mahalingam has firsthand experience in the creation of digital tools for architecture, having created software for the preliminary design of proscenium-type auditoriums. The creation of the software involved the definition of the auditorium as a virtual computational object, and an algorithmic process for auditorium design based on acoustical, functional and programmatic performance parameters.

Connecting Digital Tools

Mark J. Clayton

A decade ago, Bill Mitchell wrote "Chroniclers of our era may one day write 'What was computer-aided design?' To them, it will just be design." Because of the proliferation of digital tools for design, we are rapidly forgetting that there was ever design before computing. Ask an undergraduate student to describe the design process. There is a good chance that the student will mention using CAD and 3D modeling. Ask a contractor how to practice the profession of building. The answer will surely involve manipulating digital spreadsheets and using project management software. Ask a facility manager a similar question and most likely the answer will involve use of databases, calendaring software, web sites and email. Digital tools for those in the architecture professions have become pervasive.

Convergence is another phenomenon of the contemporary technology that has crept into our practice as researchers, educators and professionals. Communications technology and computing technology are intertwined. The two fields are rapidly becoming indistinguishable. When you communicate, there is a good chance that you are using a computer. When you use a computer, there is a good chance that you are communicating. The "back talk" that Donald Schon has described as a hallmark of the creative design process is now mediated by our digital tools. Whether communicating with external intelligences, artificial intelligences or even reflective intelligences, the computer is a participant. Our research and exploration of digital tools is increasingly inextricable from the study of design methods and cognition.

The digital tools that are described in this section are postulates. Does this software model the cognitive processes of designers? If we change the process to conform to the software, will the design artifacts improve? Can the process be expedited and improved in quality through automation encapsulated in software? We are tracing the trajectory of research laid out by Herbert Simon who noticed that computing research is not most profoundly mathematical but is rather the empirical study of how the mind works. At some point, the computer will be transparent in research about design. Within ten years, the chroniclers will ask "What was architectural computing research?" Because all design methods research will involve computing.

References

Mitchell, William J. And Malcolm McCullough. 1995. Digital design media, 2nd edition. New York: Van Nostrand Reinhold.
Schön, Donald. The Reflective Practioner. New York: Basic Books, Inc. 1983.
Simon, Herbert A. The sciences of the artificial. Cambridge, MA: the M.I.T. Press, 1969.

Mark J. Clayton has taught architectural design and computing since 1988. He is the Executive Associate Dean of the College of Architecture at Texas A&M University. Dr. Clayton earned a Bachelor of Architecture from Virginia Tech, a Master of Architecture from UCLA, and a Ph.D. in Civil and Environmental Engineering at Stanford University. He is a past President of ACADIA.

A Parametric Approach to the Design of a Tensegrity Vaulted Dome for an Ephemeral Structure for the 2004 Olympics

Katherine A. Liapi and Jinman Kim
the University of Texas, Austin

Abstract

Tensegrity, defined as “tensional integrity,” is central to the design of a semi-open exhibition space that was submitted as an entry to the international competition for the design of “Ephemeral Structures for the City of Athens,” in the context of the 2004 Olympic Games. The main feature of the proposed exhibition space is a vaulted dome composed of interconnected detachable and deployable tensegrity units. The most challenging aspect in the design of the tensegrity vault was the generation of alternative spatial configurations for form exploration and study. For this purpose a mathematical code has been developed that links all the parameters that affect the design of tensegrity vaults. The code also allows for the parametric graphical generation of the vault by displaying geometric information in a 3D environment. This paper discusses the geometric basis of the code and its usefulness in the morphological study of the tensegrity vaulted dome for the proposed ephemeral structure. The mathematical code has been shown to significantly facilitate the study of various preliminary configurations of tensegrity vaulted structures.

A Parametric Approach to the Design of a Tensegrity Vaulted Dome for an Ephemeral Structure for the 2004 Olympics

Katherine A. Liapi and Jinman Kim
the University of Texas, Austin

1 Introduction

In the fall of 2002, and in the context of the Cultural Olympiad for the 2004 Olympics, an international competition for the design of "Ephemeral Structures for the City of Athens" was held. The ephemeral structures, according to the competition programme, are to be mounted and remain in a site only for a limited amount of time; then they will be demounted and transported to another cityscape. Five different categories of ephemeral structures were identified; each category had a specific theme and was expected to generate events for cultural activities. Competitors were asked to choose among these categories and submit only one entry. The theme of the category that will be addressed in this paper is "ephemeral semi-open exhibition space."

According to the competition programme, the ephemeral structures are also expected to operate as "urban parasites," to adapt to the existing infrastructure of the cities where they migrate, and to invite citizens and visitors to participate in cultural activities. A contemporary cityscape is defined in the programme as "a site for experimentation, a site of practice, and a site of thought" (Cultural Olympiad 2002). The ephemeral structures are thus expected to promote innovation in meeting practical needs, as well as to respond to theoretical issues raised by their temporary nature.

According to the category-specific competition programme, the main requirement for the semi-open exhibition space was to design a structure in which the level of spatial enclosure varies to respond to the needs of the exhibitions or installations to be hosted. The total area of the semi-open exhibition space, in its closed form, should not exceed 50 sq m.

2 Tensegrity as the main design theme

Initially a materialization of an aesthetic quest first conceived by artist Snelson (Snelson 65), the concept of "tensegrity" (tensional integrity as coined by Buckminster Fuller) (Fuller 75), was later used to denote a novel class of structures with unique morphological characteristics and mechanical properties; deployability being one of them. Tensegrity structures are composed of struts and cables. The struts, which act as compression members, are connected only to cables, and not to each other, while the cables take only tension and form a continuous closed system. Internal tension holds struts and cables together and allows tensegrity structures to reach equilibrium at geometric configurations where bars look like floating in a network of cables. Stable configurations and related mechanical and structural properties have been extensively covered in bibliography (Emmerich 1996; Motro 1994; Hanaor 1998; Skelton 1997; Sultan 1999). Tensegrities, also defined as "kinematically indeterminate and re-configurable systems in which all parts coexist in a dynamic equilibrium" (Hanaor 1992), are characterized by an optimum relation of geometric, architectural, and structural expression (Liapi 2000).

The concept of tensegrity is central to the design development of the semi-open exhibition space that was submitted as entry to the competition for the "Ephemeral Structure for the City of Athens." The main feature of the proposed exhibition space is a vaulted dome composed of interconnected detachable and deployable tensegrity units (Figure 1). The metaphors and associations of tensegrity to the spirit of the Olympics and the ephemeral nature of the proposed structures are numerous. One explicit association is the parallel of the continuum of tension/ compression in tensegrity systems to the bone/ muscle interaction in the human body in motion.

According to the competition, the ephemeral structures are also to be seen as parasites. In this regard, the complex network of cables and nodes, inherent to the architectural expression of the tensegrity concept, generates multiple grid lines, which can be used in determining the relationship of the structure to its hosting urban context (Figure 2). The proposed structure is not intended to reside in the urban infrastructure by addressing its shape, the volume, or edge conditions, but to intrude the city's network of motion lines, align with one or more of them, and provoke the flow through it. The same system of grids will permit parasite structures, belonging to the same city network, to relate to each other with the use of sensors mounted on the nodes of the structure. As the structure migrates from one cityscape to another, the number of grid lines will keep increasing, which will allow the public to trace previous stages in its life.

At a different level of interpretation, the proposed tensegrity structure performs as a hard shell, or exoskeleton, that supports a system of re-configurable partitions/doors that extend the structure to the direction of flow through it, as well as a system of display panels, raised over the ground and attached to the tensegrity roof bar nodes. The nodes that support the panels support and penetrate a translucent and stretchable fabric covering membrane that reveals from the interior the view of the floating bars against the sky-dome. As the ephemeral structure moves to a different urban site, the tensegrity vault, as well as the space defining partitions, can change configurations to adjust to different functional or contextual requirements.

Regarding the transportability of the proposed structure, a recently developed method which is based on the rapid assembly of deployable tensegrity modules, has been proposed

Figure 1. Semi-Open Exhibit Space : Entry for the international competition on the design of Ephemeral Structure for the City of Athens.

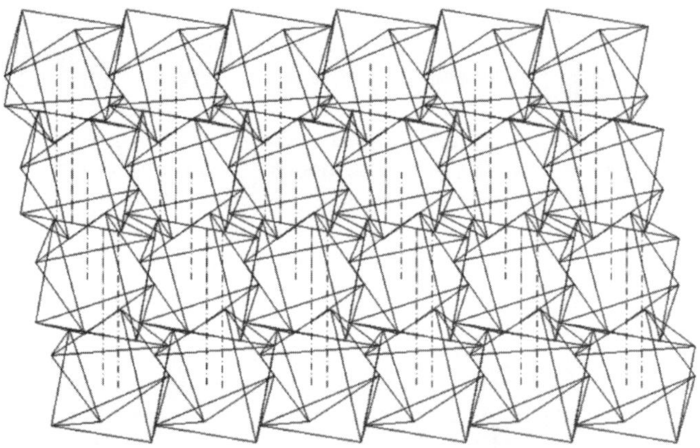

Figure 2. Grid line directions generated by the network of cables and nodes in tensegrity structures.

(Liapi 2002). In assembling the structure, tensegrity modules are not connected at nodes but by cable overlap, which, in principle, allows for variable configurations of the resulting tensegrity networks (Figure 3). The main advantage in using this feature is that, by varying the pattern of cable overlap between adjacent units, several configurations can be achieved.

3 Challenges in the design of tensegrity structures

The most challenging issue in the proposed design for the semi-open exhibition space was the generation of alternative designs of the spatial configuration of the tensegrity vault. Indeed, as already reported in relevant literature, among other critical issues in the design of tensegrity structures, geometric complexity, that is inherent to their structural and mechanical basis, accounts

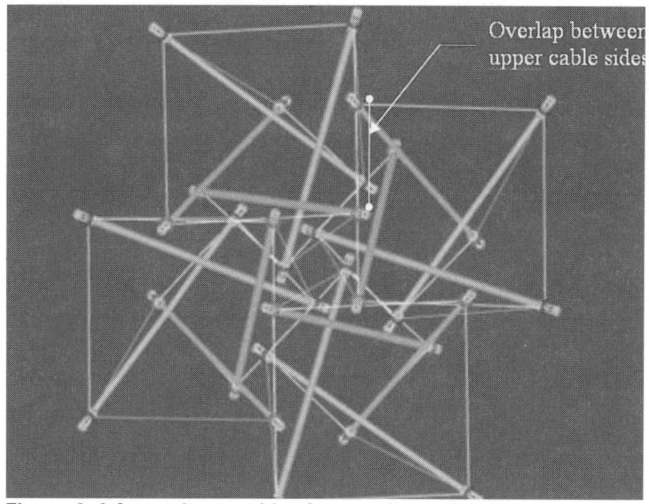

Figure 3. A four unit assembly of tensegrity modules

for significant difficulties in their study, and for their limited application in building design (Hanaor 94).

In general, the geometric configuration of double layer tensegrity networks, which are the most appropriate for building applications, depends on the configuration of the composing unit, and the method by which units are attached to each other to form a network. In order to maintain bar independence throughout the structure several patterns for connecting the units have been proposed (Emmerich 1988, Hanaor 1992). However, although patterns and general rules for the assembly of such networks exist, there is no mathematical expression that incorporates the geometric principles and parameters that determine the configuration of the network.

Unlike regular space trusses, tensegrity networks are composed of tensegrity units which are antiprismatic and therefore do not fall within the range of regular polyhedra. In addition, in order to ensure cable continuity and bar independence throughout the structure, as seen in Figure 3 that illustrates an assembly of 4 square-based units, the units do not connect end to end, but, by a partial overlap of their upper and lower base cables. Taking the above into account, the configuration of tensegrity networks cannot be addressed as a regular space packing problem. The main issue therefore is to determine the geometric basis of the problem and to come up with a geometric method and an analytic expression that takes into account the interdependence of the various parameters and constrains of the problem.

A geometric approach for the investigation of the spatial configuration of tensegrity structures of spherical shape composed of tensegrity units of square base has already been developed (Liapi, 2001). Specifically, fundamental geometric principles that govern the generation of form in tensegrity networks are demonstrated, and a method for the graphical generation of spherical tensegrity networks, based on the integration of CAD tools with Descriptive Geometry procedures, has been formulated. The method allows for the visualization of the effect of each of the interrelated parameters, such as proportions of units, overlap of upper and lower unit bases, etc., that determine the design of a tensegrity network (Liapi 2001). The method allows designers to resolve and visualize the complex geometry of such structures by following a step by step graphical procedure based on constructive geometry methods. Though the above method is of critical importance since it sets the geometric principles for the generation of any spherical network, when a number of different configurations need to be generated during design exploration, the step by step graphical representation still requires a significant amount of time, especially when the designers wish to experiment with several design parameters. In addition, for the generation of the geometry of the proposed vaulted structure for the competition, an adaptation of the geometric principles that determine the configuration of spherical tensegrity networks to address cylindrical configurations had to be developed. Accordingly, a new method to address the geometry of vaulted structures as well as the automatic generation of graphical models of vaulted configurations was needed. The main points of this approach are described in the following section.

4 Vaulted configurations: Geometry generation

Vaulted structures, in pure geometric terms, are understood as structures of cylindrical shape. They may also be referred to in this paper as single curvature networks to distinguish them from spherical, which are configurations of double curvature.
For the generation of the geometry of vaulted tensegrities the following objectives had to be met:

I) Define the geometric principles that allow for the generation of tensegrity vaulted (single curvature) networks.

II) Develop a mathematical expression that takes into account the interdependence of the various parameters and constrains of the problem.

4.1. Geometric principles that determine tensegrity vaulted configurations

Regarding the geometry of vaulted, or single curvature, tensegrity networks, the following observations were made: a) the axes of adjacent units along the axis of the cylinder are parallel to each other and perpendicular to the direction of the cylinder's axis; b) the axes of adjacent units along a cross section of the cylinder intersect at a point that lies on the axis of the cylinder; c) assuming that the upper bases of tensegrity units overlap, the lower bases of adjacent units need to overlap as well. Determining the amount of overlap of the lower bases, when the upper base overlap is given, is the main problem in this case. It needs to be reminded at this point that in tensegrity units of square base, the two cable bases are rotated with respect to each other by a 45 degrees angle that is dictated by stability requirements (Hanaor 1998).

A general geometric principle that applies to both spherical and vaulted configurations, when unit size and upper bases overlap are given, can be described as follows: When two units are placed parallel to each other and connected at the upper level only, in order to acquire the lower base overlap and the center of curvature, the units need to rotate around an axis that: a) passes through the middle point of the upper base overlap; b) lies on the upper bases' plane before rotation (Figure 4) (Liapi 2001).

Taking into account these observations and principles, it occurs that the conditions for the generation of the vaulted configuration are:

a) When unit size and proportions are given, both upper base-overlap and lower base-overlap of adjacent units along the axis of the cylinder are fixed.

b) When unit size and proportions are given, unit overlap across the vault can be varied so that different curvatures can be generated.

In the scheme in Figure 5, the position of unit overlap in a four-unit cluster of a cylindrical configuration is indicated (only upper and lower cables are shown). It is proven, and shown in this scheme, that for a vaulted structure in which the dimensions of the composing are given, the upper and lower base overlap of adjacent units along the longitudinal section of the cylinder (the axes of adjacent units are parallel to each other and perpendicular to the cylinder's axis) are fixed. Regarding the placement of two adjacent units across the cylinder axis, the scheme shows that for a given amount of upper base overlap, the two units need to rotate around an axis that passes through the mid point of the overlapping part of their bases until their lower bases meet. Accordingly, the amount of unit overlap across the axis of the cylinder determines the relative rotation of one unit in respect to the other and thus the curvature of the vault. Figure 6 shows the relative position of the 4 units of figure 5 after rotation, and the plan of a vaulted structure that results from the assembly of 24 units.

4.2. Development of a mathematical expression that generates parametric tensegrity vaults

The geometric conditions and principles that determine the form of vaulted tensegrity networks were implemented in a parametric mathematical code. Analytic geometry procedures have been followed which generate 3D coordinates of all nodes in a tensegrity network. A detailed description of the algorithm is included in a forthcoming publication.

The code has been developed in a MATLAB software environment which provides a 3D graphical interface. The code takes into account the interdependence of the various parameters and constrains and allows for input on: a) unit dimensions (bases and height); b) value of overlap between

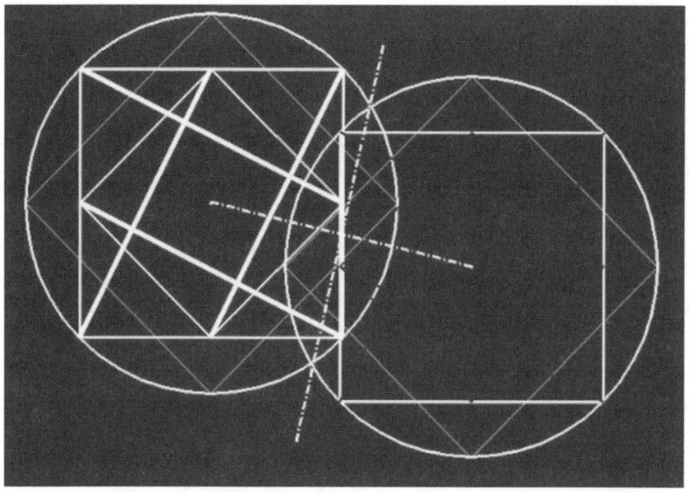

Figure 4. Overlap conditions for adjacent units of all curved tensegrity networks.

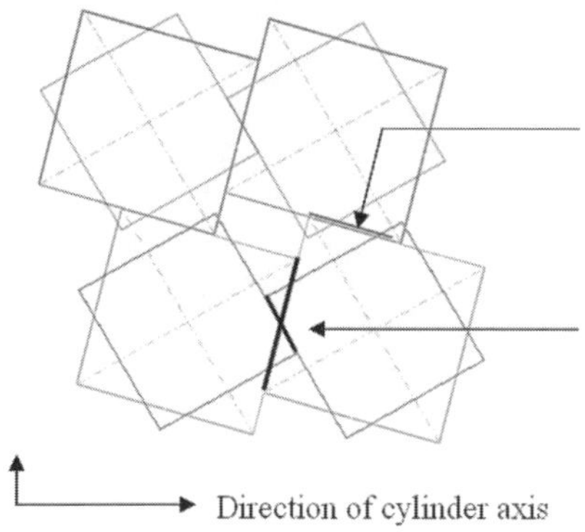

Figure 5. Overlap conditions for vaulted tensegrity networks.

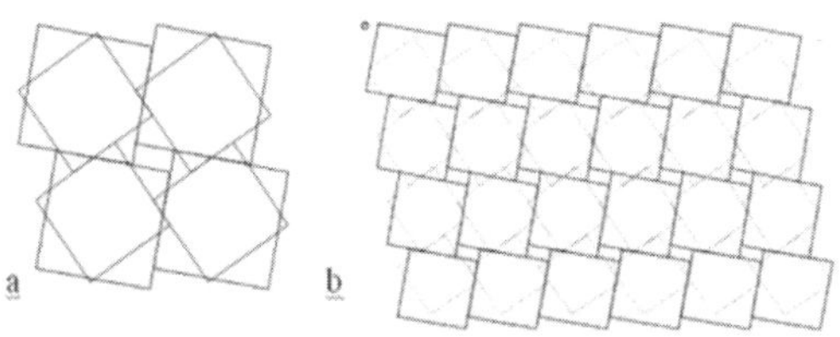

Figure 6. Four unit assembly and 24 unit vaulted structure.

upper or lower bases; and c) number of units in the longitudinal direction and across its curvature. The output provides numerical values for: a) the remaining unit dimensions (bar lengths, diagonal cables); b) radius of the structure; c) angle of rotation between adjacent units; and d) overlap of lower or upper bases respectively.

The parametric code, by displaying geometric information in a 3D graphical environment, allows for an initial form exploration of tensegrity networks. It also provides numerical values for all parameters needed for the generation of a tensegrity network. Figure 7 shows models of vaulted networks with varying curvature and number of units.

5 Tensegrity Vault: Form exploration

For the design of the tensegrity vault for the proposed ephemeral structure, various factors had to be taken into account including technical considerations such as constructability, efficiency of deployment, and structural performance. Each of the main parameters in the design of tensegriry network (number of units, proportions of unit, size of units, and overlap), as indicated earlier, is linked to the others, and any change in one parameter affects not only the form of the structure but also the above mentioned considerations. As an example, since the structure requires the on site assembly of modules, reducing the total number of units is, in principle, a desired feature. However, reducing the size of units and maintaining their proportions will significantly increase the depth of the structure. From a purely geometric point of view, to maintain the same depth of structure, when larger units are used, requires reducing unit height, and thus changing unit proportions, and possibly changing upper and lower overlaps. But, lowering unit height and keeping the same size of lower bases, will lead to units with bars at a very low angle which will affect structural performance.

Figure 8 shows two configurations that were originally considered for the design of the ephemeral structures. Both configurations are identical in terms of their basic geometric features: overall width, depth of structure, and curvature. Their main difference is that the first one consists of four units and the second of six. From a constructability point of view the first one is easier to assemble, due to the reduced number of units. On the other hand, in the second configuration bars are shorter, less prone to buckling, and at higher angle than the ones in the first one, which may result in improved structural performance. It becomes obvious at this point that additional analysis is required for determining an optimized design.

In addition to the above, since in the proposed solution space defining elements, roof membrane, and display panels are all attached to the nodes on the interior layer of the structure, any change in the system of nodes will affect space features and definition (Figure 9).

Although an optimized approach that takes into account all the above aspects in the geometric design of the network was not the objective of this study, the parametric code has facilitated form exploration and experimentation with various design parameters. After a number of alternative configurations were explored in the MATLAB environment, two different configurations of the same square footage in area, composed of 5 by 7 units, and 4 by 6 units respectively, were selected for development in a CAD environment. From the MATLAB model, angular measurements, measurements or radii and distances, as well as coordinates at the nodes were obtained. These values were used for the generation of the selected network in

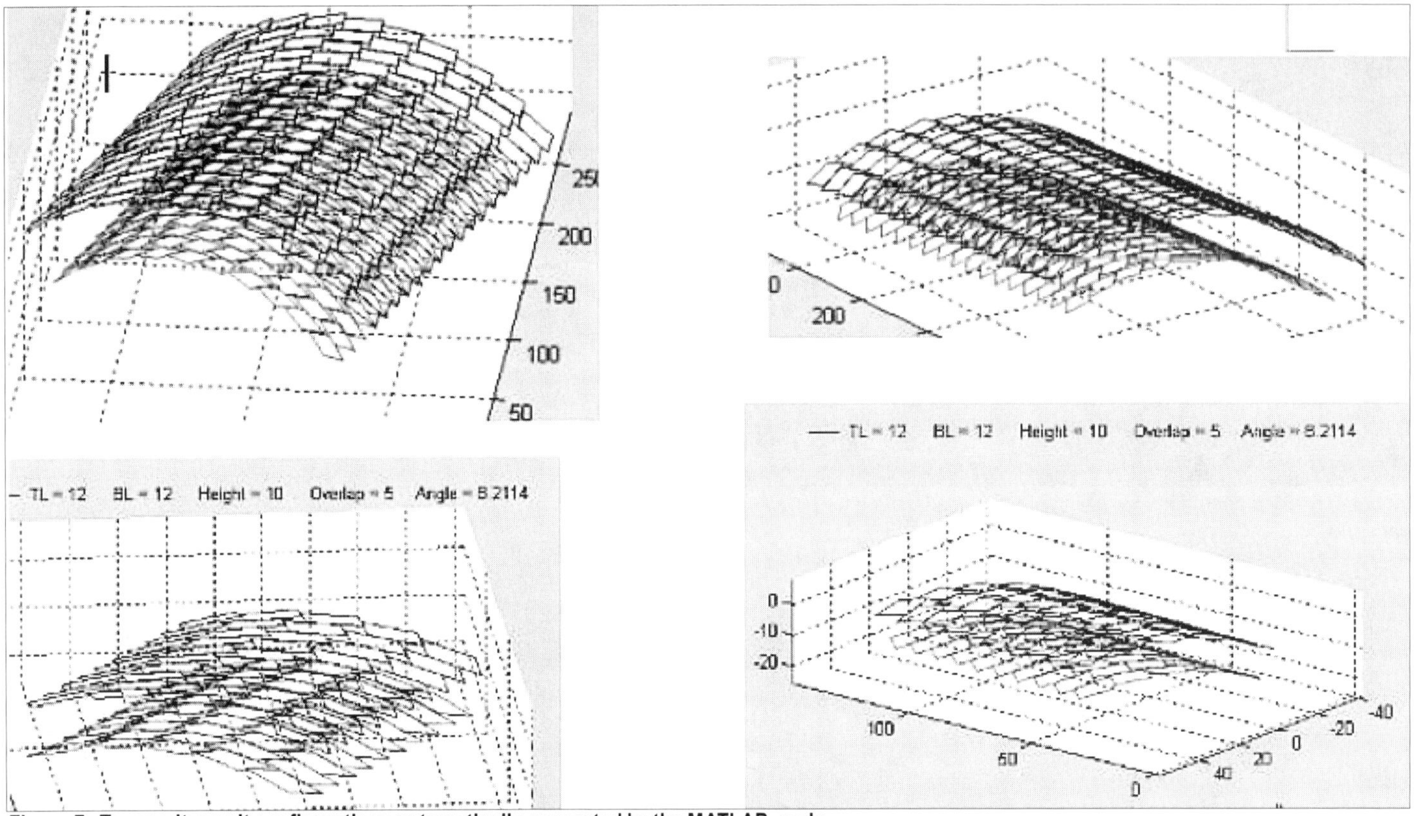

Figure 7. Tensegrity vault configurations automatically generated by the MATLAB code.

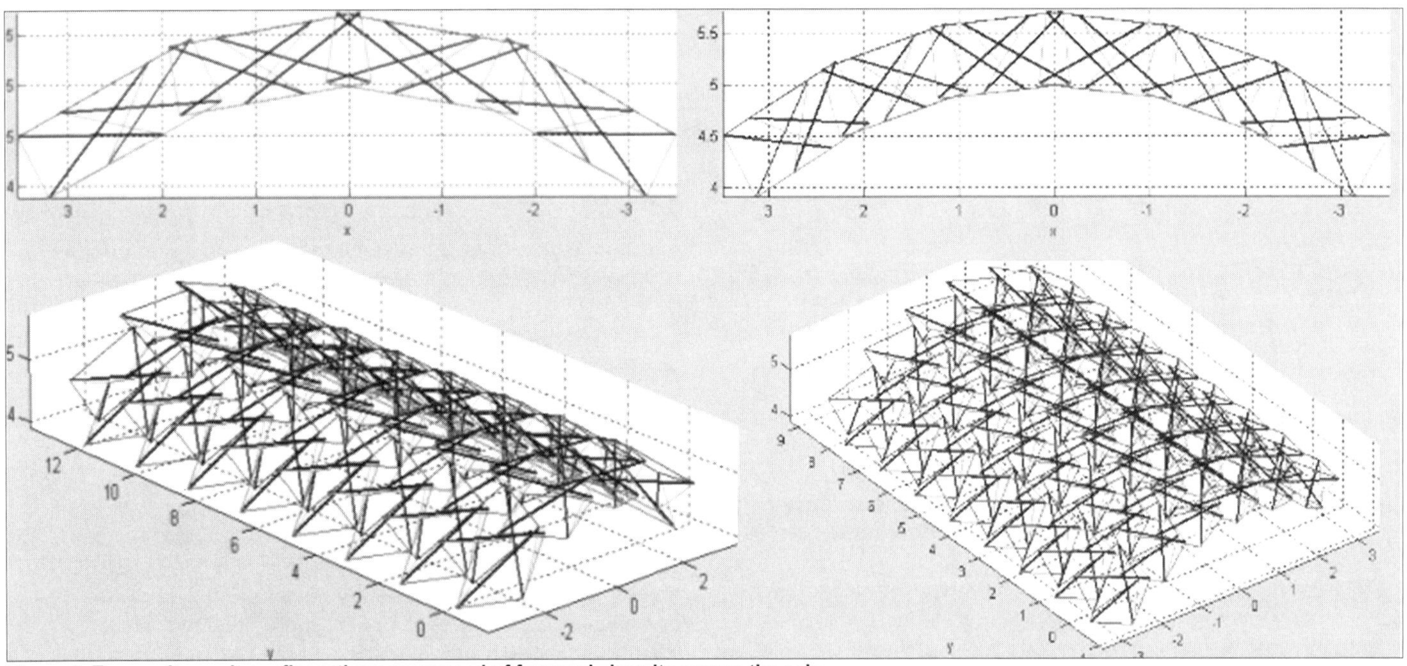

Figure 8. Tensegrity vault configurations composed of four and six units across the axis

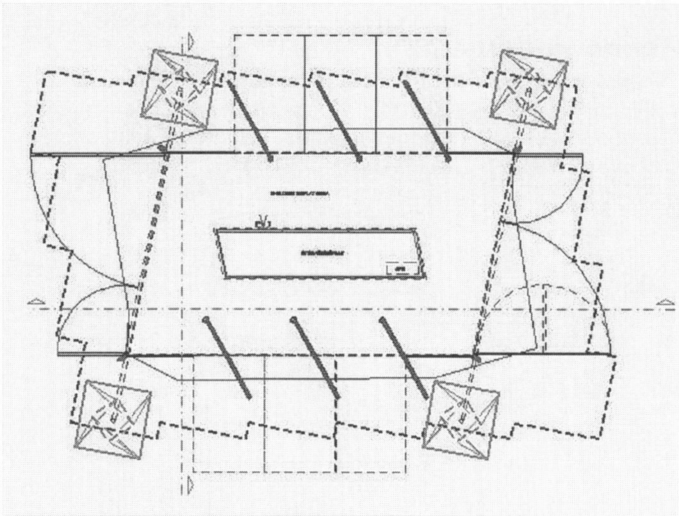

Figure 9. Ephemeral structure floor plan

the CAD environment. Figure 10 shows consecutive stages in the development of the final solution. The approach followed in the design of the ephemeral structure has also indicated that a further automation of the process is needed so that any model generated in MATLAB can be automatically recreated in a CAD environment.

7 Conclusions

The mathematical code that has been developed has successfully addressed the challenges faced during the design of a tensegrity vaulted dome of the structure that was submitted as an entry to the "Ephemeral Structures for the City of Athens" Competition. The code integrates the geometric principles that determine the form of vaulted tensegrity networks and allows for the automatic generation of a 3D model of the structure in a graphic environment. The code has been shown to significantly facilitate the study of alternative configurations that result from changes in unit proportions, unit number, or unit assembly pattern.

The code provides an initial configuration of such structures. In the actual configuration, after assembly, the square bases of each unit are composed of eight non co-planar segments. Further elaboration of the code requires some refinements and adjustments to more accurately represent the geometry of a curved structure. In general this approach has been shown to resolve issues related to geometric complexity in determining and representing the configuration of curved domical structures that have rendered the study of tensegrity structures inaccessible to architects and engineers. The approach followed in the design of the ephemeral structure has also indicated that a further automation of the process is needed so that any model generated in MATLAB can be automatically recreated in a CAD environment.

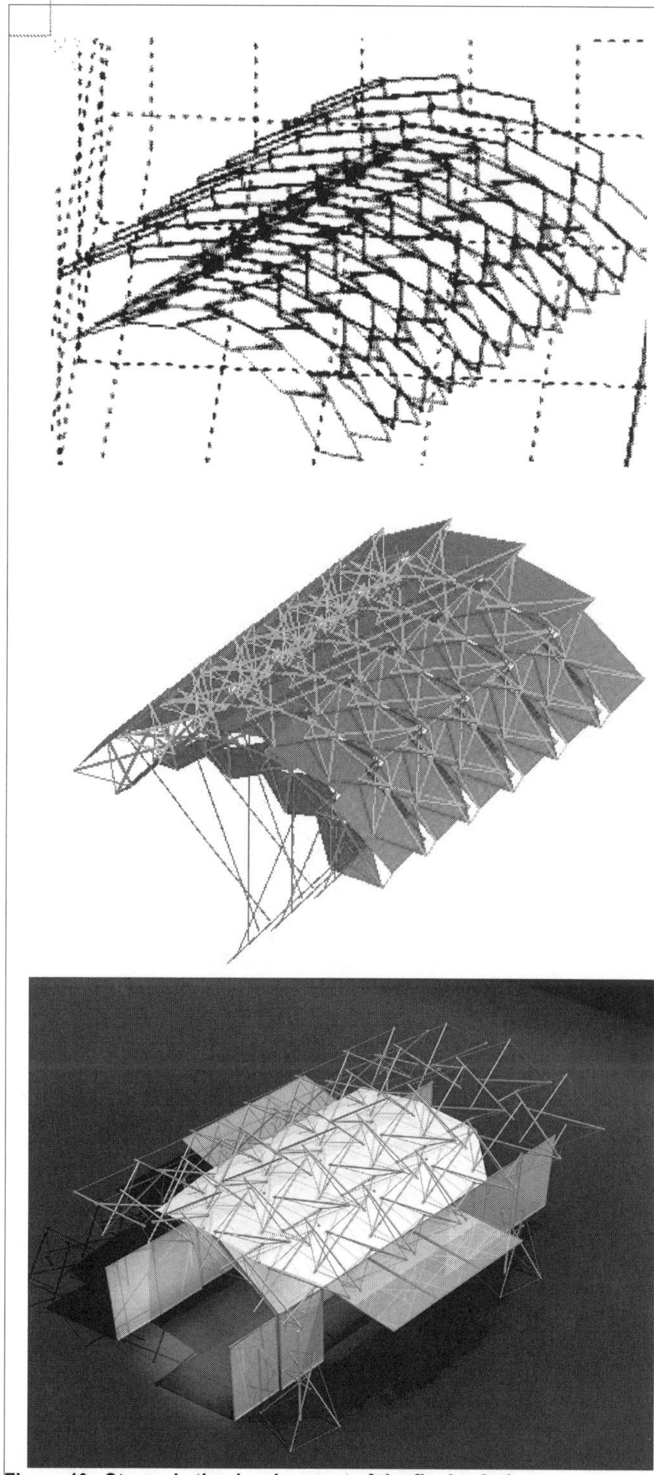

Figure 10. Stages in the development of the final solution

Acknowledgments
The authors appreciate the assistance of Brent Cutshall, M. Arch. candidate, Peter Coats, Shane Tanner, and Joan Hanson, architectural engineering undergraduate students, and Jason Charalambides, Ph.D. candidate.

References

Cultural Olympiad. (2002). *Competition programme, International competition for the design of ephemeral structures*,http: //www.cultural-olympiad.gr/ephemeral structures/index1.html ephemeralcompetition/index1.html

Emmerich, D.G. (1988). *Structures tendues et autotendantes*, Ecole d Architecture de Paris- La Villette, Paris.

Emmerich, D.G. (1996). Emmerich on self-tensioning structures. *International journal of space structures* 11(1&2):29-36.

Fuller, R. B. (1975). Synergetics: Explorations in the geometry of thinking. New York: Macmillan.

Hanaor, A. (1992). Aspects of design of double layer tensegrity domes. *International journal of space structures* 7(2):101-113.

Hanaor, A. (1994). Geometrically rigid double-layer tensegrity grids. *International journal of Space Structures.*

Hanaor, A. (1998). Tensegrity theory and application. In *Beyond the cube,* edited by J. Francois Gabriel, 385-408. New York: John Wiley & Sons, Inc.

Liapi, K. A. (2000). Tensegrity structures and structural and architectural conceptioning. In *structural morphology colloquium. Proceedings,* Delft, Netherlands, 235-240, International Association for Shell and Spatial Structures (IASS).

Liapi, K.A. (2001). A visualization method for the morphological exploration of tensegrity structures. In *Fifth international conference on information visualization* (IV 200), Proceedings, July 25-26, 2001. London: IEEE Computer Society.

Liapi, K.A. (2001). Geometric configuration and graphical representation of tensegrity spherical networks. In ACADIA 2001: *Re-inventing the discourse. Proceedings*, October 17-20, 2001, Buffalo, New York, 258-267. Association for Computer Aided Design in Architecture.

Liapi, K. (2002). A novel portable and collapsible tensegrity unit for the rapid assembly of tensegrity networks. In *Fifth international conference on space structures*, August 19-21, 2002, University of Surrey, England, 39-46. International Association of Space Structures.

Motro R. (1992). Tensegrity systems: The state of the art. *International journal of space structures*, Special Issue on Tensegrity Systems 7(2):75-84.

Motro, R. (2001). *Foldable tensegrities. Deployable structures*. New York: Springler Verlag, Wien.

Snelson, K. D. (1965). Continuous tension, discontinuous compression structures. United States Patent 3, 169,611, February 16, 1965.

Skelton, R. E. (1997). Deployable tendon-controlled structures, United States Patent 5,642,590, July 1, 1997.

Sultan, C. (1999). Modelling,design, and control of tensegrity structures with applications. Ph.D., Purdue University, West Lafayette.

SpaceMaker - Creating Space by Sketching It

Ming-Chun Lee, Ellen Yi-Luen Do
Design Machine Group
University of Washington

Abstract

Creating space is the essence of architectural design. Architects actually work with three-dimensional (3-D) space, although two-dimensional (2-D) drawings are perhaps the most commonly used design medium. It is thus valuable to help architects truly see 3-D space, while making drawings in 2-D. In addition, architects usually use symbols in their drawings to identify architectural concepts. By recognizing the symbols, it is possible to identify architectural configurations of the design. This paper introduces a symbol-based modeling tool—SpaceMaker—that allows architects to make freehand floor plans and apply symbols to identify different functional spaces. SpaceMaker then converts those floor plans into 3-D models according to the symbols.

SpaceMaker - Creating Space by Sketching It

Ming-Chun Lee, Ellen Yi-Luen Do
Design Machine Group
University of Washington

1 Introduction

1.1 Space as the Essence of Architecture

Space is the essence of architecture (Zevi 1974). Louis I. Kahn stated a clear assertion that "architecture is the thoughtful making of spaces" (Perspecta IV 1957). Berlage also argued that "the aim of our creations is the art of space, the essence of architecture" (Grundlagen 1908). The essence of architectural design is to develop and arrange spatial relationships. Architects actually create void space. Although this void space is defined by solid elements such as walls, floors, and ceilings, it is through the space that people interact, inhabit, and engage with architecture.

1.2 Activities in the Early Design Process

In the early design phases, architects usually use different types of media to explore different design concerns. Among those, 2-D drawings are the most commonly used medium for the early schematic development. Architectural drawings reveal designer's thinking graphically (Lawson 1994; Robbins 1994; Larkin & Simon 1987). By making drawings, architects have opportunities to re-examine initial ideas and further refine the ideas. The potential of graphic thinking lies in the continuous cycling of information from paper to eye to brain to hand and back to paper (Figure 1.1). Moreover, the activity of drawing includes both seeing and thinking about the subject being represented. Design drawing is an iterative and interactive act involving recording ideas, recognizing functions and meaning in the drawings, and finding new forms and adapting them into the design (Goldschmidt 1991; Schön & Wiggins 1992; Suwa & Tversky 1996). It serves as external symbol systems to facilitate thinking and support emergent ideas (Goel 1995).

Designing architecture is an action of creating space. Although architects actually work with 3-D space; drawings, however, are in 2-D. Architects see 3-D space in their mind's eye when making 2-D drawings (Figure 1.2). The translation from 2-D drawings to 3-D space is usually done by architects themselves. However, the accuracy of the translation strongly depends on architects' experience, knowledge, and capability. Novice designers might not be able to imagine space in 3-D as fluently as expert designers. Also, expert designers sometimes might enjoy seeing things in 3-D automatically without spending time to project 2-D drawings into imagined 3-D spaces. It is thus valuable to help architects see 3-D space during designing. Some architects do employ simple 3-D physical models in the early design. Architectural models are the best way to represent 3-D space (Koepke 1988). A 3-D architectural model tells a story that can be instantly understood and enables spatial relations to be perceived at a single glance (Koepke 1988; Kurrent 1999; Lucci & Orlandini 1990; Ervin & Hasbrouck 2001). 2-D drawing and 3-D modeling both have benefits to architectural design. Therefore, a tool for bridging these two design media seems important and necessary for architects developing early design concepts.

1.3 Use of Drawing Symbols

Architects usually apply symbols in their drawings to identify different design concerns such as functionality or architectural configurations (Herbert 1993; Fraser & Henmi 1994; Laseau 1989). They may use colors, different types of lines, or text to indicate different design concepts. By recognizing architects' drawing symbols, it is possible to identify their initial ideas about spatial configurations of the design (Do 1998).

1.4 Conventional 3-D Modeling Programs

Users of conventional computer 3-D modeling programs such as Form-Z or 3-D Studio usually have to insert solid objects first to define a void space that they wish to create. The space will not be created until the architects have specified all necessary enclosing elements. A space is created from outside to inside, from solid boundaries to enclosed void (Figure 1.3).

However, architects typically do not use commercial modeling programs in the early design phases, because at this stage they usually do not deal with that specific level of detail about solid elements such as dimensions, shapes, or appearance. On the contrary, architects are concerned with void space. In fact, instead of using digital modeling tools in the early design, people tend to prefer making freehand drawings or simple massing models to study architectural relationships between spaces. A freehand drawing in the early phases indicates not only a designer's decisions but also the associated degrees of ambiguity and vagueness. So a modeling tool for the early phases should also maintain the nature of early schematic design: abstraction, ambiguity, and vagueness.

1.5 SpaceMaker

In this paper, we introduce a prototype symbol-based modeling program—SpaceMaker—that allows architects to sketch 2-D floor plans to explore initial spatial layouts and draw symbols into the floor plans to identify different functional spaces. SpaceMaker then converts the floor plans into 3-D models using the drawing symbols to control the model detailing. The design of SpaceMaker is based on the study of the role of freehand

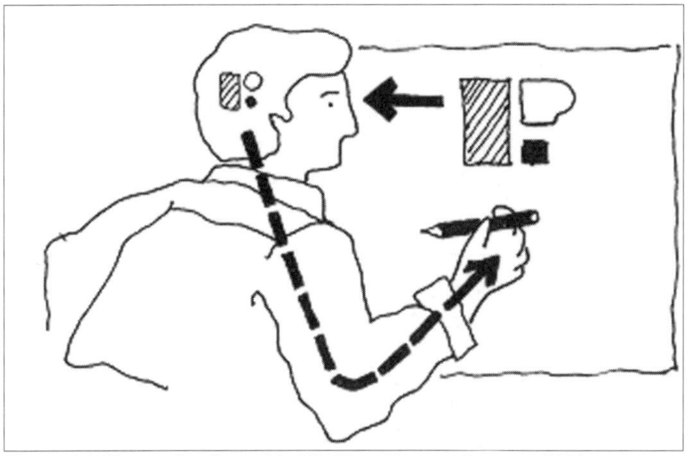

Figure 1.1. The cycle of graphic thinking. Source: Laseau, 1989.

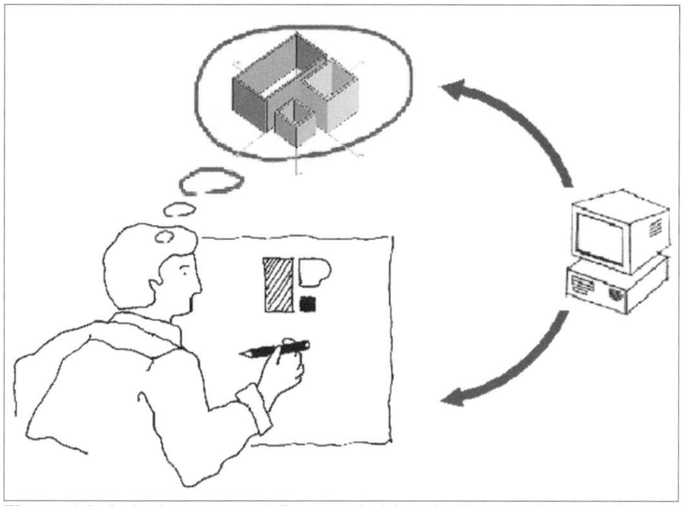

Figure 1.2. A designer sees 3-D space in his mind's eye when making sketches in 2-D. A tool for bridging the gap between 2-D and 3-D is valuable for designing.

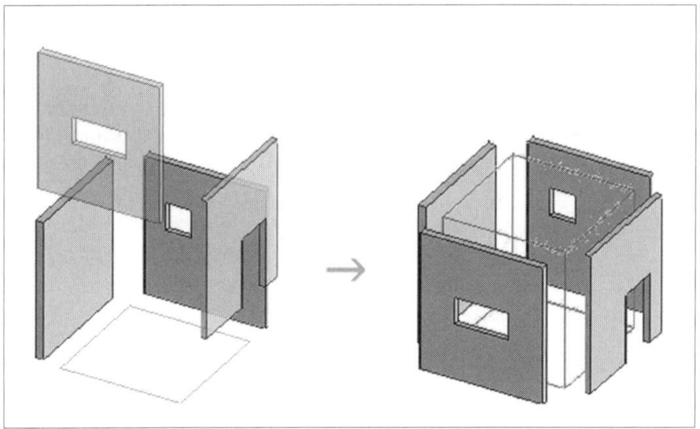

Figure 1.3. Designers assemble four solid elements in order to enclose a rectangular void space.

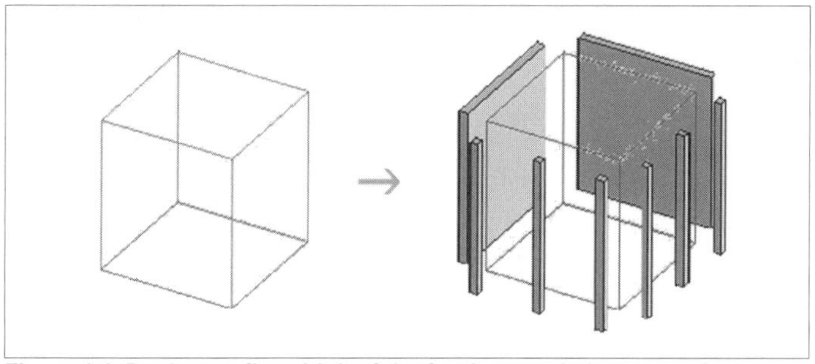

Figure 1.4. Designers first think of the fundamental character of a space, and then assemble necessary solid elements to define the space.

drawings in architectural design and the use of symbols in conceptual freehand drawings.

Compared to conventional computer modeling programs, SpaceMaker enables users to think about spaces first, to further decide the essential characteristics for each space, and then to assign appropriate enclosing elements for constructing spaces that users want to create. A space is defined from inside to outside, from the enclosed void to its solid boundaries (Figure 1.4).

2 Related Work

With the observation that drawing and modeling both play important roles in architectural design, the issue becomes how computational design tools can support freehand sketching and enable architects to generate 3-D forms easily.

2.1 Systems that Support Sketching

"Electronic Cocktail Napkin" (Gross & Do 1996), by Mark D. Gross and Ellen Yi-Luen Do, is a computer environment for making hand drawn sketches and diagrams. It aims to support freehand drawing and thinking of the sort that designers often do on the back of an envelope or cocktail napkin for creative design. Cocktail Napkin can recognize and interpret the elements and configurations of drawings made by designers, and then the system retrieves relevant information. Cocktail Napkin recognizes multi-stroke glyphs and allows designers to customize the program to recognize personally defined symbols.

Do, in her doctoral dissertation, implements a prototype computational drawing environment called "Right-Tool-Right-Time" (Do 1998). Designers use different symbols in freehand drawings to explore design concepts. She argues that an intelligent computer-aided-design environment should be able to infer designer's intentions from all drawn elements in the drawing and suggest designers with appropriate computational tools based on the inference for the task at hand.

2.2 Systems that Generate 3-D Forms by Sketching

"Digital Clay" explores the concept of the direct generation of 3-D form from freehand drawing input (Schweikardt & Gross 1998). Digital Clay derives 3-D geometry from a 2-D projected sketch. The program walks the lines of the sketch to identify convex and concave edges, then assigns 3-D coordinates to vertices, and finally generates a 3-D model that the designer can view and edit. Several similar projects are based on the same concept of deriving 3-D objects from 2-D projected drawings. Grimstead and Martin describe a method of reconstructing a Boundary-Representation (B-rep) model from a single hidden-line removed sketch of a 3-D object (Grimstead & Martin 1995). Lipson and Shpitalni introduce an Optimization-Based algorithm for reconstructing a 3-D model from a single 2-D edge-vertex graph (Lipson & Shpitalni 1996). "Quick-Sketch" by Eggli et al. also allows users to create 3-D models by making 2-D projected drawings (Eggli et al. 1995).

Do's "Sketch VR" is a pen-based computing environment that generates 3-D objects in a VRML (Virtual Reality Modeling Language) format by recognizing simple geometric shapes in a 2-D view (Do 2001). To create an architectural space designers only simply draw lines and circles in a simple "Cocktail Napkin" 2-D sketch to indicate the appearances and locations of walls and columns. Designers draw in 2-D, and a 3-D world is created accordingly. Similarly, designers can generate 3-D models of interiors by drawing diagrams to indicate furniture placements. Igarashi's "Teddy" is a sketching interface that allows users to draw 2-D freeform strokes on the screen, and then the system constructs polygonal surfaces to generate a 3-D model (Igarashi 2000). The system supports the modeling operation to construct a 3-D polygonal surface from a 2-D silhouette drawn by users. The system inflates the region surrounded by the silhouette to make wide areas fat and narrow areas thin in order to generate 3-D shapes.

2.3 Discussion

Electronic Cocktail Napkin can recognize drawn elements and configurations of freehand drawings and then retrieves relevant information for designers. Right-Tool-Right-Time infers designer's intentions by recognizing all drawn elements and identifying the task context in a drawing. Based on this inference, the system then suggests appropriate computational tools for the task at hand. Both systems focus on information retrieval based on the recognition of drawn elements and configurations. However, 3-D modeling based on the recognition of drawing symbols has not been specifically implemented into either system.

On the other hand, Sketch VR does generate 3-D objects in a VRML format by recognizing simple geometric shapes in a 2-D view. The generation of 3-D objects is accomplished by an object-oriented translation from a 2-D drawn symbol to a 3-D object. Sketch VR interprets every single drawn element as an object that will be generated in 3-D format. The same concept of the object-oriented translation is also carried by Digital Clay and Teddy, both of which deal with drawing and modeling of objects. However, when designers draw symbols into a sketch floor plan to identify either the functionality or the basic spatial characteristics, designers may think about the void space instead of any single solid element. For the early schematic development, designers need a computer modeling tool that allows them to think of the basic characteristics of a space, instead of a single element, and use a symbol to represent the spatial configuration of this space. Then the tool creates a model corresponding to the spatial configuration that the symbol represents.

3 Fundamental Features in a Freehand Drawing

Freehand drawings usually consist of simple elements such as lines, simple geometric polygons, and symbols for labeling different design concerns (Do 1998). When designers start exploring the alternatives of spatial configuration, they usually decide the exterior boundary first, and then arrange the interior spaces. Typically, designers draw envelopes to encircle an area and identify the boundary. After the boundary has been defined, designers then use simple lines or bubbles to further partition the entire floor into individual rooms. By assembling lines and bubbles, architects compose the drawings and explore the spatial layouts (Figure 3.1).

Freehand drawings can be conceived as a flexible representation of designer's thoughts about design. In a sketch floor plan, designers use a line to represent a wall, a bubble to represent an individual space, and further assemble lines and bubbles to create a floor plan that actually represents a building. Furthermore, the use of simple lines and bubbles can be a key clue of creating a 3-D modeling tool for the early schematic design. Because designers draw lines and bubbles to explore spatial configurations, a modeling tool should be able to recognize those lines and bubbles and generate a model that the designer's drawing represents (Figure 3.2).

3.1 Use of Symbols in Freehand Drawings

A space is enclosed by defining elements, such as walls and columns, with a specific spatial configuration. When arranging spatial layouts through making drawings, designers may also start exploring the alternatives of spatial configurations of architectural elements. When designers label each space with a symbol, not only do they identify the function of the space, but they also remind themselves of the proposed configuration of architectural elements. A symbol can be interpreted as a representation of the spatial configuration in designer's mind (Figure 3.3). By applying symbols into drawings, designers assign "meanings," give "characteristics," and imply "spatial configurations" to spaces.

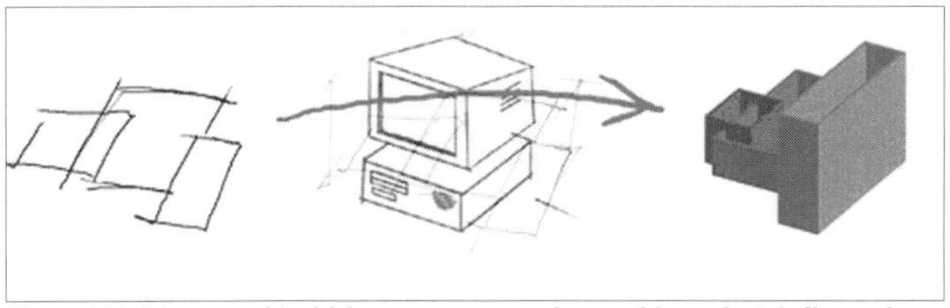

Figure 3.1. Lines and bubbles are commonly used in a sketch floor plan for designers arranging the spatial configuration. Source: Do, 1998.

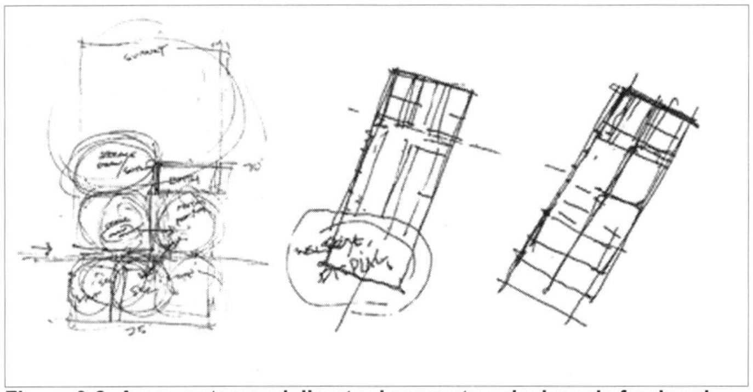

Figure 3.2. A computer modeling tool converts a designer's freehand drawings into a 3-D model by recognizing and translating drawn elements as architectural components.

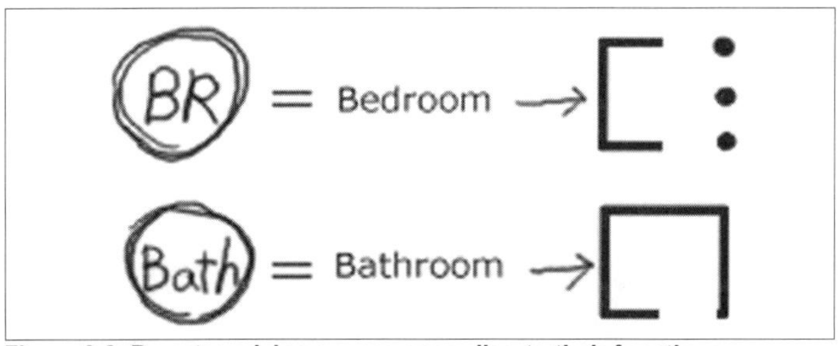

Figure 3.3. By categorizing spaces according to their functions, designers can label different spaces with different texts to indicate different configuration.

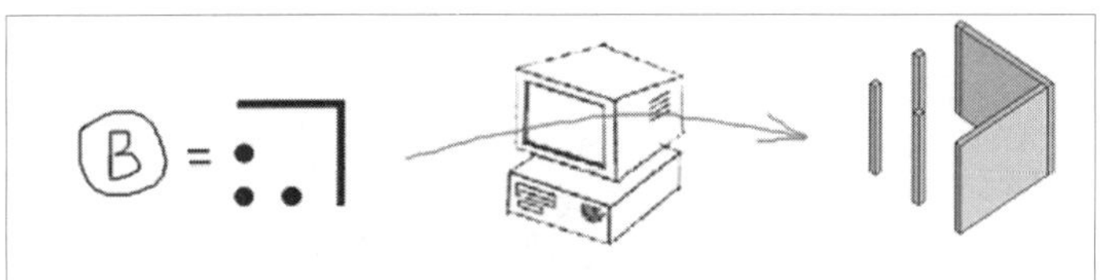

Figure 3.4. A modeling tool creates a 3-D model according to the spatial configuration that the drawing symbol represents.

This study mainly focuses on the idea that designers label interior spaces in floor-plan drawings with symbols to identify their functions and also indicate proposed spatial configurations of architectural elements. Furthermore, those symbols can make 3-D modeling easier. As discussed above, designers draw symbols to imply spatial configurations. Therefore, instead of drawing architectural elements to enclose spaces, designers can simply draw symbols and train the computer to recognize the spatial configurations that those symbols represent, and then have the computer create the appropriate architectural elements to enclose the space (Figure 3.4).

The computational implementation of SpaceMaker is mainly based on the studies of the fundamental characteristics of freehand drawings and the role of symbols in freehand sketches described in this section. SpaceMaker makes models by recognizing the fundamental features and symbols in designer's freehand drawings.

4 Implementation of SpaceMaker

4.1 Scenario / SpaceMaker in Action

This section presents a scenario of how a designer uses SpaceMaker to develop a schematic floor plan. The scenario presented here helps to clarify and demonstrate the implementation of SpaceMaker.

A novice designer, Jamie decides to develop a conceptual scheme for a small office using SpaceMaker. He starts the design by clarifying the project requirement: two staff offices, a meeting room, a storage room, and a kitchen. Jamie starts to sketch a floor plan using a digitizing pen and tablet. First, he draws a rough rectangle on the tablet to indicate the boundary of the building. SpaceMaker responds by drawing a rectangular frame on the screen. Then he draws several lines to divide the floor into five rooms. Several guidelines for indicating the boundary and partition walls appear on the screen (Figure 4.1). However, Jamie understands that still no architectural elements have been displayed. Not until he labels the sketch with symbols to identify functions of space does SpaceMaker recognize the symbols and generate the corresponding architectural elements in the building.

Jamie starts to define symbols using SpaceMaker's Symbol Definition system (Figure 4.2). After a symbol has been defined, Jamie then draws the symbol in one of the partitioned areas in the sketch, and SpaceMaker then constructs a room with the defined configuration in Space Window (Figure 4.3). Jamie continues to define other symbols for different functional spaces and goes on to complete the entire spatial layout.

After completing the layout, Jamie wants to modify the space. Jamie uses the mouse to pick a guideline in Sketch Board and move it. As a result, all rooms in Space Window aligned with this line are modified (Figure 4.4).

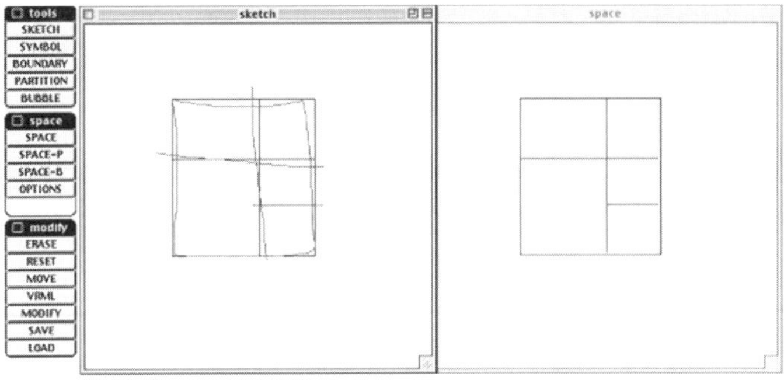

Figure 4.1. SpaceMaker generates a floor plan in Space Window (on the right) while a designer is making a sketch in Sketch Board (in the middle). The figure also shows tool palettes on the left.

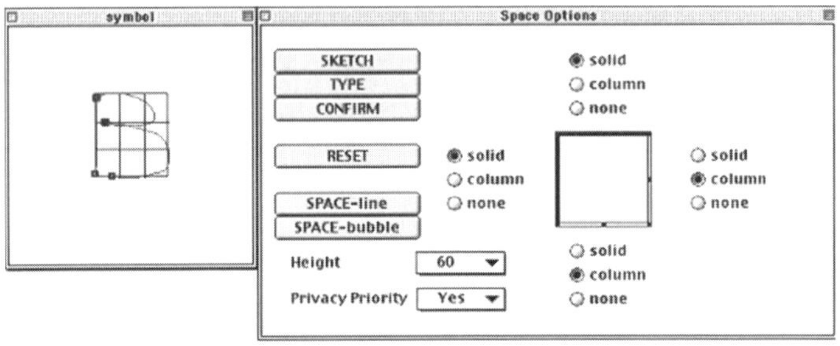

Figure 4.2, A designer draws a symbol (on the left) and defines the symbol by choosing wall elements and other parameters in Definition Window (right).

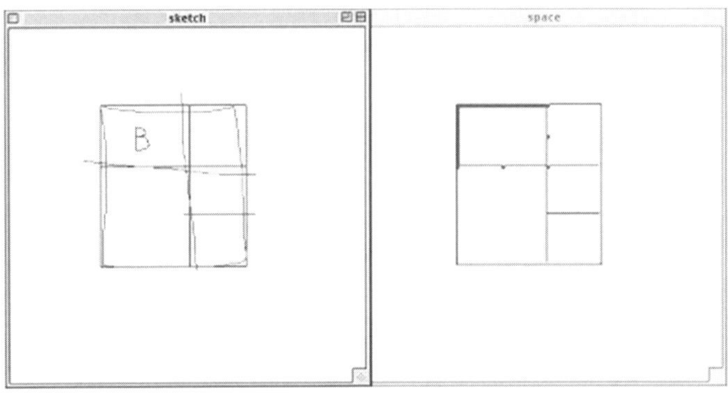

Figure 4.3. A designer draws a pre-defined symbol into Sketch Window (left); SpaceMaker then displays the setting in Space Window (right).

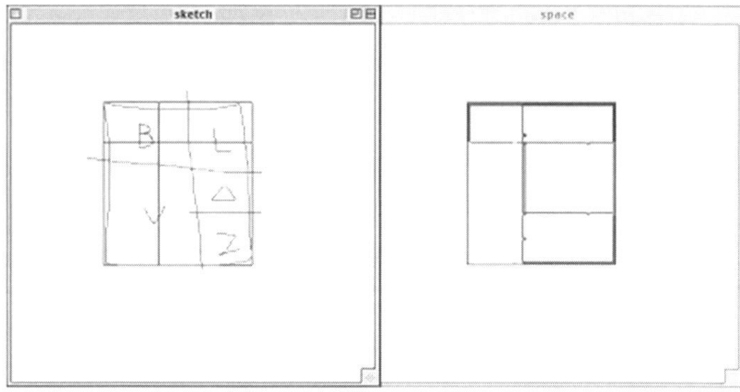

Figure 4.4 shows the result (on the right) of changing the spatial configuration of the entire building by moving guidelines in Sketch Board (left).

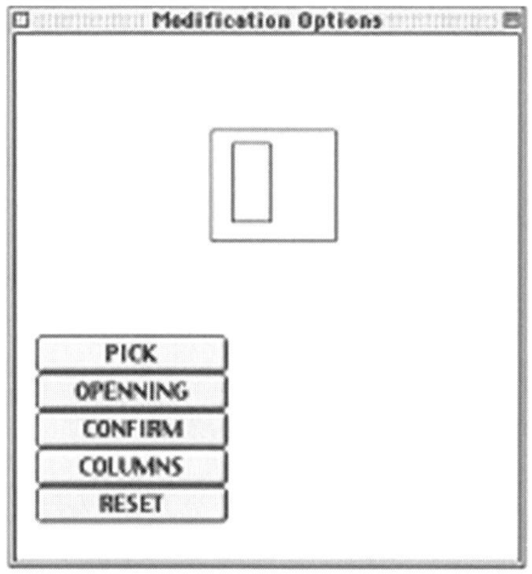

Figure 4.5. A user can change the characteristics of a wall element, for example, by opening a window in the wall.

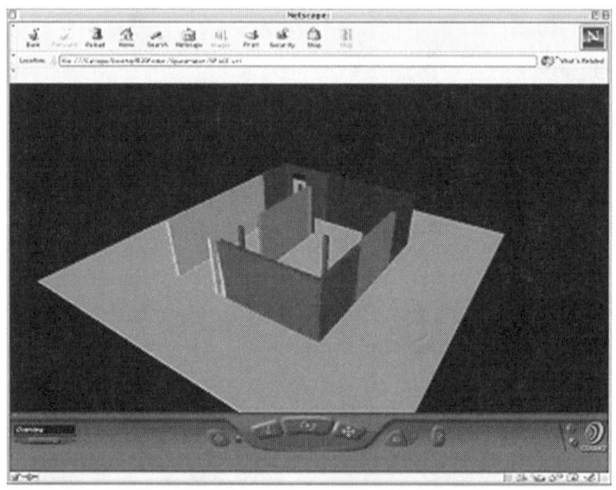

Figure 4.6. A user views the resulting model through a VRML enabled web browser.

Figure 4.4 shows the result (on the right) of changing the spatial configuration of the entire building by moving guidelines in Sketch Board (left).

Jamie wants to change the characteristics of a wall. Jamie picks a wall from Space Window and assigns the wall an opening by drawing a rectangle (Figure 4.5).

Now, Jamie is done with the spatial layout. He saves the file in VRML format, and then views this space through the VRML enabled web browser in 3-D (Figure 4.6).

4.2 System Architecture

SpaceMaker consists of several parts: a freehand drawing environment with recognition, a symbol definition system, a 3-D model conversion system, and a model modification system. Figure 4.7 illustrates SpaceMaker's system architecture.

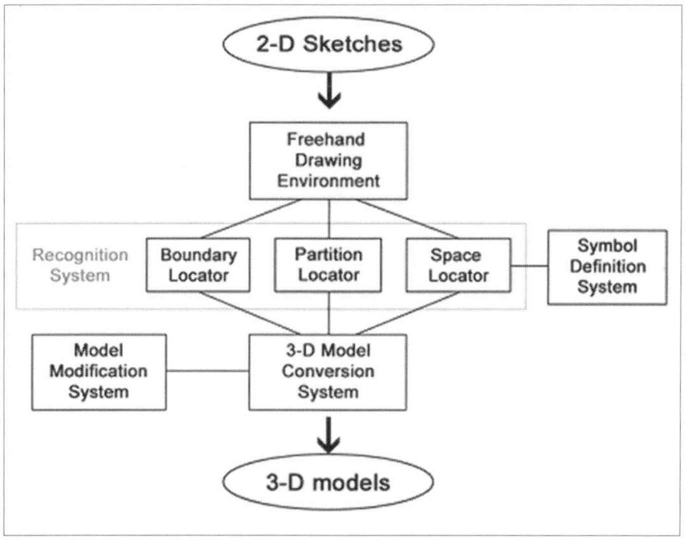

Figure 4.7 shows the SpaceMaker system architecture.

4.3 Freehand Drawing Environment

SpaceMaker is a freehand drawing environment allowing input from a mouse or a stylus with a digitizing tablet. Drawn input by users is categorized into three different types: exterior building boundary, interior partition walls, and drawing symbols. The three types of drawn input are then respectively handled by independent recognition systems: a building-boundary locator (Boundary Locator), a partition-wall locator (Partition Locator), and a symbol recognizer. The symbol recognizer also acts as an interior-space locator (Space Locator) (Figure 4.8).

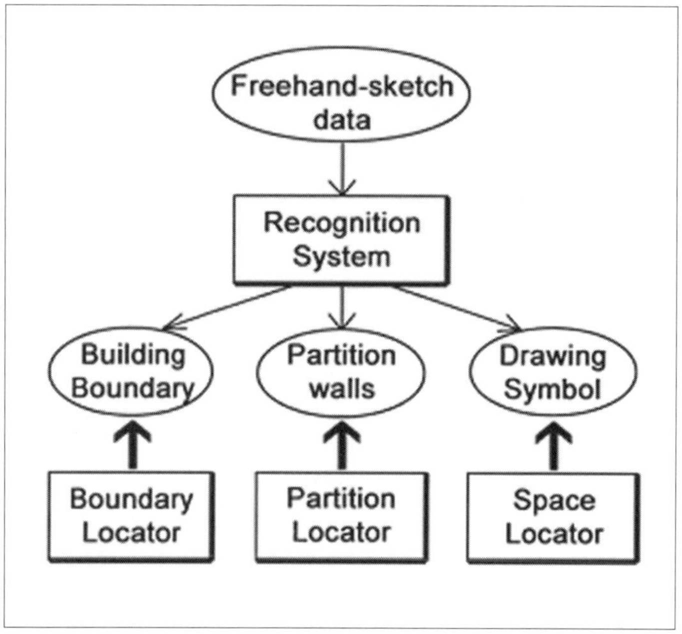

Figure 4.8 shows the structure of the recognition system. Sketching data is categorized into three types and then handled by three different recognizers.

4.4 Recognition System

4.4.1 Locators for Building Shape and Partition Walls

SpaceMaker has two simple freehand sketch recognizers, Boundary Locator and Partition Locator. Boundary Locator receives the first freehand stroke and identifies it as the boundary of a building. Typically, an architect draws a rough envelope to indicate the building boundary. SpaceMaker receives the envelope and creates a smallest rectangular frame that contains the entire freehand envelope. Boundary Locator then identifies the corners of this rectangular frame and registers it as the boundary of the building (Figure 4.9).

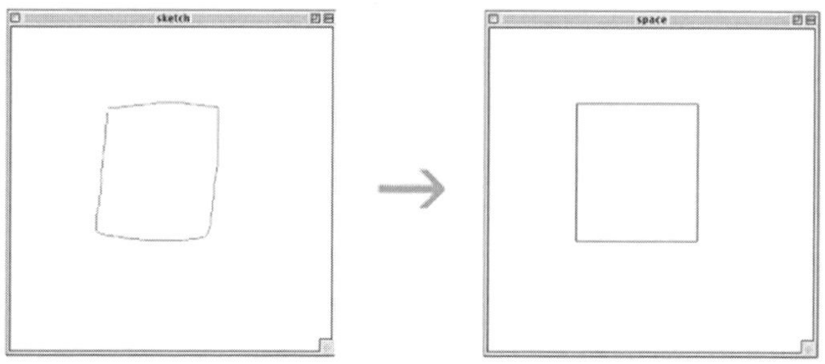

Figure 4.9. Boundary Locator recognizes a freehand envelope stroke and identifies it as the building boundary.

After drawing the boundary envelope, designers can further divide the entire floor by drawing either lines or bubbles. When a user draws a line, Partition Locator identifies the orientation and the location of the line and marks it with a guideline (Figure 4.10).

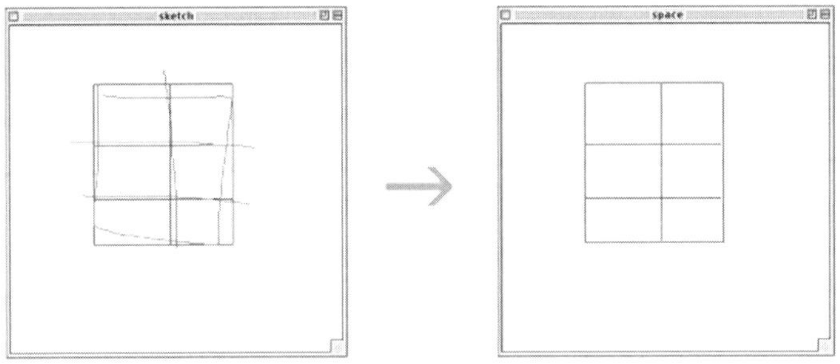

Figure 4.10. Partition Locator recognizes several freehand lines and identifies them as the interior partition walls.

Alternatively, when a user draws a bubble, Partition Locator first makes a rectangular frame to fully contain the bubble and then checks the relative location of the partition frame to the boundary frame. If the partition frame is very close to the boundary frame, then Partition Locator will automatically attach the partition frame to the boundary frame. On the other hand, if the bubble is farther from the boundary by more than a certain minimum distance, Partition Locator will consider the bubble as an individual room. The partition frame will be placed into the interior with no attachment to the boundary frame (Figure 4.11).

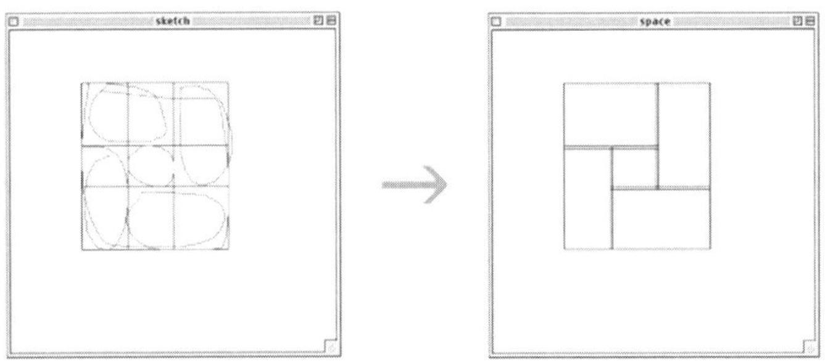

Figure 4.11. Partition Locator recognizes several freehand bubbles and identifies them as the interior partition walls.

4.4.2 Locator for Space

After users complete the layout, several interior spaces have already been identified by SpaceMaker. When users then draw a symbol into one of the blank interior spaces, Space Locator identifies the space represented by the symbol. The space is identified by finding four guidelines that enclose the labeled area (Figure 4.12).

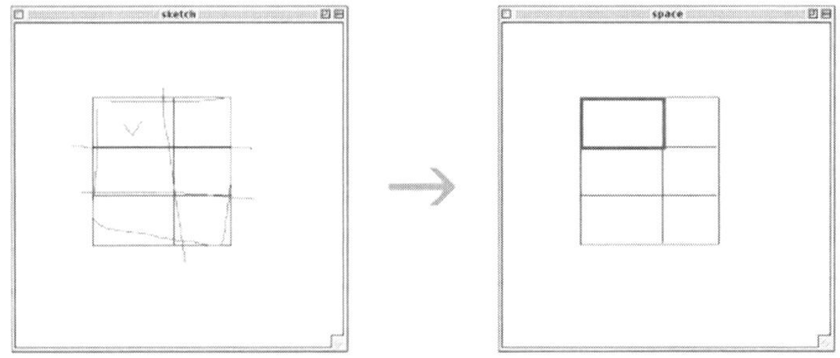

Figure 4.12. Space Locator recognizes the drawn symbol and identifies the space that the symbol represents.

4.4.3 Symbol Recognition

When designers draw symbols into the sketch, not only does Space Locator identify the location of the space, but it also tries to recognize each individual symbol. Symbol recognition is handled by Shape Recognizer, which compares the similarity of each input glyph with a set of previously defined templates created by users themselves, and then Shape Recognizer identifies the best match for the input symbol. Shape Recognizer uses basic features of the freehand input to identify symbols containing a single stroke with simple shapes, like freeform lines with limited segments, or simple geometric polygons. The features that Shape Recognizer uses include: number of corners and relative locations of starting and end points in relation to a 3x3 grid within a bounding box (Figure 4.13).

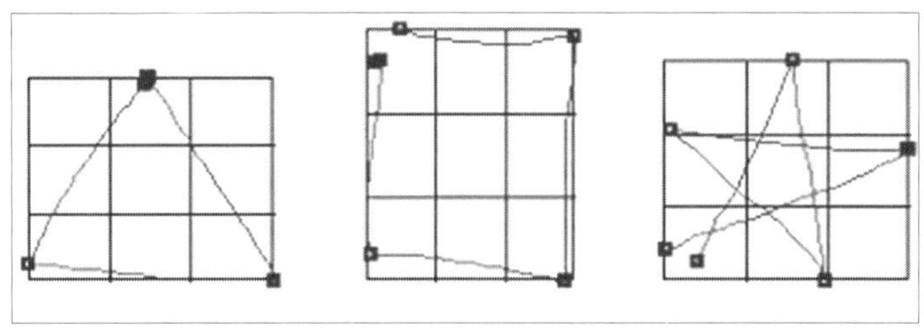

Figure 4.13. The features that Shape Recognizer uses, including number of corners and relative locations of both starting and end points in relation to a 3x3 grid.

4.5 Symbol Definition

SpaceMaker has Symbol Definition System that enables users to pre-define the architectural configuration associated with a symbol by assigning a set of four elements to the four sides of a space, the height of the space, and its condition of privacy (Figure 4.14).

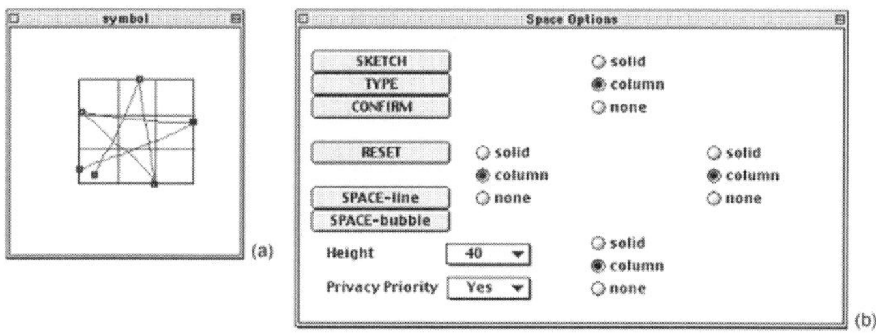

Figure 4.14. Symbol Definition System has two pop-up windows: (a) symbol-sketch window and (b) symbol-definition window. A designer can draw a symbol to represent a combination of spatial boundary conditions and privacy properties.

Users first draw a symbol and then define it by choosing different elements for each individual wall. SpaceMaker so far offers three conceptual elements: a solid wall (representing a solid element without opening), a colonnade with three columns (representing an element with relative higher degree of enclosure), and a pair of columns at two ends (representing an element without enclosure) (Figure 4.15).

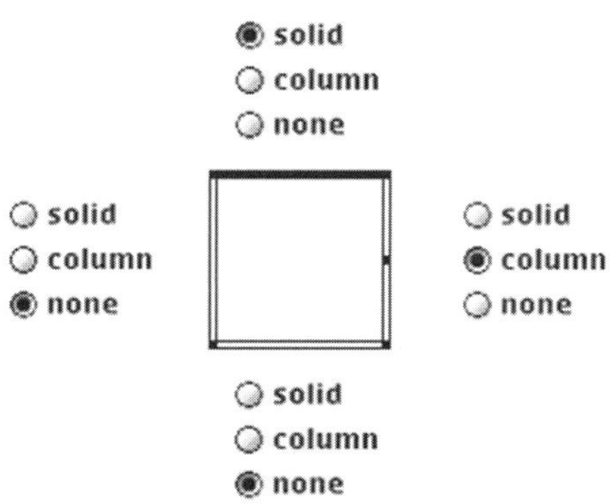

Figure 4.15 shows three different types of walls that designers can choose for defining a symbol.

After users have decided all symbol settings, Symbol Definition System associates that spatial configuration information with that particular symbol. When users then draw a pre-defined symbol into the sketch, Space Locator compares the features of the symbol to previously defined symbol templates and finds the closest match. Space Locator then retrieves the spatial configuration that this symbol carries and finally displays the space with pre-defined wall elements in the floor plan (Figure 4.16).

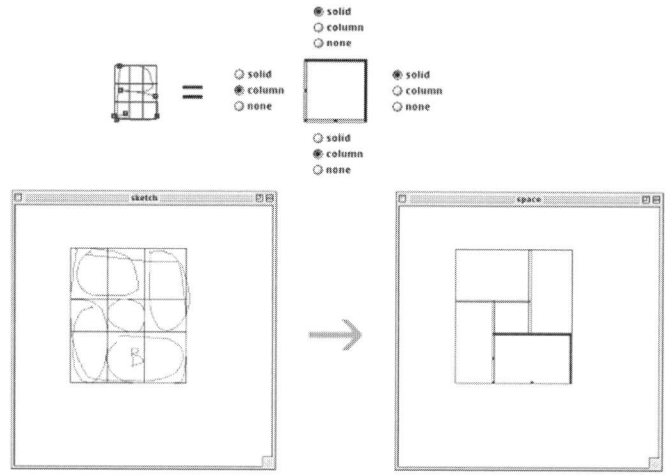

Figure 4.16. Space Locator recognizes the pre-defined symbol and inserts the elements in the Space Window according to the architectural configuration that the symbol represents.

4.5.1. Boundary Conflict

When designers draw a symbol into a sketch, SpaceMaker responds by inserting a set of four elements in the floor. However, there may be a conflict on the boundary between two adjacent spaces because two sets of four wall elements will be inserted into the floor when two symbols are applied to two adjacent spaces. The boundary between the two spaces will be specified by two potentially different elements (Figure 4.17). How do we solve the conflict?

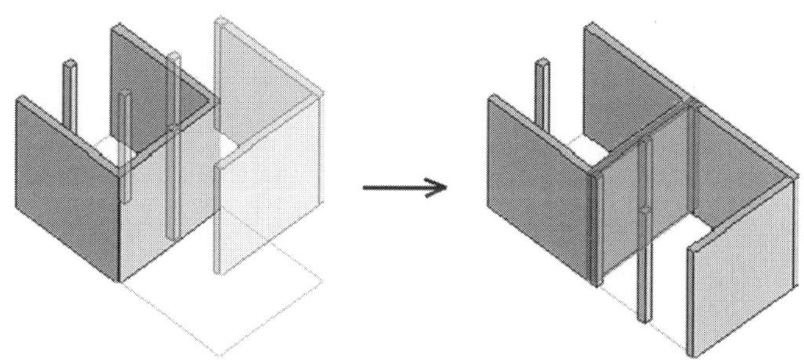

Figure 4.17 shows the boundary conflict between two adjacent spaces.

SpaceMaker has Boundary Conflict Resolver that selects a wall element for the shared space boundary based on the privacy condition of each space to deal with the conflict. SpaceMaker allows users to decide whether a space is to be assigned "privacy priority." Users must make this selection when they define a symbol. Boundary Conflict Resolver will decide which element is chosen according to the pre-defined settings of privacy priority. Basically, there are three rules with which

SpaceMaker handles the boundary conflict (Figure 4.18): (1) when one space has privacy priority, SpaceMaker picks the element containing less opening in order to maintain the privacy; (2) when two spaces both have privacy priority, the element containing more opening is chosen in order to ensure circulation between two rooms; (3) when neither space has privacy priority, the element containing more opening is picked.

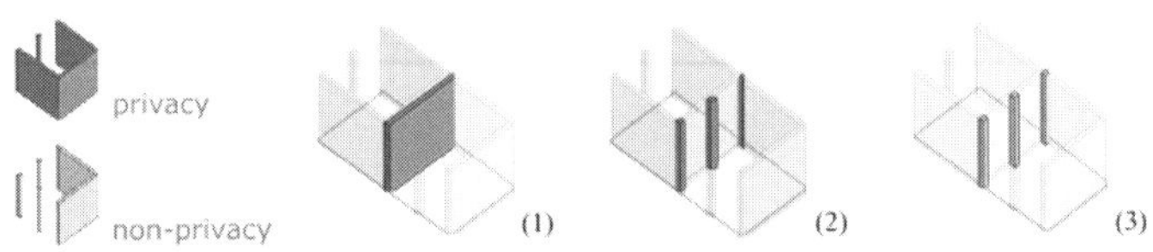

Figure 4.18 shows the three rules that Boundary Conflict Resolver uses to handle the boundary conflict.

4.6 Modification Tools for Converted Space

SpaceMaker provides two modification tools for users, Moving Tool and Opening Tool. Moving Tool allows users to modify the model by adjusting the spatial configuration in the sketch. Users can move any guideline that controls the positions of boundaries between interior spaces. All rooms aligned with this selected guideline will be modofied together (Figure 4.19).

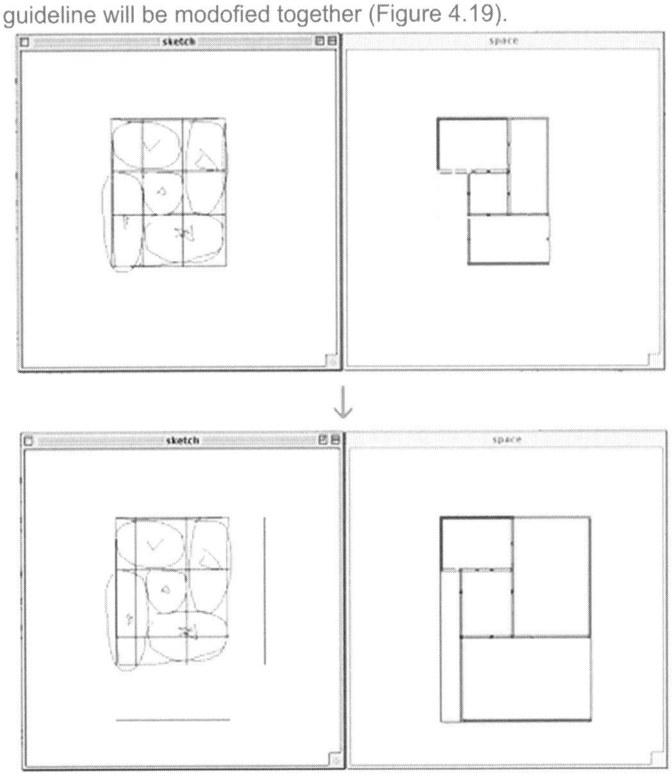

Figure 4.19. Designers can change the entire configuration of space by moving guidelines on the Sketch Board.

Opening Tool allows users to directly modify the model. Users can either add an opening on the wall or replace the wall with a colonnade. Opening Tool enables a designer to change the nature of a wall and thereby to change the nature of the spaces adjacent to that modified wall (Figure 4.20).

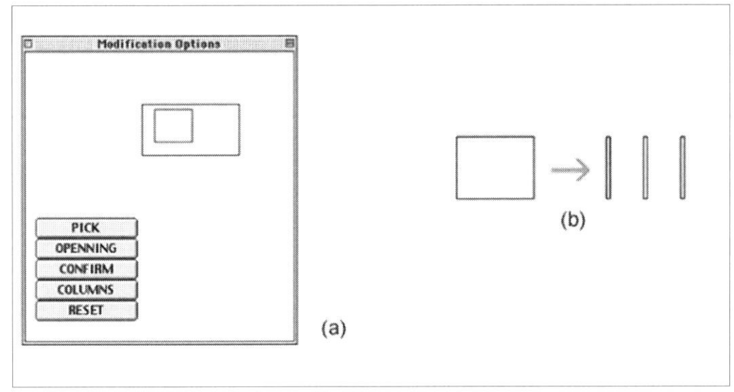

Figure 4.20. Users can change the characteristics of the partition walls by (a) adding an opening or (b) switching it to a colonnade.

4.7 Conversion to VRML Format

SpaceMaker converts 2-D sketches into 3-D models in VRML format. After designers have completed a space layout, VRML Translator outputs a standard VRML format file that any VRML enabled web-browser can read. The program assumes that the world is flat and level and that all elements will be simply extruded to a height that users have assigned while defining symbols. After creating the virtual space, users can use a VRML enabled browser to navigate the space (Figure 4.21).

5 Conclusion

We have presented a prototype 3-D modeling tool, SpaceMaker, for early schematic architectural design. The computational implementation is based on studies of the features in sketch floor plans and the use of drawing symbols. This study reveals that it is possible to quickly build 3-D models by making freehand sketches and integrating designer-defined drawing symbols into sketches. By allowing users to employ a pen-based interface to explore spatial layout, SpaceMaker enables designers to work with spatial components without specifying their precise internal structure. Using SpaceMaker, designers can arrange the spatial layout based on the fundamental characteristics of space and quickly experience the space in 3-D. On the other hand, SpaceMaker also enables designers to modify and add more precise details into the model later in the design process.

Because designers can explore spatial layout without worrying about specific details when using SpaceMaker, designers can mainly focus on "void" space instead of "solid" architectural elements. You think of the space first, and then think of the configuration of solid elements that come together with the space, and finally draw a symbol to represent this space.

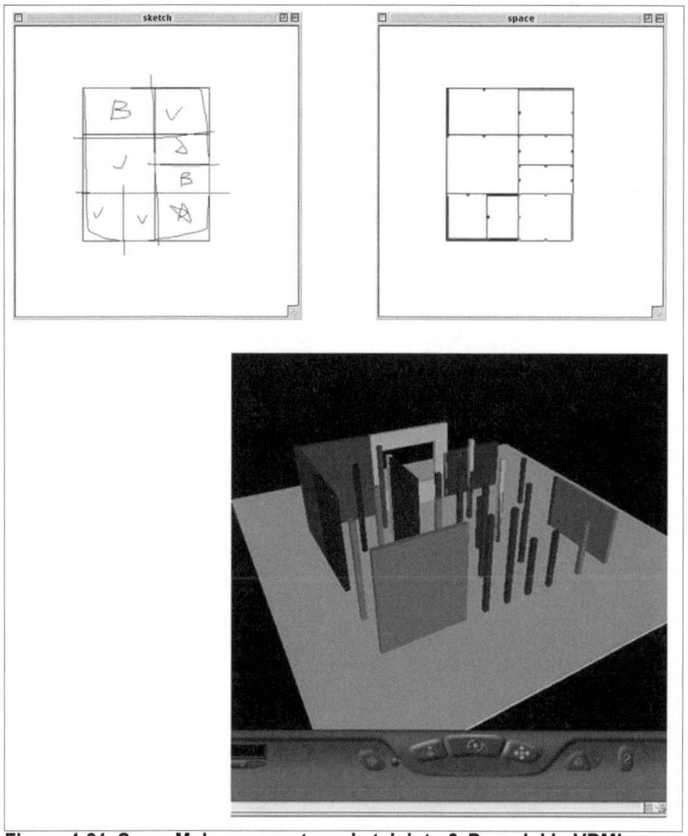

Figure 4.21. SpaceMaker converts a sketch into 3-D model in VRML format.

Designers draw to think of space, draw to explore the solution of spatial configurations, and draw to make space.

While SpaceMaker supports a convenient paper-like modeling environment, there are still some limitations due to the computational implementation. For example, the recognition systems currently only support single-stroke recognition. Users must complete any single task, such as enclosing a building boundary, partitioning the floor, and inserting a symbol, within only one single stroke input. In addition, SpaceMaker currently only recognizes a building boundary with a simple rectangular shape. It is obvious that many opportunities for extending the scope of this study remain. In the immediate future, usability tests or other formative evaluation techniques such as heuristic evaluation should be used to further refine the prototype. In addition, future versions of SpaceMaker should incorporate non-rectilinear recognition, multi-stroke input, high-level context recognition, and multi-floor layout.

SpaceMaker represents our intention to look at a different direction for establishing a 3-D modeling environment that is truly suitable to the early conceptual development for the architectural design.

References

Do, E. Y. -L. (1998). The right tool at right time: Investigation of freehand drawing as an interface to knowledge based design tools. PhD, Georgia Institute of Technology.

Do, E. Y. -L. (2000). Sketch that scene for me: Creating virtual worlds by freehand drawing. In eCAADe 2000, 265-268.

Do, E. Y. -L. (2001). VR sketchpad: Create instant 3D worlds by sketching on a transparent window. CAAD *Futures 2001*, p. 161-172.

Eggli, L., B. P. Brderlin, and G. Elber. (1995). Sketching as a solid modeler tool. *Third symposium on solid modeling and applications*, 313-321.

Ervin, S. M., and H. Hasbrouck. (2001). *Landscape modeling: Digital techniques for landscape visualization*. McGraw-Hill Professional.

Fraser, I., and R. Henmi. (1994). *Envisioning architecture—An analysis of drawing.* New York: Van Nostrand Reinhold Goel, V. (1995). *Sketches of thought.* Cambridge MA: MIT Press.

Goldschmidt, G. (1991). The dialectics of sketching, *Creativity research journal*, 4(2):123-43.

Grimstead, J., and R. R. Martin. (1995). *Creating solid models from single 2D sketches*. New York: ACM Press, 323-337.

Gross, M. D., (1996). The electronic cocktail napkin—Working with diagrams. *Design Studies* 17(1):53-69.

Gross, M. D., and E. Do. (1996). Ambiguous intentions: A paper-like interface for creative design. *ACM Conference on User Interface Software Technology*, 183-192.

Herbert, D. M. (1993). *Architectural study drawings*. New York: Van Nostrand Reinhold.

Igarashi, T. (2000). Freeform user interfaces for graphical computing. PhD dissertation, the University of Tokyo.

Koepke, M. L. (1988). *Model graphics—Building and using study models.* New York: Van Nostrand Reinhold.

Kurrent, F. (1999). *Scale models: Houses of the 20th century*. Birkhauser Verlag AG.

Landay, J. A., and B. A. Myers. (1995). Interactive sketching for the early stages of interface design. *Human factors in computing systems. ACM CHI '95*, p. 43-50.

Larkin, J. H. & H.A. Simon,(1987). Why a diagram is worth ten thousand words. *Cognitive Science Journal* 11:65-99.

Laseau, P. (1989). *Graphic thinking for architects and designers.* New York: Van Nostrand Reinhold.

Lawson, B. (1994). *Design in mind.* Oxford: Butterworth

Lipson, H., and M. Shpitalni. (1996). Optimization-based reconstruction of a 3D object from a single freehand line drawing. *CAD 28(8).*

Lucci, R., and P. Orlandini. (1990). *Product design models.* New York: Van Nostrand Reinhold.

Robbins, E. (1994). *Why architects draw.* Cambridge: MIT Press.

Schweikardt, E., and M. D. Gross. (1998). Digital clay: Deriving digital models from freehand sketches. *ACADIA '98*, 202-211.

Schön, D. A., and G. Wiggins. (1992). Kinds of seeing and their functions in designing, *Design Studies* 13(2):135-156.

Suwa, M., and B. Tversky. (1996). What architects see in their sketches: Implications for design tools. *Proceedings of ACM Human Factors in Design '96*, 191-192.

Zevi, B. (1974). *Architecture as space.* New York: Horizon Press.

Architectural Applications of Complex Adaptive Systems

Phillip Anzalone
Pratt Institute

Cory Clarke
Columbia University

Abstract

This paper presents methods and case studies of approaching architectural design and fabrication utilizing Complex Adaptive Systems (CASs). The case studies and observations described here are findings from a continuing body of research investigating applications of computational systems to architectural practice. CASs are computational mechanisms from the computer science field of Artificial Life that provide frameworks for managing large numbers of elements and their inter-relationships. The ability of the CASs to handle complexity at a scale unavailable through non-digital means provides new ways of approaching architectural design, fabrication, and practice.

Architectural Applications of Complex Adaptive Systems

Phillip Anzalone
Pratt Institute

Cory Clarke
Columbia University

1 Introduction

This paper documents findings from investigations of the application of Complex Adaptive Systems (CASs) to the practice of architecture. CASs are computational mechanisms from the computer science field of Artificial Life that provide frameworks for managing large numbers of elements and their inter-relationships. Some algorithms that are classified as CASs are Cellular Automata, Lindemayer Systems, Turing Machines, and Flocking algorithms. There are many potential applications for these systems in the architectural design process:

- Tools for the automated design of large scale buildings and urban projects;
- Techniques for the design of serialized buildings (e.g. mass housing, franchise buildings, pre-fabricated construction) that are contextually-sensitive and differentiated;
- Platforms for roboticized self-assembling and self-adjusting buildings;
- Methods for designing adaptable buildings with redundant structures with the ability to more successfully withstand damage and catastrophic events.

Critical to our investigation is the marriage of CASs with suitable geometric and structural systems. Complex computational systems have found little application in contemporary architectural practice because their effective realization is often not possible with traditional geometries, such as the Cartesian coordinate system, or with traditional structural methods, such as trabeated construction. In parallel with our investigation of applications of CASs to architectural design has been the development of formal and structural systems with geometries to match the CAS morphology.

This paper describes:

- The concept of CASs and their presentation in architectural terms, addressing ideas of context, site, program and form;
- Development of structural and construction systems that provide a means of constructing results from CAS based design systems;
- Case studies of the application of CASs in architectural design.

2 CAS concepts in architectural design

CASs are a class of dynamic systems from the field of Artificial Life. These systems typically involve sets of discrete elements that change state (typically visualized by changes in color), based on the iteration of a simple set of deterministic rules (Wuensche, Lesser 1992). The elements' states change as a function of their current state and the rules, producing an unpredictable, complex global behavior pattern.

A CAS changes its state based on the rules of the system. These rules are applied to the current state of every element in the system to calculate each element's new state. Despite the fact that these systems' behaviors are defined by completely deterministic rules, the behaviors of these systems (with sufficient elements in play) are so complex that they cannot be predicted. Since the new state of the system is determined by the current state, different initial states of a CAS can foster entirely different emergent behavior. To change the behavior of the system a CAS can merely be started with a new initial state. Different initial states in CASs will lead to different global behavior and patterns. In this way the interaction of the elements within a CAS can be thought of as a "calculator" (Neumann 1966), computing outputs based on inputs. This capacity to derive results from a complex matrix of inputs is an obvious analog to the design process—which must take the complex matrix of requirements—program, site and structure—and translate them into an architectural outcome.

There are several properties shared by CASs upon which we have focused our research. The properties listed below have provided us with a means of linking the processes and behaviors of CASs to the design and production of architecture. While these properties may not belong to all CASs, they provide a list of traits that can be combined and exploited in the production of architectural design tools. The properties are discrete composition, algorithmic relationships, exogenous control, and scalability.

2.1 Discrete Composition

The underlying substructures of CASs are discrete matrices of elements, treated as independent entities, operating in parallel. Despite the discrete nature of these systems at the local scale, they are able to exhibit global behaviors with varying degrees of continuity. The trait of having a discontinuous substructure, but varying continuity at the level of superstructure, is one of the behaviors that make CASs suitable for translation into architecture. This trait provides an analog to the way in which architecture is produced; assembled from discrete elements—

either programmatic (rooms and zones) or structural (beams and columns)—that define spaces with varying degrees of continuity (e.g. spatial, programmatic, acoustical, environmental).

2.2 Algorithmic Relationships

The behavior of a CAS is prescribed by sets of rules and algorithms that dictate the relationships between elements within the system. The relationships between elements in a CAS are iteratively re-evaluated based on these rules, providing the means for the system to adapt to internal and external changes. The clear definition of relationships between elements, and the reiteration of those relational rules over time, finds an analog in the design process—where design intentions are described in terms of relationships (privacy, lighting, proximity), and the final product emerges from the continual reiteration and refinement of these relationships.

A specific example of this can be seen in the computational algorithm described as flocking. Basic flocking systems (Figure 1) define a set of desired relationships between elements in a flock (such as ideal distance between elements and preferred position relative to other elements) and attempt to maintain these relationships by continually readjusting the positions of each element (Reynolds 1987). When the rules of proximity and position are applied to a group of elements they exhibit complex adaptive behavior similar to a flock of birds. This simple set of rules of proximity and position can find application in architecture, for example, as rules for positioning of programmatic or structural elements.

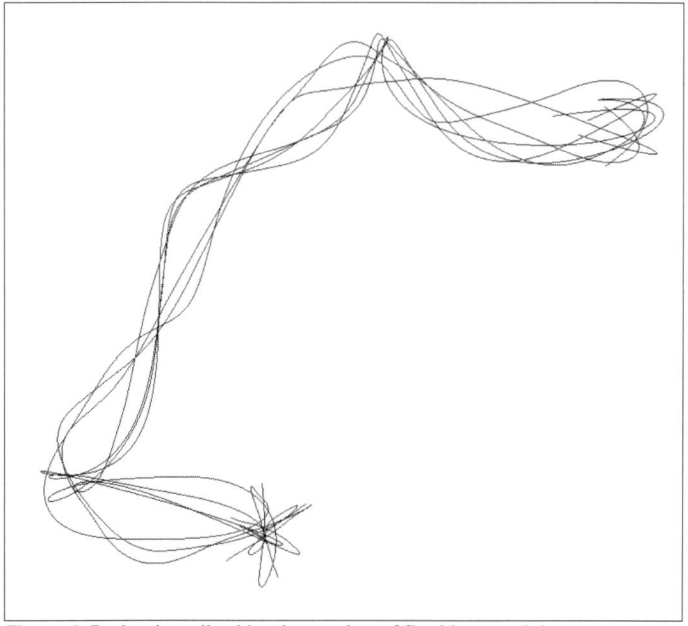

Figure 1. Paths described by the motion of flocking particles .

2.3 Exogenous Control (Contextual Awareness)

Along with the ideas of internal constraints, many CASs have the capacity to react to exogenous control, which in architectural terms can provide mechanisms for contextual and environmental awareness, and influencing the system to incorporate additional design intentions. CASs have two primary mechanisms for reacting to environment and context—initial state definition and avoidance behavior.

Since all CASs operate on a deterministic set of rules, the initial state of the system ultimately determines its outcome. Thought of in this way, the outcome of a CAS can be seen as a registration of the rules upon a particular initial state. With a simple CAS, such as Cellular Automata, the entire range of possible outcomes for every rule from a single initial state can be mapped (Wuench, Lesser 1992). In an architectural application the initial state can be defined in terms of the environment, and the behavior of the CAS would be a direct expression of the relational rules of the system within that environment.

Along with the ability to register the initial state of their environment, CASs can react to external change via mechanisms such as avoidance behavior. This behavior is comprised of basic mechanisms that monitor the incremental growth of a CAS for collisions with objects or fields in the environment and provide for additional reactions. If elements in the system are currently on a collision course, the monitoring mechanism signals for new behavioral rules to be invoked that react to the potential collision.

The obvious architectural implication of the collision detection and avoidance logic is to install the system with an awareness of surrounding buildings and landscape. However, the behavior can also be applied to more abstractly zoned volumes within the systems surrounding context as well. The growth of a system could respond to zoning envelopes, acoustical envelopes, sun and shade volumes, view corridors, program areas, and any other abstract constraints that can be represented volumetrically.

Collision detection can be further extended as a mechanism for control by inverting the logic of avoidance behavior so that the collision detection mechanism can be used as a tool for searching out attractive areas of an architectural context. If the avoidance behavior were to be changed to tend towards potential collision instead of away, the morphological tendencies of the CAS will grow towards specific areas in a site that are designated as desirable. Furthermore, the volumes of desirability and undesirability can be weighted in influence to produce a multivalent map of context.

2.4 Scalability

Many CASs exhibit a fractal behavior—the behavior of a small number of elements is congruent to the same system with exponentially more components. This scalability of behavior has two benefits to the study and implementation within architectural practice. The first is one of study and testing; since the behavior of a large system is similar to that of a small system, methods for design can be modeled in a limited capacity and still translate to the larger scale of a building or urban project. The second benefit of the scalability of CASs is their potential to be nested fractally. Their scalability makes them essentially scale-less; a particular set of rules that functions well as a global organization system could be used at the scale of an urban project, while each "cell" could in turn be filled with a smaller version of a CAS with a detailed behavior at the scale of building or dwelling unit.

3 Structural Systems

The characteristics of the organizational strategy outlined above, and the diverse range of possible complex forms that may result, require a structural solution with similar geometric and algorithmic traits. Our research focused upon the three-dimensional differential space-truss.

The traditional space-truss is a lattice structure of standard elements, typically leading to architecture of regular geometrical forms, as in the geodetic domes of Buckminster Fuller and projects such as I.M. Pei's Javits Convention Center in New York. The traditional space-truss employs standard elements because of constraints of design, analysis, and fabrication—constraints now surmountable through computer-based techniques. The differential space-truss uses non-standard elements; by allowing each element to be unique, it can take on complex three-dimensional curvilinear form as well as basic linear geometry.

During our research we built and tested several scale models of three-dimensional differential space-trusses with non-uniform elements (Figure 2). The manufacturing of the structural elements requires the use of Computer Numerically Controlled (CNC) fabrication techniques. The specific biases and limitations of these construction methods can be built into the relational rules of the CASs as further means of control. The differential space-truss has three major traits that match many of the behaviors and properties of CASs: discrete composition, lattice geometry, and scalability.

3.1 Discrete Elements

Space-truss systems are comprised of two basic components, linear struts and connecting nodes; through the manipulation of these two types of elements the system can yield a diverse range of complex three-dimensional forms. The fluid nature in which a space-truss can transition between curvilinear form and linear geometry is similar to that of monolithic structural systems such as cast concrete, yet it is constructed from repetitive discrete elements. Its range of formal expression, coupled with its discrete composition, makes the space-truss an ideal structural expression for the organizational strategies of CASs.

3.2 Lattice Configuration

The lattice configuration of a space-truss, a continuous network of nodes and struts, allows it to effectively behave as a monolithic system; load forces pass through the system on a global scale as if it were a uniform structure. The overall structural capacity emerges from the configuration of the discrete elements and their inter-connections, mimicking almost identically the emergent behavior of the coordinated elements in the CAS.

3.3 Scalability / Micro-scale Components

Structurally, the space-truss has no predetermined scale, capable of functioning equally with struts the length of 10 meters as with struts only 10 centimeters. The economies of scale behind traditional construction have led to the implementation of space-trusses only at a large scale, a single strut commonly measuring more than a meter in size. The use of CASs, which are capable of managing innumerable discrete elements, especially if they are coupled with CNC fabrication techniques and roboticized assembly methods, can allow the space-truss to be implemented at a finer scale, giving more adaptability and greater range of formal expression.

4 Case Study 1: one-dimensional Cellular Automata

We have performed several case studies applying CASs to architectural form, two of which are documented in this paper. Both case studies described here employ algorithms that are categorized in a subclass of CAS called Cellular Automata. The two specific examples are one-dimensional Cellular Automata (Wolfram 2002) and an adaptation of Conway's Game of Life (Gardner 1970). These studies focused on investigating ways of formally manifesting the behavior of the CASs via appropriate geometric systems and the differential space-truss structure. The case studies were produced by writing custom software plugins for Maxon's Cinema4D and Alias|Wavefront's Maya. The software plugins used the CAS rules to produce three-dimensional surfaces and lattice structures. The software was developed to generate forms that are able to be easily realized using CNC fabrication techniques.

4.1 Cellular Automata Rules

The structure of a Cellular Automata is a one-dimensional array of elements with variable states—typically represented as a line of black and white squares. The array is manipulated via a set of rules; in the studies done here we used 3-Neighbor Cellular Automata, which have only eight rules. The rules govern how the states of the individual elements change over time. For each discrete moment in time, the state of each element in the system is analyzed and changed based on the rules. An example of a set of rules is show in Figure 3. Typically the behavior of a Cellular Automata is visualized as a time-series plot, showing snapshots of the state of the one-dimensional array of elements at sequential moments in time all together as a two-dimensional grid.

4.2 Outcome

In translating the behavior of the one-dimensional Cellular Automata system to architectural design, the behavior of the system was treated as a series of instructions for growth in three-dimensions. Instead of interpreting the states of the elements within the Cellular Automata as white and black, the states mapped to angular directions for the development of a space-truss lattice.

Forms were generated by incrementally growing a space-truss structure where each new element within the structure was placed relative to the previous element based on the changing state of the Cellular Automata system. We discovered the forms with the most potential for architectural application resulted from the coupling of changes in state within the Cellular Automata and changes in angle within the growth of the space-truss structure. As each element was added to the truss, the angle of the new element relative to the previous element was dictated by the current state of the Cellular Automata system. A Cellular Automata pattern being translated to different surface configurations through the association between Cellular Automata states and various angles is illustrated in Figure 4. The Cellular Automata system was further studied by augmenting it with rules for exogenous responsiveness and tectonic/structural intelligence. An additional layer of behavior was added to the basic behaviors employed in the previous examples, giving it collision detection so it could respond to boundaries and environmental constraints. Figure 5 illustrates the results of the collision detection in a simple formal study.

Along with the layer of collision detection and responsiveness, a third system of behaviors was added to install proximity detection between elements. Each element within the Cellular Automata system was given additional instructions that controlled its distance relative to it neighbors during the generation of the lattice structure (Figure 5). This behavior attempted to keep the spacing between elements at an optimal distance, one that corresponded to an optimal relative length for a structural element in a differential space-truss. The mechanisms employed in maintaining optimal distance is similar to those used in the flocking behavior described earlier.

As part of the research we developed a software plugin for Maxon's Cinema4D to generate structures based on the parameters described above. The plugin has two major components, one titled "Behavior," for controlling the Cellular Automata behavior, and a second titled "Renderer" for controlling the interpretation of that behavior into form. The two components are reflected in the interface shown in Figures 6 and 7 below. The Cellular Automata rules, iterations, and initial state, as well as its flocking behavior, are all controlled via the Behavior interface. The Renderer portion allows a designer to associate the different states of the Cellular Automata with different angular directions for the interpretation into form, as shown in figure 4. The collision detection and avoidance behavior is integrated into the system

Figure 2. Fabricated prototype of differential space-truss.

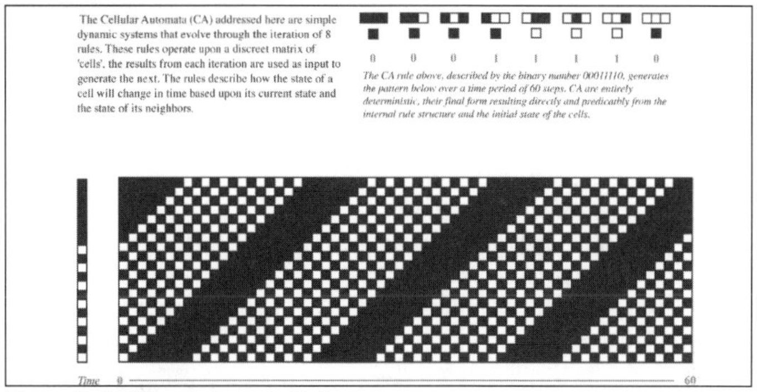

Figure 3. Cellular Automata Rules

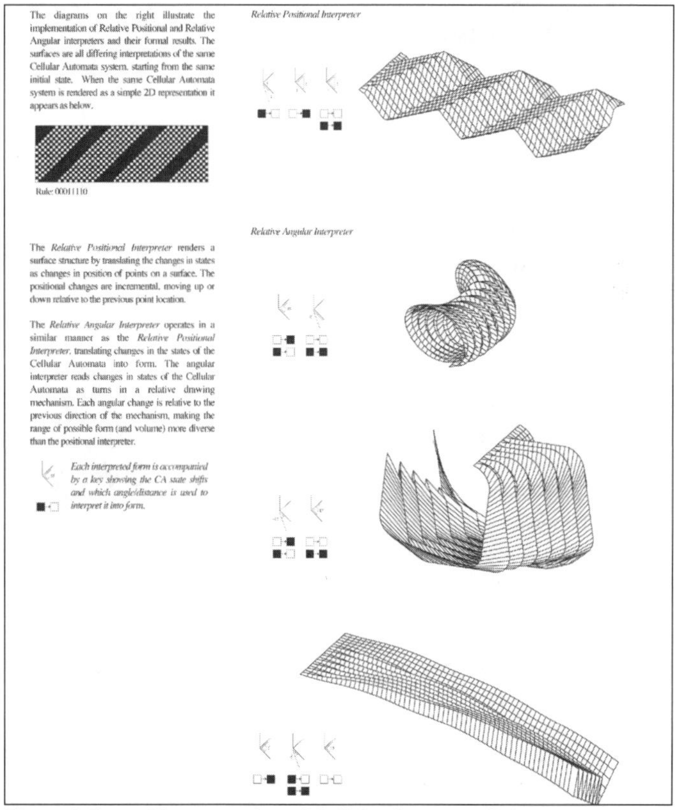

Figure 4. Formal interpretation of Cellular Automata Rules

A simple Cellular Automata using rule 0111101 to generate a folding form supported via a differential space truss structure. The Cellular Automata generates a repeating pattern that continues indefinitely, unresponsive to any external factors.

The same Cellular Automata and rule set as used above, but with an additional layer of intelligence, adding an environmental responsiveness. The structure responds to the influence of a rectangular volume in the environment. The Cellular Automata generates a folding form as above, however when it comes in contact with the volumetric obstacle in the environment it reacts by attempting to move up and out of the volume.

The third image in the series depicts the same Cellular Automata described above, but with yet another layer of intelligence added to the generative system. This layer of intelligence provides for a 'flocking' logic, preventing extreme variations in the overall form that would compromise the structural integrity. The 'flocking' logic is a communication mechanism between neighboring elements, allowing them to monitor the distance between themselves and their nearest neighbors. This allows them to adjust and maintain a consistant spacing and angle between components that is necessary for the structural behavior of the system. The term 'flocking' refers to a similar algorithm that is employed in flocks of birds, allowing the individual birds to maintain uniform distances between each other within a moving flock.

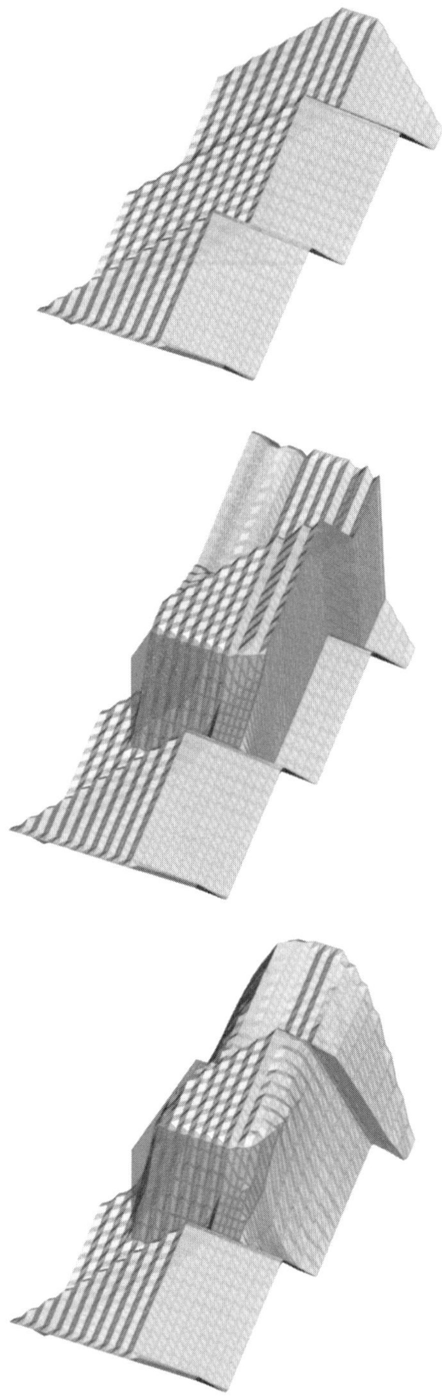

Figure 5. Flocking and Avoidance behavior applied to Cellular Automata

so that any shapes defined within the modeling environment are treated as context and avoided as the Cellular Automata structure generates itself. The plugin generates both a surface model as well as a structure of lines and curves; these curves can provide a basis for the generation of laser cut structural models.

We ran several tests of hypothetical scenarios, deploying Cellular Automata systems with specific rule sets within different urban and rural contexts. Figure 8 shows the results of one of these tests. In this test a pair of Cellular Automata, tuned towards different degrees of transparency and opacity, were deployed in an urban infill lot. The Cellular Automata plugin we developed generates ruled surfaces, which can be optimized for fabrication with linear tools such as laser cutters. Generating surfaces with a rule-based system that incorporates requirements of the fabrication method is similar to that employed in the Morphogenetic Surface Structures project from the Emergent Design Group (Testa, O'Reilly 1999).

5 Case Study 2: Conway's Game of Life Variant

5.1 System Rules

Conway's Game of Life is a two-dimensional Cellular Automata, a matrix of elements with variable states in two directions. The matrix of elements is typically arranged as a grid of black and white squares, and a set of four rules is used to change the states of the elements at each discrete moment in time. The rules for changing each element are, as with one-dimensional Cellular Automata, based on the immediate context of each element. However, since there are many more possible configurations of neighboring elements than in a one-dimensional Cellular Automata, the rules can operate on a more qualitative level. For instance, the typical rules describe conditions of loneliness, over-population, stasis, and reproduction. These rules are shown in Figure 9.

To adapt Conway's Game of Life for architectural application, we derived a variant of the rules and system that works on a three-dimensional matrix of elements. Figure 10 shows how the Game of Life can be thought of as a three-dimensional system. In this case study we extended the system of Conway's Game of Life

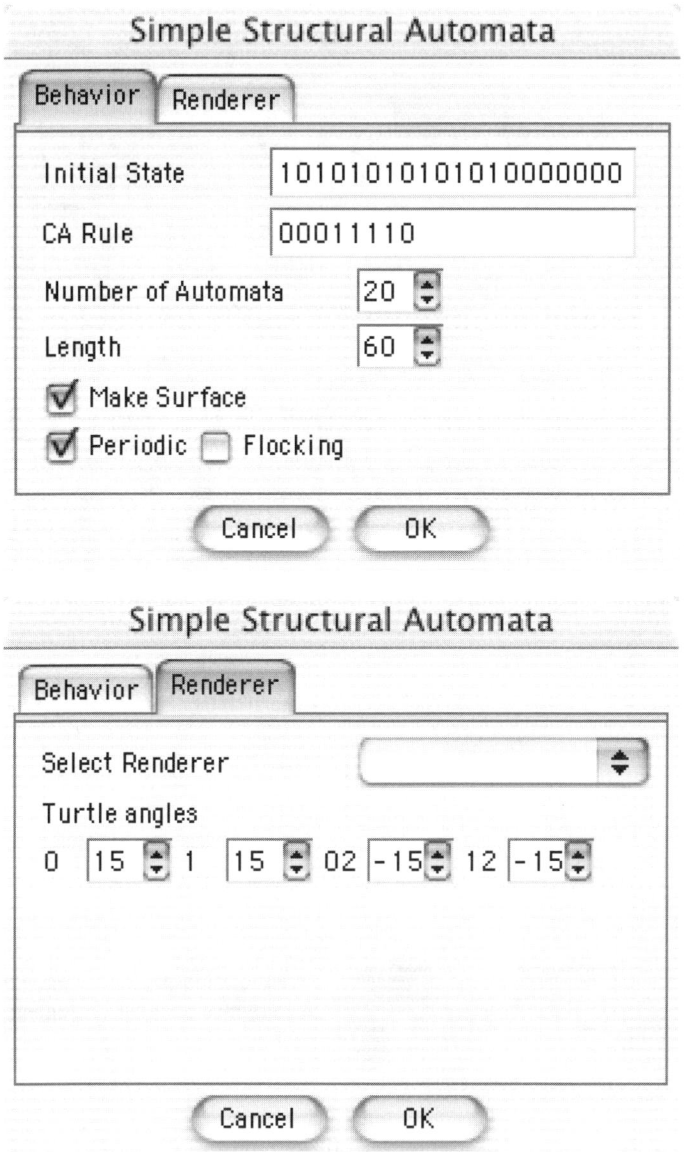

Figure 6 & 7. Interface components for Behavior and Renderer control in the Cellular Automata system

so that its implementation is not limited to a Cartesian spatial matrix so it can produce spatial conditions that are complex and more specific to the structural morphology of the differential space-truss.

5.2 Outcome

In experiments with our variant of Conway's Game of Life (Conway Variant) we sought to make the ideas of contextual awareness and structural/tectonic logic explored in the one-dimensional Cellular Automata more central to the generation of form. The basic rules of the system, those of loneliness, overcrowding, and reproduction, integrate contextual awareness without layering on additional behavioral logic as was done in the Cellular Automata studies. The architectural context is described in the same manner as the systems elements, allowing the growth of the elements to react to boundaries and environmental constraints. The forms generated by the system also act as contextual constraints for the next phase of growth, allowing the system to limit its growth in a more controlled manner.

To embed structural and formal logic into the system, studies were made in using space-filling geometries other than the typical 90-degree grid (Nooshin, Disney, and Champion 1997). With one-dimensional Cellular Automata and Conway's Game of Life, the system is typically represented as a grid of square tiles. In moving into three dimensions it is simple to mimic the behavior of these systems by extending those square tiles into three dimensions as a matrix of cubes, giving extremely limited formal possibilities and imparting no structural logic to the system. Instead, we looked towards more complex and variable space-filling geometries, such as the geometry of cells and crystals (Pearce 1990), that matched more effectively the formal logic of the differential space-truss. By coupling different space-filling geometries with variants on the rules of Conway's Game of Life, we were able to produce a diverse range of possible forms including complex spatial and structural configurations.

As with the Cellular Automata case study, we developed a custom plugin for the Conway Variant case study that would generate sample structures. The plugin provides an interface for controlling all the aspects of our variant of Conway's Game of Life rules such as "reproduction" and "overcrowding." The plugin interface is pictured in Figure 11. Instead of operating within a simple Cartesian grid, as shown in Figure 10, the system grows based on a spatial morphology of a differential space-truss. As elements within the Game of Life, the plugin uses "nodes" within a space-truss. However, instead of being located within a fixed three-dimensional grid the position and location of these nodes are determined by the "angle" and "length" parameters of the plugin. As the system grows, each node in the structure spawns new nodes and struts, or "kills" them off, based on the rules of reproduction and overcrowding from our variant on the Game of Life.

Figure 12 shows a highly constrained Conway Variant system deployed with constraints that limit its growth to a primarily vertical direction. The rules and space-filling geometry used produce a variation on a typical office tower structure with much more structural redundancy and spatial variety at the scale of the individual floor and unit.

Figure 13 shows the same system used to produce the tower, but deployed with a different initial context and geometric structure. With these different parameters the system produces a series of punctured domes with varying degrees of enclosure.

6 Future Work

We intend to further extend the rudimentary explorations in Autonomic Architecture along several different trajectories.

6.1 Geometry

The use of various space-filling geometries in Conway Variant produced a range of interesting formal results, opening up several research opportunities. As one portion of our continued research, we propose to investigate more rigorously the logic of these different spatial patterns and their formal range. We also hope to investigate these space-filling geometries combinatorially, testing applications of combinations of the geometries within a single structure to produce structures supportive of different programs and uses.

The association between ideas of structure and geometry in our case studies has remained primarily formal; in further investigations we plan to investigate "real-world" collaborative applications with structural engineers and architectural firms. There has been interest expressed within the community of practicing architects to utilize our current prototype for designing building components.

6.2 Fabrication

The application of CASs in the manner we propose offers the ability to control the size and scale of every architectural element within a structure with mathematical precision, as it is designed. This degree of control would necessitate further research in the coupling of Computer Numerically Controlled fabrication techniques with the morphology of the architectural design system. As part of our continued research we intend to develop fabrication techniques for a differential space-frame truss that would allow the limitations of the fabrication and construction process to be added as control parameters to the design system.

6.3 Algorithms

The CASs explored in our case studies, one-dimensional Cellular Automata and Conway Variant, use some of the simplest of the CAS algorithms. In further research we intend to pursue additional CAS algorithms based on the following criteria: the CAS systems we have employed so far use only two states within their organizational structure; other algorithms such as Turing Machines and 3-state Cellular Automata are capable

Figure 8. Deployment of a Cellular Automata architectural design system in an urban infill context

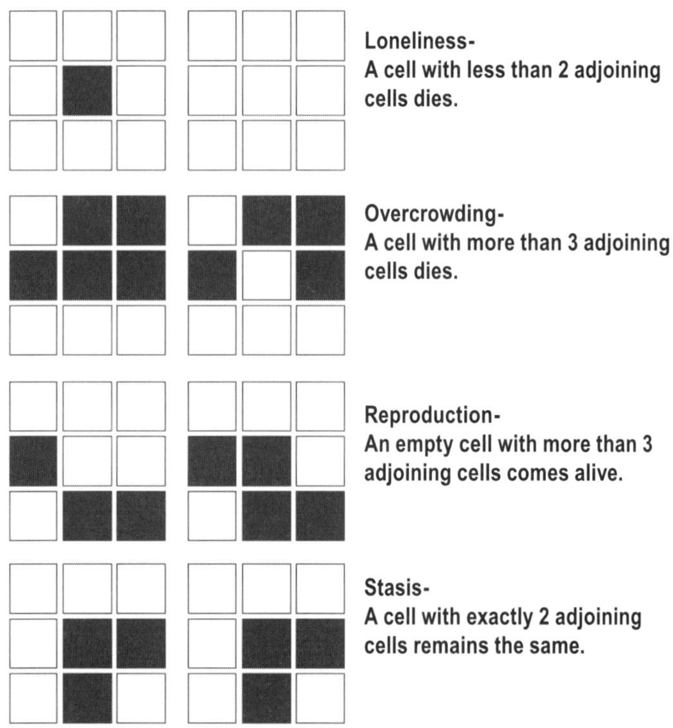

Figure 9. Rule set for Conway's Game of Life

The rule table below illustrates one set of possible rules for a 3D cellular automat based on the Game of Life. The 3D CA uses a three-dimensional grid as its matrix of cells, giving each cell a neighborhood of 26 adjoining cells. With the addition of exponentially more neighbors, the criteria for 'Loneliness' seen in 2D cellular automata is removed, leaving 3 rules. The 3 rules described below set criteria for reproduction, death from over-crowding and statis.
On the right is pictured a typical sequence of iterations of the 3D Game of Life. The entire matrix appears to pulse from iteration to iteration. Similar to the 2D Game of Life, recurring coherent organizations occur within the patterns of behavior.

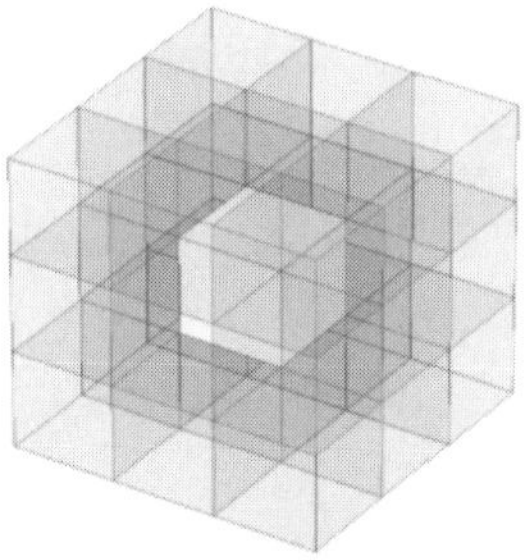

3D neighbors, comprised of the active cell and its 26 neighbors.

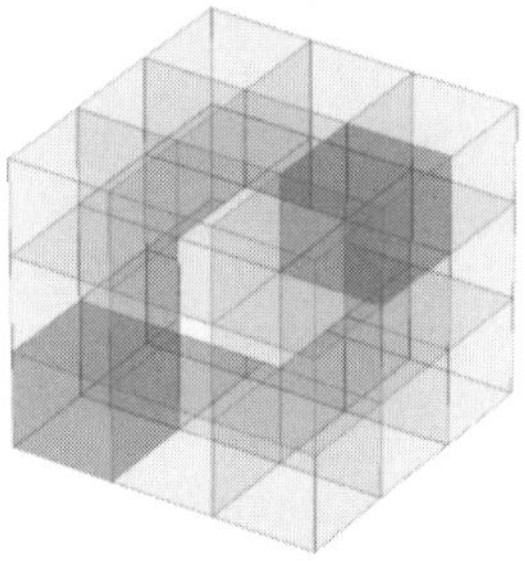

Reproduction—An empty cell with 2 neighbors comes to life.

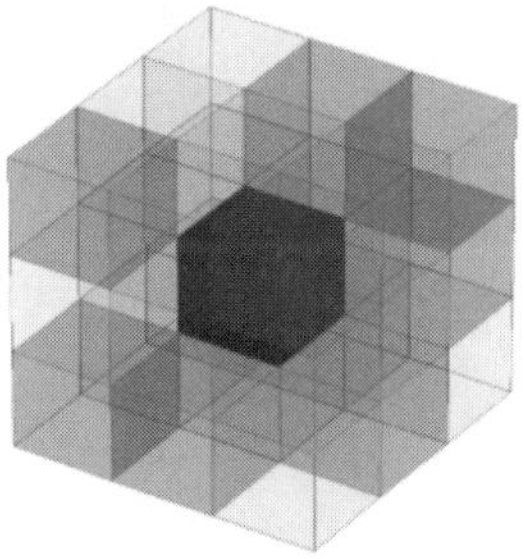

Overcrowding—A cell with more than 7 neighbors dies.

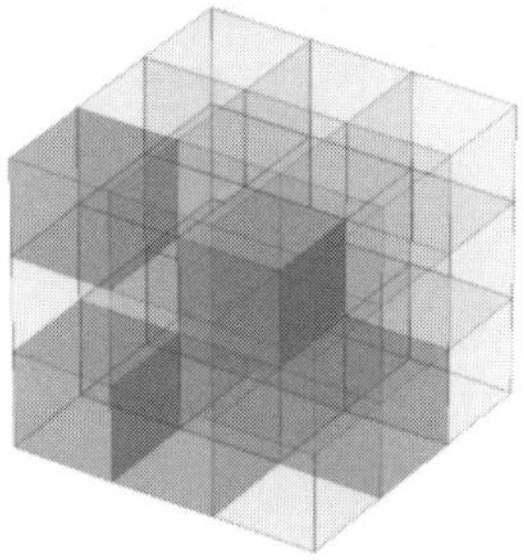

Statis—A cell with more than 2 but less than 7 neighbors continues unchanged.

Figure 10 - Rules for a 3D Conway's Game of Life.

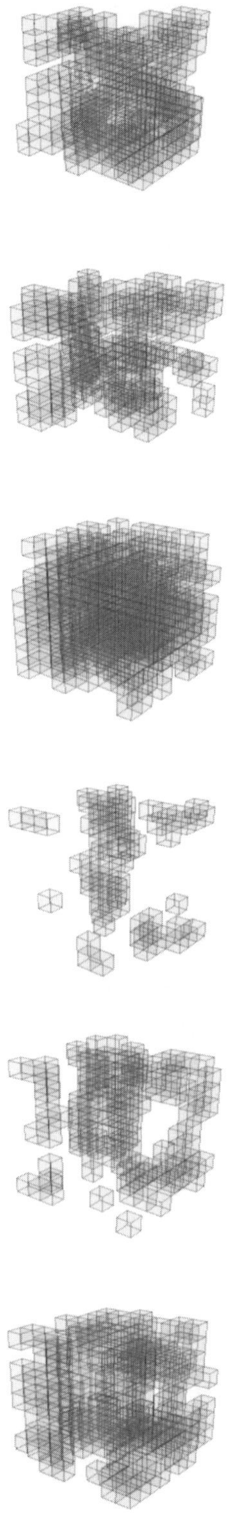

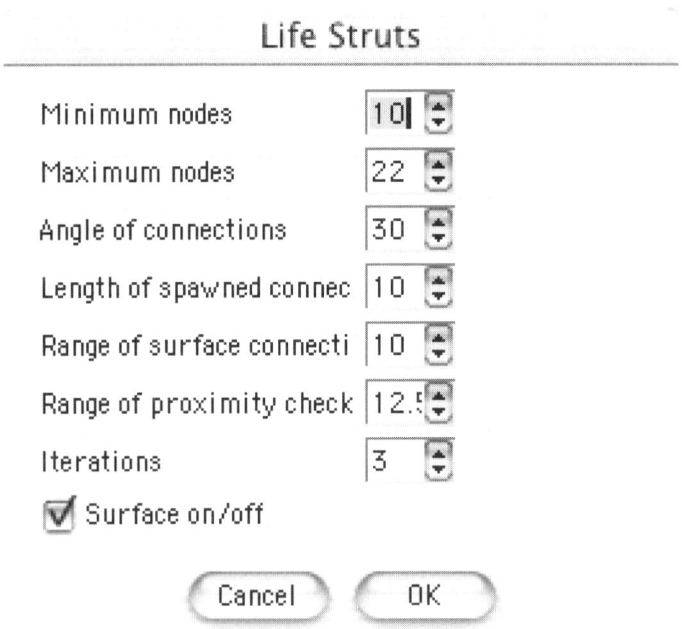

Figure 11. Software interface for generating Game of Life structures

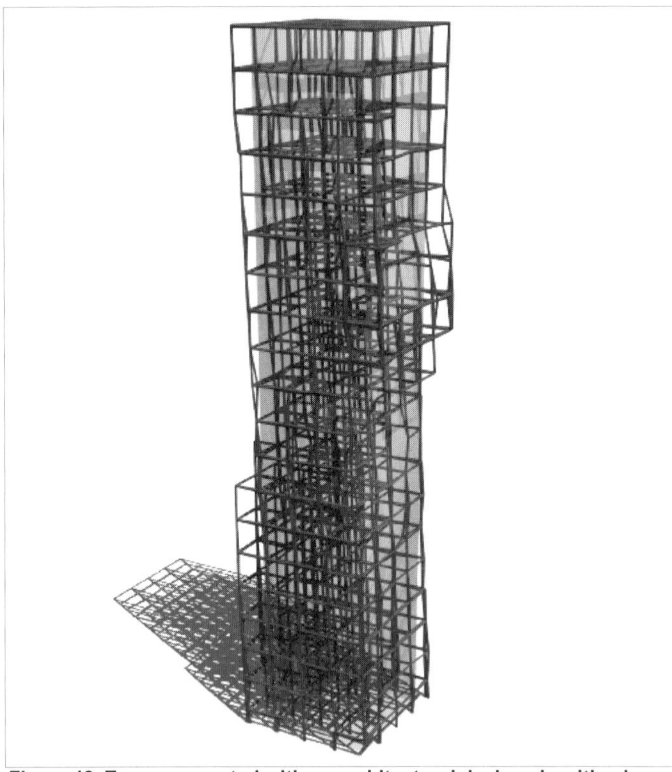

Figure 12. Tower generated with an architectural design algorithm based on Conway's Game of Life.

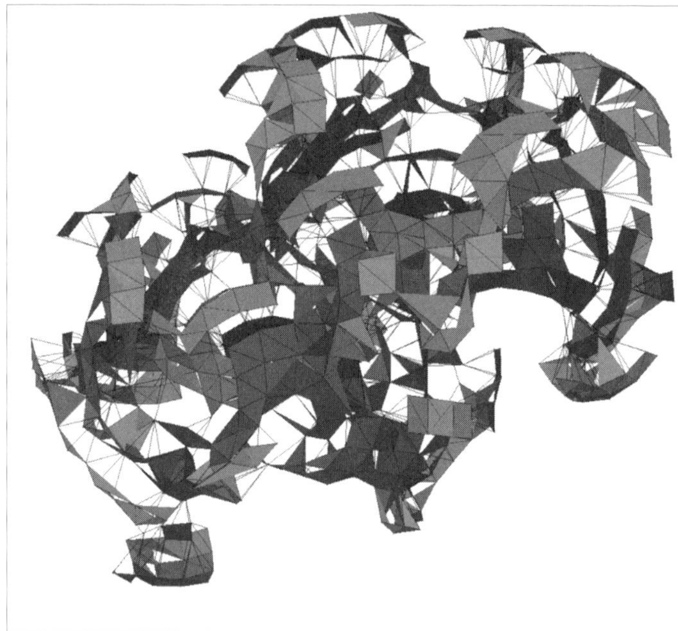

Figure 13. Structure generated within a landscape using a design algorithm based on Conway's Game of Life.

of supporting multiple states. This multi-state structure could provide for additional behaviors relating to program, site, and aesthetics—factors that have not yet been addressed in case studies.

The systems used in the case studies thus far have had limited capacity for testing local conditions. For elements of both the one-dimensional Cellular Automata and the Conway Variant, behaviors were based solely upon the state of each element's immediate neighbors. We propose to pursue methods of building behaviors based on an awareness of more than the immediate proximity, using methods similar to those developed for Neural Networks.

The environment and context of the CASs in the case studies have been described as fixed, not changing over time. To better simulate real-world applications of these systems, as well as to encourage evolution within the algorithms, we propose to pursue methods of constructing and testing these systems in continually varying environments.

References

Coxeter, H. S. M. (1973). *Regular polytopes*. New York: Dover Publications, Inc.

Gardner, M. (1970). Mathematical games: The fantastic combinations of John Conway's new solitaire game "life." *Scientific American* 223 (October): 120-123.

Hybers, P. (1997). The polyhedral world. In *Beyond the cube: The architecture of spaceframes and polyhedra*, ed. J. F. Gabriel. New York: John Wiley & Sons, Inc.

Neumann, J von, and A. W. Burks. (1966). *Theory of self-reproducing automata*. Urbana, Ill: University of Illinois Press.

Nooshin, H., P. L. Disney, and O. C. Champion. (1997). Computer-aided processing of polyhedric configurations. In *Beyond the cube: The architecture of spaceframes and polyhedra*, ed. J. F. Gabriel. New York: John Wiley & Sons, Inc.

Pearce, P. (1990). *Structure in nature is a strategy for design.* Cambridge, MA: MIT Press.

Reynolds, C. W. (1987). Flocks, herds, and schools: A distributed behavioral model. *Computer graphics* 21(4):25-34 (SIGGRAPH '87 Conference Proceedings).

Testa, P., and U. O'Reilly. (2000). MoSS: Morphogenic surface structures. *Greenwich 2000 Conference Proceedings.* London: Interscience Communications.

Wuensche, A., and M. Lesser. (1992). *The global dynamics of cellular automata*. New York: Addison-Welsey.

Wolfram, S. (2002). *A new kind of science*. New York: Wolfram Media, Inc.

LiQuID: Lighting Quality for Design

James Peng, Ben Liao, Daniel Glaser, John Canny
University of California, Berkeley

Ellen Yi-Luen Do
University of Washington, Seattle

Abstract

In this paper, we present LiQuID, a tool for seeing lighting quality in design. Photographs are useful vehicles for both describing and making assessments of architectural lighting systems. A significant barrier to using photographs during the design process relates to the sheer volume of renderings that needs to be analyzed. Although there have been efforts to produce novel visualization systems to manage large sets of photographs, this research aims to reduce the complexity by classifying data into representative prototypes. A hypothetical case study is discussed.

LiQuID: Lighting Quality for Design

James Peng, Ben Liao, Daniel Glaser, John Canny
University of California, Berkeley

Ellen Yi-Luen Do
University of Washington, Seattle

1 Motivation and Background

In the past decade, there have been significant advancements in CAAD for both describing and assessing architectural lighting. The former is about deriving numbers and rendering images to describe a lighting system. The latter deals with issues between lighting systems and occupants, energy consumption, and thermal interactions[1]. Assessment and description are not mutually exclusive activities. Lighting designers calculate daylight factors during the design process to "see light" across multiple sky positions during the design process (Erwine 1999). Moeck and Selkowitz (Moeck and Selkowitz 1995) argue the value of using photorealistic images during the analysis phase of lighting design. Performance indices may not be quantifiable upfront since, for example, precise metrics of glare are still unknown[2]. Hence, lighting design and analysis is both about imagery and numbers[3].

Generative design characterizes the approach of model building and testing under a variety of simulation conditions. Daylight varies by viewpoint, time of day, day in year, and sky condition (Figure 1). A major limitation of generative design tools is that there is "too much to describe," and analysis can be short circuited before the right data is looked at. Lighting is a complex, multivariate problem, and just generating performance graphs or images may not guarantee a comprehensive view of the data. Although certain design programs (Moeck and Selkowitz 1995), (Glaser, Voung et al. 2003), and (Papamichael, Lai et al. 2002), offer innovative ways of looking at design, they require a generate/test cycle to assess lighting performance. Due to the large parameter space, though, it is difficult to generate an effective number of test cases. For example, in most of these programs, the user would have to click a mouse button thousands of times to examine a year of data! This problem is partially overcome with more condensed or sophisticated visual representations (e.g. (Cheng and Pat-Yak Lee 2001; Glaser and Ubbelohde 2002), but they do not afford in depth analysis of lighting performance.

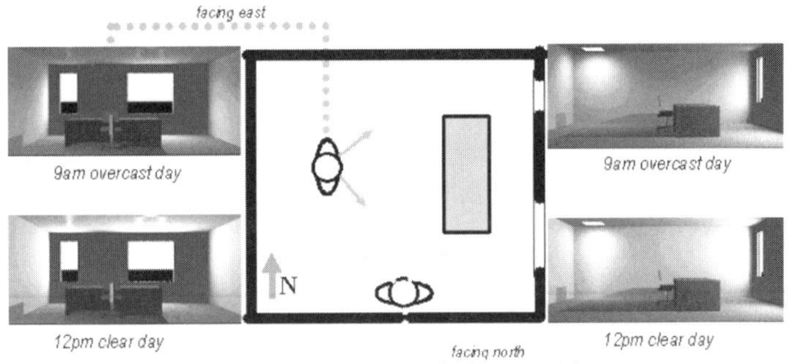

Figure 1. Lighting quality varies by viewpoint, time, and sky conditions.

We propose using clustering as a primary method for improving the process of lighting quality analysis in a generative design environment. It is based upon the theory that similar data, whether numerical or visual, can be grouped together to reduce the problem size (Aldenderfer and Blashfield 1984) (Marks, Andalman et al. 1997). Clustering does not hide important details about lighting quality that are lost with reductive performance analysis methods. Instead, it allows an architect to see the major trends in their data for focusing their description/ analysis cycle. This paper presents the design tool LiQuID (Lighting Quality In Design) which aids in the classification and visualization of lighting quality data.

2 Generating Parameter Spaces in LiQuID

LiQuID develops a comprehensive parameter space for lighting quality analysis. It starts with the room layout and deconstructs it into both abstract geometric planes and perspectives. LiQuID takes the approach that building occupant's visual needs are not limited to a single perspective, but instead will vary according to a number of factors. When the viewpoint changes, so does the geometrical region of interest. Figure 2 illustrates the four-stage process that LiQuID uses for judging lighting quality.

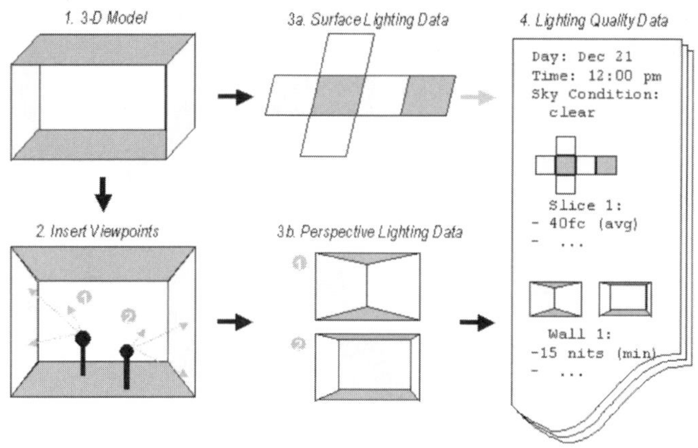

Figure 2. LiQuID generates lighting quality data in four stages. It starts with a 3D model with both electric and daylight sources (stage 1). Viewpoints are inserted at stage 2. At stage 3, both surface and perspective lighting data are generated for a range of sun angles and sky conditions and tabulated in stage 4. Note the gray arrow denotes future work.

2.1 Analysis of Geometry Files

LiQuID relies on building geometry and simulation data from the program LightSketch (Glaser, Voung et al. 2003) to perform its analysis. LightSketch is a sketch-based interface for designing architectural models with both natural and daylight features. After the user has completed the design of a space in LightSketch, the geometry of room is stored into RADIANCE (Ward 1994) compatible files. These geometry files contain information about the dimensions, layout, and locations of the various features within the building design. The size and orientation of wall surfaces are described as adjoining collections of three-dimensional coordinates. The locations and size of windows and skylights are similarly instantiated, while the geometry files regarding the luminaires also contain additional information about the luminous intensity and cutoff angle.

By examining the general layout of a building design, architects and lighting designers are able to employ certain heuristics to judge the performance and visual quality of their design. This is not a definitive measure of lighting quality, as it does not take into account individualized lighting conditions and specific concerns about the function of spaces. Nevertheless, industry standard handbooks (e.g. (Illuminating Engineering Society et al. 2000; Benya et al. 2001) provide a straightforward methodology to critique and improve upon designs. Directly from the geometry files, LiQuID can calculate the ratio of wall size and window size and note the walls with window-to-wall-size ratios of less than the recommended 20% (Illuminating Engineering Society et al. 2000). Examining the effects of luminaires upon actual viewers within a room is a complex issue, but can be partially addressed through simpler calculations. For example, LiQuID can calculate the location and range of sight from the viewer's perspective in comparison to the location and angle of a luminaire to identify direct glare.

2.2 Specifying and Locating Viewpoints

To generate luminance information, viewpoint locations and directions must be identified. This can be done either manually or automatically. Entering manual viewpoints allow for design-specific information such as identifying a place in the room that a person will likely be sitting at. Viewpoints can also automatically be generated by using the simple heuristic of looking at multiple directions at the center of the room. The emphasis on multiple views allows for a more descriptive analysis than a single view determination of lighting quality.

2.3 Surface and Perspective Data

The simulated lighting patterns within a building design are represented as a grid of luminance or illuminance values, called a slice. Each slice can represent a vertical or horizontal plane within the room, or it can represent a perspective from a viewpoint within the room. Slices derive their values from arrays of numbers in input text files or from input image files. Slices were chosen to be approximately 200x100 for images, and 20x20 for illuminance data. They are typically generated from a 12x6 sampling of a sky database, taking approximately 4 minutes with a 1.3Ghz Pentium III processor.

2.4 Lighting Quality Data

The lighting quality data that LiQuID creates allows for both formulaic and photo analysis. The quantitative analyses are still relatively basic compared with the clustering for photo analysis described in the next section. This includes determining window to wall ratios, checking sight angles for direct glare with electric light fixtures, and providing luminous intensity ranges. They are described in more detail in Section 4.

3 Clustering in LiQuID

After sketching a design and performing multiple lighting simulations across different variables, images are passed into LiQuID for analysis. A simulation is defined as the calculation of luminance and illuminance values for the design at a single specified period of time. For each simulation, images are created for all room surfaces and viewpoints within the design. Images representing one simulation are compiled into data structures called DayStructs and then fed into a clustering process. The clustering process groups DayStructs according to their similarity across a lighting quality variable, such as pattern, glare level, or uniformity of lighting. Currently LiQuID follows a data-driven approach, clustering the DayStructs according to similar lighting patterns in their image files and then performing analysis on the cluster results.

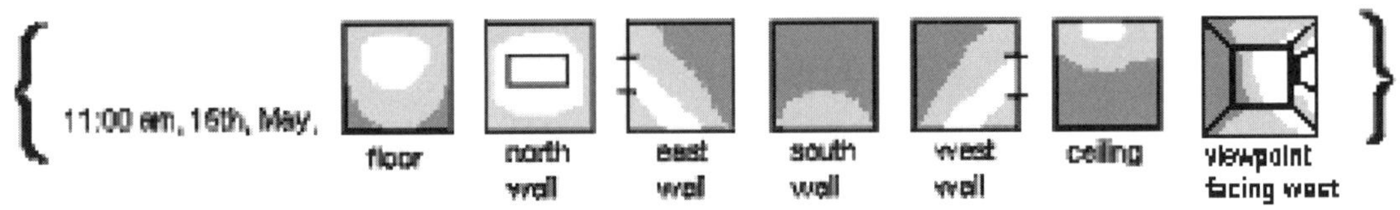

Figure 3. An example DayStruct: It is composed of a time/date header and followed by 2d planes known as Slices

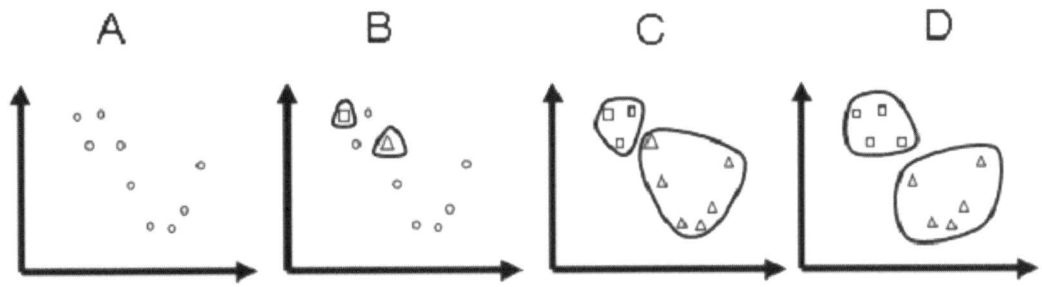

Figure 4. A) Initial Data B) Selection C) Assignment D) Reassignment

3.1 Data Structures

LiQuID stores lighting quality data in daystructs composed of multiple slices. A slice represents one viewpoint or one surface of the model for a single simulation. For example, it could represent the lighting luminance values of looking at the north side of a room March 2nd at 2 pm. A daystruct contains multiple viewpoints, luminance or illuminance values that may be pertinent for analysis of the 3D model for that period of time. It is essentially a collection of Slices with a time/date header Figure 3.

3.2 Clustering Algorithm

One of the problems that designers face is the large amount of lighting simulation data that would have to be sorted through and analyzed to accurately understand the lighting quality of their designs. Taking simulation samples randomly throughout the year to try to get a sample representation or a classification of a design's lighting quality is often tedious as well as specious, as a sample selection can be biased or not comprehensive. Therefore, the simulator program that LiQuID utilizes must uniformly and thoroughly simulate the model through different lighting conditions throughout the specified time of day, month and year, eliminating the possibility of selection bias.

To deal with a large amount of lighting simulations requires an algorithm that could take data and classify it into smaller representative units while still retaining most of the relevant information. Clustering algorithms, in general, take sets of data and partition them into groups that are "similar", as well as finding representative units for each partition. Aldenderfer and Blashfield (Aldenderfer and Blashfield 1984) have defined a clustering algorithm as a multivariate statistical procedure that starts with a data set containing information about a sample of entities and attempts to reorganize these entities into relatively homogeneous groups . For example, if a DayStruct set contained 33 simulations with extremely "high glare", 24 simulations with "uniform light", and 1 simulation which was "very dark", then a clustering algorithm would group the 33 high glare DayStructs into a "high glare" cluster, the 24 uniform lighting DayStructs into a "uniform lighting" cluster, and the 1 dark DayStruct into its very own set. Now the old set of 58 (33+24+1=58) DayStructs can instead be represented by 3 DayStructs and 3 numbers indicating the frequency that each DayStruct occurs in the set. Similarly, LiQuID clusters its simulation data and classifies them such that large quantities of similar DayStructs are represented by fewer DayStructs.

3.3 K-means Algorithm

Clustering algorithms mainly fall into two categories: hierarchical and non-hierarchical. The first type of clustering, mostly composed of algorithms known as agglomerative clustering, takes data and combines similar elements from the bottom up. In LiQuID's case, it would continuously make passes through the DayStruct set and in each pass, combine the two "most similar" DayStructs, forming them into a new cluster and thus reducing the set's size by 1. The process continues until there is only the desired number of clusters left. Agglomerative algorithms may take a large amount of time, especially in finding the "most similar" clusters to combine in each pass. Non-hierarchical clustering methods instead attempt to determine the representative DayStruct of the resulting clusters beforehand and build from there. Instead of comparing every DayStruct against each other to determine the two most similar DayStructs, each DayStruct is only compared against representative DayStructs for each pre-selected cluster. Non-hierarchical methods are often arbitrary in selecting the beginning clusters and can make unwise initial selections (like selecting extremely similar DayStructs to form two different clusters). This situation could result in bad cluster formations, but on average, non-hierarchical methods are fairly quick and relatively accurate (He 1999). Currently, LiQuID implements a non-hierarchical clustering method called K-means. The K-means algorithm is a non-deterministic clustering method. In general, the K-means algorithm initially chooses k number of DayStructs to form clusters and then slowly refines each cluster to optimize its results. One tradeoff for K-means though is that the more clusters that DayStructs are partitioned into, the more accurate and detailed the results are, but only at the cost of slower processing time. Therefore at the risk of over-allocating memory resources, more detail and more clusters may want to be generated for more detailed results.

Figure 4 illustrates the principles of his K-means algorithm. The figure shows K-means' four main steps ("A" through "D"). "A" describes the initial set of data. The pictures, stored as DayStructs, are represented by x-y coordinates on a 2d plane. This is a common technique in multidimensional scaling to manage complex data such as images. In step "B", the Selection step is to choose a specified number (K) of DayStructs as centroids. Centroids are defined as the representative DayStruct for each cluster. In the Assignment step "C", all other DayStructs are assigned to their most similar centroid. Thus the points are clustered into K different groups. During Reassignment, step "D", for each cluster, the centroids are recomputed to more accurately represent logical groups. It should be noted that steps "C" and "D" have a repetitive aspect to achieve optimal clustering (which is described in more detail in (MacQueen 1967)).

3.4 Divide and Conquer

Due to a potentially enormous size of the data sets (thousands of DayStructs of multiple images), resources have to be carefully allocated. LiQuID implements its own divide and conquer K-means clustering algorithm to avoid simultaneous management of all DayStructs. It starts by dividing the set of DayStruct into smaller subsets and clustering each subset using the K-means algorithm. Afterwards, the divide and conquer clustering algorithm is performed on the centroids of all the subsets' clusters, eventually resulting in the desired K number of clusters with each their respective centroids. This efficient use of resources allows LiQuID to manage large and complicated datasets.

3.5 Determining K

Using the K-means clustering algorithm, LiQuID runs into the problem of deciding upon the appropriate number of the K clusters. If LiQuID selects too small of a K, DayStructs that are fundamentally different may be combined into the same cluster and thus be classified the same, losing important and distinguishing lighting information. Conversely, too many clusters may defeat the purpose of clustering in the first place—namely to categorize similar data together. Currently, this problem is resolved in an ad-hoc way—with the user responsible for adding or subtracting clusters.

4 LiQuID Architecture

LiQuID is a program responsible for coordinating parameter selection with lighting quality analysis (Figure 5). By interacting with a modeler, it sets a broad range of visual and environmental parameters for daylight simulation. After the simulations are run, it serves as a processor for quantitative and visual analysis. Hence, LiQuID is positioned to capitalize on the extensive work on modeling, simulation, and analysis for lighting design.

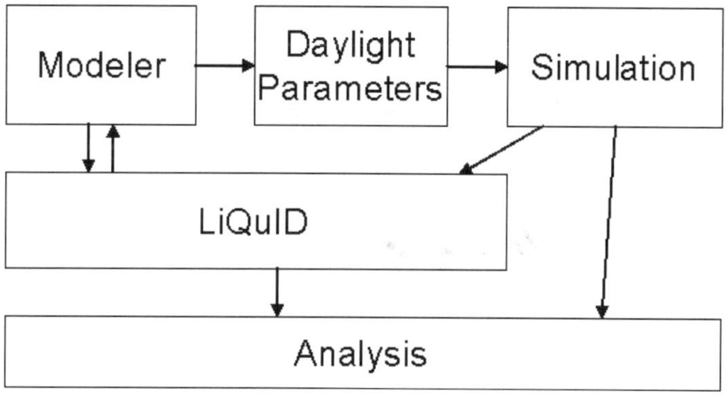

Figure 5 LiQuiD is positioned as a middleware application to coordinate the modeler with analysis components.

4.1 Modeling, Setting Parameters, and Simulation with LightSketch

LiQuID works in conjunction with the existing research program LightSketch (Glaser, Voung et al. 2003). In terms of Figure 5, Lightsketch performs the role of both modeler, parameter setter, and simulation driver. As an architectural modeler, LightSketch allows a user to quickly sketch a layout of a building and arrange the placement of windows, skylights, and various forms of luminaires. Unlike other more complex CAD programs, LightSketch only requires the understanding of a small set of architectural symbols. While the user draws and connects strokes upon the canvas, LightSketch automatically straightens out lines, which are interpreted as walls. Sketching a short line over an existing wall creates a window, while drawing small circles and boxes creates various types of luminaires and skylights in those locations. Simple to learn and use, LightSketch is intended as application for designing a building without requiring much time or technical expertise with specialized architectural software.

Aside from making 3D lighting model, LightSketch is capable of setting daylight parameters and running simulations. Multiple variables including time, date, weather, sky condition, and location can be set inside of LightSketch. The program can then drive Radiance simulations and output both luminance and illuminance data. Figure 6 illustrates a model drawn in LightSketch and illuminance data produced from it. The model is square with an east-facing window with two skylights. The illuminance data is generated though varying two time axes during clear sky conditions.

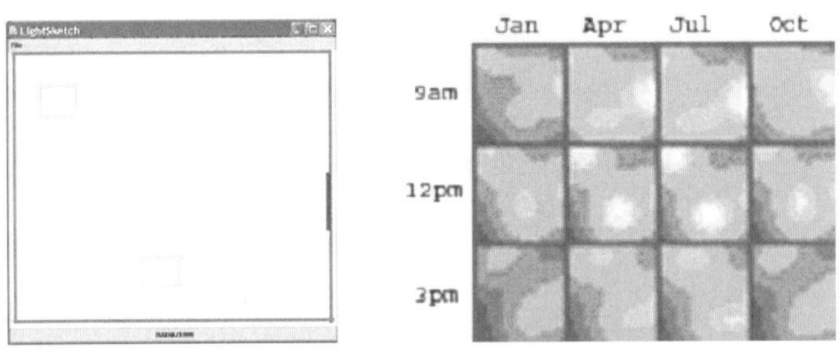

Figure 6. LightSketch showing a square room with an east window, and two skylights (left). Performance results (right), at workplane height for 4 times in the year at 3 times of day.

4.2 LiQuID

LiQuID uses a simple set of panels to aid with daylight parameter selection and analysis preferences (Figure 7). LiQuID uses this information to drive the simulation across the user specified ranges and for creating cluster sizes.

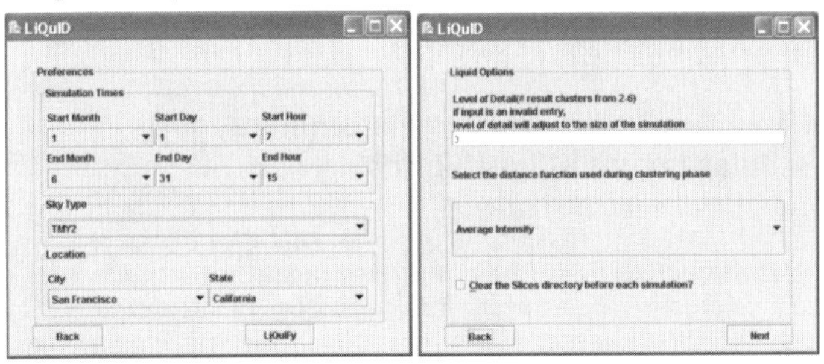

Figure 7. Portions of the LiQuID driver panel. (left) For selection of temporal, sky, and location parameters, and (right) features of the clustering utility

4.3 LiQuID Cluster Viewer and Inspector Analysis Modules

Figure 7 is a screenshot of the liquid driver panel. By modifying the level of detail requested, one can adjust the number of clusters to create. As discussed in section 3.5, this is currently done with a user input box to select the number of clusters. This flexibility is important since the data will vary in complexity (e.g. just analyzing a simple model under clear sky conditions will produce markedly different results than a complex one with measured sky conditions) and will need an appropriate number of categories to describe them. Also, the user is allowed to use two types of similarity metrics—by intensity, or a simplified glare index. Using a DG approach, the "perceptually similar" metric has been realized as comparing intensities across an image and as having similar glare effects.

The Cluster Viewer displays the results of LiQuID's clustering process. The viewpoints for each centroid (representative) is displayed along with each cluster's size (Figure 8). In this case, the 12 data points sampled were divided into three clusters of size 3, 2, and 7 daystructs respectively. The frequency of daystructs for each cluster is indicative of how often it occurs in the interval under analysis. In this case, Cluster 2 is the most frequent since 7 of 12 daystructs are most similar to its prototype. It tells us, for example, that the majority of time, the northwest skylight provides ample light across the walls it is adjacent to. Another module, the LiQuID Inpector, allows the user to see where each daystruct originates from.

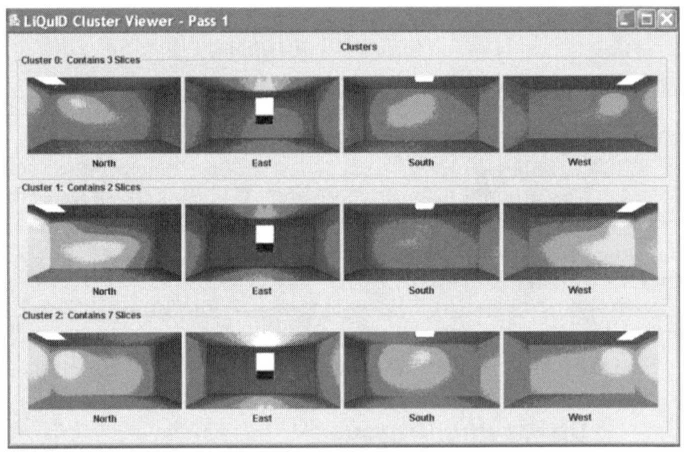

Figure 8. LiQuID's Cluster Viewer. It shows clusters (from top to bottom) and individual viewpoints for each cluster (left to right).

5 Use Scenario

Imagine that an architect, Jane, wishes to complete the fenestration scheme for an office with two exterior walls facing south and east respectively. Initially, Jane uses the program LightSketch to maximize the glazing on both exterior walls to provide for as much natural light as possible. She starts LiQuID and asks to see three clusters for lighting between 9am to 3pm. The images make clear that during this interval, under a range of sky conditions, there is far too much light. The numerical data confirms that she exceeded the recommended window to wall ratio which leads to unacceptable luminance distributions. Hence, she realizes that completely opening up the two walls would lead to a visually uncomfortable environment for most of the working day.

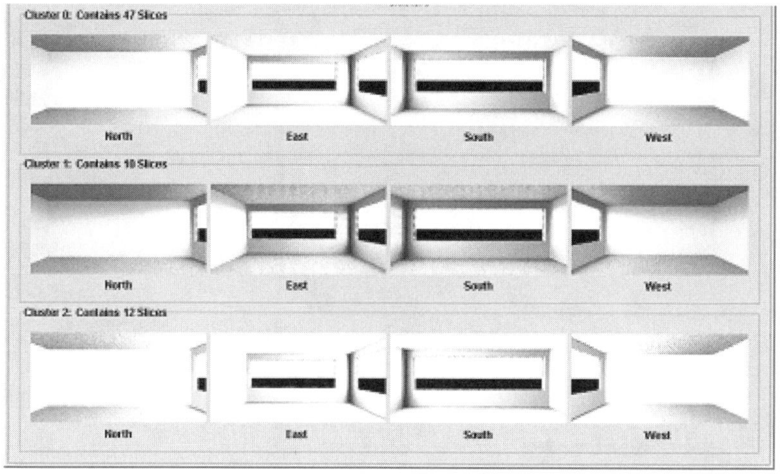

Figure 9. A sketch showing two very large windows (left) and three typical lighting conditions (right). Clusters "0" and "2" have excessive levels of glare, while the infrequent occurrence "1" is manageable.

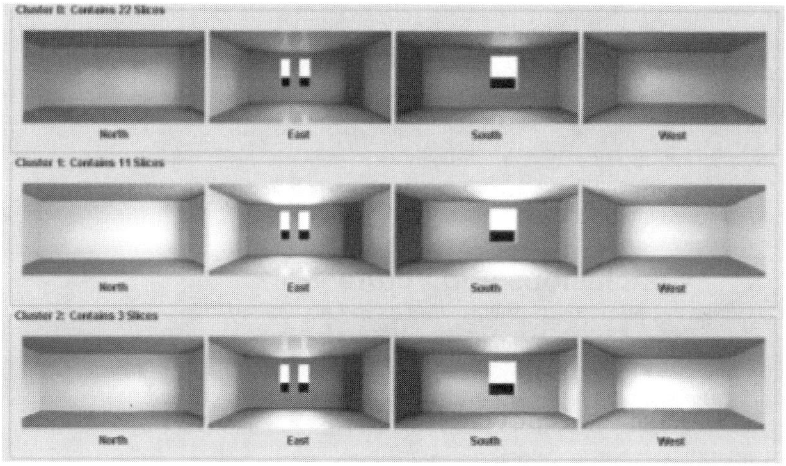

Figure 10. Using less glazing leads to a more acceptable lighting scheme. Frequently, the room appears a little dark (cluster "0"), but other times with patches of light are brighter.

Jane makes another sketch, this time using three smaller windows—two on the south side, while one on the east. She did not want to continue with her first design since she thought it would not be worth planning a shading control for the already costly large windows. She runs LiQuID on her new sketch to inspect a larger range of times (6am to 6pm) since she is more confident of her approach and is willing to wait for the additional calculations (which amount to less than a minute). Figure 10 shows the more acceptable results in LiQuID's cluster viewer. It is important to note that the relatively low light levels in Cluster 0 occur near twilight, while the high levels in Cluster 2 appear only early mornings with clear skies. The other times have generally acceptable visual quality.

Although her design does not seem to have any significant problems, Jane notices dark spots around the southeastern, and to a lesser extent, northwestern corners. Although they could be useful places for furniture, she decides to explore the possibilities of using skylight to brighten these areas. She decides to place one on its northwest and another on the southeast corners. LiQuID confirms that the apertures she draws removes the darker areas while providing more visual interest to the model without allowing for too much light (Figure 11).

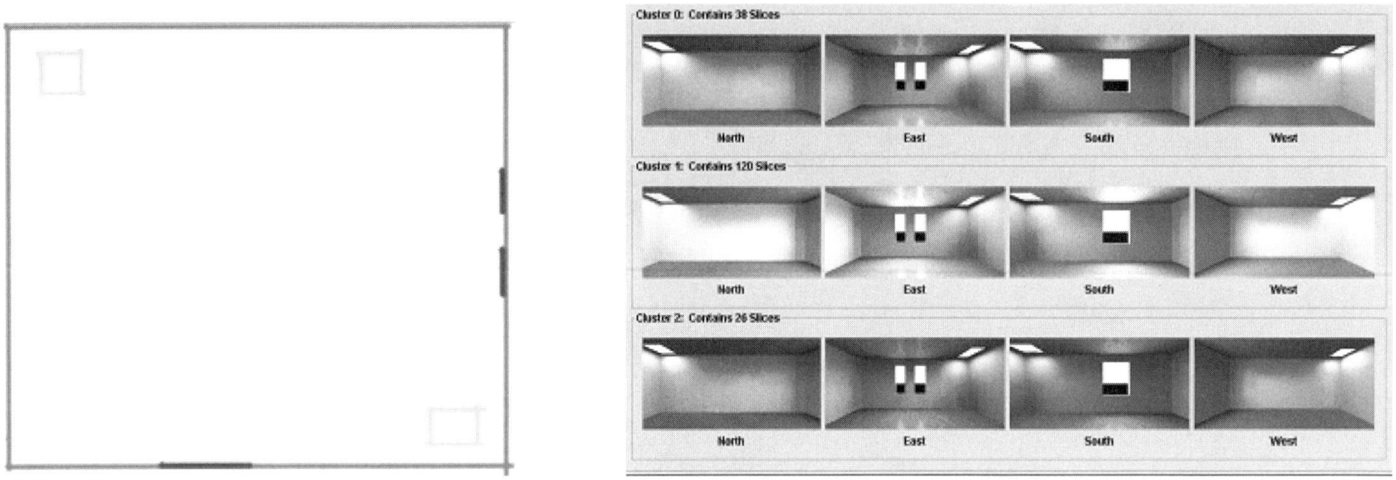

Figure 11. Adding skylights both brightens dimly lit corners and provides for more regions of visual interest.

Although it is arguable that this is a fully worked out and tested design (e.g. there is no electric lighting scheme for night occupancy, the skylights do not have diffusers, the dimensioning is still not refined, etc.), it shows how an architect could use LiQuID and LightSketch to quickly create a building design and judge its lighting quality. General trends in the data were reflected in the clusters, which were computed automatically and without a complicated interface.

6 Conclusions and Future Work

By analyzing numerous lighting simulations across multiple variables, LiQuID extracts useful lighting information from an architectural model. LiQuID aims to relieve architects and lighting designers from the tedious work required to analyze countless potential lighting situations. Also, it aims to remove some of the oversimplifications and generalizations about daylight that are utilized when evaluating lighting systems. Therefore by doing careful analysis of a comprehensive amount of simulations, LiQuID aims to provide reliable, accurate and legible feedback to building designers to encourage them to incorporate visual and environmental concerns of daylighting into their designs.

The integration of architectural modeling, lighting simulation, computer-aided classification, and lighting quality analysis is inherently a complicated issue. We are planning on improving the modeling capabilities to include more sophisticated sky descriptions and more variables for energy efficiency. More sophisticated clustering algorithms will also be employed to both improve the automation and also develop the classification system. In its current implementation, LiQuID uses a data driven process for grouping individual images for lighting simulation. Future versions will also consider classifying ranges of data to account for similarities among larger temporal units such as mornings, entire days, and weeks. The classification system can also be augmented by directly incorporating normative lighting characteristics. Lastly, links to easier to use output programs are being developed.

References

Aldenderfer, M. S. and R. K. Blashfield (1984). Cluster Analysis, Sage Publications.

Benya, J., L. Heschong, T. McGowan, N. Miller and F. Rubinstein, Eds. (2001). Advanced Lighting Guidelines. White Salmon, WA, New Buildings Institute.

Cheng, N. and E. Pat-Yak Lee (2001). Depicting Daylighting: Types of Multiple Image Display. Proceedings of the Association for Computer Aided Design in Architecture (ACADIA '01), Buffalo, New York.

Erwine, B. (1999). Daylight Models. Seattle, WA, Lighting Design Lab.

Glaser, D. and S. Ubbelohde (2002). "Techniques for Managing Planar Daylight Data." Building and Environment 37(8-9): 825-831.

Glaser, D., J. Voung, Y. Xiao, B. Thai, S. Ubbelohde, J. Canny and E. Do (2003). LightSketch: A sketch-modelling program for lighting analysis. CAAD Futures 2003, Tainan, Taiwan, Kluwer.

He, Q. (1999). Review of Clustering Algorithms as Applied in IR. Urbana-Champaign, Graduate School of Library and Information Science, University of Illinois: 33.

Illuminating Engineering Society, M. S. Rea and Illuminating Engineering Society of North America (2000). The IESNA lighting handbook : reference & application. New York, N.Y., Illuminating Engineering Society of North America.

MacQueen, J. (1967). Some Methods for Classification and Analysis of Multivariate Observations. Fifth Berkeley Symposium on Mathematical Statistics and Probability, Berkeley, CA, University of California Press.

Marks, J., B. Andalman, P. A. Beardsley, W. Freeman, S. Gibson, J. Hodgins and T. Kang (1997). Design Galleries: A General Approach to Setting Parameters for Computer Graphics and Animation. SIGGRAPH 97, Los Angeles, CA.

Moeck, M. and S. Selkowitz (1995). A Computer-Based Daylight Systems Design Tool. ACADIA, Seattle, WA.

Papamichael, K., J. Lai, D. Fuller and T. Tarik (2002). A Web-based Virtual Lighting Simulator. Proceedings of the Association for Computer Aided Design in Architecture (ACADIA '02), Pomona, CA.

Veitch, J. (2001). "Psychological processes influencing lighting quality." Journal of the Illuminating Engineering Society 30(1): 124-140.

Ward, G. (1994). "The radiance lighting simulation system." Computer Graphics 28(7): 459-72.

(Endnotes)

[1] See, for example, (Illuminating Engineering Society, Rea et al. 2000; Benya, Heschong et al. 2001; Veitch 2001) for more in depth discussion of these issues.

[2] Using images for lighting quality assessment has also been advocated by (Eissa, Mahdavi et al. 2001) for electric sources.

[3] The approach of using both photographs and quantitative results has also been advocated for teaching daylight (Hanna 1996).

08 >> Connecting Digital Data

Chairs: Julio Bermúdez, Stefano Foresti

Information Visualization

Julio Bermúdez, Stefano Foresti

Digital visualization addresses representational challenges from within and without architecture.

'Disciplinary' digital visualization is used to explore, understand and communicate architectural information associated with the production of buildings. 3D modeling, rendering, animation and VR as well as the power of digital media to permit the seamless integration of various data types are unleashing completely new ways to display architecture. As digital power continues to increase and get cheaper, portability and wi-fi networks take root, and visualization work becomes even more main stream, we can expect growing changes in the way the design process is conducted, buildings are presented and documented, and the public and 3rd party's demands from professional services. This demands a more conscious research/pedagogies aimed at developing new representation conventions.

'Interdisciplinary' digital visualization is a rapidly expanding area of expertise with competency ranging from artificial environments (e.g., Video game worlds, cinematographic stage sets, web and other cyber environments) to abstract data representation constructs (i.e., Information Architecture), this type of work has already generated quite a number of new jobs, educational programs and research projects in many industries, schools and universities. Whether or not this type of knowledge implies a different type of architect (e.g., Information Architect) is subject to debate. What is beyond argument is the fact that the need for this kind of expertise will only grow in the coming years. Therefore, it is imperative that architecture programs pay serious teaching and research attention to the areas of digital visualization.

Julio Bermúdez (M.Arch & PhD Minnesota) is an Associate Professor at the University of Utah College of Architecture & Planning. His research and pedagogic work focuses on the interaction between design process and digital media as well as the application of architectural concepts to data environments. His work has been widely published, exhibited and/or performed in the U.S. and abroad. In addition to being a member of the ACADIA and SIGradDi steering committees, Bermudez is in the advisory board of Leonardo.

Stefano Foresti is the Director of the Center for the Representation of Multi-Dimensional Information (CROMDI), and is a Senior Scientist for the Center for High Performance Computing (CHPC) at the University of Utah. He received his Doctorate in Mathematics at the Universita' di Pavia, Italy in 1987. He also served as a Post-Doctoral Fellow at the Center for Scientific and Engineering Computations at IBM in Kingston, NY, USA from 1988-1990.

Enhancing Architectural Communication with Gaming Engines

Michael Hoon, Michael Kehoe
New Jersey School of Architecture

Abstract

This paper makes a case for exploring the feasibility of utilizing the advanced graphics and sound systems of contemporary gaming engines to promote architecturally relevant work. Gaming engines, while developed largely for the PC entertainment industry, have vast potential for application in architecture. This paper will explore the depth of this potential and will outline work demonstrating the advantages and the limitations of this technology. The supporting research and observations examine the technology and reveal its potential usefulness as an instructional or depictive authoring tool. Game engines were selected that had appropriate graphical prowess, but were customizable as to allow the removal of game-specific features (to create a "professional" user interface). Projects were authored that expressed complex building details using the engine for visual depiction. The details, which included constructional components, structural assemblies, or simple design nuances, were modeled with 3D geometry and realistically textured and lighted. The game engine allowed one user or many remote simultaneous users in the virtual environment to interactively explore the presentation in real time. Scripts were developed to encourage end-users to interactively disassemble or reassemble building components as desired. Audile and/or text-based information regarding the assembly sequence were provided by exploiting the game interface features. Furthermore, interactive object scaling was provided to facilitate analysis of component relationships.

Enhancing Architectural Communication with Gaming Engines

Michael Hoon, Michael Kehoe
New Jersey School of Architecture

1 Introduction

The growing sophistication of gaming technology merits in-depth examination. Many popular computer games, while they may be seen as "casual" applications, ironically require more computational power than most business and CAD software. Optimized code, coupled with high-performance hardware graphics acceleration through OpenGL and DirectX, currently allows for high-resolution, richly textured simulations of real-time interactive spaces. Advanced spatial sound also serves to enhance user experiences. Multi-user capabilities allow several reviewers to simultaneously explore and interact within a single project through LAN or internet connections. Customizable avatars allow for user identification in the virtual environment and permit gesturing and observation of avatar-to-avatar and avatar-to-object interaction. The multi-user environment also indicates opportunities to examine such other user behaviors as way-finding, aggregation, and condition-specific reaction (e.g., overcrowding, fire propagation, prolonged elevator wait times, etc.). The results of student projects gleaned from two semesters of coursework will be used as a basis of student reaction and possible usefulness in academia. Experiences with client reaction to actual projects will also be offered. Additionally, seven years of independent research in gaming technologies will be referenced vis-à-vis its potential application in many aspects of architecture, such as design collaboration, interactive detailing, acoustics simulation, historical analysis, and life-safety simulation.

2 Early Research

Through research conducted as early as 1995, it was determined by the authors of this paper that gaming engines have credible potential as a design and presentation tool. In experimental digital design studios conducted at that time, projects were submitted in the form of animations, VRML worlds, and game environments. Research continued into the feasibility and effectiveness of these different methods. In specific regard to the observations of the use of gaming engines, the perceived impact, both positive and negative, on the development and presentation of conceptual spatial ideas will be explained. To better understand the usefulness and limitations of gaming engines in Architecture, practical experimentation was undertaken. In all, four game engines were examined *(Doom II, Quake I, Quake II, and Quake III,* all from ID Software*)* for their capacity to represent both existing spaces and conceptual spatial designs. While a range of findings were uncovered during testing with all of the aforementioned game engines, specific noteworthy aspects of potential application to architectural modeling and presentation are briefly summarized by focusing on one early project that utilized the Quake II engine.

Figure 1. Screen captures from urban residence project.

In 1998 the *Quake II* engine was used to depict a stage in the conceptual design process of an urban residence. The designer of the project agreed to consult on the game environment development while concurrently creating still renderings in *3D Studio 4* from Kinetix. Since the design had reached a developmental plateau before game modeling commenced, the work would involve only the transcribing of a conceptual design data and would not be used for design development until after presentation to the client.

The clients of the project were presented with the final results as a supplement to a traditional design proposal. The designer opened with a presentation of traditional plans, sections, elevations, and traditional digitally rendered image. The interactive game interpretation of the design was demonstrated next. Both clients demonstrated enthusiasm for the game presentation, stating that it had clarified many personally important issues, particularly in regard to material choices, spatial adjacencies, and visual accessibility. None of these issues were obscured in the traditional presentation; on the contrary, the designer conveyed these ideas quite lucidly.

In conclusion, the game model had acted to substantiate the same information that was given via traditional methods, which included both orthographic line drawings and detailed high-resolution renderings. It is not known how the clients would have reacted to the game presentation alone. Although the scope of these findings is limited, it was concluded that most laypeople will find value in interactive virtual presentations because of the diminished abstraction and the experiential nature of the depiction. Feasibility, however, was an unresolved question which needed be subjected to cost/value analysis.

The documentation of the urban dwelling design was extremely useful with regards to the clear, accessible representation of a complex conceptual design solution. Complemented by traditional tools, the game walk-through added an experiential dimension to the presentation and gave the clients valued confidence in the elapsed process, the current results, and the potential of continued design development.

Another documented experience with the *Quake II* engine is offered by Richens and Trinder, who used it advantageously in the design development of the new Computer Laboratory at the University of Cambridge.

3 Coursework

An elective course using gaming engines for the design and depiction of architectural space was developed by the authors and first offered in spring 2002, when the gaming engines and ancillary editing tools were judged to have reached an acceptable level of graphics capability and technical maturity. The purpose of the course was to introduce design students to the power of the game engines within an architectural context. While the structure of the course was based on the digital design studio paradigm, the additional capabilities of the game engine were used to exploit the potential for participant immersion, spatial interaction, and multi-user design collaboration.

Successfully negotiating the course necessitated a many-layered infusion of new skill sets for both students and instructor. Beyond new methods of 3D modeling and texture mapping, there was a need to learn new scripting conventions for object and surface behavior. While more mature 3D software can be expected to include high-level interfaces for the editing of scripted textures, or “shaders,” the script manipulations in the game interface had to be executed using text files.

There is only a cursory relationship between game engine tools and “industry-standard” architectural visualization tools. For example, there is a very limited offering of primitive geometry. The basic building block for game engine geometry is the hexagon (generally referred to as a “brush”), and higher-level geometry (including spheres) generally requires a skillful distillation of complex shapes and curves to constituent

Figure 2. Screen captures illustrating avatar and functional doors.

hexagons. Increasingly, game editors are supporting macros and plug-ins that will deliver complex shapes. However, the judicious designer must stay ever mindful of the true nature of the geometry in use, as a successfully executed wireframe model does not guarantee a successful final compilation or acceptable in-game performance. Furthermore, proper texture mapping generally requires painstaking refinement on a face-by-face level. For example, a texture which spans the multiple hexagons constituting a complex curve generally requires adjustment at the individual polygon faces for acceptable results.

Because of the limitations listed above, many experienced digital designers were easily frustrated; gratifying discoveries were often followed by difficult limitations. Comparisons to familiar modeling and rendering software were unavoidable, as students struggled to adapt to low-level techniques. Additionally, spatial designers needed to invent interfaces within the virtual environment to indicate to users the presence of "triggerable" events such as the deconstruction of a wall detail. Despite the difficulties, however, the open exploration of these issues forced designers to move beyond a static-image paradigm and consider their decision-making beyond a superficial level.

The game engines chosen for use in the course were versions of *Quake* engines. The original engines were modified to remove irrelevant gaming-specific features. Through a series of assignments within the course, students were asked to iteratively use and test the game engines for the collaborative exploration of a designed environment. After completing theoretical readings on virtual reality, the students were asked to design and create spatial environments using the 3D graphical editor *QuArK* (a freeware game level editor not to be confused with *QuarkXPress*). Students made their environments available for others to navigate in real-time and offer comments. Three design reviews were conducted during which critics were asked to enter the designed environments, explore at will, and interact with the student as well as others present in the same virtual spaces. Both local and remote reviewers participated. Communication was established through an IP voice channel and through avatar gesturing. An LCD projected image in the main critique space was periodically switched to display the first-person view of the currently speaking critic. Critics could allow their avatars to point or otherwise gesture in accordance with their voice comments.

Three major projects were required to complete the course. The first, an art gallery design proposal, accustomed the students to the interface and forced them to concentrate on circulation, lighting, and the development of custom texture libraries. In the second project, students used the scripting functions of the game application to explode a construction detail within a virtual space for abstract analysis. This also required careful consideration of how an exploding detail event should be announced to, and triggered by, those navigating a virtual space. The purpose of the final project was to express the cumulative knowledge of the semester in a student-devised project, in which each student was asked to demonstrate an accomplished understanding of the media. The projects submitted in the most recent offering of the course (which utilized a version of the Quake III engine) included a virtual museum for soft drink memorabilia, a recreation of Escher's infinite stairs, a modern day interpretation of Plato's Allegory of the Cave, several virtual spaces which adjusted their configuration according to user behavior, an enormously scaled section of a four-stroke internal combustion engine, and a poetic exploration of the threshold between real and unreal featuring disparate spaces, atmospheric soundtrack, and ambiguous movement.

Figure 3. Screen captures illustrating virtual gallery.

4 Observations

The following is a summary of current gaming technology features observed during periodic research outlined by the mentioned projects and assignments. They are intended to be specific to potential usefulness in architectural applications. Listings have been broadly categorized in terms of perceived advantages and limitations.

4.1 Advantages

- Fully Interrogative. Movement is not forcefully prescribed or scripted. By observing the directional tendencies of participants, as well as their propensity to linger or aggregate in particular spaces, architects can tailor designs changes responsively to the more efficient use of all spatial resources.
- Tactile Solidity. Solids in game environments assert their solidity. Through collision-detection, gaming engines allow for proper navigation through spaces bounded by solid elements such as walls as well as realistic navigation of staircases and ramps.
- Integrated Audio. Sounds can be ambient, or triggered by specific events in the virtual game world, complementing the visual stimuli.
- Multiple Simultaneous Users. Designed game environments can be simultaneously experienced by multiple remote participants.
- Inclusion of Avatars. Networked implementations allowing multi-participant interactions provide an enriched simulation of the human/spatial dynamic.

Figure 5. Screen captures illustrating object/avatar scale.

Figure 4. Screen captures demonstrating experiential juxtaposition.

- Simulation of Movement. The dynamic relationship of occupants to spatial boundaries allows better understanding of the ergonomic characteristics of a space. Observation of travel time further enhances the understanding of spatial juxtaposition, hierarchy, and scale.
- Simulation of Site. Environments with views of the surrounding world can be modeled using panoramic texture-mapping to simulate distant views. Support for alpha-channel texturing further allows decreased-overhead inclusion of simulated site elements such as landscaping, fencing, skylines, etc.
- Interaction with Objects. Although it is currently limited, newer engines allow for increasingly higher levels of realistic player interaction with inanimate objects set in the virtual world.

4.2 Limitations

- Comprehensiveness. The entire environment must be addressed and modeled. 'Minor' spaces and details may receive as much scrutiny as major ones. As abstraction diminishes, so do the benefits of its economy. (This can be considered an advantage of the tool.)
- Complexity. Game environment creation software currently lacks turnkey functionality and professional polish. Familiarity with traditional CAD and modeling software is often more a hindrance than a help.
- Geometry Limitations. Objects in any possible scene must be rendered in real time. Most game environments necessarily avoid excessive geometric detail opting instead for textural detail, with mixed results.
- Lack of Standardization. The finer points of the virtual depictions (textures, behaviors, sounds) do not translate very well among the various game content creation packages. File exchange with industry-standard modeling and rendering software, while improving, is still very limited.

5 Summary

Most students who used the software displayed energetic enthusiasm for the game engine as design tool. Many were willing to learn programming languages to gain better control of the appearance and behavior of textures and moving objects within the space. While undertaking the complete design and modeling of even a small building proved daunting, many students found gratification and freedom in the move away from the still-image representational paradigm. Interestingly, many of the projects deemed successful by students and critics alike were generally more experiential than spatial in nature; keen observation of circulation tendencies and an understanding of the importance of spatial sequencing became desirable skills as still-image refinement skills were shelved.

6 Future Research

Research to further refine avatar behavior within the virtual environment is planned as the next step in the evolution of this technology as it applies to architectural design. As avatars act more realistically, it is believed that designers can more confidently create spaces that better respond to their movements and behaviors. (For previously accomplished research, changes to avatar behavior were affected after observation of students walking through hallway spaces, specifically their behavior when approaching oncoming students and their need for personal space.)

Another planned research pursuit is the successful translation of game character artificial intelligence to building components within the virtual environment. In theory, this would allow building components to respond intelligently to changes in climate, lighting, structural loads, or inhabitant behavior. The potential benefits of this research were positively demonstrated by scripted object behaviors observed during coursework.

7 Conclusion

Architecture is a profession which relies heavily on the clear and accurate communication of design intent. The sophistication of recent gaming engines brings to light many capabilities that have potential within architecture to meet these needs by leveraging the power of the modern personal computer. Through practical experimentation and observation, the research outlined by this paper has attempted to determine the nature and the direction of this technology.

References

Campbell, D., and M. Wells. (1994). A critique of virtual reality in the architectural design process.

Technical Report: R-94-3, University of Washington. Retrieved March 20, 2001 from the World Wide Web: http://www.hitl.washington.edu/publications/r-94-3/

Chronis,G., and W. Knibbe. (1998). The game engines of the not-too-distant future. IDG.net
Retrieved March 20, 2001 from the World Wide Web: http: //cgi.cnn.com/TECH/computing/9808/21/gameengines.idg/

Davis, S. B., A. Huxor and J. Lansdown. (1996). The design of virtual environments with particular reference to VRML. A Report for the Advisory Group on Computer Graphics. Retrieved March 18, 2001 from the World Wide Web: http://www.agocg.ac.uk/reports/virtual/vrmldes/title.htm

Isakovic, K. (1997). Commercial 3D graphic game engines. Technical University of Berlin. Retrieved March 18, 2001 from the World Wide Web: http://cg.cs.tu-berlin.de/~ki/game_eng.html

Richens, P., and M. Trinder. (1999). Exploiting the internet to improve collaboration between users and design team.

Cambridge University. Retrieved October 21, 2002 from the World Wide Web: http://www.arct.cam.ac.uk/research/pubs/pdfs/rich99a.pdf

Student work courtesy of Akekarach Paibulkulsiri, Mark Lagunzad, Aaron Fredericks, and Brandon Amodeo.

Fluid (in)form: Influencing Design Through Dynamic Particle Simulation*

John Maze, Mark McGlothlin, Kim Tanzer
University of Florida

Abstract

"My earliest childhood memories are related to a ranch my family owned near the village of Mazamitla. It was a pueblo with hills, formed by houses with tile roofs and immense eaves to shield passersby from the heavy rains which fall in that area. Even the earth's color was interesting because it was red earth. In this village, the water distribution system consisted of great gutted logs, in the form of troughs, which ran on a support structure of tree forks, five meters high, above the roofs. The aqueduct crossed over the town, reaching the patios, where there were great stone fountains to receive the water. The patios outside the stables, with cows and chickens, all together. Outside, in the street, there were iron rings to tie the horses. The channeled logs, covered with moss, dripped water all over town, of course. It gave this village the ambience of a fairy tale."
(Luis Barragan,qtd in Ambasz 1976)

1 Premise

The early work of Christopher Alexander and Nicholas Negroponte marked the beginning of architects' selective flirtation with computational technologies. In recent years, work developed in the context of Columbia's Paperless Studio and its spin-offs has embraced the fluid form-making potential of programs such as Maya in an effort to subvert the strictures of Cartesian space. This group has also challenged the authorial will of the individual architect by assigning spatial and temporal properties to abstract concepts and setting these now-spatialized concepts in motion. The resulting interaction produces a collision of amorphous forms, currently described colloquially as "blobs."

Our project takes the same issues—the quest for an appropriate fit between computational promise and form-making and a fascination with shaping complex flows—in a different direction. We pose this architectural question: How does architecture shape and redirect one of the earth's physical "flows"—water—as it falls in the form of rain? Can we model rainfall digitally, and then shape surfaces such as roofs, terraces or landscapes to design the flow of water? Can this flow be conceived as a design opportunity, contributing to the phenomenal experience of a project as it is simultaneously shed more responsibly to the larger landscape? Can the poetic exploration of fluids prevalent within the academy be transformed into equally poetic tangible applications?

These are some of the questions we set out to explore, working in collaboration with colleagues in the University of Florida Global Information Systems Center and Digital Worlds Institute (DW). Fifteen students and three faculty members culled from our senior architecture studio met over a period of several weeks with faculty and graduate students with expertise in urban planning, engineering and fine arts. First our architecture students were required to develop a rudimentary understanding of GIS regional mapping capacity, with a particular emphasis on the study of hydrology and watersheds across our watery state of Florida. Following this regional analysis we developed a method to demonstrate the water shed by individual student's projects set within this larger landscape. Students first translated their physical models of modest (1000 sf) projects into three-dimensional digital models, then into animations to which rain could be "applied." Students' representations moved from chalk pastel to GIS to basswood to AutoCAD to 3D Studio Max and finally to Maya. Difficulties in translation and changes in material behaviors occurred at each state, and form the primary focus of this paper.

*A Digital *Work In Progress*

Fluid (in)form: Influencing design through dynamic particle simulation

John Maze, Mark McGlothlin, Kim Tanzer
University of Florida

2 Precedents

Since Renaissance theorists Alberti and Brunelleschi developed a systematic process to construct three-dimensional perspectives on a two-dimensional plane, architects and theorists have forayed into various emergent technologies of spatial representation. Rene Descartes used algebra to develop a coordinate system that removed the necessity of tools or even reference to the real world. Nearly four hundred years later, during the 1980's, a new type of spatial research and system emerged in the guise of virtual reality. Early attempts to create a multi-sensual virtual world required a pair of goggles, headphones, and a glove so that one could see, hear, and feel objects modeled in a computer environment. These interfaces were quite cumbersome, and of course inconvenient if one were to imagine working with such a situation on a daily basis. However, they did set the foundation for countless later attempts at designing an artificial world, a cyberspace as described by William Gibson in Neuromancer:

...cyberspace has a spatial and architectural form that is dematerialized, dynamic and devoid of the laws of physics; spaces in which the mind can explore free of the body; spaces that are in every way socially constructed, produced and abstract. As such, the architecture of cyberspace only mirrors that of Cartesian logic if that is how we straitjacket it.(Gibson 1984)

Arguably, a digital aesthetic has emerged in the architectural world. Those who have begun to explore the notion of an indigenous digital architectural language have come to utilize similar design elements, forms, and spaces in their work. Offices such as the UNstudio, Asymptote, Greg Lynn Form, Architectonics, and Diller-Scofidio who strive to find the architecture of cyberspace instead of simulating the architecture of the physical world have published widely their flowing, transparent, layered projects that seem quite as home in a molecular biology experiment as in a design studio context. Entranced by the idea of interconnectivity, speed, efficiency, and spatial dynamics, these designers began to explore forms only possible through the use of computer modeling technology. New formal typologies continue to emerge that challenges our understanding of the built and designed environment. As these projects begin to be built, often requiring new technologies of construction and fabrication, we start to understand the physical inhabitation of such dynamic environments as being quite different than those of the parallel and angular.

Since the early 1990s, dynamic digital forms have proliferated in graduate schools across the world, thanks largely to the efforts of young faculty members at schools such as Columbia University, Princeton, Cooper Union, UCLA, and Sci-Arc. What is important to note is that by the early nineties, graduates and recent graduates architects were the first generation to not have been educated by the giants of modernism, such as Le Corbusier, Kahn, Aalto, and Mies. The tenets of modernism were distilled through an older generation of faculty, who themselves were exploring ways to expand upon the dogma of their teachers. Hungry for a new language of design, a new way to understand urban form and space, this new generation looked to the digital revolution for inspiration.

Liquid architecture is an architecture that breathes, pulses, leaps as one form and lands as another. Liquid architecture is an architecture whose form is contingent on the interests of the beholder; it is an architecture that opens to welcome me and closes to defend me; it is an architecture without doors and hallways, where the next room is always where I need it to be and what I need it to be.(Novak 1991)

Perhaps the most noted innovator of digital architecture is Greg Lynn. Lynn began adapting software to the design of complex conceptual models in the late 1980's while at Eisenman Architects, and has continued to evolve his practice and research along with the digital explosion of the 1990's. What Lynn professes to do is typical of his generation--mapping contextual and programmatic forces of a project then modeling them in a way that allows the architecture to grow directly from the data. In this sense, the will of the architect is removed from the equation, and the design is autogenerative. For instance, he uses software such as Maya to create particle flows that simulate pedestrian and vehicular traffic in his entry for the Port Authority Gateway Competition. Particles are dispersed along routes of traffic responding to gravity and one another to create a "phase portrait" (Lynn 1998). Architectural form is then essentially derived directly from the vectors describing the motion of the particles. Many of the current generation of architects using this technology to create their formal language operate in this manner, allowing the software to create the architecture rather than simply to inform it.

One of the biggest problems with this type of design pedagogy is that it is predicated on the tool. Specifically, design possibilities are limited to a certain degree by the type of software used and the capabilities that the software has in relation to creating architectural form. Thanks to software packages such as Maya and Form Z, a new architectural language has emerged that challenges both the tenets of the discourse of architecture and standard construction means and methods. Not unexpectedly, projects built using this method tend to suffer from the abrupt translation from a digital to the physical realm.

While retaining a fascination with the fluid, we have applied the same digital parameters to understanding the dynamics of environmental forces that affect the built environment. Instead of modeling fluid forms that depict the circulation patterns of a site as Lynn does, we chose to simulate the fluid nature of water as it interacts with a building, so that the design may be improved accordingly. Ultimately we would hope to shape our chosen fluid, water, indirectly, by strategically shaping architectural form.

Process

To simulate this complex particle flow we needed tools and expertise beyond those available within our School of Architecture. At the same time, we have an interest in intensifying our school's commitment to useful and inventive applications of digital media to the architectural project. For these reasons we used this project to forge a connection between our School and one of the University of Florida's premier interdisciplinary centers, the Digital Worlds Institute currently housed jointly in the colleges of Engineering and Fine Arts. Like most large, research intensive public universities, ours has recently begun to espouse the belief that interdisciplinarity is the discipline of the 21st century. The University of Florida's Academic Mission Statement supports broad interdisciplinary programs and argues for "new avenues for research and new ways of constructing knowledge in the 21st Century." Our Genetics Institute, Institute for Aging and Center for Women's Studies—all spanning traditional departments and colleges—are sites of rich investigations and lively debates within our campus and beyond. Though proud of these initiatives, our institution struggles to map the flow of knowledge into new shapes using outdated academic structures. Departments, degrees, credit hours, FTEs, as well as physical facilities and technology interfaces all work against innovative academic exchange.

Realizing the institutional friction a formal collaboration might create, we began simply. Three architecture professors set aside a two-week segment within a design studio dedicated to building in the Florida landscape. Our climate (semi-tropical with daily rainfall all summer) makes a study of water obvious and, in retrospect, almost essential. We posed this question to the students and faculty in an ongoing special topics research seminar taught within the Digital Worlds Institute: Can the flow of rainfall onto a building and landscape be simulated in such a way that students can understand the repercussions of their designs and then work to modify their structures to more responsibly and poetically shed water?

At an introductory meeting we agreed that the DW students would investigate existing software applications and the architecture students would develop importable 3D models of their projects, some of which incorporated GIS-based site data. At our next meeting, we established a schedule for the project and set some goals for our collaboration. The Digital Worlds students reported that they believed Maya had an operation that would allow them to approximate rainfall. The operation, as it happens, is called "blobby surface."

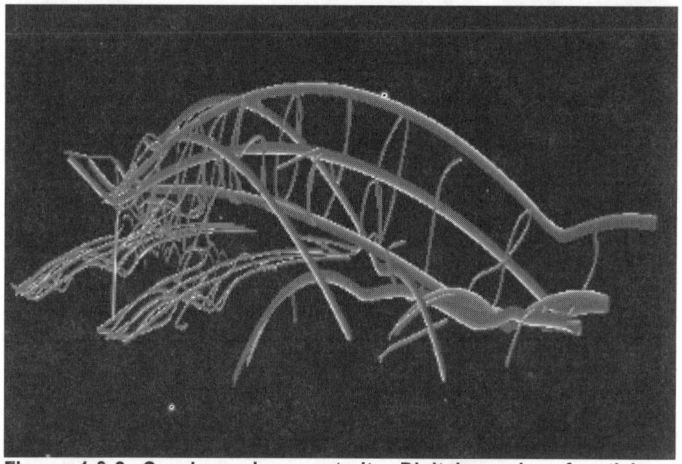

Figures 1 & 2. Greg Lynn phase portraits. Digital mapping of particle movement, subsequently translated into a system of form making.

With the assistance of the Digital Worlds Institute, the students were able to successfully import their virtual models into the dynamic animation environment found within Maya. The models were imported as .dxf files written from 3D Studio Max and required an additional parasolid plug-in for Maya to be able to correctly interpret and maintain the digital elements and their proximity to one another. Once inside Maya, the actual process for particle simulation was relatively simple. Maya allowed for the creation of a particle emitting source element placed above the model and a gravity element created below the model to control the direction of particle movement. This system established the preliminary condition of purely vertical particulate flow as an abstraction of individual raindrops falling. Density was modulated through a numerical system of randomly located particles emitted

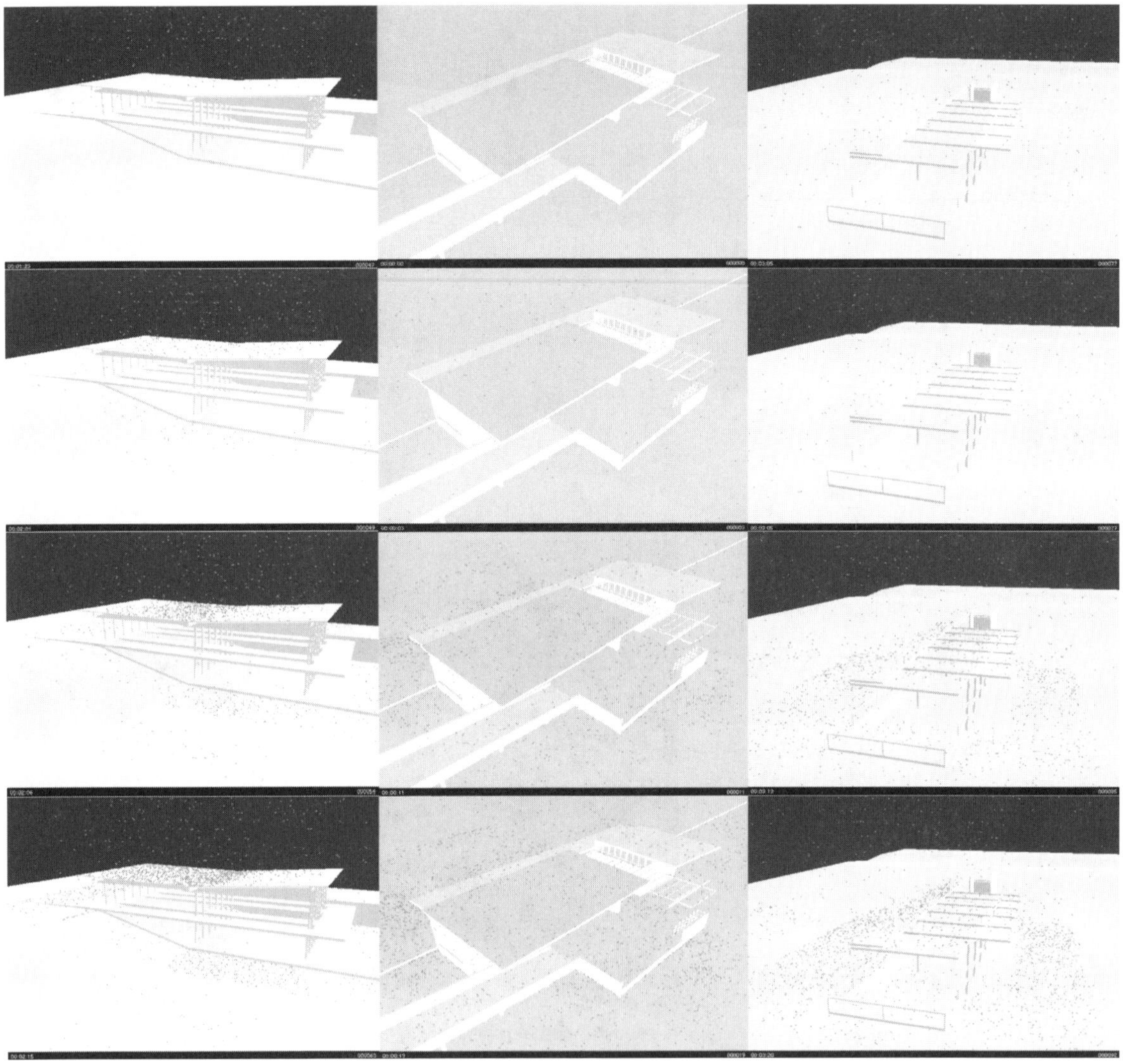

Figure 3.
Captured stills from Maya generated animations of dynamic particle simulation. Animation length ran for approximately 2 minutes. The extracted frames indicate accumulation of particles due to continued particle emission and particle flow along directional surfaces. Student projects (from left to right) – Jennifer Chue, Joe Kuehmeier, and Patrick Riddle.

with an upward limit of 500 particles/second. Adjustments with particle size accounted for the approximate size of individual drops. Modulation of the particle's dynamic response to encountered surfaces allowed for an approximation of splash. Further definition within the model itself was required in order for the particles to react to the model surfaces directly. All modeled surfaces required definition as either an active (impenetrable) or inactive (penetrable) surface. An inactive surface would have no impact on the direction or rate of travel of the particles, particles simply passed through them. Active surfaces could alter both the direction and rate of descent of particles, determined by the orientation of the surface itself as well as adjustments within the friction characteristics assigned to that surface.

The product of this simulation was a short length digital animation displaying the idealized behavior of raindrops falling onto an architectural construct and landscape. Though numerically indeterminate, the animations did allow for a visual means of analysis regarding roof and site drainage within the specific limitations of this scenario. The animations clearly delineated the fundamental principles of fluid movement across varied planes that could be used as an invaluable tool within the design process at both academic and professional levels.

The process of development for this simulation prototype also revealed numerous difficulties specific to digital media, stemming primarily from software interaction. The most dominant struggle occurred with the interface between Maya and 3D Studio Max.

The necessity of a plug-in for importing Max files was not initially known. Only after several days of struggle on the part of the DW was the software interface problem solved, and even then only with the addition of a secondary software element. Equally, the software interface appeared to only work with .dxf files written directly from Max. Though this was much less of a problem due to the relative ease of translation between the various modeling programs used by students, it still imposed an additional level of file translation as well as the possibility for file corruption or data loss.

Once the files were in Maya, a new set of challenges became apparent, ranging from software and hardware limitations to lack of familiarity by the user. Though the DW had been successful in projecting particles onto a surface and incurring an effective representation of gravitational flow, the behavior of the particles could not be adapted to fit the characteristics of fluid movement. The resulting simulations, though indicative of general flow patterns were more fictional at roof edges, where the particles followed a trajectory which was in fact noticeably longer in horizontal throw than would actually occur with liquid flow. Equally, the particles necessarily remained autonomous as elements, not interacting or combining with adjacent particles to form larger fluid bodies, which in turn allowed for only the suggestion of pooling water on a roof or a site. They never exhibited cohesion. While Maya 4.5 does have potential for the animation of fluid behavior, the lack of familiarity with the program effectively limited the collaboration to a system of particle animation. Neither the students nor DW had enough working versatility within Maya to fully take advantage of the program's potential, let alone the possibility of innovative usage to achieve a specific type of effect.

As Maya is primarily intended as animation effect software, the computational limitations became equally apparent. Though density of rainfall could be visually adjusted, rainfall intensity was effectively limited by the size and number of emitting elements. The choice to use multiple emitting elements would have increased the file size and complexity, and applied further strain to the processing capacity of the system. At the very least it would have substantially increased animation times, if it did not crash the entire system. There was also no quantifiable way to measure intensity beyond observation.

The particle emission rate was qualitatively inconvertible. Any specific calibration to a more common system of notation, such as inches per hour, could not be achieved. In addition, environmental factors such as constant wind or gusting wind could not be explored in the time we had allotted to the collaboration. The possibility of surface distinction was equally vague. Permeability of surfaces could be implied with adjusted friction, but the particles could not penetrate the surface, only move more slowly on it.

A further compounding struggle was the hardware itself. Maya's intensive operations require a powerful CPU in both processor speed and memory. Model complexity and thus

Figure 4. Designed project inserted into the particle simulation environment in Maya. Image captured from animation prior to particle emission. Student project by Jennifer Chue.

accuracy had to be kept to a minimum in order to simplify the particle simulation. In addition, once the models were imported into Maya 4.5, all operations had to be performed with this version. Preceding versions of Maya were not compatible, resulting in a reduction of the available number of viable software seats.

Conclusions

Given the prototypical condition of this proposal, there is every expectation for the continued development of accurate rainfall simulation within the Maya environment. We have identified a number of potential avenues for future work. Further exploration of particle behavior and adhesion could help to better model the unique behavior of individual droplets transitioning to fluid bodies moving on a surface. Equally, the effects of wind could be accommodated through the currently unknown effects within the program, or the subtle manipulation of multiple gravitational elements within a single model. At the same time, introduction to a different type of nomenclature for the particle density could be established, allowing for an analytical system based off of specific conditions of concern such as 50 years storms. Along a similar vein, a digital library of specific material characteristics could be developed simultaneously. This library could be imbedded with information regarding material porosity/permeability, surface friction, wicking effect or capillary action, hardness, etc. As an additional but perhaps more far reaching potential, the material library could extend to include such weathering effects as material deterioration or deformation, corrosion, and oxidation/patina.

The continuation of this collaboration will most undoubtedly occur within the studio environment. The students' willingness and enthusiasm must be embraced in order to pursue this

Figure 5. Further attempt of modeling rain by mapping blobby surfaces onto the particles to closer simulate surface tension and mutability of raindrops. A later series of models and scenes were generated applying different parameters to the particle field altering the behavior of the simulation. Gravity and friction as well as direction, wind, and reflective nature of roofing material move the modeling much further to the actualities of rainfall simulation.

endeavor, especially given the unconventional nature of this collaboration. Digital innovation has accelerated at a rate that is nearly incomprehensible, but the application of these innovations can only occur as a collaborative effort. The catalyst for these collaborations will be the participants' unfettered willingness to work around the limitations inherent within any specific software application.

The collaboration recounted here highlights the challenges of interdisciplinary exchange and the importance of intangible personal qualities noted above. For example, the architecture students would not have had access to the technologies necessary to work on the project without the good will of the faculty and students at the Digital Worlds Institute, even though the University of Florida owns all the hardware and software, and should theoretically make it available for all such educational purposes. Our students were given generous access to the DW lab because our faculty counterparts are equally eager to create collaborative ventures. Students' behaviors, knowledge bases and expectations vary across disciplines, making it essential to communicate clearly and, in some cases, to address problems from a number of perspectives to achieve consensus.

We were gratified to see an emerging collaborative ethos among our students. Although the project initially privileged the knowledge base and technology housed within the Digital Worlds Institute, the architecture students' diligence, enthusiasm and expertise turned our team from the DW's "clients" into true collaborators. By the end of the two-week experiment our students were answering as many questions as they asked.

While this modest collaboration between distinct disciplines provided some preliminary cohesion--temporarily turning particulate disciplinary studies into a fluid exchange--our primary goal remains untested. Our objective is to use dynamic particle simulation to influence design decision-making. To date we have crudely modeled a fluid condition, but we have not yet helped our students use the properties of rain, our chosen fluid, to inform design.

Finally, this project has been developed between individual faculty members outside of broader institutional support. In the long run, such collaborations can only be fully realized if they are offered stronger support from within each discipline, more fluidly integrating new proposals and investigations with existing intradisciplinary programs rather than the perpetuation of a more proprietary attitude. The potential of a truly collegial relationship between otherwise disparate disciples could help to offset the constrained fiscal environment most departments, schools, and universities operate within.

What has ultimately resulted from this experiment with modeling rainfall with help of Digital Worlds is both a grant to fund further research into such modeling with Maya and a joint graduate seminar offered to both architecture students and Digital Worlds students. The grant is funded by the Florida Roofing and Sheet Metal Association and the Earl Blank Memorial Foundation, and will hopefully result in newly authored software to plug into Alias/Wavefront's Maya animation package. The seminar will look to theoretical issues raised by the digital revolution not just in the practice and design of architecture and fine arts, but in culture at large. Faculty from both the School of Architecture and Digital Worlds will teach the course, and the students will utilize the advanced technologies of DW. The future of advanced architectural research using digital technologies such as that of DW may best be served by looking to other industries and institutions rather than attempting to facilitate it internally. This is the promise of intradisciplinary research, drawing on the strengths of all disparate parties involved synergistically.

References

Barragan, L. quoted in Emilio Ambasz. (1976). *The architecture of Luis Barragan*. New York: The Museum of Modern Art.

Dodge, M., and Rob Kitchin. (2001). *Atlas of cyberspace*. London: Pearson Educational Press.

Gibson, W. (1984). *Neuromancer*. New York: Ace Books.

Holtzman, S. R. (1994). *Digital mantras: The languages of abstraction and virtual worlds*. Cambridge: MIT Press.

Lynn, G. (1999). *Animate form*. New York: Princeton Architectural Press.

Mitchell, W. (1995). *City of bits: Space, place, and the Infobahn*. Cambridge: MIT Press.

Novak, M. (1991). *Liquid architectures in cyberspace: First steps*. Cambridge: MIT Press.

Rashid, H., and L-A. Couture. *Asymptote flux*. New York: Phaidon Press Inc.

Automated Classification of CAAD-related Publications: Conditions for Setting-Up a Keywording System

Bob Martens
Vienna University of Technology

Andre Brown
University of Liverpool

Ziga Turk
University of Ljubljana

Abstract
This paper deals with the CUMINCAD-repository (Cumulative Index on CAD), which was set up in 1998 and has served the CAAD-community since then as an important source of archived domain related information. CUMINCAD contains over 5,000 entries in the form of publications in the field of Computer Aided Architectural Design. The number has been growing steadily over the years. To date only advanced search mechanisms have been provided to access these works. This may work out well for a just-in-time location of a reference, but is inadequate for just in case browsing through the history of CAAD. For such applications, a hierarchical browsing interface, like one in Yahoo or DMOZ.org is envisioned. This paper describes how the keyword categories were defined and how a moderate, distributed effort in defining the categories will allow machine-identified classification of the entire data set. The aim of the paper is to contribute to building up a wide spread consensus on what the appropriate keyword categories in CAAD are, and what sub-topics should sit below the main keyword categories.

Keywords
Web-based Bibliographic Database; Searchable Index; CAAD Research; Classification

Automated Classification of CAAD-related Publications: Conditions for Setting-Up a Keywording System

Bob Martens
Vienna University of Technology
Andre Brown
Universityof Liverpool
Ziga Turk
University of Ljubljana

1 Introduction

In a very direct and astute paper Maver (1995) noted seven principal shortcomings in contemporary CAAD research: what he referred to as "seven deadly sins." Amongst the major failings that he identified were déjà vu (repeating research already undertaken by others), the failure to validate, and the failure to evaluate. There is such a rich body of research in CAAD that there was, and still is, a clear need to allow researchers ready access to that body of work, so that they can minimize the commitment of those sins. But access alone, though a significant problem, is not enough. What is needed is a way of interrogating the research information in an efficient and effective way. The research entities need to be stored and classified in a way that will allow optimal access, browse and search routines.

One starting point would be to ask, "How does a traditional library handle classification of recorded entities?" Human expertise is used ("manually"), and this is rather cost-intensive as well as time-consuming. As we are dealing with a specific field of knowledge—CAAD—we may assume that those looking for information in a related Digital Library will have some previous knowledge of the domain and thus will achieve a satisfactory search result. Taking into account the fact that thousands of published pages are archived in CUMINCAD, one can hardly expect that this documented scientific knowledge can be handled autonomously. Using advanced search techniques will deliver a generally reliable result, as various fields of the database entries can be investigated simultaneously. Not all records, however, have keywords submitted by the author. The keywords are invented by the authors (rather than being chosen from a list), and their relevance has sometimes to be considered with a little scepticism.

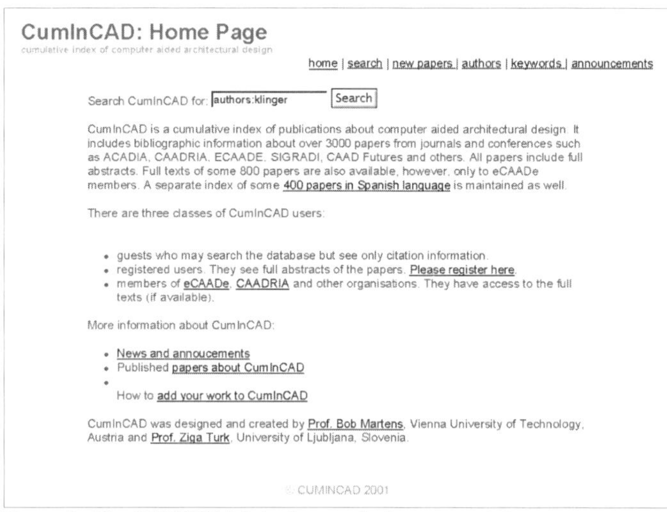

Figure 1. The CUMINCAD interface: entering a search term

The added value of keywording based on a common taxonomy is obvious, even when many other bibliographic fields are searchable. There is a direct relationship between the added value of keywording and the number of searchable documents: the more documents you keep, the more you need keywording. Having each paper tagged with a simple subject allocation cannot be satisfactory in the long term. Subjects need to be refined until they actually reach the precision and consensus of a thesaurus. The continual increase of papers available in CUMINCAD will lead to a poor performance for information retrieval if an effective classification is not undertaken.

Classification by subject specialists is by the far the most effective method, but it is costly in terms of time, and it requires well-qualified people to do it. The question arises as to whether one could achieve a useful result by some automatic procedure based on the text of the title, the summary, or the full text document.

2 Previous work on the indexing and interrogation of CAAD research

The searching of general web-based data and ways of optimizing such search activities has a relatively recent history. Brin and Page (1998) described a very well conceived system for general web searching, called Google, and that system is now in wide general use amongst researchers in all disciplines. Brin and Page noted that at the time they wrote, "despite the importance of search engines on the web, very little academic research has been done on them."

However, in contrast to general web-based information, the field of research in CAAD represents a relatively well-controlled and homogeneous collection of information. Research on information retrieval systems for more controlled bodies of data goes back to around 1993-4 (Witten et al. 1994), and presents a somewhat different problem in terms of information structuring and searching to general web searching problems. CAAD research has an effective history of less than five decades, and in that time there has been an explosive increase in research and development in the field. However, there are common themes and activities that characterize the research: identifying those themes would enable increased efficiency in interrogation. In order to address this matter, attempts have been made to establish context ontologies, rather than broad global ontologies, in order to make information retrieval more efficient and effective (Chiang et al. 2001). In the field of CAAD, this kind of approach is likely to prove very useful.

Based on CUMINCAD dataset, Turk et al. (2001) applied text-learning techniques to automatically generate classes of CAAD papers. In spite of the fact that making sense of the categories created is based on intelligent human interpretation, the results were less than satisfactory—they were found very different to human classification of the same works in conference sessions. A similar conclusion has been drawn from a similar analysis of the construction IT papers (Turk 2003).

Chiu et al. (2002) took the research publications of CAADRIA conferences from 1996 to 2001 as the source data with which to develop a data mining system. The system that was developed had the goal of applying "data mining techniques to study the current research paradigms and their relationships based on a research orientated database of collected papers."

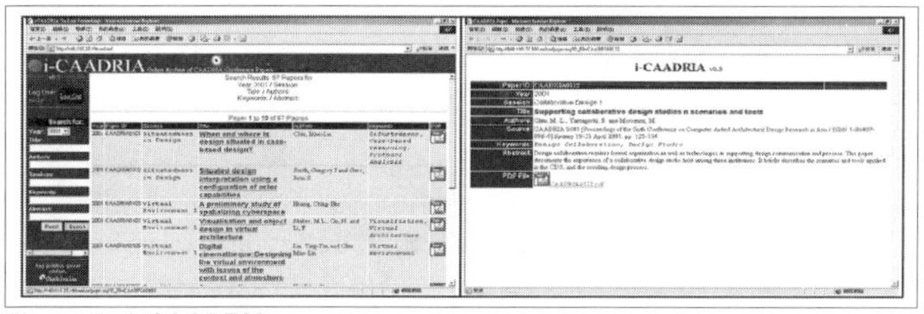

Figure 2. i-CAADRIA

What has come out of this research is a very elegant and enlightening research tool called i-CAADRIA, which has great potential. It is implemented using JAVA, ASP, and HTML, and the data is stored in an ACCESS database. Arising from their analysis, Chiu et al. were able to identify 13 cluster-of-paper domains as follows:

- Design Methods and Models
- Design Cognition
- Collaborative Design
- Information systems
- Design Media and HCI
- Precedents and Prototype
- Shape Studies and knowledge representation
- Generative Systems
- VR and VE
- Simulation
- Prediction and Evaluation
- Regional Information
- Design Education

Obviously these areas are somewhat subjective and are likely to be driven by a particular set of conference themes and culture, given the source of the data. But the areas do provide an interesting foundation for discussion of sub-themes within CAAD research.

In a more detailed study of research themes and sub-domains Martens and Turk (2002) have conducted a detailed analysis of the content and subject areas addressed in CAAD research publications. The work extends and augments the work of Chiu et al. and begins to establish an extensive and informed taxonomy of domain specific terms.

A more focused study by Kosovac et al. (2000) looked at the problem of keywording though the automatic analysis of construction industry documentation. The study focused on a subset of data; that referring to information on roofing of buildings. Concluding from the study, the authors suggested that the "methodology used was found to be highly useful, although it was not sufficient by itself for constructing a thesaurus for the architecture, engineering, construction and facilities management industries [. . .] a considerable human intervention was required." Ciftcioglu and Durmisevic (2001) considered the problem of data mining in the context of construction industry work and have developed a technique that enables data reduction, through clustering, of the large dataset that is produced from an initial analysis.

In the 1980s there was a relatively large body of research undertaken in Artificial Intelligence and Expert Systems. As a necessary part of this research, it was often needed to analyse text based information to provide the database of material with which the systems being developed could interrogate and interact. For instance, Robinson (1981) reports on the use of tree structures to address the problem of retrieving multikey records via range queries form a large, dynamic index in the field of CAD.

It is worth concluding this section by noting the caveats to which some of the researchers in data interrogation techniques have drawn attention. In particular Chiu et al. (2001) note that, with reference to keywords, there are linguistic problems (such as synonymies) as well as the technical problems (devising algorithms). For instance collaboration and cooperation are not exactly the same, but sometimes can be, and are interchanged. Added to that, many authors use key phrases rather than keywords. Are those key phrases used consistently by others? Some are. Ones like *Human Computer Interaction* are established, but how do we identify significant differences, if there are any, between collaborative design, design collaboration, design, and collaboration in keywording? There are also other subtle problems, such as differences in British English and US English. An example would be modeling and modelling, a word that is used frequently in the CAAD domain. These and similar problems require attention when refining the system.

As we mentioned earlier in the paper, the source archive used in this paper is the CUMINCAD system. The creation of CUMINCAD in 1998 was based on the knowledge, that no (web-based) repository existed to support further dissemination of research work in the field of CAAD and Construction IT. Outside Journals, the main channel of exchange has been in the format of annual conference meetings with proceedings as a tangible result. More than 70 CAAD conferences have been organized to date, and many additional conferences have CAAD related papers submitted to them. In total, about 3,200 CAAD conference (organized by the associations mentioned in this report) papers can be identified in the period 1981-2001. It has to be said that the level of professionalism has increased significantly in the last five years. Also, the process of annual production of papers has been improved substantially, and this has generally happened in tandem with a more rigorous blind reviewing procedure. In 2001, 410 papers were published in conference proceedings. However, this annual production level seems to be a number that will not grow in the near future. The current increase, on a annual basis—without the biannual CAAD futures—is approximately 350 papers. CUMINCAD, which developed on a shoestring budget, supports the important task of information management, as no other similar initiative could be identified so far for this field of research. The associations in charge are established on a non-profit base and have no commercial interest in “making money” from the conference activities.

3 Bibliographic Databases and Aspects of Searching

Bibliographic databases were developed from the traditional library card catalogue in order to enable users to access library documents via various types of bibliographic information, such as title, author, series, or conference date. In addition, these catalogues sometimes contained some form of classification by subject, such as the Universal (or Dewey) Decimal Classification used for books. With the introduction of e-print archives, huge collections of documents in several fields have been made available on the World Wide Web. These developments however have not yet been followed up from a keywording point of view.

3.1 Searching Documents by Subject

Database search engines may offer some features that are designed to improve the precision of the search. Words can be strung together as a phrase, and this phrase searched for. However, searching for a phrase of more than three words is likely to result in a low recall factor because of the flexibility of natural language (particularly English) in representing nuances of meaning by variations in word order. In another approach, limits can be placed on the maximum number of intervening words that are allowed to occur between a pair of chosen words (proximity searches). Of course it is not just the search strategy that counts, but the result of the search strategy when applied to the data. Therefore, exactly which data for a given document are available for searching influences the search result. There are two main uses of a bibliographic database. The first one is to search for a specific item which one already knows about and wants to find out if the digital library has it and, if so, to get access to the document. This is the so-called “referral” approach, a bit like looking up a piece of information in an encyclopaedia. The other main use is when one has a specific problem in mind and wants to find documents that address that problem. It is only with this second type of use that we are concerned in this paper. Basically, this leads to a subject-based approach to the digital library collection.

3.2 Subject connections via references

There is already a system of searching academic literature in a thematic way without any kind of intermediate database. This is via the references to other work or works that have been an accepted and established part of scholarly publications in the subject area. Starting from a core document, one can gradually widen the scope using the references and hopefully arrive at some fairly complete set of relevant documents. The electronic age has again enhanced such an approach without, however, changing it in principle. References in an electronic document can be links to the electronic versions of the documents referred to. The main obvious drawback in this approach is that authors may not have referred to all the relevant material, either due to deliberate omission or just because they do not know about it. Another possible disadvantage is that by definition one can only refer to what already exists at the time of writing a document. From the original document past documents will be reached, but all new documents will be missed. However, this could theoretically be solved through a database of such references, by forward searching from a document to retrieve all other documents that have referred to it later. In practice, the connections via references is not an adequate approach for users needing an exhaustive list of available documents related to a given topic. The process takes too long, and the full coverage is far from guaranteed. The other solution—querying a bibliographic database directly—is potentially much faster, but it may still result in an incomplete result.

At the time of writing, a citation database with nearly 20,000 references (collected from previous CAAD conference papers) has been connected to CUMINCAD.

3.3 Data from the record itself which are available for searching

Here we are only really concerned with data relating to the subject matter of the recorded document, so data like author names do not play a role. Of course, searching for an author can result in retrieving a certain subject, but it is almost never the case that this author is involved with all the documents in that subject area. Traditionally, the title is the item of bibliographic information that expresses the subject content. However, a title is usually far too short to contain a complete description of the subject area in a way that can be used efficiently by a search engine. A specialist reading the title may understand what the document is about, but that specialist is using all sorts of prior knowledge into which context the new title can be. Therefore the recall factor of a title-based search is likely to be low.

Sometimes titles are misleading. They can be guilty of overestimation concerning the real content, or the title simply promises too much. Furthermore, as the number of documents in the database steadily increases with time, the precision of title-based searches is likely to decrease as well. An extension of this, which has become much easier to realise for electronic documents, is that more of the text than just the title can be used for searching. Ideally this would relate to an extended abstract that summarises all aspects of the work covered in the paper, but it still remains that it is very time consuming to read all this information.

3.4 Subject Indexing

The grouping of source material by subject is called subject indexing or keyword enhancement. When we say "keyword," this could of course mean a phrase of two or more words. There are two very different ways of doing this: to choose terms from a fixed thesaurus or to use free keywords that can be chosen by the indexer at will. The strategy of assigning keywords will obviously depend on which parts of the document itself (title, abstract, full text) are also available for searching. It has to be stated that CUMINCAD has been focusing on conference papers; in many cases the supplementary addition of keywords simply did not take place.

Allocating keywords on a free basis could also use terms that are not present in the document, but in practice this technique is mainly used for adding useful words or phrases taken from the text, such as section headings and other specific words that could help in improving the recall factor of the search. Free keywords can also be useful for indexing terms containing special characters that would not be completely recognised if they appeared in the title or abstract. Free keywords can also be a useful way of adding synonyms of terms that appear in the text. But it would be better in general to handle synonyms at the search input end rather than adding them to each record when they occur.

The efficient allocation of keywords from a fixed thesaurus makes the most demands on the indexer, as the documents have to be well understood. The indexed terms may not appear in the same way in the text at all, which can give this method a big advantage over any strategy that just uses the text of the document. Of course, such a method requires the existence of a complete, precise, and up-to-date thesaurus, which is quite difficult to achieve in a rapidly-changing specialized research area like CAAD.

In practice, these two forms of indexing are extreme cases. Real approaches have aspects of both, even though they may be closer to one than the other. Thus, the drawback of having a fixed thesaurus is that the thesaurus itself has to be modified to keep up with developments in the field. On the other hand, free keywording can be chosen to conform to a minimum set of rules, instead of being completely free and just taking the words as they appear. For example, it could be decided to choose singular forms instead of plurals. In fact, after a period of use, listing the terms which have been given as free keywords does give an empirical thesaurus, that can then be used to standardize the keywords which are subsequently assigned, in order to improve consistency.

4 Beta version of a System for establishing Topics and Associated Keywords

The reasons specified above encouraged us to take a closer look at the possibilities of setting up a system of keyword categories for the area of Computer Aided Architectural Design. The range of tasks was limited to three key measures:

(i) compilation of a list of no more than 30 primary topics (key categories) within the domain

(ii) definition of 5-10 subtopics each per keyword category, and

(iii) selection of up to 10 relevant typical papers from the database associated with these topics.

Given the existing CUMNICAD repository as the source, first of all a provisional list was established based on the frequency of entries in the CUMINCAD-database field "keywords":

- 2D Representation
- 3D City Modeling
- 3D Modeling
- Animation
- Artificial Intelligence
- Case Based Reasoning
- Collaborative Design
- Communication
- Computer Integrated Construction
- Constraint Based Design
- Database Systems
- Design Methodology
- Design Process
- Digital Design Education
- Digital Media
- Environmental Simulation
- Generative Design
- Human-Computer Interaction
- Image Processing
- Interactive Design
- Knowledge Modeling (KM)
- Learning Environment
- Object Oriented Modeling
- Performance Simulation
- Shape Grammars
- Virtual Design Studio
- Virtual Environments
- Virtual Reality
- Visualization
- Web Design

For the definition of related subtopics and typical publications expert-help within the CAAD-community was requested. In order to avoid additional workload, the experts did not see the whole set of keywords, but only one category. As this is work in progress, the inquiry is not yet completely finished. To give an impression of the result one example is displayed here:

- Collaborative Design
  - Collaborative Teamwork
  - Collective Authorship
  - Computer Supported Collaborative Design
  - Computer Supported Collaborative Work
  - Distributed Modeling
  - Distributed Workgroups
  - Groupware
  - Groupwork
  - Information Sharing
  - Multi-User Workspace

The provisional list is covering a vast amount of information in order to feed the bibliographic database. Naturally a specialized field like CAAD does not consist of fixed topics, and thus the systematics introduced above are to be adjusted in line with current developments. On completion of a “Betaversion 1.0” tests with clustering processes can be initiated. The user community might be particularly interested in hints as to comparable publications.

Even in a list like the one above we see potential problems that are outlined in Section 2. There are terms such as “distributed modeling,” where there is potential ambiguity and confusion on at least two counts: firstly the British and US spellings of modeling/modelling, and secondly the use in a phrase and singly as just “modelling.”

Also there may be overlap across subtopic groups. For instance, distributed modelling can be a subtopic of Collaborative design. It could easily be a subtopic of a different primary keyword: modelling. Hence the generic structure that is identified for keywords and subtopics is not a pure tree structure; the branches of the tree intermesh. Hence the idea of a rationalised and strict hierarchy of terms is neither realistic nor possible.

At least at present, it is not reasonable to consider that we could impose a lexicon of standard terms on the CAAD research community. New terms will be added by researchers, and other terms will become unused or redundant as the research field develops. One of the interesting aspects of the research reported here is to track and reflect that evolution; so imposing a lexicon would be unduly restrictive and artificial. The problem, then, is one of dynamically tracking the evolution, but also we hope that there will be scope for introducing the idea of commonly used core terms in a standard form so that we can all search for research in a particular sub-topic area.

5 Text Learning and Clustering

The result of the effort of human experts is a list of 30 or so topics, each with about ten subtopics and about 10 related papers. It can be seen that for the sample groups of around 300 papers (out of over 5000) we have a manually defined the topic to which a paper belongs. We also have lists of 300 keywords, each associated with one topic. This data will be used to classify the 5000 papers in two ways:

1. keywords related to the topics will be used as learning set to train a classification tool. Based on this training, the 5000 publications will be classified.
2. papers, identified as typical for a topic, will be used as a training set to train a classification tool.

The results of the classification will then be combined and compared. Human experts will be asked to review the resulting classes and:

1. Identify papers also typical for a topic.
2. Identify papers clearly classified into a wrong topic.

Based on these comments, and a review of the effectiveness of performance of the system, the classification engine will be trained again. After a couple of iterative cycles the categories should be quite well established. The classification engine and the system to suggest a different classification will be part of an on-line knowledge management service which is part of the SciX system and which has the goal of providing technologies for low maintenance efforts and self-organisations of digital libraries such as CUMINCAD. After the bulk of the papers have been categorised it is envisaged that each new paper will be classified by the system automatically.

6 Conclusions

The number of recorded publications in CUMINCAD has grown year by year and growth has reached a steady state. A need for setting up a framework concerning the classification of stored knowledge in this extensive Digital Library has now become clear, and this fact defined the starting point of the work reported here. The procedure for gathering keywords and related sets of subtopics has been described in this paper, and the clear distinction is made between this activity and the implementation of an automated classification system, which is planned to follow at a later stage within the CUMINCAD development process. It will be interesting to see how efficiently the automated process that is planned for the next stage of development, will prove to be. An irony occurs to us. That is, that in this paper in indexing and searching data on CAAD research we may well have missed referencing, and drawing on, work by others on the subject of indexing and searching. Apologies are due if this is the case, but also it is reassuring that the CUMINCAD system was very useful in tracking down certain relevant work in this area.

Acknowledgements

The topics, associated keywords, and related typical papers were compiled in the framework of the Scix-Project. Invaluable input in the course of development was made by the eCAADe-council and individual experts, to whom we extend our sincere thanks.

References

Brin, S., and L. Page. (1998). *The anatomy of a large-scale hypertextual web search engine*. Stanford, CA: Computer Science Department, Stanford University.

Chiu, M. L., C. J. Lin, T. S. Jeng, and C. H. Lee. (2002). Re-searching the research problems with CAAD: Datamining in i-CAADRIA. *CAADRIA 2002: Proceedings of the 7th International conference on computer aided architectural design research in asia cyberjaya (Malaysia).* 18–20 April 2002, pp. 031-38.

Chiang, C., and Story. (2001). A smart web query method for semantic retrieval of web data. *Data & knowledge engineering*, Elsevier, 28:63-84.

Ciftcioglu, Ö., and S. Durmisevic. (2001). Knowledge management by information mining, *Proceedings of the ninth international conference on computer aided architectural design futures*,533-545,Eindhoven 8-11 July 2001.

Kosovac, B., D. J. Vanier, and T. M. Froese. (2000). Use of keyphrase extraction software for creation of an AEC/FM thesaurus. *ITcon* 5.

Maver, T. W. (1995). CAAD's seven deadly sins. In *Sixth International Conference on Computer-Aided Architectural Design Futures* Singapore,21-22, 24-26 September 1995.

Robinson, J. T. (1981). The K-D-B-tree: A search structure of large multidimensional dynamic indexes. *CADline* 22.

Turk, Z., T. Cerovsek, and B. Martens. (2001). The topics of CAAD: A machine's perspective. In *Proceedings of the Ninth international conference on computer aided architectural design futures*,547-560,Eindhoven. 8-11 July 2001.

Turk, Z., and T. Cerovsek. (2003). Mapping the W78 papers onto the construction informatics topic map. *Proceedings of the 20th CIB W78 conference on information technology in construction.* Waiheke Island, Auckland, New Zealand. 23-25 April 2003 (forthcoming).

Witten, I., A. Moffat, and T. Bell. (1994). *Managing gigabytes: Compressing and indexing documents and images*. New York: Van Nostrand Reinhold.

Online Database for Structural Details – DeTra

Robert Pahle
Arizona State University

Friedhelm Stein
University of Siegen

Abstract

DeTra is a research project that arose from the question: "How is it possible to assist students and professionals in architecture, dealing with structural details?" Our solution is a structural detail database, which assists by presenting example solutions of similar designs. This research was conducted in two overlapping parts. The first part of the research included the definition of a structure and a language to describe structural details—flexible enough to enable complex computer based queries, simple enough to be understandable. Major problems were the inclusion of vague terms, different meanings for the same word, and different words for the same fact. The second part was to create internet-based computer software, which utilizes the developed concepts and allows their evaluation. Thereby the system can be used with different access methods to the same data collection.

This approach intends to present both standard detail examples and project-related detail examples. For that reason the structural connections will be presented including all available project data. The information includes texts, sketches, drawings, photos, animations, and the database description. Our implementation handles this content. According to the holistic presentation of the search results a strong tool for evaluation is given to the user.

Online Database for Structural Details – DeTra

Robert Pahle
Arizona State University

Friedhelm Stein
University of Siegen

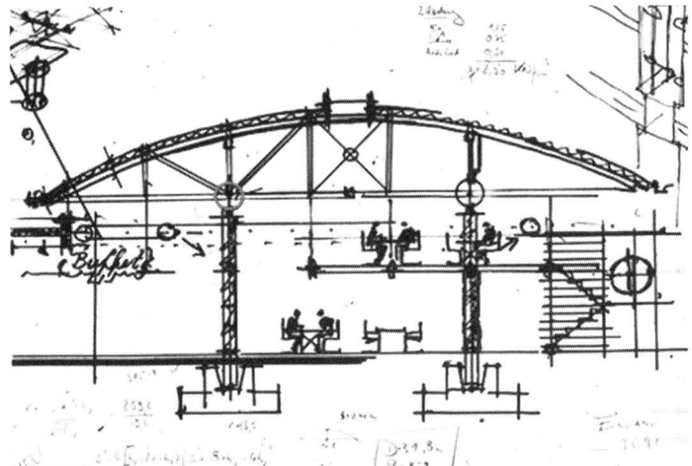

Figure 1. Sketch of a preliminary design of a café.

1 Introduction

In illustration 1 you find a sketch of a preliminary design. In order to realize such a concept, it is necessary to make decisions on many different aspects, such as structure, building construction, and design. One of these aspects is the detailed design of the structural junctions. At first glance, it looks like a simple structured problem. There are a limited number of trusses joining together in one point, each one with a well-defined angle and profile. But, in real life you can find thousands of different solutions for the same "simple" problem. Apparently, there must be a lot more of additional aspects which determine the final design of each structural junction. Unfortunately, many of the additional aspects are not precisely definable. For instance: "How does it fit to the neighborhood?"

How do architects normally handle such a situation? They screen journals, books, or papers. There are books on steel construction, books on frames, and articles on specific projects, but you won't find books about structural details dealing with the complete array of structural junctions. That's why it is quite difficult for students of architecture to deal with the design of structural details.

Such problems are quite often in architectural education. Therefore, the methodology "learning on examples" is well established in teaching for architects and designers and has proven to be very efficient.

In a joint research project of the structural design departments of Aachen University of Technology and the University of Siegen our research group aims to use this methodology for structural details. The projects name is DeTra, a combination of the first letters of the German words "DEtails von TRAgwerken" It is financially supported by the "Universitätsverbund Multimedia NRW."

2 Idea

As per description, there are huge numbers of details with similar functions. To handle such a large quantity of information fast and reasonably, it is suggested to use a computer based database. Since there will be consistently new details to put into the database, it's advisable to use a central data management to access the up-to-date information at all times. The internet as a worldwide computer network is a perfect tool for such a task. In order to use such a database very easily, it makes sense to develop several different methods of access. Self-evident is the access via a website for finding relevant details with appropriate criteria. Many of the relevant criteria are already available in programs for statical calculations. Therefore, it makes sense to use this existing information directly for the request—the second method to access the database. A third version is a teaching tool for aspects of constructional design or structural design, which stresses the content with examples of the database.

To give the person who is seeking the right impression of the located details, it is important to utilize a good and logical extract of the given information. Therefore it is the idea to present a detail preferably in the connection with the building in which it is used. Only on a special request should all information of the database be displayed.

3 Related Work

Within the context of classification of structural details a large amount of work has been done to describe and classify structural details (Ackermann 1988; Ackermann & Dersch 1982; Ballast 2000; Becker 1987; Ewald 1975; Newman 1993; Roth 1994, 1996, 2001; Williams 1999). But to come up with a concept for storing structural connections in a database, there are some parts missing. First and most obvious are the vague descriptions of design. Architects especially like to describe their work in vague terms like "compact," "solid," or "flexible." Second, the language between customers, architects, and structural engineers is not always clear cut. There are misinterpretations and misunderstandings among them. For that reason, it is not easy to define a description for a specific detail which is definite. Third, classifications of structural connections do not follow one scheme. Therefore, the design of a database which suits all possible designs is extremely complex.

There are some commercial products available which allow searching for structural details (Architectural Details Inc. 2003; Detail 2003; Newman 1997). These products provide a data collection and a predefined way to approach the information, but they are lacking any possibility to describe the anticipated detail exactly and then search for appropriate solutions. Another problem with these commercial products is the aim to find exactly one solution for a problem. Often this solution is available in a drawing format like AutoCAD's DXF or DWG and can be integrated into a drawing immediately. Our approach tries to find as many as possible examples to a given problem. The architect or student is encouraged to adapt his own detail from many different solutions presented in a comprehensive manner with respect to the project where they have been used.

4 Description of structural details

The implementation of a highly detailed structural connection search is only possible if there is an adequate descriptive language for structural details. As seen in the discussion of related works, there are only few attempts to standardize terminology and descriptive patterns for structural details. This problem is even more difficult since vague terms like "a heavy junction," describing the architectural design, are very important communicative elements in the description of a detail. On the other hand, there are a lot of predetermined terms like purlin structural situations. Count and measurable descriptions like materials, stress, etc. are a third possibility.

Many details are created by specific persons for specific projects. This information is also very important for a potential search, since an architect is able to assess structural details with regard to a build project. Furthermore, it should be possible to search for other details of the same project to evaluate the overall implementation of details, as well as a search of details, which belong to a specific architect to compare differences between projects. Therefore, an appropriate description should include each of these three aspects in a computer interpretable version in order to support flexible and detailed search queries and an easy possibility for implementation.

The categorizing of the different aspects led to four major groups.

- Detail Features
- Detail Elements
- Projects
- Persons

The information in these four major groups can be further structured in subgroups, and the subgroups can be composed of other subgroups up to the level of a single information piece. This realization led to the idea to organize all information hierarchically in a way that avoids redundancy. Figure 2 shows a part of the hierarchical structure.

The example address can be used for both, projects and persons, which could have an address. It is a tree, which can

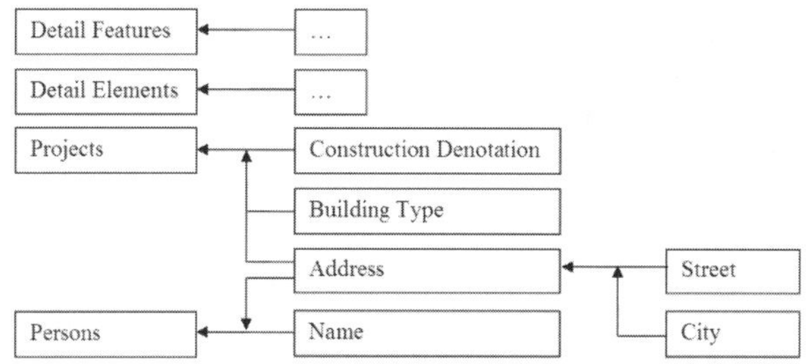

Figure 2: Part of the hierarchical description structure

Figure 3: Different connections at the same building

have cross connections at different levels. In the following sections we describe briefly our classification:

4.2 Detail-Features

The classification detail-features describes structural and design information, which is based on the complete detail, such as the adjacency of a connection to a wall or a ceiling.

4.2.1. Component Features

Component features describe that the connection is adjacent to a wall, ceiling, roof, or façade. For each component it is possible to specify points like a bottom connection, a middle connection, or a head connection of a façade or a wall, as well as to specify specific points for the roof like a purlin or rafter support. This specific way of description is used to include well known professional language.

4.2.2. Structural Features

The classification structural features is a description of a junction through structural components like frame, arc, truss, cable supported structure, beam, column. It is also possible to specify points like bottom or top of a column.

4.2.3. Stress Features

Structural junctions can also be described by the kind of stress (e.g. tension, or pressure). There are specific terms like tensile bar or tensile rope, which specify indirectly how the junction acts.

4.2.4. Design Features

Design features are very important for the implementation of the final junction. It is the desired visual effect, which gives the architect the possibility to distinguish the specific detail from general solutions to make it more individual. There are often overlaying design themes, which are for instance used to create similar layouts for junctions in the same building, although the structural needs of each junction are different. In figure 3, there are two junctions of the same building, which could be characterized as accentuated, which is the description of the visual effect of the junction. Often there is a range of descriptions like accentuated, less accentuated, and not accentuated. Another way to distinguish junctions is if the parts are fit together directly (e.g. welded), or if there is another element in-between like the bolt in figure 4.

4.3 Detail-Elements

The second general approach is to look at a detail by describing the elements of which it is made. For instance, in figure 3 left image there are two elements that are connected together. Each element has its own characteristics.

4.3.1. Number and Angular Arrangement

In a first step, it is important to name the elements exactly. Therefore, it is the easiest way to count the connected elements. There are many ways to count and to start counting the elements. After many discussions, our research group decided, referring to a Cartesian coordinate system, to start the counting at the positive x-axis and go counter clock wise beginning with element 1 as seen in figure 4. Angles are also counted in the same way, starting always from the positive x-axis. Since many angles are not exact known, there are 8 different angles we consider for the search [0°, between 0° and 90°, 90°, between 90 and 180°, 180°, between 180° and 270°, 270°, between 270° and 360°]. Thereby between 0° and 90° means an element can be located somewhere between these angles. The major reason for this model is stress, which differs strongly between different angles. For instance, a column (usually oriented vertically) has a quite different load and stress than a beam (usually oriented horizontally), and there is also a difference between a vertical element and an element not just vertically oriented. A second reason is practicality. In order to easily describe the angular properties, it should be easy enough to do (e.g. without a tool). On the other hand there is a loss of exactness, but our tests have shown that the results based on a geometry search are still very good.

4.3.2. Element-Type, Cross-Section Type, Materials, Stress, Connection-Information

Since we have defined a way to name each element of a structural junction it is possible to describe each element in a detailed manner. In many cases the specific purpose of elements can be extracted by their element-type name, like column or beam

A second classification is the cross section type. Figure 5 summarizes some of the most popular types. The last icon [Figure 5, bottom left] symbolizes a free form, where it is not possible or not easy to specify a cross-section type.

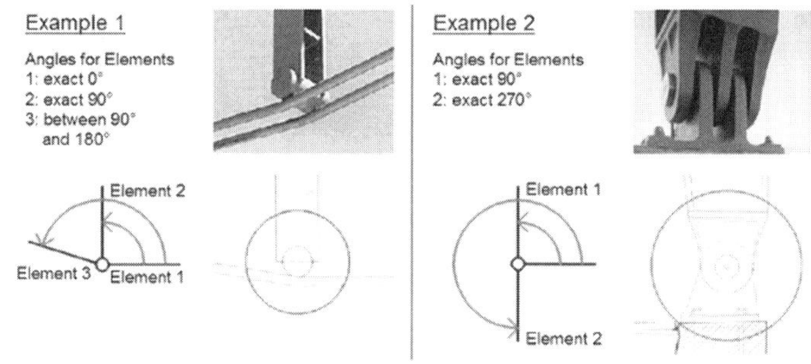

Figure 4: Counting and angular arrangement of elements.

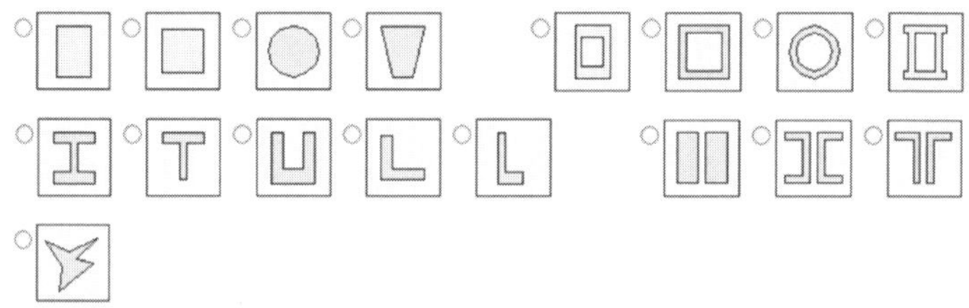

Figure 5: Most popular cross section types.

Each element is made of one or more materials; thereby the building-material has to be another classification.

The stress of each element can be defined as pressure, tension, bending moment, or a combination of these. So, each element—not only the complete junction—can be classified using stress.

It is also esthetically and structurally important how each element is connected to the joint. First, we can look at the static information: bending resistant or pin-jointed. And second, it is possible to define the way a specific junction is joined (e. g. welded joint or a bolt etc.).

4.4 Projects

Another criterion, which specifies a structural junction, is the building or the buildings where it is used. This information is interesting because different junctions of the same building often have overarching visual layout. Sometimes junctions are designed specifically for one building. It should be possible to describe all junctions of the same building, and therefore projects are a classification.

Sub classifications of projects for instance are the denotation, address, and the building type such as stadium, school, or theater.

4.5 Persons

Many structural junctions can be related to the architect or engineer who developed the joints. Architects often tend to create their own “hand writing” in design. For instance, many buildings of Richard Meyer or Frank O. Gehry are interrelated through design singularities such as white tiles or amorphous metal structures. If one searches for a specific design type, it can be really useful to consider structural junctions of the same architect.

4.6 Complete description – a combination of classifications

Each of the given classifications can be combined to describe the complete structural detail. The description can be increased gradually depending on how much information for a structural detail is available.
Example:

- 3 Elements
- Element 1 = Steel
- Element 1 = between 0° and 90°
- Element 1 = T-Beam
- Element 2 = Steel
- ....

Such a very detailed description is necessary, specifically if one wants to search for an example of a structural junction based on a drawing (see section 5.3).

4.7 Vagueness and Misinterpretation

Since there are often many terms for the same information or one term which can have different meanings, the idea comes up to standardize the language of the different professionals. For our project such an approach was far too difficult. We decided to try a different approach. For a specific criterion (e.g. material), we can determine which information (e.g. steel, wood etc.) is used in the database. For querying a specific criterion only the available data is displayed either in a list box or as an image. Thereby it can be easily determined which term was used to describe a specific detail, and so the search query is much easier. A future version of the descriptions could also include a thesaurus to enable different terms with the same meaning to have the same search results.

Another problem can be the mirroring of a structural junction. Our description (specifically numbering and angles) starts always from the same side, but usually a structural connection can be used also in a mirrored version. We decided to leave that problem as is and to rely on the judgment of the user to understand this issue. We will consider integrating a mirroring of search criteria for a future version.

5 User Interface

In order to find a user interface which is easy to handle, different possibilities were tested. As a result, both internet based queries and input could always be divided into three steps. Primarily, the criterion to be edited has to be chosen. Secondly, information is attributed to this criterion. In the final step, the issue is illustrated for examination.

The interface of each part of the program is discussed succinctly in this paragraph.

5.1 Data Input

In order to enter records into the database, the user has to authenticate in the input area, typing in his username and password. Then it is possible to start the input on a specific internet page.

The system implementation separates groups of information, such as projects, elements, materials, etc., and objects (the actual structural junctions). If one wants to give certain information to an object, this information is only assigned through a pointer. That guarantees that information is not redundant and simplifies the process of inputing the data, because e.g. information about an architectural project is only typed once and can be assigned as often as necessary.

An object being filled with information is illustrated in figure 6, inside the green border. The input of data takes place in the three main areas starting from the left side. First, a branch of criteria is specified on the left side [Figure 6, blue border]. All sub criteria will now appear in the second area [Figure 6, middle]. These are information pieces, which can be attached to an object and which later will allow the search for a specific object. For each criterion a list box turns up, offering all acceptable entries. By selecting appropriate entries of the list boxes and clicking "save" the selected information is attached to the object and shows up on the right side [Figure 6, red frame].

In the case that desired information fails to appear in the list box, a respective input field is provided, available by clicking on the sub criterion that is created as a link. Besides, in the opening window, existing entries can be deleted [Figure 7, red frame], or can be modified and completed [Figure 7, blue frame]. Modified data is automatically updated for all references.

When editing is finished, the window can be closed; all necessary data will be updated automatically. On the right side of the main entry page [Figure 6, violet frame], the complete data that is available for a certain object will appear self-controlled. The X [Figure 7, red frame] is used to deallocate. With the described procedure, any information can be collected to an object, whereby a single junction is regarded as an object.
Such an object will only be free for querying after assigning presentation data to it. This can only be done by storing suitable images and texts in the database, assigning them to a certain detail, and completing the procedure by reassigning them in the presentation area of the input page. Henceforth, the detail will be ready for querying.

5.2 Search over the Internet

The start page, which appears via Internet whenever DeTra is started http://detra.architektur.uni-siegen.de, is the query interface. At this place the user gains the possibility to search for details that suit his personal requirements. Again, the procedure is divided into three sections. First, a relevant criterion is chosen from the criteria tree in the left field [Figure 8, blue frame]. Depending on that selection, he either can input search values, or, when the database is already able to determine possible

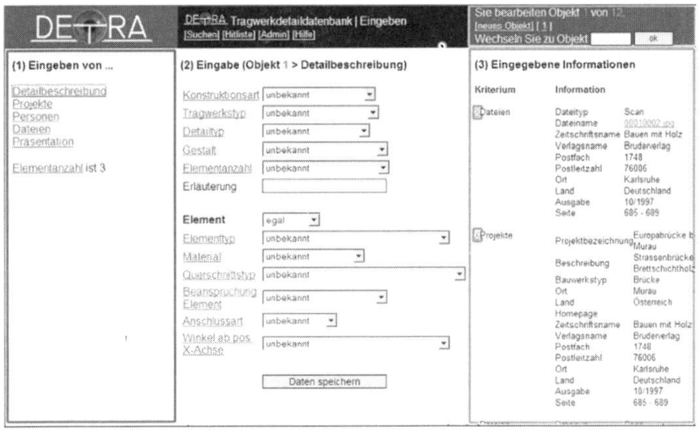

Figure 6: The form to allocate information to an object

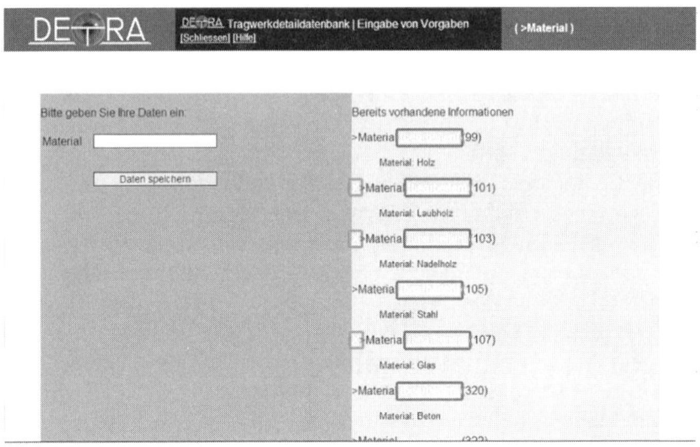

Figure 7: The form to enter information

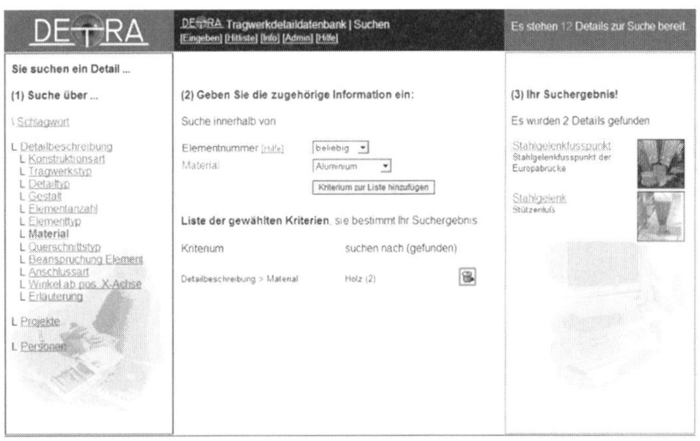

Figure 8: Search form

values, choose from a list of records [Figure 8, middle field]. Depending on the requirements, selections will be displayed either in a list of text information or in a list of small diagrams. The element number, referring to a single element that is meeting the queried junction, can optionally be given, generating a relation between the search criterion and the specified element.

Whenever search criteria are chosen, they are listed on the lower part in the middle of the screen. Simultaneously, a query is performed generating a list of result-records in the right field [Figure 8, violet frame]. The list of criteria is linked as an AND-conjunction. By clicking on the respective trash button, a criterion can be removed from the criteria list [Figure 8, red frame].

By clicking on the title or thumbnail of a search result in the right frame [Figure 8, blue frame], a new window opens with a detailed description of the corresponding record. The detail is presented in the context of the respective project, accompanied with images and explanation texts. This presentation complies with the presentation area in the data input section. Additionally, an outright view with all accessible information can be obtained.

5.3 Search with Structural Information of a Graphical-Static Software

In order to simplify the input of search criteria, a procedure has been developed, allowing direct data assignment from a example-static program to DeTra. This program has been created as an LISP application in AutoCAD, and has been expanded with respective program modules. First, a sketch of the structural system is drawn, and values are assigned to material, profiles, support, and load [Figure 9]. By hitting the command button "Search connection examples," all information is read and sent to DeTra, and the query is performed immediately. The data transfer is achieved by sending the data from Auto-LISP via command line to the Internet Explorer to the respective web page, which prepares the received data and forwards it to the actual query [Figure 10]. In the help menu, the functionality of querying is accurately described on the basis of examples. As already mentioned, the current prototype allows adjusting the list of criteria, even with a filled database. To relieve future decisions upon suitable criteria, each query is logged in an anonymous hit list.

6 Implementation

At the time being, the Internet offers one of the easiest ways to distribute information. In order to provide a widely spread accesibility for students, the research group decided early to use standardized hard- and software and, regarding issues of access and of updating the database, implement a centralized version of the system (Client-Server Principle).

For storing and searching the structural details we use the mySQL database, available for Windows, UNIX and Macintosh; PHP scripting language is used to prepare the data for distribution in HTML format—both free available for our prefered

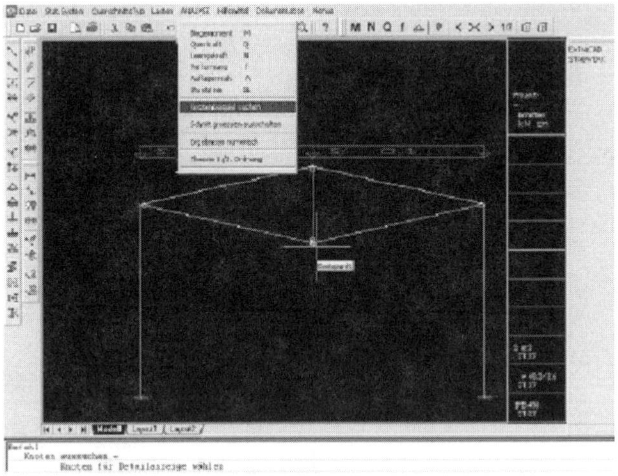

Figure 9: Example of a graphical query.

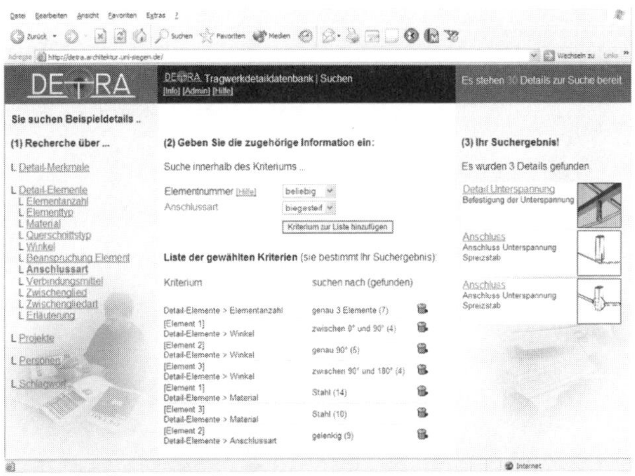

Figure 10: Query results.

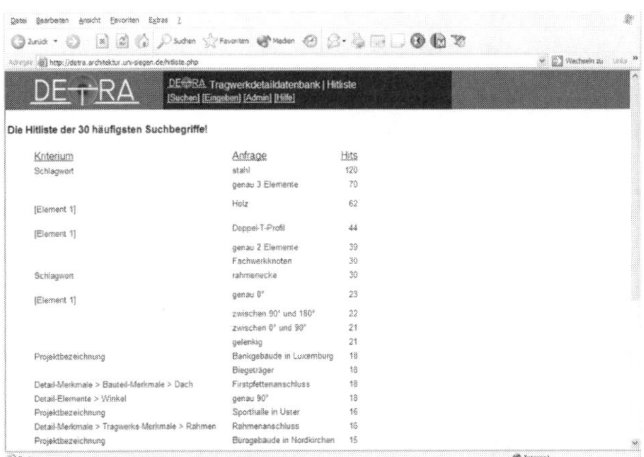

Figure 11: Hit list of the queries.

computer platforms.

Of the many possible web-server-combinations we chose a Windows 2000 Server—Internet Information Server 5.0 and a RedHat Linux 7.1—Apache 1.32 combination. Clients too can choose between several operating systems and browsers, like Linux/MacOS/Windows and InternetExplorer/Netscape/Mosaic; due to the lack of time we tested only the Internet Explorer for search queries.

As our example-static-program is an AutoCAD-application (see section 5.3). Windows-environment is needed for its use.

7 Evaluation

Evaluating DeTra was a difficult and time-consuming task—and it has not yet come to its end.

In a first step, the research team presented the language and its structure to professional architects, teachers, and lots of students. Due to this process, an efficient way to select appropriate and graspable criteria was found. In the second step, professionals and students tested different versions of the user interface. Here, a multi page oriented version, where criteria and the results appeared on different web pages, was discarded in favor of a single page version where criteria and search results appear on the same web page. We learned that starting the search at any odd search criterion is more flexible, but at the same time more difficult, than a guided approach over many web pages. There seems to be a trade off between search-flexibility and ease of use.

Finally, we decided on the more flexible solution. The current version allows the listing and the manipulation of search criteria generated through this automatic process.

Very interesting information for evaluation is gathered by maintaining a hit list of the most often searched criteria [Figure 11]. This hit list allows analyzing which criteria were selected properly and which approach for searching the data base is preferred by the users. This enables the optimization of search criteria.

Another approach to evaluation was made by asking students to acquire and input more structural junctions for the search. In their seminar, the students had the task to choose buildings and to analyze and describe structural junctions from different perspectives such as structure, construction, and design. The results of this experiment were that the needed abilities to understand the structural implications, as well as the professional language were not adequate to the detailed needs of the data input. Thereby a member of the research team had to review all given details to verify the appropriate description. We came to the conclusion that for a final version a specifically trained professional should input the data.

8 Limitations and Outlook

The research at hand is the approach of the authors to handle a complex database system. Due to the high flexibility of the system, there is a leak in query, since it needs a lot of queries to determine the correct result with a high number of restrictions to the structural detail search. The intended solution to this problem is a completely different search algorithm, which is subject for further implementation, leading to very high search speeds even with a large amount of users at the same time.

Already within the development phase of the project, ideas for supplementary functions occurred. For example, the situation may appear that a certain search criterion in the keyword query will not lead to any results because the database uses a synonym. So it would be an excellent upgrade to check the full-text search word based criteria with a thesaurus.

Another difficulty resulting from the query is geometry. The current version is not able to find mirrored details, although usually it is possible to use the same detail in a mirrored version. A possible future development is the transition from 2D to 3D geometry. In view of the great complexity of such a development, a new research application would be necessary. It is also very difficult to realize an input module that is easy to use and still can handle the full 3D information.

9 Conclusions

The online structural detail database DeTra is an approach to create a tool which is able to find example junctions for architectural and structural design using different and flexible ways for the description of the anticipated detail. The authors explored different ways of describing structural details, as well as the effectiveness of different search methods and result visualizations. DeTra is designed to work over the internet and has the ability to adapt quite flexibly to future conditions.

References

Ackermann, K. (1988). *Tragwerke in der konstruckiven architektur*. Stuttgart: Deutsche Verlagsanstalt.

Ackermann, K., and R. Dersch. (1982). *Grundlagen für das entwerfen und konstruieren: Das fügen tragender bauteile.* Stuttgart: Universität.

Architectural Details Inc. (2003). High quality construction details for the AEC industry. Retrieved 2003.03.10, from http://www.details-details.com/home.html

Ballast, D. K. (2000). *Architect's handbook of construction detailing.* Washington, D.C.: BNI Publications.

Becker, G. (1987). *Tragkonstruktionen des hochbaues.* Düsseldorf: Werner Verlag.

Detail. (2003). Detail - Deutscher baukatalog. Retrieved 2003.02.10, from https://www.detail.de/Archiv/En/Details

Ewald, O. (1975). *Lösungssammlung für das methodische konstruieren.* Düsseldorf: VDI-Verlag.

Newman, M. (1993). *Standard handbook of structural details for building construction* (2nd ed.). New York: McGraw-Hill.

Newman, M. (1997). *McGraw hill electronic structural detail library* (CD-ROM ed.). New York: McGraw-Hill Professional.

Roth, K. (1994). *Konstruieren mit konstruktionskatalogen, Band I konstruktionslehre.* Berlin, Heidelberg: Springer Verlag.

Roth, K. (1996). *Konstruieren mit konstruktionskatalogen, Band II konstruktionskataloge*. Berlin, Heidelberg: Springer Verlag.

Roth, K. (2001). *Konstruieren mit konstruktionskatalogen, Band III verbindungen und verschlüsse*. Berlin, Heidelberg: Springer Verlag.

Williams, D. R. (1999). *Structural details manual.* New York ; London: McGraw-Hill.

9 >> Works in Progress

Chair: Loukas Kalisperis, Penn State University

digital works in progress – juried

An Insight into the Freedom of Using a Pen: Pen-based System and Pen-and-paper

Chor-Kheng Lim
National Chiao Tung University

Abstract

In earlier researches on freehand sketching, the cognitive behavior of designers was studied. In recent years, some researchers began to look into this area from the design media aspect. The pen-based system, developed by Gross, Landay and other researchers, used the pen as an input device, allowing sketches to be freely drawn in a computer environment. The importance of the freehand sketch lies in its ability to freely represent various drawing projections using ambiguous sketches. However, as for the various drawing projections, such as diagrams, symbols, plans, elevations, sections, perspectives, etc., how are they interrelated to a designer's thinking process and the cognitive behavior? Different media have different abilities to represent different projections. Would they affect the designer's design thinking as well? Targeting different media, i.e., conventional freehand sketches vs. the computer pen-based system, this research uses case studies and think-aloud protocol analysis to present an analysis and discussion. Research results show that there is a relationship of gradual embodiment that is mutually complementary, going from a whole perspective to being the dissected into sections between the different projections. In addition, these projections restrict the designer's various design thinking processes, while the use of different media may somewhat change the actual design thinking of the designer

An Insight into the Freedom of Using a Pen: Pen-based System and Pen-and-paper

Chor-Kheng Lim
National Chiao Tung University

1 Introduction

The conceptual stage is the most critical stage in the design process. In recent years, extensive studies have been done on the characteristics of sketches resulting from this stage and the designers' cognitive behavior. Studies relevant to the design aspect presented analyses and discussions on the drawings' characteristics and classifications (Faruque 1984; Robbins 1994; Fraser & Henmi 1994; Goel 1995; Herbert 1993). These studies explain how the sketches possess such qualities as convenience, freehandedness, and the ability to represent ambiguity. Thus, they are an excellent tool used by designers to express their ideas outwardly. Designers are accustomed to representing ambiguous concepts and complex objects using simple, abstract drawings. These drawings are composed of many annotations or various projections, such as diagrams, symbols, plans, elevations, sections, perspectives, etc. However these drawings are not the complete and concrete drawings found in the final designs, so they possess such qualities as abstraction, ambiguity, and imprecision (Goel 1995). Faruque (1984) used examples to explain the different levels of abstraction in these drawings, from simpler drawings to the more complex: annotations, symbols, plans, elevations, and perspectives, shading, and rendering (Fig. 1). These drawing projections can be used to aid the design thinking process.

Figure 1. Level of abstraction (after Faruque, 1984)

Other researchers studying sketches from the cognition aspect target in on the interaction between the designers and their sketches while analyzing the designers' cognitive behavior. This type of research emphasizes the characteristics of visual thinking or visual reasoning and can be classified into three types: 1. How designers look at sketches (Goldschimidt 1991, 1992, 1994); 2. What the designer sees in a sketch (Suwa & Tversky 1997); 3. How the designers draw and what do they draw (Van Sommer 1984). Schon argues that the designer frequently interacts with or communicates through the chosen design media in the design process. Laseau (1987) likewise pointed out that between the drawings in the sketch and the designer, there is a cycling process going on among the brain, hands, sketch, and eyes. Based on the dialogue between designer and sketch, the designer will derive some visual feedback from the sketch, which contains dense and ambiguous lines, and then reinterprets the sketch or experiences an unexpected discovery from the sketch (Schon & Wiggins 1992; Suwa & Tversky 1997).

In addition, the new computer medium came up with the Computer-Aided Design (CAD) systems. Utilization of CAD is different from traditional methods; therefore, certain impacts and influences are expected to happen to design behaviors. Earlier CAD systems emphasized the final presentation that takes place in the final stage of design. In recent years, however, in order to comprehensively assist designers to produce more stimuli for their designs in the conceptual stage, Computer-Aided Conceptual Design (CACD) was gradually developed (Lipson & Shpitalni 1996; Gross 1996; Van Dijk 1995; Elsas & Vergeest 1998; Won 2000; Wong 2000). These cognitive research and related theories regarding the computer medium for the conceptual stage, however, focused mainly on the development of mouse-based CACD. For example, the shape molding system, Fast Shape Designer (FSD) developed by Van Dijk (1995), was a drawing system capable of transforming two-dimensional sketches into three-dimensional models. The Displacement Feature Function (DFF) proposed by Elsas and Vergeest (1998) utilizing interactive windows and real-time visual feedback was another example. In addition, Wong and Wong's (2000) discussion on design cognitive behaviors through comparing traditional and computer based media explained the theory that uses of different media change the designers' design behaviors and visual thinking.

However, when researchers came to a real understanding of designers' behaviors during the initial sketching stage, they discovered that behaviors are fast and ambiguous yet creative, and most of the designers were still relying on the conventional medium: pen-and-paper (Gross 1996; Landay & Myer 1995). Since this mouse-based computer medium is incapable of supporting the functions of pen-and-paper during initial sketching, many researchers, like Moran (1994 1995), Gross and Do (1996), and Landay (1996), turned to the research and development of a pen-based system. Their purpose was to provide the CACD system with conveniences and functions: fast expressions of images in designers' brains, ambiguity, resolution, gesture, and notions through related peripherals like the stylus and tablet touch-screen display; or combining virtual reality to simulate traditional pen-and-paper functions.

2 Problem Statement and Objective

The pen-based system has improved the CAD operating

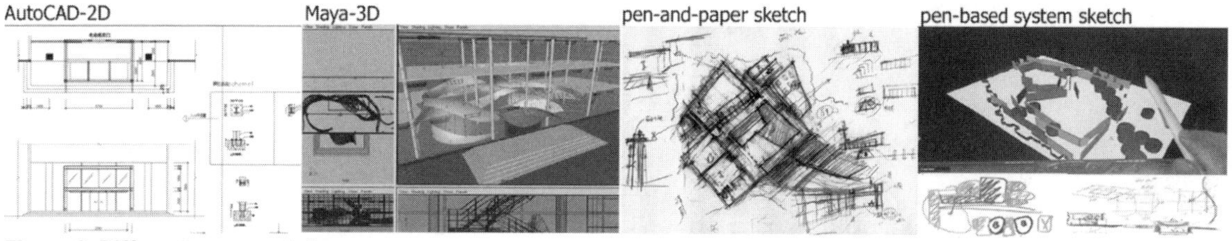

Figure 2. Different representation

interface to enable designers to complete the whole course of design in a computer environment. Currently, developed pen-based systems can be classified into three categories:

1. Projection drafting systems that combine physical pen-and-paper to aid in group communications (Wellner 1993; Moran & Chiu 1995).
2. Systems that translate two-dimensional sketches into three-dimensional models (Igarashi 1999; Schweikardt & Gross 2000; Do 2001).
3. Systems that function mainly as graphic recognition engines for sketches (Landay 1996; Gross & Do 1996; Plimmer & Apperley 2002).

The main purpose for developing these systems is to simulate the characteristics of pen- and-paper, thereby achieving the cognitive design behavior found in designers who use conventional pen-and-paper for sketching. Such characteristics include the simulated touch sensitivity of a pen, of coloring, and of semi-transparent tracing paper (Gross & Do 1996; Pilmmer & Apperley 2002). However, the most important feature is that it allows the designer to use the pen as the design medium. The motion involved in drawing out sketches can be even more freehanded and convenient. Pen-based systems allows sketches with ambiguous and dense lines to be drawn freehanded as if using conventional pen and paper. It also allows doodling, which integrates various drawing projections on a sketch - such as diagrams, symbols, plans, elevations, sections, and perspectives - to aid the design thinking process. Faruque (1984) categorized these various projections into different levels of abstraction. Yet, what is the relationship between the different levels of abstraction during the process of drawing, as proposed by Faruque (1984), and the designer's thinking process? What relationship is there between these different approaches to drawing?

While both use a pen-like device as an input tool, a pen-based system and conventional pen-and-paper are actually two different types of design media. The drawing environment for and the representation of drawing projections by these media are also different. The characteristics of the projection representations by the various media will vary with the mechanisms of the media themselves, as shown in Figure 2. Especially for the computer-based media, some represent 3-D perspective projections more easily, while others are better at 2-D projections, such as plans, elevations, and sections. However, freehand sketches can represent various projections freely, primarily because the drawings are made with a pen, which affords a greater degree of freedom in representing various projections. In light of the above considerations, would the differences between pen-based systems and the conventional pen-and-paper have an impact on the representation of projections? Would this then lead to differences in the design processes by designers?

Based on the questions raised here, this research will focus on freehand sketches by two different kinds of media: conventional pen-and-paper and a computerized pen-based system, and will provide in-depth analysis and discussion based on the different levels of abstraction drawings and differences in the cognitive design behaviors. Lastly, some aspects regarding the differences between the two media will be discussed.

3 Case studies

As undeterminable and divergence issues often arise alongside with proposed research fundamentals and its experimental methodology, in addition to the ambiguity of predetermined analytical criteria versus the achievable objectives, the lack of understanding of design cognition has repeatedly become the primal obstructions of experimental actualization. Hence, in order to further integrate the systemization and feasibility of the cognitive experimental scheme conscientiously and thoroughly, the research was commenced by case studies with initial attempts of analyzing and categorizing the possibilities of preliminary and phenomena occurrences as the essence of experimental hypothesis and analytical configuration.

3.1 Procedures

The procedures were carried out with the specific topic "Tied-up Sketch," targeting on the experimentations on sixth, seventh, or eighth grade architecture students to come up with freehand sketches and answer some questions. The design processes are described in detail as below.

The subjects began with freehand sketch to initiate each of their design concepts; the task was to be accomplished within a given time or preset extensions. The key was that the design concept must be completed. The subjects were then to answer five questions. The topics of the design task comprised aspects on functionality and criterion within similar scopes of very simple design. All design tasks were limited to certain degree of representation (Table 1), and each type of representation was categorized into 4 representative figures of level of abstraction (Faruque 1984), from simple to complex:

A. Only use annotation, diagram or symbol
B. Only use plan, elevation and section
C. Only use perspective
D. Only use perspective + rendering or shading

	Design topic	Representation (drawing projections)	Time (min)
A.	Personal working space	Only use annotation, diagram or symbol	10-15
B.	An observatory	Only use plan, elevation, section	10-15
C.	Bus stop	Only use perspective	10-15
D.	Lavabo near the beach	Only use perspective + rendering or shading	10-15

Table 1

Questions-

1. What would you think about the perfection of your concept? (%)
2. What did you think about when you are drawing? (e.g. Spatial relationship, form, functions etc.)
3. What is the limitation of this way of presentation?
4. What do you want to draw next step?
5. Do you feel have to change the drawing projections?

3.2 Discussion and Findings

Sketches of the case studies

A: Only use annotation, diagram or symbol

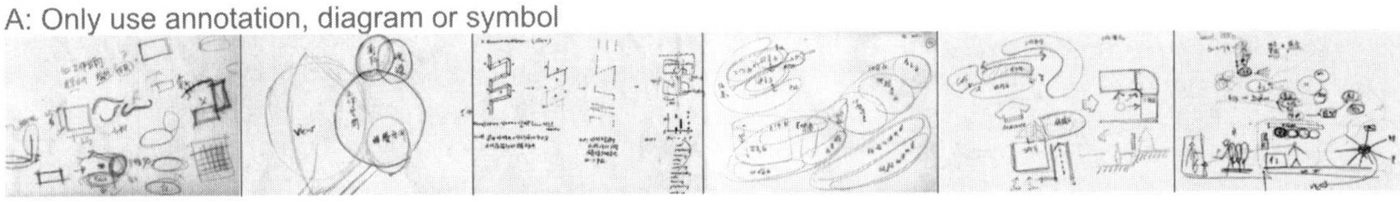

Figure 3

B. Only use plan, elevation and section

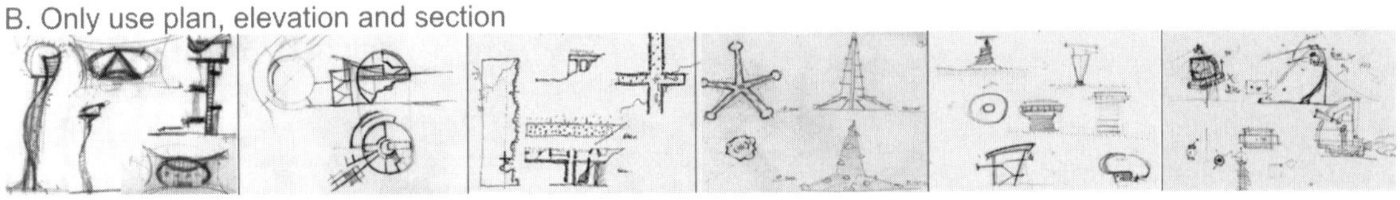

Figure 4

C. Only use perspective

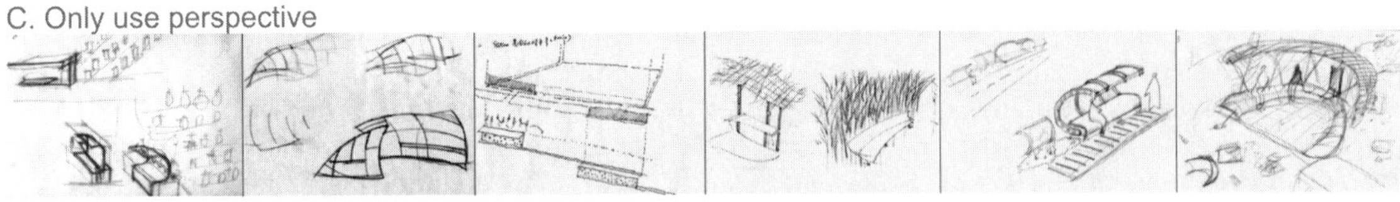

Figure 5

D. Only use perspective + rendering or shading

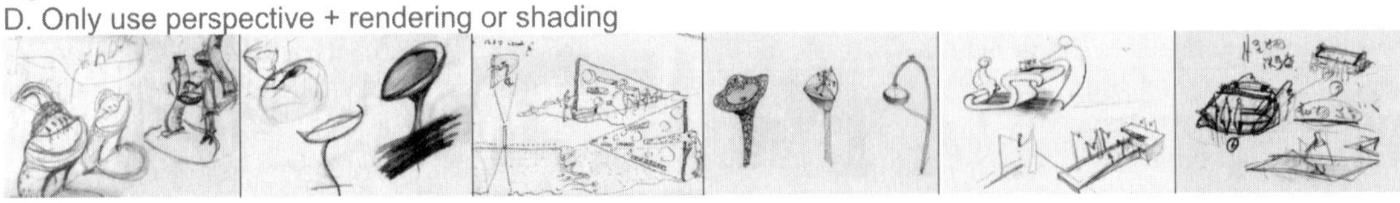

Figure 6

From subject's interpretations, the sketches in aspect of design factors and considerations were then concluded and classified into visual features including shapes, sizes, textures; spatial relativity as well as relations to spaces and environments and spatial configurations; functionality design and design concepts. Suwa's (1998) theory was consequently used to guideline these factors into three levels of action categories:
Perceptual level --- visual feature, spatial relation, organization
Functional level --- function
Conceptual level --- concept

As table 2 shows, we can find out that there are some relationships among levels of abstraction and action categories:
1. When using annotation, diagram or symbol, most designers (5 persons) considers spatial relation.
2. When using plan, elevation and section, most designers (6 persons) consider design function, design concept, and also consider environment relationship (5 persons).
3. When using perspective, most designers (6 persons) consider design function, and also consider shape and environment relationship (5 persons).
4. When using perspective + rendering or shading, most designers (6 persons) consider design function and shape. Secondly, they consider the texture and environment relationship (5 persons).

At the same time, it is also evidently obvious that the more precise and visual the drawings are (e.g. perspectives), the more design factors were put into consideration. Simple-formed drawing projection such as diagrams had only led the subjects to focus on the factors of spatial relationship and conceivably on functionality aspects. However, with slightly more complex perspectives, the subjects were able to focus not only on functionalities, but also form, environmental relation and textures. When applied upon different action categories, we could capture that: when sketches were done in projections of plan, elevation or section representations, and more considerations in accordance to Conceptual category. In category of Functional, projections of plan, elevation, section, perspective and rendering greatly involve in the relatively considerations. Visual features, spatial relation and configurations are the three sub-categories of Perceptual categories. In this category, diagram, symbol and annotation are mostly considering the spatial relation (5). Moreover, projections such as plan, elevation, section and perspective representations acquire supplemental and powerful visual features (5) and spatial relations (5). The perspective with rendering also creates more visual features especially textures consideration (5).

Meanwhile, different drawing projections could create relativities amongst its individual procedures and reciprocal, as the following procedure:
1. When using annotation, diagram or symbol, next step hope to draw plan (5 persons).
2. When using plan, elevation and section, next step hope to draw perspective (5 persons).
3. When using perspective, next step hope to rendering (4 persons).
4. When using perspective + rendering or shading, next step hope to draw section (5 persons) and also need annotation, diagram or symbol to assist. (4 persons).

From the above consequential relativities, we can easily comprehend how these sketches from four different levels of abstractions interact with one another. The design concept steadily developed into more concrete systems from initial abstractions; and so on the drawing sketches represent the

Table 2

	perceptual						functional	conceptual	next step					
	visual feature			spatial relation					different projections					
			texture		environment	layout	function	concept	Symbol, Annotation, diagram	plan	elevation	section	perspective	rendering
Annotation Diagram, symbol	0	1	1	**5**	2	3	4	1	----	**5**	2	2	2	0
Plan Elevation, Section	**5**	2	2	1	**5**	1	**6**	**6**	2	----	----	----	**5**	1
	5	1	3	2	**5**	0	**6**	4	3	3	4	3	---	4
Rendering	**6**	1	**5**	1	**5**	0	**6**	3	4	4	3	**5**	---	---

The Numeral is the amount of the designers

gradually concretizing sequential relationship. Moreover, when designers have rendered the perspectives, they sometimes hope to continue designing by taking advantage of the deployment of other abstract concepts. From the drawing it is shown that most designers would hope to use section representations to consolidate the overall design physique, whereas some also use simple diagram or texts to support their concepts. (From the Sketches of the case studies, textual descriptions and simple diagrams were drawn next to the main design body to represent the less crucial fundaments of the design.) These approaches show that different projections of drawing hold relationships of:
1. The gradually concretizing sequential relationship.
2. The mutually complementary relationship.
3. The relationship of going from a whole perspective-drawing to a dissected section-drawing.

As a result, the hypothesis of relativity between different levels of abstraction and design attempts can be concluded as follows: Different levels of abstraction such as texts/ symbols/ diagram, plans/ sectional/ elevation, perspectives and renderings will lead to the different design action categories, Perceptual, Functional, and Conceptual. Meanwhile, there is a relationship of gradual concretizing sequential, mutually complementary, and going from a whole perspective-drawing to a dissected section-drawing between the different projections.

4 Protocol analysis

4.1 Procedures

The experiment is proceeded by constructing a Think-Aloud Analysis to prove the preliminary hypothesis from the first part of case studies and to enable further analytical progress. The subject was an architect with 10 years professional experience. Warm-up session: The subject was first given a one-month period to get familiar with hardware and software, equipment that would be utilized during the experimentation. The subject had to become accustomed to operating software, Electronic Cocktail Napkin, and hardware such as portable LCD Interactive Pen Displays without any problem. Besides, prior to the official kick-off of the experimentation, the subject was given 30 minutes to warm up with a small design exercise.

Think-Aloud design session: the subject went through two design tasks, conventional freehand sketch (Experiment A) and pen-based system sketch (Experiment B). When Experiment A was completed, the subject was then given a week long Experiment B. Each test took 90-120 minutes in total. During both experimentations, complete scenes including the produced sketches and think aloud protocol data were recorded.

4.2 Coding Scheme

Segmentation

The protocol data was first categorized by different levels of abstractions; each level of the dividend data was carried out for segmentation. The definition of segmentation adopt the definition of Goldschmidt's (1991), Design Moves, implicating a series of coherent or subordinate reasoning actions originated from the design essence. The beginning of a new segmentation often occurs when a designer shifts its design concepts or comparative actions such as drafting notions. An individual segmentation may contain one or more protocols.

Coding Scheme

The coding schema was the proposed target on the level of abstraction, upon which to construct a process oriented coding schema. It was set on the basis of the analytical structure developed from the first part of Case Study, delving into the relativity of the application of different design medium such as conventional sketches and pen-based system versus representations of different levels of abstraction such as annotations, symbols, diagrams, plan, elevations, sections, and rendering perspectives.

Level of abstraction: Four coding ranks were divided by different abstract sketches:

Table 3

3	perspective + rendering or shading / VR
2	perspective
1	plan, elevation and section
0	annotation, diagram or symbol

4.3 Analysis and Result

A. Conventional pen-and-paper sketch (indicate as SK)
Duration: 85 Minutes

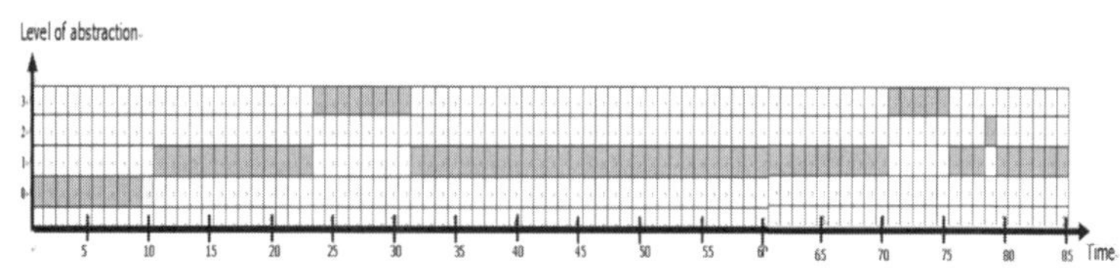

Figure 7

B. Pen-based system (indicate as ECN)
Duration: 136 Minutes

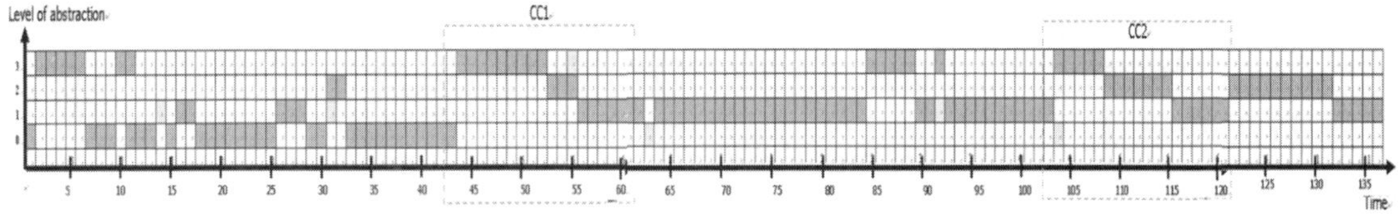

Figure 8

Divergence of Timeline
From the above two figures, we can clearly see the distinct difference between the application of the two design mediums. The Pen-Based System took almost 60% of the time to complete as that of the conventional pen-and paper sketch. As a matter of fact, in both mediums, the actual times taken for the experimenter to complete the sketches were relatively similar, yet with the additional VR features Pen-Based System (Figure 9), the designer spent more time on viewing and examining the drawings. From Figures 7 and 8, we can see that the proportion of time taken was largely consumptive, spent merely reviewing the 3-D drawing generated by VR.

Hypothesis Verification
From the two Figures (7 & 8), we can also monitor the progressive procedure relativity, which was formed by the drawing projection's relationship to the freehand sketch (0-->1-->3). This relativity then continued at the 2nd level (plan, elevation, and section) from the transferal of the 3rd level (perspective). The dismantlement of overall perspective drawings into two-dimensional representations of plans/sections/elevations would also be recorded during the course of using ECN. Moreover, almost all kinds of sketches, whether plans, sectionals or elevation representations, would be additionally supported by simple diagrams or annotations (Figure 10). Such a result had perceptibly verified the three hypotheses from the previous case study. However, during the ECN experiment, as the variations of the levels of abstraction were somewhat unsteady, the progressive procedure relativity became somewhat obscure, yet emphasized the relativity amongst different figures.

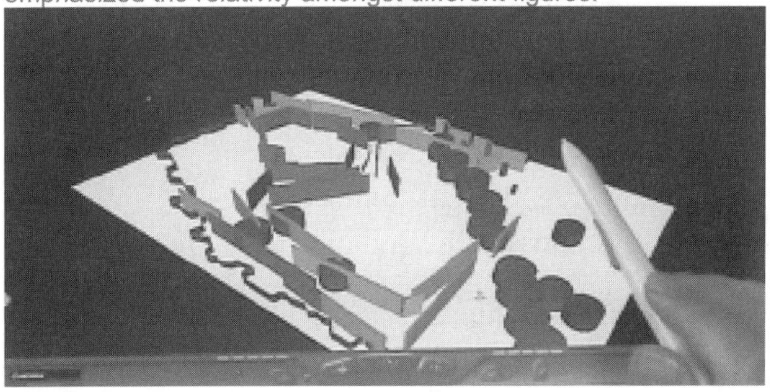

Figure 9. Look and inspect the VR

From figures 7 and 8, we can determine the following phenomena:

1. Different levels of abstraction have steadier variables in an SK (conventional pen-and-paper sketch) but a higher variable frequency in ECN.
The timeframe in the SK experiment progressed steadily from 0 to 3 in the first third of the overall time, simple diagrams or symbols gradually progressed into plans, elevations, and sectional representations followed by the completion of the final rendering perspective. The concept development again returned to level 1 (plan, elevation, and section) of two dimensional representations and remained steady until the completion of the perspectives of level 3 (perspective).
However, in ECN, the design concept progression is somewhat unsteady at the beginning, bouncing between levels 0, 1, 2 and 3. As the figures gradually transform, the progression became more constant yet still adjusting occasionally amongst levels 3, 2 and 1 (3-->2-->1-->3-->1-->3-->2-->1-->2-->1) with a longer retaining period for each individual figure formation.

2. Consequential progression from the level of abstraction 3-->2-->1 was formed in CC1 (45-85 minutes) and CC2 (105-120 minutes) of the ECN experiment.
As the software consists of a VR depiction function, level 3 of the ECN experiment was frequently presented by a VR illustration. The subject had come up with the perspectives (level 2) by tracing the 3-D images generated by the VR function (level 3). After inspecting the drawing, they revised it by shifting to section, elevation or plan (level 1).

3. During ECN experimentation, level 3 (VR) had appeared in the early stages of the sketch design, shifting erratically amongst Levels 0, 1 and 3, in contrast to the consequential progression that was occurring in the SK experimentation.
This occurrence was a result of the VR function of ECN. As the subject was able to easily transform 2-D diagrams into 3-D VR representations right from the beginning of the sketching stage, enabling a clearer and more visible milieu quality, the VR

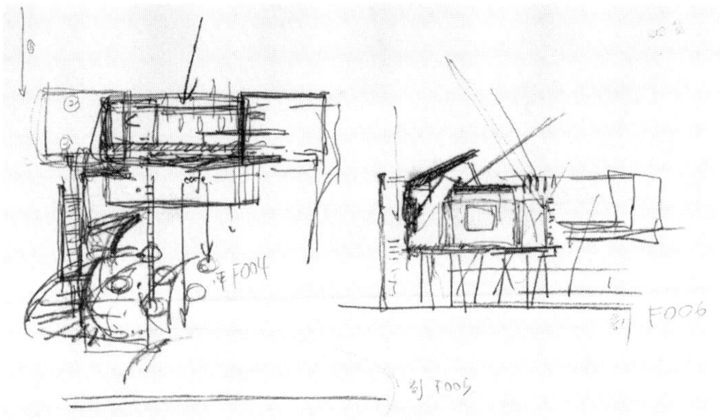

Figure 10. Plan, section (associated with diagram & annotation)

function was recurrently activated and utilized.

From Table 4, we can distinguish clearly that Level 1 had been mostly employed by the utilization of the SK and ECN. Nevertheless, the difference between the two experimentations in the time spent on different levels of abstraction (0, 1, 2, 3) is far greater in SK than in the ECN. During the SK design scheme, Level 1 took up 72% of the entire conceptual development period, while only 0.9% is used in Level 2. However, when designing with ECN, the overall time spent on each level during the design process is closer to being the same. This experiment proved that even when a designer uses a pen as the primary sketching tool, different design mediums can impact greatly on the usage frequency of the figure deployment.

5 Conclusions and Limitation

The following conclusions can be drawn from the above analysis: In freehand sketches, there are close relationships between the different drawings that possess varying levels of abstraction: 1. the gradually concretizing sequential relationship, 2. the mutually complementary relationship, and 3. the relationship of going from a whole perspective drawing to a dissected section drawing. However, these relationships may change with the use of different media, which present varying degrees of difficulty in performing the task of representation. From case studies, it is also known that the various projections restrict the designer's design thinking in different action categories (perceptual, functional and knowledge). Therefore, the utilization of various projections and the varying frequencies of their occurrence will lead to differences in design thinking during the design process.

In addition, from experiment results it is seen that pen-based systems can perform freehand sketches just as well as conventional pen-and-paper. However, due to the former's special functions, such as VR mode, pen-based systems allow a designer to inspect a 3-D view during the sketching stage. This characteristic allows the drawing and inspection of concrete images (e.g. 3-D models) to be performed in the early sketching stage, which in the past was only possible in the later stages of the design. This gives the designer more opportunities during the sketching stage to carry out the design thinking process based on ambiguous 2-D projections and more concrete 3-D images, as well as offering more opportunities for visual feedback.

The limitation of this research is in its lack of in-depth analysis of the cognitive process applied to the drawings with varying levels of abstraction. From the case studies only a preliminary conclusion was drawn about the relationship between the action categories (perceptual, functional and conceptual) and the various drawing projections. More exact studies must be done using protocol analysis. This research only explains how the two entities mutually limit each other, without explaining the content-oriented relationship within.

6 Significance and Future Studies

As pen-based systems possess the characteristics of conventional pen-and-paper, they play a critical role in representing the ambiguous nature of CAD design and are gradually giving a tangible form to the conventional pen-and-paper method, while linking the gap between the designer's conceptual stage and the CAD designs generated by the present-day computer-based media.

1. Research on Sketch Recognition

This research presents detailed analyses and discussions on the levels of abstraction in the designer's drawings during the conceptual stage, which may be used to help understand the precise and important visual reasoning process followed by the designer. If the designer's need to represent differently during freehand sketching is understood, then the most suitable design media can be selected and given to the designer for use as an excDot representation tool.

2. Research Methodologies on Design

When sketches become digitized information, there will be a major breakthrough in terms of research methodologies,

Table 3

Level of abstraction	SK (drawing time/total time)	ECN (drawing time/total time)
3	796 /5078 = 0.15	1543 /8141 = 0.19 ** **(inspect)**
2	47 /5078 = 0.009	1324 /8141 = 0.16
1	3667/5078 = 0.72	3452 /8141 = 0.42
0	568s/5078 = 0.11	1822 /8141 = 0.22

especially for the study of sketches. The cumbersome data processing required in the past for protocol analysis experimentation can now be recorded or dissected using the computer's powerful storage and computational capabilities. From here the experimentation steps can be made more precise and efficient.

3. The Integration of Design Media Means

Because pen-based systems allow designers to perform freehand sketches in a computer-based environment, the designer may integrate or combine the sketches with other computer-aided systems. This bridges the gap made by the use of different media for initial-stage freehand sketching and for later-stage design and development. The freehand sketch not only plays the role of a communication tool for the designer, it also serves as an excellent computer based media tool for consolidating and accessing other design-assisting software.

As the cognitive behaviors displayed when using the pen-based system and when using conventional pen-and-paper are different, future researches will, one hopes, use these derived phenomena to consolidate relevant research results, and then make inferences about a theoretical model for an improved pen-based system. Further studies can then be done to see if the computational drawing environment based on cognitive design behavior may be helpful to a designer's creative behavior and how it may impact the design outcome. In addition, the hope is to take the research a step further and study how to integrate the designers' personal idiosyncrasies into the pen-based systems, thereby providing the designers with more stimulation.

References

Do, E. Y.-L. (2001). *VR Sketchpad*. CAAD *Futures*. Eindhoven, 161-172.

Elsas, P. A. and J.S.M.Vergeest,(1998). New functionality for computer-aided conceptual design: The displacement feature. *Design studies.* 19: 81-102.

Faruque, O. (1984). *Graphic communication as a design tool.* New York: Van Nostrand Reinhold.

Fraser, I.,and Henmi, R. (1994). *Envisioning architecture - an analysis of drawing.* New York: Van Nostrand Reinhold.

Goldschmidt, G. (1991). The dialectics of sketching. *Creativity research journal.* 4(2): 123-143.

Gross, M. D., and E.Do. (1996). Ambigious Intensions: A Paper-like interface for creative design. *Proceedings ACM conference on user interface software technology.*

Gross, M. D. (1996). The Electronic Cocktail Napkin - a computational environment for working with design diagrams. *Design studies.*17(1): 53-69.

Goel, V. (1995). *Sketches of thought.* Cambridge, MA: The MIT Press.

Herbert, D.M. (1993). *Architectural study drawing.* New York: Van Nostrand Reinhold.

Igarashi, T.,S. Matsuoka, and H.Tanaka, (1999). Teddy: A sketching interface for 3D freeform design. *ACM SIGGRAPH.* Annual Conference on Computer Graphics, 409-416.

Landay, J., and B.A. Myers, (1995). Interactive sketching for the early stages of user interface design. *Proceedings of CHI'95,* 43-50.

Laseau, P. (1987) *Graphic thinking for architects and designers.* New York : Van Nostrand Reinhold.

Lipson, H. and M.Shpitalni, (1996). Optimization-based reconstruction of a 3D object from a single freehand line drawing, *Journal of computer aided design* 28 (8), 651-663.

Moran, T. P. and P.Chiu, (1995). Implicit structures for pen-based system within a freedom interaction paradigm. *Proceeding CHI'95.*

Plimmer, B. E. and M.Apperley, (2002). Computer-aided sketching to capture preliminary design. Australian User Interface Conference (AUIC2002).

Purcell, A. T., and J.S.Gero, (1998). Drawings and the design process. *Design studies.* 19(4): 389-430.

Robbins, E. (1994). *Why Architect's Draw?*,Cambridge, MIT Press.

Saund, E. and T.Moran, (1994). A perceptually-supported sketch editor. *Symposium on user interface sortware & Technology,* 175-184. N.Y.

Schweikardt, E. and M. D.Gross, (2000). Digital clay: deriving digital models from freehand sketches. *Automation in construction* 9: 107-115.

Suwa, M., and B.Tversky. (1997). What do architects and students perceive in their design sketches? A protocol analysis. *Design Studies.* 18(4): 385-403.

Van Dijk, C. G. C. (1995). New insights in computer-aided design. *Design studies,* 16(1): 62-80.

Wellner, P. (1993). Interacting with Paper on the DigitalDesk. *Communications of the ACM,* 36, 87-96.

Won, P.-H. (2000). The comparison between visual thinking using computer and conventional media in the concept generation stages of design. *Automation in construction* 10: 319-325.

Wong, C.-H. (2000). Some phenomena of design thinking in the concept generation stage using computer media.*CAADRIA*, 255-264. Singapore.

Physical Simulation in a VR Tool for Urban Design

Frieder Schubert and Philipp Lurz
University of Stuttgart

Constantin Boytscheff, Bernd Jödicke,
Martin Merkler and Jens Wiesner
University of Applied Sciences, Konstanz

Abstract

Physical influences on a city, such as noise, light, air flow, and solar energy quantities, can already be simulated on computers; however, these simulations are usually not embedded into the urban planning process. Regarding a broad field of these influences and their correlations will improve the quality of the design. The use of simulations in the sketching stage provides the possibility of reacting accordingly for the urban planner, which is essential for sustainable design.

This paper describes the development of a virtual reality tool for the early urban design process, in which we realized a network connection between a software package calculating noise propagation in urban spaces and a virtual reality design environment. In this dynamic VR design tool, it is possible to experiment with simple geometric forms and objects (these objects can be added to constructions, removed, and transformed). Interactively, with each action of the planner, simulations are generated and visualized in the VR environment in real-time.

The last part of the paper describes our concept, how this VR design tool should be integrated in the study of urban planning, and how we want the students to get a sense for the impact of their design on physical phenomena in an urban scale.

Physical Simulation in a VR Tool for Urban Design

Frieder Schubert and Philipp Lurz
University of Stuttgart

Constantin Boytscheff, Bernd Jödicke,
Martin Merkler and Jens Wiesner
University of Applied Sciences, Konstanz

1 Concept

Next to esthetics, there are many aspects which have to be considered in architectural and urban planning. Planning becomes a very complex task and requires a broad knowledge in different scientific disciplines. The quality of the solutions resulting from the planning process increases with the number of criteria that are considered. But, even a well experienced designer gets to the limit of his ability by the number of aspects, their variability, and correlation that have to be regarded.

Computers are able to process a large amount of information through predefined algorithms in order to reduce the information to results that can be handled. Physical phenomena like the propagation of noise in urban spaces, air pollution, air flow, areas of light and shadow, and daylight and solar energy quantities can be simulated with the help of computers in that manner.

It is hard to foresee e.g. the distribution of noise in urban spaces. Architects and urban planners usually do not have extensive experiences and knowledge of the correlation between their design and the consequences for the spatial propagation of sound in urban spaces. Noise simulation software is able to improve this situation and can assist planners. In the context of this project, we decided to simulate the noise propagation in urban spaces with the aid of a special software package.

Usually just specialists have the know how that is necessary for the application of simulation software. These programs fit their particular needs, and they are almost the only ones using simulation software in a professional way. The application of simulation software is too sophisticated for the usual needs of architects and urban planners. That way, planning aspects which have to be simulated are not taken into consideration in the early design process or just at a later date when the boundary conditions are already defined.

In order to integrate computer simulation into the design process, it is necessary to simplify their application and to make the results and correlations among different aspects visible and understandable for architects and urban planners—especially when they are not observable without any simulation technology. The result of a simulation process is much easier to understand if it is visualized. By the simulation of physical phenomena in urban spaces, it is reasonable to treat them spatially in simulation and visualization. A suitable medium for 3D visualization is Virtual Reality (VR). VR is already established for scientific data visualization in disciplines like civil engineering and medicine technology. In architecture and urban planning, VR is only used occasionally and almost never serves just as an immersive presentation tool for CAD-models. But VR is also appropriate as a design tool. In distinction from the representation on paper or on screen, which is limited to two dimensional projections, VR features many benefits known from physical model making.

A significant advantage of VR in comparison to physical modeling is the ability to integrate design relevant information like simulation results within the early design process. This can not be realized with conventional models. This integration can be achieved by connecting the simulation and the VR environment, so that by each change of design parameters, actual simulation results are provided in real-time.

We suppose that in consideration of the technological development current CAD-workstations will be at least partially displaced by Augmented Reality and VR in architecture and urban planning within several years. This is not only true for those planning phases in which CAD is already used, but also for the early design process.

In spite of several already realized innovative VR-projects, the establishment of VR in architectural teaching and profession could not yet be achieved. But VR systems became simplified and significantly cheaper within years, which enables an easier application in teaching and practice.

Programs that are able to provide comprehensible and evaluable information on ecological questions are appropriate to assist teaching. They open up the possibility of integrating ecological aspects into the design process, which may affect the design itself. Therefore, the programs should fit the needs and abilities of designers and facilitate their practice. Designers should be able—similar to sketching and physical modeling—to create several alternative design variations quick and easily.

"r.Vipar" was established, so that the integration of simulation software into the design process will lead to a new chance for the application of VR in teaching and practice. If this chance is used, the quality of architectural and urban planning solutions designed with the help of VR will at least improve in terms of ecological aspects. The promoted tool, which is still under construction, will make its contribution to this evolution.

2 Simulation

There are different kinds of simulation routines that can be used in architecture and urban planning. With the help of computers, wind fields, cool air discharges, the propagation of air pollutants along the road, the distribution of daylight or artificial lighting in street spaces and buildings, solar energy quantities on building facades, and the propagation of noise in the city can be be simulated, among other things.

Depending on the kind of simulation and the applied

algorithms, the effort of computation varies, and the time of calculation differs accordingly. The calibration of initial parameters required for computation may also have a significant influence, but can more or less be optimized for fast computation times depending on the kind of simulation. Only if the simulation routine reacts on design changes within the shortest time and immediately supplies updated results, can it be used within the draft process. A simulation is appropriate for real-time application if the calculation period does not exceed some seconds. Naturally, the hardware should be as new and as fast as possible. However, computing time does not only depend on the technical conditions of the hardware, but can also be accelerated by different software-technical principles.

2.1 Acceleration of RT-Simulations

Simulation results can become less accurate through acceleration. In other words: at the expense of precision, simulations can be accelerated. One principle of acceleration, thus is the use of algorithms that provide rounded values. Simulations can also be accelerated if their algorithms are optimized or simplified, and if the dissolution of computed points is reduced within a certain area. A further acceleration principle is called "nesting-procedure." Here, the resolution of simulation is gradually increased. With the skillful arrangement of the area that has to be computed, in more or less important zones, the simulation can be divided hierarchically in several computation cycles. An initial rough calculation output is refined gradually in its accuracy at relevant spots. However, the "nesting-procedure" cannot be realized with some kinds of simulation—or just with a huge effort.

Still another principle is the parallelism of simulations. Parallelism means that a simulation run is split into a certain number of packages that will be assigned to different processors. The number of packages is approximately inversely proportional to the computation time of the entire simulation. In extreme cases, only one individual point is computed per package.

Even an excellent simulation can illustrate reality only approximately. Therefore, a fundamental assumption for the realization of real-time simulations within the "r.Vipar"-project is that designers do not need absolute accurate simulation results during the draft process. It is adequate if the simulation computes and shows tendencies at this point. The planner should be able to observe how changes in his design correlate with improvements or degradations in the simulation result. More accurate simulations can still be performed optionally later.

2.2 Selection of the simulation

For this project, we chose a simulation method which can be accelerated by as many of these principles as possible. On noise simulation all of the principles were applicable, and the goal of our project, to develop a tool which provides simulation results in real-time, seemed to be easily realizable. In comparison to other computable phenomena, noise propagation can be calculated quickly. Therefore, we decided to work with Soundplan, a professional simulation software for the computation of noise propagation in urban spaces developed for "MS Windows."

2.3 Controlling of the Sound Simulation

The company Braunstein & Berndt developed an interface in cooperation with us, so that Soundplan can be controlled by external programs. With the help of this interface, simulation parameters, three-dimensional geometry, points of emission and immission, and the simulation results can be transferred. If buildings are e.g. created, transformed, or removed during a planning session, this will be communicated to the simulation software. The simulation routine starts a new computation procedure after the transmission and provides updated results.

Two calculation proceedings, the "noise-map run" and the "single-point run," can be released with this interface. During the "noise-map run" the noise levels are simulated for all points of the predefined, structured grid. For the "single-point run" any point in space can be defined, and the noise level at that point will be computed. These two calculation methods differ nearly only in the definition of the points of immission and, therefore, are combinable with each other. The computation of such a single point just takes the fraction of one second on an average PC.

3 Visualization Techniques

Through visualization huge amounts of data become comprehensible easier and faster, and their analysis and evaluation can be accelerated. The kind of visualization has substantial influence on the designer's perception and can affect his decision making. Therefore, different methods of data visualization and the correlations between data visualization and the process of decision making of architects and city planners have to be examined and tested in the context of this project.

Common forms for the visual representation of noise propagation are horizontal and vertical sections or shades of color on building facades. However, a three-dimensional model of noise immission offers a more comprehensive impression. Especially for people who have to deal with the results of noise propagation but are not familiar with the procedure of their calculation, a three-dimensional representation may be a crucial assistance. Depending on the question, it serves as an indication of critical zones in a scenario. They can be recognized quickly by the user, and thus help to develop a feeling for the behavior of noise propagation. This kind of application of visualization is called "Explorative Analysis." It should obtain an understanding of the structure of the data and an insight into its correlations. "Scientific Visualization" is the umbrella term for the visualization of complex data records in order to get a better sense for their underlying structure.

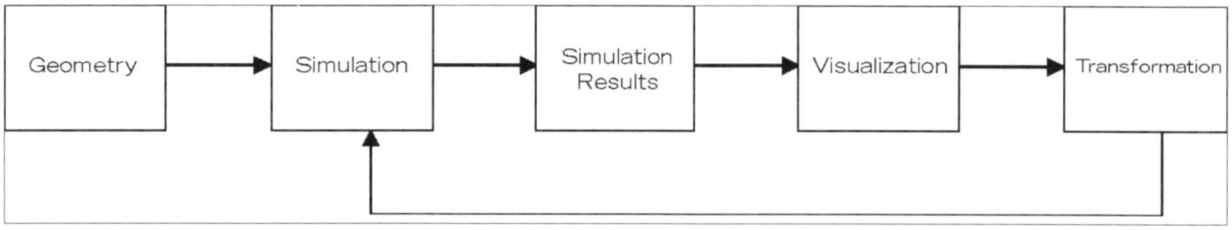

Figure 1. Simulation and Interaction

3.1 Visualization of Noise Propagation in Urban Spaces

Noise propagation in urban spaces is visualized on PC screens as two-dimensional sections through the three-dimensional area of investigation so far. This can be quite reasonable for noise nuisance plans of large areas. If an urban space is to be examined, the vertical structure and the spatial propagation of noise becomes relevant. This can only be examined with a program that offers the ability of simulating and visualizing noise propagation in the third dimension as well.

For the creation of an expertise about the noise level distribution in the city, the noise propagation is usually just computed for one horizontal level at a certain height. For the three-dimensional representation, either several horizontal or vertical sections must be simulated, or a three-dimensional structured or unstructured grid has to be defined that can also be simulated by "single-point runs." The resulting model can be supplied to a visualization software.

A competent facility with much expertise within the range of "Scientific Visualization" is the visualization department of the High Performance Computing Center Stuttgart (HLRS) at the University of Stuttgart, which is participating in this project. Numerous projects in cooperation with international firms and other research establishments or universities were already accomplished successfully. As a major result of their research and development activities, the HLRS developed a software called COVISE (Collaborative Visualization and Simulation Environment). COVISE was particularly developed for the visualization of three-dimensional simulation data. This program running under the operating system Linux is intended for data visualization on screen and for different kinds of virtual reality media.

3.2 Function Mode of COVISE

Since COVISE is developed with a modular structure, it is easily extendable with Plug-Ins and offers open interfaces for the connection of different simulation programs. We interactively connected Soundplan and COVISE with a particularly developed Plug-In. Some functions of the VUI (Virtual User Interface) of COVISE were extended to a simple VR-Modeler that can be adapted to our desired needs.

3.3 Employment of the VUI

The VR-Modeler is conceived consciously simply. Only a few modeling functions are needed. For example, simple building cuboids (boxes) can be created or removed. They can be transformed (moved, rotated, and scaled) afterwards. Optionally, with each change of the VR model the noise propagation is computed again by the connected sound simulation interactively (Figure 1). The ergonomics of the Modeler should enable sketching in VR in a similar, simpler way than working with e.g. PS (expanded polystyrene) foam which is commonly used by city planners for sketch models within the design phase.

4 Technical Implementation – Status Quo

The software-technical realization is based on the connection of already existing programs. They were linked with each other through the development of extensions and Plug-Ins in order to create an extended, interactive design environment. The developers of the respective programs provide support for the project "r.Vipar" in terms of their know-how.

For the connection of the noise simulation program Soundplan running under MS Windows and the virtual reality software COVISE developed for Linux we had to create a control and data interface with appropriate I/O filters connecting both operating systems. The sound simulation and the VR software are thus running with two different workstations. Controlling is currently based on an SSH interface and will be gradually replaced by an internal protocol.

Geometry and other attributes can be transferred over the interface to the simulation and the result values from the simulation in reverse. It is possible to save conditions of intermediate design results, including all individual settings made, and to export the building geometry as well as the model of the noise propagation as vrml-file. Thus, different situations can be compared with one another later again.

The model of the surrounding area can be optionally created with any CAD-program. Over a DXF interface it can be imported into the sound simulation software. COVISE is able to import DXF-files as well, but can also handle vrml 2.0 format. Any objects created in VR, like buildings or points of immission, will be accounted in the simulation run. They can be picked up and freely moved in space (Figure 3). A new computation of the simulation is started currently by pressing a button in

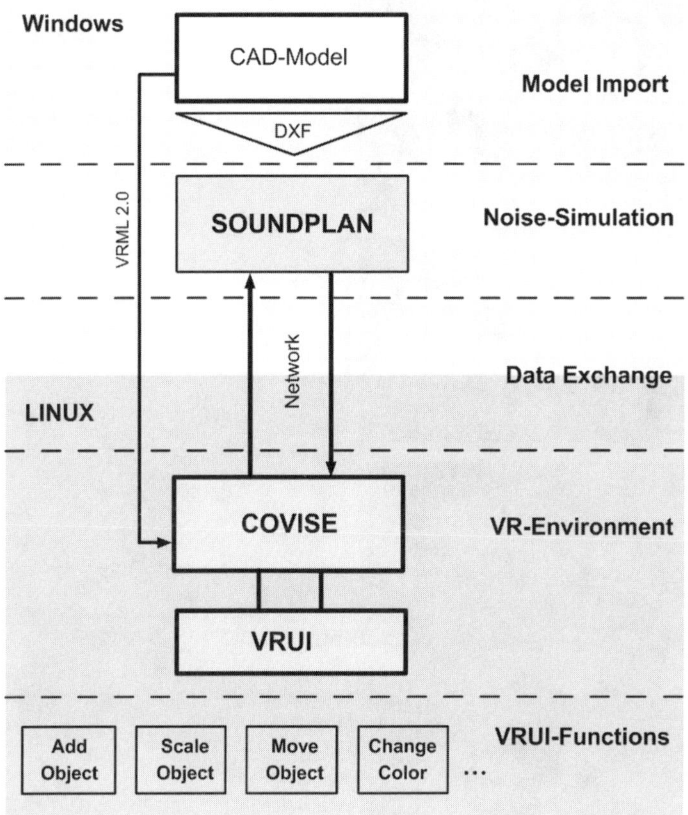

Figure 2.

the VRUI. For the representation of the noise propagation different visualization techniques, like ISO-surfaces or volume rendering, can be used. The shades of color and limit values can be changed over an VRUI interface interactively among other visualization parameters.

5 Intended employment in teachings

5.1 Didactical Concept: the "Open VR"

The faculty of architecture and urban planning at the University of Stuttgart runs a computer pool with approximately 100 CAD workstations over all. Within this pool a "One-Wall" VR installation is going to be set up. This includes a stereo projection wall together with a tracking system that will be operated with similar technology as used in a "CAVE" (Cave Automatic Virtual Environment). This facility should be freely accessible like all the other workstations for collegiate studies. Through this direct access working on VR projects should become more natural. The basics of how to use and work within a VR environment will be taught in classes. Some seminars will concern specific questions regarding the field of architecture, city planning, and virtual reality. Under these conditions the VR-tool developed in the context of "r.Vipar" is to be employed for small design tasks concerning city planning.

5.2 The practice in basic teachings

The developed tool should also be usable for teaching first and second year students. Therefore, a goal is to sensitize them for the topic of scientific simulations through e.g. the simulation of noise propagation in urban spaces. They will learn how to consider ecological aspects within their design process.

6 Outlook

In the further progress of the project, "r.Vipar" the on-line interface will be optimized first. Parallel to that, visualization techniques will be examined, and the VR Modeler will be adapted to the required needs. In the VRUI, it should be possible to define single points of immission as well as structured or unstructured grids. Afterwards, a prototype of the design environment developed in "r.Vipar" is to be used in teaching and thus tested by students.

A next step will be to expand the prototype through an interactive connection with the light simulation program "Lightscape." With the help of this software, it should be possible to integrate the simulation of daylight and artificial light situations into draft planning. A converter has already been developed. It summarizes several output files from "Lightscape" to a "Vrml 2.0" file that can be imported into COVISE. It should become possible to examine shading processes of buildings and to create e.g. zoning plans for city lighting in VR.

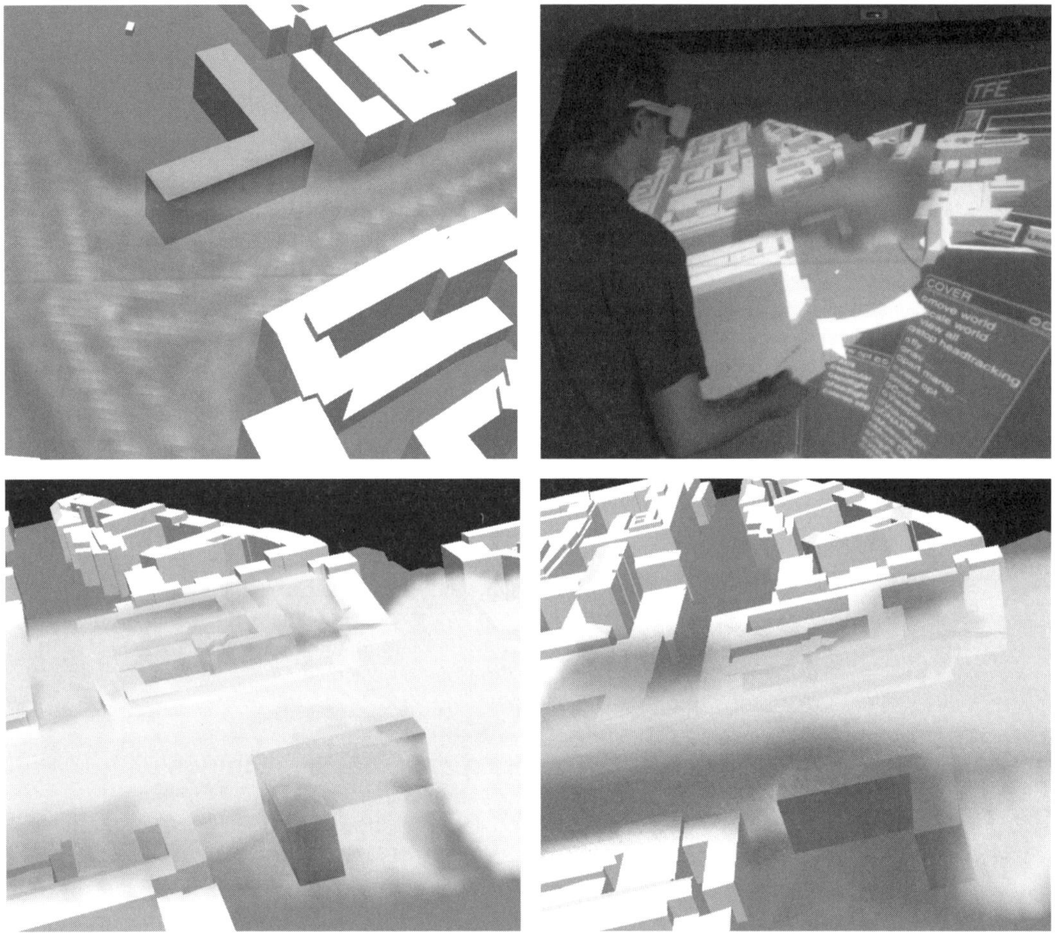

Figure 3.

References

Besser, T., and R. Schildwächter. (2000). VRML in der Bauleitplanung und im städtebaulichen Entwurf, *CORP 2000*, 7. Symposium zur Rolle der Informationstechnologie in der und für die Raumplanung.

Fritz, O. (2002). Programmieren statt Zeichnen? - Vom Einfluß digitaler Technologie auf den architektonischen Entwurf, in: *archithese 4/02*, 14-19, Internet:http://www.caad.arch.ethz.ch/CAAD-Extern/665

Lehmkühler, S. (1999). Computergestützte Visualisierungstechniken in der Stadtplanung – Bedingungen und Potentiale des Ersatzes traditioneller durch computergestützte Visualisierungstechniken in der Stadtplanungspraxis, *Blaue Reihe, Dortmunder Beiträge zur Raumplanung 91*, Dortmund 1999.

Lang and Rantzau. (1998). *Virtual Reality usage at HRLS*, HLRS, Rechenzentrum Universität Stuttgart. Stuttgart: Internet: http://www.hlrs.de/organization/vis/

Preim and Ritter. (2002). *Techniken zur interaktiven Hervorhebung von Objekten inmedizinischen 3d-Visualisierung*, MeVis, Center for Medical Diagnostic Systems and Visualization, University of Bremen.

Schweizer, S. (2000). WUMS - Modellierung auf lokaler Ebene, *SI Universität Stuttgat*, Stuttgart: http://www.architektur.uni-stuttgart.de/WUMS/einl.html

Töllner, M. (2000). Die Arbeit mit Unschärfen im städtebaulichen Entwurfsprozess, *CORP 2000*, 7. Symposium für „Computergestützte Raumplanung."

Tsou, J.Y., Y. Zhu, and S. Lam. (2001). Improving air quality of public transport interchanges desing – Strategies to integrate CFD simulation in early design process. *Proceedings of the eCAADe 2001*, 54 – 59, Otaniemi: Otaniemi Oy.

G Pen: An Intelligent Designer's Playmate

Chor-Kheng Lim
National Chiao Tung University

Abstract

In the field of design the pen-based system is a newly developed computer interface that provides the designer with the convenience of a pen in freehand sketches. But these pen-based systems only focus on an interface familiar to the designers and the application of the hardware and software that go with it, treating the pen only as a mouse-like input device. As pen and pad are devices for the pen-based system, the hope is that they can be endowed with more intelligent characteristics to let them interact with designer's gestures and become a creative source for the designers, while simultaneously preventing the design fixation encountered by designers during design process. This research utilizes the unintentional hand gestures made by designers, such as the designer's grip of the pen or movement involved in playing with the pen, putting it down, knocking it, twisting it or shaking it, during the thinking process or when running into a design fixation. From the interaction between the pen and the pad, certain actions may be generated to stimulate the designer's thinking process. This research uses a neural network as the main learning mechanism for the eventual development of a prototype of a pen-based drawing system that provides timely visual stimulation: a G Pen system.

G Pen: An Intelligent Designer's Playmate

Chor-Kheng Lim
National Chiao Tung University

1 Introduction

In 1965 Mr. Sutherland, a computer graphic pioneer, devised the interactive drawing program called Sketchpad. Sketchpad enabled users to touch or draw directly on a cathode-ray tube image by using a light pen. However, since the 1970s when the mouse was universally adapted, this type of stylus device became relatively unpopular until the beginning of 1990, in which year pen-based systems and PDAs were introduced and marketed. Stylus devices once again became the focus of discussion, especially in the design field, due to the importance of input devices to a designer. Stacy (1996) pointed out that a good Computer Aided Conceptual Design system (CACD), should provide an environment for designers without any system limitations so that designers' ideas can flow freely. Due to the complexity of the operating interface in mouse-based CACD systems, researchers turned to designing a pen-based drawing system that would be suitable for designers in the conceptual stage (Gross 1996; Gross and Do 1996; Landay 1996; Trinder 1999; Plimmer and Apperley 2002).

Besides having such advantages as being convenient and easy to use, the pen-based system also has powerful added features: research-based features such as gestures and drawing characteristics, the application of transparent tracing paper, the simulation of the touch sensitivity of a pen, colors and the ability to edit. Given that such an application interface, which offers a natural design medium, has been tried and even found suitable in the conceptual design stage, the pen-based system, with the exception of the aforementioned intelligent assisting features, has a real chance to become something that sparks the imagination and stimulates creativity.

2 Problem and Objective

During the drawing process, designers may encounter a state of design fixation for a period (Jansson et al. 1991). It is at this time that the design media utilized can be a very important factor to a designer due to the frequent interaction or communication through the chosen design media (Schon and Wiggins 1992). The problem of design fixation can be solved if both ends in a communication process can carry out a bi-directional active or passive interaction.

A designer's gesture in a pen-based system expresses his/her intentions. The most common situation will be when a designer puts down the pen as he/she is tired of drawing at the moment. This gesture represents the state of design fixation. Other gestures, like playing with the pen, are also common occurrences in a design process. From this, we derive that a pen is not only an input device; it is also a "playmate" to a designer. Therefore, other than providing multi-functional features and extensive memory capacity, a pen-based system should also be equipped with intelligent interactive mechanisms to provide designers with creative or imaginative visual stimuli. This research focuses mainly on how to make the interactive relationship between a designer and design media more interesting. Solutions for the question of how to provide a designer with appropriate visual stimuli should be found in order to solve the problem of design fixation. The objective of this research is to devise a prototype of a pen-based sketching system, or G Pen, that is able to provide timely visual stimuli. This system utilizes the Neural Network (Coyne and Newton 1990; Haykin 1999) as the main learning mechanism (Figure1).

3 Previous Works

3.1 Development of computers' User Interface

The computer's user interface (UI) has been modified and invented to fulfill the demands of different fields, such as mouse-ware and light pen devices development in the early periods. Nowadays, due to advanced technology, various devices have been developed. These can be categorized as:

1. General input devices: mouse-like devices (mouse, wheel mouse, trackball, etc); keyboards (QWERTY, Dvorak, Maltron, chording keyboard); pen-based devices (pressure sensitive, tablet computer, palm-top).

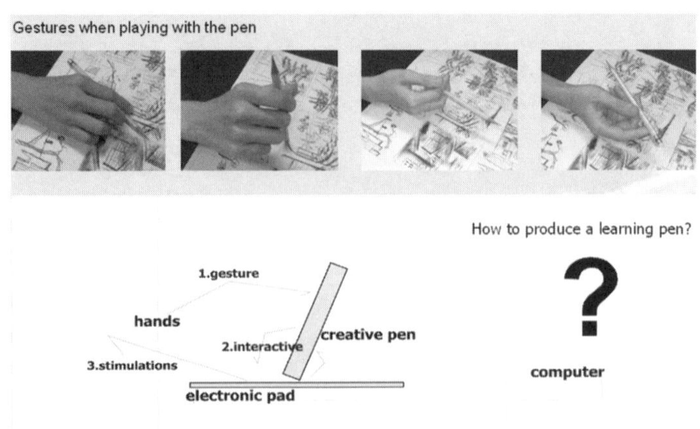

Figure 1. System concept

2. 3D input devices: mainly gesture-based like electromagnetic tracker, acoustic-inertial trackers, optical trackers, gloves and motion capture.
3. Output devices: divide into two parts-Classification-Stereo & Degree of immersion, such as desktop (vector display, CRT, LCD); semi-immersive desktop (rear projected, typically in stereo); immersive (CAVE, stereo shutter glasses).

The development of these devices attempts to be more useable and interactive to the users, especially in correlation to the human behavior or human gestures.

3.2 User Interface in Design Field

During the design conceptual stage, the designer gives a tangible form to the inner thought process via the design media. The design media therefore must be something that the designer is accustomed to using. The speed with which they operate must also be unencumbered by complex commands. Since 1990, many researchers labored hard to find suitable interfaces for designers to draw with. Gross, Landay, Trinder and other researchers all proposed pen-based systems as a suitable interface which can overcome the cumbersome movement required to operate a mouse. With the pen-based system hand drawing or handwriting replaces keyboard entries while gestures replace the keys and buttons on a physical device.

The pen-based system is suitable as a drawing interface, because pen-and-paper is thoroughly familiar to the designers, and the pen-based system is derivative of the pen-and-paper. Other than to serve as a natural input interface, it can also couple the system's functions with more functions like gesture-based, transparency, adaptability of the pen and knowledge based systems to form a total intelligent design-assisting system.

3.3 Development of pen-based system

The pen-based system has improved the CAD operating interface to enable designers to complete the whole course of design in a computer environment. Currently developed pen-based systems can be classified into three categories:

1. Projection drafting systems that combine physical pen-and-paper to aid in group communications (Wellner 1993; Moran and Chiu 1995).
2. Systems that translate two-dimensional sketches into three-dimensional models (Igarashi 1999; Schweikardt and Gross 2000; Do 2001).
3. Systems that function mainly as graphic recognition engines for sketches (Landay 1996; Gross & Do 1996; Plimmer & Apperley 2002).

For the 1st category, Digital Desk proposed by Wellner (1993) integrates the physical table and the projection of the computer to constitute the table as a digitized workstation. The 2nd category enables the translation from two-dimensional sketches into three-dimensional models. Igarashi (1996) had developed the Teddy system which is generally used in the industrial field. As an example of the 3rd category's system, Gross (1996) proposed a graphic recognition system—Electric Cocktail Napkin for the architecture field in order to be used in the conceptual design stage.

In addition to these software developments, pen-based systems attempt to explore the input interface. For example, Nabeshima (1995) developed a memo pen which integrate some components to a pen such as lenses, a CCD, a stress sensor, a micro computer, a memory and a battery to enable recording naturally the process of writing (figure 2). Furthermore, Hennessy (1992) proposed a drawing tool in the industrial field called IDEATOR which is constituted by the LCD tablet and various functional electronic pens (figure 3). These pen-based systems extend the current pen-and-paper's characteristics; especially attach more computational function to it.

3.4 Method

This input and output device of the G Pen system is no longer a simple input/output device; rather, it is now a mechanism to interact with the designer. It is designed mainly on the designer's unintentional gestures, such as putting the pen down, touching and knocking with the pen, and twirling and shaking the pen (Figure 4), and the interaction between the pen and pad to produce stimulating visual feedbacks.

This research proposed a preliminary prototype of the system. Due to the differing gestures of the different designers, the G pen system needs a learning mechanism to recognize these gestures. The manipulation of the G pen system is divided into two stages (Figure 5):

1. External tracking process—to detect various gestures as the input data for the second stage.
2. Internal training system—utilizing the Neural Network for learning and training in the recognition of the different gestures, and then reacting into the proper assigned feedback actions.

The system operational procedures are as the following:

1. Tracking:

Two light points (point A and point B) are installed on each end of the pen as trackers. After continuously filming the designer's gestures when drawing, coordinates of the light points are marked in a 7x7 grid. The purpose of tracking is to detect various gestures.

As Figure 6 shows, different gestures can be detected from the key frame of the continuous film as it records the track of the light point trackers (A & B): when putting down the pen, it is static and idle, hence we can obtain the coordinates of A and B (AX1,AY1)(BX2,BY2); while knocking with the pen is a continuous action, and the track is vertical, so we can derive the coordinates of A(AX1,AY1)(AX2,AY2) or B (BX1,BY1)(BX2,BY2); shaking the pen has two different gestures, shaking with one end of the pen and both ends of the pen. Both of these tracks are curved; nevertheless it can be differentiated by the amount of the

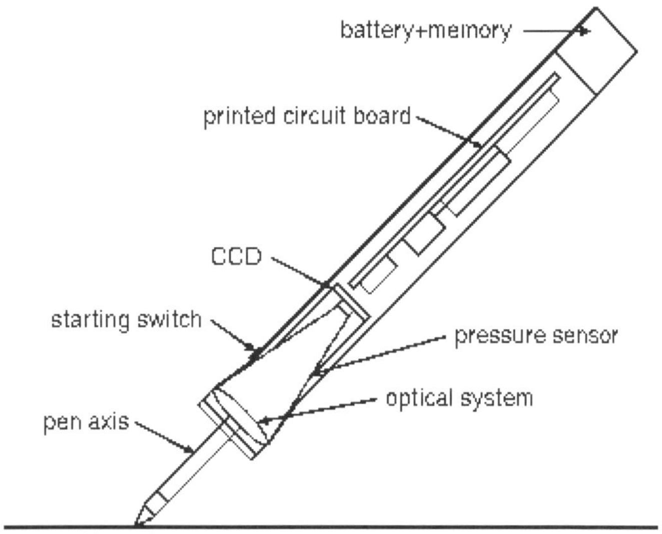

Figure 2. Memo Pen

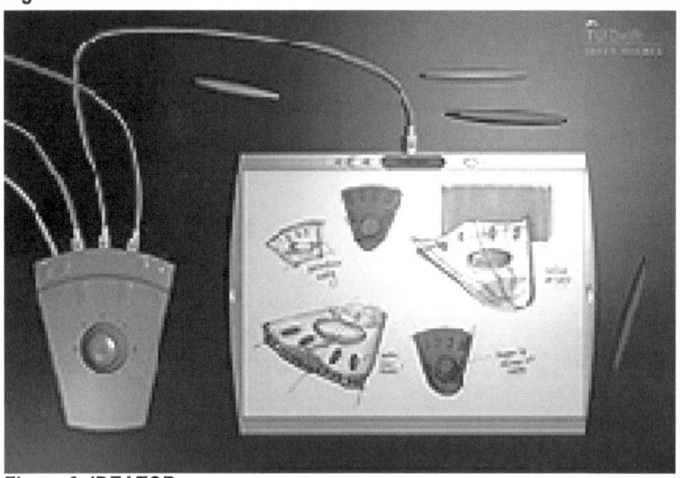

Figure 3. IDEATOR

light point trackers, one point or two points. Lastly, twirling the pen has a horizontal track, and obtains the two trackers (A & B) coordinates (AX1,AY1)(AX2,AY2) (BX1,BY1)(BX2,BY2). All these coordinate values will conduct input data for the next training stage.

2. Training:

The neural network is utilized as the training and learning mechanism. The coordinates data derived from tracking is used as object-oriented input data for the neural network system, and assigned feedback actions are used as the output data (Figure 8).

• Input data: In addition to the data of the coordinates data from the tracking phase, it incorporates another two attributes to constitute the input data for the neural network system: 1. The amount of the light point trackers. 2. The track figures of the key frames, such as: point A, point B, vertical track, horizontal track and curve track.

• Output data: Various feedback actions are used for the output data, such as idle, edit, zooming, and image display and rotate (Table 1). However, so far the operating system now is using some symbols to represent these actions (Figure 7).

Table 1: Feedback actions

	Gestures	Feedback action
1.	Put down the pen	IDLE
2.	Knocking	Edit
3	Shaking (single light point)	Zooming
4.	Shaking (two light points)	Image display
5.	Twirling	Rotate

• Training data: Draw 20 different sets of gesture coordinates from the films to be used as neural network training data (4 sets of data each from the 5 gestures data, Figure 9). Then configure the neural network software system with 63 input data, 49 output data, and two 25 hidden layers [63-25-25-49] (Figure 10). These 20 sets of data proceeds the training process until the value of training error is less than 0.01, which is called "well train." Use this "well train" network to test the input data, finally it obtains an exact assigned output data.

• Testing data: After the above stated training data is well trained, draw another 20 sets of coordinates from the film as testing data (Figure 11). This testing data will be tested by the "well train" network to confirm that the outcome is exactly true.

3.5 Results

After the neural network is well trained and tests have been done with the testing data, derived results are stated in figure 12 and 13. Although the output data of the fourth and fifth groups are not as intact as the previous three, they can still be easily identified. Due to the fact that this research is still in progress, the system uses the symbols to represent the outcome feedback actions instead of reacting to the proper actions by the display device. However, from the derived results of the network, it can prove that the utilized neural network as the learning mechanism is feasible. Therefore, we conclude that the prototype may have the opportunity to be developed into a better interactive pen-based system for design purposes. This system does not have the difficulties in using the interface, and the neural network learning mechanism learns and trains to adapt to different gestures of different designers. Therefore, it will become a new design media equipped with intelligent creativity assistance.

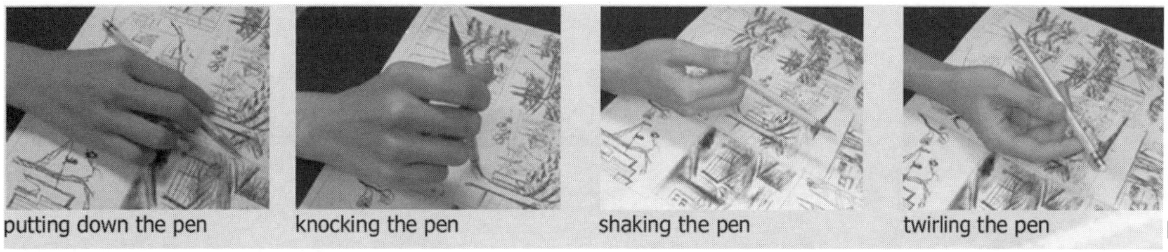

Figure 4. Gestures

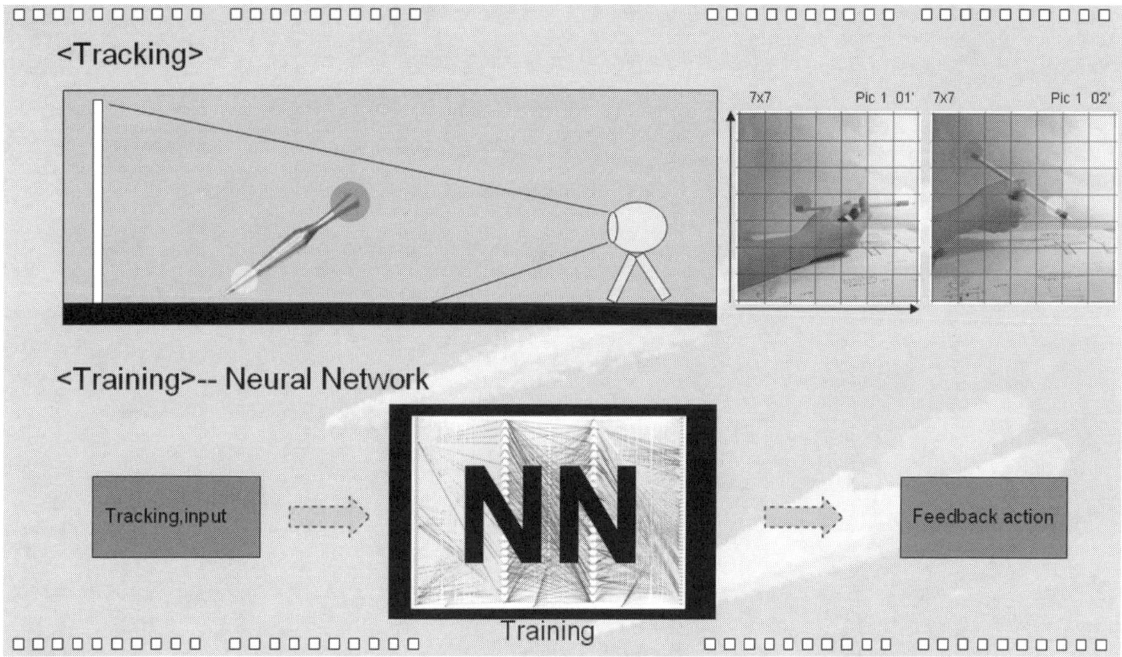

Figure 5. Mechanism

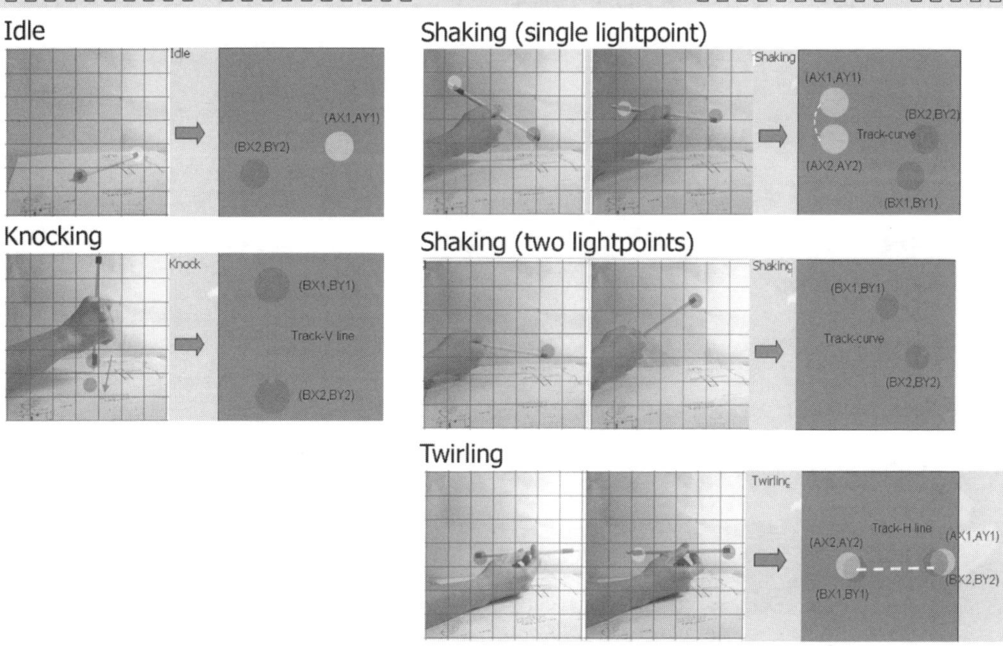

Figure 6. Tracking

3.6 Significant and Future Studies

The G pen system proposed by research is an interactive design media, destined to provide designers' with visual stimuli and solve the design fixation encountered by designers while drawing. It can encourage designers to think of a new idea or experience some unexpected discoveries. Meanwhile, designers will become accustomed to it naturally as it is a pen input device which is convenient to most people. Further more it can become a good design "playmate" to the designers and can be used by them in general.

For future studies, it is hoped that this prototype of the system can enhance its learning and training mechanism in order to provide designers with the ability to set the feedback actions or different gestures more freely. Moreover, the feedback actions must be revised so that they provide a good interaction between designers and their drawings instead of influencing the design process.

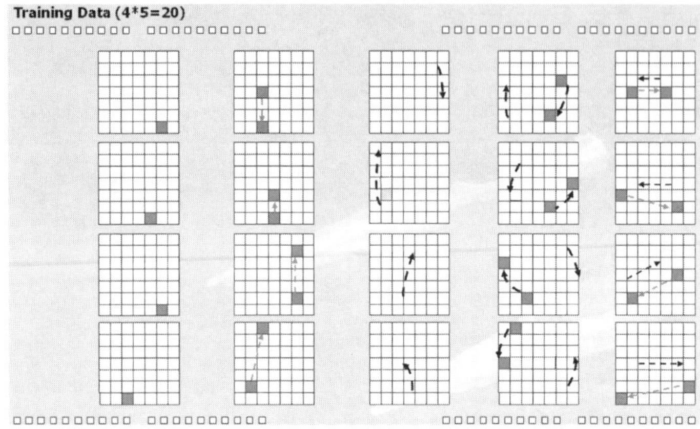

Figure 9. Training Data

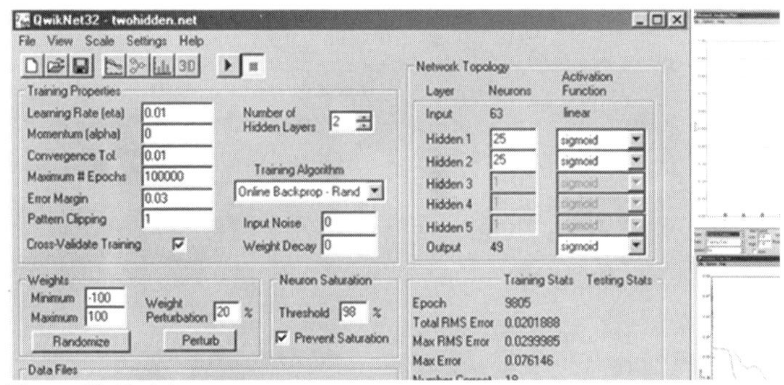

Figure 10. Training

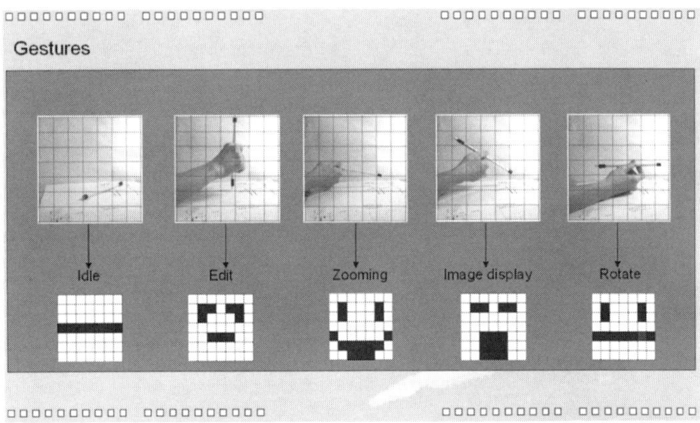

Figure 7. Feedback actions

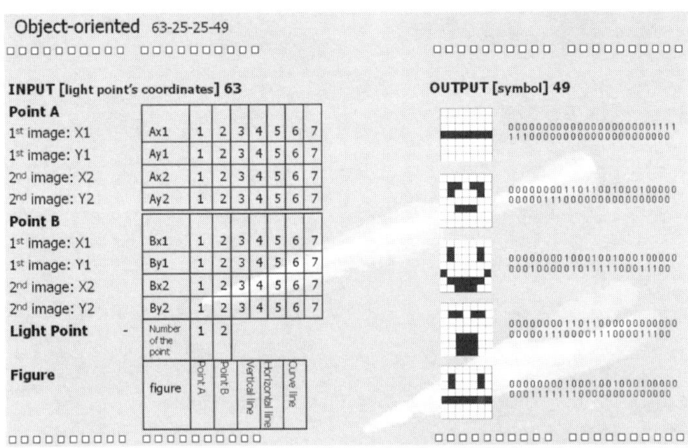

Figure 8. Input & Output Data

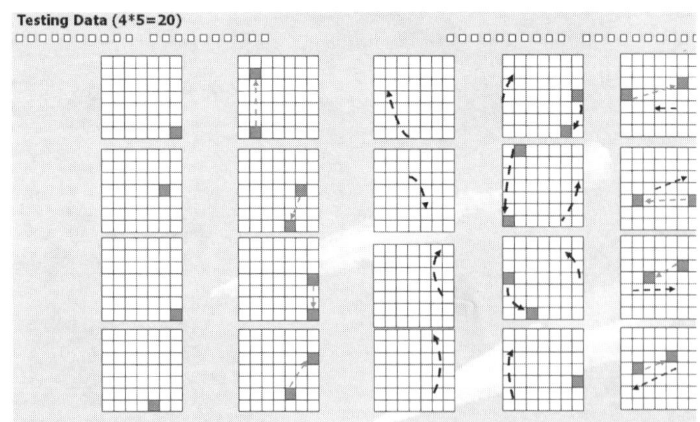

Figure 11. Testing Data

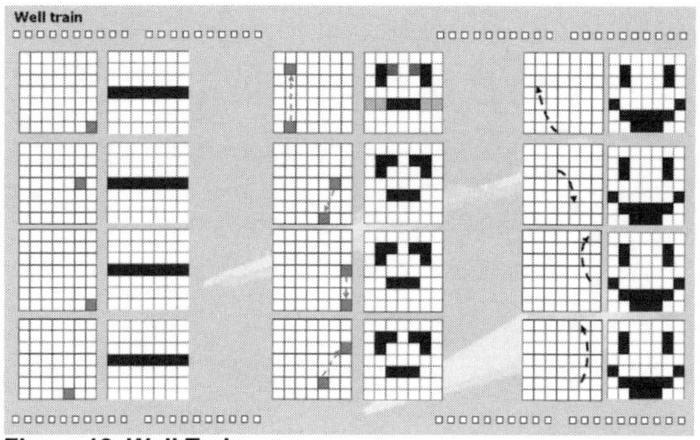

Figure 12. Well Train

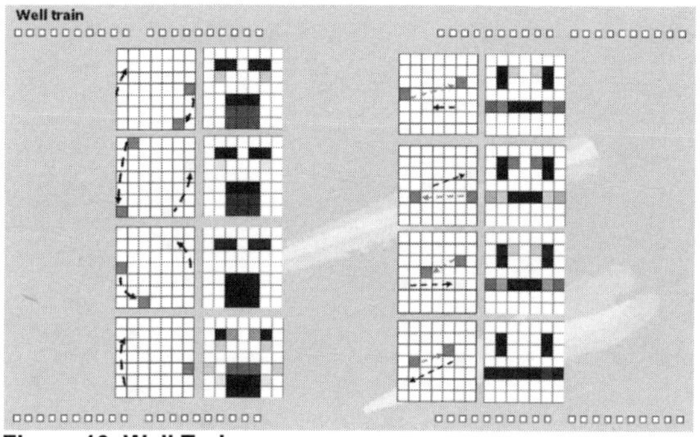

Figure 13. Well Train

References

Coyne, R. D. and S. Newton, (1990). Design reasoning by association. *Environment and planningB: Planning and design*. 17: 39-56.

Do, E. Y.-L. (2001). VR Sketchpad. *CAAD FUTURES*. Eindhoven. 161-172.

Gross, M. D. (1996). The Electronic Cocktail Napkin - a computational environment for working with design diagrams. *Design studies*. 17(1): 53-69.

Gross, M. D. and E.Do. (1996). Ambiguous Intensions: A Paper-like interface for creative design. *Proceedings of ACM conference on user interface software technology.*

Haykin, S. (1999). *Neural networks: A comprehensive foundation:* Prentice Hall.

Hennessey, J. M. (1992). The IDEATE project: Exploring computer enhancements for conceptualising. Edited by T.White and A Tzonis, *Automation based creative design.* Elsevier, Amsterdam.

Igarashi, T., S.Matsuoka, and H.Tanaka, (1999). Teddy: A sketching interface for 3D freeform design. *ACM SIGGRAPH*. Annual Conference on Computer Graphics. 409-416.

Jansson, G, D. and S.Smith, (1991). Design Fixation. *Design studies* 12(1): 3-11.

Landay, J. A. (1996). SILK: Sketching Interfaces Like Krazy. *Human factors in Computing. CHI96.*

Moran, T. P. and P.Chiu, (1995). Implicit Structures for Pen-Based System within a Freedom Interaction Paradigm. *Proceeding CHI'95.*

Nabeshima, S.,Yamamoto,K.Agusa,T.Taguch (1995) MEMO-PEN: a new input device.*CHI'95 Conference Companion* 1995: 256-257.

Plimmer, B. E., and M. Apperley. (2002). Computer-aided sketching to capture preliminary design. *Australian user interface conference* (AUIC2002).

Schon, D. A. and G.Wiggins (1992). Kinds of seeing and their structures in designing. *Design studies,*13: 135-156.

Schweikardt, E. and M. D. Gross, (2000). Digital clay:deriving digital models from freehand sketches. *Automation in construction* 9: 107-115.

Trinder, M. (1999). The computer's role in sketch design: A transparent sketching medium. *Proceedings of CAADfutures'99.*

Wellner, P. (1993). Interacting with paper on the DigitalDesk. *Communications of the ACM*. 87-96.

SolCAD: 3D Spatial Design Tool Tool to Generate Solar Envelope

Manu Juyal, Arizona State University

Karen Kensek, University of Southern California
Ralph Knowles, University of Southern California

Abstract

In this research the concept of Solar Envelope has been used to develop a 3D Spatial Design Tool tool, SolCAD, for generating an envelope over a given site based on various design parameters. The solar envelope can be imagined as a container, whose boundaries are derived from the sun's relative motion. Buildings within this container will not overshadow their surroundings during critical periods of solar access for passive and low-energy architecture. The solar envelope is a space-time construct. Its spatial limits are defined by the parameters of land parcel size, shape, orientation, topography and latitude. It also depends on the time or the period of the time for which it is designed. Its time limits are defined by the hours of each day and the season for which solar access is provided to the land parcel (Knowles 1981). This tool intends to generate an envelope over a site of any shape, size and orientation and for different boundary and height conditions of shadow lines. It is suitable for initial stages of building design process to determine the shape of the building even before the design has been conceptualized.

SolCAD: 3D Spatial Design Tool Tool to Generate Solar Envelope

Manu Juyal, Arizona State University

Karen Kensek, University of Southern California
Ralph Knowles, University of Southern California

1 Introduction

Solar access has become a critical issue around the world with an increasing number of common people looking at the sun as a source of energy. Solar Access has therefore become a legitimate area of public policy. Its main objective is to regulate the conditions that will restrict or allow the neighbors to shadow one another (Knowles 1981). There should be a constant honest effort on part of the architects and planners to make sure that the building does not infringe the solar rights of adjacent properties. Pioneering efforts to solve these issues were made by Ralph L. Knowles by developing and testing the concept of solar envelope over the period 1976-1993. Solar envelope is a container within which a designed building will not cast a shadow on surrounding (Figure1). The solar envelope is a space-time construct. The shape and the size of an envelope are defined by the geometry, orientation, topography, location of the site and its urban context. It also depends on the time or the period of the time in a day for which it is designed. Its time limits are defined by the hours of each day and the season for which solar access is provided to the land parcel (Knowles 1981).

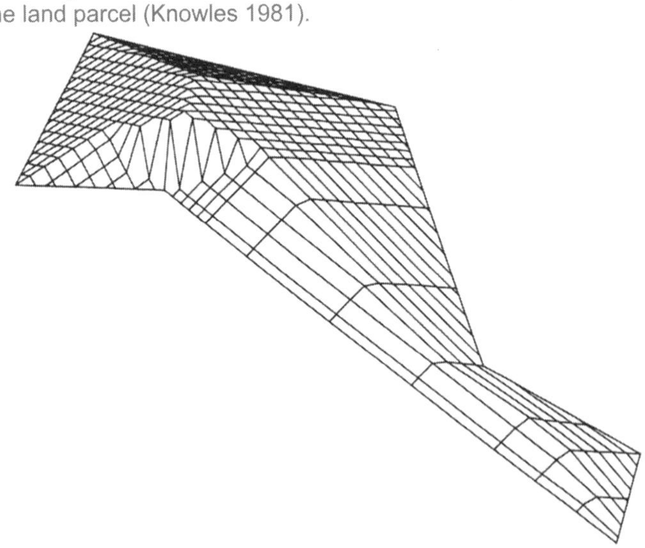

Figure 1. Solar envelope for winter solstice. (Knowles 1981)

The solar envelope helps conserve energy and improve the quality of life by guaranteeing access to sunlight during critical insolation period of a day. It can be used to give the guidelines to control building height and shape so that an appropriate amount of sunlight in the city for a particular time period can be insured. Ralph Knowles has been testing this concept in upper division design studios at the School of Architecture at the University of Southern California. The results of his research have been published in *Energy and Form*, *Solar Energy, Building and the Law*, and *Sun Rhythm and Form.*

In USC design studios, solar envelopes are constructed manually. All the calculations are done graphically and the results are presented using physical models. The tedious and time-consuming work involved in manual method of constructing does not leave students with enough opportunity and willingness to explore other useful issues related to solar envelopes. Even for most practicing architects, this process would be too long and time consuming to be implemented in the practice (Yeh 1992). To be effective as a design tool and a zoning instrument for urban solar-access, the solar envelope needs a computer tool for quick calculations and visualization. The most important step in this direction will be to develop a CAD tool which can not only check the validity of a given design but can also provide guidelines or suggestions to the designer for further amendments of a design.

Past attempts to develop such a tool have not been entirely successful due to their inability to include some desirable spatial and temporal constraints on the envelope's size and shape. There are various factors. The most important being the inability to generate the envelope for a complex geometrical shape and for varying shadow conditions at site boundaries. There was also a need for compatibility with the existing CAD programs so that the drawing data can be exchanged between them. Also, the past programs allowed the analysis of one set of data but failed to compare different set of data, i.e., failed to compare the solar envelope for different times of years.

2 Objective

The aim of this study is to develop a new tool that will have the ability to handle more envelope conditions without overly burdening the user and thus discouraging planning and architectural applications.

The solar envelope technique is widely accepted and acknowledged, but due to its complexity it needs an expertise in the understanding of basic geography and descriptive geometry. Moreover, the process of constructing a solar envelope manually using physical models can sometimes be very tedious and time consuming, especially for the site with a complex geometry. Furthermore, it does not allow the comparison of different time periods, based on weather and sun availability. The development of SolCAD is a step in the direction of making this process simpler for users, both experts and beginners. With the use of

SolCAD the construction of solar envelopes can be completed in a few seconds against doing it manually where it can take days and weeks to construct an accurate envelope.

The aim is to make SolCAD work for sites with complex geometry and to make it compatible with the widely used CAD tools, e.g., AutoCAD and Form_Z. It should allow users to compare the data for different time periods and for different shadow conditions. The purpose of this tool is not to undermine the importance of manual method of generating the envelope but to facilitate it with its quick calculating abilities. SolCAD by its interactivity and quick calculations will make the process of generating solar envelopes fast and accurate.

3 Existing Tools and Methods

3.1 Physical Method

So far the most commonly used method to design the envelope is by building physical models. Knowles (1981) suggested various methods to draw a solar envelope physically. He used both solid and surface geometries to generate the envelope. The physical method of generating solar envelops uses descriptive geometry, hand calculator, protractors and physical models. Students calculate solar altitude and azimuth to physically generate the solar envelope. Physical models are built to assist the solar design. Using physical models and a sun-simulating machine, the students could actually visualize the effect of the sun's movement on a building and neighborhood (Kensek and Knowles 1997).

Researchers have also proposed and implemented a number of computer-based tools to generate a solar envelope. Arumi (1979) developed a computerized model to determine maximum permissible height of a building that does not infringe the solar rights of adjacent properties. Schiler and Yeh (1992) developed a computer program, *SolVelope*, to generate solar envelopes for flat-rectangular sites with graphical and numerical output. Kensek and Knowles (1997) explain in detail a computer tool, "CalcSolar," that has been developed at the University of Southern California, Los Angeles.

3.2 SolVelope

SolVelope is a computer-based tool to generate solar envelope developed in 1992 by Uen-Fang Patricia Yeh as her thesis for the Master of Building Science degree at USC. This program allows users to test the envelope for different latitude, times and dates, site size and orientation and neighboring site conditions such as streets, parks and the adjacent buildings. However, this tool is limited to only rectangular flat sites; gives ambiguous results for the corner conditions; and also lacks compatibility with the existing CAD tools (Schiler and Yeh 1993).

3.3 CalcSolar

One of the major steps forward in computer generated solar envelope is CalcSolar program, which is written in AutoLisp by Karen Kensek at the University of Southern California. CalcSolar uses the geometric modeling and graphics engine of AutoCAD. It uses AutoCAD to draw sites and shadow constraints. The main advantage of this program is its interactivity and AutoCAD environment, with which most of the architects and planners are familiar. The use of AutoCAD engine has allowed this program to use its interactivity and graphical features. However, the application of this tool is also limited to rectangular sites. Inspite of this shortcoming, CalcSolar tool has been a vast improvement over SolVelope and the developers have resolved some of the computing issues raised by SolVelope.

Numerous attempts have been developed to computerize the sun path diagram and shading mask protractors to analyze the shading devices. The most prominent of them were SolrPath (Haberl and McWatters) at Texas A&M University, Solar Masking Calculator and Shading Analyzer at Building Science Program, University of Southern California. But the solar envelope discussed in this paper looks into the overall shape of the building and not the parts of the buildings, e.g., fenestrations etc. It provides the designers with a form or a framework of the building to start the designing process. Its main aim is to optimize the shape of a building.

4 SolCAD

The program is written in Java programming language and has used Java3D library for graphics display. The main reason for Java as the programming language of choice is its portability. As a result it can be read and run by interpreters on many platforms including Windows 95, Windows NT, and Solaris 2.3 and later. Also, Java3D is a 3D scene-graph-based graphics programming API for the Java language. Using Java3D library developers can easily incorporate high-quality, scalable, platform-independent 3D graphics into Java.

The application has been divided into two steps. In the first step the user draws the site boundaries and shadow boundaries in AutoCAD and in the second step solar envelope is constructed using SolCAD. The mode of communication between the two steps is DXF files generated by AutoCAD.

4.1 Creating the Input File in AutoCAD

Graphical input for the application will come in the form of DXF files using AutoCAD. The site boundaries and the shadow boundaries will be drawn in two separate layers, "Site" and "Fence" respectively. The lines should be closed 3D polylines, represented by appropriate x, y and z coordinates. SolCAD assumes that on AutoCAD screen the north will always point up. Therefore, the site has to be drawn relative to screen's north direction. Once the site boundaries and shadow boundaries are created, the drawing is saved as DXF file.

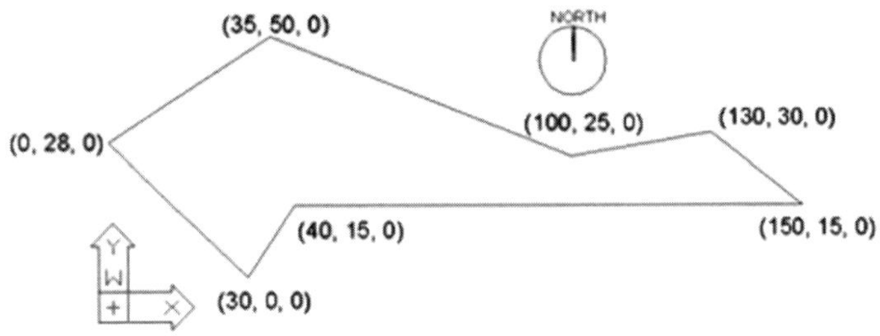

Figure 2: Sample site drawn in AutoCAD. (Knowles 1981)

4.2 Inputs in SolCAD

SolCAD allows the user to construct two types of envelopes, *Single Day Envelope and Composite Envelope.* The single day envelope allows users to generate the envelope for a given time period in a day, e.g., envelope for the time period between 9:00AM and 3:00PM on 21st September. The composite envelope allows the generation of optimized solar envelope for different time periods in a day and also for different times periods in a year, e.g., if users want to see the optimized solar envelope for the entire year, the composite envelope will calculate the envelopes for summer solstice, equinox and winter solstice and will give the optimized result.

To construct Single Day Envelope, users need to select the Select *"Single Day Envelope"* menu item from the control menu. In the dialog box that appears (Figure 3), the desired DXF file is chosen. The variables for the input are month, day, cut-off times, latitude, and grid size. Month represents the month for which the envelope is desired and day represents the day in that month. The cut-off time is a set of times that defines the start and the end of a time period, where start time represents the time of a day from which the envelope is valid and end time represents the time until the envelope remains valid for that day. Grid size decides the density of the mesh representing the envelope, i.e., the distance between the grid points. Maximum permissible height is the height a structure can have in the given area or on the given site as per laws. The north latitudes are given positive values while the south latitudes are given negative values.

The construction of the composite envelope is relatively simpler. The main inputs are the two DXF files having geometric information about solar envelope for two different conditions (Figure 5). Once the program is executed, it compares the information in both the files and calculates the optimized result. The two DXF files, which are used as input, are basically single day envelopes constructed for different time periods or different days or both. One of the highlights of this method is that we can compare and optimize the envelopes for any number of cases simply by first constructing single day envelopes for individual cases and then comparing them with one another.

4.3 Algorithm

There are two approaches for constructing solar envelopes: solid modeling and surface modeling. SolCAD uses the surface geometry method to construct the envelope. Using surface geometry every object is identified to be composed of a number of planes or lines. As a result, clipping is faster and more accurate in surfaces than in solids.

The main idea is to define a cut-off plane for each edge at a regular interval. The edges of each of these planes are defined by the lines drawn from sun's position to the start and the end points of an edge of the site. These cut-off planes are then used for further clipping operations.

The site is divided into a grid based on the grid size provided by the user (Figure 7). Vertical lines are drawn from each grid intersection points and also from the intersection points of grid lines and edges. These vertical lines are clipped for each plane separately and the intersection of each line with the plane is recorded every time clipping is performed on it. Each vertical line should have the minimum height at the end of the calculations in order to optimize the envelope.

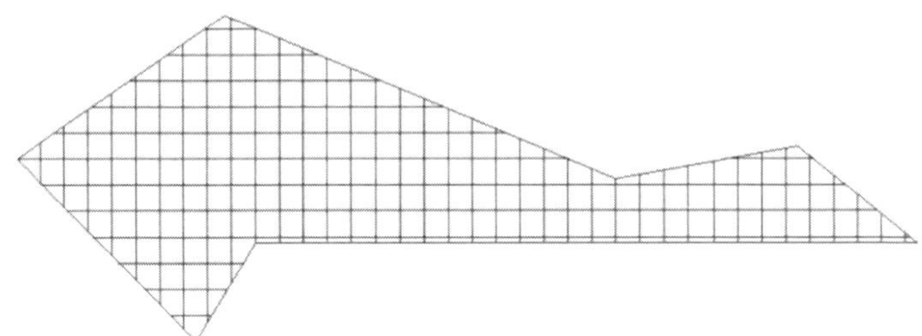

Figure 7: Grid layout on the site

SolCAD uses parametric equations for determining the planar surfaces. The parametric equation of planar surface defines infinite plane, which gives ambiguous results because if a plane is infinite then every line will have an intersection with it. The first check determines if the grid intersection point lies within the plane defined by the edge and sun's position, projected on the ground, i.e. if z=0. If the point is within the plane, then the clipping is performed on the vertical line at that point. In the second check, height of the vertical line (z-value of the end point of the line), which is obtained after clipping, is compared with height that is currently stored. If the new height is found to be less than the current height then it replaces the current height. Thus, at the end we have a set of vertical lines at each grid intersection point with minimum height (z-value).

At the end, the final shape is set by the shortest height attained for each vertical line. Endpoints of these lines can be joined with each other to draw the envelope (Figure 4-11). The accuracy of the envelope depends on the fineness of the grid. A greater degree of precision can be achieved by making the grid dense.

4.4 Output

The output is in the form of a sloping mesh, which defines the solar envelope. Each point on the mesh gives the height or the elevation of the envelope at the envelope at the corresponding point on the ground. This mesh is connected to edges/boundaries of the site at the height derived from the calculation. The end points of these are then joined to form a mesh. The user has an option to view the mesh in SolCAD or to save the file in DXF format and view it in AutoCAD (Figure 8) (Figure 9) (Figure 10).

4.5 Test

The tool was tested for various site conditions, shadow conditions as well as for various temporal conditions. Different shadow conditions were taken into account. The possible shadow conditions that emerged were:

1) No shadow should fall beyond the site boundaries, i.e. shadow height is zero on boundaries.
2) Shadows of certain height will fall either on neighboring properties or on streets or on site boundaries. The heights for the shadows can be provided by placing shadow lines at appropriate positions (section 4.1).
3) Shadows of varying heights fall on the neighboring properties in the form of a pattern.

The sites' conditions were mainly related to the shape and the topology of the sites. The conditions tested were:

4) The sites with irregular shapes (both convex and concave polygonal shapes).
5) The sites with generalized slopes.
6) Width of the surrounding street.
7) A courtyard inside the proposed building on the site.

The temporal conditions were tested for 34° N latitude (Los Angeles).

8) Three different days in the year summer solstice (21st June), Equinox (21st September), winter solstice (21st December). The days can vary with the place and the discretion of the users.
9) The cut-off time was taken to be 9:00AM-3:00PM for June and September, and 10:00AM-2:00PM for December.

5 Future Improvements

There are some limitations with the current version of SolCAD. The current version is not completely a CAD tool yet. It doesn't allow the user to draw the site and boundary inside the program and depends on the input in the form of DXF files. Efforts are being made to enhance the interactivity of the program, which include providing drawing and editing capabilities inside the tool, a better user interface where the user can interactively select the options or the parameters, e.g., providing an interactive world map for selecting the latitudes of the location of the site.

The current version recognizes the continuous slope in one

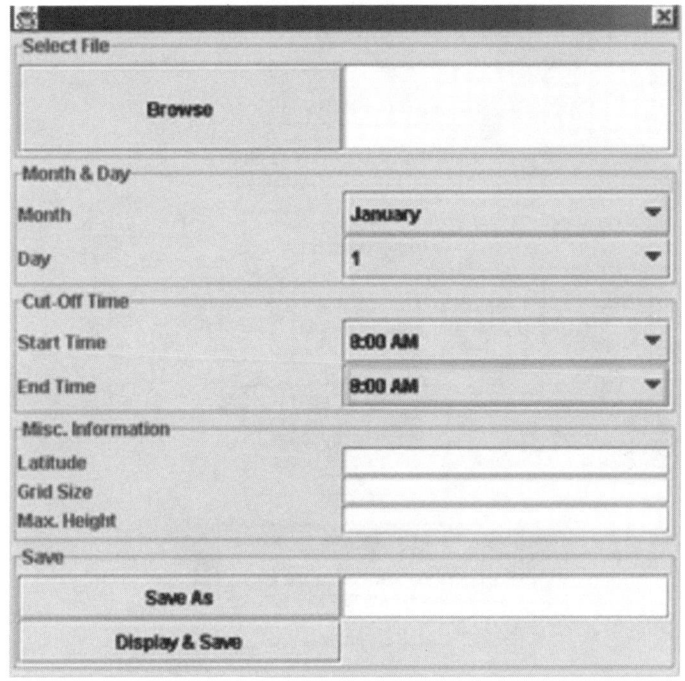

Figure 3. Dialog Box for Single Day Envelope

direction. It will be improved to read more complex topography. The program can also be improved to share the data with related programs like DOE, SOLSHADE and SHADOW. This will widen the scope of its application and will give the user more options. Not only will it increase the usability of the program but will also make many tasks that have become very complicated due to the use of DXF files because many programs have limited capabilities with DXF format.

To widen the application of the tool, it will be upgraded to support the GIS systems. This will extend is utility to an urban design and city planning level.

6 Conclusion

The solar envelope not only protects the solar rights of adjacent buildings but also determines the shape of the building. It helps in designing environmentally responsive buildings to improve living conditions.

The objective of SolCAD is accurate calculation and quick generation of solar envelopes. It is a 3D Spatial Design Tool

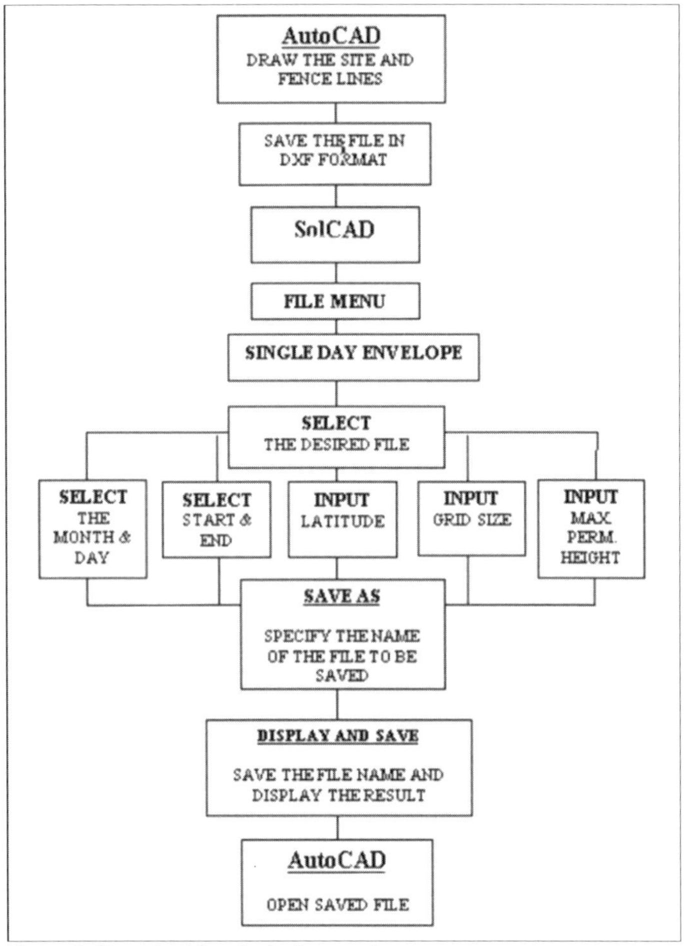

Figure 4: Flow chart for single day envelope

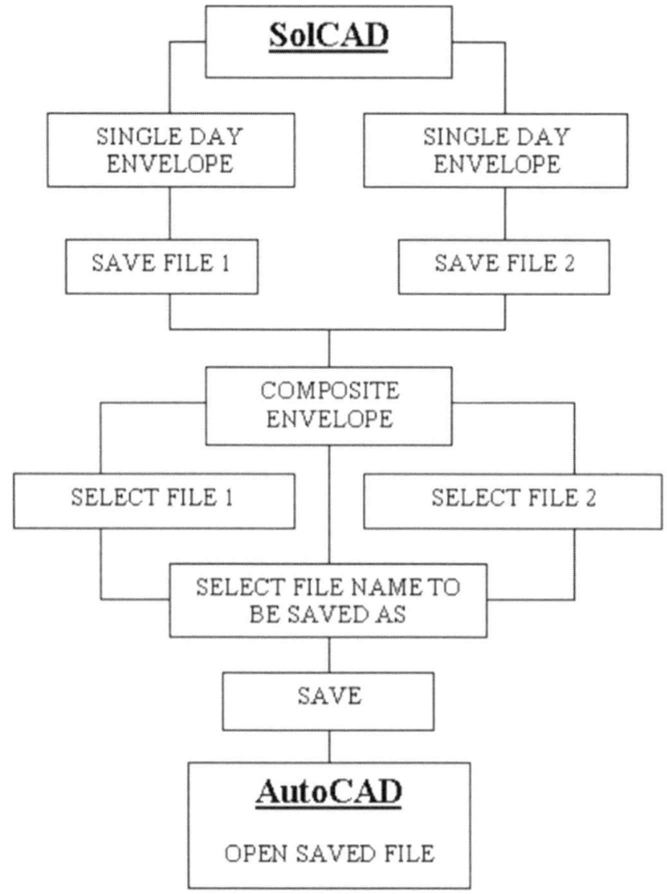

Figure 6: Flow chart for composite envelope

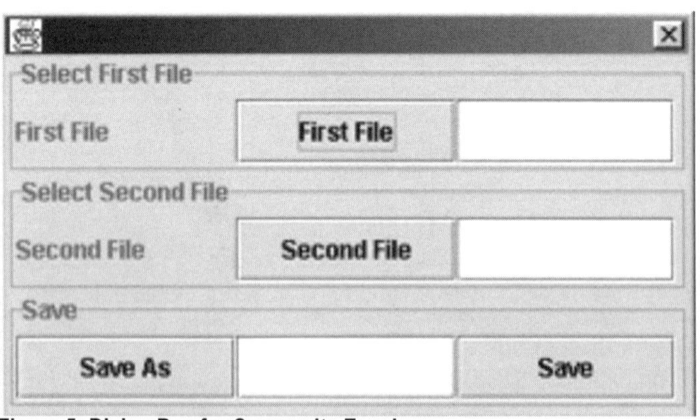

Figure 5: Dialog Box for Composite Envelope

tool for architects, designers, building services engineers and planners. It is suitable for initial stages of building design process to determine the shape of the building even before the design has been conceptualized. It provides design as well as the zoning guidelines in terms of an envelope around the site so that if a building conforms to the shape of solar envelope or remains within the envelope, it will not infringe on the solar rights of the neighboring properties.

SolCAD, has vastly improved upon the shortcomings of earlier tools. It has the ability to read and write DXF files. This has made the tool compatible with popular CAD tools such as AutoCAD and Form_Z. It can analyze sites with different polygonal shapes. It can analyze sites with generalized slopes. SolCAD can read

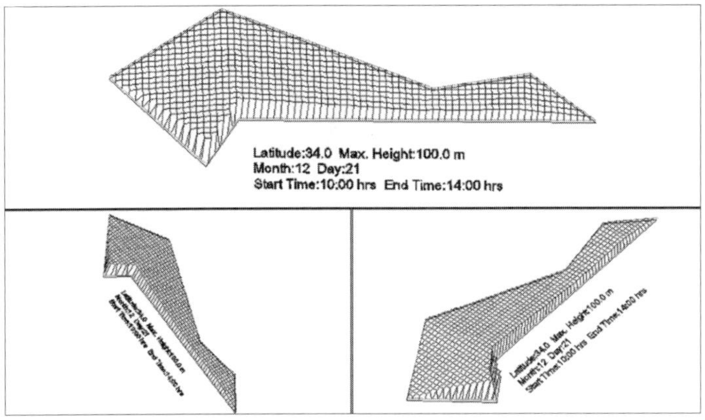

Figure 8. Single day envelope on 21st December

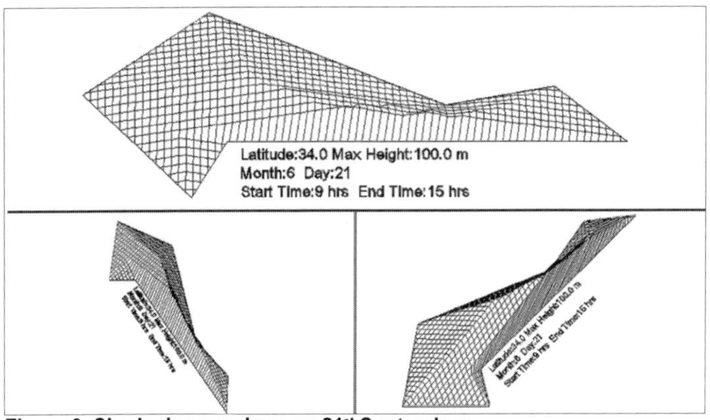

Figure 9. Single day envelope on 21st September

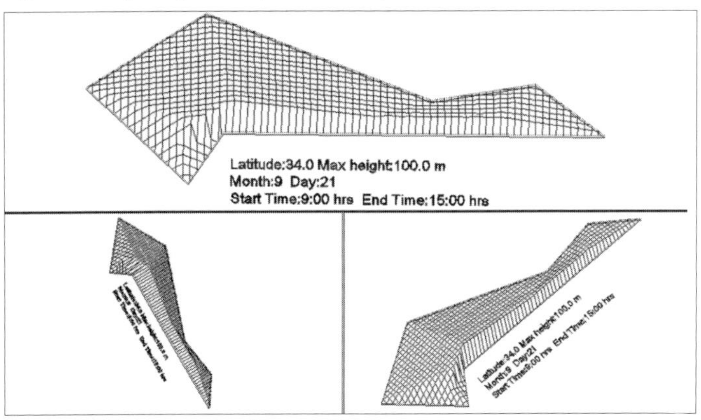

Figure 10. Single day envelope on 21st June

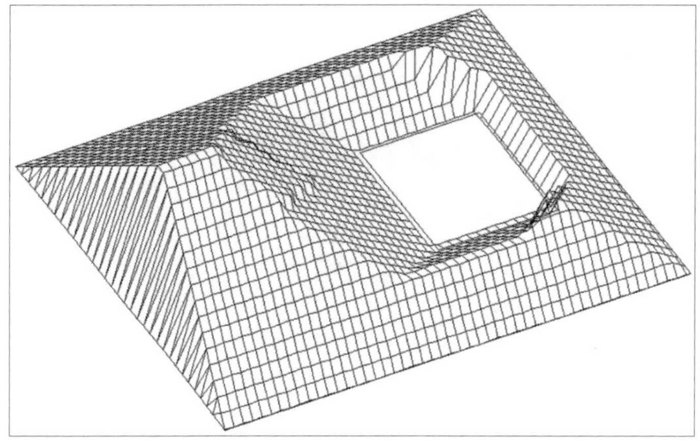

Figure 11. Solar envelope for building, having a courtyard, on a site

the shadow constraints with varying shadow-height conditions inside the site boundaries, over the site boundaries and outside the site-boundaries. It can very well recognize the courtyards within a building. It can also recognize the outlines of shadow-patterns on adjacent properties. Not only can we analyze the solar-envelope for a single day as in the past tools but we can also compare the solar-envelopes between different time periods to get an optimized envelope, called a composite envelope. The program has a user friendly Graphical User Interface (GUI) that allows easy input and shows the results as three-dimensional graphical output. SolCAD takes much lesser time than other similar tools to complete the task of same complexity.

7 Acknowledgements

The authors would like to thank Building Science Program, the University of Southern California, where the idea was originally conceived as part of the Master's thesis. I would like to thank Ralph Knowles and Karen Kensek, School of Architecture, the University of Southern California, for their support.

The authors are also thankful to the PhD program, Environmental Design and Planning for their resources and encouragement to work on this paper.

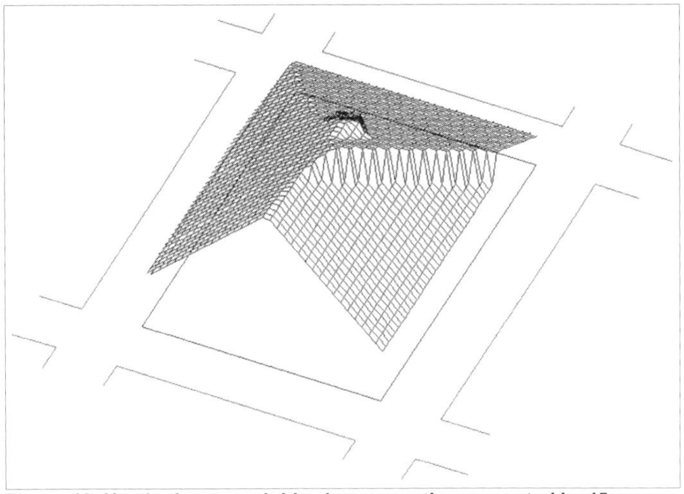

Figure 12. No shadow on neighboring properties separated by 15 m

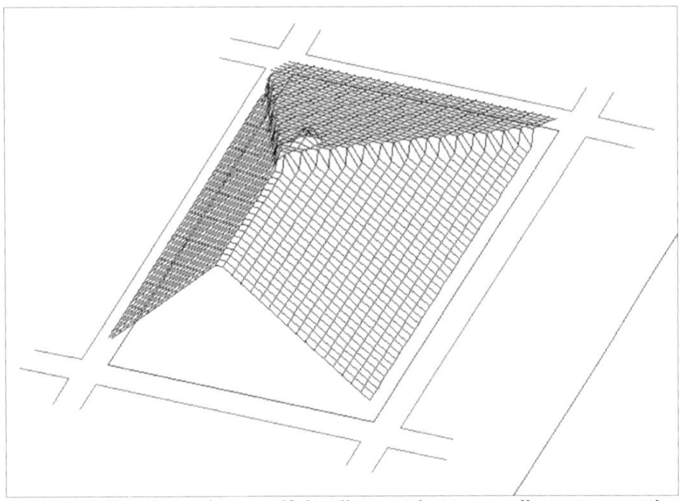

Figure 13. Envelope changes if the distance between adjacent properties changes

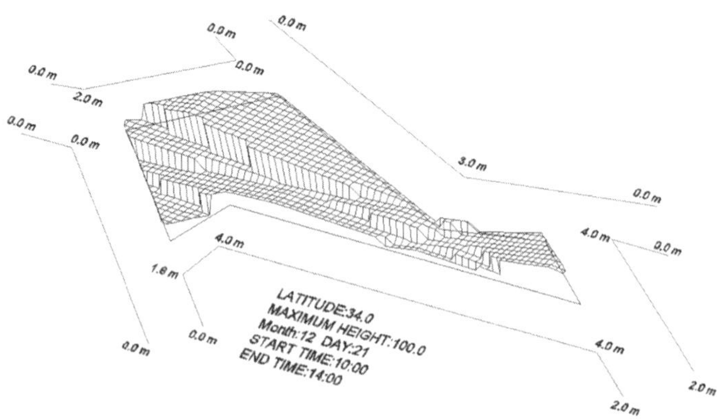

Figure 14: Envelope for shadow lines of varying height on adjacent properties

References

Arumi, F. (1979). Computer-aided energy design for buildings.In ed by D WAtson,141-160.NY: McGraw-Hill *Energy conservation through building design.*

Foley, J. D.,A.V.Dam,S.K. Feiner, and J.F.Huges,(1996). *Computer Graphics: Principles and practice, Second Edition. In Solar access zoning:computer generation of the solar envelope* edited by C.A Wesley,K.M. Kensek and R.Knowles,ACSA Southwest Regional Meeting. University of New Mexico, Albuquerque, *New Mexico.*

Knowles, R. L. (1974). *Energy and form / An ecological approach to urban growth.* Cambridge: The MIT Press.

Knowles, R. (1981). *Sun rythm form.* Cambridge:The MIT Press.

Knowles, R. L. and K.M.Kensek, (2000). The interstitium : A zoning strategy for seasonally adaptive architecture. *PLEA 2000, Cambridge, UK,* 773-774.

Mazria, E. (1979). *The passive solar energy book, expanded professional edition.* Rodale Press.

McWatters, K. (1994). Development procedures for computerized plotting of a sun-path diagram and shading mask protractor. *ASME solar energy conference. San Francisco, CA,* 483-491.

Narang, V. (1999). Solar masking calculator, building science program, University of Southern California, Los Angeles.

Schildt, H. (2001). *The Complete Reference JavaTM 2*, 4th edn:N.Y. McGraw-Hill.

Schiler, M., and P.Yeh, (1993). Solvelope: An interactive computer program for defining and drawing solar envelopes. *18th National Passive Solar Conference, ASES. Washington D.C.*

Tripathi, A. (1999). Shading analyser, Building Science Program, University of Southern California, Los Angeles.

Yeh, U.-F. (1992). Computer Aided Solar Envelope Design, *Building Science*, University of Southern California.

Multidimensional Presentation Environments with Integrated Intelligent Agents

Gregory More (SIAL), Lin Padgham (CSIT), Ian Mathieson (CSIT), Mark Burry (SIAL)
RMIT University

Abstract

A Multidimensional Presentation Environment (MPE) is defined here as a digital environment containing spatially located data that can be navigated by a presenter. Given an array of data types and the potential infinity of the associated datascapes, there is an opportunity to develop systems that assist the presenter in the navigation and analysis of complex information scenarios. This research reports on the utilisation of intelligent agent based software for a better understanding of spatial information representation within the MPE. This is achieved by utilising intelligent agent software to aid the presenter in the searching, retrieving, and articulation of datasets, and the application of such technologies in the generation of time based 3D graphical and audio presentations.

Multidimensional Presentation Environments with Integrated Intelligent Agents

Gregory More (SIAL), Lin Padgham (CSIT), Ian Mathieson (CSIT), Mark Burry (SIAL)
RMIT University

1 Introduction

This paper reports on research in progress into the development of a digital prototype 'presentation landscape' that explores the integration of intelligent agents in relation to visual and sonic arrangements of information. This research develops from a successful Australian Research Grant (ARC) application entitled: *Sharing Complex Systems Information by Challenging the Orthodoxies of Linear Presentation.* The project team spans two disciplines: spatial information architecture and computer science, connecting the information of space with the space of information. The objectives of the larger research effort are the human and social issues effecting decision making processes informed by spatial visualization and sonification with integrated computational support, especially in complex systems environments such as design collaboration, weather prediction, and disaster management situations. This paper reports on the developments to date of establishing the presentation prototype and the integration of Intelligent Agent support, and not the 'effectiveness' testing of such solutions.

1.1 Background

Comparative research of presentation orthodoxies has shown that digital media can assist where previous technologies were formally limited. Research at University of Maryland for example, at the Human-Computer Interaction Lab, has produced a software product (Counterpoint, http://www.cs.umd.edu/hcil/counterpoint/) that integrates zoomable user interfaces (ZUIs) to navigate 2D information. As an adjunct to MS PowerPoint™ this software reveals the advantages of simple panning and zooming through a ZUI to allow nonlinear navigation of information. This is described as a 2.5 dimensional presentation system (Good and Bederson 2002). Since the early 90s, researchers at Xerox PARC - User Interface Research Group have examined 3D approaches to digital arrangements of information http://www2.parc.com/istl/projects/uir/publications/project/index.html#uiiv). These explorations are related to single user navigation through components of information rather than presenter and audience presentation environments. Much of the pedagogy of architecture is based on the information of space and, in turn, spatial information. In the last decade architects have begun to explore the bridge between digital information spaces and constructed physical space, especially in museology. The Virtual New York Stock Exchange project by Asymptote (Couture and Rashid 2002) is one example that provides a digital simulation of a physical stock exchange with an overlay of continually updating information represented digitally. If this example succeeds on one level, utilising new media to deliver content to the requirements of the NYSE, it nevertheless offers little in the realm of digital spatial reconfiguration. Rather, it reinforces spatial concepts that mimic the physical world through a static model. The freedom of presentation media such as Counterpoint questions the need for strictly determined spatial constructs when dealing with information representation. Our research examines the role of dynamic systems for information presentation – with a specific case study of generic design based presentation information: images, movies, and sound. MPE and their navigation are inherently nonlinear with regard to user interaction and, as such, raise issues of the kind of decisions the user makes when traversing or altering these information spaces in a less determined manner than simply moving forwards or backwards. Intelligent agents are a leading edge technology that assist in the development and evolution of a range of complex systems – particularly systems that need to operate in real time in a dynamic and complex environment. Intelligent software agents incorporate the ability to reason about ways to achieve a desired goal in any current environment, and are able to adjust their behaviour to changing environmental conditions. The presentation of complex information in a flexible manner which can adjust to the specifics of an individual situation is a complex task with many specialised situations, different mechanisms available for different types of users, and different adjustments necessary to deal with environmental issues such as lack of sufficient information, inconsistency in information, unexpected information, etc. In this paper we explore in more detail how intelligent agent systems can assist in the kind of presentation tasks described, and we present the current MPE prototype and its three main components (visual, audio, data) before discussing the integration of intelligent agent support with this system.

2 Intelligent Agents

Intelligent agents are a new software paradigm, for which the terms of the initial research ideas (e.g. Georgeff and Lansky 1986, Bratman 1987) date back to the mid 1980s. During the 1990s the technology has been successfully used in a number of challenging applications such as air traffic control and space shuttle monitoring. In a number of papers at the Agents in Design 2002 conference (Gero and Brazier 2002), Gero et al. explored cognitive aspects of software agents in complex design processes. We are particularly interested in goal directed agents using pre-specified plans, such as those supported by the agent development frameworks JACK (AOS 2000), dMARS

(Kinny 1993), PRS (Ingrand, Georgeff and Rao 1992), JAM (Huber 1999), etc. These are referred to as "BDI" (Belief, Desire, Intention) agents, because of the way that they represent and work in terms of these kind of concepts. (In particular we use JACK, an industrial strength system for developing BDI agents, developed by Agent-Oriented Software in Melbourne, Australia). The plans in these systems describe a particular way of achieving a goal (or sub-goal) in a particular situation, known as a "context". The goal directed nature of the agent execution mechanism provided by the system ensures that if an agent fails to achieve its goal using a particular plan, it will search its plan library and try an alternative plan if one is available. Appropriate plans for use are decided only when the agent is ready to achieve the sub-goal. Thus the choice is always made with the current situation in mind. Plans can also contain sub-goals, which allows for a hierarchical approach where goals are broken down into sub- goals, which may themselves be further broken down. At each level the appropriate plan for the current situation is chosen from the library of available plans. The combination of reactivity and goal-directedness of BDI agent systems make them an excellent candidate for complex applications operating in dynamic environments. In addition to this run-time flexibility, BDI systems are highly scalable. As new situations are identified and ways of behaving in those situations developed, additional plans can be added to the agent's repertoire, with a description of the applicable situation. The area of complex information presentation is one where it is highly likely that new situations and new ways of presenting information in those situations will be discovered as the application develops. Thus this modularity and scalability is an extremely important characteristic for the application area. There are many aspects of preparing and delivering a presentation that could potentially be supported by an intelligent agent system. If we conceptualise a presentation as achieving a goal, we can see different kinds of presentations as achieving somewhat different kinds of goals, with varying sub-goals. For example we may have a goal to deliver a short introductory presentation in an area, which may have some alternative plans made up of sequences of sub-goals such as below:

Plan 1:	Plan 2:
Introduce area	Provide example
Provide example	Provide another example
Investigate one aspect	Summarise research question
Summarise research questions	Sketch possible solution
	Overview review

The intelligent agent system could then explore the space of possible sequences of images (assuming appropriately annotated sequences arranged by concept) and produce a suitable presentation, taking into account elements of the environment such as the interests of the audience, or the time available. Alternatively the agent system could interact with the user, suggesting options at different steps along the way. Agent systems provide an excellent framework for developing this kind of support – and doing so in a modular and scaleable way. However additional information must be represented and maintained in order for the agent to do its reasoning. The exact nature of that information is of course determined by what support one decides to prioritise.

3 Presentation Prototype

The prototype to date combines representations of datasets within a realtime 3D digital space. In this environment the presenter can navigate through a dataset arranged in a variety of spatial configurations with an accompanying soundscape. The software based interpretation requires the following capabilities: to interpret input from presenter, retrieve information, reconfigure visual and sound-scapes relative to information, and track the systems events.

3.1 Visualization and Audio Techniques

The MPE prototype is developed with a propriety software product Macromedia DirectorTM. This software has constituent

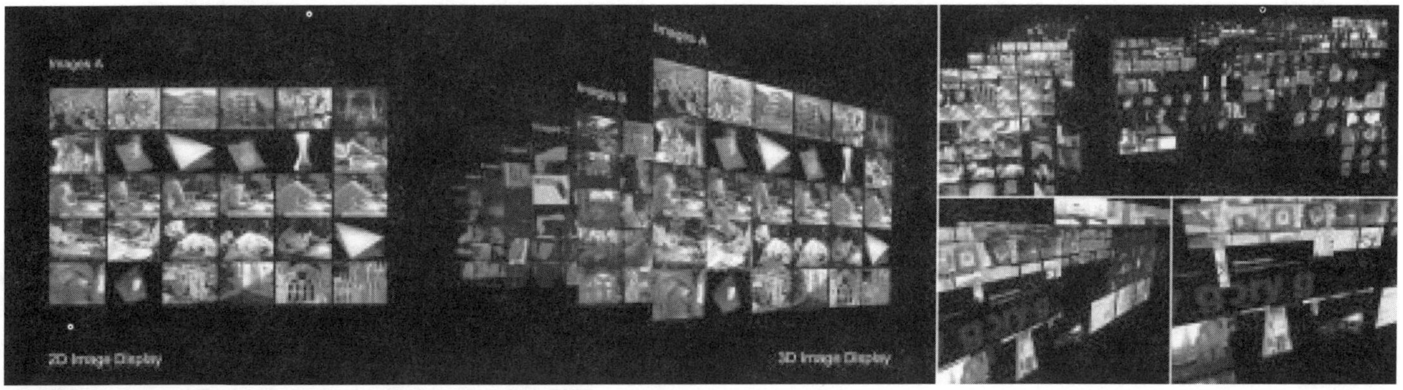

Figure 1. 2D thumbnail and 3D spatial arrangements within MPE

tools for dealing with digital media (text, image, digital video) and user interaction. Since July 2001 Macromedia (http: //www.macromedia.com/) DirectorTM has included 3D components that incorporate OpenGL and DirectX graphics support. These components are controlled by the Director native language LINGO, and provide a similar environment to VRML (mesh geometries, bitmap texturing, lighting capabilities), but in a stable browser independent platform.

The MPE explores the nonlinear potential of image layout and navigation via the realtime graphics capabilities of Macromedia DirectorTM. Figure 1. displays two developed methods of image cataloguing. The 2D 'thumbnail' array allows lecture content to be accessed in nonlinear fashion, jumping from image to image, or sequentially. The alternative 3D arrangements allow for rapid recognition of content by an informed presenter, and context by the audience. The images are retrieved from a database and the representations are generated on startup of the MPE application, allowing easy exchange of content information. The configuration of the images is also flexible allowing for images and associated elements, titles, movies, links, to be arranged in a series of formations, be they orthogonal screens, or any transformation of coordinates, rotation, and scale. These arrangements are transmutable, so the space can be animatedly reconfigured between differing compositions of information elements. The audio component of the prototype integrates the concepts of spatialising sound relative to various datasets. Audio within the environment is critical to increased user understanding of their informational field. This research is interested in the development of acoustical environments that aid the user in two main areas; for thematic and navigation concerns. The sound components of this research develop from several key themes presented in the International Community for Auditory Display "Sonification Report: Status of the Field and Research Agenda " (Kramer et al. 2001). With additional reference to extant research on the role of non speech audio for the representation of data dimensions (Walker 2000).

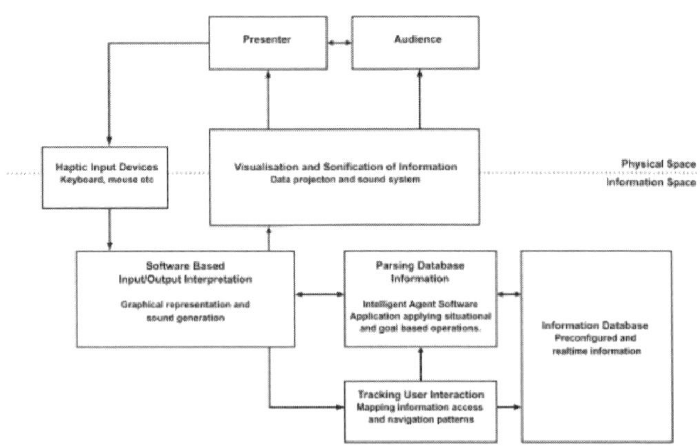

Figure 2. Schematic diagram of the MPE

3.2 Data Capturing and Intelligent Agent Connections

The current MPE prototype utilizes a series of external preferences and tracking systems to obtain user intentions and interactions. These form the primary source information in the dialogue between Director and JACK. At start up, preferences are (pre)defined for the initial criteria of the lecture (e.g. length of presentation, number of possible images, etc). Subsequent interaction data can be stored in an external database and exchanged with JACK via XML.

4 Integrating Intelligent Agent Support into the MPE

The fundamental elements to utilise and manipulate are: the data items for presentation, including descriptive metadata; historic records of past use, including presentation sequences and intents; and the current (or future) presentation plan – also sequence(s) and intents. This plan is a model of the presenter's intent, but we may additionally need to model audience/user intents (or capture/infer them on the fly). The key question will be how accumulated history (experience) influences agent behavior. Items will need unique identification, since (planned) sequences can be reordered. On the other hand, how can one revisit a point in a stream of dynamic data? Must such data be explicitly recorded into the history, for later reference/use? The history should record for each item in the actual sequence presented, its duration (time on view), as well as "why" i.e. the specific concepts intended by the presenter. The latter could possibly be inferred from conceptual overlaps with adjacent items, unless the presenter intended contrast. A presentation plan will nearly always involve time bounds. It may simply be a list of high-level concepts and durations, or may involve more explicit sequences or subsets of individual items and durations. Plans may also include weights indicating the relative importance of particular items or concepts. Where a presentation plan includes time bounded concept sequences and the item database contains appropriate metadata, the agent can determine whether the items actually used conform to the plan. When too much time is spent on one concept, subsequent sections may be adjusted by proposing the removal of briefer or less important items. Conversely, when running ahead of time, additional items or even entire related concepts may be proposed. In the absence of relevant history, such suggestions must be constructed afresh from the conceptual graph of items.

5 Conclusion

The MPE prototype is an exploration into understanding the consequences of multidimensional information delivery aided by intelligent agent support. The questions that remain to be answered within this research include the degree to which presenters of the future are willing to be aided or guided by such intelligent agent support to design their information pool. The outcome of this research is to develop what plans the agents may undertake to assist a presenter within a spatial information environment, in turn generating a better understanding of decision making processes for presenters within complex informational scenarios.

References

Bratman, M.E. (1987). “Intentions, Plans, and Practical Reason”, Harvard University Press, Cambridge, MA.

Couture, L. and Rashid, H. (2002). FLUX. New York: Phaidon Press Inc,.

Georgeff, M. P. and Lansky, A.L., (1986). Procedural Knowledge, in Proceedings of the IEEE Special Issue on Knowledge Representation, vol 74, 1986.

Gero, J.S. and Brazier, F. (eds.) (2002). Agents in Design 2002, Key Centre of Design Computing and Cognition, University of Sydney, Australia, p. 279.

Huber, M. J. (1999). “JAM: A BDI-theoretic Mobile Agent Architecture”, Proceedings of the Third International Conference on Autonomous Agents (Agents’99), Seattle, WA, May, 1999, pp. 236-243.

Ingrand, F.F, Georgeff, M.P. Rao, A.S. (1992). “An Architecture for real-time reasoning and system control”, in IEEE Expert”, 1992, vol. 7, number 6.

Kinny, D. (1993). “The Distributed Multi-Agent Reasoning System Architecture and Language Specification. Australian Artificial Intelligence Institute, Melbourne, Australia.

Kramer G., Walker, B.,T. Bonebright, P. Cook, J. Flowers, N. Miner, J. Neuhoff, (1997). Sonification Report.Melbourne, Australia,Status of the Field and Research Agenda, ICAD 1997. http://www.icad.org/websiteV2.0/References/nsf.html

Walker, B. (2000). Magnitude Estimation of Conceptual Data Dimensions for Use in Sonification, Phd Thesis, Rice University.

TOSU

SANDbox Urbanism suggestions for deserting the city

Andrew Hume and Amy Schultz
Senior Design Studio, Arch 441+442
The Ohio State University

Studio Professor: Lisa Tilder

The Las Vegas Experience: Representation, Image and Identity Construction (project b)

...(see p. 429)

This studio sought to examine the unique representational phenomena of the city through the design proposal of a Hotel + Experience for Las Vegas. Students were asked to craft their own "realities" - project and program - from research on a series of topics: From all-things-Disney to corporate branding; from World's Fairs to themed environments and utopian communities; from simulation and synthetic environments to surface, skin and computer graphics concepts. Students drew upon Vegas culture and the particularities of site (and non-site) to develop proposals which further explored issues of identity construction, consumption and production, and image in popular culture.

It has finally all come together: the lunar theatrical landscape of the Strip and the casino hotels, the amusement park and the shopping mall, themed and prefabricated, available as a package vacation for all.

- Ada Louise Huxtable

Timothy Breihan, John Cerone, Greg Dutton, Nicholas Faehnle, Rachel Huss, Jason Ivaliotis, Malika Kirkling, Bridget Kline, Andrea Knoch, Naosuke Nemoto, Evan Williams, Jonathan Yang

3rd and 4th Year Studio, ARC 301/401
University of Miami Ohio

Studio Professor: Sergio Sanabria
Media Advisor: Murali Puranandi

The Tower of Babel
a transformation of vladimir tatlin's monument to the third international as a new headquarters for the united

UMO

Description of Project + Digital Design Process

This studio, subsidized by a grant from the Havighurst Center for Russian Studies, focused on a collective investigation of a visionary early soviet project of 1918-20 by Vladimir Tatlin for a Monument to the Third International. The twelve students in this studio decided to use Tatlin's project as a starting point for a new and greatly expanded headquarters for the United Nations, to be sited on the Upper Bay of New York City–as a climactic intermediate between the Varrazano Narrows bridge, the Statue of Liberty, and the profile of Lower Manhattan. The political aspirations metaphorically embodied in this monument seemed appropriate to the lofty goals of the United Nations.

The mixed-use building, with 5,000,000 square feet of space, rises 110 stories, commemorating the destroyed WTC, but proposing potentially safer redundant circulation systems. The building presents to the public the work and ideals of the United Nations, accommodating a plurality of functions and activities, and addressing environmental concerns through a clearly "revealed' production of clean energy through solar and wind power, and the deployment of garden. The building provides space for the organs, agencies, and organizations of the United Nations headquartered in New York, and also includes commercial rental space, a cultural center comprising a library, a research college, exhibition spaces, and a variety of music, performance, lecture, and cinema halls. Housing for staff, special visitors and dignitaries is provided, as well as a major hotel.

This project could not have been done within the timeframe if it were not for the 3D computer model. Clearly form•Z facilitated this process in the conception and concoction stages.

Conception: The Project, designed by a team of 12 students was coordinated by maintaining a computer file of the design decision that had to be clearly agreed upon by the studio as a whole.

Concoction: In order to build the large stainless steel sculptural model of our final design, with its complex three dimensionally torqued connectors, the model was essential to obtain actual dimensions and angles for fabrication. The students could not have fabricated this installation in the timeframe, given that every one of the truss members has a distinct length or pitch or yon.

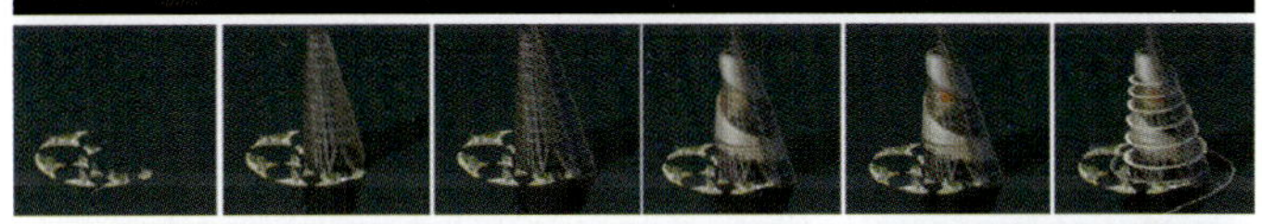

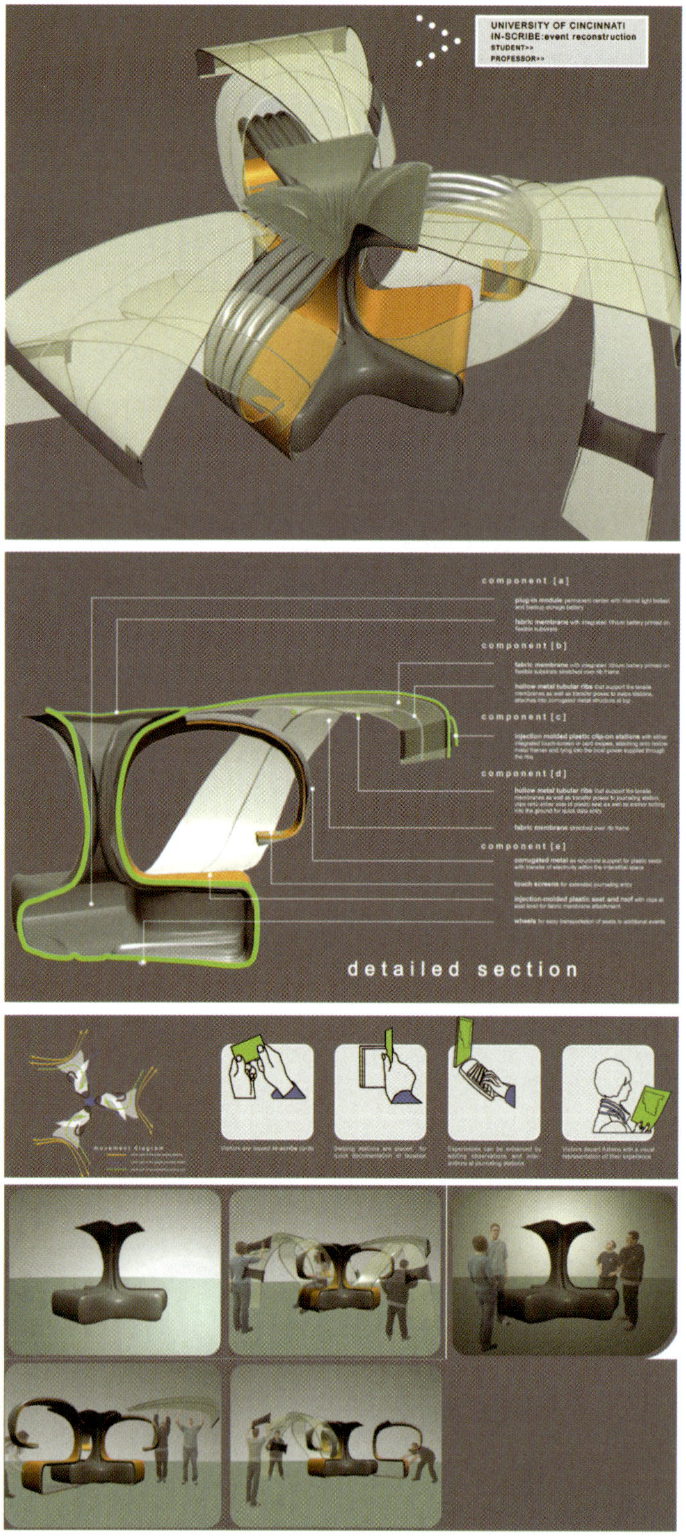

INSCRIBE

Mandi Hoskins and Melissa Williams
Graduate Level
The University of Cincinnati

Studio Professor: Marc Swackhamer

Inscribe: Questions + Answers

Q: What does it mean to generate activity?

A: The majority of visitors to the Olympics are most commonly the spectators of the various competitions who not only observe the sports, but are also part of the larger experiences of the crowd and the activity associated with that venue in particular. By mapping the conglomeration of a multitude of experiences at differing sites, the visitor can be located within the larger collective dynamic of the city and the spectacle of the Olympic event. The mere act of documentation and recording text enables an inscription of a memory, thus translating a singular notion into a tangible, visible object that is infinitely linked to the city of Athens. While allowing for multiple variables of user groups and ranges of time, this activity encourages both individual and group patronage, as well as supporting three levels of interaction varying from quickly citing a location to a more private journaling session. With an issued card, the visitor can electronically document themselves within the Olympic park at a multitude of sites by swiping the card, or have the option for journaling briefly or for an extended period of time. At the very least, the visitors depart Athens with individualized representations of their experiences, mapped within the physical context of the city. While every visitor would receive a completed document, the experience could be enhanced through additional journal entries of descriptions, observations, and perceptions.

Q: How is the form of in-scribe generated?

A: The systems of movement that are created by the varying speeds of the users were combined with the programmatic requirements of the activity to suggest the formal response. The placement of both the seated station in relation to the other two functions of the structure were important in establishing varying zones of activity and indicating their respective queuing locations. Similarly, the flexibility of the tensile membrane allowed for subtle contouring to either envelope the user, thus creating greater privacy while journaling, or make adjustments in height to support quickly moving groups on the more public exterior edges. Ultimately, the resultant form is tailored to provide a more accommodating human oriented-scale in relation to that of the venues and vastness of the landscape.

Q: How is the placement of this system determined within the landscape?

A: In-scribe anticipates and thrives off of the activity generated by the groups of people attending the Olympic venues. The system's core module is located within the landscape in anticipation of an event, and when the need becomes manifest, the remainder of the system is brought into place. As the activity level dissipates and the spectacle of the crowd wanes, the system becomes no longer of use and is moved to another active site. That which is left behind, is a visual representation of the strength of the activity that was once present. The varying intensity of the light, shone within the cavity of the remaining core module, illuminates aspects of the site immediately surrounding it and continues to reflect the persistent memory of what came before in the context of the ever-changing city.

UC

URBAN FURNITURE:
from gazebo to digi-booth

Charlotte Hunt
interdisciplinary design studio
University of Cincinnati

Studio Professor: Udo Greinacher / Urban Design
Elizabeth Pincus, studio critic
Professor Patrick Snadon / Interior Design

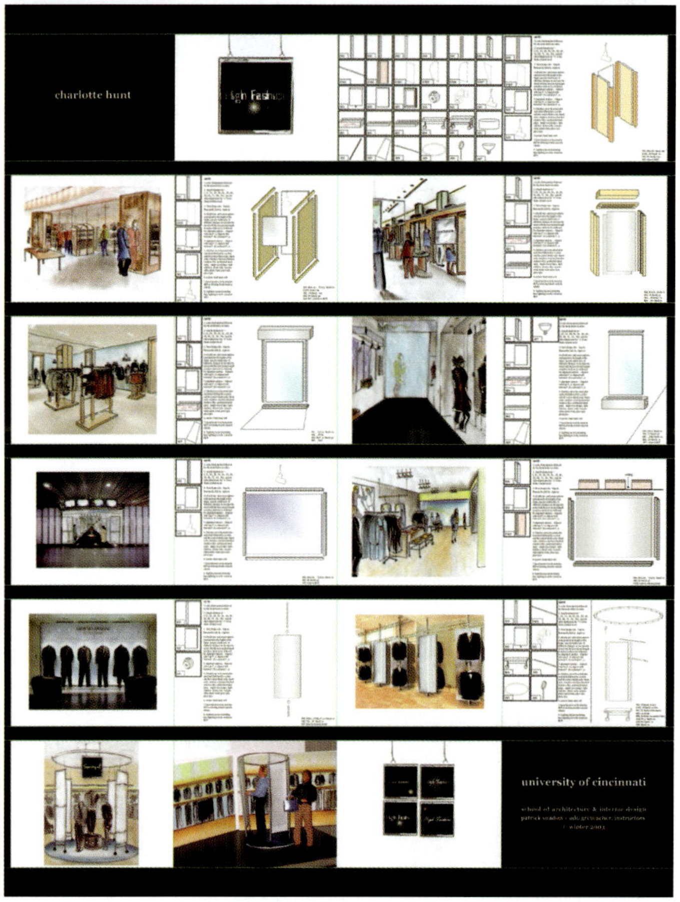

URBAN FURNITURE: from gazebo to digi-booth

Recent years have seen the steady increase of automated kiosks and temporary structures that begin to replace traditional building types. In this course we studied and analyzed the development of the gazebo/kiosk in urban/rural settings both inside and outside over time, assessed its value for commerce and social equity, proposed a forward projection regarding the role digital info-booths/commercial kiosks will play in our urban environment, and developed new spatial models that can become an integral part of our daily experience.

The kiosk, "High Fashion" takes a futuristic look at shopping. Pressure, time, and options are some reasons why people can shop at home from their computers rather than go to a store. This kiosk explores the convenience of virtual shopping and brings this experience back into the store so that it is both "virtual" and "social." Body scanning technology creates a full-size replica of you that can be manipulated on a screen. You can try on clothes without trying on clothes! Added features allow the customer to adjust the light levels, pick their own background, and combine outfits with accessories throughout the store.

"High Fashion" is the answer for mothers with small children, for students in a hurry, and for those who are just looking for a different shopping experience – not to mention fashion advise! The environments that may be created from the "High Fashion" kit of parts are endless. By combining frames, lasers, screens, and accessories, "High Fashion" can fit into the most high-class boutique or the most simple chain. It's easy, it's fun, it's "High Fashion".

Design Proposal - The Problem Identified:
I walk into a store (with partial intention of buying something)…I am trying not to make eye contact with that sales clerk who is about to ask…."is there anything in particular I can help you find today?". (Darn, she caught my eye), I respond…"no thanks, just looking". The truth is, I am looking, looking for ideas…so I head to the dressing room with a few potentials, making sure not to exceed the limit of six items per dressing room. I exit the dressing room, give the clothes to the attendant as she says, "So, none of these worked for you today" (with a sigh of course)…and I think to myself, "god forbid that someone actually made you do your job"… guess I won't try on that other stuff after all.

This scenario applies not just to buying clothes, but to cars, furniture, or anything that can be "bought". In most cases, when you are really interested in buying something, the information is not available or the sales person is nowhere to be found. This proposal will alleviate the pressure that is attached to buying by introducing the concept of "automated browsing" inside the store, within a kiosk prototype.

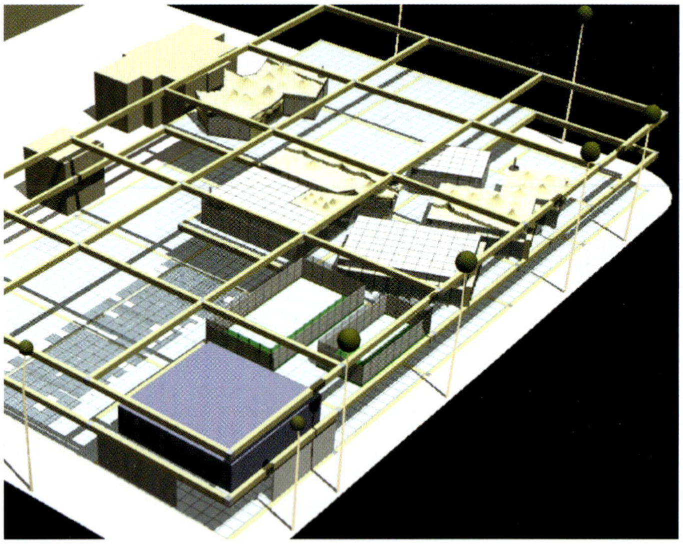

Ecological Elementary School

John Cerone
Senior Design Studio
University of Miami Ohio

Studio Professor: Scott Johnston
Critic/Media Advisor: Murali Puranandi

Elementary School: The Design Process

Although the final presentation documents were all either generated or processed by computer, the steps leading to a final product were the result of constant interaction between computer and paper. The process began on paper with quick sketches of the main grid elements—the most fundamental pieces of the "kit of parts".

The move was then made to the computer, creating a "sketch" model comprised of the grid in a simplified form (the origins of a symbol library) and rough volumes representing the buildings, streets, sidewalks, trees, and people of the actual site. This model allowed for walkthroughs and fly-bys helping to visualize and better understand space arrangement and orientation.

The views created by the computer were then converted to quick paper sketches to allow for quick documentation of thoughts on special arrangements and relationships of masses.

The computer was used to lay out space arrangement with rough volumes. More walkthroughs and fly-bys were used for greater visualization of the interaction of spaces, and again, more paper sketches were used to document thoughts of possible detail.

Large steps were taken on paper to conceive the "feeling" of the spaces. Quick perspectives of classroom spaces, interior and exterior, allowed for rapid documentation of many simultaneous decisions—quickly rendering allowed for rapid experimentation with material and scale. Quick gesture-sketches was congruent with my process of thinking and decision making. I began sketching details of the components of which spaces would be comprised.

The kit of parts was then refined to great detail on the computer, extensively expanding and detailing the symbol library. Each symbol was created in several levels of detail to aid in the "construction" process. Once the parts were created, I began fitting them together, roughly mimicking the actual construction method of such a structure. When placing symbols and the navigation of views, low levels of detail were used in the interest of expediting rendering time. When detail was important to a rendering, detail levels of necessary elements were increased.

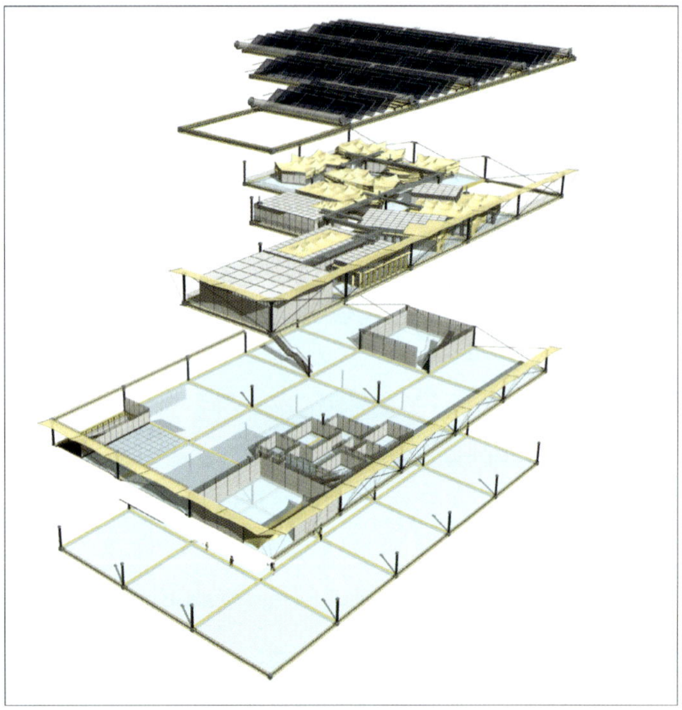

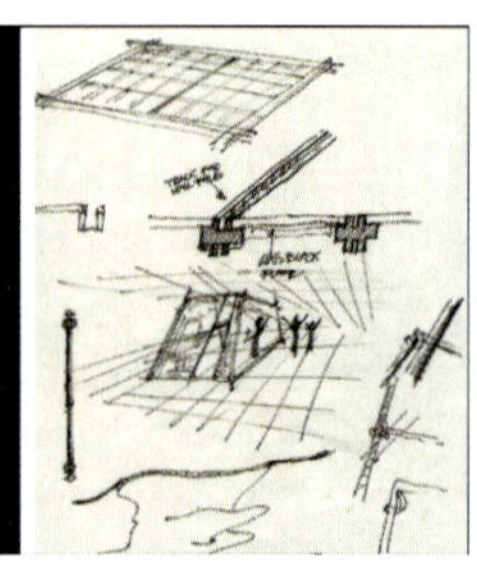

OSU

Las Vegas Incorporated: experience +/- commodity = identity

Andrew Colopy
Senior Design Studio, Arch 441+442
The Ohio State University

Studio Professor: Lisa Tilder

The Las Vegas Experience: Representation, Image and Identity Construction (project a)

All fakes are not created equal; there are good fakes and bad fakes. The standard is no longer real versus phony, but the relative merits of the imitation. What makes the good ones better is their improvement on reality.

- Ada Louise Huxtable

In a society dominated by image and the production and consumption of fantasy, Vegas is a modern Mecca. It is in Las Vegas that the image-copy improves upon the referent - with increased entertainment value and merchandising opportunities. The image of Vegas is everything, an adult theme park super-sized menu, with no going back to the value meal.

Even its own history has been repackaged for consumption: Jerde's conversion of Fremont Street into The Freemont Street Experience is only one example of many so-called unique image-experiences for sale. Vegas represents a new American geography, at once everywhere and nowhere, where for a few days all things might be possible. The Las Vegas Experience embodies a fluctuating condition of continuous reinvention.

(see p.424)...

UK

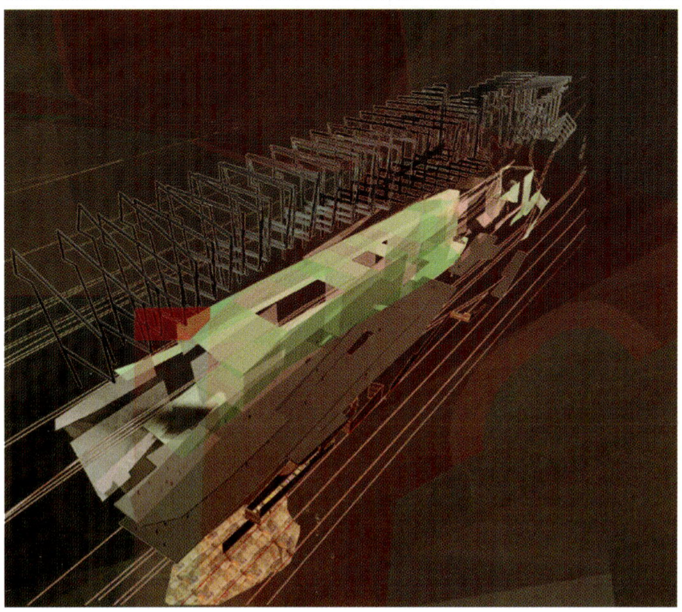

Virtual Raves in Synthetic Landscapes Hybrid Rave Space

Aaron Anderson,KoshiKawakami,Kristy Van Zant
Digital Design Studio
University of Kentucky

Studio Professor: Greg A. Luhan

Virtual Raves in Synthetic Landscapes

Project Description: The typology of public event spaces has transformed substantially over centuries. Ranges of spatial configurations have been developed with numerous instances and adaptations; many have occurred in our own century as the information needs of the modern society evolved. Bernard Tschumi denotes these phenomena as architectural urbanism where city-generators, functions, and programs combine and intersect in spaces of endless cross programming. Today, derelict industrial spaces [terrain vagues] have become social places that accommodate public activities. New technologies, particularly those associated with electronic media have radically influenced the program and typology of these event-spaces. Yet, in spite of social, technological, and material changes, the essence of the event-structure has not changed, it remains a place of interaction.

The students investigated the history of rave revealing origins couched in the dance rituals associated with the Black Plague. Today, the rave has developed into an event-space characterized by its anti-capitalist notions and techno-music rage as generated from a digital environment. The result of this paradigm shift is an environment fraught with electronic pulsation. These pulsations are technologically enhanced and thus accelerated to levels that can not only simulate but also stimulate the human heartbeat. At the center of the rave is the techno-shaman. The techno-shaman is the architect of the event that controls color, light, space, tempo, and ultimately, the crowd.

Once the students understood the rave vocabulary, they began to intersect the idea of ruin and the possible implications of inserting a rave into one of the industrial sites. Through a close reading of these spaces, a series of analytical intentions emerged. The selected sites are abandoned structures that were initially used for communal gathering or distribution. The functions of the sites were steel manufacturing plants, tobacco warehouses, train stations, and railyards. The research of the individual site led to a unique and active synthesis between the idea of rave and the space of the ruin. Similarities between all of the sites were then used to augment the relationship between the non-apparent structure of rave and the physical site and the possible effects that such a union might have on its urban context. From this juxtaposition emerged a pliable condition that mitigated between the container and the contained. The space between these two forces became a wall fragment that defines the boundaries between things and a space of occupation.

In an effort to simulate more closely the tension between the two spaces, Regal Plastic, a plastics fabrication and distribution company, was invited to participate in our studio. Regal Plastic was sought after because of their recent innovations into the realm of virtual constructions. Based in Kansas City, Missouri, Regal Plastic is currently fabricating the Virtual Reality Center at Iowa State University in Des Moines, Iowa. In order to narrow the boundaries between the digital environment and the construction process, the students worked closely with Robert McFarlane and Jack Smith Tyler of the Nashville Branch of Regal Plastic. The use of the synthetic material, plastic seemed 'natural' to our process. Not only were the students successful in realizing their projects through digital representations, but also they were equally successful in narrowing the gap between their imagination and the final constructed process.

UIC

Block 37

Jeff Morgan + Josse Popma
MArch Design Studio
University of Illinois, Chicago

Studio Professor: Doug Garofalo

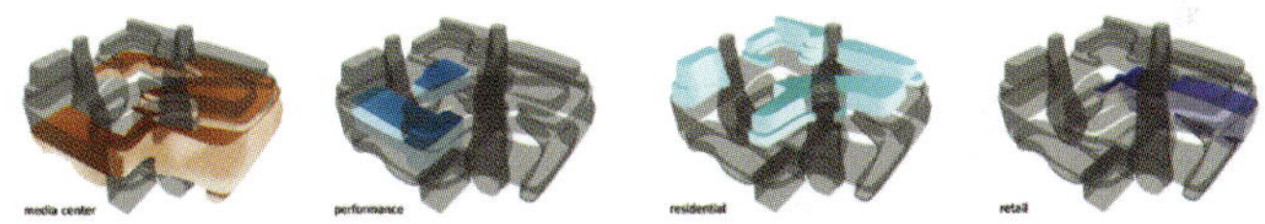

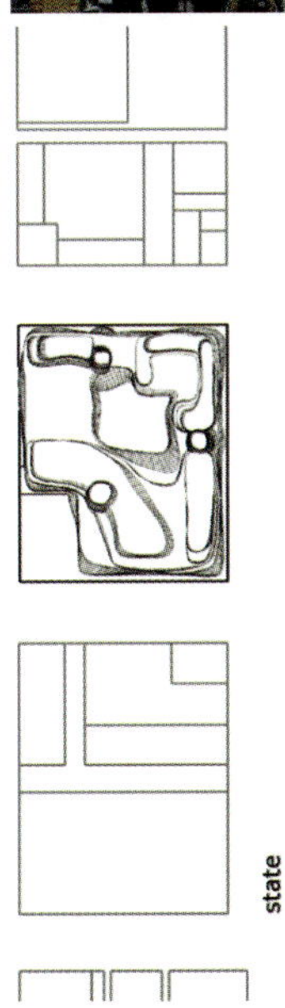

Block 37

The proposal for Block 37 was envisioned to anchor the north end of State Street, forming an implied axis between the Harold Washington Library and the New Media Center. The two buildings share similar educational responsibilities for the public, offering a variety of programs and facilities. In addition, they also assume a related physical presence on their respective sites, due to a similarity in the size of the building programs.

The controversial history of the site raised many issues concerning the typology of the building. In general, the building considered a multiplicity of programs with the intention of mixing and shifting them throughout the space. The context of the site also provided several interesting elements to take into consideration. For instance, the pedway running between the Red and Blue Lines of the subway bisected the site with a transfer tunnel. The ComEd power utility building needed to remain on the without interfering with its operations.

Block 37's location in an urban fabric is extremely unique for the fact that almost an entire block in the middle of the city has been left untouched for such a length of time. Its relationship to Daley Plaza and the retail of State Street position it between a significant portion of commercial buildings and a number of civic buildings including City Hall, the State of Illinois building, and Daley Center.

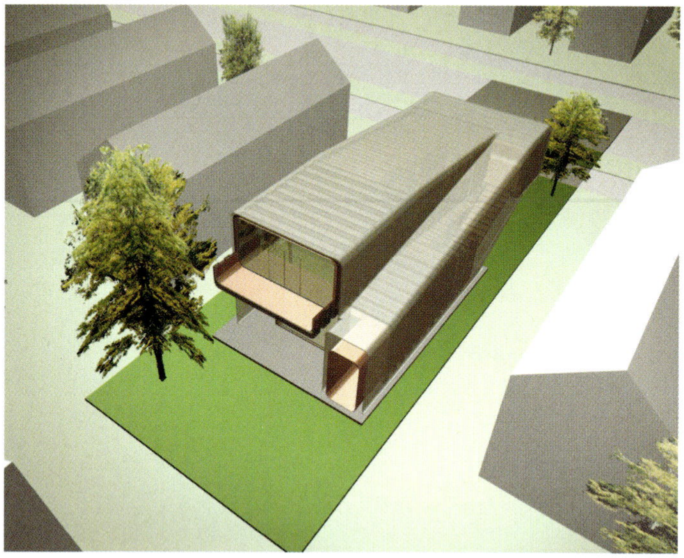

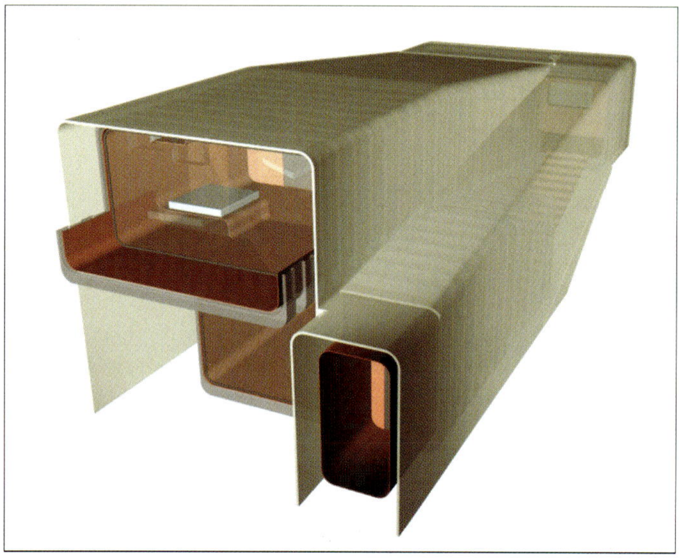

housemc

Adam Fure
Design Studio
University of Michigan

Studio Professor: Karl Daubmann

Mass-Crafting
Numerical instructions for construction

Craft oriented culture was eventually displaced by mass-production, and it was not until the early 1990's when a new paradigm began to emerge, one of infinite customer driven flexibility. Mass customization promises a flexible and efficient mode of production for customized parts or services at low cost. The catalyst for such a revolution has been computer-aided design and computer controlled manufacturing.

This new mode of production is typified in the US Department of Defense's Joint Strike Fighter program, which in 1996 awarded both Lockheed-Martin and Boeing contracts. The JSF program began with a logical but radical proposition: instead of creating three different airplanes for three different users, one design approach would be used to build a single family of aircraft that could achieve economies of scale in production and support. The three users in this case were to be the Navy, Air Force, and Marines. The family of aircraft designed shared 90% of the same parts, yet their performance remained incredibly varied. Both Lockheed-Martin and Boeing satisfied the requirements of their contracts because of their efforts in research, computation, and advanced manufacturing techniques. The Joint Strike Fighter is first top-of-the-line fighter to be virtually designed, built, and flown before a single piece of metal was cut.3

Such innovations in manufacturing have always influenced the making of buildings. The materials that are available, the methods of erection, and the pool of people constructing buildings evolve based on the paradigmatic shifts in the culture of making. These issues consequently influence every aspect of building, from the interaction permitted between designer and fabricator to the format of instructions and specifications issued for the purpose of making.

Although mass-customization is feasible for manufacturing (typically at small dimensional scales) it is still not fully available for the construction of buildings. Computer driven manufacturing has affected high-end buildings, making difficult things possible, but the promise of high variability for low cost is still not affordable. And in the end, architect designed buildings are typically custom made, based on a clients needs and desires. Architects provide high variability for medium range cost within the current model of making without all the CNC manufacturing. A model that emerged from the work of the Wallenberg studio was that of "mass-crafting" which employs strategies of the three production models mentioned (craftspeople, mass-production, and mass-customization). In the mass-crafting model the design process exploits computation to develop a parameter based procedural model allowing for a repetitive fabrication process that not only allows for variation but also seeks to create it.

(see p. 433)...

Variations + Versioning

Lindsay Wai
Design Studio
University of Michigan

Studio Professor: Karl Daubmann

...(see p. 432)

A major holdover from the previous culture of making is that of repetition and modularity. It is true that it is always cheaper and faster to make the same part, component, or building over and over again but then again cheaper is not necessarily better. Through computer driven manufacturing, we can now provide more customization and variation for minimal economic investment as opposed to the repetitive quantitative benefits afforded by mass-production. For many decades architects have used their time during design development to standardize the form, dimensions and materials to fit available parts, products, and methods. Many architects fear mass-customization because it offers no perceived resistance, removing the standardization phase of the design process, and ultimately the necessity to think critically about making. Mass-crafting looks for the criticality not within the specification of available parts but in the restrictions provided by the new tools in the manufacturing process. Even if an architect designs a building employing components of standard sizes, a water-jet cutter will not make any distinction between rectangular or freeform cuts. Water-jet cutting, as just one possibility for cutting, has limitations of sheet size, depth of cut, and file input format. The price of the panel is not based on the complexity of shape but instead will be based on machine time and material cost. The designer can now engage the process directly, using the computer file to potentially cut a panel that takes less time to cut, is pre-drilled for assembly, conserves material, and creates a building façade with a desired effect. Resistance and limitations of making exist but they are not only opportunities for designers to reclaim aspects in the building manufacturing process but they are ways to be critical about making.

1. Lux, David S., "The History of American Technology - Small Arms in Revolutionary and Early National Eras". Course taught at Bryant College. http://web.bryant.edu/~history/h364material/musket/index.htm

2. MODEL T FORD PRODUCTION (Compiled by R.E. Houston, Ford Production Department, August 3, 1927)

3. Hoffman, Carl. "The X Wars", Wired Magazine Issue 9.07 July 2001.

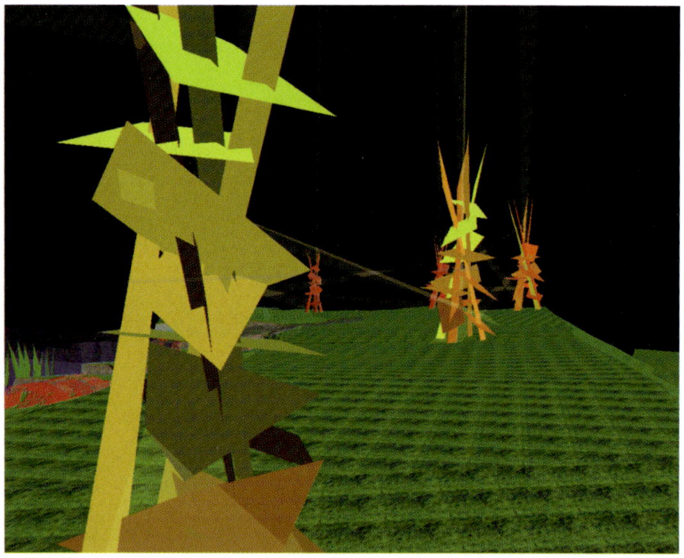

Make No Little Plans: Designing the Chicago Lakefront in a Virtual Reality Environment

Andrew Cockrell , Elizabeth Kolzow, Emma Smith
Kalev Leetaru, (NCSA) Computer Science Student Assistant
Graduate Studio
University of Illinois at Urbana-Champaign

Studio Professor: Joy Monice Malnar

Immersive Virtual Reality

Architects have always needed somewhere to draw. History has seen dirt, stone, wood, and paper each serve in turn as the architect's medium. Every technological advance has helped to manifest these exploratory visions in ever-increasing fidelity, while influencing the way in which the design process is conducted. Computer technology is the latest step in this progression, adding a third dimension to the architect's drawings. Programs like form•Z, 3DS max, etc. allow the architect to build lifelike models and take clients on fly-throughs. Now, virtual reality has advanced architectural drawing to "full body design", letting architects experience their creations, rather than just seeing those creations in front of them. ShadowLight-Mirage offers a unique environment in virtual reality in which to create rich ambiances of vibrancy, vitality and vigor.

The Virtual Future?: ShadowLight-Mirage allows architects total freedom to focus on design by temporarily removing the real-world restrictions of gravity and structure. Instead of being limited by these concerns at the conceptual stage, the architect is free to express the creation in its entirely. Once the design has been fully manifested, the architect can go back and constrain the design in a global context. By addressing gravity and structure in a second stage, the designer sees the big picture, and can potentially make a different set of design choices than if the concept had been materialized in a contemporary bottom-up fashion. ShadowLight-Mirage is now in its second generation and is constantly evolving to forge the future of architectural design in virtual reality.

UK

The Space of an IDEA: Ideas for Living

Lisa Neidhardt
Digital Design Studio
University of Kentucky

Studio Professor: Gregory A. Luhan

Studio Issue: The space of an idea resides in the connection between thinking and making. The studio explorations reveal the tension between the private experience and the public perception and investigate new methods of architectural assemblage. By uniting thinking/drawing with seeing/making, an effectual palette engenders a new way of looking at the individual and thus narrows the normative boundaries associated with actualizing ideas.

The challenge of the project is to transform the philosophical questions pertaining to digitalization into an operative condition to adequately address the issues of modern living. How do we live as individuals? How do we live as a community? How do we move? What is our grounding device? Is it possible to address the issue of memory and occupation on a particular site? What are the types of traces left behind in computer-space? Is it possible to derive a new method of connecting object-space to landscape-ground based upon these philosophical constructs? Would these ideas prove to be a suitable foundation for an actualizable architecture? One answer may lay in the transfiguration of the insight, imagination, and idea of inhabitation. How do the sequential acts of the everyday define space?

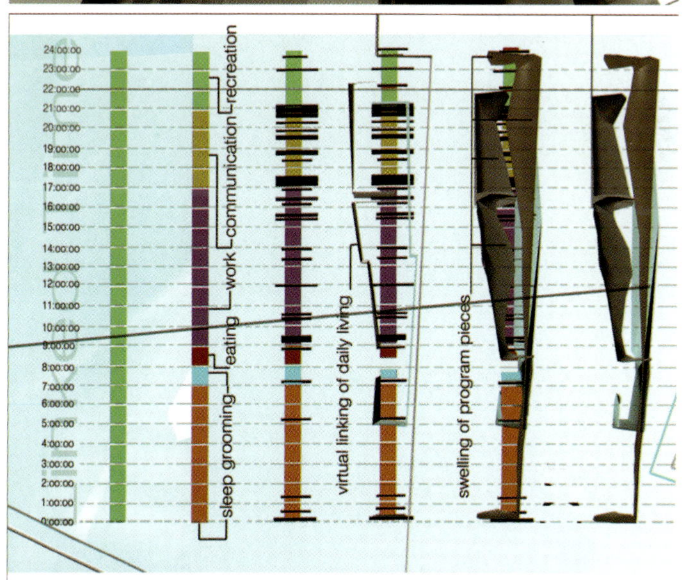

Project Description: A Diagram for Conceptual Development
[The diagram is based upon OBSERVATION. The goal of the diagram is to ENABLE and STIMULATE the imagination.] In architecture, the diagram is historically understood in two ways: as an explanatory device or analytical device or as a generative device. In its analytical role, the diagram REPRESENTS in a different way than a sketch or plan of a building. As such, the diagram attempts to uncover latent structures of organization even though it is not a conventional structure itself. As a generative device in a process of design, the diagram is also a form of representation. As a generator, a diagram mediates between a tactile or tangible object, a real building, and what can be called architecture's interiority. The diagram acts like a surface that receives inscriptions from the memory of that which does not yet exist; this is to say the potential architectural object. This provides traces of function, enclosure, meaning, and site from the specific conditions. Eisenman, Diagram: An Original Scene of Writing (23.27 - 23.29)

TRANSLATE/INTERPRET vs. TRANSMUTE/TRANSPOSE/TRANSFORM
Transform the functional conditions of the diagram in spatial terms and into a pliable structure that can be used for inhabitation. In order to convert the diagram, one must actualize the architect's intuition and imagination as a framework of architecture. In this way, the architect's process of making is imprinted into the realized building. The transformation of the diagram into architecture should inform the spatial order of the structure, the site and its context, and its tectonics, construction or in our case its fabrication.

BSU

Mountain Deflection Reflection

Zachary Hilleson
3rd Year Design Studio
Ball State University
(With John Brown, University of Calgary)

Studio Professor: F. Stacy Norman

Studio Focus: Digital Design and Collaboration

The focus of this studio was to understand the impact of digital media on the process of design, collaboration, and fabrication. This design studio brought together Ball State University and the University of Calgary in a joint venture opportunity. The use of digital tools provided fertile ground for the exploration of collaborative methods in design and fabrication.

There were two primary questions raised over the course of the term. The first question was related to distance collaboration, while the second is related to digital design and fabrication. The distance between each of the universities was substantial and the creation of a design environment that brought together collaborators in a "real" sense were grounds for exploration. The second question lay in the ability to push the use of the computer beyond a tool for design visualization and into a realm of making. Digital information allowed us to visualization an object or a space but the real question was one of fabrication—how digital can inform how we make objects or construct space. Emergent technologies are late in coming to the field of architecture, the use of CNC (computer-numerically-controlled) devices now offer the ability for mass customization and can push beyond digital visualization and into new methods of fabrication.